Fun with Mommy and Me

Fun with Mommy and Me

*More than 300 Together-Time Activities
for You and Your Child:
Birth to Age Five*

Dr. Cindy Bunin Nurik
with Jane Schonberger

Dutton

All fingerplays, rhymes, poems, and songs printed in *Fun with Mommy and Me* either have been written by the authors of this book or compiled from early childhood educational materials. A diligent effort has been made to research and trace the ownership of any and all materials in order to seek permission of publication and or make proper acknowledgment of their use. If any errors have occurred, they shall be immediately rectified and full credit acknowledged in future editions upon notification of the publisher.

DUTTON
Published by the Penguin Group
Penguin Putnam Inc., 375 Hudson Street, New York, New York 10014, U.S.A.
Penguin Books Ltd, 27 Wrights Lane, London W8 5TZ, England
Penguin Books Australia Ltd, Ringwood, Victoria, Australia
Penguin Books Canada Ltd, 10 Alcorn Avenue, Toronto, Ontario, Canada M4V 3B2 Penguin Books (N.Z.) Ltd, 182-190 Wairau Road, Auckland 10, New Zealand

Penguin Books Ltd, Registered Offices: Harmondsworth, Middlesex, England

Published by Dutton, a member of Penguin Putnam Inc.

First Printing, September, 2001
10 9 8 7 6 5 4 3 2 1

For permission to use material in this book, grateful acknowledgment is made to the following publishers and authors:

Where Is Thumbkin?, © 1993 by Pam Schiller and Thomas Moore Price $14.95. Published by Gryphon House, PO Box 207, Beltsville MD 20704.

Everyday Circle Times, ©1983 by Liz and Dick Wilmes Published by Building Blocks, 38W567.

"You Are My Sunshine" by Jimmie Davis and Charles Mitchell, Copyright©1940 by Peer International Corporation. Copyright Renewed. International Copyright Secured. Used by permission. All Rights Reserved.

"Three Little Fishies" by Saxie Dowell, ©1939 (renewed). Chappell & Co. All Rights Reserved. Used by permission. Warner Bros. Publications U.S. Inc. Miami, FL 33014.

Fun with Mommy and Me in its entirety (including, but not limited to, narration and compilation):
© Mommy and Me Enterprises, Inc. 2001

REGISTERED TRADEMARK—MARCA REGISTRADA

LIBRARY OF CONGRESS CATALOGING-IN-PUBLICATION DATA
Nurik, Cindy Bunin.
    Fun with Mommy and Me: more than 300 together-time activities for you and your
child, birth–age five / by Cindy Bunin Nurik and Jane Schonberger.
        p.cm.
    ISBN 0-525-94620-9 (acid-free paper)
    1. Child development. 2. Early childhood education—Activity programs. 3. Child rearing. 4. Mother and child. I. Schonberger, Jane. II. Title.

HQ767.9 .N87 2001
649'.5—dc21   2001017345
Mommy and Me™ and *Fun with Mommy and Me*™ are marks and names owned by Mommy and Me Enterprises, Inc.

Produced by Bumpy Slide Books
Interior design by Nanette Yawitz
Cover design by Lane and Lane Design
Photography by Anthony Nex Photography
Clothes provided by Baby Guess and Mamiye Brothers, Inc.

This book is dedicated to four very special people in my life. First and foremost, my parents, Kitty and Murray Bunin. Although they have passed on, they still play a very important role in every aspect of my life. Their unconditional love as parents and their lessons about life have helped me on my own life's journey. Without their love, wisdom, and support, I never would have been able to reach my goals.

Second, my loving husband, Marc. Our twenty-three years together have taught me the true meaning of respect, perseverance, admiration, and love. Without his constant support and solid belief and understanding of the importance of *Mommy and Me*, I never could have finished. I will forever be grateful.

And last, but not least, my wonderful daughter, Kacey. The gift of motherhood over the last ten years has filled my life with a joy that is unsurpassed. Kacey has taught me patience and humility. Her antics have given me many hours of fun and laughter along with the typical concerns that accompany parenthood. I would not change one minute of my experience with this incredible little person. All my dreams came true the day she came into my life. So, my darling child, thank you from the bottom of my heart for being you.

Cindy Nurik

To my mother, Marcia Schonberger, who battled physical challenges to play with me in her own special way, and who still reminds me to wear my rubbers when it rains; to my one-in-a-million husband, George, who supports me in every way; and to my daughters, Alex and Maddie, who make me proud to be called "Mommy."

Jane Schonberger

CONTENTS

ACKNOWLEDGMENTS

I would like to take this opportunity to acknowledge the many special people who contributed to, and assisted in, the completion of *Fun with Mommy and Me*.

To Jane Schonberger, for her perseverance, experience, guidance, and friendship.

To Larry Bracco, my friend and partner, for taking my phone call, and for believing in the *Mommy and Me* project from the very beginning.

To Stella Bunin, my aunt, for all her nurturing, love, dedication, great craft ideas, poems, and delicious recipes. And thanks to Jerry Bunin, my uncle, for understanding and supporting the many hours of work Stella put into this project.

To Barbara Lazar and Laurie Berman, my colleagues and friends, for sharing their teaching experiences and knowledge.

To Dr. Jeffrey Greiff, for his faithful support, and contribution of medical advice.

To Barbara Yannucci, my dear friend, for her incredible patience, dedication, and the loving relationship with my daughter, Kacey.

To Sami, for his unconditional love.

To Lee Paseltiner, my first mentor and lifelong friend, for his constant encouragement throughout my life, and for teaching me at a very young age that I could do anything I set my mind to.

To Dr. James Drake, my second mentor, for all his inspiration throughout the years.

To Dr. Sinai Waxman for his professional input and support.

To Dr. Harvey Parker, for his experience and enthusiasm, from the beginning.

To my immediate family, for their love, support and encouragement.

To Ed Goldberg and Alan Gardner for all their brotherly love and advice.

To each and every person who contributed by nurturing and teaching me what is truly important in life—enabling me to achieve my goals and follow my dreams—my deepest gratitude.
  C.N.

Special thanks also go to our agent, Betsy Amster, whose advice was invaluable.

To our editor, Brian Tart, and former editor, Lori Lipsky, who understood the need for a book that helps make parenting fun.

To our Mommy and Me Enterprises colleagues—George Morency, Shelley Miles, Melissa Segal, Casey Sipes, Nina Wishengrad, and Marcie Ersoff—who read, and reread the manuscript.

To wordsmith Lynette Padwa who helped give the project a voice.

To Lisa Marsoli and Jon Rosenberg of Bumpy Slide Books whose organizational skills were unsurpassed.

To talented designer Nanette Yawitz.

To photographer extraordinaire Anthony Nex.

To the models who shared special moments with us on-camera.

And to the many *Mommy and Me* participants over the years who have contributed ideas, songs, games, and activities that celebrate the joys of together-time.
  J.S.

FROM THE DESK OF DR. CINDY NURIK

Welcome to the world of *Mommy and Me.*™ You and your child are about to embark on a special adventure filled with laughing, loving, learning, and togetherness. *Mommy and Me* was created for parents who want to make the most of the precious time they spend with their children. This time is but a whisper—just ask anyone with grown kids.

I've been a child-development specialist and educator for more than twenty years and have seen firsthand the benefits of sharing time with your young child. In my early clinical work, I studied the magical connection that can develop between parent and child. Convinced of the importance of this bond, I opened the Parent-Child Enrichment Center in Coral Springs, Florida, in 1979 where I developed a unique *Mommy and Me* curriculum. Over time I taught hundreds of classes and watched the program evolve and the children flourish.

In 1990 I became a mother. The moment my daughter, Kacey, was put into my arms and we made eye contact is one that will be etched in my memory forever. I realized then the responsibility that my husband and I had taken on, and I began to focus on the same issues as the parents in my classes: how could I make Kacey feel loved? How could I promote self-esteem and a love of learning? How could we make the most of the time we spent together?

I quickly discovered that the activities I'd created for my classes could help us enjoy our time together at home. Whether you have thirty minutes a day or thirty hours a week to devote to your child, *Fun with Mommy and Me* can help you take full advantage of that time. The collection of activities included here has been enjoyed by millions of parents and children over the years. They are designed to exercise young bodies, stimulate young minds, and help children have fun as they grow. Most of all, by sharing these *Mommy and Me* activities with your child, you are giving him or her a very precious gift—the gift of your time. I know from experience that your child will blossom in front of your eyes.

Wishing you fun-filled times together,

Dr. Cindy Nurik

Dr. Cindy Nurik

"The journey
of a thousand
miles begins
with a single
step."

—Lao Tzu

GETTING STARTED

1

*F*or the first five years of life, children live to play and play to learn. When your baby mimics the nursery songs you croon to him, he's not only bonding with you, he's trying out your language. When your daughter rolls a ball, she's not just having fun, she's discovering shape, light and shadow, and basic physics. Through play, children learn about themselves, other people, and the world around them.

Scientists now believe that the period from birth to age three is more important than any other in terms of brain development. It is during the first three years of life that the brain establishes its basic circuitry, literally wiring itself for the future. Stimulation—light, color, sound, and touch—encourages brain synapses to form, creating this crucial wiring. Then, between the ages of three and five, children's intellectual capabilities begin to bloom. By understanding the unique contributions you make to your child's development, you'll be able to nurture his growth during these critical first years. The best way to do this is by introducing games and activities that systematically build on the skills children acquire at each new stage.

NATURAL ABILITIES

And what will *you* gain from playing with your child, besides the obvious pleasure of it? Play offers a window into your child's soul. You'll find out what makes her laugh and what holds her attention. As you spend uninterrupted time together, away from telephones and TV, you'll discover how she reacts to triumphs and disappointments and the bond between the two of you will grow stronger. If you do the activities in this book on a regular basis, you're more likely to appreciate important developmental milestones in your child's life, such as drinking from a cup for the first time or following simple verbal directions.

Because this book offers a wide range of activities, you'll also be able to identify your child's aptitudes and passions much sooner than you might think. In one of my classes, a young mother was puzzled by her toddler's fascination with mud, water, and juice. As the weeks progressed and we completed a number of different projects, the little boy's motivation became clearer: he appeared to be a budding artist. He wanted to make pictures long before he had the words to tell his mother about it. "I had plenty of trucks and blocks for him at home," she told me, "but he never played with them for long. Last week I bought him some finger paints and sat him in the backyard on a big sheet of butcher paper. He went wild! It never would have occurred to me without your class.

Mommy's Memo

Watching how your child reacts to various challenges tells you a great deal about her temperament and problem-solving skills.

Mom, Did You Know?

The average weight of a newborn is 7½ pounds (3.4 kilos) with boys slightly heavier than girls. Ninety-five percent of full-term newborns weigh between 5½ and 10 pounds (2.5–4.6 kilos).

I thought painting was for older kids." That's the beauty of *Fun with Mommy and Me*—it gives mothers a chance to expose their children to all sorts of experiences they otherwise might not have at this young age. Along the way, parents begin to understand their child's unique potential.

As you play with your baby, you'll often catch her gazing at you intently. Few people will hang on your every word as much, or be as hungry for your touch as your infant or toddler. It's not just that she relies on you for nurturing, it's that she's getting to know you, too. The way you play with her will lay the foundation for a lifetime of trust and closeness.

WHY MOMMY AND ME?

The advice and activities in this book evolved from the thousands of hours I've spent with mothers and children in my *Mommy and Me* classes over the past twenty-five years. You've probably heard of *Mommy and Me* or know someone who attends a parent-child playgroup. These groups have sprung up all across the country over the past two decades, a direct result of the times we live in.

In past generations, moms stayed at home to raise their children. There were no such things as playgroups or play dates because kids played with other children in the neighborhood. Many new mothers could also count on an extended family to help raise their children. If Mom couldn't remember the words to "This Old Man," Grandpa could. If she wasn't sure when to start teaching her child manners, her own mother was there to offer an opinion, which could then be weighed against the opinions of the other moms on the block.

This built-in support system is a thing of the past for many of us. In its place, parent-child playgroups are there to offer a haven where new moms can spend time with one another, compare notes about their babies, and relearn the games and songs of childhood. Most important, the classes give moms an environment where they can interact with their children with no distractions. A mother who was in one of my groups a few years ago recalled how she had felt when she returned to work just three months after her daughter was born: "At first I could hardly stand being separated from her, but every Saturday morning we went to Dr. Cindy's *Mommy and Me*. We both knew that whatever else happened during the week, we'd have that time to reconnect. As little as Jenny was, I could tell she looked forward to it as much as I did."

I've written this book so that you'll be able to duplicate the most valuable parts of my *Mommy and Me* classes in your own home. In many ways, playing at home offers the best of all possible worlds: you can choose any hour to embark on an activity, you don't have to pack up and drive somewhere, and the fun takes places in the environment where your baby feels most comfortable. After reading this book, you may decide to start your own *Mommy and Me* group with friends. Whether you're home alone or with other moms and children, the basic elements of my *Mommy and Me* experience remain the same: a mother, a child, and a game or activity enjoyed together with no distractions.

FOCUSED TIME

When I first greet a new group of mothers and children, I tell them, "This class is about getting back to basics. Maybe you've heard that your child should be playing computer games by age two and practicing piano by four in order to get a head start in this competitive world. I feel differently. My parenting groups aren't about competing, they're about building strong emotional bonds with your children. Your children will develop on their own natural timetables. And the supplies we use are low tech—you can buy them at any market or drugstore. The real investment is your time, and the payoff is the relationship you'll have with your kids. As an extra bonus, you'll get some wonderful memories, too."

Time and emotional commitment go hand-in-hand when building a strong bond with your child. Over the years, I've

Mom, Did You Know?

The average length of a newborn is 20 inches (50 centimeters). Ninety-five percent of full-term newborns are between 18 and 22 inches (44–55 centimeters).

Mommy's Memo

Get down on the floor with your baby. You are the ultimate plaything, and any activity will seem more fun if your baby can share it with you.

Safe and Sound

When you're playing on the floor make sure you have some small quilts, beach towels, mats, or area rugs for comfort and safety. Wool rugs can be irritating, and a sensitive baby may react adversely. Synthetic, stain-resistant area rugs are a good alternative.

watched as overworked, pressured parents stress out their children by overscheduling them, too. I've seen how these children become emotionally deprived of their parents, while the parents struggle with feelings of guilt and inadequacy. Time together with your child is the best remedy for this situation. A cornerstone of my *Mommy and Me* philosophy is the use of *focused time*, time devoted exclusively to your child.

In my classes, focused time means that the mothers concentrate on their kids and refrain from chatting with one another about shoe sales or recent movies. When you're doing the activities at home, focused time means being there for your child. No answering the phone, feeding the cat, or sneaking a peek at the newspaper. No setting up an activity and then leaving your child to her own devices. No hurrying to finish and clean up the mess. While self-guided play has many benefits, the activities in this book were designed for two people. They work best when you're down on the floor, eye-to-eye with your little one, encouraging her curiosity and cheering her efforts.

BE COMMITTED

By spending focused time together early on, you'll lay the groundwork for a lifelong relationship based on mutual respect and understanding. Your child will face many hurdles as she grows up, from peer pressure to scholastic or sports anxiety. You'll want her to feel that she can confide in you, and you'll want to be able to communicate honestly with her when she does. To get to that point, you must invest the time now, when she's young. Although it's never too late to start building trust, the sooner you begin, the stronger the bond between you and your child will be.

The mothers who come to my classes are well aware of the challenges of raising children today. "I want to be a good mother," they'll announce. "How do you do it? What's the secret?" I tell them that I agree with the renowned child psychologist D. W. Winnicott, who said that there is no such thing as a perfect parent but that most of us are "good enough." Instead of trying to be perfect, I encourage parents to aim for emotional commitment by following these simple guidelines:

- Say "I love you" to your child at least once a day. Remember those bumper stickers that asked, "Have you hugged your kid today?" Live by that rule!
- Encourage your child's efforts and praise him frequently.
- Observe your child. Notice his likes and dislikes, and talk to him about them.
- Help your child cultivate new skills and interests. With so much media available, it's up to parents to make sure their children have hobbies that don't require a mouse or a remote control. Children who can't entertain themselves are easily bored, and bored children often get into trouble. The activities in this book are a good way to foster self-reliance and a love of learning.
- Involve yourself in your child's life—learn the names of his day-care friends, get to know his teacher, ask what happened on his favorite TV show. Show him that you're interested in his world.
- Most of all, listen to your child and give him eye contact for at least a few minutes every day.

None of us is going to be a perfect parent. We'll all yell at our child (sometimes in public), make promises we can't keep, and tally up our mistakes in the dead of night. Think of these guidelines, then, as preventive medicine. They aren't hard to practice, and they'll keep your relationship healthy.

HOW TO HAVE FUN WITH MOMMY AND ME

*E*ach activity in *Fun with Mommy and Me* is designed to help build important learning skills and nourish the parent-child bond. The activities are grouped by chronological age for babies and by calendar month for children ages two through five.

Mommy's Memo

Actions speak louder than words! While praise is wonderful, it's not as important as your undivided attention. It's when your child sees that you are truly interested in what she's doing that she feels valued.

Mom, Did You Know?

The average head circumference of a newborn is 14 inches (35 centimeters). The circumference of a baby's head increases by nearly 3 inches during the first eight months.

Daddy and Me

Although moms generally

spend more time with their

children than dads, it's

important for a child to

bond with both parents.

All of the activities

featured in this book

can be undertaken by

dads as well as moms

(or any other caregiver).

For babies, the activities are geared toward developing basic skills such as gross and fine muscle coordination, understanding and forming words, shape and color recognition, and comprehending cause and effect. Children ages two through five are treated to a monthly curriculum with a wider variety of games and activities.

MOMMY AND ME ACTIVITIES

Arts and crafts projects encourage creativity, hone fine motor skills, and teach children to stay with a task. It takes patience for little fingers to cut and paste or to fashion a puppet out of a paper bag and felt. These projects are also ideal for teaching educational concepts. Holidays, customs, spatial relationships, family history, and much more are explored through the arts and crafts in these pages.

Children universally adore cooking. It's also one of the most versatile activities you can share with your little one. Very young children love to pour, stir, and touch the ingredients, especially flour. Older children can learn basic weights and measures and can crack eggs, roll out dough, and use cookie cutters. Of course, everyone loves to decorate cakes and cookies. And as children begin to recognize letters, they can read the labels on food packaging. Associating the pictures with the words is a terrific way to get them to practice reading.

One of the most profound and beneficial forms of play involves music. As a registered music therapist, I've had many opportunities to observe its positive effects on children. Whether it's because of the exhilaration a toddler feels beating on a bevy of kitchen pots or the way a familiar tune can soothe a crying infant, music is a powerful force in every child's life. In addition to the joy it brings, music is also important to a child's development. It strengthens the ability to concentrate, which assists in learning. When children dance, they get exercise and improve their coordination. While listening to music, they learn new words and word patterns such as rhymes and alliteration. Above all, music brings you closer to your child. When you bathe him to the tune of "Baby Beluga" or hum "My Darling Clementine" as you stroll down the supermarket aisle, your song communicates love. For all these reasons, this book contains plenty of lyrics, and the activities often involve singing or some type of musical expression.

The traditional fingerplays and nursery and action rhymes in the book will delight your child and spur his intellectual growth. The words, actions, rhymes, and repetition are entrancing to babies and toddlers. In their first year, babies devote much of their time to two objectives: movement and speech. Fingerplays—"The Eensy Weensy Spider" is a classic example—helps develop these two basic skills. Children find fingerplays fascinating because they can immediately participate in the fun. The rhymes encourage mimicry, and repetition is essential to the development of speech and other cognitive skills. Nursery rhymes also appeal to all young children, who love to experiment with sounds and words. Toddlers learn language from your repetition and enunciation, and preschoolers learn syntax and practice memory skills by chanting the rhymes on their own. Many of us have a favorite action game or fingerplay from childhood, and you may recall the chants and rhymes found on these pages.

Reading is widely acknowledged to be the most beneficial thing a parent can do with a child in terms of bolstering language skills and imagination. In each chapter of this book, I direct you to fairy tales and contemporary favorites that will excite and entertain young listeners. These stories are excellent vehicles for expanding your child's awareness and exposing him to different places and people. As they listen, children will also learn about fundamental rules of good citizenship such as sharing, telling the truth, respecting adults, and standing up for what's right. When reading to a young child, the golden rule is to *go slowly*. Children need time to comprehend the words and build mental pictures of what's been said.

Along with the activities in *Fun with Mommy and Me*,

Mommy's Memo

Very young children don't really care what you're saying, they just love to hear your voice. So go ahead and make up all the silly rhymes you can think of. Before long you'll hear "More, Mommy, more!"

Mom, Did You Know?

In newborns, the head is larger, the face is rounder, and the jaw is smaller than in an adult. The chest is rounded, the abdomen is relatively prominent, and the extremities (arms and legs) are relatively short.

Mommy's Memo

It's a good idea to put everything you might need for one activity in a box or plastic bin. This helps you keep a variety of things ready for your baby to play with. You might have a Sand Toy Box, a Dress-Up Box, an Art and Crafts Box, and a Musical Activity Box.

I've included some of the other elements that have made my Mommy and Me classes so successful over the years. In the pages that follow, I give developmental guidelines that will help you know when to introduce your child to new activities. I provide tips on child safety and discipline, and I reveal my favorite strategies for relaxation.

TEN RULES OF THE ROAD

The activities in this book have complete, step-by-step instructions, and all the supplies and equipment you need are clearly listed. Try to make sure your schedule provides for both outdoor and indoor play, and aim for a balance of quiet time and active time. Before you begin, read the rules below. They apply to all the activities in *Fun with Mommy and Me*.

1. Choose a time and place where you and your child will not be interrupted.

2. Plan ahead. Decide which part of the curriculum you'll be working on and have all the necessary materials ready.

3. Make eye contact with your child. Let him know you are paying attention.

4. Don't rush. If you can't complete an activity, don't worry. Tell your child you will finish it tomorrow (and do it!). It's the quality of the time, not the quantity, that matters.

5. Don't overstimulate your child. If he or she gets fussy during an activity, stop. Have realistic expectations before you start, and remember, this is supposed to be fun.

6. Feel free to substitute words, colors, or ingredients in any activity in the handbook. After all, we're teaching children to be creative.

7. Don't compare your child's progress with that of other children. Each child grows and learns at his or her own pace.

8. Encourage other family members to join in the activities. The more the merrier. Your child will really enjoy the extra attention.

9. Be patient. If your child is unable to do a specific activity, give him several chances to feel successful by encouraging him. And don't forget to praise him for trying!

10. Let your child know how much fun you had and how proud you are of his efforts.

Now, let's begin!

Mommy's Memo

Many of the games, songs, and activities featured in this collection require only your time and enthusiasm.

Mom, Did You Know?

By age two, a child's head is 90 percent of its adult size.

"Every child is
born a genius."

—Richard Buckminster Fuller

BUSY
BABIES

2

HOW BABIES LEARN

Babies have an extraordinary drive to explore and discover their environment. After spending nine months in a dark, confined place, it must be an awesome experience to be thrust into a world of light and colors, smells, sounds, and touch. A speck of lint, a sunbeam, or a simple smile is endlessly fascinating to a new baby. The plethora of stimuli is exhausting, however, and newborns sleep a lot in order to recharge their batteries and process more of their surroundings.

When babies are awake, they spend every moment exploring and responding to their amazing new environment. Never again will the learning curve be as intense as it is during the first few months of life. As each day passes, they try to assimilate their new surroundings into their world. Babies use all their faculties to do this. Something is real only if it can be touched, seen, smelled, tasted, or heard. Placing an object in their mouths is just one way babies learn what's real. This oral exploration allows them to discover the taste and texture of different objects. Banging a toy on a table, shaking a rattle, or painting with pudding are also ways to process information. Interact with your baby as he interacts with his environment and you'll help stimulate cognitive development.

You can encourage your baby's learning in a number of ways. Stimulate her sense of touch with materials such as silk, tissue, felt, and terrycloth, or read *Pat the Bunny*, which makes touching part of the reading experience. Touching and massaging your baby are powerful ways to relax her and may even increase her alertness and attention span. Vocalize as much as possible by singing, reading, and talking to increase the aural connection between you and your baby. Let her delight in the scent of freshly baked bread, a whiff of vanilla, or a recently peeled orange, and offer visual stimuli whenever possible.

At first a baby uses his or her senses independently of one another. For instance, a newborn may listen to a sound but not use her eyes to see where it's coming from. Eventually the baby will use her senses simultaneously and begin associating them with people, events, and certain comforts. These skills develop naturally, but there are things you can do to encourage them and help your eager infant gain a grip on her environment.

A great way to encourage your baby is to bring her into your universe. Many parents think they need to manufacture constant stimuli, but that's not true. It's enough just to allow your baby to become part of your world in simple ways. When our daughter, Kacey, was small, I used to place her

Mommy's Memo

One of the hardest things for new moms to remember is to SLOW DOWN! Remember, your child is seeing things for the first time. Make sure you take time to linger over them with her.

Mom, Did You Know?

At birth, an infant's brain houses 100 billion nerve cells or neurons. A newborn's brain is about twenty-five percent of its approximate adult weight.

in her infant seat and set her on the kitchen table. Whether we were cooking, eating, or talking on the phone, she was there to observe her family's interactions. She was constantly fascinated by her surroundings and eager to interact with her environment.

YOUR BABY'S ENVIRONMENT

Decorating the nursery is one of the first opportunities you have to make an impact on your baby's life. It's important to make her surroundings stimulating and comfortable, but sometimes in our excitement we tend to go overboard and the room becomes a gigantic toy store. A good rule of thumb is, less is more. If a room is too cluttered with things for baby to see, touch, and hear, she can become overwhelmed and confused. I once had a neighbor who combined so many different colors, characters, and styles that the nursery was transformed into a theme park. Here are some basic tips for creating a pleasant environment:

- Hang simple pictures, snapshots, or wall hangings near the baby's crib and changing table so that she will be visually stimulated during changes and while in the crib.

- Place colored stars or shapes on the ceiling. After all, babies spend a great deal of time on their backs looking up. Why not make it interesting?

- Use colorful curtains, wallpaper, bumper pads, and bedding to make the room "come alive" and be more fun for the baby. Newborns respond best to sharply contrasting images, so feature some black and white toys and patterns during the first three months.

- Hang a mirror securely on the wall so the baby can look at herself. There are also crib toys on the market that contain mirrors. This will aid baby in developing a sense of self.

What all children need during the first months is love, warmth, comfort, and consistency. Try not to worry whether you have the latest, greatest baby merchandise on the market and concentrate on the greatest asset of all—your time.

- For auditory stimulation, attach a musical mobile or wind chimes to your baby's crib or playpen. This will encourage her to become aware of sound and movement.

A few carefully chosen decorations and toys are all it takes. Babies don't know the difference between expensive or inexpensive, and they're too young to differentiate between Target and Neiman Marcus. All they need is love, warmth, comfort, and consistency. So use your instincts, relax, and, above all, have fun!

THE MAGIC OF MUSIC

Infancy is a great time to expose your child to different forms of music. Just as an upbeat tune helps you fend off the blues or a soothing song helps you relax, your baby reacts to music in similar ways. Classical lullabies have been used to calm babies down for generations, and they often associate these melodies with sleep time. When babies are alert and active they respond to everything from reggae to rock and roll. Infants can definitely recognize a tune and will be able to distinguish favorites from a very young age.

With music boxes, CDs, cassettes, and musical instruments, you can introduce varying styles of music throughout the day. Try listening to classical composers such as Debussy or Mozart during dinner, waltz around the house to Chopin, or play Brahms softly when your baby is in his crib. Early Beatles songs are certain mood-lifters and Broadway or Top 40 tunes are great energizers. Of course there's also a large repertoire of children's recording artists who sing simple, catchy melodies that children like. But the music your baby will like best of all is you singing to him. The rhythms and melodies will help facilitate language development, and learning to recognize musical patterns is an important pre-math skill. (Don't underestimate the power of music!) So, get up, put on some music, and dance with your baby. He'll enjoy the rhythmic movement and will develop lifelong skills as well as an appreciation for all forms of music.

"Music and rhythm find their way into the secret places of the soul."

—Plato

Mom, Did You Know?

Vision is the slowest sense to develop. For the first few months, babies don't perceive color or focus on objects more than 15 inches away. Vision approaches 20/60 by age two.

LANGUAGE DEVELOPMENT

Research links verbal intelligence to how many words a child hears in the first year of life. Even if your baby is too young to talk back, talking to her stimulates brain development. You can lay a strong foundation by introducing your baby to verbal communication in a variety of ways. She might not be able repeat words yet, but she's definitely storing all the information in her rapidly developing memory.

The first months of life are a sensitive time, when verbal stimulation is particularly important for your baby. When my daughter was first put into my arms, I looked at her and immediately started chatting: "Hello, Kacey, I'm your mommy." I began to tell her all about myself and her daddy and how happy we were to finally see and hold her.

The nurse looked at me like I was crazy, saying "She doesn't understand a word you're saying." Rather than debate the issue I just smiled and continued the conversation with my little daughter. I knew that this chatter would make her feel secure and wanted. Even if I weren't familiar with the research, I could see for myself how intently Kacey reacted to the sound of my voice.

One of the first skills a newborn learns is that of listening to sounds in her environment. Watch your baby. If she had previously been active, when she hears a sound she will become quiet. If she's quiet and she hears a sound, she will become active. If she is sucking her thumb or a bottle when she hears a sound, she will stop in order to listen.

After she learns to listen, your infant will begin to look for the source of the sounds, and eventually she'll turn her head toward it. By cooing or making noises at your baby, by describing even the most mundane household chore, you're not only connecting with her but also encouraging her to listen. Your voice will become the familiar sound she listens for daily. Take advantage of every opportunity to engage her with a variety of words and sounds. When you're with friends, keep your baby nearby so she can hear the richness of human interaction.

Mommy's Memo

A baby in a bilingual home will get double the language training if she regularly hears both languages spoken. If you'd like her to learn more than one language, try to repeat each phrase in both languages, or have each parent speak to her in a different language.

Babies learn things about language before they ever understand words. Very early on, they begin to comprehend that spoken words have consequences. When I called out to my husband, Kacey understood that Daddy would come into the room (and he usually did!). As soon as a baby starts to listen to speech, she begins to learn the rhythm of language. Soon she'll start to coo and babble, and within the first two years, she'll try to imitate your speech.

HOW TO TALK TO YOUR BABY

Some people are naturally chatty. For them, it's easy to carry on a cheerful, one-sided conversation with an infant. Others aren't quite so loquacious and might even feel a little silly talking to a newborn. If you're wondering what to talk to your baby about, the answer is anything and everything. Think about all the things you hear, see, touch, and smell during the day. Share these experiences with your baby by talking and naming objects and describing your actions. Try to observe where she's looking and what interests her at the moment, then talk about whatever seems to be attracting her attention.

Here are some "baby-talk" topics:

- PEOPLE—When talking to your baby about people, speak in the third person to help clarify things. For example, instead of "I am going to put your diaper on," say, "Mommy is going to put Johanna's diaper on." Always call your baby by his or her name. The more you say it, the earlier the baby will learn it. "Peek-a-Boo" is a good game to play with your baby to reinforce this skill. (See page 36)

- BODY PARTS—When you're bathing your baby, name each body part as you wash. This will help him develop body awareness. Give him eye contact and smile, then

Mom, Did You Know?

Newborns demand as many as ten or more feedings a day; feeding frequency declines by nearly half during the first few months as the digestive system matures.

gently repeat, "This is (baby's name) head, shoulders, tummy, arms, legs, eyes, nose," and so on. You may even want to sing a song like "Head, Shoulders, Knees, and Toes."

- CLOTHING—As babies learn about their bodies, they will start to notice their clothing. When you're changing your baby's clothes, name each article of clothing as you pull it on or off. Be sure to incorporate verbs, such as *button, snap, lace, zip,* and *tie.* Allow your baby to feel the texture of the clothing, using descriptive words such as *soft, silky, fuzzy.* Name the colors, too.

- OBJECTS—If you're doing chores around the house, tell your baby exactly what you are doing. If you're cooking, talk about pots, pans, stove, oven, salt, butter, milk. When you're washing the dishes, name them. If you're in the mood to risk getting a little wet, let your baby play with the suds while you serenade her with "This is the way we wash the spoon. . . . " (See page 71)

- OUTINGS—Even a trip to the supermarket can be a chance to stimulate your child. As you roam the aisles, point to objects and identify them by name. At the doctor's office, the park, or your friend's house, keep your baby in the loop. While you don't want to wear her ears out with constant chatter, for the most part she will find your voice reassuring and will absorb the language more quickly if she hears it often.

There is one very special form of talking to your baby— reading. No matter how young he is, reading to your child will pay off. Long before he can understand the story, reading will help your baby develop an ear for the cadence of language. There are plenty of good books to read to babies — such as *Goodnight Moon* and *Guess How Much I Love You,* and the chapters that follow list many of these. Choose board books with large, bright pictures and simple text, or even wordless books with pictures for you to narrate. Books designed for older children with clear images and bright colors can also captivate a baby. Or you can read poetry originally written for adult ears. What your baby doesn't understand will nonetheless delight him because of the sound of your voice and the rhythm of the words.

ACTIVITIES AND MILESTONES

The "Busy Baby" activities on the following pages are divided into chronological stages. These divisions are made with specific developmental goals in mind. As your baby acquires more muscle control, her range of activities will increase. Each activity is simple and easy to follow, allowing you to be an active participant in your child's growth.

While observing your baby's development, remember not to judge her too harshly. I've had moms who asked for an appraisal after a couple of classes and seemed truly disappointed when I wasn't able to assure them of their child's entrance into Harvard or Yale. You and your child will grow together, and in time each of you will gain essential experience and the necessary skills to succeed in life.

While I've included monthly milestones in each section, it's important to remember that babies are unique individuals who develop at their own pace. From rolling over, to sitting up, to taking those first steps, *normal* is a relative term.

Whether a baby reaches developmental milestones early or late bears little relation to either their cognitive skills or their future proficiency, so there's absolutely no reason to push. Even those destined for Ivy League schools may be slow starters in some areas. My developmental guidelines are general, therefore, and will not apply to every baby. If you're concerned about whether your baby is reaching appropriate milestones, talk with your pediatrician.

Mommy's Memo

Look before you leap— to conclusions, that is. The more you observe your child, the better you will get to know him. He won't do things the way you do, but then again, why should he? He's his own little person.

Mom, Did You Know?

There are thirteen natural reflexes that newborns have, including sucking, grasping, and blinking.

In the first three months of life, babies absorb everything around them. The world is brand new and every bit of it is fascinating. Toward the end of the first month, your baby will become more alert and start to focus on external stimuli.

By two months of age, she'll be able to differentiate between her mother and father. By the third month, she'll become quite social. She'll start to reach out with her hands and explore the world in dramatic new ways. Every time you play a game, sing a song, or recite a rhyme, you teach your baby something new and strengthen the bond between you. There's no need, however, to push your baby to learn. She'll develop skills naturally through trial and error. All you need to do is provide a stimulating and nurturing environment where she can develop at her own pace.

0-3 MONTHS
Newborns

MONTHLY MILESTONES

0 to 1 Month
Sucks
Startles at loud noises
Moves arms and legs rapidly
Cries when wet or hungry
Makes some throaty noises
Can focus on objects 8–12 inches away

1 Month
Likes to stare at faces, especially eyes
May be able to visually follow an object
Responds to voices, rattles, and other sounds
May vocalize in ways other than crying
If held in standing position, may step reflexively

2 Months
Smiles, coos, and laughs
Looks at hands
May hold a rattle briefly
Rolls from side to back
Attempts to hit or kick objects nearby

3 Months
Can reach for objects
Lifts head when placed on stomach
Holds head erect when held in sitting position
Kicks legs actively
May suck thumb
Puts objects into mouth
Looks at fingers and hands
Laughs out loud when happy

FUNNY FACES AND SILLY SOUNDS

Discovery Game

Your Baby Will Learn

Voice recognition

Face recognition

Gross motor skills

Bonding

Mommy's Materials

Your face, mouth, and voice

*S*tudies show that the human face is far more interesting to a baby than fabricated designs and patterns, so why waste money on expensive toys or decorations? Your baby will look adoringly at you whether or not you're wearing makeup, your hair is washed, or you've got bags under your eyes from lack of sleep. And your voice is alluring whether you're tone deaf or have a five-octave range. Vocalizing in fun and interesting ways makes the aural connection between you and your baby that much more stimulating.

STEP BY STEP

1. Move in close to your baby (approximately 8–12 inches away).

2. Try singing a song in a high voice and then repeat the same song in a low voice. Watch the reaction of your baby to the two different sounds.

3. Make funny faces—stick out your tongue, raise your eyebrows, wiggle your ears if you can, wink or blink your eyes, scrunch your nose, and so on.

4. Give your newborn a chance to imitate your facial expressions. (She may not do anything yet but she's definitely watching).

5. Repeat the sounds your baby makes. Add sounds of your own: blow raspberries, hum, buzz, whistle, shush, click your tongue, speak with accents.

6. Puff out your cheeks and press your baby's hands or the soles of her feet against them; let the air rush out with a whoosh.

MORE MOMMY AND ME FUN

A Staring Contest: Engage your baby in a time-honored ritual of seeing who'll blink first. He may surprise you. Chances are that before he gets bored you'll have dropped your gaze, wondering where he got that amazing dimple, those full lips, or whether his nose looks like yours or his father's.

Baby Faces: Babies love looking at other babies. Glue photos or pictures of baby faces (old parenting magazines are a good source) to a piece of poster board and prop it up so your baby can see. You'll be amazed to see him coo and smile as he "converses" with his new friends.

Silly Songs: From "Ta Ra Ra Boom De Ay" and "Polly Wolly Doodle" to "Mairzy Doats" and "John Jacob Jingleheimer Schmidt," there are loads of silly songs to sing. Lose any inhibitions you have about singing out loud and put on a private, silly-inspired concert for your little one.

Mommy's Memo

Your baby will react to everyone, but your face will always launch the biggest smile.

Mom, Did You Know?

Beginning in the womb, babies are able to distinguish the sound of human voices. Brain research indicates that when a baby hears a high-pitched voice, his heart rate increases and he feels cheerful. A lower-pitched voice makes him feel calm and content.

• 0–3 MONTHS ACTIVITIES •

25

EYE CANDY
Visual Tracking

Your Baby Will Learn

Observation

Concentration

Visual stimulation

Spatial relationships

Shapes and color

Head and eye muscle
development

Mommy's Materials

A small colored ball or
a toy

As you observe your young baby, you may be surprised at the clarity of his gaze and how well he can lock on to an object within his field of vision. Even newborns can locate and stare at an object, particularly a sharply contrasting pattern or design, if it is held at the right distance—8–12 inches (approximately the distance at which a nursing infant sees his mother's face). By providing visual stimulation, you'll get to see how well your baby can control his vision and you'll discover what signals he uses to look at and track various objects.

STEP BY STEP

1. Place a ball or toy in your hand about 9 inches away from your baby's eyes and move it back and forth. You may jiggle it a little to get his attention.

2. Wait until the baby's eyes lock on to the object. Then move it very slowly and watch him track it. If you go too fast, he'll lose it. The object will hold his gaze like a magnet as long as it remains within his range of vision.

3. At the beginning, your baby may only be able to track the object for a very short period. Keep doing this daily and you will see him progress. By about three months, he will probably be able to follow an object from side to side as well as track vertical motion.

MORE MOMMY AND ME FUN

Rattle: Use a rattle instead of a ball or toy and see if your baby responds to the noise it makes. Many babies use their hearing to locate and track an object.

Fingers: Slowly wiggle your index finger in front of your baby's eyes to get his attention. Wiggle your finger to the left and to the right, and see if he continues to follow with his eyes. Create a starburst with your hand.

Mobile: Dangle a brightly colored or sharply contrasting mobile or object a foot in front of your baby's face. Try to stay out of his visual range as you move the mobile slowly from side to side. See if your baby can lock on to it. You may see him lose control of his eyes once the mobile has gone beyond his visual-spatial range. Continue practicing and keep track of his range of focus.

Flashlight: Slowly move a flashlight back and forth and watch your baby track the beam of light on the wall. Make sure not to shine the light directly into your baby's eyes.

Mommy's Memo

Your baby has his own language to tell you how appropriate a visual stimulus is for him. If the object is dull or uninteresting, he'll turn away from it. If it has too much contrast or too much color, it may be too stimulating and he will avoid it.

Mom, Did You Know?

When an infant looks at a moving object, a neuron from his retina connects to the visual part of his brain, helping to develop his vision.

BABY MASSAGE
Sensory Stimulation

Your Baby Will Learn

Bonding

Body awareness

Listening/Language skills

Sensory awareness

Relaxation

Mommy's Materials

Changing pad or
soft surface

Relaxing music

Baby lotion or oil (optional)

Safe and Sound

Make sure to test all oil or lotion on a small patch of skin first for allergic reactions.

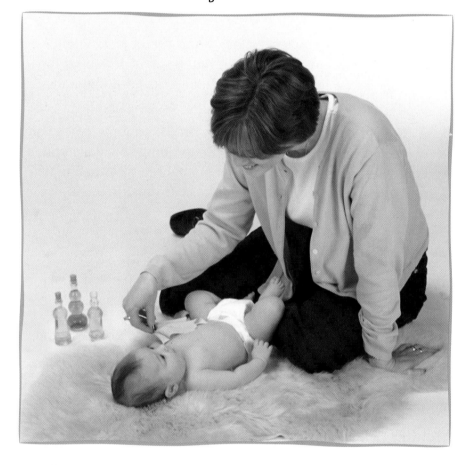

One of the best ways to bond with your baby is through massage. Just as it does for adults, massage can release a baby's tension and help her relax. Baby massage can improve circulation and sometimes relieve colic. It also stimulates the digestive and respiratory systems. Most important, baby massage establishes a level of physical intimacy that helps with the process of bonding. Through nonverbal communication your baby begins to understand how much you love her. She'll learn to trust you and will feel safe and secure when she feels your touch. This pleasurable activity has great benefits for both participants.

STEP BY STEP

1. Undress your baby, leaving only her diaper on. Be sure the room is a comfortable temperature.

2. Lay her down on a bed, changing pad, or the floor.

3. Gently massage your baby's arms and hands, legs and feet. Move from the shoulder down the arm to the hand and from the thigh down to the foot. At the hands and feet, be sure to massage your baby's toes and fingers.

4. Massage your baby's chest and shoulders. Turn her on her tummy (or lay her across your knees) and massage her back. Start from the shoulders and move down toward the buttocks.

5. As you massage, sing or talk gently to your baby or play soft music.

MORE MOMMY AND ME FUN

Tickle Time: When your baby is resting on the changing table or bed, blow air gently through a straw and tickle your baby. As you direct the air to her stomach, arms, legs, and feet, be sure to mention each body part.

Silk or Satin: Use different objects to stroke your baby. A silk or satin scarf, a feather, washcloth, a piece of velvet, or a cotton ball are good choices. Name the parts of the body that you touch.

Hand Rub: Use different hand motions—firm strokes with your palms, gentle kneading, or finger taps. Massage your baby's head by making soft rhythmic circles along the cheeks and temples. Slide your thumbs from the forehead down the sides of your baby's face.

Aromatherapy: The rich aromas of aromatherapy massage oils trigger physical and emotional responses in both adults and babies. Essential oils such as lavender, eucalyptus, and rosemary can relax and soothe little bodies. Warm the scented oil or lotion in your hands before applying and gently rub into your baby's skin (avoiding the face and eyes).

Mommy's Memo

Try not to massage your baby when she's ready for a meal or has a full tummy.

Mom, Did You Know?

Baby massage and touch has been shown to improve the growth and development of premature babies. Skin-to-skin contact, sometimes referred to as "kangaroo care," is the practice of "pouching" an infant against a parent's bare chest.

• 0-3 MONTHS ACTIVITIES •

29

DIAPER PARTY
Sensory Stimulation

Your Baby Will Learn

Bonding

Body awareness

Sensory awareness

Mommy's Materials

Diaper

Small squeak or stuffed toy, or mobile

Changing pad

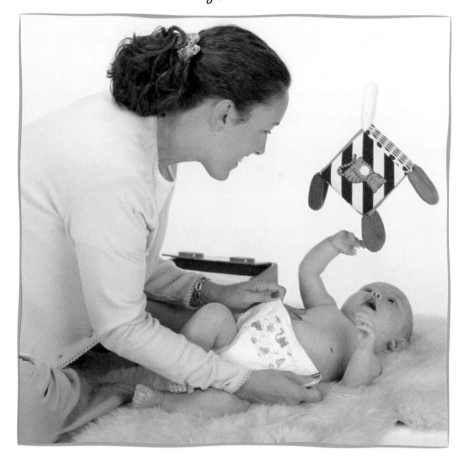

*S*ome babies lie on their backs and happily wave their chubby legs in the air as you change their diaper. Others kick, cry, and flail, making the procedure stressful for both of you. If your baby is one of the latter, don't worry. There are plenty of ways to make diaper changing a more enjoyable experience for you and your child. Being able to transform diaper changing into a positive experience helps foster a good relationship with your infant. The skin-to-skin contact will help her relax, and many babies are so comforted by this activity that they will stop crying and be ready for play.

STEP BY STEP

1. Place your child gently on a changing table or soft surface.

2. Give her a diaper or small toy to inspect while you're changing her (if her hands are busy, she might be less active).

3. Talk to your child while you are moving her and changing her diaper. Describe what you are doing. Use an exaggerated voice so she keeps her attention on you.

4. If it helps, sing a song. Try this to the tune of "Row, Row, Row Your Boat."

> *Change, change, change your diaper.*
> *Wow, it's really smelly!*
> *Take it off, wipe and wash,*
> *Now, I'll kiss your belly!*

MORE MOMMY AND ME FUN

Sights and Sounds: A wind-up mobile over the changing table can help provide visual stimulation (hang it slightly to the side). Pictures hung at eye level to the changing table will also entertain your baby.

Bangle Break: A bangle bracelet on your wrist is sometimes a good distraction. You can also take the bracelet off and let your baby hold it while you change her.

Live Entertainment: If your baby has older siblings, have them help you keep the baby entertained while you're at the changing station. Recite nursery rhymes. Sing songs. Smile and coo back at baby when she smiles and coos. Try giving simple directions. Ask your baby to "smile" and then smile at her.

Tickle Time: When all else fails, try tickling. Start at her head and tickle each part of her body as you work your way down to the Velcro or pins. Switch to the other side and work your way up, naming the body parts as you tickle.

Mommy's Memo

The trick to changing diapers without a fuss is to involve baby, be quick, and provide plenty of distractions. Take heart. You won't be changing diapers forever.

Mom, Did You Know?

An average baby goes through 10,000 diaper changes.

Safe and Sound

Try using alcohol-free wipes if possible. Baby wipes that contain alcohol tend to make your baby's bottom too dry.

From four to six months your baby is babbling, cooing, laughing, and interacting. You'll notice him becoming an active participant and making a real effort to be social. Often referred to as lap babies, infants this age can support their heads but may not be able to sit up by themselves yet. Still, their increased muscle development allows for a larger reper-toire of games and activities. During this stage, mimicry becomes an important element of play. As your baby's throat and facial muscles mature, his "talking" will become more sophisticated. As early as four months, your child will begin to use many of the tones and patterns he hears you using. He may experiment with repeating one sound for a whole day or even days at a time before trying a new one. In addition to sound recognition, games and activities for this age group start to integrate new skills such as eye-hand coordination, motor development, and body awareness.

4-6 MONTHS
Lap Babies

MONTHLY MILESTONES

4 Months
Rolls from back to side
Kicks
Laughs, talks, and coos to people and toys
Makes funny noises
Plays with fingers
When lying on tummy, can support chest and head with arms
Will follow objects with eyes
When pulled to a sitting position, can keep head straight
May start eating solid foods
Uses both hands to reach
May make consonant sounds such n, d, p, or b

5 Months
Will be able to sit briefly with support
Rolls from stomach to side
Recognizes family members
Uses hands to put food into mouth
Likes looking at self in the mirror
When held in a standing position, will bounce up and down
Grasps small objects with both hands
May make several sounds—*oo-ee-ah*

6 Months
Drinks from cup with help
Plays by banging things
Drops toys on purpose and looks for them
Can sit briefly without support
Transfers objects from one hand to the other
Will imitate sounds
May add more sounds—*v, sh*
Will be able to show pleasure and displeasure

Your Baby Will Learn

Observation

Eye-hand coordination

Listening/Language skills

Sound recognition

Social skills

Cause and effect

Mommy's Materials

A small, colorful, lightweight, nontoxic rattle

SHAKE, RATTLE, AND ROLL
Playtime

The very first games you play with your baby will probably involve a rattle. Available in all shapes and colors, rattles are sure attention-grabbers that will delight your child. Just reaching for an object like a rattle helps the brain develop eye-hand coordination. When your baby first grabs and shakes his rattle, he might not realize that he is the one making all the noise. Be patient—eventually he'll figure it out, and before long he'll clutch the rattle with both hands and really shake things up.

STEP BY STEP

1. Sit your baby on your lap or in an infant seat.

2. Hold the rattle directly in front of him so that he sees it.

3. Shake the rattle several times while saying, "See the rattle? Do you hear the sound it makes?" When he responds to the sounds, be sure to praise him.

4. With encouragement, he will eventually reach for the rattle (and probably try to put it in his mouth).

5. While he holds the rattle, move his hand back and forth and watch him try to follow the sound.

MOMMY-MADE

You can create your own rattles by filling small plastic cups, plastic eggs, or film canisters with various small objects. Different items create different sounds. Experiment with rice, beans, seeds, or macaroni. Oversize noise-makers (for two hands) can be made from resealable containers such as coffee cans or food storage boxes filled with beads, dried pasta, or marbles.

MORE MOMMY AND ME FUN

High and Low: Shake the rattle on one side of your baby and then the other. Shake it high and low. Encourage him to search for the sound. If he doesn't reach for the rattle, take his hand and put his little fingers around it. He will instinctively hold on to it, shake it, and inevitably drop it. As he gets older, he'll learn to pass the rattle from hand to hand. When you shake the rattle, sing this song to the tune of "Mary Had a Little Lamb."

> *Shake your rattle,*
> *Shake, shake, shake,*
> *Shake, shake, shake,*
> *Shake, shake, shake,*
> *Shake your rattle,*
> *Shake, shake, shake,*
> *Hear the sound it makes!*

Mommy's Memo

Playing with a rattle provides one of the first lessons in cause and effect. When your baby shakes the rattle, it makes a sound. Once he makes that connection, your baby gains a sense of power and control.

Safe and Sound

Make certain that homemade rattles are securely fastened so your baby can't open them and swallow what's inside.

PEEK-A-BOO!
Classic Game

Your Baby Will Learn

Object permanence

Voice recognition

Eye development

Anticipation

Social interaction

Mommy's Materials

Your face and hands

Blanket, cloth diaper, or
puppet (optional)

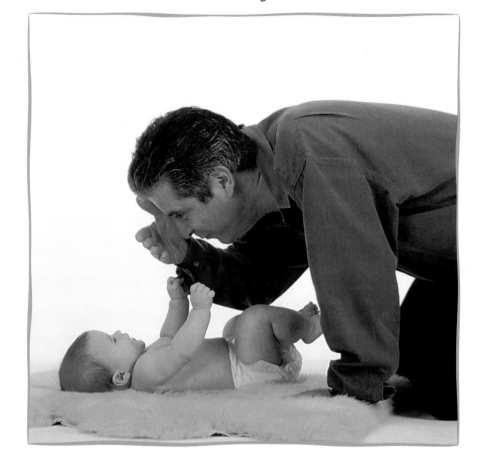

*P*eek-a-boo is magic. You can play it anytime, anywhere, and it never fails to amuse. The delight your baby expresses comes from seeing you disappear and magically reappear. Peek-a-boo is a game babies never seem to tire of, so be prepared for numerous variations in the coming months. With every version, thousands of neural connections are formed or strengthened, adding a bit more development to the complex "wiring" that takes place in your child's brain. You'll find yourself playing over and over again as your baby delights in rediscovering your face.

STEP BY STEP

1. Move your face in and out of your baby's visual range as you say "peek-a-boo." His eyes will follow you and you may even get a smile or two.

2. Cover your face with your hands and ask, "Where's Mommy or Daddy?" Wait about three seconds before taking your hands away. Your baby will laugh with joy when he sees your face again.

3. Hold a blanket, a cloth diaper, or a napkin between you and your baby and ask, "Where's Jonathan?" Reveal his face and say, "Peek-a-boo, Mommy or Daddy sees you!" (Use proper names whenever possible since babies don't yet understand pronouns.)

MORE MOMMY AND ME FUN

Peek-a-Boo Plus: Play peek-a-boo when you come around the corner into the room or when you're waiting in a restaurant or at the supermarket. You can use a menu or a box of cereal to hide your face, or you can play peek-a-boo with a puppet. You can even play when pulling a shirt over your baby's head or with a towel when drying off after a bath.

Peek-a-Boo Plate: Draw or glue a large colorful face onto a paper plate or large lid. Show your baby the face. Turn it over and show the blank side. Turn it back over and say, "Peek-a-boo," as the face gradually comes into view.

Peek-a-Boo Window: Glue a photo of a face (if possible use a picture of your baby) on a piece of poster board. Cut a peek-a-boo window flap on a plain piece of paper and tape over the picture. Play peek-a-boo by lifting the flap and revealing the baby picture.

Rhyme Time: Try this traditional rhyme—

> Peek-a-boo, peek-a-boo,
> Who's that hiding there?
> Peek-a-boo, peek-a-boo,
> (Child's name)'s behind the chair!

Mommy's Memo

When playing peek-a-boo, your baby is learning a concept known as object permanence: objects (and people) have a permanent existence even when they can't be seen. Babies find this a reassuring experience as well as a funny one.

Mom, Did You Know?

A newborn has a visual memory of about three seconds.

FUNNY FINGERS AND TICKLY TOES
Fingerplay

Your Baby Will Learn

Motor skills

Listening/Language skills

Social skills

Anticipation

Body concepts

Mommy's Materials

Your hands

Finger puppets (optional)

Safe and Sound

Toys given to infants should be at least 1⅝" in diameter. Make sure toys have no small pieces or sharp edges and can be easily sanitized.

*O*nce they discover them, babies are especially intrigued with toes and fingers. I've seen four- and five-month-olds become literally hypnotized looking at their own hands and feet. With finger games, you'll find recognizable, repeatable patterns that babies love. Add tickling to the activity, and you'll get hours of pleasure. Babies love to anticipate the tickling part, making rhymes like "This Little Piggy" perennial favorites.

STEP BY STEP

1. Place your baby in front of you and start wiggling your fingers. Follow the action as the rhyme indicates:

> *I have ten little fingers*
> *And they all belong to me.*
> *I can make them do things.*
> *Would you like to see?*
> *I can shut them up tight*
> *Or open them wide.*
> *I can put them together*
> *Or make them all hide.*
> *I can make them jump high,*
> *I can make them jump low,*
> *I can fold them quietly*
> *And hold them just so.*
> *And I can tickle baby*
> *Let's go, go, go!*

2. For a toe game, try "This Little Piggy." After your baby learns the rhyme, slow down on the last line to build anticipation.

> *This little piggy went to market* (hold big toe),
> *This little piggy stayed home* (hold second toe).
> *This little piggy had roast beef*
> (or tofu, or pizza—hold third toe),
> *This little piggy had none* (hold fourth toe).
> *And this little piggy cried "wee, wee, wee,"*
> *all the way home.*
> (tickle all the way up to the belly)

MORE MOMMY AND ME FUN

Finger and Toe Art: For a great art project, place your baby's feet or hands in a tray of nontoxic paint and then on a large sheet of paper. Try to save the prints and date them. Repeat every two months to document your baby's growth. You can even frame the prints and give them as a gift.

Mommy's Memo

Fingerplays are often regarded as the perfect activity for a young baby. They combine two of the fundamental skills of babyhood—movement and speech—into an entertaining game.

Mom, Did You Know?

A baby's nervous system develops from head to toe and physical milestones follow suit. Head control comes first, followed by arm and hand movements, body control, and finally walking.

WEE WORKOUT
Exercise

Your Baby Will Learn

Coordination

Awareness of body parts

Listening/Language skills

Gross motor skills

Bonding

Social skills

Mommy's Materials

Changing table, flat padded surface, or soft mat

*E*veryone loves a good workout, and babies are no exception. Even before they have control of their own movements they enjoy exercising their arms and legs. Guiding their movements helps babies develop muscle coordination and allows them to become acquainted with the parts of their body. Head turns, leg lifts, stretches, and kicks are all necessary for proper muscle development. A daily exercise routine will be both stimulating and entertaining for your little one. Before long, he'll be rolling, kneeling, and crawling all by himself.

STEP BY STEP

1. Lay baby on his back on a soft mat, blanket, or bed.

2. Place your thumbs in baby's fist. He'll grasp your fingers. (This is one of the thirteen natural reflexes of newborns.)

3. Wrap your fingers around his to be sure you have a secure grip.

4. Now say to baby, "Hang on—up we go, up, up, up!" Gently pull his arms up toward you, and his head should lean toward you a little off the floor. (If he is unable to hold his head up, wait until he has better head control.)

5. Now gently place your baby back down. "Down we go. Down, down, down."

6. Do this procedure several times. As your baby gets stronger, you can pull him up higher (remember to pull gently, though). Make this a daily exercise routine with your baby and just watch him grow.

MORE MOMMY AND ME FUN

Stretching Exercises: Limber up your baby with stretching exercises. Raise his arms over his head or rotate his legs in a lateral motion. Bring one arm and the opposite leg together. Gently cross his arms over his chest, letting him hug himself. Then stretch his arms out wide.

Batter Up: Encourage a baby who loves to kick to do target practice with his feet. Or hang a toy within reach and let him bat at it with his hands.

Young Cyclist: With your baby on his back, hold his feet and move his legs toward his body one at a time in a cycling motion. As you're cycling, sing to the tune of "Row, Row, Row Your Boat."

> *Move, move, move your legs,*
> *Like a little bunny.*
> *Faster, faster, faster, faster*
> *(Baby's name)'s so cute and funny!*

Mommy's Memo

Once your baby can support the weight of his head well, balance his body on your palms and then carefully curl him or bench-press him. Both your biceps and your baby will love the exercise.

Safe and Sound

Once your baby can roll over, be certain you don't leave him alone and in danger of falling off a bed, sofa, or changing table.

WHITE HOUSE TOUR
Language Development

Your Baby Will Learn

Listening/Language skills

Vocal patterns

Awareness of environment

Mommy's Materials

You and your voice

Household objects

To an infant, your home is as wondrous as a theme park, and if you pay attention you might be able to discover her favorite rides—the rooms, colors, and smells that are especially appealing to her. The more she can touch or physically interact with, the better. Turn on the tap in the kitchen and put her hand under cool running water. Open and close the blinds. Turn on the sprinklers outside and watch the rainbows that appear in them. Once you're tuned in to the possibilities, you'll be surprised at how entertaining your home can be.

STEP BY STEP

1. Go from room to room and describe each location: "The kitchen is for cooking food—mmmmm," "The bedroom is for sleeping—ooooooh, nice," and so on. Be sure to describe shapes, colors, smells, and sounds.

2. Every time you pass a mirror, tap on it, and your baby will turn her head toward it. Say "Look at the baby. See Jen. What a cute baby!" This assists baby in self-awareness.

3. When you pass a painting or picture, stop. Hold your baby in front of it and describe it.

4. Be sure to draw attention to the items you have put on the walls or ceiling. Point or snap to get the baby's attention. Blow on a wind chime or mobile to get it moving.

5. Go out in the yard and point out trees, flowers, cars, birds, and of course, your neighbors.

MORE MOMMY AND ME FUN

Road Trip: Whether you're running errands, going to a doctor's appointment, or visiting friends, point out all of the sights and sounds you encounter along the way. At the supermarket point out the colors and shapes of the produce; a visit to a friend presents a new display of home furnishings to describe; and a ride in the car offers up opportunities to talk about landmarks and signposts along the way.

Art Gallery Tour: Visit a museum or art gallery to describe new shapes and colors. Talk about the paintings and sculptures that you see. Children's museums often have hands-on exhibits where you can discuss what things feel like.

Reporter: You can report on the weather, recite the sports scores, announce the stock market quotes, or read the newspaper aloud. Provide a running account of your day: "Mommy is changing your diaper," "Mommy is making your lunch," "Here comes the mail," and so on. By keeping your baby in the loop, you're acknowledging her importance in your life.

Mommy's Memo

Speak clearly and slowly and enunciate well to give your baby an opportunity to distinguish individual words. Talk face-to-face whenever possible.

Mom, Did You Know?

At first, a baby speaks vowels and consonants randomly. Real words usually appear sometime around the first birthday.

• 4–6 MONTHS ACTIVITIES •

At seven, eight, and nine months old, babies are crawlers. They've mastered sitting up and are ready to explore the world around them. With mobility comes increased danger, so babyproofing your home is essential. Cognitive development continues to take place as the baby learns about spatial relationships and cause and effect. She'll be able to pick up and drop objects with both hands and solve problems such as how to pick up a third toy when she's already clutching playthings with both hands. With increasing physical coordination, your baby is no longer as dependent on you. She's beginning to develop self-awareness and her own personality. As your baby continues to develop control of her body, and as her verbal understanding increases, you'll be able to add activities that focus on sound and movement as well as creative play.

7-9 MONTHS
Crawlers

MONTHLY MILESTONES

7 Months
Sits alone for short intervals
May start combining sounds—*mamaa, bababa, dedede*
Is able to get into sitting position
Holds two objects, one in each hand, and transfers
Will rock when on hands and knees
Rolls from back to stomach
Is able to briefly bear weight on feet

8 Months
May show fear of strangers (stranger anxiety)
Is able to chew and bite
Uses thumb and two of four fingers to pick up objects
Responds to his or her name
Will babble and imitate your mouth movements
Can pivot body while lying on stomach
Can sit alone for longer periods of time

9 Months
Attempts to crawl
Sits without support
Screams to get attention
Will not share toys
May point to nose, eyes, and so on
Uses furniture to pull up on
Reacts to the word *no*
Continues to babble

BOUNCING BABY
Exercise

Your Baby Will Learn

Rhythm

Anticipation

Listening/Language skills

Balance

Gross motor skills

Mommy's Materials

Your lap

A chair

Once your baby sits up well, she's ready to straddle your knees while you bounce her up and down and sing a rhyming song. In fact, your lap is sure to become one of your baby's favorite spots—a secure sanctuary where she'll enjoy many special moments, including lively lap games. The songs, movements, and musical games you play on your lap are part of the brain exercises that introduce children to speech patterns, sensory motor skills, and essential movement skills.

STEP BY STEP

1. Sit your baby on your lap facing you, or outward.

2. Hold her under her arms.

3. Sit on the edge of the chair and lift your heels so your baby gets a good bounce.

4. Try this pair of bouncing rhymes to get started:

"Down By the Banks"

> *Down by the banks of the hanky panky*
> (bounce baby)
> *Where the bullfrogs jump from bank to banky,*
> (move from one knee to the other)
> *They went oops, ops, belly flops,*
> (open your knees)
> *One missed the lily pad*
> *And went kerplop!*
> (while holding your baby securely, let her slide down to the ground)

"Duke of York"

> *The grand old Duke of York,*
> *He had ten thousand men.* (bounce baby)
> *He marched them up to the top of the hill*
> (march your legs higher)
> *And he marched them down again.*
> (march your legs down)
> *And when you're up, you're up,*
> (raise both legs or lift baby)
> *And when you're down, you're down.*
> (drop both legs or sit baby back down)
> *And when you're only halfway up*
> (raise legs halfway or lift baby halfway)
> *You're neither up nor down.*
> (move legs up and down or lift baby up and down)

Mommy's Memo

When you recite a rhyme, you're introducing important language skills. Speak clearly and allow your baby to see your mouth. Enunciate and accentuate the rhyming words. You can even exaggerate your diction for added emphasis.

Safe and Sound

Be sure to support your baby's head and neck at all times.

PUPPET PARTY
Creative Play

Your Baby Will Learn

Eye-hand coordination

Listening/Language skills

Social skills

Imagination

Mommy's Materials

A puppet or stuffed animal

Creative play is an important aspect of intellectual and social development. Playing pretend opens the door to all sorts of possibilities and can keep some children occupied for hours. Throw a Puppet Party and watch your child's facial response. Does he smile? Does he react to the puppet as if it were a real person? The more you talk with the puppet, the more your child's verbal communication skills will grow. You'll provide a good foundation for language development while having fun at the same time.

STEP BY STEP

1. Put your baby on your lap or beside you and put the puppet on your hand.

2. Sing songs, recite poems, make the puppet come to life.

3. Change the pitch of your voice for different characters or puppets. Experiment with different emotions. Pretend to be happy, sad, tired, or timid.

4. Watch your baby's face light up with laughter as you move the puppet from side to side and animate it with your hand.

5. Try moving the puppet up and down and in a circle to see if your baby can follow the movement.

MOMMY-MADE

You don't need an expensive store-bought puppet or doll for this activity. You can use old socks, mittens, a pillowcase or a paper bag to create fun puppets. In a pinch, you can even turn your hand into a puppet or draw an entire cast of characters on your fingertips. Try drawing a face on the back of a wooden spoon, a tongue depressor, or a paper plate.

MORE MOMMY AND ME FUN

Bye-Bye: Puppets can also help teach nonverbal communication. Waving bye-bye is a good example. Your baby actually learns to associate a gesture with a word. First, have the puppet wave bye-bye. Then say, "Can you wave bye-bye?" Practice this over and over and pretty soon your baby will be waving bye-bye to everyone.

Role-Play: For older children, role-playing with puppets is an effective way to help them express their feelings. It's sometimes easier to express anger or fear through a puppet than it is to confront a problem head on. And you can help demonstrate how to handle difficult situations. You can also ask your child to tell you about the puppet. Does he have a name? A family? An adventure to share? Sit back and listen as your child's imagination kicks into high gear.

Mommy's Memo

During playtime, be aware of your baby's temperament. If he is frightened of a puppet, try again another time.

Safe and Sound

Be sure puppets are nontoxic and the eyes are securely attached so that they cannot come off.

SPLISH SPLASH
Bathtime/Waterplay

Your Baby Will Learn

Gross motor skills

Listening/Language skills

Body parts

Cause and effect

Sensory stimulation

Mommy's Materials

Bath seat (if baby feels more comfortable with support)

Washcloth and towel

Bath toys

Top Bath Songs

"Rub a Dub Dub"

"Row, Row, Row Your Boat"

"Splish Splash"

"This Is the Way We Wash Our Ears (Toes, Hands)"

Leaning over the tub to wash your baby can leave you with soggy clothes and a sore back, but it can also be a wonderful chance to bond with your baby and discover the benefits of water play. Once he can sit up by himself, it's time for your baby to graduate to the big tub, where he'll delight in tactile sensations such as splashing and slapping the water. The bath also offers a chance to experiment, as babies discover which objects float and which sink. Watch your baby catch a bobbing toy and you'll witness a powerful look of mastery on his face.

STEP BY STEP

1. Test the bath water to make sure it's comfortably warm.

2. Make sure you have everything you'll need—including towel, washcloth, soap, shampoo, and bath toys—*before* you put your baby in the tub.

3. Gently dip your baby in the bath so he can feel the water and the security of your hands at the same time.

4. Once he's soaking, encourage him to "pat the water" or "splish splash." If he needs a demonstration, show him how. Allow him to explore on his own terms.

5. Teach your baby body parts as you bathe him: "This is the way we wash our ears. . . ." Substitute toes, hands, and so on.

6. Experiment with various bath toys such as a rubber duck or sponge blocks. Bath activity centers often have water wheels or spouting whales. Vinyl bath stickers stick to the side of the tub and can be peeled off again. And of course, babies love anything that pours: plastic watering cans, Tupperware containers, and measuring cups.

7. If you're worried about getting wet, wear a plastic apron and a shower cap.

MORE MOMMY AND ME FUN

Double Clean: Try bathing with a young baby who is still acclimating to bathtime.

Rain Shower: A baby who can hold a small cup can pour water through a strainer and create a rain shower in the tub. She can even shower a doll that is in the tub with her.

Kitchen Sink: Babies unable to sit up well usually fit nicely into a large kitchen sink. The sides provide a perfect backrest for babies who are just learning to sit up on their own, and the countertop position is wonderful for parents' backs, too. Just make sure that you've moved any kitchen utensils and appliances far away from the sink.

Mommy's Memo

If you have to pick just one bath toy, a plastic cup is the most versatile. It floats when it's empty and sinks when it's full. You can poke holes in it and turn it into a rainmaker. And like most plastic bath toys, it can be run through the dishwasher.

Safe and Sound

Don't ever leave your baby unattended in the bath, even for a second.

SHADOW PLAY
Visual Tracking

Your Baby Will Learn

Visual acuity

Concentration

Observation

Imagination

Mommy's Materials

A lamp or flashlight

Hands

*S*ometime between six and nine months, your baby will discover shadows. You can encourage this discovery by creating and pointing out various shadow designs. My best friend's son was so fascinated by shadows he used to lie in his crib hypnotized by the silhouette of the swaying tree outside his window projected on his wall. The best thing about playing with shadows is that you can usually count on them to be there when you need them. Just orient yourselves properly with respect to the sun or a light and you're set to amaze.

STEP BY STEP

1. Begin by showing your baby his own shadow as well as your own.

2. Move around to show that as you move, so does your shadow.

3. Watch for other shadows: the dog's, the stroller's, the mailman's, and so forth.

4. Learn to make shadows with your hands: hopping bunnies, barking dogs, butterflies, and so on.

MORE MOMMY AND ME FUN

"My Shadow"
by Robert Louis Stevenson

I have a little shadow that goes in and out with me,
And what can be the use of him is more than I can see.
He is very very like me from his heels up to his head;
And I see him jump before me when I jump into my bed.

The funniest thing about him is the way he likes to grow—
Not at all like proper children, which is always very slow;
For he sometimes shoots up taller like an India-rubber ball.
And he sometimes gets so little that there's none of him at all.

He hasn't got a notion of how children ought to play,
And can only make a fool of me in every sort of way.
He stays so close beside me, he's a coward you can see;
I'd think shame to stick to nursie as that shadow sticks to me!

One morning, very early, before the sun was up,
I rose and found the shining dew on every buttercup;
But my lazy little shadow, like an arrant sleepy-head,
Had stayed at home behind me and was fast asleep in bed.

Selected Stories

The Little Book of Hand Shadows
by Phila H. Webb and Jane Corby

Fun with Hand Shadows
by Sati Achath and Bala Chandran

Shadow Games:
A Book of Hand and Puppet Shadows
by Bill Mayer and Peter Foy

Hand Shadows and More Hand Shadows
by Henry Bursill

DAWN TO DUSK
Sing-Along

Your Baby Will Learn

Routines

Bonding

Self-awareness

Listening/Language skills

Mommy's Materials

Your voice

MORNING

Some babies wake up with their batteries completely charged and an amazing amount of energy. Others are sleepyheads who are capable of dozing all morning long. For a musical wake-up, this variation of "Frère Jacques" is a great way to start off the day. Instead of the traditional "Brother John," say "Baby (child's name)."

English:
Are you sleeping, are you sleeping
Baby (name)? Baby (name)?
Morning bells are ringing, morning bells are ringing
Ding, dang, dong. Ding, dang, dong.

French:
Bebe (name), Bebe (name),
Dormez-vous, dormez-vous?
Sonnent les mantines, sonnent les mantines
Ding-dang-dong. Ding-dang-dong.

German:
Saeugling (name), Saeugling (name),
Schlaefst Du noch, schlaefst Du noch?
Morgenglocken laeuten, Morgenglocken laeuten,
Ding-dang-dong. Ding-dang-dong.

Spanish:
Niño/niña (name), Niño/niña (name)
¿Duermes tu, duermes tu?
Tocan las campanas,
Tocan las campanas
Tan, tan, tan.
Tan, tan, tan.

NIGHT

For many parents, helping baby develop good sleep patterns at night is a great (and exhausting) challenge. The most important thing to do is maintain a consistent "sleep environment." As part of your bedtime routine, you might put some of your child's favorite dolls or toys to bed each night. Tuck them in, kiss them good night, and wish them sweet dreams. You might also sing a lullaby each night or hold and rock your child in a particular way when it's time to go to sleep. Try singing "Rock-a-Bye Baby", "Brahms Lullaby", or "Hush Little Baby", part of every mother's repetoire.

"Hush Little Baby"

Hush, little baby, don't say a word.
Mama's gonna buy you a mockingbird.
If that mockingbird don't sing,
Mama's gonna buy you a diamond ring.
If that diamond ring turns brass,
Mama's gonna buy you a looking glass.
And if that looking glass gets broke,
Mama's gonna buy you a billy goat.
If that billy goat don't pull,
Mama's gonna buy you
A cart and bull.
And if that cart and bull turn over,
Mama's gonna buy you
A dog named Rover.
If that dog named Rover won't bark,
Mama's gonna buy you
A horse and cart.
And if that horse and cart fall down,
You'll still be the sweetest
Little baby in town.

Mommy's Memo

By four months, many babies will sleep six to eight hours each night. By six or seven months, many will sleep through the night. Be patient—you, too, will get a full night's sleep eventually.

Safe and Sound

As your baby becomes more mobile, be sure to babyproof your home and eliminate all potential hazards.

The end of your baby's first year is an amazing time. Language development, spatial relationships, and motor skills are all being fine-tuned. At ten to twelve months, babies are pre-walkers. They climb, crawl, cruise, try to balance, often take their first steps, and are into everything. Most spend a good part of the day playing around with sounds that vary in tone, pitch, and intensity. With a new sense of self, babies this age also communicate better and may even speak a few words. Separation anxiety may kick in, which is an indication of a maturing memory. And as ten- to twelve-month-olds explore themselves and the world around them, they are drawn to activities that whet their insatiable curiosity.

10-12 MONTHS
On the Move

MONTHLY MILESTONES

10 Months
Crawls
Curious about contents of boxes and containers
Will put objects in containers
Attempts to scribble
Will look at books
Will play pat-a-cake and other simple games
Interested in television and music
Can go from lying down to sitting on his own

11 Months
May stand alone
May speak a few words—*mama, dada*
Loves to play ball
Walks by holding on to furniture
May drink from cup
Separation anxiety—doesn't like you to leave

12 Months
Can point with index finger
May be able to undress self
Can climb and crawl up and down steps
Practices words he knows—*mama, papa, bye-bye*
Can imitate sounds—such as *bow-wow, quack*
Babbles short sentences
Can remember events for longer periods of time
May be able to group things by shape and color
Can distinguish self from others
Prefers to self-feed
May only take one nap
May have tantrums

MIRROR MAGIC
Self-awareness

Your Baby Will Learn

Eye-hand coordination

Listening/Language skills

Body parts

Self-awareness

Imitation

Mommy's Materials

A large mirror

Various playthings: hats, towels, scarves, and so forth

All babies love to gaze at themselves in the mirror. They never seem to tire of looking at the most adorable face in the world—their own. Not only is it fun, it also helps babies develop a sense of self-awareness. By looking at his reflection, your baby will begin to distinguish himself as an individual and start to understand that he has his own identity. Distinctive facial features are especially interesting to a young baby, and you'll find he can entertain himself (and you) for long periods of time with just his own blinks, smiles, and funny faces.

STEP BY STEP

1. Place your baby in front of the mirror and say, "Look at (child's name) in the mirror."

2. Point out various body parts. Ask your baby to touch his head, nose, and other body parts.

3. Put different hats on your head, then his head, or let him do it himself.

4. Make funny faces and ask him to do the same. Move left, move right, and have your baby mimic you.

5. Hold a favorite doll or stuffed animal in front of the mirror and make it move.

MORE MOMMY AND ME FUN

Imitative play: Stick out your tongue and make a noise at the same time. Your baby will try to imitate you by opening his mouth and putting his tongue out, too. Try moving your tongue up and down and side to side, and see what your baby does.

Self-guided play: For self-guided play, place an unbreakable mirror in your baby's crib. This provides endless opportunities for mirror play even when you're not around.

Rhyme Time:

> *Mirror, mirror*
> *On the wall,*
> *Who's the cutest*
> *Baby of all?*
> (Child's name) *is!*

Self-Awareness: Babies won't realize they're gazing at themselves in the mirror until they're about nine months old. To tell if he's grasped the concept, put a spot of lipstick on your baby's cheek. If he looks in the mirror and tries to wipe it off his face and not the reflection in the mirror, he's got it. You can also put a toy behind him as he is looking in the mirror—if he turns around to touch it, he's figured it out.

Mommy's Memo

For extra fun, find three-way mirrors in department or clothing stores and play some mirror games.

Safe and Sound

Make sure that you use an unbreakable mirror for this activity.

FOOD, GLORIOUS FOOD
Mealtime

Your Baby Will Learn

Fine motor skills

Eye-hand coordination

To follow directions

Mealtime rituals

Mommy's Materials

Nutritional, bite-size pieces of food

High chair

Fun Finger Foods

(Cut in bite-size pieces):

Cooked macaroni
Tofu
Peas
Diced cooked vegetables
Sliced banana
Dry cereal (e.g., Cheerios®)
Chicken nuggets
Cubed cheese
Pieces of Jell-O®
Chunky mashed potatoes
Whole grain bread or toast
Rice cakes

The kitchen is likely to be your baby's favorite room in the house. It's full of interesting sights, sounds, and smells. Capitalize on your baby's interest by engaging her senses as you prepare meals. Let her smell a freshly peeled orange or bang her spoon on a plastic bowl. Once lunch is served, don't worry if she plays with her food. To a ten-month-old, food is a sport as much as a meal. She's not concerned with getting the appropriate balance of carbs and protein; she only wants to know if the food squishes like clay or flies like an airplane.

STEP BY STEP

1. Once your baby is able to sit comfortably in a high chair, you can start offering her small pieces of food to pick up. Start out by showing her a small cracker.

2. Pick it up with your thumb and index finger. Explain that you are going to eat the cracker. Put it in your mouth.

3. Speak to your baby while you are doing this so she understands.

4. Eventually, your baby will get the idea and grasp the food with her own chubby fingers and put it in her eager mouth.

5. Try holding out your hand and see if your baby will pick up a piece of food and place it in your palm.

6. Praise your baby for a job well done.

7. As your baby gets older and is able to chew with her molars, you can add other items to the menu.

MORE MOMMY AND ME FUN

Rhyme Time: Try this trio of classic favorites—

Jack Sprat could eat no fat,
His wife could eat no lean,
And so between the two of them
They licked the platter clean.

Peas porridge hot, peas porridge cold,
Peas porridge in the pot, nine days old.
Some like it hot, some like it cold,
Some like it in the pot, nine days old.

Oh have you seen the Muffin Man,
The Muffin Man, the Muffin Man,
Oh have you seen the Muffin Man,
Who lives on Drury Lane?

Mommy's Memo

Add dipping sauces like applesauce or yogurt for more food tasting fun.

Mom, Did You Know?

For most children, the ability to utilize the pincer grip (thumb and forefinger) develops between nine and twelve months. Until the molars appear and your child can chew, foods should be soft enough to be gummed.

Safe and Sound

Avoid popcorn, nuts, grapes, raw vegetables, hard candies, and raisins.

• 10-12 MONTHS ACTIVITIES •

PLAY BALL
Game

Your Baby Will Learn

Eye-hand coordination

Bonding

Gross motor skills

Timing

Mommy's Materials

A ball

Types of Balls

Beach ball

Basketball

Soccer ball

Volleyball

Kickball

Rubber ball

Rugby ball

Football

Wiffle ball

Softball

Baseball

Tennis ball

Hand ball

Ping Pong ball

Most parents don't realize the trust that is involved in a simple game of catch! Think about the emotional dilemma. Your child is giving up her special ball—something she adores. She thinks to herself, "Will I get my ball back?" At that defining moment you start on a lifetime journey of earning her trust. Every time you throw or roll the ball back, you reinforce that trust. This is one of the first games in which baby is an active, reciprocal participant, so the next time your little one asks you to play ball, remember, it's not just a simple game.

STEP BY STEP

1. Sit facing your baby, in a straddle position if possible.

2. Roll a ball back and forth between the two of you.

3. Try using balls of various sizes and textures. For little ones, be sure to use a big ball so they can handle it. Graduate to smaller balls.

4. Talk through the motions: "Mommy is rolling the ball to (child's name). Roll the ball back to Mommy."

5. Count out loud as you roll the ball back and forth.

MORE MOMMY AND ME FUN

Basketball: Show your baby how to roll a ball into a box or bucket or toss it into a laundry or wastebasket.

Bouncing Ball: Show your baby how to drop or bounce a ball.

Rock-a-ball: If you have a giant inflatable ball, you can hold your baby firmly on top and roll her back and forth.

Bowling: Try bowling, using empty plastic soda or detergent bottles for pins.

Catch: As your baby gets older (around twenty months), try playing catch. A partially deflated beach ball is easy to grasp and good for a beginner. Instruct her to hold her hands out, then gently toss the ball into her arms. Demonstrate how to cradle the ball and hold on to it. Show her how to toss it. Don't expect perfect aim. Throwing and catching a ball takes considerable coordination. You can also try batting a balloon back and forth.

Rhyme Time:

A little ball, (hands together like a ball)
A bigger ball, (hands curved into a bigger ball)
A great big ball I see. (arms curved to form a giant ball)
Now let's count the balls:
One, two, three. (reverse movements)

Mommy's Memo

Learning to let go of a cherished object happens at about nine months of age. Your baby is probably ready to play this game if she easily tosses things out of her crib.

Mom, Did You Know?

The origins of baseball are unknown but most historians agree it's based on the English game of "rounders." Baseball, as we know it, first became popular in the early nineteenth century.

TUMBLING TOWER
Discovery Game

Your Baby Will Learn

Eye-hand coordination

Following directions

The concept "down"

Balance

Cause-and-effect

Mommy's Materials

Four (or more) unbreakable objects (such as wooden blocks or plastic containers)

Stacking objects and watching them fall down is one of a baby's greatest joys—and when your baby finds something he likes, he'll do it over and over and over again. Why the seeming obsession? Because this kind of repetition is what helps him learn new skills. Knocking down towers of blocks will help your child develop his powers of concentration, manual dexterity, and coordination. The feeling of power that comes from triggering the tower tumble is addictive—watch out!

STEP BY STEP

1. Stack the objects into a tower and knock them down while your baby is watching.

2. Repeat several times.

3. Encourage your baby to knock them down himself.

4. Use the word *down* as the objects fall down.

5. Encourage your baby to experiment. Let him stack the objects and knock them down again.

6. Praise him when he succeeds.

MOMMY-MADE

Create your own blocks from clean, cut-down milk or orange juice cartons. You can also make oversized blocks by stuffing a brown paper grocery bag halfway with shredded paper or old newspaper. Fold over, tape closed, and decorate with markers. Make a bridge, tunnel, or castle with containers and introduce other playthings like toy cars or dolls into the environment.

MORE MOMMY AND ME FUN

Stacking: Find other objects to stack and knock down. As your baby grows you can assemble additional objects and build a higher stack. Use margarine or yogurt containers, egg cartons, diaper wipe containers, or empty cereal boxes. Stack nesting cups and knock them over. Use rectangular blocks to show how the domino effect works.

Pyramids: Take a box of small paper cups, stack them like a pyramid or castle, and let your baby knock them down.

More Cause-and-Effect: Other popular cause-and-effect activities include squeak toys, jack-in-the-boxes, rattles, and banging a pot with a spoon. Social cause-and-effect involves the reactions baby gets when he smiles, cries, or waves bye-bye.

Mommy's Memo

A real awareness of cause-and-effect relationships begins at about seven months. At around nine months a baby will experiment on his own with causal relationships. Letting him repeatedly turn on the water or lights will delight him more than most store-bought toys.

Mom, Did You Know?

Between birth and age two, a baby's brain triples in size.

After the first year, your baby's developmental milestones are not so narrowly defined. You'll still notice new traits on a daily and weekly basis, but your baby will also be fine-tuning the skills she has developed over the last year. She'll become more dexterous with her hands and fingers, and as she learns how to grasp and manipulate tools, she'll be both proud of her achievement and frustrated that she can't do more.

At about one year, your baby will start walking (wobbling like Frankenstein) and you'll spend much of your time running after her. She will also be developing her sense of humor, her performance abilities, and her independence. Shouts of frustration may erupt when you try to do something for her that she wants to do herself. Have patience. Her language skills are also developing, and although she may not talk in sentences yet, she can now communicate effectively in many ways.

13-15 MONTHS
Walkers

MONTHLY MILESTONES

13-15 Months
Able to use fingers
Can take objects in and out of containers
Able to turn pages of a book
Walks holding an adult's hand
Imitates adult actions
Fills and empties a pail
Throws and rolls a ball
Scribbles
Helps dress and undress himself
Stands alone; perhaps walks
Drinks from a cup
Attempts to use utensils
Shows many emotions, such as anxiety and jealousy
Plays alone for a short time
Enjoys participating in games
Tries to achieve a sense of self identity
Follows simple commands and will wait momentarily
    for a response
Able to stack two blocks
Able to turn pages in a book
Enjoys running around
Throws objects
Able to point to specific pictures in a book, when asked
Able to pound pegs on a workbench

MINDING TABLE MANNERS
Mealtime

Your Baby Will Learn

Eye-hand coordination

Listening/Language skills

Independence

Socialization

About food

Mommy's Materials

A baby spoon

Soft food

Plastic cup (with or without handles)

Plastic or newspaper (to put under the high chair)

A bib (for sure!)

As your baby gets older she'll want to feel grown-up at the table. With your help, she'll soon become more competent. Teaching table manners may be messy, but it's also great fun. No matter how careful you are, however, there will be plenty of spills. To control the chaos, keep a few paper towels or a sponge nearby. Don't hover too closely though—you want your child to be focused enough to master these new skills, and wiping her face every five seconds might interfere with her concentration. Watch closely as she masters each step, and keep a camera nearby, because the process also makes for great photo opportunities.

STEP BY STEP

1. Place baby in a seated position (in a high chair if possible).

2. Show her how to put the spoon into the food and then to her mouth. Talk her through the activity as you go.

3. Demonstrate how to use a cup. Guide your baby to drink from her cup with your help.

4. Repeat these activities over and over until your baby can use the cup and spoon properly.

MORE MOMMY AND ME FUN

Dinner Party: Turn mealtime into a lunch or dinner party. Try having your child's favorite doll or teddy bear join you at the table. Set a place and talk about what you're doing: "Here is Teddy's dish. Here is Teddy's cup and spoon." Ask questions: "Is Teddy thirsty? Does Teddy want pasta for dinner?"

Food Art: Cookie cutters turn many foods into works of art. Use them on anything flat and thin, such as bread, sliced turkey, or cheese. Cut out a variety of shapes and try playing a matching game for lunch.

Table Tips: Use child-size utensils—you can't expect your baby to eat neatly if she's wrestling with a spoon as long as her forearm. Make certain she's sitting high enough above the table to see her food. If her chin is resting on the table, it will be difficult for her to gauge distances or manipulate the utensils.

Rhyme Time: Try this mealtime favorite—

> *Pat a cake,*
> *Pat a cake,*
> *Baker's man,*
> *Bake me a cake as fast as you can.*
> *Roll it and pat it*
> *And mark it with a B,*
> *And put it in the oven*
> *For baby and me.*

Mommy's Memo

Teach your child good mealtime manners by your own example. Put aside phone calls, chores, and other interruptions and encourage conversation and interaction.

Mom, Did You Know?

When your baby drops her spoon over and over again she's learning cause-and-effect (as well as loving the sound and mess it makes).

Safe and Sound

Avoid tying food to issues of control or emotion, and try not to use food as a reward or a pacifier.

A KITCHEN CONCERT
Music and Rhythm

Your Baby Will Learn

Motor skills

Auditory discrimination

Coordination

Rhythm/Patterns

Cause-and-effect

Spatial ability

Mommy's Materials

Music: radio, tape, or CD

Instruments (store-bought or Mommy-made)

Babies love to make music. You can start a concert simply by clapping your hands. Follow up by pulling out some pots, pans, and a wooden spoon and you have a drum set. Add an empty paper towel tube and you have a trumpet. Hit two metal lids together and you have cymbals. When you create fun rhythms for your child to mimic, you help improve her patterning skills, which are necessary for comprehension of beginning math and reading. Clap your hands in a pattern and encourage your child to repeat the pattern. Making music helps develop your baby's creativity and fosters her independence.

STEP BY STEP

1. Put on some great music with a steady beat, and start clapping your hands to the beat. Encourage your child to clap her hands to the music.

2. If your baby needs help, put her hands together and show her how to clap. Say, "Good job! Terrific! Great clapping."

3. Add pots, pans, plastic bowls, wooden spoons, and more to the band. Sit on the floor with your child and bang spoons and hit pots together. Encourage your child to make her own music.

4. Clap, chant, or bang out a rhythm (one, two, three, or rum, tum, tum). See if your child can imitate you and repeat the rhythm. Give her a chance to create a pattern for you to learn and repeat.

MORE MOMMY AND ME FUN

Stop and Start: Stop and start the music. This is a great way to develop your baby's sense of anticipation.

Musical Modes: Try different tempos and styles including marches, waltzes, polkas, reggae, and so on.

Sing-along: As you're washing up, try engaging your little one with song (sing to the tune of "Mulberry Bush"):
> This is the way we wash the spoon,
> (fork, knife, plate, cup, and so on)
> Wash the spoon, wash the spoon.
> This is the way we wash the spoon,
> Before we eat our meal.

MOMMY-MADE

Shakers: Make rhythm instruments by filling paper bags with rice or dried beans. Shake the bags to the music. Make shakers by filling film containers or cake tins with rocks, beads, beans, rice, or buttons. Or put a handful of small, crunchy cereal between two paper plates or aluminum pie plates and staple them together. (Use duct or electrical tape over the staples so there are no sharp edges.)

Mommy's Memo

Stock a kitchen cabinet with pots and utensils that can be played. It gives kids their own space in the kitchen and allows them to become active family participants.

Mom, Did You Know?

Many cultures place special importance on the ceremonial drum. Native Americans decorate their drums with special symbols from nature such as birds, bears, or wolves.

• 13–15 MONTHS ACTIVITIES •

HAPPY HANDS
Fingerplays and Action Rhymes

Your Baby Will Learn

Fine motor skills

To follow directions

Listening/Language skills

Self-esteem

Social skills

Mommy's Materials

Words to the rhymes

Hands and fingers

There are a myriad of games to help your baby develop coordination and build language. Some of the most fun are action rhymes. Even if your baby hasn't spoken her first word yet, she'll find the rhymes amusing and will want to follow along. As she becomes more and more familiar with the material and rhythms, you'll find her becoming actively involved. This leap from passive to active is an important step in childhood development. These simple action games are tremendous for building social skills, and they help young children gain confidence. Introduce them as early as you can and play them often.

STEP BY STEP

1. "Open, Shut Them"
Open, shut them, (open and close fists)
Open, shut them,
Give a little clap, clap, clap. (clap three times)
Open, shut them,
Open, shut them,
Put them in your lap, lap, lap. (hands in lap)
Creep them, crawl them, (walk fingers up body)
Creep them, crawl them,
Right up to your chin, chin, chin.
Open wide your little mouth, (touch lips)
But do not let them in. (run fingers downward, tickling)

2. "Wheels on the Bus"
The wheels on the bus go round and round,
Round and round, round and round.
The wheels on the bus go round and round,
All through the town.
(roll hands and arms in circular motion)

The doors on the bus, they open and close,
Open and close, open and close.
The doors on the bus, they open and close
All through the town. (hands apart and together)

The windows on the bus go up and down,
Up and down, up and down,
The windows on the bus go up and down
All through the town.
(hands up and down)

Alternate verses:
The driver on the bus says, "Move on back..."
The horn on the bus goes beep, beep, beep...
The wipers on the bus go swish, swish, swish...
The babies on the bus go "Waa, waa, waa..."
The mommies on the bus go "Ssh, ssh, ssh..."

Mommy's Memo

Repeat the fingerplays and actions, asking your child to join in. When possible, encourage other members of the family to chant along.

Mom, Did You Know?

Research indicates that exposure to songs and rhymes improves a baby's vocabulary development.

•13–15 MONTHS ACTIVITIES•

TELEPHONE TALK
Language Development

Your Baby Will Learn

Listening/Language skills

Imagination

Role-playing

Telephone etiquette

Social skills

Mommy's Materials

Toy telephone (or a real one that is unplugged)

The gift of gab is learned behavior. Pretending to talk on the phone is a good way to introduce both language and social skills. You can make believe that you are talking to Grandma, Daddy, a neighbor, or a friend. Some children like to hear you chat, while others grab for the phone and want to "talk" themselves. My daughter used to imitate my phone behavior by holding a play phone to her ear, pacing the floor, and "talking." Seeing her interpretation of my phone habits was a real eye opener and it wasn't long before she began imitating my other behavior as well.

STEP BY STEP

1. Sit with your baby on your lap or beside you and hold the phone to your ear as you talk. Pretend the phone is ringing and answer it. "Hello, _____ (child's name)."

2. Hold the phone to the baby's ear and repeat the same sentence.

3. After you have done this a few times, pretend to have a longer conversation of two or three sentences. Use the baby's name in the conversation and other words that he understands, such as *Daddy*, *dinner*, and *bye-bye*.

4. Put the phone to the baby's ear and see whether he will talk into it.

5. Praise your child by saying, "Good talking!"

6. When you're finished, be sure to say "good-bye" and hang up the phone.

MORE MOMMY AND ME FUN

The Name Game: Walk around the house and describe what you see—colors, shapes, objects, and so forth. You can play the Name Game anytime and anywhere. As your child's vocabulary grows, it can extend from a repeating game to a question-and-answer game: Can you touch your head? The teddy bear's head? Where is the red balloon? Can you show me the yellow flower?

Can We Talk? In learning the conversational process, babies respond to how language starts and stops. As your baby tries repeating sounds and says his first words, engage him in conversation. Repeat the sounds and words back and introduce new ones. Establish a dialogue. Ask questions. Though it may not yet be a recognizable conversation, you're establishing that you hear what your baby has to say and that it's important.

Mommy's Memo

Be certain your child knows the difference between toy phones and real phones. There is nothing more aggravating to a caller than a young child who answers the phone and is unable to communicate.

Safe and Sound

Be careful of phone cords; they are a potential danger and should be placed out of child's reach. Toy phones should have a cord less than 6 inches long.

*B*oundless energy, fierce independence, and nonstop talking typify your baby at this point in his development. He wants the freedom to experiment but gets frustrated or overstimulated when things don't work out his way. As he struggles to control his world and actions, he also thrives on exploration and creativity. In terms of activities, he probably likes playing games, scribbling, doing puzzles, pulling and pushing toys, and figuring out how things work. Songs and rhymes are especially appealing and reading books with a parent is an enjoyable pastime. Now you have more opportunities to participate in play where you and your child both develop new boundaries of trust and confidence. Relish these moments and feed your child's boundless curiosity.

16-18 MONTHS
Walkers/Talkers

MONTHLY MILESTONES

16-18 Months

Walks steadily
Stacks three or four objects
Recognizes body parts
Helps get dressed—raises arms, puts on hat
Able to use spoon and cup fairly well
Points to objects when asked to
Walks up and down stairs
Understands directions and words
Vocabulary up to twelve words
Very dependent on familiar adults
Short attention span
Does not share
Curious about the world around him
Learns cause-and-effect
Moody
Can solve problems
Scribbles with crayons
Able to throw overhand
Does a great deal of exploring
Eager to become involved in the world
Loves to listen and dance to music
Will become more independent of you
Carries objects from one place to another
Able to march to music
Tries to refine fine motor skills

PUZZLE FUN
Learning Game

Your Baby Will Learn

Fine motor skills

Pincer grasp

Shapes and colors

Problem-solving

Sharing

Self-esteem

Mommy's Materials

Various puzzles

Optional:

  Pictures

  Cardboard

  Nontoxic glue

  Safety scissors

*P*uzzles are endlessly fascinating for your child. Every time she puts one together, her problem-solving abilities get better. She's also building the skills needed to read and write, as well as learning that the sum of parts can make a whole—a concept that will help in math later on. Start with simple puzzles. When she masters one level, graduate to more complex puzzles. Remember to give positive reinforcement when working with your child. Instead of saying, "No, not that piece," say, "Let's try again and see if the piece fits here." When your child fits the piece, say, "Great job. You did it!" This will help build her confidence and self-esteem.

STEP BY STEP

1. Pick a puzzle that is age-appropriate and features familiar objects or people.

2. Start by removing one piece from a completely assembled puzzle and allowing your child to replace it.

3. Take out two or more pieces and demonstrate how to put the puzzle together again.

4. See if your child is able to place pieces back in the appropriate places.

5. Talk about the theme of the puzzle and extend the experience by asking questions.

6. When your child has mastered the puzzle, move on to a new one.

MOMMY-MADE

It's easy to make your own puzzles. Glue a photograph or picture to a piece of poster board, or have your child draw a design with crayon or marker. Cover with transparent contact paper, then cut into three or more pieces (depending on your child's abilities).

MORE MOMMY AND ME FUN

Animal Puzzles: Cut animal pictures into two or three easily recognizable parts (such as head, body, and tail) and have your child reassemble them.

Food Puzzles: Make puzzles out of sandwiches or pieces of cheese. Create puzzles that have different textures, numbers of pieces, colors, and sizes.

Choosing a Puzzle: Buy puzzles new, or look for them at yard sales, or in resale stores. When choosing a puzzle, make sure it's suited to your child's age and abilities. The younger the child, the more she will benefit from large, recognizable pieces. For toddlers, more complex puzzles may show pictures of people, cars and trucks, animals, or scenes from storybooks.

Mommy's Memo

Quality puzzles are a good investment because children can use them over and over again. Color code or mark the back of each puzzle piece so you'll know which pieces go with which puzzle.

Safe and Sound

Be sure puzzle pieces are large enough so they can't be swallowed.

ANIMAL ANTICS
Learning Game

Your Baby Will Learn

Animal sounds

Animal behavior

Social skills

Imagination

Creativity

Matching

Mommy's Materials

Toy or stuffed animals

Pictures of animals

Animal costumes (optional)

Children love to make animal sounds. Even better, they love to watch *you* make animal sounds. When you trumpet like an elephant, buzz like a bumblebee, or growl like a tiger you're teaching valuable lessons about animal behavior. Your child's imagination kicks into full gear when she pretends to be a cat, a dog, a worm, or a frog. Watch her hop, wiggle, or crawl on all fours as she imagines himself a wild creature from the animal kingdom.

STEP BY STEP

1. Show your child an animal picture or toy.

2. Make the corresponding sound—quack like a duck, oink or snort like a pig, cluck like a chicken, moo like a cow.

3. Ask your child to copy the sound.

4. Talk about each animal—where it lives, what it looks like, what it likes to eat, whether it sleeps during the daytime or at night, and so on.

MORE MOMMY AND ME FUN

Animal Matching: Make animal sounds and see if your child can point to and match the sound to animal pictures or toys.

Animal Outing: Take a trip to a zoo, farm, or pet store to look at real animals. Point out various animal body parts and how they differ from yours. Notice body parts that people don't have such as an elephant's trunk, a kangaroo's pouch, or a dog's tail.

Mom and Baby Animals: Find books at the store or library that show animal babies and their moms. Talk about what the different babies are called (cats and kittens, dogs and puppies, kangaroos and joeys).

Walk Like an Animal: Move like an animal and ask your child to copy your actions. Jump like a frog, slither like a snake, or hop like a rabbit.

Sing-Along: Try this classic song—
"Old MacDonald Had a Farm"
Old MacDonald had a farm, E-I-E-I-O.
And on his farm he had some chicks, E-I-E-I-O.
With a chick, chick here, and a chick, chick there,
Here a chick, there a chick,
Everywhere a chick, chick.
Old MacDonald had a farm, E-I-E-I-O.
Add sound of other barnyard animals, such as:
a duck—*quack, quack*; a cow—*moo, moo*; a turkey—*gobble, gobble*; a pig—*oink, oink*; a donkey—*ee-aww*

Mommy's Memo

For young children, pets make gratifying companions. They're entertaining and provide unconditional love. Pets also introduce children to the circle of life in relevant ways. As children share in the care of a pet, they develop a sense of responsibility.

Selected Stories

How Animals Live
by Anne Civardi and
Cathy Kilpatrick

Make Way for Ducklings
(Caldecott Medalist)
by Robert McCloskey

Peter Rabbit
by Beatrix Potter

FAMILY ALBUM
Arts and Crafts

Your Baby Will Learn

Fine motor skills

Listening/Language skills

Family history

Visual memory

Self-awareness

Mommy's Materials

Pictures of family members or pets

Construction paper

Yarn

Nontoxic glue

Sharing memories is as important to a young child as to an adult. It's fun to let your child look through your old photo albums, and even more gratifying to make one together. As you fill the album, point out the pictures and identify the various people: "Here's Daddy" or "Look! There's your grandma." This type of observation helps a child reinforce familial relationships. Ask your child to identify and point out different family members: "Show me your grandpa" or "Where is Mommy?" Include pictures of your child as a baby: "Look how small you were. You're so big now!" Your child will soon attach labels and names to members of your family.

STEP BY STEP

1. Fold sheets of paper in half to make at least four pages.

2. Glue one large picture of a family member or group on each page.

3. Punch two holes in the fold. Thread yarn through holes, tie, and crease.

4. Sit with your baby and point to each picture as you name the person.

5. Once your baby is familiar with the names, ask him to point to Grandma or some other family member.

6. Laminate the cover of your handmade family album and preserve as a keepsake.

MORE MOMMY AND ME FUN

Family Story Time: If you have an older child, let him dictate a story to you about the family. Write the words on each page of his book. Leave room for your child to add photos or illustrate his story.

Family Magnets: Glue or tape family photos onto flat magnets and display them on the refrigerator.

Pet Scrapbook: Since pets are family members too, make a photo album of the family pet. You can take photographs and draw pictures for the book and even include such items as their certificate from obedience school.

Family Tree: Make a family tree to illustrate your child's place in the family unit. Cut a tree out of construction paper, then glue on pictures of different members of your family.

Family Finger Game: Cut out a small picture of each family member's face: Mom, Dad, sister, brother, dog, cat, etc. Tape one to each of your fingertips. To the tune of "Where is Thumbkin?" sing: "Where is Mommy, where is Mommy? Here she is," and so on. Do a verse with each family member. Your child will love it!

Mommy's Memo

Be sure to write names and dates on all your photos. Memories fade more quickly than pictures.

Mom, Did You Know?

Pictures of friends and family can help ease separation anxiety and aid in coping with personal changes such as the birth of a sibling.

• 16-18 MONTHS ACTIVITIES •

SAND STRUCTURES
Creative Play

Your Baby Will Learn

Creativity

Measuring

Sensory stimulation

Fine motor skills

Gross motor skills

Concepts of "full" and "empty"

Mommy's Materials

Sandbox or pit

Kitchen utensils

Watering can

Small shovels

Pail

Cups or molds

At the beach, a park playground, or in your backyard, most babies and toddlers find romping in the sand their favorite outdoor activity. It's easy to see why—perhaps no other medium invites play and nourishes the imagination as much as sand does. Making designs in the sand and building castles is a creative process that also enhances learning. By scooping and pouring sand, children learn how to measure and are introduced to a variety of important pre-math skills. Children can also dig in it, draw in it, and hide toys in it. Take off your shoes to join them and you'll find yourself remembering the sandbox games that used to be your favorites.

STEP BY STEP

1. Show your child how to fill a cup with sand and turn it over.

2. Add some water to the sand to make it damp.

3. Scoop sand into various-size cups or molds and pat down.

4. Turn a large cup or mold over first, then turn a smaller cup of sand over on top of the large one.

5. Continue to build one- and two-cup-high structures to create a castle or series of buildings.

MORE MOMMY AND ME FUN

Super Sand Play:
- Bury toys and try to find them in the sand.
- Place a magnet on a string and "fish" for metal washers and bolts.
- Build a "sand cake" and other make-believe edibles.
- Add seashells to the sandbox for a beach experience.
- Make designs in the sand with various utensils.
- Create roads in the sand for toy cars or trucks.
- Make a "drip castle" with wet sand.
- Hide ice cubes in the sandbox. Encourage children to locate them. Use adjectives such as *wet* and *cold*.
- For indoor fun, a cornmeal box or baking pan filled with salt provides many of the same opportunities as a sandbox.

Sand Sculptures: Mix 2 cups of sand and 1 cup of cornstarch in a saucepan. Stir in 1 cup of water. Heat mixture while stirring. When thick, remove from heat and cool. You can now sculpt the sand into anything you want and it will harden as it dries.

MOMMY-MADE

There's no need to buy expensive sand toys. Look in your kitchen cabinets and you'll find all you need: spatula, cookie cutters, slotted spoon, measuring cup, colander, plastic bowls, a strainer, a sifter, and more.

Mommy's Memo

If you have a sandbox, fill it with washed play-sand (usually found in garden centers) that is clean, weed-free, and a nice grade with which to build sand sculptures and castles.

Safe and Sound

Remind children not to throw sand and to play with the sand below eye level. Also, never use glass or other breakable materials in the sand.

PLAY HOUSE
Creative Play

Your Baby Will Learn

Fine motor skills

Gross motor skills

Concepts of "inside" and "outside"

Listening/Language skills

Role playing

Mommy's Materials

A large box from a furniture or appliance store

Nontoxic markers

Scissors or carpet knife (for adult use)

Masking tape

Nontoxic glue

There is nothing quite like a giant box to inspire imaginary play. For most children, the box is far more interesting than whatever came inside it, and it immediately becomes a plaything. Turn a box into a playhouse and your child will soon be carrying objects back and forth to his new abode. He'll pretend it's his own special place, and when he gets tired he may even take a nap in it. You can also turn an oversize box into different kinds of buildings. The box can become a storefront, a post office, or even a take-out restaurant. If you have multiple boxes, set up a whole community.

STEP BY STEP

1. Cut a door in the box, large enough for your child to go in and out of easily. If you want the door to open and close, leave one side of the door intact.

2. A doorknob can be made by gluing a spool to the door. Alternatively, cut a round hole that will substitute for a doorknob.

3. Draw and cut out two or more windows. If you want, leave attached at the sides for shutters.

4. Encourage your child to help decorate the inside and outside of the house with felt markers or crayons. The outside of the house can have grass or a picket fence along the bottom portion. Inside you can paste or tape pictures cut out of magazines.

5. Invite your child to move into his new house. He'll probably move his favorite dolls and stuffed animals in too.

MORE MOMMY AND ME FUN

Construction Site: While building your playhouse, wear construction hats and a pretend tool belt. You can cut off the bottom and top flaps of an oversize carton and use them to create window boxes, a mailbox, chimney—even a pitched roof.

Maze: Link several boxes and create a maze for your child to crawl through. Construct tunnels by draping sheets between structures; add an obstacle course using pillows or cushions, alternating between enclosed and open areas.

Camp-out: Pretend the box is a tent (or set up a real tent) and camp out together. Put a sleeping bag and flashlight inside the tent. Scatter stuffed animals around the area and pretend you're on a safari!

Play Car: Turn an oversize box into a fire truck, race car, or train. Try to find the appropriate hats to complete the picture. A firefighter's hat, a racing helmet, or a conductor's cap may encourage your child to better play his part.

Mommy's Memo

Instead of discarding worn linens, create a make-believe house by draping a sheet over a card table or between two chairs. Cut a window or door opening to add realism to your playhouse.

Safe and Sound

Remove any staples that could hurt a child, and use masking tape to cover over any rough edges. Make sure an adult is the one responsible for any of the cutting and taping.

*N*o longer a baby, your child is walking, running, and jumping. His voracious curiosity sometimes puts him in jeopardy, but rather than reprimand him, try explaining appropriate options and behavior. Your child's vocabulary is also increasing. His use of the word "no" is probably becoming more frequent, and he may become bossy and try to take control of situations. This is the start of what's sometimes referred to as the "terrible twos," but I prefer to call it the "trying twos" when children begin to assert themselves; it's a sign of positive emotional growth.

As your child segues from two naps a day to one, you'll have more time to fill. Musical games, reading, sorting, physical or pretend play, and sensory games are all good. You'll probably notice that your child likes to play the same games over and over again—this is because it feels good to know how to do these things. Repetition helps build important skills, so have patience when your child begs "Again!"

19-24 MONTHS
Toddlers

MONTHLY MILESTONES

19-24 Months

Able to sit down in chair

Throws and kicks ball clumsily

Begins to run

May be willing to start toilet training

Develops grasp and stance

Plays alone

Able to help with simple tasks

Resists sharing

Shy with strangers

Short attention span

Recognizes some pictures in book; names body parts

Remembers places he has been

Able to deal with some abstractions, like discussing people,
    ideas, and objects when they're not physically present

Can find a lost object, or plan a visit to friends

Vocabulary increases to twenty to 200 words

Understands simple questions

Sings and hums

Eager to figure out how things work

Able to place a circle and square in a sorting box

Able to unscrew lid of jar

Able to imitate a verticle stroke on paper

Engages in parallel play

Able to direct own play

Can pound, roll, and squeeze clay

Able to string beads together

Able to remove clothing

Able to kick a ball forward without losing balance

Walks up and down steps alone

CLOTHESPINS AND THE BASKET
Learning Game

Your Baby Will Learn

Gross motor skills

Eye-hand coordination

Colors and numbers

Following directions

Concept of "in" and "out"

Mommy's Materials

Old-fashioned wooden clothespins

Nontoxic markers

Construction paper, markers, stickers, and other decorations

A large coffee can or pail

*S*ometimes the simplest games are the most fascinating to a young child. The most common household items can provide hours of entertainment, as this favorite activity proves. I once had a twenty-month-old in one of my classes who wanted to play the clothespin game the entire hour. There are a number of variations to keep the game fresh and appealing, and as your child's skills improve, you can make the game more challenging. It's inexpensive and easy fun!

STEP BY STEP

1. Have your child color the clothespins with the markers.

2. With your child, decorate the coffee can or pail with construction paper, markers, stickers, or whatever else you have on hand.

3. To start the game, have your child stand over the coffee can and see how many clothespins he can drop in. Have him take a step backward every time he makes it in, and see how far back he can go before he misses.

4. Another variation is to have your child sit, kneel, then stand, even get up on a chair, to see how high he can get before the pin misses the can.

MORE MOMMY AND ME FUN

Clothespin Drop: Stand above the container and keep score of how many clothespins your child drops into the container. Reinforce the number by saying, "You put two clothespins into the container, that's three clothespins" and so on.

Fill 'Er Up: Use an empty two-liter soda bottle and show your child how to push the clothespins through the top. When shaken, the clothespins make a rattling sound (cause-and-effect). Your child will also begin to understand the concepts of "in" and "out" and "full" and "empty."

Colored Clothespins: Place some colored clothespins on a table. Count the clothespins aloud and identify the colors. Separate them into piles according to color, and count the number in each pile. Identify both color and number: "There are three red clothespins in this pile," and so on.

Mr. Posh Hangs up His Wash: Collect a few small items of clothing including socks, bibs, a napkin, a washcloth, perhaps some doll clothes. Show your child how to clip a clothespin on a line. Allow him to try clipping the clothespins. Once he has the hang of it, let him pin up the clothing.

Mommy's Memo

Hanging clothes on the line may seem old-fashioned, but it is good for our environment. By using natural resources—sun and air—to dry our clothes, we're saving electricity.

Mom, Did You Know?

The more repetition that occurs, the more a baby's brain grows in its under-standing of an activity.

BUBBLE BLAST
Discovery

Your Baby Will Learn

Gross motor skills

Eye-hand coordination

Listening/Language skills

Following directions

Cause-and-effect

Mommy's Materials

Water

Large plastic bowl

Straws

Liquid soap (Dawn works well)

Bubble solution (store-bought or Mommy-made)

Bubble wands

Children love blowing. Add bubbles to the equation and you double the fun. Bubbles are fascinating, festive, and free-floating wonders that bring a smile to everyone's face. Chasing and catching bubbles is a great way to stimulate eye-hand coordination, and popping them offers an introduction to physics. Blowing bubbles also helps strengthen mouth muscles, which aids in language development. Best of all, bubbles are bliss for little ones.

STEP BY STEP

1. Let your toddler practice blowing air through a straw into a large cup or bowl of water.

2. Add a little liquid soap (about 2 tablespoons to a cup of water) and have your toddler blow again. Recite the rhyme: "Bubbles, bubbles, everywhere. See them blow into the air."

3. Use a bubble wand to make bubbles, blowing and waving the wand through the air.

4. See how many bubbles your child can catch on the wand.

5. Try counting the bubbles and catching them before they touch the ground.

6. Show how to keep a bubble in the air by blowing it from underneath.

MORE MOMMY AND ME FUN

Big and Little: Use different size wands. Use commercially available bubble blowers that create showers of tiny bubbles or fill a wading pool with bubble mixture and make an oversized bubble using a hula hoop.

Hot and Cold: Have your child hold a bubble up to the sunlight to see its colors. Try blowing bubbles outside on a freezing cold day. What happens? Do they freeze?

Bubble Painting: Catch bubbles tinted with food coloring on a white sheet of paper and see what kind of designs you can create.

MOMMY-MADE

In addition to the basic bubble recipe above, you can make a "better bubble" by mixing 1–2 tablespoons of glycerin (available in most drugstores and supermarkets), 2 tablespoons of mild dishwashing detergent, and a cup of water. (Use Karo or corn syrup if you can't find glycerin.) Pour the mixture into margarine tubs. Add a light tint of food coloring, if you like.

Mommy's Memo

As the bubbles float through the air, distinguish between big and little, high and low, and describe the round shapes.

Safe and Sound

Make sure to supervise your child at all times and warn him about getting bubbles or bubble solution in his eyes or mouth.

Selected Stories

Bubble, Bubble
by Mercer Mayer

Bubbles, Bubbles Everywhere
by Melvin Berger and Dwight Kuhn

The Bubble Factory
by Tomie de Paola

CLAY DOUGH
Arts and Crafts

•19–24 MONTHS ACTIVITIES•

Your Baby Will Learn

Creativity

Shapes and colors

Motor skills

Sensory stimulation

Following directions

Mommy's Materials

Nontoxic modeling clay

Airtight container
(for storage)

Modeling tools such as a
cookie cutter, rolling pin,
empty spool, comb, or any
other household item that
will leave an interesting
pattern in the clay

Sculpting clay into various shapes adds another dimension to your child's playtime. In addition to encouraging her creative abilities, she is learning about shapes, colors, and textures. When your child plays with a hunk of clay or dough she has the whole world in her hands, a world that she can create, destroy, and re-create whenever and however she chooses. Be sure to set up the clay in an area where it won't matter if your child drops some on the floor—it's hard to get out of carpets. The kitchen is the best place in the house; outside is better yet.

STEP BY STEP

1. Roll a piece of clay (or Play-Doh®) on the table.

2. Squeeze it, pound it, poke it, roll it into a snake, mold it into a ball, stretch it, pull it apart, poke holes in it.

3. Give your child some tools, such as cookie cutters or plastic utensils, to make patterns on the flattened clay.

4. Form shapes like circles, balls, triangles, squares, and letters of the alphabet.

5. Mix the colors together and see what happens.

6. When done, store all clay or Play-Doh in a cool, dry place in airtight containers.

MORE MOMMY AND ME FUN

Clay Detective: With older children, you can play Clay Detective by making impressions of various objects and textures and asking your child to guess what objects made them.

MOMMY-MADE

Easy Dough: For an easy make-it-yourself clay recipe, mix 3 cups flour, ½ cup salad oil, and about ½ cup of water. Knead well and add food coloring if you want colored dough.

Microwave Dough: Mix 2 cups flour, 2 cups water, 1 cup salt, 2 teaspoons cream of tartar, and 2 tablespoons cooking oil in large microwave-safe bowl and microwave for 5 minutes. Stop every minute to stir. Cool and knead well. Add food coloring for colored dough.

Edible Dough: To make up a batch of edible clay, mix ¼ cup creamy peanut butter, 1 tablespoon wheat germ, 1 tablespoon honey, and 3 tablespoons nonfat dried milk in a bowl until it sticks together. Chill, then model the clay into anything you want. You can add shoestring licorice, gumdrops, pretzel sticks, or other edible decorations.

Mommy's Memo

There is no right or wrong way to create or experience art—only the exploration of what's possible.

Mom, Did You Know?

Making homemade clay dough is a great way to develop your child's measuring and motor skills.

•19-24 MONTHS ACTIVITIES•

PICTURE THIS
Arts and Crafts

Your Baby Will Learn

Creativity

Colors and shapes

To follow directions

Fine motor skills

Kinesthetic awareness

Mommy's Materials

Easel

Nontoxic water-based paints

Large white paper

Soft brushes

Smock

Newspaper or butcher paper

Plastic cups with water

A glue stick (helpful for adding other materials)

This activity gives kids the chance to do their favorite thing—get messy! Whether smearing finger paint or applying colors with a brush at an easel, your child gets his creative juices flowing and is able to create his own masterpiece. From marble and straw painting, to painting with pudding, there are lots of opportunities for artistic experimentation. You'll find that colors are most intense when they're wet, so if you want to photograph the artwork, do so while your child is still in the midst of creating his tour de force. Be sure to give him time and not rush him. Who knows, you could be the proud mother of the next Picasso!

STEP BY STEP

1. Set up art supplies in a contained area or outside.

2. Place newspapers under the easel on the floor, or on the table.

3. Place paint in plastic cups with brushes and water.

4. Suggest what to paint if your child needs inspiration.

5. Try different techniques—use a toothbrush or sponge instead of a paintbrush, or splatter the paint instead of brushing.

6. Hang painting to dry.

MORE MOMMY AND ME FUN

Musical Painting: Play a tape or CD and ask your child to paint to the music. Begin with gentle, rhythmic music. Watch to see how he interprets the music through his movements. After a while, switch to faster-paced music and encourage him to match his movements to the new selection.

Color Chemistry: Combining colors can create intense and beautiful new shades. Start with dry paper, where the color stays in a fairly limited area. Then try wet paper, where the color fans out. Tip the paper and watch the color spread even farther. One drop goes a long way!

Marble Painting: Place a piece of paper inside a shoebox top. Drop marbles into different colors of paint and roll them across the piece of paper to create a design.

Straw Painting: Put some paint thinned with water on a piece of paper and blow on it with a straw. See what happens when you add additional paints and combine colors.

Finger Paints: Dampen some paper (special finger-paint paper, available at art stores, is expensive and can be replaced with shiny shelf paper or freezer wrap) and allow your child to use his hands and fingers to make different designs using thumbs, fingertips, fingernails, heels of the hand, and knuckles.

Mommy's Memo

Food painting is great fun for young children. Whipped cream (with food coloring) or flavored pudding make great finger paint that cleans up easily and can be tasted. For portable, no-mess finger painting, place colored whipped cream in plastic bags, seal, and make designs with your fingertips.

Mom, Did You Know?

Roll-on deodorant bottles filled with liquid tempera paint make a huge ballpoint pen that children really love.

• 19–24 MONTHS ACTIVITIES •

WHAT'S MISSING?
Discovery Game

Your Baby Will Learn

Eye-hand coordination

To follow directions

Names of objects

Visual memory

Problem solving

Object permanence

Mommy's Materials

Three or four common child-safe objects (such as a toy, a book, a stuffed animal, a crayon, or a shoe)

Your child may never want to stop playing this game of discovery. In fact, it's fun for adults and older siblings, too. With its simple concept, you can vary the game for kids of different ages and abilities. For the youngest players, use a limited number of distinctly dissimilar toys or other objects. To make the game more difficult, increase the number of objects, and choose items that are more similar in size and shape. If you start out easy, your child will gain confidence and with each success will want to move on to more complex variations.

STEP BY STEP

1. Place two or three objects on a tray or table.

2. Name all objects. Repeat for younger children.

3. Tell child to close his eyes.

4. Quickly remove one object.

5. Ask, "What's missing?" Encourage your child to guess.

6. Repeat. Have your child remove an object and quiz you as well.

MORE MOMMY AND ME FUN

Missing Toy: A younger child (twelve–fifteen months) will love to play this variation. Show him one of his toys, then place it in a bag and see if he can discover where you hid it. When he's successful say, "You found it. What a fantastic job!"

Which Hand? For an older child, hide the toy in one of your hands and have him guess where it is. You can use this game to introduce the concept of left hand and right hand.

Which Cup? Increase the level of difficulty for older children by hiding a small toy under one of three cups while your child is watching. Move the cups around and ask him to find the toy.

Missing Picture Part: Draw a familiar picture with missing parts and see if your child can identify what's missing (for instance, an animal without a tail or a car without wheels).

Classic Hide-and-Seek: One of the most enduring games of discovery is hide-and-seek. It stimulates your child's curiosity while helping to ease separation anxiety. To play, hide yourself and call out, "I'm hiding. Come find me." Allow your child to listen for the direction of your voice. If he can't locate it, call out again. Let your child find you and act surprised at his sleuthing skills. Finding you gives your toddler quite a sense of accomplishment, and the game is a great social activity because it involves taking turns.

Mommy's Memo

Introduce games when your child is rested and in a good mood. If your child is tired and cranky he won't be nearly as receptive to new activities.

Safe and Sound

When playing "What's Missing?" beware of using small parts that a child may choke on. When playing "Hide and Seek," warn children to stay out of closets, or confined spaces where they may suffocate.

MATCH GAME
Learning Game

Your Baby Will Learn

Eye-hand coordination

To follow directions

Shapes and colors

Critical thinking

Memory

Categorization

Shape and size relationships

Mommy's Materials

Poster board

Nontoxic glue

Safety scissors

Magazine pictures of real objects such as fruit, utensils, or small toys

Matching items such as an orange, an apple, a spoon, fork, rattle, toy car, or doll

Children enjoy making and playing their own matching games. They enjoy the challenge, and establishing the link between pictures or objects provides immediate gratification. Understanding one-to-one correspondence and shape and size relationships is an important concept for young children to grasp. When playing the matching game, choose pictures that are rich in sensory images (fine art) or emotion (family photos). You'll find your child endlessly fascinated with corresponding objects and images.

STEP BY STEP

1. Find pictures of real objects and mount them on large pieces of cardboard to make playing cards.

2. Place real objects that match the photos around the room.

3. Hand a card to the child and say, "This is a picture of an orange. Can you find an orange in the room?"

4. Have the child match the card to the real object.

MORE MOMMY AND ME FUN

Seeing Double: Find two identical sets of pictures (art museum brochures are good), postcards, playing cards, or photographs. Give your child one set of pictures and ask her to find the matches that you have hidden around a room. Choose just a few pairs for younger children, more as children get older.

Concentration: Older children can play a memory game with multiple sets by turning pictures over and trying to make a match. Once a match is made, remove both pictures and continue on with remaining pictures.

Mix and Match: Use everyday objects to play a simple matching game. Separate pairs that normally go together and see if your child can match them up. For example, separate a pot from its lid or shoes from a pair.

Matching Shapes: A shape-sorting box (store-bought or Mommy-made) provides a simple matching activity in which objects of various shapes and sizes are matched to the shapes on the lid of a box.

MOMMY-MADE

A homemade shape sorter can be made by choosing three or four shapes or objects and tracing them on the lid of a shoebox. Cut the shapes (adults only, please) and replace the lid. Now invite your child to match the objects to the cut-out shapes.

Mommy's Memo

Younger children may not be developmentally ready to match items. You can simplify by limiting the number of objects or shapes.

Mom, Did You Know?

Understanding one-to-one correspondence and size and shape relationships is a good introduction to mathematics and scientific reasoning.

• 19-24 MONTHS ACTIVITIES •

TEDDY BEAR PICNIC
Playtime

Your Baby Will Learn

Animal behavior

Creative expression

To follow directions

Role playing

Mommy's Materials

Teddy bears

Snack food

A "Beary" Good Snack

Using a bear-shaped cookie cutter, cut bread into bear shapes and make sandwiches with honey or peanut butter in the middle.

For bear milk, add a dash of cinnamon to a cup of milk and stir. Finish off with some Teddy Grahams or blueberry ice cream.

Teddy bears are familiar creatures to most young children; they become both friend and family and are loved by girls and boys, as well as most adults. Introduced through stories, picture books, and songs, a stuffed teddy bear is most likely a companion during both playtime and sleep time. Invite your child to a special Teddy Bear Picnic and you're both in for some fun. There are enough variations so that this can become a favorite activity—and you can finish up each picnic with a great big bear hug.

STEP BY STEP

1. Have your child bring his favorite bear (or stuffed animal) to a pretend picnic.

2. Set out play cups and saucers for the bears and have them sit at a small table or on a blanket.

3. Read stories about teddy bears.

4. Eat bear snacks (see opposite).

5. Play the Teddy Bear Activity Game (see below).

6. Take pictures of your child and his teddy bear at the picnic for the family album.

MORE MOMMY AND ME FUN

Make-Believe Bear: Use a large blanket or tablecloth to make a cave, and pretend you're hibernating bears. Explain that baby bears are called cubs and they like to snuggle up to their furry mothers to stay warm.

Bear Bop: Play some music and dance with teddy. When the music stops your child and teddy have to freeze. Try moving like a bear (bend at the waist, hands on the floor).

Teddy Bear Activity Game: This action rhyme is an all time favorite—

Teddy Bear, Teddy Bear, (sit on floor, clap hands twice)
Turn around. (spin around)
Teddy Bear, Teddy Bear, (clap hands twice)
Touch the ground. (tap the ground)
Teddy Bear, Teddy Bear, (clap hands twice)
Reach up high. (reach up)
Teddy Bear, Teddy Bear, (clap hands twice)
Wink one eye. (wink)
Teddy Bear, Teddy Bear, (clap hands twice)
Slap your knees. (slap knees)
Teddy Bear, Teddy Bear, (clap hands twice)
Be still, please. (sit still).

Mommy's Memo

Use your child's interest in bears to pique his curiosity about other animals.

Mom, Did You Know?

The teddy bear probably takes its name from the twenty-sixth president of the U.S., Theodore Roosevelt. On one of his many hunting trips, Roosevelt refused to shoot a bear cub, inspiring toymakers to create a toy bear and name it after him.

Selected Stories

Blueberries for Sal
by Robert McCloskey

Corduroy
by Don Freeman

"Every child is an artist. The challenge is to remain one once he grows up."

—Picasso

TODDLERS AND PRESCHOOLERS

3

*I*f you thought the first twenty-four months of your child's life were amazing, buckle up and get ready for an even more incredible journey. At two years old, your child has mastered an array of skills and is more eager than ever to learn new things and explore his world. As he gets older, his play will become more imaginative and complex. Playing is a way for your child to stretch himself and practice his independence, creativity, curiosity, and problem-solving skills. Playtime activities can also promote moral values, social skills, and "emotional intelligence"—a term coined by author Daniel Goleman that refers to traits such as self-awareness, empathy, personal motivation, and altruism. For instance, long before your child feels comfortable sharing her favorite toy with a sibling, she may offer it to a stuffed animal or doll. Her first "please" or "thank you" may slip out at an imaginary tea party. And what parent can resist wasting a Band-Aid the first time her child demonstrates compassion and wants to administer to her hurt teddy bear?

Playtime also helps toddlers and preschoolers find answers to their endless stream of questions, particularly "Why?" Children ask "why" for a lot of reasons. Sometimes they want an explanation, other times they're angling for a topic that will require a lengthy answer from you—in other words, they want your attention. Although the "why"s can be trying, be patient with your child. You don't want to suppress her curiosity or interest in communicating. If you're not in a talkative mood, try turning the tables on your little inquisitor: "Why do *you* think the cat ran away?"

Constant questions are a signal that an intense phase of intellectual growth is beginning. The month-by-month *Mommy and Me* curriculum that follows is designed to encourage this growth and engage your child's sense of wonder and discovery.

THE MOMMY AND ME CURRICULUM

*D*ivided into month-long units, my *Mommy and Me* toddler and preschool program takes you and your child through an entire year of laughing, learning, and sharing. Each month, you'll find seasonal activities, holiday art projects, relevant educational concepts, and musical activities. I've made an effort to introduce multicultural concepts since one of the best ways to combat racism and bigotry is to teach young children about various cultures. This allows them to grow up respecting and appreciating the differences among us. The

Mommy's Memo

Playtime is a way for your child to stretch himself and practice his independence, creative curiosity, and problem-solving skills.

Mom, Did You Know?

At about two years of age, your toddler may lean toward using one hand over the other. About 10 percent of the population is left-handed and about 20 percent is ambidextrous.

curriculum is meant to be a springboard for spending time with your child. You don't need to follow the instructions to the letter—feel free to improvise or devise alternative games and activities. Be creative!

The best part of the curriculum is that it can be used over and over again. Every child will enjoy and learn from the lessons at her own developmental level, and as your child grasps more concepts, you can customize the activity to suit her. Tips for extending or varying the activities are included for just this purpose. In addition, because the activities are "expandable," you can use this book for several years in a row. It's the "Mommy" part of the *Mommy and Me* equation that makes this year-to-year, level-to-level customizing possible. Your child will delight in recalling the activities she did the previous year, and remark on what she's able to do now. Best of all, these family traditions are a great source of comfort to young children and will be remembered for years to come. Look for specific information in the following subject areas:

COLORS

Colors are an important part of our environment. To heighten your child's awareness of color, each monthly section includes one or more colors that are chosen for their prominence in nature during that time of year. September's red and yellow represent fall foliage; October's orange and black stand for Halloween; July's red, white, and blue emphasize Independence Day, and so on. To reinforce your child's grasp of the concept, point out the colors of the month when you are out and about. Name colors of foods, clothes, toys, and more whenever you can. You can even dedicate one day as a "yellow" day or a "green" day and try to wear clothing and eat foods that are the chosen color. You might also go on a color hunt and search for things that are one color, or create a color book of pictures cut and pasted from magazines.

Selected Stories

White Rabbit's Color Book
by Alan Baker

Colors Everywhere
by Tana Hoban

If You Want to Find Golden
by Eileen Spinelli

A Color of His Own
by Leo Lionni

The Purple Coat
by Amy Hest

Little Blue and Little Yellow
by Leo Lionni

Harold and the Purple Crayon
by Crockett Johnson

Encourage talking about colors, i.e.: "The coldest color I can think of is . . . The warmest color I can think of is . . . The softest color I can think of is . . . When I think of yellow, I think of . . . When I think of blue, I think of . . . My favorite color for a house is . . . My favorite color for a flower is . . . The funniest color I can think of is . . . The color that makes me the happiest is . . ." and so on.

SHAPES

Windows, tables, bowls, a slice of pie, an egg—shapes are everywhere. The concept of shapes, however, is not easy for children to grasp, so I have made it an integral part of the curriculum. Each month, I've chosen shapes that coincide with what is going on in the world around us: heart shapes for February, a circle for October, and so on. Be sure to reinforce the lessons by playing games with your child. Point to a window and say, "Can you tell me what shape that window is?" You might also serve snacks in shapes: sandwiches cut into triangles, round melon balls, cucumber slices, rectangle wafers, or graham cracker squares. Shape-sorting boxes are a perennial favorite with children, or create tactile shape pieces out of felt, carpet pieces, or sandpaper and have your child sort by feel. By the age of three, a child can usually sketch recognizable shapes, including circles, rectangles, and triangles, and you can integrate this new skill into many daily activities by encouraging him to draw objects he sees. You can also try incorporating shapes into music by singing songs about shapes. Sing to the tune of "The Muffin Man":

> *Do you know what shape this is?*
> *What shape this is, what shape this is?*
> *Do you know what shape this is,*
> *I'm holding in my hand?*

Mommy's Memo

Place shapes in a "feely bag" and ask your child to choose by touch the shape that matches the one you're holding.

Mom, Did You Know?

A child's introduction to geometric shapes begins in infancy with blocks, mobiles, puzzles, and sorting toys.

KEY CONCEPTS

The educational concepts of each month may tie in with holidays, seasons, animals, recurring events, or aspects of human nature. For example, in February we'll explore the concept of love and in November we'll learn about harvests and being thankful. At the beginning of each month, I offer a list of relevant concepts that you may find interesting and appropriate to introduce to your child. To encourage your child's understanding of these concepts, try to talk to her about them whenever the opportunity arises.

ART ACTIVITIES

Creating art projects is more than just a fun way to hone fine motor skills. Arts and crafts also help children develop other key skills such as following directions, recognizing shapes and colors, and understanding spatial relationships. The ability to draw begins sometime during a child's second year, and around his fourth birthday your child will begin to create representative images such as stick figures and scenes. To encourage his interest in art, provide a place to draw freely, and praise his efforts. Each art activity in our monthly curriculum lists the materials you'll need for the project and easy-to-follow directions. It's a good idea to set up all the art supplies before you begin the activity. Have fun—and don't be afraid to make a mess.

CREATIVE COOKING

Cooking up simple recipes with your child is a delicious way for him to help out and for you to have fun together. This part of the curriculum provides easy-to-follow recipes that coincide with other monthly activities. Cooking together teaches concepts such as cutting and rolling (small and large motor skills), measuring and sorting (math skills), and nutrition. Not only do you have fun, you also have a finished product you can eat. After you're done cooking, have your child help you clean up so he'll understand that cleaning is part of the process. This will teach him about taking responsibility for himself and his home. Praising your child as a "good helper" will encourage him to be helpful as he grows up.

As you cook, you'll discover that the kitchen is a virtual learning laboratory. Sorting and categorizing is important for your child to learn, as it reinforces observation and classification skills. Kids enjoy knowing the differences between different objects and being able to group them accordingly. Try opening the silverware drawer and letting your child group the spoons, forks, and knives (butter or plastic knives only!). Ask him to compare the different sizes and shapes of the flatware and describe the differences to you. Kitchen chemistry is the science of mixing ingredients and creating new food with different properties. Edible art is the practice of combining ingredients to make new and visually interesting creations. If you look at your work in the kitchen as a chore, then you're missing out on heaps of fun.

SING-ALONGS

Without music, life would be awfully quiet and extremely boring. The music in my *Mommy and Me* curriculum will help fill your head with tunes that are proven child pleasers and may bring back wonderful childhood memories of your own. Sing the songs with your child and share them with your entire family. Don't worry if you can't carry a tune—your child will be too swept up by the experience to realize you're singing out of key. Even if your child doesn't exhibit spectacular musical gifts, keep the joy of music alive by introducing various genres and styles. Your interest and commitment to music will make the difference in how your child "hears" the world.

Mommy's Memo

Young children generally love helping out around the house. Cooking and cleaning up can become memorable together-time activities.

Mom, Did You Know?

Research studies indicate that learning to play an instrument increases spatial-temporal reasoning. Though musical training has its benefits, don't introduce formal lessons before a child is four or five years old.

Two-year-olds like listening to music and love singing games and musical play. By the age of three most children can combine rhythm, words, and basic pitch; by five years of age, a child can usually beat time at regular intervals and sing a song. But the vocal instrument isn't the only means of making music. Banging out a rhythm on a drum, shaking maracas or a tambourine, or strumming a guitar are all great ways to integrate music into your child's life. Whenever possible, expose your child to live music. A concert, parade, or children's ballet are all good musical experiences.

As a musical supplement, I've included numerous fingerplays and action rhymes. These are little poems, chants, or rhymes that you act out with your fingers and hands. You and your child will love doing them everywhere. They're a terrific help when you're passing the time in waiting rooms, on planes, standing in line, or even in the bathtub. The fingerplays and action rhymes correspond with holidays, seasons, and other educational concepts featured in each chapter, and all are accompanied by easy-to-follow directions.

PHYSICAL FUN

*Y*oung children love to move, so helping them develop their coordination and gross motor skills is easy. The sense of achievement that comes from mastering physical movements increases a child's self-esteem and aids in socialization. In addition to the fun you'll have when you "get physical" with your child, there are good reasons for you to help direct her play. Running, jumping, swimming, and playing ball prepare children for playing sports and other activities. Even galloping like a horse or jumping like a frog aid in developing necessary gross motor skills. What's more, active kids tend to become active adults, so the encouragement you give them when they're young is a sound investment in their future health.

Some parents are so afraid their children will hurt themselves that they never give them a chance to discover what

Mommy's Memo

Songs are more meaningful when they're made personal. Whenever possible, introduce your child's name or events from his own experience into your singing. ("Are you sleeping, are you sleeping, Little Meg, Little John?")

they're physically capable of. Better to cheer them on and intervene if necessary than to clip their wings too closely. For each month, I'll feature at least two fun physical activities that you can do with your child. Not only will your child have fun, but you will feel like a kid again, too. An extra bonus: at bedtime, everyone will be ready for a good night's sleep.

TERRIFIC TRIPS

*G*etting out of the house is good for everyone. Every month I recommend one or two terrific trips for you to take with your child. These mini-adventures correspond to other activities that are part of the monthly curriculum. Be sure to plan ahead and tell your child about the outing a couple of days in advance to add to the excitement (as long as there is very little chance that you'll have to cancel). If possible, take along the whole family. Whenever possible, I've included specific tips and activities that complement the trip and help extend the experience.

MOMS ONLY

*W*ritten exclusively for parents, these pages focus on some of the important issues you may face while raising a toddler or preschooler. Included will be sections on the following:

Discipline Do: Learning how to discipline your child is one of the hardest aspects of parenthood, especially once your child reaches age two and begins to develop a will of his own. Each month, I offer disciplinary tips you can implement in your household. From learning how to limit sugar intake during the holidays to developing positive reinforcements for acceptable behavior, I provide concrete ideas for making life around your house easier.

Daddy and Me

Dad should have an individual relationship with his child and going on a weekly outing is one way to accomplish this. Whether it's a trip to the barber shop, bowling alley, or a ball game, this focused time together will be memorable for both of you.

Relaxation Rx: Every mother needs time for herself. Each month, I share some ideas on how to get some much-needed relaxation. Whether it's sharing a romantic dinner with your partner or treating yourself to an afternoon at the spa or beauty salon, finding leisure time for yourself is essential if you hope to maintain a loving and patient attitude toward your family.

Toddler Tidbit: Your child is growing quickly and learning new skills each day. Each month brings new challenges and new opportunities to introduce developmental concepts. From bicycle safety in June to beating the winter blues in January; from dealing with feelings and learning how to express love in February; to preparing your child for pre-school in the fall, you'll find an abundance of useful information in these sections.

Medical Message: Tips from pediatricians and other medical experts will help get you through the trials and tribulations of childhood health care. The curriculum covers insect bites and sunburn during the summer months, frostbite in the winter, controlling sugar consumption around Halloween, and more.

SELECTED STORIES

Whether it's before bedtime or while the two of you are snuggled up on the couch, your child will always be eager to hear you tell a story. Children learn language through reading, which is why it is an essential part of our curriculum. Each month I suggest a number of stories— both traditional and contemporary—for you to read to your child. They can all be found at the library or your local bookstore (if you have trouble finding them, check our Web site www.mommyandme.com). When reading together, always sit quietly in a place with no distractions. And remember, read slowly!

Storytelling doesn't always have to come from books. You can also make up stories or tell your children family stories. Every child should know his or her roots and telling stories about your family's past creates a healthy sense of belonging. Oral interpretation through dramatic activity or storytelling is regarded as an effective method of promoting enjoyment of literature, developing oral expression and increasing reading comprehension. This can be as easy as pulling out old photo albums and scrapbooks and relating stories about the faces staring back at you or remembering family stories or rituals from when you were a child. As your child becomes more verbal, encourage her to tell stories about herself. Some of the best stories evolve from family lore. To help your children develop a love for storytelling and reading help them start their own library, give books as gifts, and spend part of every day looking at illustrations, reading, and telling stories.

READY, SET, PLAY

*T*he *Mommy and Me* experience continues in the pages that follow. Whether it's mom, dad, grandmother, grandfather, nanny, aunt, or uncle participating in the activities, make sure that the focus remains on having fun together. Remember to take your time, improvise, be creative, and enjoy the special time with your child. They're only this age once, and at least for now, you are the most important person in their life.

Mommy's Memo

Different holidays offer children a glimpse of the cultural, racial, and religious diversity they'll encounter in the world outside their homes.

White is

the Color of

the Month.

A Circle is

the Shape of

the Month.

JANUARY

Happy New Year! As we hang a brand-new calendar we pause to reflect on the months ahead. January marks a fresh start, with hopes and plans for an exciting year. The holiday rush is over, and our January curriculum offers loads of winter fun as well as games that will help your child learn about the season. From making paper snowflakes and popcorn snowmen to hitting the ice rink and taking a winter walk, January is filled with new beginnings and new things to enjoy. There's a lot to do, so bundle up and let's get started!

KEY JANUARY CONCEPTS:

1. Snow is white.

2. Calendars help people keep track of passing time.

3. A year is divided into twelve months; a month is divided into four weeks; a week is divided into seven days.

4. A year has four seasons. Cold and snow are signs of the winter season.

5. The Chinese New Year, based on the lunar calendar, falls sometime between January 21 and February 21.

6. Dr. Martin Luther King was a famous African-American who taught brotherhood and peace among all people. (The third Monday in January marks Martin Luther King Day.)

"Free at last! Free at last! Thank God Almighty, we are free at last!"

—Martin Luther King

TIME CAPSULE
Art Activity • 15 Minutes to 1 Hour

Your Child Will Learn

Fine motor skills

Listening/Language skills

Number recognition

Concept of "time"

Family history

Critical thinking

Creativity

Mommy's Materials

Family photos

Mementos

Airtight canister with lid (such as a container used for potato chips, oatmeal, coffee, etc.)

Safety scissors

Markers and/or stickers

Tinfoil

Nontoxic glue

*C*reating a time capsule can become an annual tradition that your family looks forward to each New Year's. As young children examine their own lives and the world around them, they begin to understand the concept of history. Dig out old pictures and show your child how he's grown. Share your own childhood pictures, too, and point out how various members of your family, such as grandparents or aunts and uncles, looked when they were children. In choosing mementos to include in his time capsule, your child will learn about his family history, neighborhood, and the time period in which he lives.

STEP BY STEP

1. Gather up personal items such as photos of family, friends, and pets. Be sure to label names and vital statistics (e.g., height, weight); add artwork, child's handprint, a toy, and/or newspaper and magazine headlines.

2. Cover the canister with tinfoil and decorate any way your child desires, using markers, stickers, or other items. Put your child's name and the date on the time capsule.

3. Place personal items inside the capsule. After replacing the lid, explain that the capsule is to be hidden away until a certain date. Help your child decide when the capsule should be opened: next New Year's? in five years? in ten years? in twenty-five years?

4. Choose a place to hide the capsule (a basement or attic works well) and conceal it with a note specifying the opening date.

CHOOSING ARTIFACTS

Collect artifacts that describe your children's life and times. In addition to original art or photos, you can add a creative story, newspaper article, political campaign buttons, and baseball or sports cards. Try adding mint-fresh coins and first-issue stamps or a listing of movies currently playing at the theater. Another fun idea is to record some of your child's favorite songs and place the tape in your time capsule.

MORE MOMMY AND ME FUN

Time Talk: Discuss the fact that things change over time. Talk about when you were a child. Look at books with pictures from past eras. Ask your child to imagine what life was like before videos, computers, and television. Encourage him to imagine what the future will be like.

Make Time Count: Mark a specific time on your calendar each week when you and your child will have a date. Ask your child for suggestions on how you should spend this special time together.

Mommy's Memo

Talk to your child about the passage of time by showing him a clock or a calendar. He may not be able to tell time until he's five or six, but he'll have a natural sense of time relative to his daily activities such as mealtime or bedtime.

Mom, Did You Know?

The 365 days in a calendar year reflect the length of time it takes the earth to orbit the sun.

SNOWFLAKES
Art Activity • 10 to 15 Minutes

Your Child Will Learn

Fine motor skills

Shape recognition

Eye-hand coordination

Concept of "winter"

Mommy's Materials

White paper to use for cutting circles of different sizes (coffee filters work well, also)

Plate or bowl

Safety scissors

Nontoxic glue

Dark-colored construction paper

*S*nowflakes are one of the most beautiful creations in nature, but most children have little knowledge of what a snowflake actually looks like. This art activity provides an opportunity to learn about snowflakes and make one. Though all are six-sided symmetrical crystals, no two are the same. As you make your folds and cuts, you'll discover limitless ways to make your own distinctive snowflakes. And when you're finished, create a whole snowstorm by hanging them for the entire family to see.

STEP BY STEP

1. Lay the plate or bowl upside down on the white paper. Trace around the rim and cut out the circle.

2. Fold white paper circle in half and then in thirds as shown in diagram.

3. Begin cutting the design of the snowflake. Use scissors to cut out small shapes but don't cut away all the folds or the snowflake will fall apart. (Remember, it's not important to make perfect folds or cuts. Your child will still be fascinated with the end result.)

4. Gently open the snowflake to see what kind of design you've created.

5. Glue snowflakes onto the dark paper or string all the artwork from the ceiling.

MORE MOMMY AND ME FUN

Tissue Snowflakes: Colored tissue paper or wrapping paper makes vibrant snowflakes. You can layer several tissue snowflakes and get different see-through effects by turning the different layers slightly like a kaleidoscope.

Tortilla Snowflakes: Use the same technique as cutting out paper snowflakes to make snowflake shapes out of flour tortillas. Then put a touch of oil in a pan and fry the tortilla until it is crisp. Sprinkle on powdered sugar.

Soapy Snowmen: Mix up faux snow by combining 2 cups of Ivory Snow with ½ cup water. Combine in a blender or whip with electric beater until doughy. Shape damp soap into three balls and stack them by gently pushing a toothpick through. Add twig arms, clove eyes, shirt buttons, and a felt scarf.

Snowflake Globe: Fill a small jar (a baby food jar works well) with iridescent glitter, confetti pieces, and water. Glue the rim of the lid (adults only, please) and secure to the jar. When finished, children can shake their jar and make it snow whenever they want.

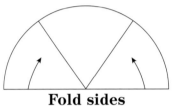

Fold sides

Mommy's Memo

Explain to your child that just as each person is unique, so is each snowflake.

Mom, Did You Know?

When water freezes inside clouds, ice crystals join together to form snowflakes. As they fall, snowflakes connect to make bigger snowflakes. The largest on record measured more than 12 inches in diameter.

• JANUARY ACTIVITIES •

SNOW ICE CREAM
Creative Cooking • 10 to 20 Minutes

Your Child Will Learn

Color concepts

Fine motor skills

Counting

To follow directions

Taste discrimination

Mommy's Materials

Clean snow or crushed ice (approx. 4–5 cups)

½ cup sugar (confectioner's sugar works better than refined, but either will suffice)

¼ tsp. vanilla extract

Flavored syrup (optional)

1 cup milk or cream

*f you're lucky enough to live in an area where you can find clean snow, your kids will love making ice cream out of it. This recipe is mounds of fun and even a very young child can help in the preparations. Once you've collected a container of fresh snow, you can either mix up a big batch of ice cream or each child can make his own individual serving in a cereal bowl. Snow ice cream is best eaten at one sitting, so when it's ready, scoop it up and enjoy one of life's simple pleasures.

STEP BY STEP

1. Collect some freshly fallen clean snow and put in a bowl.

2. Sprinkle the sugar in and add some vanilla extract (not too much—it's very strong). If you have bottles of flavored syrup like raspberry or licorice, use a dash instead of the vanilla extract.

3. Mix the ingredients together until the sugar is dissolved. Add just enough milk to make a nice slushy texture.

MORE MOMMY AND ME FUN

Snow Cones: Besides being yummy, snow cones can help teach your child about the cold, even if you live in a warm climate. Place cracked ice cubes in a blender and crush. Pour in a small amount of fruit juice and blend together. Scoop the finished product into your child's cup. For added fun, allow your child to play with the extra blended ice and make a snowball.

Popcorn Snowmen: No snow? No worries. To make scrumptious snowmen, pop about 15 cups of popcorn and set aside. Melt ½ cup of butter or margarine in a saucepan over medium-low heat. Add two-10 ounce packages of marshmallows, stirring constantly. Once melted, pour over the popcorn and stir to coat. When cool enough to touch, rub margarine on your hands and form popcorn balls. Stack three balls using white frosting for glue. Add pretzel-stick arms, raisin eyes, and a candy-corn nose. Arrange candies into a broad grin. For buttons, use gumdrops or red hots. For scarves, cut rectangles out of a fruit "roll-up," or fruit leather.

Marshmallow Snowman: For a noncook version of a snowman, have your child place three large marshmallows on top of one another and secure with a toothpick. Decorate with raisins, mini candies, and pieces of cereal. (Be sure to take out the toothpick before eating this wonderful winter creation).

Mommy's Memo

In honor of Chinese New Year, try eating some foods with chopsticks this month.

Mom, Did You Know?

Legend has it that the Roman emperor Nero discovered the first frozen dessert. Runners brought snow from the mountain, which was then mixed with nectar, fruit pulp, and honey.

Safe and Sound

For snow ice cream, a fresh snowfall offers the best chance to find ingredients free of dirt or other undesired contaminants.

Selected Stories

The Snowman
by Raymond Briggs

The Snowy Day
by Ezra Jack Keats

The Snow Queen
by Hans Christian Andersen

Snowflake Bentley
(Caldecott Award Winner)
by Jacqueline Briggs
Martin and Mary Azarian

Snow
(Caldecott Honor Book)
by Uri Shulevitz

Just a Snowy Day
by Mercer Mayer

Selected Songs

"Frosty the Snowman"
Performed by Gene Autry

"Let It Snow"
Performed by Vaughn
Monroe

"Sleigh Ride"
Performed by Leroy
Anderson

SING ALONG
Music, Fingerplays, and Action Rhymes

"I'M A LITTLE SNOWMAN"

I'm a little snowman short and fat,

Here is my nose, my eyes, and hat.

When the sun starts shining—oops, watch out!

I will melt—without a doubt.

"NO MORE SNOWMEN"

Five little snowmen,
(hold up five fingers)

Riding on a sled.
(wiggle fingers pretending to sled)

One fell down and bumped his head.
(use your finger to bump your head)

Frosty called the doctor
(pretend to dial a phone)

And the doctor said, "No more snowmen
(shake your forefinger)

Riding on that sled!"
(repeat)

Count down "four little snowmen, three little snowmen," and so on until "No more snowmen riding on that sled."

"SNOW"
(Sing to the tune of "The Farmer in the Dell")

The snow is on the roof,
(point hands over head)

The snow is on the ground,
(point to the floor)

The snow is on the window,
(make a window with your hands)

The snow is all around.
(make large circles with hands)

"FIVE LITTLE SNOWMEN"

Five little snowmen sitting on the ground,
(pat hands on floor)

The first one said, "Oh, aren't we round."
(make circle with arms)

The second one said, "There are snowflakes in the air."
(wiggle fingers above head)

The third one said, "But we don't care."
(shrug shoulders)

The fourth one said, "Let's run and run and run."
(pat hands quickly on the floor)

The fifth one said, "I'm ready for some fun."
(smile)

Whew went the wind,
(blow)

And out came the sun,
(make circle with arms over head)

And the five little snowmen knew their fun was done.
(pretend you're melting)

Mommy's Memo

January songs and fingerplays help develop counting skills through repetition as they reinforce the concepts of winter.

JANUARY ACTIVITIES

"Building a snowman together will surely melt your heart."

—Unknown

125

ICE-SKATING
Physical Fun

Your Child Will Learn

Gross motor skills

Balance

Spatial relationships

Coordination

Concept of "cold"

Mommy's Materials

Warm clothes

Thick socks

Gloves or mittens

Safety gear

Ice skates

*T*here are few activities more exhilarating than skating outside on a frozen pond in crisp winter air amid beautiful scenery. Falling is part of the fun, and if you approach it with good humor and lots of padding, there's no reason why even a very young child can't enjoy this invigorating pastime. If you live in a warm climate, don't despair—check out the Yellow Pages for a convenient indoor ice- or roller-skating facility.

TIPS FOR A GREAT SKATING EXPERIENCE

1. If you are skating on an outdoor pond, be sure to check with the local authorities to make sure the ice is safe to skate on.

2. Safety gear is a must! Hockey or bike helmets should be used. Knee and elbow pads are strongly advised for extra protection. Many indoor rinks have safety equipment available for rental.

3. A child should be at least three years old before she learns how to skate on single blades. For children under three, double blades allow them to get accustomed to the feel of the ice.

4. Under no circumstances should a child who is not yet walking be skating.

5. For beginners, there is a wonderful device called an "Easy Glider," which helps support a child's body on the ice. It is available at most ice arenas and helps save a parent's back and arms. (If unavailable, a lightweight chair works well.)

6. Ice arenas are cold, so warm clothing such as jackets, sweaters, pants, hats, and mittens are a must. If you don't have mittens, socks are a great substitute. For warm feet, thick socks are especially important. (That goes for grown-ups as well as kids.) Bring along an extra pair or two.

7. Be sure that the ice skates fit your child properly. The rule of thumb is that the skate size should be one size smaller than the shoe size.

8. The skate should fit securely around the ankle. Even though your child may be able to tie her own shoe, do it for her to be certain it's tied tightly enough for support.

9. When your child says she is tired, be sure to listen to her. Ten minutes on the ice can be an eternity. Rest awhile, then go back and try again.

Mommy's Memo

For faux skating, slide across a bare-floored room on pieces of 8½ x 11-inch paper while listening to music such as "The Skater's Waltz" by Emil Waldteufel. If you have carpets, use two pieces of wax paper or cover your stocking feet with plastic bags.

Safe and Sound

Make sure your child wears a hat when the temperatures are below freezing. Most of a person's body heat is lost through an uncovered head—an important consideration for young children.

WINTER TRACKS
Terrific Trips

Your Child Will Learn

Animal behavior

Critical thinking

Shapes and patterns

Following directions

Great National Parks

Yosemite National Park: Winter treats include ranger-led walks, ice-skating, cross-country skiing, and hiking.

Yellowstone: Winter snow makes the steaming hot springs, geysers, fumaroles, and mud pots look even more supernatural.

Grand Canyon National Park: During the winter, you'll get the park's great overlooks almost to yourself—and the splendor of this 277-mile-long canyon is better than ever.

When the excitement of the first snowfall wanes, children often get restless and cabin fever sets in. Fortunately, there are plenty of outdoor activities to keep them busy in the short, cold days of January. A winter walk holds many secrets for those willing to venture out to the forests, riverbanks, parks, and fields. Beginning trackers can look for signs of animal life as well as observe winter constellations, identify tree branch patterns, and study life in frozen ponds. You can instill a lifelong love of nature in your child by introducing him to the many secrets that a winter landscape holds.

CRITTER CLUES

Check for the "critter clues" that the wildlife in your area leaves behind. Clues include track patterns (each species has a characteristic way of moving), browse (evidence that the animal has eaten), and scat (which can yield information about what an animal has eaten). Keep your eyes peeled—you never know what clues you might find along the way.

The more remote your location, the more likely you are to find prints of wild creatures. Challenge yourselves to identify squirrels, chipmunks, deer, grouse, or wild turkey tracks. The woodland community is particularly active. You might find evidence of deer, raccoons, foxes, or rabbits. If you don't live near the woods, you can still do plenty of tracking: prints of a neighborhood dog, a stray cat, or a tiny field mouse will prove equally fascinating to your child.

Your young scientist can also help identify and gather all types of data. Older children can keep records and charts graphing the details they've found. And after an exhilarating winter walk, it's fun to regroup indoors with a warm drink and talk about all you've seen and learned.

MORE MOMMY AND ME FUN

Winter Dress-up: We all know how long it takes for little ones to put on their winter garb. To speed up the process, gather up all the items—boots, coat, hat, mittens—and make a game of it. Sit on the floor together and have a race to see who can get dressed and undressed quicker.

Snowflake Sleuth: During a snowfall, bundle up your munchkin and go outside. Bring along a magnifying glass and dark piece of construction paper or velvet to catch snowflakes. Quickly, before they melt, examine the flakes with the magnifying glass. Many snowflakes are "broken" so you don't see the whole six-sided crystal, but with persistence you'll find some beautiful examples. This activity is easiest during a warm snowfall when the flakes are big and fluffy.

Mommy's Memo

You don't need to be a naturalist to teach your children about the winter world. Children are naturally inquisitive, and generally just need some guidance. Check out a book from your local library on animal tracks and look at guidebooks or children's stories that may help.

Selected Stories

Big Tracks, Little Tracks: Following Animal Prints by Millicent E. Selsam

In the Snow: Who's Been Here? by Lindsay Barrett George

Animals in the Snow by Margaret Wise Brown

• JANUARY ACTIVITIES •

MOMS ONLY
Advice, Tips, and Suggestions

Selected Stories

My Dream of Martin
Luther King
by Faith Ringgold

A Picture Book of Martin
Luther King, Jr.
by David A. Adler

Happy Birthday, Martin
Luther King
by Jean Marzollo

DISCIPLINE DO

Teamwork: Parents who don't share the same ideas when it comes to discipline can wreak havoc on a family. I remember a young boy on a ski vacation who was told by his parents not to go down a specific trail alone. When he did, his mother didn't want to allow him to ski the next day. The father thought his son was just being adventurous and shouldn't be punished. There was a major disagreement in front of the child, and the parents didn't talk to each other the rest of the evening. This situation could have been avoided had both parents established clear ground rules beforehand. In this case, the parents could have agreed that if their son broke any safety rules, some of his skiing privileges would be revoked. This type of teamwork helps tremendously, and not surprisingly, children respond better to parents who work together. If you're wondering which parent prevailed in the example above, the answer is neither—there was a blizzard the next day and the slopes were closed!

RELAXATION Rx

A Warm Bath: After spending your day outside playing in the snow or helping to shovel the walk, you need to set aside some time and take care of yourself. When the kids are finally sleeping, run a steaming-hot bath, put some soothing music on a cassette player, and light beeswax or scented candles on a small table near the tub. Leave out clean towels and a washcloth, a back scrubber, and a few magazines. Finally, sprinkle in some scented bath oil, sip a glass of your favorite beverage, and be sure to put a "Do Not Disturb" sign on the door! If you want a really quick fix on a cold night, warm up and relax without the fuss of a bath. Throw some big towels in a dryer, turn it on high, and five minutes later wrap yourself up in them as you unwind in a big chair or on the bed.

TODDLER TIDBIT

Diversity and Equality: It's never too early to teach young children about diversity, tolerance, and equality. In honor of Martin Luther King, January is a good time to remember the freedom and dignity of all races and peoples. To illustrate Dr. King's message, show your child a brown egg and a white egg. Observe the eggs together before breaking them open. The message is clear. While the eggs are different on the outside, they are the same on the inside, just like people. You can also show several dolls of different colors. Have your child point out all of the things the dolls have in common and all of the things that are different. Try some playacting with your dolls. Ask questions such as, "Do they all feel sad sometimes?" "If they all fell down, would they all feel hurt?" Finish off the discussion by explaining Dr. King's dream of equality and filling in the following blank with your own words: "I have a dream that one day all people will _____."

MEDICAL MESSAGE

Kids and Frostbite: Kids love to play outside in the snow. However, a winter wonderland can be treacherous. Overexposure to cold can cause frostbite, which injures the skin and the tissues beneath. Children get frostbite more easily than adults because they're often too busy playing to realize that they should go inside to dry off and warm up. Extremities such as ears, nose, fingers, and toes are at greatest risk. Children with frostbite will have a loss of feeling in the affected area. The frozen areas can appear purplish, mottled, yellow, or waxy. The affected area should not be massaged or rubbed with snow. If your child shows symptoms of frostbite, find a warm area as quickly as possible. Remove clothing from frostbitten areas and cover with warm blankets or use your own body heat to rewarm the skin. Frostbite is a medical emergency and your doctor should be called if it is severe. "Frostnip," on the other hand, is a tingling or numbness that goes away with rewarming (try using warm water, about 100 to 104 degrees). The best defense is dressing warmly and keeping dry.

Mommy's Memo

Although some of us live in mild climates, every young child needs to understand the four seasons and the special delights that winter brings.

Mom, Did You Know?

It's a myth that your child will catch cold if he goes outside without a hat or mittens. Germs cause sickness, not clothing choices. Of course, keeping your child warm improves resistance to germs and helps keep him healthy.

Red is
the Color of
the Month.

A Heart is
the Shape of
the Month.

FEBRUARY

Valentine's Day is wildly popular with children. The theme of love is one they can easily grasp, and they adore the bold, bright colors and heart shapes they see in store windows. Our February curriculum is full of activities designed to help foster compassion in young children. Explain to your child the meaning of Valentine's Day and how love is a wonderful sentiment to share. Give him or her lots of hugs and kisses and demonstrate affection. When children feel loved, they feel happy. February also brings other holidays and celebrations, from Groundhog Day to Presidents' Day to Black History Month. So besides a lot of love being shared, there is a potpourri of activities for all to enjoy.

KEY FEBRUARY CONCEPTS:

1. The shape of a heart and the color red are symbols of Valentine's Day.

2. Black History Month honors African Americans who have made contributions to U.S. history.

3. Valentine's Day is when people exchange cards, flowers, and gifts as an expression of love and friendship.

4. Love is a special emotion that reflects deep affection.

5. Presidents' Day marks the birthdays of two great U.S. presidents: George Washington and Abraham Lincoln.

6. The Groundhog Day forecast indicates whether winter will be over soon.

"A mother holds her children's hands for a while — their hearts forever."
— Unknown

HANDS ON HEART
Art Activity • 15 to 20 Minutes

Your Child Will Learn

Fine motor skills

Valentine's Day traditions

Colors and shapes

Eye-hand coordination

Mommy's Materials

Glue

White paper doily

Two sheets of construction paper (pink and red)

Safety scissors

Pencil

Crayons

Valentine's Day is one of my favorite holidays. It belongs to everyone and is usually a huge lovefest. Your child probably has quite a few people he's sweet on, from Grandma to his favorite teacher or best friend. When February 14 rolls around, it's nice for him to be able to share a homemade gift with the most treasured people in his life. This art activity requires little more than a few materials and your child's touch to make it truly heartfelt.

STEP BY STEP

1. Glue paper doily to red construction paper.

2. Fold pink paper in half and cut into a heart shape slightly smaller than the doily. If your child can't manage scissors yet, you can precut the heart.

3. Place your child's hand on the pink heart and trace it (or paint your child's hand red and make a handprint).

4. Glue the heart on the doily.

5. Write an "I Love You" message from your child on the hand.

MORE MOMMY AND ME FUN

Tissue Paper Love Leaves: There is a rare type of tree that only blooms on Valentine's Day. Instead of water to help it grow, all it needs is love! Cut out various size heart shapes from red and white construction paper. Tear or cut small pieces of red tissue paper, crumple them up, and glue them on the hearts. Make a small hole in the top of each heart and loop a string through. Now bundle up, take your beautiful love leaves outside, and hang them on trees in the yard.

Heart Animals and People: Make heart animals and people by pasting different shaped hearts together and adding facial features with chalk, crayons, glitter, lace, or ribbons. For example, you can use one large heart for a head and smaller hearts for ears, eyes, nose, mouth, etc.

Heart Prints: Cut a potato in half. Press a heart-shaped cookie cutter into the potato. Cut around the cookie-cutter line, leaving a raised heart. Put a thin layer of red tempera paint on a paper plate. Demonstrate how to stamp the potato in the paint and then onto a piece of paper.

Heart Rubbings: Cut out different sizes of hearts from sandpaper. Tape hearts down and lay a sheet of thin white paper over them. Use the side of a red crayon to rub over hearts lightly, making a pattern on paper.

Mommy's Memo

Handmade valentines are a great gift of love. Your child can repeat this activity several times to make valentines for the whole family. Grandparents really love these handmade treasures.

Mom, Did You Know?

There are many legends surrounding Valentine's Day, but the most popular suggests the holiday of love originated in the third century to commemorate Saint Valentine, who performed secret marriages.

GROUNDHOG SHADOWPLAY
Art Activity • 15 Minutes

Your Child Will Learn

Groundhog Day traditions

Fine motor skills

To follow directions

Light and shadow

Weather

Mommy's Materials

Brown construction paper

Safety scissors

Popsicle® or craft stick or straw

Cotton balls or white felt

Flashlight

Paper cup (optional)

Selected Stories

It's Groundhog Day
by Steven Kroll

Gregory's Shadow
by Don Freeman

According to legend, if a groundhog in Punxsutawney, Pennsylvania, peeks his head out of his burrow after hibernating all winter and he sees his shadow, he'll return to his hole and there will be six more weeks of winter. Even if it's not Groundhog Day, you can vary this activity for other times of the year. Create turkey shadows in November and bunny pop-ups for Easter. Regardless of the shape of your shadow puppet, your child will be fascinated with the play possibilities.

STEP BY STEP

1. Help your child cut a groundhog out of brown construction paper using safety scissors.

2. Attach to a Popsicle® or craft stick or straw and shine the flashlight on a blank wall.

3. Place the groundhog in front of the flashlight and make his shadow appear.

4. Explain that objects that get in the way of the sun or a bright light cause shadows.

5. If you like, you can cover a paper or Styrofoam cup with brown construction paper for the burrow (you can even add cotton balls or white felt around the top edge for snow). Then use the craft stick or straw to make the groundhog pop up out of his "burrow" when winter is over.

MORE MOMMY AND ME FUN

Shadow Play: Let your child experiment with making his own shadows. Ask him to make big shadows, little shadows, animal shadows, and moving shadows. For more shadow play, trace your child's shadow at different times of the day. See page 53 for the classic Robert Louis Stevenson poem "My Shadow."

Groundhog Box: Find a box large enough for a child to crawl in and let him decorate it like a groundhog's home. Paint it, draw trees on it, and then let him pretend to be a groundhog crawling in and out of his "hole."

Rhyme Time: Here's a fun rhyme for Groundhog Day—

> *Here's a little groundhog,*
> *Furry and brown.*
> *He's popping up to look around.*
> *If he sees his shadow, down he'll go,*
> *Then six more weeks of winter. Oh no!*

Mommy's Memo

On February 2, ask everyone in the family to make a prediction about whether the groundhog will see his shadow.

Mom, Did You Know?

The groundhog, also known as a woodchuck, is a shy, burrowing, and hibernating mammal that has excellent eyesight and eats seeds, roots, and plants.

JELL-O® HEARTS
Creative Cooking • 15 Minutes Prep

Your Child Will Learn

Fine motor skills

Valentine's Day traditions

The color red

Heart shapes

Numbers/Counting

Mommy's Materials

1 pot for boiling

1 box of instant Jell-O®
(raspberry, cherry, or
strawberry flavor)

1 shallow baking pan

Heart-shaped cookie
cutters (various sizes if
possible)

Since our color of the month is red and our shape is a heart, our cooking fun will combine the two. All kids love Jell-O, and these ruby red hearts are as pretty as jewelry. Through mixing, pouring, and cutting, your child's fine motor coordination will improve, and after you've both worked up an appetite you can enjoy these Valentine treats and share them with friends and family.

STEP BY STEP

1. Follow instructions on box of Jell-O and pour it into the baking pan.

2. Allow the Jell-O to cool (which can take a couple of hours).

3. Once the Jell-O is cool, wash your hands and use heart-shaped cookie cutters to cut out shapes and lay them out on another plate. (Dipping the cutter in hot water first helps make a cleaner shape).

4. You can also use the heart-shaped cookie cutter to stamp hearts out of other types of food, including pancakes, bread, and slices of cheese.

MORE MOMMY AND ME FUN

Strawberry Heart Muffins: A perfect Valentine breakfast. Cut an English muffin in half (toast it if you like). Spread some cream cheese on the muffin halves. Cut 3 or 4 strawberries in half (show your child that strawberries cut in half are heart-shaped). If they're out of season, use frozen ones. Put heart-shaped strawberry halves on the muffin and serve.

Strawberry Milkshake: Combine 8 ounces of fresh or frozen strawberries and 2 ounces of milk in a blender. Garnish with a slice of strawberry and enjoy.

Heart Sandwich: Cut a large heart from a slice of bread. Spread with butter or cream cheese and put a little red jelly in the center before serving.

Rhyme Time: Try a Valentine's Day version of this classic poem—

> Roses are red,
> Violets are blue,
> You are sweet,
> And I love you!

Mommy's Memo

While waiting for Jell-O to cool, pull out some magazines and have your child point out all the items that are red. Not only will this pass the time, but it will help teach your child how the color red is incorporated into the world.

Mom, Did You Know?

Heart-healthy menus, (low in fat, cholesterol, and sodium) can help prevent heart disease.

SING ALONG
Music, Fingerplays, and Action Rhymes

Your Child Will Learn

Language acquisition

Auditory development

Rhythm

Sensory exploration

Bonding

Selected Stories

Guess How Much I Love You
by Sam McBratney

A Book of Hugs
by Dave Ross

Love You Forever
by Robert Munsch

I Love You With All My
Heart
by Noris Kern

The Valentine Bears
by Eve Bunting

Arthur's Valentine
by Marc Brown

"IF YOU'RE HAPPY AND YOU KNOW IT"

If you're happy and you know it,
Give a hug! (hug your child)
If you're happy and you know it,
Give a hug!
If you're happy and you know it,
Then your face will really show it.
If you're happy and you know it,
Give a hug!
If you're happy and you know it,
Throw a kiss! (throw a kiss)
If you're happy and you know it,
Throw a kiss!
If you're happy and you know it,
Then your face will really show it.
If you're happy and you know it,
Throw a kiss!!
Alternate verses:
Stomp your feet
Clap your hands
Touch your nose, etc.

"DAY FOR LOVE"

Pretty red hearts,
(trace outline of heart in air with index fingers)
And two-by-two. (hold up two fingers of both hands)
Holding hands, (clasp hands together)
And "I love you." (clasp hands to heart)
Scented flowers (hand "holds" flower to nose, sniff)
From garden vines,
A day for love, St. Valentine's.

"FIVE LITTLE VALENTINES"

Five little Valentines (hold up five fingers)
From the corner store.
I gave one to Mommy, (pretend to hand one off)
Now there are four. (hold up four fingers)
Four little Valentines, (hold up four fingers)
Pretty ones to see.
I gave one to brother, (or sister, or friend's name),
(pretend to hand one off)
Now there are three. (hold up three fingers)
Three little Valentines, (hold up three fingers)
Pink, red, and blue.
I gave one to Grandma, (or Grandpa, or aunt, or uncle),
(pretend to hand one off)
Now there are two. (hold up two fingers)
Two little Valentines, (hold up two fingers)
My poem is almost done.
I gave one to Daddy, (pretend to hand one off)
Now there is one. (hold up one finger)
One little Valentine. (hold up one finger)
Wow! We've had fun!
I gave it to me, (point to self)
Now there are none! (hands up in the air)

"YOU ARE MY SUNSHINE"

You are my sunshine,
My only sunshine.
You make me happy
When skies are gray.
You'll never know, dear,
How much I love you.
Please don't take
My sunshine away!

by Jimmie Davis and Charles Mitchell
©1940 by Peer International Corporation.
Used by permission. All Rights Reserved.

Mommy's Memo

My mother sang "You Are My Sunshine" to me when I was little and I have carried on that tradition with my daughter. I even recorded myself singing it so when I'm away, she can listen to my voice and feel comforted by it.

Mom, Did You Know?

Research shows that children who can easily express their feelings have an easier time handling conflicts.

VALENTINE BEANBAG TOSS
Physical Fun

Your Child Will Learn

Gross motor skills

Listening/Language skills

To follow directions

Shape concepts

Color concepts

Mommy's Materials

Beanbags

Basket or bucket

Red construction paper

Tape

Kids love playing beanbag toss. It's easy and they feel a real sense of accomplishment. You'll need a wastepaper basket or bucket and beanbags for this activity. You'll also need to cut a heart out of red construction paper with a hole in the center large enough for the beanbags to go through. Tape it over the wastebasket. Now—ready, set, aim. As your child becomes more confident, move the basket farther away to challenge her. If the activity is too difficult, move it closer. The last thing you want to do is frustrate her. Score!

MOMMY-MADE

Why not make your own heart-shaped beanbags? They're easy to make out of scrap material filled with rice or beans. First, cut two heart shapes out of red felt. Next, glue (or sew) the hearts together at the edges, leaving a small hole so you can pour in the beans after the glue dries. Glue the hole together and, when it dries, you have your own set of beanbags! Be sure to supervise small children during this activity to prevent them from choking on any beans that might fall out.

MORE MOMMY AND ME FUN

Beanbag Games: Find beanbags of different shapes, sizes, and colors. Using masking tape or cut poster board, create various shapes on the floor. Ask your child to toss the red beanbag onto the heart shape. Or have the child toss the small blue beanbag onto the large yellow square. The game will help your child make associations between different colors and shapes. You can also write the numbers 1 through 5 in the shapes and see who can throw his beanbag on the highest number.

More Beanbag Games: Use the beanbags to help identify different body parts by asking your child to put a beanbag on his or her head. Have him find various body parts and balance the beanbag on those parts (elbow, hand, and so on). For older children, ask them to hold the beanbag between their knees and try to walk around.

Pin Cupid's Heart: On a large piece of poster board, draw a flying Cupid with his arrow, or buy a cut-out Cupid and glue it onto the poster board. Cut out a small red heart. Stick a piece of tacky tape on the back of the heart. Take turns being blindfolded and pinning the heart on Cupid's arrow.

Musical Hearts: Cut out and laminate giant paper hearts for a Valentine version of musical chairs. When the music stops, everyone must stand on a heart. Take away a heart each round until there is one player left.

•FEBRUARY ACTIVITIES•

THE LIBRARY
Terrific Trips

Your Child Will Learn

Vocabulary

Art through illustrations

Book types

Reading skills

Responsibility

Selected Stories

Freedom's Fruit
by William H. Hooks

Pass It On: African-
American Poetry for
Children
selected by Wade Hudson

Follow the Drinking Gourd
by Jeanette Winter

Arthur Meets the President
by Marc Brown

Hail to the Chief
by Don Robb

How many presidents are there? Who invented peanut butter? Where is Punxsutawney? No question needs to go without an answer if you have a library nearby. A visit to your local library is inexpensive, fun, and educational. And the joy of sharing books is a priceless gift you can give your child. Most libraries offer a wealth of materials to stimulate and amuse all ages, including Mom and Dad. Many have music-listening stations, video equipment, story cassettes, and computers. Every time you share a story, a book, a game, or a song with a child, you have a chance to light a flame that will last a lifetime.

LIBRARY TIPS

1. Plan to visit at a time when you are both fed and well rested.

2. Choose comfortable clothes that allow you to get down on the floor and play or read a book together.

3. Ask if your child can get his own library card. The American Library Association suggests that you register your child for his own card as soon as he demonstrates interest, and make it a special event by telling grandparents, friends, and so on.

4. Bring a large, sturdy book bag that is comfortable to carry when full. Be certain to explain that the books you bring home are on loan and must be returned so that some other children can share in reading them.

5. Don't view the staff as caregivers. Invite another mom to visit the library with you, and while one of you browses the adult section the other can stay with the kids.

6. If your library is computerized, ask for a printout of the books you checked out. Stick the list on the refrigerator so on return day you'll know which books you're looking for.

MORE MOMMY AND ME FUN

Presidents' Day Game: While reading books about Presidents' Day, show your child coins and bills with pictures of Abraham Lincoln and George Washington. Have your child sort pennies and quarters. You can also ask questions like: If you could be president for a day, what would you do? What do you think the president does all day?

Research and Read: Get a list of African American inventers and what they invented. For example, Garrett Morgan invented the traffic light and George Washington Carver invented peanut butter. Talk about the stories and, when you're home, have your child make a collage with pictures of the inventions.

Mommy's Memo

Keep a list of all your child's questions and take it with you to the library to help your child find the answers.

Mom, Did You Know?

Nearly 200,000 people in the U.S. and 4.1 million people in the world are Leap Day babies born on February 29.

MOMS ONLY
Advice, Tips, and Suggestions

Safe and Sound

Regular immunizations are a vital part of keeping your child healthy. Vaccinations against infectious diseases such as hepatitis B, rubella, and polio help protect against life-threatening sicknesses. Be sure to check with your pediatrician on available inoculations and immunization schedules.

DISCIPLINE DO

Love Bites: When a child bites, most parents are stunned. As with all disciplinary issues, parents should approach the situation with love and understanding. First of all, it is important to understand why children bite. Usually it is out of anger, frustration, trying to be powerful in a group, fear, insecurity, and not getting their way. Once you look at the big picture and try to analyze the situation, it will be easier for you to control your child. Here are some helpful hints:

● Never, ever bite your child back! This shows that it's okay to bite, which will hurt your disciplinary efforts in the long run. ● Do not put soap in your child's mouth, lemon juice on his lips, or give him a taste of Tabasco sauce. ● Tell your child that biting and hurting others is unacceptable behavior. If you catch your child in the act of biting, verbally scold him by saying, "This is not acceptable behavior."
● Turn your attention to the victim (the child who has been bitten) so that your child will realize that biting does not gain him attention. ● Teach your child other ways to express his anger, such as jumping up and down or hitting a pillow, and be sure to praise him if he expresses his anger in an appropriate manner other than biting.

RELAXATION Rx

Romantic Dinner: After working, making art projects, cooking, cleaning, and playing, it is now your time! Why not order in a nice romantic dinner for you and your husband? Splurge on some gourmet cuisine from your favorite restaurant, put the kids to bed early, and open a good bottle of wine. You could even save some of those Jell-O hearts you made for dessert. Valentine's Day shouldn't be the only day for revitalizing your relationship; make dates and romantic dinners a regular part of your week. After all, you and your spouse also need special time together!

TODDLER TIDBIT

Together Time: None of us can be told often enough that we are loved and special. If you were made to feel loved as a child, you're fortunate. Many people aren't so lucky, and may need to learn techniques for demonstrating love to their children. The best way is through "together time." Try to set aside at least fifteen minutes each day when you can sit and play with your toddler or preschooler. Give your child plenty of eye contact and let nothing else distract you. Listen to him or her. Ask questions and touch your child often. Make a date for lunch or to read a special book together. Many children will want to spend the entire time on your lap or cradled in your arms like a baby. The important thing is to focus solely on your child for these few minutes.

MEDICAL MESSAGE

The Overly Concerned Parent: There is such a thing as being overly concerned when a medical problem arises. New parents are notorious for this, myself included. Every time my baby had a sniffle or cough I would call the pediatrician. It's often difficult to know when aches or pains are serious or when children just need Tylenol or chicken soup. While it's important to bring any symptoms that concern you to the attention of your doctor, here are some guidelines for the ones that require medical attention:

- Blood in the urine or stool
- Diarrhea that has a strange odor and mucus in it
- Sweaty and clammy skin
- Vomiting
- Constipation
- Ingestion of a foreign object or poisonous substance
- A head injury
- Convulsions
- Lethargic behavior
- Difficulty breathing
- Severe cough
- An unusual rash
- Unusual discharge from the eyes, ears, or nose
- Burns
- Possible broken bones
- A severe cut
- High fever

Mommy's Memo

If your child has difficulty dealing with a situation or has a concern, don't interrupt or try to minimize the problem.

Mom, Did You Know?

At about age three, children start to distinguish gender. Once they make the distinction, it's common for toddlers and preschoolers to prefer to play with other children of the same sex.

• FEBRUARY ACTIVITIES •

147

Green is
the Color of
the Month.

A Diamond and
a Clover are
the Shapes of
the Month.

MARCH

March's dramatic weather conditions provide a nice springboard for introducing your child to the concepts of weather and seasons. Wind, clouds, rain, fog, sunshine, and sometimes snow may frustrate your attempts to choose the right clothing, but it's worth it—the chaotic weather signals that springtime is near. The first signs of spring are small but graphic: a flower bud, a leaf on a tree, shoots of grass, the tips of leaves from the bulbs you planted in the fall. With luck, there will be enough green in the landscape to put you in the mood to celebrate St. Patrick's Day. Keep an eye out for leprechauns and be sure to read your child a tale or two about these mischievous creatures. This month neither wind, hail, rain, or snow can keep us from having fun, so let's go!

KEY MARCH CONCEPTS:

1. There are many weather changes in March. Wind, rain, sunshine, clouds, and hail all represent different types of weather.

2. Spring begins the third week in March.

3. Kites, birds, and airplanes all fly.

4. St. Patrick's Day, March 17, honors Ireland's patron saint and is celebrated by Irish people all around the world.

5. There are numerous St. Patrick's Day legends about very small people called leprechauns who have magical powers.

6. The color green is symbolic of St. Patrick's Day and spring.

"O, wind, if Winter comes, can Spring be far behind?"

— Percy Bysshe Shelley

BLOWING IN THE WIND CHIMES
Art Activity
30 Minutes Prep • 30 Minutes Assembly

Your Child Will Learn

About wind and weather

Concepts of "up" and "down"

Eye-hand coordination

Fine and gross motor skills

Listening/Language skills

Shapes and colors

Mommy's Materials

Waxed paper

Rolling pin

Air-dry modeling clay

Cookie cutters and/or plastic knives

Tempera paints

Paintbrushes

Colored skeins of wool or fishing line

A dowel

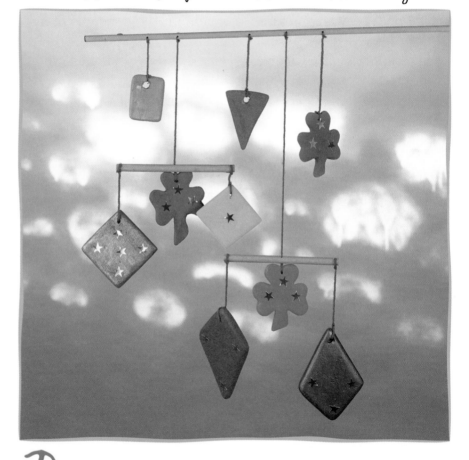

Did you know that wind can make music? When it blows, you not only feel it, you can hear it. A wind chime alerts you to a breeze with a melodic jingle. Making a wind chime with your child introduces several skills and concepts, including fine motor coordination, creative expression, and understanding weather patterns. It takes more than one sitting to complete this wind chime, but that's part of what makes it extra special when it's finished. Hang it outside and enjoy listening to the wind's special song!

150

STEP BY STEP

Part One:

1. Put waxed paper on the table and roll the clay into thick slabs with the rolling pin.

2. Using a blunt knife or cookie cutter, cut shapes from the clay, such as diamonds and clovers, to reinforce our shapes of the month.

3. Make a hole at the top of the shape with a pencil point, so the string will be able to fit through.

4. Let the clay dry for a day or two.

Part Two:

5. When the shapes are dry, paint them any way you desire. (Try to include green, the color of the month.)

6. Thread colored yarn through the hole in each shape and tie with a knot.

7. Secure the shapes to the dowel by tying with the yarn.

8. Hang the wind chimes outside on a tree, where the wind will catch them.

MORE MOMMY AND ME FUN

Easy Wind Chime: Attach three strings to an embroidery hoop (or wire hanger stretched into a circle shape) so it hangs evenly. Suspend four to eight additional strings and tie on anything that makes noise (beads, bells, etc). When finished, hang outside where it can blow in the wind.

Wind Sock: To make a wind sock, cut off the bottom of a paper lunch bag. Decorate the bag with glitter, green paint, clover- and diamond-shaped stickers, etc. Attach green crepe-paper streamers to one end of the bag. Fasten a construction paper or pipe cleaner handle to the other end of the bag and hang it outside to catch a breeze.

Mommy's Memo

Go outside on a windy day and watch how clouds float in the sky, flags flap in the air, trees sway, and hair blows. Have your child listen for sounds like leaves rustling and windows rattling. This heightens your child's senses and helps with expressive language.

SHAMROCK COOKIES
Creative Cooking • 15 Minutes Prep

Your Child Will Learn

The color green

Shape recognition

St. Patrick's Day traditions

Fine motor skills

Measuring

Counting

Mommy's Materials

1 cup sugar

14 tbsp. butter

1 egg

1 tsp. vanilla

2 cups flour

½ tsp. salt

Green food coloring

On St. Patrick's Day, when people celebrate by wearing green, invite your kids to dress up and share some green cuisine. Start with a tasty breakfast of green eggs. If you're ambitious, you can eat green cuisine all day by serving a leafy salad or pea soup for lunch, celery snacks for appetizers, pesto pasta for dinner, and limeade for a beverage. Or you can add a bit of green food coloring to any of your favorite foods. Of course, the best green cuisine of all is shamrock cookies. May the luck of the Irish be yours.

STEP BY STEP

1. Cream 1 cup sugar and 14 tbsp. butter together until pale and fluffy.

2. Beat in 1 egg and 1 tsp. vanilla.

3. Sift together 2 cups flour and ½ tsp. salt.

4. Stir the flour gradually into the creamed mixture and add green food coloring.

5. Wrap the dough and refrigerate it for at least 30 minutes.

6. Roll the dough out and cut with a shamrock-shaped cookie cutter. (Note: The dough can be frozen or kept refrigerated for about seven days.)

7. Place on a lightly greased baking sheet and bake in oven preheated to 350 degrees for 8–10 minutes. Frost with green icing, or green candy sprinkles if desired. Makes around 40 cookies.

MORE MOMMY AND ME FUN

Green Eggs (Without Ham): Turn the stove on medium heat and spray a frying pan with cooking spray or add butter or margarine. Crack 2 eggs and beat them in a bowl with a fork (you can use only the whites if you prefer). Add a drop of green food coloring. Scramble the eggs in a frying pan to your desired taste. Serve with a sprig of parsley.

Green Deviled Eggs: Slice 6 hard-boiled eggs in half and scoop out the yolk. Mix the yolks with 3 drops of green food coloring, then add 1 teaspoon prepared mustard and 1 tablespoon mayonnaise. Mix with a fork until smooth. Scoop the yolk mixture into each egg white half. Makes 12.

St. Patrick's Punch: Put 1 liter of lime sherbet in a punch bowl (it works best if it is half melted). Next, add ¼ cup of pineapple juice. Whisk them together, making a smooth texture. Last, add a 2-liter bottle of Sprite slowly, mixing continuously, until the punch bowl is full.

Mommy's Memo

For fun, put a drop of green food coloring in a glass of milk, and dunk the shamrock cookies before eating.

Mom, Did You Know?

A shamrock is a green, cloverlike plant that grows in Ireland and is traditionally associated with St. Patrick's Day. Many people believe that a shamrock with four petals represents good luck.

• MARCH ACTIVITIES •

153

SING ALONG
Music, Fingerplays, and Action Rhymes

•MARCH ACTIVITIES•

Your Child Will Learn

Colors

Fine motor skills

Rhythm

Creative expression

Listening/Language skills

Holidays and seasons

Selected Stories

Green Eggs and Ham
by Dr. Seuss

St. Patrick's Day in the
Morning
by Eve Bunting

A Leprechaun's St. Patrick's
Day
by Sarah Kirwan Blazek

St. Patrick's Day
by Gail Gibbons

"OH, I WISH I WERE A LITTLE LEPRECHAUN"

(Sing to the tune of "If You're Happy and You Know It")

Oh, I wish I were a little leprechaun!
Oh, I wish I were a little leprechaun!
I'd dance around all day, get in everybody's way.
Oh, I wish I were a little leprechaun!

Oh, I wish I were a little leprechaun!
Oh, I wish I were a little leprechaun!
I'd play hide and seek with you,
and have lots of fun, it's true.
Oh, I wish I were a little leprechaun!

Oh, I wish I were a little leprechaun!
Oh, I wish I were a little leprechaun!
I'd give gold and treats to you,
I would dress in green, not blue.
Oh, I wish I were a little leprechaun!

"THE WIND"

Feel the strong wind, it almost blows me down,
(bend over, almost falling)
Hear it whistle through the trees and all around.
(cup hand to ear)
Try to see the wind as it howls and blows,
(hands over eyebrows)
But what the wind looks like? Nobody knows!
(shrug shoulders, palms up)

"THE GREEN GRASS GREW ALL AROUND"

Oh, in the woods there was a tree,
The prettiest tree that you ever did see.
And the tree in the ground,
And the green grass grew all around, all around,
And the green grass grew all around.
And on this tree there was a limb,
The prettiest limb that you ever did see.
And the limb on the tree,
And the tree in the ground,
And the green grass grew all around, all around
And the green grass grew all around.
(alternate verses)
And on this limb, there was a branch,
And on this branch, there was a twig,
And on this twig, there was a leaf,
And on this leaf, there was a bird.

"THE KITE"

See the kite way up high,
(pretend your hand is a kite)
Sailing, dancing in the sky.
Turning, twisting, and swirling around,
When the wind stops
It comes fluttering down.
(bring hands slowly down)

"LITTLE LEPRECHAUN"

I'm a little leprechaun dressed in green,
The tiniest man that you've ever seen,
If you ever catch me, so it's told,
I'll give you my pot of gold.

Mommy's Memo

Put on some Irish music and have your child hunt for a pot of gold (rocks or bottle caps that you've spray-painted gold), a blarney stone, a four-leaf clover, or objects that are green.

Mom, Did You Know?

History and legend are intertwined when it comes to St. Patrick. Many people believe he drove the snakes out of Ireland. While it's true there are no snakes in Ireland, chances are there never have been since the island was separated from the mainland at the end of the ice age.

GO FLY A KITE
Physical Fun

Your Child Will Learn

Colors

Shapes

Fine motor skills

Gross motor skills

Wind and weather

Mommy's Materials

Safety scissors

Poster board or oak tag

Five pieces of ribbon cut 8 inches in length

Two pieces of yarn cut 18 inches in length

Crayons or markers

Hole punch

Paper ring reinforcements (the kind you use on paper in binders)

Tape

Kite string

The best thing about the wind is that it knows how to play. When the March wind blows and the sun is brightly shining, we know springtime is not far away. While waiting for milder weather, use the windy days of March to have some fun making and flying a kite. All you need is an open space, a breezy day, your child, and a kite. You'll feel a bit anxious before the kite rises off the ground, but once it does, both you and your child will feel victorious. Making a kite is a breeze, and when you see it fly way up in the sky you will feel really proud knowing you and your child made it together.

STEP BY STEP

1. Help your child cut the poster board into the shape of a diamond.

2. Make the kite's tail (for stabilization) by tightly tying the strands of ribbon to a piece of yarn at various intervals.

3. Have your child decorate or draw pictures on the kite using his imagination.

4. At one corner of the kite, punch a small hole where you will insert the tail and secure with tape or ring reinforcers.

5. At the other end of the kite, punch a similar hole for the other strand of yarn (or kite string) with which to pull the completed kite.

Kite-Flying Tips:
Despite the classic image from childhood, running is not always the best way to launch a kite. Instead stand with your back to the wind, release the kite from your hand as you slowly let out the line. If there is sufficient wind, your kite will sail and you can start to pull on the line so it will climb. If the kite spins and dives, try lengthening the tail.

MORE MOMMY AND ME FUN

Paper Bag Kite: Punch four holes in the top of a paper bag—one in each corner—and add paper ring reinforcements. Create two handles using lengths of string about 30 inches long. Cut another piece of string and tie it to the two loops you created. Glue crepe paper or ribbon streamers to the bottom of the bag as kite tails. When finished, hold on tightly to the string handle and let the wind catch the kite. When the bag fills with air it will float and flutter behind you.

Streamer Kites: Colorful crepe-paper streamers tied to a short stick provide endless fun for a toddler on a windy day. This streamer version is easier to handle than a full-size kite but it flutters just as happily in a strong breeze. A preschooler with two long streamers will be twice as happy when a gust of wind blows by.

Mommy's Memo

Diamond kites, good for light to medium winds, are among the easiest to fly because they adjust easily to wind shifts.

Mom, Did You Know?

In 1752, Benjamin Franklin began experimenting with kites and discovered that lightning is electricity.

Safe and Sound

When you fly your kite, be sure there are no obstructions such as roads, high electrical wires, or trees. If you're at a beach, be sure to stay clear of the water and never fly in rain or lightning.

• MARCH ACTIVITIES •

VISITING A SENIOR CENTER
Terrific Trips

Your Child Will Learn

Compassion

Listening skills

About families

Respect

Selected Stories

Abuela
by Arthur Dorros and
Elisa Kleven

Mr. Putter and Tabby
by Cynthia Rylant

Mrs. Katz and Tush
by Patricia Polacco

Just Grandma and Me
by Mercer Mayer

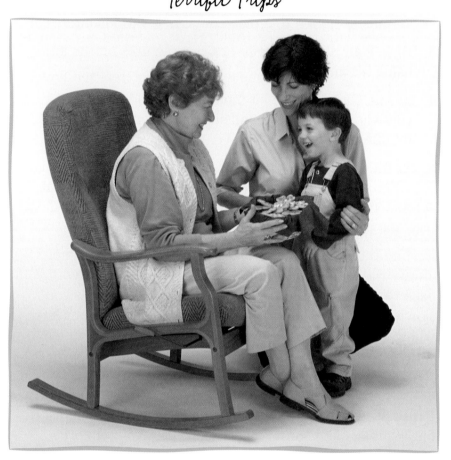

Although the changing weather patterns offer beautiful seasonal changes, the end of winter can be a bleak time of year for some people. For a great way to brighten up someone's day, plan a visit to a residence facility for seniors. Many of the residents at these centers have few or no visitors. Talking with an eager, happy child cheers them up tremendously. Call ahead of time to plan your visit with the coordinator of a nursing home in your area. You and your child can pick one special person to visit, or make the rounds.

TEACHING EMPATHY

Teaching your child to be empathetic is an integral part of helping him to become a thoughtful and caring person. Have your child help you bake some shamrock cookies, or make a special craft or card to bring. This is an important learning experience with great rewards for all concerned. My daughter used to love visiting our local senior center because she got a lot of attention. As she grew older, she realized how much the seniors looked forward to our visits. She began to understand loneliness and to appreciate how fortunate she was to have family.

MORE MOMMY AND ME FUN

Spring Walk: Once old man winter lets go, we all develop a little spring in our step. When the weather turns mild, why not go for a spring walk. Together, look for signs of spring. See if you can find branches with buds beginning to appear. Listen for birds. Smell the air. Find new blades of grass or leaves shooting out of bulbs planted last year. Ask questions. Point out all the green objects you see and talk about the color green. This helps with expressive language.

St. Paddy Parade: Many communities host annual St. Patrick's Day parades that promote Irish culture. From the grand parade down New York City's Fifth Avenue with marching bands and elaborate floats, to local events with school children waving flags, St. Patrick's Day is a day to get out and celebrate.

Irish Dance Festival: Not everyone can find a stage production of *Riverdance* or *Lord of the Dance* nearby, but there are usually numerous Irish dance festivals performing at this time of year. From traditional step dancing to *ceilidh* to set performances, you'll quickly be swept away by the sound of pounding feet and swirling Irish music. Check your local listings or try enrolling in some Irish dance classes together with your child.

Mommy's Memo

Visiting a senior center can extend well beyond the month of March. Why not turn it into a regular activity? Not only will you have fun but your child will become a more compassionate person.

Mom, Did You Know?

Research shows that elderly people who have social interaction and are involved in activities that challenge the mind tend to live longer.

• MARCH ACTIVITIES •

MOMS ONLY
Advice, Tips, and Suggestions

Mommy's Memo

Be aware that your behavior can influence your child's behavior. If you are good, fair, honest, and respectful, chances are your children will be too.

DISCIPLINE DO
Reinforcing Good Behavior: After a day of kite flying and parades, take the time to reinforce your child's good behavior. This can be done with a smile, a hug, a kiss or "What a good job! You listened so well at the park! You should be so proud of yourself!" This positive reinforcement and encouragement have an impact on your child's sense of self-worth far greater than you might imagine. Specific praise, rather than general comments, seems to get the best results. Don't limit your encouragement to one area of development but provide positive attention in a variety of contexts. This will go a long way in building strong self-esteem. For a hundred ways to praise your child, check out our Web site: www.mommyandme.com.

RELAXATION Rx
Massage Therapy: Bet you're using some muscles you haven't exercised in a while! Running after a kite, or roughhousing with the kids can contribute to aches and pains. There's nothing like a good back rub for working out the kinks. In many areas, you can find a day spa or a masseuse who will come to your home. If you can't see a massage therapist, recruit your husband or significant other for the job. It won't cost a penny and it will do wonders for both of you. The human touch has long been acknowledged as a powerful healing tool, and although a massage may not be the cure to all that ails you, it can help alleviate a variety of maladies, from stress to pain. If you haven't had a massage in your home before, here are a couple of tips to get you started. Unplug the phone, and eliminate bright light, noise, and drafts. Set out oils, scents, pillows, towels, and anything else you might want to use before you start. Most important, be sure to relax and enjoy the comforting reprieve.

TODDLER TIDBIT

Stranger Danger: Every time I go on an outing with my daughter, I give her a little talk about strangers. She has probably heard the speech a hundred times—and will hear it a hundred times more. Here are some important tips for explaining stranger danger:

● A stranger is a person you don't know. ● Most people love children, but there are some who have bad intentions. Sometimes the bad ones look like good ones. They may even look like Mommy or Daddy. ● Never open the door for *anyone* unless an adult is with you. ● Never play outside by yourself. Always have an adult with you to supervise. ● If a stranger tells you Mommy or Daddy sent him to get you, scream and run away. ● Don't get into a stranger's car even if they tell you they have a cute puppy to show you, or a piece of candy to give you. ● Always stay with your parents when you are at the park, in an airport, or in a mall. If you get lost, go to the nearest counter and ask for help.

MEDICAL MESSAGE

The Wild Wind: March is here with a vengeance and a wind that just blows and blows. Dirt and dust can easily lodge in a child's eye. While eyelashes are designed to keep foreign matter out of the eye, sometimes they fail. Should you treat the problem yourself or call the doctor? First, stop your child's natural rubbing response to minimize the risk of embedding the dirt into the eyelid lining or the eyeball. Allow some time for good tears and blinking, which may dislodge the object. Try checking under a light for small specks of dirt on both the lower and upper lining. If possible, remove the dirt with the moistened corner of a tissue. If you suspect that a foreign body remains and there is the possibility of injury to any part of the eye, call your doctor or an ophthalmologist. If an injury exists, the eye should be covered with a shield such as a cone-shaped piece of cardboard that rests on the bone around the eye, not on the eye itself. Immediate treatment will lessen the chance of permanent injury to those baby blues (or browns or greens).

Mommy's Memo

Your child may not understand all the subtleties of stranger danger at a young age, but it's important for her to grasp the idea that she should stay within your sight when in a public place.

Mom, Did You Know?

The incidents of stranger abductions are actually quite rare. Most kidnappers are known to the child—usually an estranged parent—and most kidnappings are not arbitrary incidents.

The Colors of
the Rainbow
are the Colors
of the Month.

An Oval is
the Shape of
the Month.

APRIL

April may bring a few showers, but there's no denying it—spring is here. Our activities this month will focus on the reawakening of the earth. You and your child will have the opportunity to interact with nature by feeding ducks, making bird feeders, walking in the rain, planting seeds, and watching seedlings grow. We start the month off with April Fools' Day. This is the ideal time to clown around, plan surprises, and read funny jokes and stories. Easter and Passover also take place in April, and you'll find activities that celebrate the two holidays. Both are rooted in ancient traditions that have endured through the centuries. As we teach our children about religious customs, we begin to expose them to the variety of cultures that coexist in our society. There are lots of reasons to celebrate this month, so let's start the festivities!

KEY APRIL CONCEPTS:

1. The first day of the month is April Fools' Day, a day set aside for silliness.

2. Spring is the season when the earth renews itself.

3. Colors of a rainbow include red, orange, yellow, green, blue, indigo, and violet.

4. Birds are feathered animals with wings. They build nests and lay eggs. An egg is oval shaped.

5. Rain plays a necessary role in the natural cycle of life.

6. Earth Day, celebrated on April 22, focuses worldwide attention on preserving the earth's natural resources.

7. Easter and Passover are important religious holidays, with their own traditions and customs.

"April hath put a spirit of youth in everything."

— William Shakespeare

FOR THE BIRDS
Art Activity • 30 to 45 Minutes

Your Child Will Learn

Fine motor skills

Eye-hand coordination

To follow instructions

Language acquisition

Bird behavior

Color concepts

Shape concepts

Mommy's Materials

Empty ½-gallon milk or juice carton (rinsed out)

Safety scissors

Thin wire, 8 inches in length

Popsicle or craft sticks

Tempera paint

Stickers

Birdseed

*C*hances are if you step outside and are very quiet, you'll hear the sound of birds—pigeons cooing, crows cawing, ravens whistling, sparrows chirping, and mockingbirds boasting. Because of their great variety, birds help heighten a child's appreciation of the natural world. And since birds don't know the difference between a fancy, store-bought bird feeder and one that's homemade, you can recycle some items you may have around the house to create an inviting bird bistro in your own backyard.

STEP BY STEP

1. Cut out large openings on opposite sides of the carton (adults only, please).

2. Punch two small holes on top of the carton. Thread wire through the small holes, twisting the ends together to form a loop.

3. Glue Popsicle or craft stick shingles onto the roof (or use paint stirrers). For a perch, poke holes below the openings and slip a dowel through the holes.

4. Paint the carton or decorate with stickers.

5. Fill the bottom of the carton with birdseed. (You can make your own mix by combining a variety of nuts and seeds, such as sunflower seeds, millet, thistle seeds, and yellow corn.)

6. Hang the feeder in a spot that's easy to view but far enough away from fences or posts to thwart predators (especially cats).

MORE MOMMY AND ME FUN

Pinecone Bird Feeder: For another bird feeder, go outside and find a pinecone. Get some peanut butter and sprinkle sesame seeds or raisins on it. Dip your finger in and try some. Now, roll the pinecone in the mixture and hang it from a tree.

Play Ornithologist: Go to the library and find books on birds. Make a list of the different species. Keep a chart with the pictures of each type and check them off when they come. Graph the number of each species that feeds at the feeder over time and compare. This will help your child with discrimination and matching skills.

Birdbath: Believe it or not, water is just as important as food for birds. They need water year-round to drink and to bathe in (so they can keep their feathers in good shape and retain warmth). You can make some simple birdbaths with a clean garbage can lid or plant saucer set on two bricks. Remember to refill often with clean, soap-free water.

Mommy's Memo

Spring is the season when new life is born. Talk to your child about the oval shape of the egg and discuss the creatures that hatch from eggs, such as ducks, chickens, and other birds.

Mom, Did You Know?

It is not true that a mother bird will desert her nest or babies if they have been handled by humans. Birds have no sense of smell and therefore no way to detect that their chick's been touched.

RAINBOW RAIN STICK
Art Activity • 20 to 30 Minutes

Your Child Will Learn

Rainbow colors

Sound discrimination

Earth Day

Recycling

Mommy's Materials

Paper rolls (mailing tubes are good)

Packing tape

Nontoxic tempera paint, crayons, stickers, or rainbow wrapping paper

Toothpicks

White glue

Rice, seeds, corn kernels, or dried peas

pringtime showers help rejuvenate the planet. During the month of April, Earth Day reminds us that we need to protect our natural resources. A great way to combine the two concepts is to recycle cardboard tubes to make a tropical rain stick. Legend has it that the Chileans invented the rain stick. The unique interior mazelike structure was originally formed with cactus spines, bamboo, or slivers of palm. Use the stick to create the sound of rain and to introduce cycles of nature. When the stick is finished, shake it and twist it to mimic the sound of rain falling on leaves, and wait for the sound of thunder.

STEP BY STEP

1. Poke holes (a lot of them) in paper rolls.

2. Cover one end of the roll with tape.

3. Decorate the roll with rainbow colors or rainbow wrapping paper. You can tape three or four crayons together and demonstrate how to draw a rainbow with one stroke.

4. Put toothpicks through one hole and out another. (The idea is to have the toothpicks going in at different angles to make the required sound.)

5. Glue both ends of the toothpick and cut off any protruding ends (adults only, please).

6. Fill the roll with rice or dried peas. Experiment with how much to use. (It won't take a lot.)

7. Tape up the other end and there you have it—a rain stick!

MORE MOMMY AND ME FUN

Recycled 3-D Art: Collect all types of recyclable items, including newspapers, aluminum foil, plastic cups, egg cartons, etc., and make a sculpture. Be sure to display your child's creation where everyone can admire it.

Rainbow: Fill a glass bowl with cold water and place it half off and half on a table. Put a piece of white paper on the floor and be sure the sunlight shines directly through the bowl and onto the paper. Magically, a rainbow appears right in front of your eyes. On a sunny day, use a garden hose to spray a fine mist of water across the sun's rays. Have your child stand with her back to the sun and look for a rainbow in the mist.

Rainbow Crayons: Recycle crayons by turning old, broken ones into colorful new ones. Remove all paper and melt used crayons in an empty pie tin. Place in a saucepan filled with water over low heat on the stove. Pour melted wax in candy molds or paper cups. Wait for wax to cool (you can place in freezer) and pop out the new crayons when set.

Mommy's Memo

Put on rain gear and boots and go puddle stomping during a spring shower. Float leaves down the gutter. Study reflections in the puddles. Measure the depth of puddles. With older children you can discuss the rain cycle. Why is rain good? What would happen if it didn't rain?

Mom, Did You Know?

Earth Day was started in the 1970s as a movement led by college students and has since become an international media and educational event.

CHOCOLATE-COVERED MATZOH
Creative Cooking • 30 Minutes Prep

Your Child Will Learn

Holiday traditions

Fine motor skills

Counting/Measuring skills

Language acquisition

Following directions

Mommy's Materials

½ cup margarine

1 cup brown sugar

5 to 6 pieces plain matzoh

12 oz. bittersweet chocolate bits (kosher for Passover)

½ cup crushed almonds or other nuts (optional)

*T*he traditional Passover dinner is called a seder. During the meal, the story of Moses and the Jewish exodus from Egypt is retold through words and symbolic foods. Children are a big part of the seder ceremony, and when they get involved with the preparations they learn a lot about the meaning of the holiday. Involve your children in all kinds of holiday preparations and create traditions they can pass on to their own children.

STEP BY STEP

1. Melt margarine with brown sugar in saucepan; boil until mixture coats a spoon.

2. Line a cookie sheet with foil, lay matzoh on sheet, and brush with brown sugar mixture. Bake for 3–4 minutes (watch closely, it burns easily), until the mixture starts to bubble.

3. Cover with chocolate chips and put back in the oven until the chips start to melt.

4. Spread the chocolate with a spatula to cover the matzoh. If you want, sprinkle crushed almonds over the top.

5. Let the chocolate-covered matzoh harden in the refrigerator for a couple of hours.

6. While the chocolate is cooling, clean up the mess. (You can start by licking the pot!)

7. Break into pieces and serve. Makes 10–12 servings.

MORE MOMMY AND ME FUN

Getting Ready: The day of the first seder, bring your child into the kitchen to prepare his own seder plate using small portions of everything included on the main seder plate. The *Haggadah* (Passover storybook) explains the symbolism of the bitter herb, *charoset* (relish made with chopped apples and nuts), green vegetable, shank bone, and roasted egg.

Find the *Afikomen*: Traditionally, after the seder meal is eaten, the family patriarch hides a piece of matzoh, *Afikomen*, as a symbolic dessert. The child who finds it receives a small prize. Try hiding the *Afikomen* and see who can find it first.

***Afikomen* Cover:** To make a matzoh cover, sew or glue pieces of blue and white felt together along three edges (leaving the top edge open). You can decorate by making a six-sided star with white glue and covering with sparkles. Let dry and shake off excess glitter. Place the matzoh in the cover.

Mom, Did You Know?

Throughout the Passover holiday, Jews eat matzoh, an unleavened bread, to commemorate the fact that their ancestors had no time to bake raised bread during their flight from Egypt.

Selected Stories

Miriam's Cup: A Passover Story
by Fran Manushkin

Matzo Ball Moon
by Lesléa Newman

The Four Questions
by Lynne Sharon Schwartz

The Carp in the Bathtub
by Barbara Cohen

Let My Babies Go! A Passover Story
by Sarah Willson

EGG-CELLENT EASTER EGG FUN
Holiday Bonus • 20 to 30 Minutes

• APRIL ACTIVITIES •

Your Child Will Learn

Holiday traditions

Shapes

Colors

Fine motor skills

Patterns

To follow directions

Mommy's Materials

Smock

1 cup hot tap water

1 cup white vinegar

Food coloring—rainbow colors

Small plastic bowls

1 dozen hard-boiled eggs

Spoons

1 egg carton

Crayons, paint, and stickers

The celebration of Easter is considered to be the most important event in the Christian religion. The holiday celebrates new life through a variety of rituals, including worship, songs, stories, and the giving of gifts. Fittingly, many of these are representative of the signs of rebirth that spring brings. For little children, Easter signifies more than a religious holiday; it means the Easter bunny, colorful Easter eggs, and Easter baskets full of delicious candy! For many families, the Easter egg hunt is the most popular part of the celebration.

STEP BY STEP

1. Combine the hot tap water, white vinegar, and a few drops of food coloring in a plastic bowl. (You can also buy an egg-dyeing kit.) Repeat process using various colors.

2. You can wrap rubber bands around the eggs before you dye them to create a swirl pattern.

3. Have your child decorate the hard-boiled eggs. Place one egg at a time into the various bowls of colored dye.

4. Remove the eggs with a spoon, place the eggs to dry in the egg carton (or make an egg-drying stand out of a small piece of paper towel tube).

5. Place in an Easter basket for a holiday decoration or use in an Easter egg hunt.

MORE MOMMY AND ME FUN

Easter Egg Hunt: If several children are participating in an egg hunt, give each child a specific color of egg to look for. The children will collect only the eggs that are their color, limiting the competitive factor. Each child receives the same number of eggs, and this version of the egg hunt also reinforces color identification.

Bunny Hop: With two or more children, you can have a bunny hop race. Divide the group into two teams and have a relay. Each child has to hop like a bunny, drop a plastic egg into the basket, and tag the next runner in line. The first team to get all the eggs in the basket is the winner. To make this even more fun, have the kids wear bunny ears.

Confetti Eggs: Also known by the Spanish name *Cascaron*, confetti eggs are a great Easter tradition. Hollow out a raw egg by blowing or draining the insides through a small hole. Rinse and drain. Once dry, paint or glue small squares of colorful tissue paper to the egg shells. Then, fill eggs with brightly colored confetti and tape hole closed. During an Easter party, break the eggs over guests' heads and wait for squeals of delight. Olé!

Mommy's Memo

Point out the oval shape of the eggs and ask your child to look for other objects around the house and yard that are oval.

Mom, Did You Know?

The custom of decorating eggs actually predates Easter by hundreds of years. Egyptians placed them in tombs as symbols of birth and resurrection. Later, in the second century A.D., the Romans gave them as gifts—the wealthy would adorn them with gold leaf; peasants boiled them in dyes made from flowers, leaves, and insects.

SING ALONG
Music, Fingerplays, and Action Rhymes

• A P R I L A C T I V I T I E S •

Your Child Will Learn

Language acquisition

Listening skills

About rain and rainbows

Creative expression

Colors

Selected Stories

A Rainbow of My Own
by Don Freeman

The Rainbow Fish
by Marcus Pfister

Peter Spier's Rain
by Peter Spier

Rain Feet
by Angela Johnson

Selected Songs

"Raindrops Keep Falling on
My Head"
Performed by B.J. Thomas

"Singin' in the Rain"
Performed by Gene Kelly

"Water Music"
by Handel

"IT'S RAINING, IT'S POURING"

It's raining, it's pouring,
The old man is snoring.
He went to bed and
Bumped his head
And he couldn't get up in the morning.

"IF ALL THE RAINDROPS"

If all the raindrops were lemondrops and gumdrops
Oh, what a rain that would be!
Standing outside, with my mouth open wide
Singing La la la la, la la la, la la la.
If all the raindrops were lemondrops and gumdrops
Oh, what a rain that would be!

If all the snowflakes were candy bars and milkshakes
Oh, what a snow that would be!
Standing outside, with my mouth open wide
Singing La la la la, la la la, la la la.
If all the snowflakes were candy bars and milkshakes
Oh, what a snow that would be!

If all the sunbeams were bubble gum and ice cream
Oh, what a sun that would be!
Standing outside, with my mouth open wide
Singing La la la la, la la la, la la la.
If all the sunbeams were bubble gum and ice cream
Oh, what a sun that would be!

"WE PLANT THE SEEDS"

(Sing to the tune of "The Farmer in the Dell")

(Child's name) *plants the seeds,*
(Name) *plants the seeds.*
Hi ho, the dairy-o,
(Name) *plants the seeds.*
Alternate verses:
The sun comes out to shine, (hold arms up)
The rain begins to fall, (fingers flutter down)
The seeds begin to grow.
(stand on tiptoe and put hands in the air)
(Name) *digs them up,* (pretend to use a shovel)
Now we get to eat. (pretend to eat)

"IT AIN'T GONNA RAIN"

It ain't gonna rain no more, no more,
It ain't gonna rain no more.
How in the heck will we wash the neck
If it ain't gonna rain no more?
It ain't gonna thunder, it ain't gonna pour,
It ain't gonna rain no more.

"FUNNY BUNNY"

I'm a funny little bunny
(make bunny ears on top of head)
Sitting on a stump.
(pretend to sit)
I flap my floppy little ears
(flap the bunny ears)
And then I jump, jump, jump.
(hop and jump around)

Mommy's Memo

Use the senses to discuss the rain: the sound it makes drumming against the roof and dripping from the trees; how it feels; what it tastes like. Are the drops big or small? Are they falling gently or are they beating down hard?

Mom, Did You Know?

A rainbow is an arch of light that forms when sunlight falls on tiny drops of water in the air. The natural spectrum of colors always appears in the same order: red, orange, yellow, green, blue, indigo, and violet.

• A P R I L   A C T I V I T I E S •

173

PLANTING A GARDEN
Physical Fun

Your Child Will Learn

Colors

Shapes

Patterns

Science

Math

Natural cycles

Selected Stories

The Tiny Seed
by Eric Carle

Garden
by Robert Maass

The Carrot Seed
by Ruth Krauss

Flower Garden
by Eve Bunting

Planting a Rainbow
by Lois Ehlert

Jack and the Beanstalk
by various authors

Gardening can be a great together-time activity for your family. Help your children plant a garden and you'll harvest their appreciation for the wonders of the natural world. From seed selection through planting and tending the garden, children learn about the cycle of life firsthand and develop a sense of pride and responsibility. When the work is complete, the whole family can enjoy the fruits of their labor. Gardening may be the most kid-friendly activity there is: dirt and water aren't off-limits, surprises lurk beneath every leaf, and it's okay to get your clothes dirty.

STEP BY STEP

1. Pick an area on the edge of the yard to plant your garden, out of high-traffic zones.

2. Begin by finding out which plants and flowers will grow best in your geographic location. (Make a visit to your local nursery or the library.)

3. Herbs are a good choice for a family garden. They generally grow from late spring through fall, are easy to grow, and many of them are perennials. Plant several varieties: basil, chives, dill, parsley, oregano, rosemary, thyme, sage, and cilantro.

4. For a flower garden, marigolds, petunias, and impatiens are good choices.

5. For a vegetable garden, try beans, radishes, lettuce, or cherry tomatoes, which kids seem to love.

6. Be sure to teach your child the proper way to water so the plants don't drown. Morning or afternoon is usually the best time to douse them.

7. Wear the proper gear, including gardening gloves and a hat for shade.

8. Kids love to pick what they've grown. After they do, let them help you cook dinner with the fresh ingredients.

MORE MOMMY AND ME FUN

Rainbow Garden: A rainbow garden can be grown with plants grouped according to color. For younger children, take them to a garden center and let them choose flowers in each color of the rainbow (e.g., lavender, yarrow, artemisia, and roses).

Potpourri: Leave cut flowers out to air dry and make gifts out of dried rose heads and petals with a few greens and dried pods added in. You can add rose essential oil if you wish. Place in a basket or bowl, or fill a sachet with dried lavender.

Mommy's Memo

Let children begin by doing simple tasks. A two-year-old might not be able to plant seedlings, but she can help water and put stones in the bottom of pots for drainage.

Mom, Did You Know?

If you gently rub the leaves of herbs in the garden, the scent is released.

Safe and Sound

Be sure your child understands that she shouldn't taste the seeds you're planting. Many are chemically treated and could be harmful.

• APRIL ACTIVITIES •

NURSERY OR BOTANICAL GARDEN
Terrific Trips

APRIL ACTIVITIES

*A*h, winter is finally over. A special time of year has arrived. Take a trip to your local wildflower field, botanical garden, greenhouse, or nursery to see and enjoy the blossoms that welcome spring. Sometimes the people who work at the nursery, or garden, have interesting information to share, especially if you go on a weekday when they're not as busy. There are plenty of little prizes to buy your toddler at the end of the outing: a tiny cactus plant, a garden wind toy on a stick, or a child's watering can are all great choices.

SPRING FLING

At this time of year many gardens have plantings of tulips, hyacinths, and other lovely spring-blooming bulbs. Here, you'll find the colors you've been craving all winter. Learn the names of the different types of plants, and take along a camera. If you can, buy some seeds to plant at home, either in the yard or on a windowsill. Help your child water the seeds each day, and watch for the first sprouts to poke through the soil. If there isn't a nursery or garden nearby, it's a great time of year to visit your local florist. Colors, floral varieties, and wonderful fragrances are all there to enjoy. Talk to your child about the names and colors of different types of flowers. Ask older children to describe them to you. If you are really lucky, the florist may be making arrangements. Your child can watch the creation of a miniature "botanical garden" in front of his eyes. Be sure to take some flowers or plants home to brighten up the house or use as a centerpiece at dinner.

MORE MOMMY AND ME FUN

Nature Center: Nature centers exist in most local park systems, and they usually feature some sort of nature program for children. They teach kids about the local plant and animal life, ecosystems, and environmental concerns. Also, the Sierra Club, which has chapters around the country, sponsors family nature walks and other outdoor activities.

Duck Pond: Plan ahead for this one by saving some bread for your outing. A few morsels carefully thrown to one duck in the pond is sure to bring the others paddling your way. If you are really lucky, tiny fluffy baby ducks will be greeting you, too.

Wildflower Celebration: Across the country Mother Nature's color creations are welcomed with special celebrations. Wildflower displays, tours of areas abundant in colorful flowers (often led by expert naturalists), and gardening demonstrations provide an exciting opportunity to photograph, enjoy, and learn about the wonderful world of wildflowers. Check local listings for events in your area.

Mommy's Memo

No matter what time of year it is, don't forget to stop and smell the roses. Be patient as your child sniffs flowers, compares scents, touches fuzzy leaves, and becomes acquainted with the great green outdoors.

Mom, Did You Know?

Botany is the branch of biological science that deals with the study of plants. Horticulture is the science or art of cultivating fruits, vegetables, or flowers.

• A P R I L   A C T I V I T I E S •

MOMS ONLY
Advice, Tips, and Suggestions

DISCIPLINE DO

Respect Nature: As a parent, it is your job to teach your child to respect the environment by being gentle with the plants and animals he comes into contact with. Instruct him not to rip at plants or tear up grass just for the fun of it. Instead, gently pick a flower or a few blades of grass and investigate. A big magnifying glass makes a terrific gift for children and helps shift their focus from destroying nature to exploring it.

It's even more important to teach your children to be gentle—and cautious—with animals. The proper way to approach a neighborhood dog or cat is slowly, with the back of your hand extended toward the animal. Give the pet a chance to sniff your hand, then let it come closer. If it seems friendly, you can gently stroke its back or scratch between its ears. Of course, you should never approach a stray or unfamiliar animal. When a dog is being walked, always ask the owner if it is friendly before you pet it.

RELAXATION Rx

April Foolishness: "He who lives without folly is not so wise as he thinks" goes an old saying. One of the best ways to relax is to get silly. For April Fools', there are a variety of absurd or outrageous pranks to play that will help break up your daily routine. You can go out of your way to tell jokes, wear your clothes "inside out" for the fun of it, or plan your day "end to the beginning." Try serving dinner in reverse order. Start with dessert first, then the main dish, the salad, and finally the appetizer. Mix up the containers. Place the soup in a casserole dish, place the sugar in the relish dish, put the gravy in the sugar bowl and get ready for some laughs. Breaking up your routine is not only liberating but great fun for the entire family.

TODDLER TIDBIT

Where Do Babies Come From? Spring is an appropriate time of year to discuss the birds and the bees. Most parents are not sure how to begin dealing with a preschooler's curiosity about sex. Answer your child's questions with a clear signal that you are willing to talk—"I'm really glad you asked me that," or, "What a great question." This lets her know that you are comfortable with the subject. It's also best to give simple, honest answers and always use the proper anatomical names for the body parts. Talk in a way that fits the age and stage of your child and don't worry about knowing all the answers; what you know is a lot less important than how you respond. If you can convey the message that no subject, including sex, is forbidden in your home, you'll be doing just fine. Fortunately, there are a number of books available that can help you out. Check out *Where Do Babies Come From?* by Angela Royston and *How Are Babies Made?* by Andrew Andry and Steven Schepp.

MEDICAL MESSAGE

Spring Allergies: If your child sneezes, coughs, or has a runny nose that never lets up, he may be allergic to elements in the environment. In the springtime, allergies are especially troublesome because of all the pollen in the air. Allergies can be difficult to distinguish from all the colds, flu, and other viruses around, but chances are if you're a sufferer, your child might be too. The good news is that most allergies and asthma are manageable once properly diagnosed and treated. There are several allergy medicines, including antihistamines in both tablet and liquid form, that can relieve symptoms such as itchy eyes and runny noses. Prescription nasal sprays can also help reduce symptoms. For the severely allergic child, a trip to the allergist may be in order for shots that will eventually minimize allergic reactions. The most successful treatment for allergies, however, is removal of the offending allergens. During peak pollen season, for example, stay indoors when possible (particularly on windy days). Daily baths and shampoos also help remove pollen and serve as an effective treatment.

Mommy's Memo

This is the time of year when many zoos and aquariums have baby animals on exhibit. Call your local zoo to find out if there are any new occupants to view. If you live near a farm you might also check there for permission to visit.

Mom, Did You Know?

Up to 80 percent of children with asthma develop symptoms before the age of five. Some allergies disappear as a child grows older and some return under different guises.

Purple, Pink, and Yellow are the Colors of the Month.

A Circle is the Shape of the Month.

MAY

May is a special month for mothers. I remember my first Mother's Day as if it were yesterday. My husband showered me with flowers and gifts, and even the baby gave me a little something. (My husband was *really* on the ball that year!) In addition to the well-deserved accolades from our spouses and kids, Mother's Day gives us an opportunity to show our children how we honor the older generation. After I had a child, I had a deeper appreciation for all my own mother had done for me over the years. Although she's no longer alive, I still remember her each Mother's Day and I make sure that my daughter hears stories about her grandmother. But there's more to May than Mother's Day. Spring is finally in full bloom, the weather is mild, and the heat of summer is still a month or two away. It's the ideal time to teach your child how to ride a bike, go to the circus, or simply to enjoy the sights, sounds, and smells of spring. So let's head out and make some memories!

KEY MAY CONCEPTS:

1. Colors of spring include purple, pink, and yellow.

2. Mother's Day, the second Sunday of May, is set apart every year to honor motherhood.

3. May Day, traditionally the first day of May, is Labor Day in most European and Latin American countries.

4. Cinco de Mayo commemorates the Mexican victory over the French at the Battle of Puebla, and celebrates Mexican unity and freedom.

5. Memorial Day honors America's armed forces killed in wars.

6. Springtime often signals the start of the circus season.

"Mothers are like fine china. As the years go by, they increase in value."

— Unknown

FLOWER POWER
Art Activity • 15 to 30 Minutes

Your Child Will Learn

Fine motor skills

Creative expression

Parts of a flower

Patterns

Colors and shapes

Mommy's Materials

Tissue paper

Construction paper

Pipe cleaners

Crayons and markers

Nontoxic glue

Safety scissors

Small flower pots

*E*verything's coming up roses—and pansies, tulips, and zinnias. It's a great time to spring into the season with all kinds of seasonal art projects. Flowers enchant everyone with their fragrance and colors, and they especially fascinate young children. Their drawings are usually festooned with flowers, so when you show them new ways to make art with their favorite subject, they'll be eager to learn. The sunflowers, handprint tulips, and 3-D blossoms described here can be combined to make a fabulous Mother's Day bouquet or a vibrant work of art.

STEP BY STEP

1. Cut out three different-size paper circles and fringe the edges.

2. Put the circles together, largest on the bottom, smallest on top.

3. Add a small yellow circle or yellow dot sticker to the middle.

4. Create other flowers by bending pipe cleaners into the shape of petals.

5. Fasten together layers of colored tissue paper cut in circles.

6. Attach Popsicle or craft sticks, straws, or pipe cleaners for stems.

7. Once a bouquet is created, put the flowers in a vase or a hand-painted terra-cotta pot.

MORE MOMMY AND ME FUN

Sunflowers: Use a round paper plate as the center of the sunflower. Cut yellow petals out of construction paper and glue them around the edges of the plate. Glue sunflower seeds to the center. Take a piece of green construction paper and roll it up lengthwise to form the stem. Attach the sunflower to the stem and finish off by adding cut paper leaves.

Tiny Tulips: Paint the palm and fingers of your child's hand, excluding the thumb, using one of the month's colors. Place hand firmly on one end of a piece of construction paper. Repeat the process with remaining colors. With a green crayon or marker add stem, leaves, and grass.

Tongue-Depressor Flowers: Color or paint tongue depressors green. Cut petal shapes from construction paper and glue the petals to the top of the tongue depressors. Cut leaf shapes from green construction paper and attach a couple to the stem.

Mommy's Memo

Add a little perfume to the paper or tissue you're using to make the pretend flowers smell nice.

Selected Stories

Sunflower
by Miela Ford

Backyard Sunflower
by Elizabeth King

Sunflower House
by Eve Bunting

Gift of the Sun
by Dianne Stewart

MOTHER'S DAY TEA
Creative Cooking • 20 Minutes Prep

Your Child Will Learn

Mother's Day traditions

Manners

Setting a table

Sharing

Mommy's Materials

Mother's Day Cake:

8 tbsp. sweet, unsalted butter, softened

¾ cup sugar

2 eggs, beaten

Grated rind from 2 lemons

¾ cup flour

Pinch of salt

6 tbsp. milk, room temperature

Topping:

Juice of 1 lemon

3 tbsp. sugar

If you can, turn your Mother's Day celebration into a multi-generational affair by honoring your own mother as your child honors you. A great way to do this is with a tea party. Make the setting gracious and elegant. A pretty tablecloth and napkins, fine china, fresh flowers, and doily-lined platters all set the stage for a delightful afternoon of light conversation and delicious food. Serve cookies, baked goods, tea, and coffee. If your own mother is not around, get together with some other moms in the neighborhood and use the occasion to get to know one another better.

STEP BY STEP

1. Cream butter and sugar together until light and fluffy.

2. Add eggs a little at a time, beating well after each addition.

3. Mix in grated lemon rind, flour, and salt. Beat thoroughly, add the milk, and beat again.

4. Pour into 8-inch greased and floured loaf pan and bake about one hour in a preheated 325-degree oven.

5. To make topping, combine lemon juice and sugar in a small bowl and set in a warm place until sugar dissolves.

6. Remove cake from oven (it should spring back when pressed gently in center) and immediately prick the top with a thin skewer and pour lemon topping over until completely covered. Cool in pan.

MORE MOMMY AND ME FUN

Tea Sandwiches: For a luncheon tea, serve tomato and fresh dill sandwiches or cucumber sandwiches (kids may enjoy PB & J or cheese versions). Flatten the bread lightly by using a rolling pin. After making the sandwiches, cut the crusts off and cut into triangles, squares, or rounds using a cookie cutter.

Reading Tea Leaves: Make tea, using loose tea leaves. While drinking, make a wish or think of a question. Leave about a teaspoon of tea in your cup along with the tea leaves. Hold the cup in your left hand and swirl it counterclockwise three times. Gently turn the cup upside down on the saucer to drain, then turn it right side up. The pattern the leaves form will be the response to your wish or question. Some patterns to look for: Circle = trust and love; Crescent moon = changes; Heart = love; Rainbow = good luck.

Mother's Day Crown: Cut a strip of colored construction paper, 2 inches wide and about 2 feet long. Tape or staple the ends to make a circle and punch holes around the top edge. Decorate it by threading fresh or paper flowers and leaves through the holes.

Mommy's Memo

Loose tea tastes the best. The rule is one heaping teaspoon of tea for each cup of water, plus one teaspoon "for the pot." Try Earl Grey, Darjeeling, English Breakfast, Ceylon, Orange Pekoe, or Jasmine.

Mom, Did You Know?

Mother's Day dates back to the ancient Romans and made its way to the United States in the early twentieth century. On May 8, 1914, President Woodrow Wilson proclaimed the second Sunday in May an annual day of celebrating mothers.

• MAY ACTIVITIES •

Your Child Will Learn

Language acquisition

Gross motor skills

Creative expression

Rhythm and melody

About May Day

About spring

Selected Stories

The Rainbow Tulip
by Pat Mora

On the Morn of Mayfest
by Erica Silverman

Spring Story
by Jill Barklem

SING ALONG
Music, Fingerplays, and Action Rhymes

"HERE WE GO ROUND THE MAY DAY POLE"

(Sing to the tune of "Here We Go
'Round the Mulberry Bush")

Here we go 'round the May Day pole,
May Day pole, May Day pole,
Here we go 'round the May Day pole,
To celebrate the spring!

"THE DAYS OF SPRING . . ."

(Sing to the tune of "The Farmer in the Dell")

The days of spring are here.
Warm, sunny days are near.
Birds in trees, flowers and bees,
The days of spring are here.

"IF I COULD BE A FLOWER"

(Sing to the tune of "The More We Get Together")

If I could be a flower,
A flower, a flower;
If I could be a flower, what kind would I be?
A daisy, a pansy, a tulip, a lilac,
If I could be a flower, I'd be a (fill in the blank).

"A TISKET, A TASKET"

A tisket, a tasket,
I made a May basket.
I filled it up with flowers bright
and hung it on the door just right.

MOMMY, MOMMY

1-2-3, (hold up and count three fingers)
Won't you give
A kiss to me?
(pretend to throw a kiss)

AMIGOS (for Cinco De Mayo)

(Sing to the tune of "Ten Little Indians")

Uno, dos, tres amigos,
Quatro, cinco, seis amigos,
Siete, ocho, neuve amigos,
Diez amigos aqui.

MORE MOMMY AND ME FUN

May Pole: One of the traditional customs of May Day is joyful dancing around a pole decorated with brightly colored ribbons. Dancers hold streamers hanging from the May pole as they circle the pole celebrating the wonders of spring. Some of the children run in one direction, some in the other, lifting their streamers as they pass one another. The streamers become entwined, wrapping the pole in colorful braids.

May Basket: Celebrate the first day of May with an age-old tradition—a May basket. Fill a basket with fresh flowers, then surprise a friend by leaving it on her doorstep.

Mommy's Memo

How about a walk to see if those April showers have brought May flowers? If you've planted bulbs in the past, you should have some lovely blooms by now.

Mom, Did You Know?

May Day has been celebrated among Latin and Germanic cultures for centuries. Today, May Day is observed as a festival for children to celebrate the growth of flowers in the spring. In many European countries, May Day is also observed as a labor holiday.

· MAY ACTIVITIES ·

187

CINCO DE MAYO
Physical Fun

Your Child Will Learn

Mexican traditions

Shapes

Colors

Fine motor skills

Gross motor skills

Selected Stories

Cinco de Mayo
by Lola M. Schaefer

Fiesta: Ethnic Traditional
Holidays
by June Behrens

Selected Songs

"Fiesta Musical"
(Warner Bros. Records)

"Best Latin Party Album in
the World—Ever!"
(Virgin Records)

"All the Best from Mexico"
(Madacy Entertainment)

Cinco de Mayo is a potent symbol of Mexican unity and national pride and is celebrated these days on both sides of the border. It's a time to listen to the mariachis, watch the señoritas whirl, inhale the aroma of sizzling tacos *al carbon*, participate in a Mexican hat dance contest, and dance the Jumping Bean. Breaking open a piñata filled with candy or treats is an activity enjoyed by kids of all cultures. Traditional piñatas are most often shaped like stars or animals, but you can easily make a simple round one out of papier mâché.

MOMMY-MADE

For a do-it-yourself piñata, mix one part water and one part flour to make a paste. Dip newspaper strips in the paste, and then spread over a good-size inflated balloon. When the newspaper has dried, pop the balloon and cut a slit in the top for filling with candy and prizes. Using a hole puncher, make two holes equidistant from each other, and tie string to create a hanger. Cover with more strips and let it dry completely. Decorate with tissue paper. Once you're ready to play, hang the piñata on a hook or over a tree branch and pull on the rope to move the piñata around. Each child in turn will get a chance to break the piñata. Blindfold the child, spin her around once or twice, and let her whack at it with a long stick until it breaks, releasing the candy and prizes.

MORE MOMMY AND ME FUN

Mexican Hat Dance: The Mexican hat dance is a traditional dance done around a hat called a sombrero. To do the dance, place a large sombrero on the floor and play some Mexican music. (Look for a sombrero in a costume or party store.) It's best if you have a group of children sitting in a circle around the sombrero. As you call each child's name, the child goes into the circle and dances around the sombrero to the music.

The Jumping Bean: Explain to your child that a Mexican jumping bean has a type of caterpillar pupa inside it. When the caterpillar gets warm, it twitches or jumps and makes the bean move. Play Mexican music and, as the music plays, have the children jump like Mexican jumping beans. When the music stops, have each child freeze. Anyone who moves after the music stops is out. Play until one winner remains.

Where is Mexico? Bring out a globe or a map of North America. Show your child where you live and where Mexico is. Discuss how long it would take to get to Mexico by car and by airplane. Talk about what the climate is like there, the food, and so on.

Mommy's Memo

Children love parties, so why not have your own fiesta to celebrate Cinco de Mayo? Sample foods like hot chilis, beans, rice, and tortillas and afterward, take a nice long siesta!

Mom, Did You Know?

Cinco de Mayo commemorates the Mexican victory at the Battle of Puebla on May 5, 1862. Today, Mexicans and Mexican Americans celebrate their heritage by enjoying fiestas, or festivals, with traditional Mexican music and dance.

THE BIG TOP
Terrific Trips

Your Child Will Learn

Names of animals

Circus traditions

Social skills

Humor

Selected Stories

Bopo Joins the Circus
by Lisa M. Rodriguez

If I Ran the Circus
by Dr. Seuss

Paddington Bear at the
Circus
by Michael Bond

Selected Circuses

Ringling Bros. and
Barnum & Bailey

Big Apple Circus

UniverSoul Circus

Cirque du Soleil

May brings the circus to town, a springtime tradition the entire family can look forward to. There's something for everyone at the circus: clowns, trapeze artists, animals, weight lifters, tightrope walkers, contortionists, and much more. With multiple rings and hundreds of performers, today's circuses are thrilling the public with a blend of traditional big-top acts and theatrical pieces inspired by trailblazing groups such as Cirque du Soleil. The look on your child's face as he or she is mesmerized by performing pachyderms or high-flying trapeze artists is more than worth the price of admission.

MORE MOMMY AND ME FUN

Clown Alley: For a homegrown version of the circus clown, try dressing your child up in your silliest old clothes. Your sneakers or slippers will feel like clown shoes on little feet. Find a pair of old trousers and suspenders, some floppy fake flowers, an old pair of gloves. Paint your child's face like a clown using nontoxic, hypoallergenic face paint (available in most party or beauty stores). When you're done, let your child paint your face.

Circus Sideshow: Create your own circus sideshow with toys your child already owns. Use hula hoops for circus rings, and enlist stuffed animals as performers. Collect balls for juggling and have your child ride his bike (or trike) while tooting on a horn. Place all your child's toy instruments in a line and instruct him to play the music for the Clown's Parade. Funny hats and costumes are a must. If you own a small trampoline, put that into action, too.

Circus School: Turn a trip to the circus into a learning experience by asking lots of questions. "T is the first letter of tiger. Can you find the tiger? What sound does a tiger make? M is the first letter of monkey. Where's the monkey? Can you move like one? The word elephant begins with E. So does the word ear. Can you point to the elephant's ears?"

Animal Act: Pretend you are different animals by jumping, hopping, and growling. Ask your child to guess what type of animal you are. Then, you try to guess what animal she is!

Rhyme Time: Recite this fun rhyme together—

> *I'd like to be a circus clown*
> *And make a funny face,*
> *And have the people laugh at me*
> *As I hop around the place.*

Mommy's Memo

It is not uncommon for small children to be frightened of clowns. Point out that under a clown's face is a real face with eyes, nose, mouth, and so on. This will make your child feel at ease and be able to enjoy the clown's antics!

Mom, Did You Know?

The most famous American circus, the Ringling Bros. and Barnum & Bailey Circus, was founded by P. T. Barnum in 1841.

MOMS ONLY
Advice, Tips, and Suggestions

Safe and Sound

Helmets are the key to preventing serious head injuries. All children under twelve years of age are required by law to wear a helmet when riding a bicycle. Set a good example and wear one yourself when you ride.

For more information write:
National Safe Kids
Campaign
111 Michigan Avenue NW
Washington, DC,
20010-2770

DISCIPLINE DO

Expectations: Having unrealistic expectations is a common malady among parents. Try not to set up unattainable goals for your child's development, skills, and behavior. For example, when teaching your child to ride a bike, know her limitations. Many kids don't master a two-wheeler until they are six or seven years old. Start with a trike or a bicycle with training wheels, and don't expect your child to immediately be able to join the Tour de France.

It's easy to create a win-win scenario. Learn what is age-appropriate for your child so you won't set her and yourself up for failure and frustration. Don't ever push your child beyond the point of confidence and remember that the decision to graduate from a tricycle must be her own. Everyone, both parent and child, will be happier if expectations going into the situation are well thought out and practical.

RELAXATION Rx

The Gift of Time: Mother's Day is a day to show love. Why not show yourself some and take some time off? You need to take care of yourself, too! To keep yourself mentally and emotionally healthy, take time for personal rituals: exercise, meditation, eating well, and just relaxing. You'll have more energy, be able to accomplish more, and engage in life more fully. The more you can reduce stress in your life, the more time and money you will ultimately save. So make sure you regenerate regularly, not just one day a year. Find your own special place to relax and visit it regularly. Meditate. Rediscover how to play. Try something you've always wanted to do, like take piano or tango lessons. Dress up in something other than sweats or jeans and go out. Think back to the things you used to do for fun and try some of them again. In order to be a good mom, sometimes it's necessary to mother yourself, too!

TODDLER TIDBIT

Cycle Safety: Today's parents know that bicycle safety must be taught right along with braking and balancing. Here are some important tips to remember:

● A bike helmet is a must—certain states even have laws requiring them. When purchasing a bike helmet make sure it has a label approved by the Snell Memorial Foundation for the American National Standards Institute. Ask the salesperson to help you adjust the helmet properly on your child's head. ● The brakes on a bike should be checked every year, as should its overall condition. ● Be sure to choose the proper size bike for your child, not one that he will grow into. Do this by making sure he can place both feet on the ground while sitting on the seat and that he is able to reach the handlebars. While standing flatfooted over the bike, he should be able to lift the front wheel two inches off the ground.

MEDICAL MESSAGE

Head Injuries: Kids are constantly having accidents, and head injuries are the most serious. That's why it is imperative for children to wear helmets when participating in sports such as biking, rollerblading, ice- and roller-skating, skiing, and playing baseball. Any head injury that results in a loss of consciousness, severe bleeding, or a change in the scalp (such as a large bump) should immediately be seen by a doctor. The first twenty-four hours after the injury are the most critical, so keep your eye out for warning signs that may indicate serious injury. Even if your child doesn't have any of the symptoms, she should be awakened several times during the night following the accident. Remember, it's always better to be safe than sorry. If you are unsure, don't hesitate to call your doctor. You should take your child to the doctor if he has any of these symptoms following a head injury:

- Projectile vomiting
- Convulsions
- Severe headache
- Confusion or restlessness
- Unequal pupils
- Double vision
- Blood or fluid oozing from ears or nose

Mommy's Memo

Remember your whole identity is not based on the fact that you're somebody's mother—so take time for yourself!

Selected Stories

Are You My Mother?
by P. D. Eastman

On Mother's Lap
by Ann Herbert Scott

Love You Forever
by Robert N. Munsch

· M A Y   A C T I V I T I E S ·

Yellow and
Black are
the Colors of
the Month.

A Rectangle
is the Shape of
the Month.

JUNE

Summer officially arrives in the northern hemisphere on June 21. What does this mean? Warmer weather and more daylight hours in which to enjoy outdoor activities. Talk to your child about the sights, sounds, and sensations of summer; the types of clothes and shoes we wear, the fruits and vegetables that are available, the chime of the ice-cream truck, and the buzz of insects. Most children are fascinated with bugs, from the shimmering beauty of butterflies to an army of ants swarming over a melted sweet. This month's curriculum will teach about the diversity of insects and the strange, sometimes astonishing transformations that are part of their life cycles. We'll also learn about nature, history, and family, with a variety of activities that are fun and enlightening for parents as well as kids.

KEY JUNE CONCEPTS:

1. Yellow and black are the colors of a bumble bee.

2. Summer is the season between spring and autumn.

3. The solstice (when the sun is at its farthest point from the equator) marks the first day of summer.

4. Father's Day, the third Sunday in June, is a special day to show dads how much we love and appreciate them.

5. Flag Day, June 14, commemorates the anniversary of the adoption of the American flag.

6. The red, white, and blue of the American flag signifies valor, purity, and justice.

> "There are two lasting bequests we can give our children. One is roots. The other is wings."
>
> — Hodding Carter, Jr.

BETTY THE BUTTERFLY
Art Activity • 30 Minutes

Your Child Will Learn

About butterflies

Colors

Shapes

Fine motor skills

To follow directions

Creative expression

Mommy's Materials

Black marker

Clear contact paper

Safety scissors

Several colors of
tissue paper

Yarn

Pipe cleaners

Glue

Butterflies possess a beauty and mystery that have captivated men and women for thousands of years. They've been celebrated throughout history in art and literature as symbols of creativity, freedom, and the splendor of nature. The life cycle of the butterfly is fascinating to everyone, but it's particularly magical for children. These art activities will take you through the entire life cycle, from egg to caterpillar to chrysalis to butterfly. Be sure to explain the entire process to your child. Older children can comprehend the details more easily, but all children can appreciate the wonder.

STEP BY STEP

1. Draw a butterfly shape with marker onto the front of clear contact paper. You can use a pattern, but it is more fun to create an original shape.

2. Peel off the back of the contact paper and lay it on the table sticky side up. (Don't cut the butterfly outline yet.)

3. Cut tissue paper into 2–inch squares. Cut, tear, or crumple the small pieces and press them onto contact paper. Decorate interior of butterfly, leaving as much or as little space clear as desired.

4. Lay another piece of contact paper on top, placing the sticky sides together so the tissue is "sandwiched" in between.

5. Cut out along your predetermined outline.

6. Make a hole at the top of the butterfly and insert yarn to hang your masterpiece. Glue on pipe cleaners as feelers.

7. Trim with pipe cleaners to finish off.

8. These butterflies look beautiful hanging in windows as sun catchers and lend themselves to discussions of light, shadow, transparency, translucency, opaqueness, and color.

MORE MOMMY AND ME FUN

Kacey the Caterpillar: Cut an egg carton (Styrofoam works best) lengthwise so there are two six-section halves. Take pipe cleaners and stick one through each cup so they hang out on either side to form legs. Take two pipe cleaners, and stick them through the front of the first cup for antennae. Put glue on the edges of the carton and seal the carton. Let dry and decorate. Be sure to draw or glue beads on the head for eyes.

Mommy's Memo

Most butterflies only live two or three weeks, so when you see one, be gentle and admire from afar.

Mom, Did You Know?

Butterfly eggs hatch into larvae called caterpillars. When a caterpillar reaches its full size, it is ready for its big magic trick. It spins a chrysalis (the correct term, as opposed to cocoon), lies dormant for a while, then emerges as a butterfly ready to spread her wings and soar away. This is called metamorphosis.

DADDY'S DAY TREASURE BOX
Art Activity • 30 to 40 Minutes

Your Child Will Learn

About giving

Fine motor skills

About Father's Day

Shapes

Colors

Mommy's Materials

Pictures

Empty cigar box (or other hinged box)

Glue

Varnish

Pen

Tissue paper

Ribbon

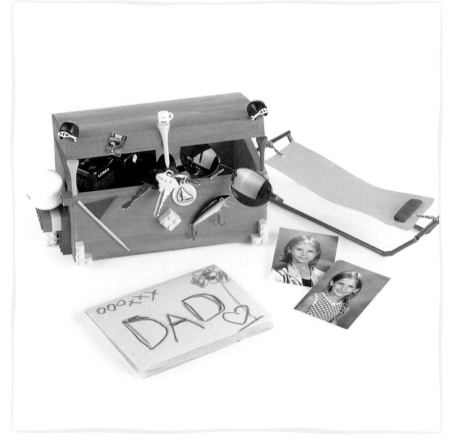

*F*ather's Day is celebrated on the third Sunday of June. It's a day when Dad doesn't have to work, mow the lawn, repair something around the house, or wax the car (busy guy, isn't he?). And when it comes to gifts, Dad deserves more than a striped tie and store-bought card. While power tools and electronic toys may look appealing, every parent knows that a gift made of tape, glue, and a piece of construction paper with "I Love You" marked in fat red crayon melts a father's heart faster than the sun melts ice on a hot summer day.

STEP BY STEP

1. Clip out letters, pictures, or photos that Dad might like. If he's a golfer, find or draw pictures of golf clubs. If he loves sports, collect pictures of his favorite events.

2. If you're stuck for ideas, make handprints on a piece of construction paper and cut them out.

3. Glue the pictures, drawings, or prints on the cigar box or hinged box.

4. Have your child glue a photo of him- or herself onto the box lid.

5. Finish by covering with a glaze or white glue that dries clear.

6. Add this note: "Daddy, Daddy, I love you. Daddy, Daddy, loves me true. We run, we jump, and play ball, too. These are the things we love to do!"

7. Wrap in tissue and tie with ribbon.

MORE MOMMY AND ME FUN

Father's Day Card: Talk to your child about things he can do around the house to help his dad. Then help make a "Helping Hands" Father's Day card. Paint your child's hand with tempera paint and have him make handprints on four sheets of white paper. When dry, make a cover out of construction paper and staple your child's handprint papers inside. Dad can tear out the pages of the card and present them when he needs a "helping hand."

A Wallet-Size Collage: So Dad can remember you through-out the day, cut a credit card–size rectangle out of poster board and have your child decorate both sides with mes-sages, stickers, drawings, and glued-on photographs. To make the card sturdier, cover it on both sides with clear contact paper or have it laminated. Dad can keep the card in his wal-let and take it with him wherever he goes—a reminder of who loves him best of all.

Mommy's Memo

Pick an activity you know Dad likes and make sure that on this day Dad and his children are part of each other's lives.

Selected Stories

My Dad Takes Care of Me
by Patricia Quinlan

I Love My Daddy Because . . .
by Laurel Porter-Gaylord

Just Me and My Dad
by Mercer Mayer

Lots of Dads
by Shelley Rotner and Sheila M. Kelly

Owl Moon
by Jane Yolen

• JUNE ACTIVITIES •

HONEY GRANOLA BARS

Creative Cooking • 15 to 20 Minutes Prep

Your Child Will Learn

Cutting

Measuring

Shape reinforcement

Taste discrimination

Mommy's Materials

3 cups low-fat granola

¾ cup dried fruit (such as dried cranberries, finely chopped dried apricots or dates)

½ cup honey

¼ cup vegetable oil

¾ tsp. vanilla extract

3 egg whites, lightly beaten

Safe and Sound

Don't serve honey to infants under the age of twelve months. It contains spores that may cause botulism in infants.

*N*early everyone has a taste for honey—in fact, people have been collecting it since prehistoric times. Ancient Egyptian tombs are illustrated with pictures of servants smoking bees out of their nests and, until the Middle Ages, honey was the sweetener of choice throughout Europe. Today it remains popular for its unique flavor. To satisfy a sweet tooth, here is a fun and yummy recipe kids love to make and eat.

STEP BY STEP

1. In a large bowl, mix granola and dried fruit together.

2. Heat honey, oil, and vanilla over medium heat in a small saucepan, stirring until the honey is dissolved.

3. Pour honey mixture over granola and mix until well coated.

4. Pour egg whites over granola mixture and mix well.

5. Pack firmly into an 8-inch-square nonstick baking pan.

6. Bake at 325 degrees for 40 minutes or until golden brown.

7. Cool and cut into rectangular bars.

MORE MOMMY AND ME FUN

Honey Pot: Eating honey in its purest form is an event in itself. Combining honey with fruit is an extra special and healthy treat! Cut up a variety of fruits—apples, bananas, pears—and dip them in a dish of honey. How sweet it is!

Banana Caterpillar: Start with a not-too-ripe banana and create legs and antennae by poking pretzel sticks into the peeled fruit. Use peanut butter for eyes and for gluing on a raisin spine—then watch your kids devour the bugs, one leg at a time.

Ants or Bugs on a Log: Fill a stick of washed celery with peanut butter (or cream cheese) and place raisins (ants) or prune pieces (bugs) on top. Then eat up!

Honey Dip: Mix 1 cup peanut butter, 1 cup carob, and 1 cup honey in a bowl. Combine well. As an option, add ½ cup each of chopped walnuts and shredded coconut. Chill in refrigerator for at least one hour. Use as a dip for crackers, pretzels, or fruit.

Honey Shake: Combine 1½ cups milk, 1½ cups sliced strawberries, 1 cup vanilla yogurt, and ¼ cup honey in a blender. Add 4–5 ice cubes and blend until smooth.

Mommy's Memo

Honey granola bars reinforce the shape of the month: rectangle. You can also point out other rectangular shapes around you, including doors, windows, sandwich halves, crackers, and so on.

Mom, Did You Know?

Butterflies and moths drink nectar from flowers for food. Their taste buds are at the bottoms of their feet.

SING ALONG
Music, Fingerplays, and Action Rhymes

Your Child Will Learn

Language acquisition

Gross motor skills

Creative expression

Rhythm and melody

Selected Stories

Where Butterflies Grow
by Joanne Ryder

Butterfly Boy
by Virginia Kroll

Waiting for Wings
by Lois Ehlert

Charlie the Caterpillar
by Dom DeLuise

"SLEEPY CATERPILLARS"

"Let's go to sleep," the little caterpillars said
(wiggle fingers)
As they tucked themselves into their beds.
(make fists)
They will awaken by and by,
And each one will be a lovely butterfly.
(open hand, one finger at a time and hook thumbs
together with fingers forming "wings")

"BUTTERFLY"

Bright colored butterfly
(connect thumbs and wiggle fingers)
Looking for honey, (pretend eyeglasses)
Spread your wings and fly away,
(separate hands and wiggle fingers)
While it's hot and sunny. (arms into round sun)

"BABY BUMBLEBEE"

I'm bringing home a baby bumblebee.
Won't my mommy be so proud of me?
I'm bringing home a baby bumblebee.
"Ouch," it stung me!

"BEE HIVE"

(Put your hands together like a bee hive and say . . .)
This is my bee hive, but where are the bees?
Hidden inside where nobody sees,
One, two, three, four, five, they flee,
(pop fingers up while counting)
Buzzing off busily, a way to the trees!

"CATERPILLAR TO BUTTERFLY"

A fuzzy caterpillar wiggled down a tree.
He wiggled long, he wiggled short,
he wiggled right at me.
I put him in a box. "Don't go away," I said.
But when I looked again I saw a butterfly instead.
Now I could never make one, even if I tried.
'Cause only Mother Nature can make a butterfly.

"THE ANTS GO MARCHING"

The ants go marching one by one, hurrah, hurrah.
The ants go marching one by one, hurrah, hurrah.
The ants go marching one by one,
The little one stops to suck his thumb,
And they all go marching down
Into the ground
To get out of the rain.
Boom! Boom! Boom!
two—*tie his shoe,* three—*climb a tree*
four—*shut the door,* five—*take a dive*
six—*pick up sticks,* seven—*pray to heaven*
eight—*shut the gate,* nine—*check the time*
ten—*say "THE END."*

Mommy's Memo

For ideas of songs and action rhymes to sing on Flag Day, refer to Independence Day activities in the July curriculum.

Mom, Did You Know?

There are over 20,000 species of bees in the world. The most familiar is the honeybee. Just like ants, honeybees live together in colonies called nests or hives. Bees are not only black and yellow, but can also be gray, red, and metallic blue and green.

INSECT BOOGIE
Physical Fun

Your Child Will Learn

Gross motor skills

Creative expression

Rhythm

Movement

About insects

Mommy's Materials

Scarves

Puppets

Crepe-paper rolls

Selected Stories

A Very Quiet Cricket
by Eric Carle

Alpha Bugs: A Pop-Up
Alphabet
by David A. Carter

Ladybug's Birthday
by Steve Metzger

After you and your child have the chance to observe insects, it's time to get wild and act like them! Creep like a spider, scramble like an ant, crawl like a caterpillar, curl up like a chrysalis, buzz like a bee, jump like a grasshopper, and fly like a butterfly. Give children colorful scarves or crepe-paper streamers and show them how to use the props to imitate butterfly movements.

MORE MOMMY AND ME FUN

Flight of the Bumblebee: Talk about bees with your child—how they love honey, help flowers grow, and can sting if you annoy them. Then have some fun. Play "Flight of the Bumblebee" by Tchaikovsky and have your child buzz around the room like a bee. Bees dance to communicate, so tell your little one to dance to communicate, too: feelings (happy, sad, excited); desires (for food, sleep, louder music); or other suggestions (let's go outside; I'm tired). This is a great way to burn off a little energy.

The Ant March: Pretend you're ants at a picnic, ready to eat. Play and sing "The Ants Go Marching" and march like soldiers. Get some drums and march to the beat!

Ant Life: Discuss the life of ants with your child. Describe how they live in anthills and work together as a community. Take a magnifying glass outside to see how big they can look. (Don't let the sun shine directly through the glass or the ants will fry!) If you wish, you can even feed the ants by leaving a few flakes of cereal or drops of maple syrup or soda on the ground. Watch them come running!

Ant Print: Using a black ink pad, take your child's fingerprint and make all three parts of the ant (head, thorax, and abdomen). Finish by drawing six legs and the antennae.

Ant Farm: In toy or hobby shops you can find ant farms, which will let you observe the movements and activities of an ant colony on a daily basis.

Busy as a Bee: Honey bees are social insects with every member of the colony working on special jobs that help each other. Think of the chores you can do to help out your family and get to work. Even young children can contribute by picking up games and toys, helping to set the table, and cleaning up their bedroom. While this may not seem like fun at first, the image of busy bees may help make these chores more enjoyable.

Mommy's Memo

There's nothing better at bringing out ants than a picnic! Even if you'd rather not share your food, this is the perfect time of year for eating outside.

Mom, Did You Know?

Ants are strong for their size; they can carry fifty times their body weight. Also, some scientists believe that ants make up 30 percent of the animal biomass of the Amazon Basin—and 10 percent of the world's biomass.

• JUNE ACTIVITIES •

BIG-TIME BUG HUNT
Terrific Trips

Your Child Will Learn

Observation

Insect facts

Motor skills

Listening/Language skills

Colors and shapes

Patterns

Selected Stories

The Very Hungry Caterpillar
by Eric Carle

The Grouchy Ladybug
by Eric Carle

The Caterpillar and the
Polliwog
by Jack Kent

Fireflies
by Julie Brinckloe

Daddy Is a Doodlebug
by Bruce Degen

Snappy Little Bugs
by Claire Nielson

As long as it's bug season, why not go on a bug hunt? Although your backyard probably has plenty of bugs, you can turn the hunt into an expedition by going to a park or wilderness area, preferably one with water. A creek, pond, or riverbank will attract insects that you won't find in your own backyard. When you and your child go critter catching, bring along tongs or tweezers, and wear garden gloves if you plan to use your fingers. Be sure to look under leaves and rocks, where insects love to hide. Remember to be gentle when you pick them up, and after you observe them, set them free.

BUG BITS

- If you put a creature in a jar, place a slightly crumpled, damp (not wet) paper towel into the jar with it. In addition to moisture, the paper towel will provide cracks and crevices for your creature to hide in and cling to.
- To make a suitable lid for a jar, use a piece of cloth held in place with a rubber band. Plenty of air passes through cloth. Plastic peanut butter jars (quart size) are perfect because they won't break if dropped.
- If you don't know what to feed your insect, don't keep it for more than a day or two.
- When you observe your insect, you'll see that it has three main body parts: the head, the thorax, and the abdomen. Insects have six legs attached to the thorax, and usually one to two pairs of wings. The head has a pair of antennae. These act as sense organs to detect smell or movement. Insects have compound eyes. Many insects have several other sense organs, such as special ears on their legs.

MORE MOMMY AND ME FUN

Bug Hotel: Decorate a large oatmeal box with tempera paints. When dry, cut windows in the oatmeal box (adults only, please). Cut pieces of screen larger than the windows and tape over the opening from the inside of the box with heavy tape. Make a handle by punching a hole in each side of the top of the box and threading a piece of heavy string through. Once your bugs are safely checked in to your Bug Hotel, check them out with a magnifying glass. Point out the colors and patterns on the insect. Count the legs, wings, and antennae.

Firefly Fun: On a warm, calm summer night, you might see a yellow light dart in the air from bush to tree. Go get a jar with a lid that's tight, and try to catch fireflies for a unique night light. *A-hunting we will go, A-hunting we will go, We'll catch ourselves a lightning bug and then we'll let it go!*

Mommy's Memo

Provide your child with a pocket-size spiral notebook to use as a bug diary. If your child enjoys drawing, he or she may also want to attempt to sketch the bugs you see.

Mom, Did You Know?

More than half of all living things in the world are insects. (Note: Spiders are arachnids, not insects, and have eight, rather than six, legs.)

Safe and Sound

Watch out for harmful insects such as red ants and bees, which can bite or sting.

MOMS ONLY
Advice, Tips, and Suggestions

Safe and Sound

Ticks, may attach them-selves to the body and bite, causing a rash, blister, fever, nausea, or vomiting. If your child has an encounter with a tick, take him to the doctor. Parents should watch for Lyme disease in certain regions of the country, particularly New England.

DISCIPLINE DO

For Safety's Sake: Far too many times I've observed a parent attempting to warn a child about imminent danger such as swarming bees or an oncoming car by screaming or hitting. Whatever the reason, it's never okay to hit a child! It violates his dignity and has long-term detrimental effects on his self-esteem. Warning your child about dangerous activities—such as going near a pool without an adult, touching insects, or not running into the street—must be handled differently from typical reprimands for talking back or misbehaving. In these cases it is important to signal to your child that this is a serious situation and he must stop the behavior *now*. Rather than hitting or screaming wildly, simply yell "danger." Withdraw your child from the situation, and then calmly explain why the action is dangerous and shouldn't be repeated. You'll find your child will respond better when you target your forms of discipline and refrain from hitting.

RELAXATION Rx

Cocoon to Butterfly: Now that summer is here, it's time to get into shape. Exercise is the best way. Whether it's aerobics, kick-boxing, or tennis, find something that you enjoy. When you exercise, natural chemicals called endorphins are released into your body that make you feel wonderful and, in turn, help you relax. The YMCA and other health centers often have free or inexpensive on-site childcare, so there are no excuses. Although there's no denying that exercise is a wonderful way to relieve tension, you can also use the Y as a means of getting a little rest. Take yoga instead of aerobics, swim a few lazy laps in the pool, or take a sauna. Some Ys and health clubs have rooftop or outdoor areas where you can just lie in the sun. Even poking along on the recumbent bike while reading a magazine for an hour is welcome relief. All winter long you have been in a cocoon, and now it's time to shed your skin and blossom into a beautiful butterfly.

TODDLER TIDBIT

Summertime Transition: The end of a school year triggers many emotions, not only for adults but for kids as well. If you plan to take your child out of preschool for the summer, there's a good possibility he will experience the same confusing emotions that older children do when the school year ends. He'll be changing his daily routine, saying good-bye to friends and teachers, and leaving familiar surroundings. Many children don't know how to express their unease or unhappiness about all these changes, so as parents we need to be aware of signs that our children may be having trouble with the transition. Here are some things you can do to help:

● Talk to your child by easing into the subject. "When I was young, I felt sad when school was over because I missed my friends." This may help validate his feelings. ● Have your child write a note to the teacher. This can help with closure. ● Make sure you have a picture of the teacher and classmates so your child can have it to refer to when needed. ● Host an end-of-the-year party to assist in closure. ● Keep your child's routine as similar as possible, with the same bedtime, mealtime, and so on.

MEDICAL MESSAGE

Insect Bites: The best treatment for insect bites is prevention. During the summer, children should wear white, green, or tan loose-fitting clothing. Bright colors and flower prints often attract insects. Insect repellent made specifically for children is also helpful. Calamine lotion, antihistamines, or steroid creams may relieve itching. An ice pack can decrease swelling. A raw onion or potato slice applied to the bite has been found to help, too. Bites from black widow or brown recluse spiders and multiple stings from bees, wasps, or hornets can be dangerous, as can bites from an insect to which your child has had a bad reaction in the past. Once you know a certain kind of bite causes a severe reaction, you should carry a special kit with a syringe and medication to help reverse the reaction. Better safe than sorry! If there is an emergency, do not hesitate to call 911.

Mommy's Memo

Try to communicate your expectations clearly to your child and help him prepare for a change in structure by making suggestions on how to deal with transitions.

Mom, Did You Know?

A bedbug is a small, flat, reddish-brown bug that hides during the day and comes out during the night. Bedbug bites look like little red bumps and are generally itchy but are rarely serious.

Red, White, and
Blue are
the Colors of
the Month.

Stars and
Stripes are the
Shapes of
the Month.

JULY

Happy Birthday, America! Fireworks, cookouts, lemonade stands, family vacations, fresh fruit pies—that's what July is all about. Our July curriculum is filled with exciting activities and projects to help celebrate Independence Day. We'll learn about boats and parades and we'll make our own pretend fireworks. On a stroll around the neighborhood, we'll look for signs of summer: wading pools, dogs panting, bathing suits, picnics, flowers blooming, flags waving. And we'll bake up some delicious summer recipes, including blueberry pie, lemonade, and red, white, and blue cake. Come on—let's celebrate summer!

KEY JULY CONCEPTS:

1. Symbols associated with America and its birth as a nation include the American flag, the Statue of Liberty, and the Liberty Bell.

2. Red, white, and blue are the colors of the American flag.

3. The American flag is made up of stars and stripes.

4. America celebrates her birthday on July 4, the day the United States declared independence in 1776.

5. Canada celebrates her birthday on July 1. The Canadian flag is red and white with a maple leaf in the center.

6. A boat is a vessel that travels on water; paddles, motors, and wind can all power boats.

"A happy childhood is one of the best gifts you can give your child."

— Unknown

SHIPS AHOY
Art Activity • 15 to 30 Minutes

Your Child Will Learn

Fine motor skills

Eye-hand coordination

To follow directions

Science concepts

Shapes and colors

Mommy's Materials

Sponges

Safety scissors

Paper for sails

Crayons, markers, or stickers

Drinking straws

Tape

Safe and Sound

If you go out on a boat or near water, make sure your child wears a life preserver for safety.

When the weather is hot, our waterways are busy with boats. Most towns and cities are situated near a lake, river, or ocean where you and your child can see floating vessels such as rowboats, sailboats, tugboats, steamboats, airboats, motorboats, cruise ships, or barges, to name a few. To reinforce your child's understanding of various types of boats, gather up magazines with pictures or visit the library or bookstore. Then try this boat-building project, which will teach your child about the many different ways to power boats and the physics of floating.

STEP BY STEP

1. Assist your child in cutting sponges into shapes of boats.

2. Make a sail by cutting a small square or triangle out of construction paper.

3. Decorate the sail with crayons, markers, or stickers. Try using red, white, and blue, and star-shaped stickers for a festive look.

4. Cut straw in half lengthwise for the mast.

5. Tape sail to the straw.

6. Cut a small hole in middle of sponge and insert the mast.

7. Float the boats in a tub of water. Bon Voyage!

MORE MOMMY AND ME FUN

Bonus Boats: Other materials for boats can include foil, wood, styrofoam containers, or milk cartons. It's also fun to build boats from Duplos, then try to sink the boats with pennies, toy people, keys, etc. You can also find an origami book and make a paper boat.

Sink or Swim: For older children, create a Floating and Sinking Chart to graph items that float in water and those that do not. Let your child place various items in a tub of water and record whether or not they float. Discuss the results of the experiment.

The Unsinkable Egg: Here's a trick that will demonstrate why it's easier to float in the ocean than in fresh water. Fill a large glass with hot tap water. Use a spoon to ease a fresh egg into the water. It will sink to the bottom because it has a greater density than water. Next, stir some table salt into the water until the egg rises. The salt increases the water's density, making it heavier than the egg. Like magic, the egg now floats.

Mommy's Memo

Ivory Soap floats! Poke sharpened pencil through a piece of paper for the sail, then poke the pencil into a bar of Ivory Soap.

Selected Stories

The Boat Alphabet Book
by Jerry Pallotta

Boats
by Byron Barton

Paddle to the Sea
(Caldecott Medalist)
by Holling Clancy Holling

Rupert's Big Splash
by Bob Graham

Sing Along

Row, row, row your boat,
Gently down the stream.
Merrily, merrily, merrily, merrily,
Life is but a dream!

RED, WHITE, AND BLUE CAKE
Creative Cooking • 20 to 30 Minutes Prep

Your Child Will Learn

Red, white, and blue

Stars and stripes

Measuring

To follow directions

Sensory exploration

Mommy's Materials

Rectangular cake pan

White cake mix and specified ingredients such as eggs and oil

White frosting

Blueberries

Strawberries

Whipped cream

All across America, on the Fourth of July, families pause for a day to celebrate their freedom. And after they commemorate the founding of their country, they sit down to indulge in a festive feast. With a little planning and a lot of red, white, and blue, it's easy to create a fabulous menu bursting with the colors of summer. Serve up an edible flag for dessert and you'll have all the kids in the neighborhood feeling like patriots.

STEP BY STEP

1. Follow directions on box of white cake mix and bake in rectangular pan.

2. Cool and frost with white frosting.

3. In the upper left corner, form the blueberries into the shape of a square.

4. Place the strawberries in a row to make seven stripes across the cake.

5. Use the tip of a whipped-cream dispenser to make little stars on the blueberries.

MORE MOMMY AND ME FUN

Blueberry Pie: Line a pie tin with a prepared pie shell. To make the filling, mix 2 tablespoons of cornstarch and ¼ cup of water together until smooth, and then blend with ⅔ cup of sugar. Let the mixture stand for 15 minutes, then blend in 4 cups of blueberries (washed and drained). Pour into the pie shell, dot the fruit with 2 tablespoons of butter or margarine, cover with crust or lattice, and bake in a preheated oven at 350 degrees for 40–45 minutes.

Lemonade: Squeeze juice from 5 fresh lemons with a hand or electric juicer. Pour into pitcher and add 4–5 cups of water to dilute. Add the sweetener of your choice to taste. The best sweetener is sugar water made from ½ cup sugar melted in 1 cup of hot water.

Red, White, and Blue Shake: Put 2 scoops of vanilla ice cream and about 2 cups of milk into blender. Blend for about 30 seconds. Add a couple of ice cubes and a few drops of blue food coloring. Pour into tall clear glass. Add a layer of whipped cream and top off with a red maraschino cherry.

Sailboat Sandwiches: Slice the tops off crescent rolls and hollow them out. Fill the rolls with tuna or egg salad (or any other filling). Cut slices of cheese into triangles. Insert a toothpick into each triangle to make little sails and plant in the sandwiches.

Mommy's Memo

Setting up a lemonade stand develops a myriad of skills and teaches many concepts. From cognitive development (measuring ingredients) to abstract relationships (money) to fine and gross motor skills (counting out coins and pouring drinks into the cups) to social skills (salesmanship and manners), this activity has it all!

Mom, Did You Know?

The red, white, and blue of the flag signify valor, purity, and justice.

· JULY ACTIVITIES ·

SING ALONG
Music, Fingerplays, and Action Rhymes

Your Child Will Learn

Listening skills

Creative expression

Language acquisition

American history

Selected Stories

The Flag We Love
by Pam Muñoz Ryan

Happy Birthday, America!
by Marsha Wilson Chall

Hurray for the Fourth of July
by Wendy Watson

Hats Off for the Fourth of July!
by Harriet Ziefert

"YANKEE DOODLE"

Yankee Doodle went to town
A-riding on a pony,
Stuck a feather in his hat
And called it macaroni.
(chorus)
Yankee Doodle, keep it up,
Yankee Doodle Dandy,
Mind the music and the step
And with the girls be handy.

Father and I went down to camp
Along with Captain Gooding,
And there we saw the men and the boys
As thick as hasty puddin'.
(chorus)
And there was Captain Washington
Upon a slapping stallion,
Giving orders to his men,
I guess there were a million.
(chorus)
"Yankee Doodle" is a tune
That comes in mighty handy.
The enemy all runs away
At "Yankee Doodle Dandy."
(chorus)

"FIVE LITTLE SOLDIERS"

Five little soldiers standing in a row. (hold up five fingers)
Three stood straight, (hold up three fingers)
Two stood low. (hold two fingers folded down)
Along came the captain. (opposite index in front)
What do you think?
They all stood straight as quick as a wink!
(hold up five fingers)

"THE FLAG"

We love our flag,
(draw an imaginary rectangle with fingers)
The red, white, and blue.
We stand at attention, (stand up straight)
And salute her, too. (salute)
We pledge our allegiance (hands over heart)
To our country big and strong.
(arms opened wide, and make fists)
We are tall and straight like soldiers (stand up straight)
As we march along. (march in place)

"WAVE, WAVE, THE FLAG"

(Sing to the tune of "Row, Row, Row Your Boat")

Wave, wave, wave the flag,
As we march around.
Hold it high to show our pride,
It must not touch the ground.
Wave, wave, wave the flag,
Dear red, white, and blue.
Stars and stripes forever bright,
America to you!

• JULY ACTIVITIES •

Mommy's Memo

"Yankee Doodle" is an all-time favorite for kids. I loved it when I was young, and I'll bet you didn't know there were so many verses! After the celebrations, sit back, relax, and watch the movie Yankee Doodle Dandy starring James Cagney. The networks usually broadcast it this time of year, or you can find it at the video store.

Mom, Did You Know?

The stars on the American flag represent the fifty states and the stripes symbolize the original thirteen colonies.

JULY FOURTH PARADE
Physical Fun

Your Child Will Learn

Gross motor skills

To follow directions

To have fun

American history

Mommy's Materials

Flags

Streamers

Noisemakers

What Fourth of July would be complete without a parade? Before you go to your town's big parade, let your children and the other boys and girls in the neighborhood create one of their own. Tell everyone to dress in red, white, and blue and to grab their rhythm instruments or noisemakers. Get out some pots and pans and wooden spoons to create your own drum corps. Play marching music from a tape recorder (try the marches of John Phillip Sousa). Start the parade around the playground or down the sidewalk. When it's over, treat everyone at your house to red, white, and blue Popsicles.

MORE MOMMY AND ME FUN

Parade Floats: Decorate tricycles or other riding or pulling toys for a parade. Some decorating ideas: weave red, white, and blue crepe paper through bicycle spokes; tie balloons or streamers to handlebars; make a float in a wagon; hang noisy cans or pie plates from the bikes.

Marching: Have older children march in different directions: backward, forward, left, right, diagonally. Also different speeds—fast, slow, really fast, really slow! This helps improve coordination and listening skills.

Birthday Party: Set up a birthday party for America. Ask what games your child likes to play at birthday parties and play some of those games. Play patriotic games, too, like Pin the Star on the Flag or Musical Chairs to marching music. Sing "Happy Birthday" and substitute "USA" in place of someone's name.

Noisemakers: Glue, paint, collage, or color on white paper plates. Fold plate in half and put beans or whatever makes noise inside of the plate. Staple shut, leaving a small opening at bottom to put streamers in so they hang out, then staple closed. You can also make your own shakers. (See page 71)

Sidewalk Chalk: Bring out your artistic side by getting out colored chalk and drawing a Fourth of July sidewalk mural. Try your hand at creating colorful fireworks, or draw a giant red, white, and blue American flag. Preserve the art by spraying with hairspray.

Fantastic Fireworks: You can make dazzling pretend sparklers by taping gold and silver curling ribbon on the end of straws and twirling them like fireworks. Your child can also create firework art by drawing tiny circles on dark colored construction paper with white chalk and then drawing lines radiating outward from the circles with glue. Sprinkle glitter over the glue and shake off any excess.

Mommy's Memo

Look at the American flag and discuss the patterns. Count the stars and stripes to reinforce the colors and shapes of the month.

Mom, Did You Know?

The founders of our country had big plans for the Fourth of July. Patriot Samuel Adams wrote, "There will be celebrations by succeeding generations, as the great anniversary festival, and it ought to be commemorated as the day of deliverance with pomp and parade, with guns, bells, bonfires, and illuminations, from one end of the continent to the other."

• JULY ACTIVITIES •

SUMMER PICNIC
Terrific Trips

Your Child Will Learn

Sharing

Manners

Traditions

Gross motor skills

Mommy's Materials

Blanket

Picnic basket

Food and drinks

Sunscreen

Cups and utensils

Selected Stories

Biscuit's Picnic
by Alyssa Satin Capucilli

Boats, Boats, Boats
by Joanna Ruane

A Summer Picnic
by Richard Scarry

Some of my favorite childhood memories stem from picnic outings with my family. While the eighteenth-century French and English aristocracy may have enjoyed servant-attended formal picnics with chairs and table settings of fine china and crystal, modern picnics are usually more casual affairs. Today, picnics can be as simple or as festive as you like—all that matters to children is that they get to eat outdoors. One of the great warm-weather pleasures, picnics can take place anytime and anywhere, from the lawn in front of the library or a favorite museum to a mountaintop or beach.

Problem-Free Picnics

The first consideration for your picnic is location. Pick a site that is comfortable with nearby restroom facilities if possible, and some shelter from the sun. A theme helps everyone get involved. A beach-party picnic, a safari picnic, or an all-American picnic are all good ideas. If you're into sports, a portable party or tailgate party can be a nice change from entertaining in your dining room or backyard. Even if you live in the city, an urban picnic can take place on a park bench where the entertainment is free and nonstop.

The most difficult thing about having a picnic or cookout away from home is remembering everything! If you plan on grilling, make sure you have charcoal or wood chips, fire starter, matches, tongs, and barbecue seasonings (in addition to the grill or hibachi). Other essentials include a sharp knife, trash bags, bottle opener, napkins or paper towels, plates, utensils, and blankets. And don't forget the sunscreen, insect repellent, and wet wipes or antibacterial lotion to clean your hands before lunch.

To keep kids entertained there's a plethora of picnic activities from bocce ball—a lawn bowling game—to face painting, a scavenger hunt, relay races, or a balloon toss. Definitely bring a camera so you can put together a summer scrapbook!

MORE MOMMY AND ME FUN

Going on a Picnic: With older kids you can play a progressive memory game. Start with the phrase "I'm going on a picnic . . ." Add objects in alphabetical order and see who can remember the longest list. "I'm going on a picnic and I'm bringing an apple." "I'm going on a picnic and I'm bringing an apple and a banana" and so on (cupcake, doughnut, egg, french fries, a grapefruit).

Historic Landmarks: On your way to a picnic, why not stop for a visit at the State Capitol, the Governor's mansion, the Mayor's office, or a famous historical landmark? Some historic attractions offer special children's programs or opportunities to dress up in period costume. You might even be able to picnic on the front lawn after your visit.

Mommy's Memo

Put foods in the cooler in the opposite order you'll be using them. The food you'll need last should be packed first, at the bottom, so you can take out the food only as you need it.

Mom, Did You Know?

July 4, 1776, marks the day the United States declared independence from Britain.

Safe and Sound

Store all picnic food in a cooler filled with freezer packs or bags of ice to prevent spoiling.

MOMS ONLY
Advice, Tips, and Suggestions

Safe and Sound

For information on the use

of fireworks, contact:

The National Council for

Firework Safety,

4808 Moorland Lane

Suite 109

Bethesda, MD 20814

301-907-7998.

www.fireworksafety.com.

DISCIPLINE DO

Asserting Their Independence: As children get older, they start asserting their independence by not listening to you. Even the most well-behaved, easygoing child will begin to test the waters, and parents are usually unprepared for it. The key to successfully dealing with this difficult stage is to be proactive, not reactive. My experience both as a mother and as a family therapist has taught me that one of the best behavior-management tools is a simple sticker chart. Children can see what is happening and know they are working toward a goal and pleasing you. This is how it works: Buy or create a sticker chart to encourage positive behavior. Employ an "if/then" message, for example, "You will get a sticker if you behave at the picnic. However, if you misbehave then you will not get a sticker." When your child gets five stickers on his chart, he gets a treat. This technique teaches children that there will be consequences to their behavior. You'll be surprised with the positive results.

RELAXATION Rx

Your Own Independence Day: Declare your own independence by taking an afternoon off. I remember what a friend of mine (and mother of two) told me before my daughter was born. She said, "You need at least one afternoon a week just for yourself. Find a sitter now!" Try to give yourself at least four hours a week—Mom's afternoon off—and try to arrange it so that you don't have to spend that time doing errands. If possible, you can trade off babysitting chores with friends or members of your playgroup. Force yourself, if necessary, to relax: take a book to the park, visit a friend, get in the car and take a little drive, get a facial or a free makeover at the department store, whatever works for you that does not involve taking care of anyone or anything else. This afternoon or morning of independence will do wonders for both you and your relationship with your family.

TODDLER TIDBIT

Fireworks Safety: Nothing is more spectacular than watching fireworks light up the nighttime sky, but the pyrotechnics do carry a certain risk. The safest way to enjoy these displays is from a distance. Here are some rules that will help make your July Fourth fireworks both thrilling and safe:

- Stay away from illegal fireworks and explosives. Buy them only from legitimate stores.
- Do not carry fireworks in your pocket.
- Never give fireworks to small children.
- When storing fireworks, keep them in a cool dry place.
- Always have an adult present when setting off fireworks.
- Never make or experiment with fireworks.
- Always read and follow directions carefully.
- Only ignite fireworks outside.
- Light one firework at a time.
- Never relight a dud firework.
- Keep a bucket of water nearby.
- Wear eye protection, and after you light the firework, step away.
- Teach children to hold sparklers at arms' length.
- Never, ever throw a firework at another person.

MEDICAL MESSAGE

Burns: Fireworks, barbecues, the sun, and kids can sometimes spell disaster. Despite our diligent warnings, children don't really understand the danger these things pose. If an accident should happen, how should you treat a burn? First remove the heat source. Then place the burned area under a cold-water faucet, hose, or into a cooler with ice if there is one readily available. Very small burns can be treated with an over-the-counter antibiotic burn ointment and a gauze bandage. A doctor should see any burn that blisters and extends over an area greater than a couple of inches. If the burn appears severe, call 911 immediately.

Mommy's Memo

If you decide to celebrate the Fourth of July with fireworks, check with your local police department to determine what kind of fireworks can be legally discharged in your area.

Mom, Did You Know?

Nearly 30 percent of all injuries associated with fireworks are caused by illegal explosives or homemade fireworks. Some of the most dangerous are M-80s, M-100s, and cherry bombs.

Green, Orange,
Blue, and Yellow
are the Colors of
the Month.

A Circle

and a Star

are the Shapes

of the Month.

AUGUST

Whew! It's August and the heat is on! Since it's the height of summer and temperatures are soaring, it's definitely time to start thinking about a trip to the beach. Even if you don't live near an ocean, you'll find a lake, river, city pool, or water park that will cool you off. Since oceans make up nearly three-quarters of the earth's surface, it's important that your child learn about this ecosystem. Why not plan a vacation to the beach and make the trip both a time for family fun and a learning experience? To make the most of your visit to the seashore, this month's curriculum includes many seaworthy projects and activities. Learning about fish, the ocean, colorful shells, and water safety will encourage everyone to have fun in the sun. If you can't get to the beach, these projects will bring the spirit of the beach to you!

KEY AUGUST CONCEPTS:

1. The world under the sea is a vast ecosystem and home to millions of species of marine life

2. Oceans cover nearly three-quarters of the earth's surface.

3. A starfish is shaped like a star and a sand dollar is the shape of a circle.

4. Fish ruled the ocean before dinosaurs ruled the land.

5. Pool and water safety are important for children and adults.

6. The sun, which is the center of our solar system, is the closest star to earth.

"When I was down beside the sea,
A wooden spade they gave to me
To dig the sandy shore.
My holes were empty like a cup,
In every hole the sea came up
Till it could come no more."

—Robert Louis Stevenson

BEACH IN A BOTTLE
Art Activity • 20 to 30 Minutes

Your Child Will Learn

Fine motor skills

Creative thinking

About marine life

Colors and shapes

Mommy's Materials

Clear glass or plastic jar
(a mason jar or large
mayonnaise jar works well)

Sand

Shells

Fishing lure, starfish,
seahorse, etc. (optional)

Water

Blue food coloring

In the oceans—and other bodies of water such as rivers and lakes—there are magnificent creatures ranging from starfish, jellyfish, and electric eels to freshwater seals, giant squid, and whales. From your local library, check out picture books with photographs of these wondrous animals. Talk to your child about the many different types of marine life. Ask questions: What colors are these creatures? What do they look like? How are they different from one another? This type of dialogue helps enhance expressive language skills and creative thinking.

STEP BY STEP

1. Put about 1 inch of sand in the bottom of a clear jar (you can also use a plastic water or soda bottle).

2. Add some small seashells.

3. Embellish with colorful rocks, pieces of coral or driftwood, a starfish, or a seahorse.

4. Add water and color the water blue with a drop of food coloring.

5. Finish off with a fish-shaped fishing lure and glue the cap on, or cover tightly.

MORE MOMMY AND ME FUN

Fishy Feet: Use a paintbrush to paint the bottom of your child's feet with tempera paint (orange, green, and yellow are good choices). Have him step on a piece of blue construction paper, making two footprints. Wash off, change colors, and repeat. When the prints dry, use a marker to make a nose, eyes, and fins on the feet prints. Don't forget to clean your child's feet or those fishy prints will be all over the house.

Sponge Painting: Use safety scissors to cut sponges into different shapes—stars, circles, squares, and even a fish shape. Pour tempera paint into aluminum pans and dip the sponge shapes into them. Once they're coated with paint, imprint on blue paper to make different marine-inspired designs.

Fishbowl: Take a sheet of white paper and cut into the shape of a fishbowl. Glue sand onto the bottom and then draw or cut and glue various images of sea life onto the scene. If possible, glue small seashells onto the sand. Finish by covering the fishbowl with a piece of blue cellophane.

Fishy Facts: Share some fun facts such as these— Fish are the most diverse vertebrate group (animals with backbones). They have gills for breathing, fins for swimming, and streamlined bodies to help them move with ease through the water.

Mommy's Memo

Many sponges you buy in stores are made of fake materials. Real sponges may live several thousand feet below the surface of the ocean.

Mom, Did You Know?

Seawater is salty because rivers carry minerals (including salt) found in soil and rocks to the ocean. Since this has been happening for millions of years, the oceans now have a lot of salt—about 1 cup per gallon!

SUN CATCHERS
Art Activity • 15 to 30 Minutes

Your Child Will Learn

About the sun

Colors and shapes

Fine motor skills

Creative expression

Mommy's Materials

Round paper plates or plastic lids

Safety scissors

Colored tissue paper, plastic wrap, or cellophane

Glue

Hole-puncher

Yarn

Selected Stories

The Sun
by Seymour Simon

The Sun Is My Favorite Star
by Frank Asch

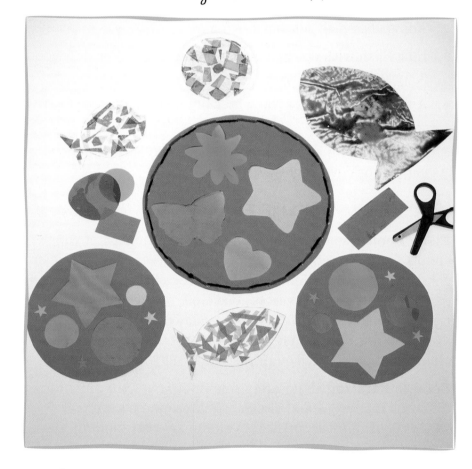

Have you and your child ever looked out the window at night and wondered about the stars and planets? Although it may not look like it, our sun is a star just like all the other stars in the sky. The difference is that we are much nearer to the sun than the other stars so it looks much bigger and brighter. By creating a device that hangs in a window where the sun illuminates it, we can catch the sun's rays and turn them into a colorful design. So grab some rays and let them help you make beautiful art.

STEP BY STEP

1. Cut designs—like a star, circle, heart, or triangle—in a paper plate or lid.

2. Glue different colored tissue paper to the back of shapes.

3. Punch holes along the edges of the paper plate.

4. Lace the yarn through the holes.

5. Hang in your window. When the sun shines through your sun catcher, the colors will come alive!

MORE MOMMY AND ME FUN

Fish Sun Catchers: Cut two identical fish patterns from clear contact paper (flip the pattern so you have a front and back piece). Peel the backing off the contact paper of one fish and lay it on the table, sticky side up. Place small pieces of colored tissue paper all over the contact paper. Experiment with color mixing such as combining blue and yellow to make green. When done, peel the other fish and place it on top (sticky sides together). Punch a hole near the edge, string a piece of yarn through the hole, and hang near a window.

Magic Sun Pictures: Place several small items (a cup, a block, a doll) on pieces of black construction paper. Place outside in direct sunlight on a very hot day. At the end of the day, remove the items and observe what has happened to the paper.

Plastic Sun Catcher: Punch a hole near the rim of a clear plastic lid. Glue designs cut from colored tissue paper to the center of the lid. Tie a string through the hole and hang the sun catcher in a window.

Crayon Sun Catcher: Using a vegetable peeler, shave crayons into small thin pieces. Place a sheet of wax paper onto newspaper and sprinkle with crayon bits. Place another sheet of wax paper on top and press with a warm iron (adults only, please) for a few seconds. Cut into fish or other shapes and hang in a window.

Mommy's Memo

Kaleidoscopes are wonderful for introducing your child to the beautiful interplay of light and color.

Mom, Did You Know?

The sun is 93 million miles from earth and it would take seventeen years to fly there in a jet plane.

Safe and Sound

Even though the sun is our source of light and warmth, it can be extremely dangerous. Children should never look at the sun too long, or without protection, and they should always use sunscreen.

EDIBLE AQUARIUM
Creative Cooking • 10 Minutes

Your Child Will Learn

Fine motor skills

Colors and shapes

Creative expression

Language acquisition

Social skills

Mommy's Materials

8 oz. softened cream-cheese bar

Blue food coloring

Bowl and spoon

A few large rectangular-shaped crackers

2 cups small fish-shaped crackers, such as Goldfish crackers

An aquarium is great fun to watch—but to eat? Why not! Here are a couple of quick fishy snack ideas that are not only yummy but also loads of fun to make. Allow your child to assemble his own creations. Encourage new ideas and let him use his imagination. He'll have so much fun he won't realize that by spreading ingredients he's developing fine motor coordination and by talking about his creation he's developing language arts and social skills. But this edible aqua art won't last long—it tastes as good as it looks!

STEP BY STEP

1. Add a few drops of blue food coloring to the cream cheese and stir.

2. Spread cream cheese on large, rectangular crackers to look like waves.

3. Place a few fish-shaped crackers on top of the blue cream cheese to look like they're swimming.

4. Optional: Take a few Cheerios and stick them above the goldfish to make air bubbles or use thin sticks of celery or green fruit leather to replicate seaweed.

MORE MOMMY AND ME FUN

Starfish Cookies: Use a star-shaped cookie cutter to cut sugar-cookie dough (available ready-made in most markets). Bake according to directions, and when the cookies are almost done, sprinkle with sesame seeds, place back in the oven, and finish baking.

Starfish Sandwiches: Use a cookie cutter to cut slices of bread and make starfish-shaped sandwiches. Serve with cooked shell macaroni for a truly ocean-themed lunch.

Sand Dollar Cookies: Heat ¾ cup sugar, ½ cup of butter or margarine, and a dash of baking soda in a small pot until it comes to a boil. Add 2 cups uncooked oatmeal and blend. Roll mixture into small balls and place on a well-greased cookie sheet. Bake at 350 degrees for 10 minutes. When done, use the side of a toothpick to make petal-like marks in a circular pattern. Now you have your own oatmeal sand dollars!

Jell-O Gummy Aquarium: Buy a fishbowl or clean a large glass bowl and prepare enough blue-colored Jell-O to fill the container at least three-quarters full. When partially set, mix in gummy fish. Let it set in the refrigerator and serve.

Mommy's Memo

Put ten Goldfish crackers in a cup. Take them out one at a time, counting from one to ten. Now invite your child to eat the crackers one at a time, counting until you have none left.

Mom, Did You Know?

Fish can be tiny or huge. They can be round, box-like, or long and slim. They can be any color of the rainbow, striped, spotted, or luminous. The smallest fish is the Gobi, which measures 0.4 inches long. The largest is the great white shark, which can reach 40 feet in length!

SING ALONG
Music, Fingerplays, and Action Rhymes

Your Child Will Learn

Language acquisition

Auditory skills

Musical expression

About fish

About oceans

Selected Stories

The Rainbow Fish
by Marcus Pfister

A Day at the Beach
by Mircea Vasiliu

Spot Goes to the Beach
by Eric Hill

Just Grandma and Me
by Mercer Mayer

Swimmy
by Leo Lionni

"MY BONNIE LIES OVER THE OCEAN"

My bonnie lies over the ocean.
My bonnie lies over the sea.
My bonnie lies over the ocean.
Oh, bring back my bonnie to me.
Bring back, bring back,
Oh, bring back my bonnie to me, to me.
Bring back, bring back,
Oh, bring back my bonnie to me.

"A SAILOR"

A sailor went to sea, sea, sea, sea,
To see what he could see, see, see,
But all that he could see, see, see,
Was the bottom of the deep blue sea, sea, sea!

"FISH"

1, 2, 3, 4, 5,
I caught a fish alive,
6, 7, 8, 9, 10
I let it go again.
Why did you let it go?
Because it bit my finger so.
Which finger did it bite?
The little finger on the right.

"FISHING"

Have you ever gone fishing (pretend to fish)
On a bright and sunny day? (make a sun with your arms)
With all the little fishies swimmin' up and down the bay.
(put hands together and move like fish)
With your hands in your pockets, (slap pockets)
And your pockets in your pants, (slap hips)
All the little fishies do the hoochy coochy dance. (dance)
BaDa DaDa Da BaDa DaDa (clap while singing)
BaDa DaDa Da BaDa DaDa
With your hands in your pockets, (slap pockets)
And your pockets in your pants, (slap hips)
All the little fishies do the hoochy coochy dance. (dance)

"SAILING SAILING"

Sailing, sailing,
Over the bounding main.
For many a stormy wind shall blow
'ere Jack comes home again.

"THREE LITTLE FISHIES"

Down in the meadow,
In a little bitty pool,
Swam three little fishies
And a mama fishie too!
"Swim," said the mama fish, "swim if you can!"
And they swam, and they swam,
All over the dam!
Boop-boop, dittem dattem watten chu!
Boop-boop, dittem dattem watten chu!
Boop-boop, dittem dattem watten chu!
And they swam, and they swam,
All over the dam!

by Saxie Dowell
©1939 (Renewed) Chappell & Co.
All Rights Reserved. Used by permission.

Mommy's Memo

Talk about the way different sea creatures move and try imitating them yourself, or use tub toys to demonstrate. Fish swim fast, turtles and crabs move slowly, the octopus undulates, jellyfish float! Have your child pretend to be each animal and move accordingly.

Mom, Did You Know?

There are billions of fish in the ocean—more than 25,000 species.

BEACH PARTY
Physical Fun

Your Child Will Learn

Gross motor skills

To Follow directions

Number recognition

Creative expression

Imitative play

Mommy's Materials

Beach ball

Sunscreen

Bathing suit

*E*ven if you don't live near the beach, you can still throw a great *Mommy and Me* beach-themed party. Dress in beach attire, get out the beach balls, and snack on tropical fruits. Hang travel posters on the walls to provide that hot-fun-in-the-sun feeling. Pretend to surf while listening to the Beach Boys. Set up a wading pool and lounge in beach chairs beneath a beach umbrella. Wear Hawaiian leis. Fill a giant bucket with sand and add seashells to the top. And for some physical fun, play versions of these classic games. Most can be adapted so they will work in your backyard, at a public pool, river, lake, or park.

BEACH GAMES

Beach Volleyball: Try a kid-friendly version of this California-inspired game, using a real volleyball or substituting a beach ball. The basic rule is to keep the ball in the air. You can hit it with your hands, fists, arms, or any part of your body from the waist up. Catching the ball is not allowed. See how many times you can pass the ball back and forth without it hitting the ground.

Beach Ball Fun: Blow up a beach ball and, with a permanent marker, write a number on each section. Roll or toss the ball to your child, and have her tell you the number. If the number is three, tell her to jump three times or clap three times. Now, you do the same. Let her choose what activity you must do: hop, clap, jump, run in circles, and so on. Kids love seeing their parents do silly things!

Sand Tic-Tac-Toe: Make a nine-square grid in the sand and draw the Xs and Os with a stick, your finger, or driftwood.

Hopscotch: Draw a hopscotch board in the sand with your finger or a stick. Each player finds a beach-related marker to toss: a clamshell, plastic shovel, or piece of driftwood all work well. Make it more challenging by having children jump, or hop on one leg.

Darts: Draw a dartboard in the sand with six concentric circles and give each ring a point value. Each player should choose three markers that look the same (three clamshells, three rocks, etc.). Take turns tossing the markers at the dartboard and keep score in the sand.

Sand Sculptures: Instead of building sand castles, why not try sculpting animals, cars, and other things? Suggest a theme and encourage your child to use shells and other natural elements to add details to their works of art, such as shells for eyes and ears; driftwood for whiskers, antlers, or tusks; seaweed for fur, manes, tails, and so on.

Beach Bowling: Make ten pins by filling a cup with moist sand and turning it over. Take turns rolling a ball to knock the pins over. Keep score in the sand.

Mommy's Memo

Don't forget that all-time favorite: burying Mommy in the sand! Let your child pile on the sand until your body (not head, please!) is completely hidden, then burst out of the sand and give your child a hug.

Safe and Sound

Not all glass you find on the beach is well-worn beach glass. Warn your child not to pick up any glass until you have had a chance to inspect it.

COLLECTING SHELLS
Terrific Trips

Your Child Will Learn

Categorization

Patterns

Colors and shapes

Marine life

Selected Aquariums

Aquarium for Wildlife
Conservation
(Coney Island, NY)
Aquarium of the Americas
(New Orleans, LA)
Aquarium of the Pacific
(Long Beach, CA)
Ak-Sar-Ben Aquarium
(Omaha, NE)
Monterey Bay Aquarium
(Monterey, CA)
Mystic Aquarium (Mystic, CT)
National Aquarium
(Baltimore, MD)
New England Aquarium
(Boston, MA)
Seattle Aquarium
(Seattle, WA)
Shedd Aquarium (Chicago, IL)
Steinhart Aquarium
(San Francisco, CA)
Tennessee Aquarium
(Chattanooga, TN)

The seashore lures us with its classic images—rolling waves, blue skies, and gulls soaring overhead. But for many kids, the best views can be found at ground level. Here they snatch gems tossed up from the bottom of the ocean—smoothly polished pebbles, ancient fossils, driftwood, and periwinkles. These discoveries can be saved as they are or used for sandcastle decorations, game pieces, make-believe currency, or the beginnings of jar collections. Spend a morning or afternoon searching the shoreline for sea treasure, and you'll both go home happy as clams!

MORE MOMMY AND ME FUN

Shell Fun: After collecting shells, let your child sort them into groups by kind, size, texture, and so on. Have him count the number of shells in each group. Continue by asking him to find the smallest and largest shell. Take turns balancing the shells in each hand to see which is heaviest and which is lightest. You can add other pattern and categorizing games if your child seems to like these kinds of activities.

Listen to the Ocean: Hold a conch or similar seashell to your ear and hear the ocean. The smooth hard interior acts as a tiny echo chamber. Outside sounds ricochet throughout the empty shell, so when you put it to your ear, you hear white noise that sounds like crashing surf.

Inland Beach: If you don't live near the beach, set up a small kiddie pool and fill it with sand. Let your child take off her shoes and socks and explore it. Provide buckets and shovels. If you have any seashells around, bury them in the sand and let your child try to find them.

Treasures from the Sea: Cover the bottom of an empty shoebox with sand. Place seashells or items you've found at the beach on top of the sand. Cover the top of the open box with clear plastic wrap and secure shut with tape.

Aquarium or Fish Store: Take your child to the local pet store and visit the tropical fish tank! Talking about the kinds of fish you see helps reinforce learning. Why not take a few fish home and set up an aquarium? Try finding ones that are green, orange, blue, and yellow to reinforce the month's review of the colors.

Tongue Twister: Remember this one? I bet you can't say it five times fast!

> *She sells seashells by the seashore.*
> *She sells seashells by the seashore.*
> *She sells seashells by the seashore.*
> *She sells seashells by the seashore.*
> *She sells seashells by the seashore.*

Mommy's Memo

Collecting shells (or stamps, or coins) is a great hobby that teaches valuable skills about responsibility, organization, and goal setting.

Mom, Did You Know?

There are more than 100,000 varieties of seashells. Hinged pairs come from bivalves (like clams); spiral shells are from gastropods (like snails). The giant marine clam can be up to 4 feet across and more than 700 pounds, while the rare coin-shell, .047 inches across, would fit on the head of a pin.

MOMS ONLY
Advice, Tips, and Suggestions

Safe and Sound

When outside enjoying summer activities and water play, use waterproof sunscreen (SPF 15 or greater) that won't rub or wash off while swimming. Be sure to apply fifteen to thirty minutes before going outside. For a free guide on sun protection for children, call the Skin Cancer Foundation at 1-800-SKIN-490.

DISCIPLINE DO

Pool Etiquette: I will never forget the time my family and I were vacationing at a resort, having a wonderful time in the luxurious swimming pool, when all of a sudden the lifeguard blew her whistle signaling everyone to exit the water. We were told the pool needed to be cleaned and would be out of commission for at least three hours. Why? Because a child had used the pool as a toilet. I don't blame the child—he probably wasn't old enough to understand. I blame the parents. By being unrealistic about their child's ability to control himself, they endangered the health of others. E-coli bacteria, which can be found in fecal matter, is very dangerous. While swimming diapers may help, the truth is if it's in the diaper, it's in the pool. So parents, please, be considerate. If you have any doubt, don't let your child swim in a public pool until they're potty-trained.

RELAXATION Rx

Water Therapy: Feeling stressed from all the summer activities? Probably. Remember that day at the beach with your family? Great, wasn't it? How about treating yourself to a day at the beach sans kids? Water has amazing soothing qualities. Listening to the ocean is incredibly calming. Looking at water is also relaxing, almost mesmerizing. If you don't live near a beach, go to a lake, river, or a spa. Large, upscale hotels often have beautiful grounds with fountains—there's nothing wrong with visiting for an hour or so, maybe having a cup of tea or a drink. If you want to use the pool, many hotels will allow you to do so if you get a massage, facial, or some other type of spa service there. The warm water found in therapy pools, mineral springs, and spas improves your circulation, increases flexibility, and is a great stress buster. If all else fails, buy a CD or tape with sounds of the ocean, close your eyes, and just drift away.

TODDLER TIDBIT

Water Safety: According to the American Red Cross, drowning is the second leading cause of death for young children. To prevent accidents, it's important to be vigilant about water safety and provide continuous adult supervision any place where there is water. Here are some swimming safety tips:

● Research and observe different swim programs in your area. Select one that teaches safety before fun. Ask what skills will be taught in the program, and check the qualifications of the instructors. ● Do not allow your child to be thrown into a pool, as this can cause both physical and emotional trauma. ● Don't encourage your child to use a flotation device as this adds a false sense of security. ● Be sure the program teaches critical survival techniques such as being able to float on the back, learning to rest and breathe, and rolling over and swimming to the wall. These skills can save a life! ● No one is drown-proof, not even people who know how to swim. Always be sure that someone else who can swim is there while you and your child are in the water.

MEDICAL MESSAGE

Summertime Colds: Even though it's 90 degrees outside, the whole family might be sneezing and coughing, victims of the dreaded summer cold. There is no cure, and summer colds seem to last longer than winter ones. A number of over-the-counter remedies can ease symptoms, but some may be dangerous for children under six months. Always read the labels, and if in doubt, check with your pediatrician. Decongestants and antihistamines are often the first line of defense. Nose drops and sprays can decrease nasal secretions and swelling, but should not be used for more than three days. Saline nose drops, followed by gentle suctioning of mucus with a bulb syringe, can be helpful for young children. Make sure your child gets lots of rest and fluids, and use children's acetaminophen or ibuprofen for fever. It's best to avoid aspirin, which has been linked to Reye's Syndrome. Sucking candy lozenges may help ease sore throats, and don't forget the chicken soup!

Mommy's Memo

If your child is afraid of the water, try to understand his specific concerns so you can help him overcome them. Frequent exposure to fun water activities, positive experiences, and appropriate praise will usually help him gain enough confidence to conquer his fears and enjoy himself.

Mom, Did You Know?

Children can drown in as little as 1 inch of water. Vigilant supervision is the best defense against accidents.

Red, Green,
Yellow, Orange,
and Brown are
the Colors of
the Month. Leaf Shapes
and Circles are
the Shapes of
the Month.

SEPTEMBER

*A*utumn is one of the most colorful seasons, boasting magnificent reds, yellows, and oranges. Of course, nothing beats fall in New England, where the trees blaze with color. But no matter where you live, you'll find signs of autumn and pastimes that offer a nice change of pace in this season of changes. A simple walk in the woods or park becomes a treat for the senses. The sights, sounds, and smells of autumn hold many wonders for little ones, who'll pepper you with questions like "Why are the leaves falling? What are the squirrels doing with all those nuts? When can we pick the apples off the tree? Why does the moon look so big and bright?" These and other questions will be answered with September's seasonal activities and projects.

KEY SEPTEMBER CONCEPTS:

1. Red, yellow, orange, and brown are typical colors of fall foliage.

2. Apples can be red, green, or yellow.

3. Autumn officially begins on September 23.

4. For many children, the school year begins in September.

5. The harvest moon is a full moon occurring near the autumnal equinox.

6. Labor Day, the first Monday in September, is a holiday honoring America's working men and women.

7. The Jewish New Year, or Rosh Hashanah, is the first of the High Holy Days, which end ten days later with Yom Kippur.

"We do not inherit the earth from our ancestors, we borrow it from our children."

— Native American saying

LEAF PLACEMATS
Art Activity • 15 to 30 Minutes

Your Child Will Learn

Colors

Shapes of leaves

Fine motor skills

About autumn

Mommy's Materials

Autumn leaves

Construction paper

Photograph of child

Tape and glue

Crayons

Acrylic paint (optional)

Clear contact paper

*N*ature provides an abundance of arts and crafts supplies, and leaves are some of the easiest to find. From leaf pressing and collages to colorful leaf rubbings, there are a variety of fall art activities that are not only fun, but also help teach about different kinds of trees. Before you get started on your leaf art, you'll need to collect some leaves. Show your child all the lovely colors the leaves have turned. Have him point out the wonderful oranges, reds, yellows, browns, and greens. Pick the leaves together and try to gather a collection that varies in size, texture, smell, color, and shape.

STEP BY STEP

1. Press leaves under newspaper and heavy books for several days.

2. When dry and flat, glue onto construction paper, leaving a blank border.

3. In the center you can add photographs of your child (perhaps jumping in a pile of leaves).

4. Decorate the border with drawings or leaf prints (lightly paint the back of a leaf with acrylic paint, then press onto the paper).

5. When finished, cover with clear contact paper or laminate at a copy shop.

MORE MOMMY AND ME FUN

Leaf Scrapbook: Put fresh leaves on absorbent paper towels and press them in a heavy book, drying them for a day or two. When you take them out, tape them onto blank pages in your own nature scrapbook. Try to identify the different varieties of leaves and label them if you can. You can also create a fall eco-journal by collecting other seasonal artifacts and writing your child's thoughts on each page.

Autumn Window Decoration: Using a low setting, iron a pretty leaf between two pieces of waxed paper (adults only, please). Use a sheet of plain paper or cloth on top. After the leaf is secured between the waxed paper, hang in a sunny window for decoration.

Lovely Leaf Rubbings: Glue various leaves onto a piece of drawing paper. Cover the leaves with another piece of thin drawing paper or tissue paper. Be sure to tape the edges so the paper will not move. Choose crayons and chalk and then rub them gently across the paper until you see the shape of the leaves showing through. The rubbing should reveal the leaf's outlines, stem, and veins.

Mommy's Memo

If you don't know an oak or maple from an alder or locust, you may want to obtain a guide to help you identify the tree leaves.

Mom, Did You Know?

Ever wonder why leaves change colors in the fall? A pigment called chlorophyll makes leaves appear green. During the fall, the production of chlorophyll decreases due to the change in temperature. This is when the other pigments such as red and yellow appear, and the leaves display brilliant colors.

PAPIER MÂCHÉ APPLES
Art Activity • 30 to 40 Minutes

• SEPTEMBER ACTIVITIES •

Your Child Will Learn

Colors and shapes

Eye-hand coordination

Fine motor skills

To follow directions

About apples

Mommy's Materials

Apple (for reference)

Several sheets of
newspaper or tinfoil

Masking tape

Flour and water

Twig

Red, green, or yellow paint

Paintbrush

Green felt

Autumn is a time for collecting and storing food for the winter. Explain to your child what harvesting is, and that animals such as squirrels do it, too. For example, we collect apples, and they collect nuts. In America, the apple can be traced back as early as 1630, according to records of the Massachusetts Bay Colony. The early settlers brought the seeds with them from Europe. Apple trees became widespread due to the work of John Chapman, better known as Johnny Appleseed, and today we can find apples growing in every corner of the country.

STEP BY STEP

1. Roll the newspaper up into balls the size of an apple. (Alternatively, you can ball up some tinfoil.)

2. Tape the newspaper together. Fashion a dent at the top for the stem and a small, flat area on the bottom so the apple will look more realistic.

3. Mix flour and water together to form a paste.

4. Dip strips of newspaper or paper toweling into the mixture, and make sure to wipe the excess between your fingers. Lay the paper over the ball until it is totally covered. While the apple is still wet, insert a real twig for the stem.

5. Let it dry overnight, add felt leaves, and then paint. Show your child how apples can be solid colors as well as combinations such as yellow-green and yellow-red.

MORE MOMMY AND ME FUN

Apple Printing: Cut an apple in half lengthwise. You should be able to see the "star" that the core forms in the apple. Put some red or green tempera paint in a shallow container (a pie tin works well) and show your child how to dip the apple in the paint and press onto a piece of paper, creating an apple print. Finish up by having your child dip his thumb into green paint and press onto the top of the apple for leaves.

Dried Apple Face: Peel apples with a vegetable peeler (adults only, please), but leave the skin on the bottom. Using a plastic knife, carve a face into the apple. First hollow out deep-set eyes, then make a triangle nose, and finish by making a slit for the mouth. Put apple faces in a warm place to dry for at least two weeks. Make periodic observations of changes as the apple dries and shrinks.

Mommy's Memo

Show your child an apple and compare to other fruits and vegetables. Talking about the shapes, colors, and textures enhances observation and language skills.

Mom, Did You Know?

Apples float in water because 25 percent of their volume is air.

• SEPTEMBER ACTIVITIES •

CARAMEL-COATED APPLES
Creative Cooking • 20 to 30 Minutes

Your Child Will Learn

Fine motor skills

Creativity

Pre-math skills

Shapes and colors

Mommy's Materials

1½ tbsp. butter

1½ cups light brown sugar

6 tbsp. water

8–10 apples (Macintosh, Granny Smith, or Red Delicious work well)

Dried fruit and candy (optional)

Remember the old saying "An apple a day keeps the doctor away"? Today we know that apples really do deserve their reputation as symbols of good health. They contain almost no fat or sodium, are rich in dietary fiber, are a good source of pectin (known to reduce cholesterol levels), contain vitamin C, and potassium and other vital nutrients, including calcium, iron, vitamin A, thiamin, magnesium, and phosphorus. Each year, my family returns from our fall apple-picking outings with a little too much of a good thing. That translates into lots of homemade applesauce, pecan baked apples, apple frosties, and my daughter's favorite, caramel-coated apples.

STEP BY STEP

1. Melt butter in a saucepan.

2. Add light brown sugar and water. Stir until it has a smooth consistency. Gently bring to a boil, then cover and simmer for 3 minutes, until the mixture is thin but somewhat sticky.

3. Remove from heat.

4. Pierce the centers of the apples with a Popsicle or craft stick, then swirl in the syrup until coated.

5. Place apples on a greased cookie sheet to harden. Refrigerate for 1 to 2 hours.

6. Optional: Decorate with small pieces of dried fruit and candy before refrigeration.

MORE MOMMY AND ME FUN

Apple Frosty: This quick and delicious drink is not only yummy, it's also healthy. Combine 1 peeled and diced sweet apple, ¼ cup of milk, and 3 ice cubes in a blender. Mix until smooth and serve.

Applesauce: Peel and core 6 tart apples, then cut them into chunks. Place the apples in a large saucepan, and add the juice of one lemon and ½ cup water. Stir in ¼ cup sugar. Bring the mixture to a boil, then reduce the heat to low. Cover the pot and cook for 30 minutes or until the apples are soft. After removing the mixture from the heat, add 1 teaspoon cinnamon and raisins, if desired. Stir lightly for a chunky sauce and rigorously for a smooth sauce. Makes 2½ cups.

Apples and Honey: A traditional Rosh Hashanah (Jewish New Year) treat is sliced apples dipped in honey. Rosh Hashanah, which falls in the Jewish month of Tishri, usually occurs sometime in September or October. It is a day of remembrance and a time when friends and family gather together to celebrate the new year, which is ushered in by the blowing of a ram's horn, called a *shofar.*

Mommy's Memo

Why not have an apple tasting? Choose a few from the following list:

Cortland
Delicious
Fuji
Gala
Granny Smith
Jonathan
Macintosh
Red
Rome Beauty
Stayman
Wealthy
York Imperial

Which are sweet? Which tart? Your child will no doubt have a favorite—or two!

Mom, Did You Know?

Apples are high in complex carbohydrates, giving a boost of energy that lasts longer than the temporary effect of sugar.

SING ALONG
Music, Fingerplays, and Action Rhymes

• SEPTEMBER ACTIVITIES •

Your Child Will Learn

About autumn

Fine and gross motor skills

Rhythm

To follow directions

Listening/Language skills

Selected Stories

When Autumn Comes
by Robert Maass

Fall
by Chris L. Demarest

Autumn Days
by Ann Schweninger

Safe and Sound

Be sure to teach your
child never to approach
squirrels. Even though they
appear adorable and fluffy,
they are wild animals and
can bite, so beware!

"APPLE TREE"

Way up high in the apple tree,
Two little apples smiled at me.
I shook that tree as hard as I could.
Down came the apples.
Ummmmmmm! They were good!

"LEAVES ARE FALLING"

(Sing to the tune of "Frere Jacques"/ "Are You Sleeping?")

Leaves are falling,
Leaves are falling,
To the ground,
To the ground.
Rustling, rustling, rustling,
Hear the leaves crunching.
Crunch, crunch, crunch,
Crunch, crunch, crunch.

"FALLING LEAVES"

Pretty little falling leaves, (both hands high)
Falling, falling down, (hands fall down)
Tumbling over each other, (roll hands)
Until they reach the ground.
(place hands and body on floor)

"10 LITTLE LEAVES"

(Sing to the tune of "10 Little Indians")

1 little, 2 little, 3 little leaves,
4 little, 5 little, 6 little leaves,
7 little, 8 little, 9 little leaves,
10 little leaves blow away!

"LITTLE LEAVES"

Little leaves fall gently down,
(fingers wiggling from high to low)
Red and yellow, orange and brown;
(raise hands and lower them, fluttering like falling leaves)
Twirling, whirling, around and around,
(repeat above motions)
Quietly without a sound;
Falling softly to the ground,
(lower bodies gradually to floor)
Down and down and down.
Falling, falling, slowly falling,
Nearly to the ground,
Twirling them around. (quickly raise all your fingers)

"GRAY SQUIRREL"

Gray Squirrel, Gray Squirrel, (hop like a squirrel)
Swish your bushy tail. (shake your behind)
Gray Squirrel, Gray Squirrel, (hop like a squirrel)
Swish your bushy tail. (shake your behind)
Wrinkle up your funny nose. (wrinkle up your nose)
Hold an acorn in your toes. (bend down and touch toes)
Gray Squirrel, Gray Squirrel, (repeat from above)
Swish your bushy tail! (repeat from above)

Mommy's Memo

Select a musical piece such as "The Blue Danube" by Strauss or any other flowing type of classical music. Then suggest to your child that he is a leaf hanging from a tree. Tell him to close his eyes and pretend that the wind is blowing, blowing, blowing, and suddenly the leaf starts to whirl around and around, tumbling, tumbling, to the ground. Faster, slower, round and round, and to the ground.

COMMUNITY HELPERS
Physical Fun

Your Child Will Learn

Language acquisition

Gross motor skills

Role playing

Creative expression

Social Studies

Mommy's Materials

Dress-up clothes

Toy props, such as a doctor's bag, cash register, or tools

*C*elebrate the historic holiday of Labor Day by commemorating the huge contributions workers have made to the strength, prosperity, and well-being of our nation. Talk about some of the country's early laborers such as John Henry and sing songs like "I've Been Working on the Railroad." Look at books and magazines, and make a collage of doctors, fire fighters, pilots, construction workers, artists, and dancers. Discuss what each worker does. Put out lots of dress-up clothes, have a play store register, items for a restaurant, and other objects such as police hats, doctor kits, fire hats, and teacher supplies that will inspire dramatic play.

Assembly Line Production Race: This is a fun activity for developing a basic understanding of how an assembly line operates. This race is done with groups of "workers" given identical tasks to perform. The first group to complete their work is the winner. To begin, choose a few age-appropriate items for the workers to assemble that require at least as many steps to make as the number of participants in each group. For example, you can have the kids assemble goodie bags. Give the first worker a box of sandwich bags; the rest of the workers can each have pieces of candy, balloons, toys, and so on. Give the last two workers ribbons to tie the bags closed and a basket to put them in. Encourage them to work together as a team.

MORE MOMMY AND ME FUN

Factory Tours: Many factories offer a behind-the-scenes look at how products are actually made. The tours can be an interesting and inexpensive activity where you often get a chance to sample the goods. Sometimes promoted as tourist attractions, you may find some noteworthy industrial facilities in your own community. For more information, try searching the internet (use "factory tours" as keywords) and be sure to call ahead to make sure that the factory not only welcomes visitors, but is child-friendly.

Factory Favorites: Some factory favorites include Hershey's Chocolate World in Pennsylvania where you can see how the famous candy is processed (800-HERSHEY) and the Boeing factory near Seattle where you can observe the final assembly of jumbo jets in one of the world's biggest buildings (800-464-1476). Also check out Vermont's Ben & Jerry's Ice Cream where you can view the ice-cream making process and observe the lucky workers whose job it is to invent new flavors (802-244-8687), and the Louisville Slugger Factory where baseball fans can smell freshly cut wood as a new bat is carved every fifteen seconds (502-588-7227). At the Jelly Belly factory tour you can see how a variety of creative confectionaries, such as Pet Gummi candies and gourmet Jelly Belly beans, are made (707-428-2838).

Mom, Did You Know?

The first Labor Day parade was held on September 5, 1882. In 1884 the U.S. Congress voted Labor Day a federal holiday, and it's now celebrated the first Monday of September.

Selected Stories

John Henry
(Caldecott Honor Book)
by Julius Lester and
Jerry Pinkney

Mike Mulligan and His
Steam Shovel
by Virginia Lee Burton

The Bobbin Girl
by Emily Arnold McCully

Building a House
by Byron Barton

• SEPTEMBER ACTIVITIES •

APPLE ORCHARD

Terrific Trips

Your Child Will Learn

Shapes and colors

Sharing

Gross motor skills

Fine motor skills

Categorization

Selected Stories

The Giving Tree
by Shel Silverstein

Red Leaf, Yellow Leaf
by Lois Ehlert

Apples and Pumpkins
by Anne Rockwell

The True Tale of Johnny
Appleseed
by Margaret Hodges

Before you lug home a 10-pound bag of apples from the supermarket, consider a family outing that takes you straight to the source—an orchard where you can pick your own. Whether you pick a peck or a bushel, you may want to top off the trip with a picnic under the trees. Of course, there's no need to pack dessert, but remember to wash any apples you eat after lunch. Commercial farms generally use pesticides. Once home, wrap your apples in newspaper and store them in a cool, dry place. Remove any that become mushy. One bad apple really *can* spoil the whole bunch.

MORE MOMMY AND ME FUN

An Autumn Hike: Take your child on a walk in the woods. Give her a paper lunch bag in which to place the treasures she finds along the way: fallen acorns, red and yellow leaves, interesting sticks, and other odds and ends. Later, at home, take a stiff piece of cardboard or oak tag and help your child glue her treasures around the outer edges to make a frame. In the center of the frame, glue a favorite snapshot of your child. Write the date and the child's name at the bottom. Hang with magnets on the refrigerator. This is a fun craft for kids of all ages, and it makes a nice keepsake as well.

Harvest Moon: On September evenings, the moon takes center stage, appearing larger than it does the rest of the year. Do you remember the song "Shine On Harvest Moon"? The harvest moon is a real astronomical event: a full moon that occurs near the autumnal equinox, on or near September 23. For several nights the moon rises at almost the same time, near sunset, and is extremely bright. This bright harvest moon is helpful to farmers in northern latitudes because it gives them more light to harvest crops. Now that you know when the harvest moon will rise, be sure to take your child out to see this glorious sight. If you have a telescope, even better! Many cities have local observatories that have special harvest moon programs, so check your local listings.

Fall Fairs and Festivals: The end of summer inspires both small towns and big cities to celebrate everything from harvests to arts and crafts to Native American culture. Some of the fair games you may find at these gatherings include pig- calling contests, bake-offs, and pie-eating competitions. You may also be able to go on a ponyride or hayride. Carnivals, rodeos, and crafts fairs can all be found this time of year, so plan an afternoon or weekend around nearby end-of-summer festivities.

Cider Mill: During Autumn, cider mills across the country come alive. Tours allow visitors a behind-the-scenes look at the cider-making process and they usually provide tasty samples.

Mommy's Memo

To locate an orchard near you, call your state agriculture department, check your local paper, or go online.

Mom, Did You Know?

Apple cider is simply the fermented juice of an apple. If you sample apple cider, make sure it is pasteurized, so it is safe to consume. The real hard stuff, applejack and cider brandy, is distilled from fermented cider and has a high percentage of alcohol, so keep it away from the kids.

MOMS ONLY
Advice, Tips, and Suggestions

Selected Stories

The Berenstain Bears Go
to School
by Stan & Jan Berenstain

Arthur Goes to School
by Marc Brown

Franklin Goes to School
by Paulette Bourgeois

DISCIPLINE DO

Time-Out: Time-out is one of the most effective tools for managing misbehavior. If done correctly, it can produce quick behavior changes. Time-out means that your child is removed from a reinforcing situation and asked to spend quiet time in a non-reinforcing environment. It should be a quiet, unexciting place, void of toys, TV, books, and people—a place he won't enjoy, such as an extra bedroom, or a time-out chair in a corner. Don't pick a frightening place, such as a cellar or closet, but don't pick a place he likes either.

There are three steps in the use of time-out: First, tell the child once to stop misbehaving. Second, warn the child that if he doesn't stop misbehaving, he will go to time-out. And third, if the child does not listen and continues to misbehave, immediately put the child in time-out. Up to about four or five years, the length of a time-out should equate to a child's age: one minute per year. Always tell your child clearly why he is getting the time-out. Then, as soon as you let him off the time-out, ask him to repeat the reason. If your child is told specifically what the rules are and specifically what the consequences will be if they're broken, he'll eventually get the point.

RELAXATION Rx

Autumn Walk and Leaf-Jumping: When was the last time you went for a brisk walk by yourself? Although it's tempting to want to share the fall colors with your little one, do yourself a favor and take a solo walk or hike this month, taking in the smells, sights, and sounds of magnificent autumn. No matter where you live, this season of change is a great time for reflection. And why not have some fall fun? When no one's looking, jump in a big pile of leaves! Brings back some great memories, doesn't it? It's a tradition, like apple picking, that the young and young-at-heart anticipate every autumn.

TODDLER TIDBIT

Preparing Your Child for School: As exciting as the first day of school can be, it can cause stress and anxiety for all involved. I can't guarantee you won't cry (I did), but I can provide some tips for preparing your child:

● Check out the school thoroughly. Be sure it is certified by the state and meets all state requirements. ● Make sure the school has an "Open Door Policy," allowing you to come any time to observe. ● Bring your child to the school before classes start to see his classroom and, if possible, meet the teacher. Find the names of classmates and get the kids acquainted beforehand. ● Walk around the halls and playground, and be sure to show your child the bathroom. ● Explain the schedule and activities to your child. Reassure him that someone will always pick him up. ● Allow your child to take a transitional object such as a small stuffed animal with him for security. ● Make sure you are allowed to stay in the classroom until your child is settled down. Never let a teacher pull your child away from you!

MEDICAL MESSAGE

Head Lice—Not My Child! School is here, and so are the head lice. Even in the cleanest of schools and day-care centers, all it takes is one child with lice to start an epidemic. Lice are small insects that live on human heads, laying eggs (nits) that attach to the hair shaft. A diagnosis can be made by viewing the eggs or the actual insect under a microscope. Sometimes they can be seen by the naked eye. Medicated shampoos such as Kwell, Rid, and Nix are available for treatment. Be sure to carefully remove all nits from the shaft of the hair. It's not necessary to cut your child's hair, but it does take patience and perseverance to eliminate them. Items such as combs, brushes, hats, and bedding should be soaked for one hour in an alcohol-based solution and then washed in hot water. The house should be thoroughly vacuumed. All stuffed animals should be placed in a sealed plastic bag for two weeks. Family members and other close contacts should be searched for nits.

Mommy's Memo

Separation is a frightening experience, and crying is normal for the first day, or even week of school. However, if your child continues to cry after one week, you might want to discuss with the teacher whether the child is ready to begin school.

Mom, Did You Know?

Head lice can strike anyone, but are most common among school-age girls. Communal closets, where the parasite moves easily among clothing, promotes the spread of lice.

Black and
Orange are
the Colors of
the Month.

A Circle and
a Triangle are
the Shapes of
the Month.

OCTOBER

Spiders and pumpkins and bats—oh my! What a spooky month we have ahead of us. October is filled with Halloween fun, such as decorating pumpkins and playing witch games. And all those sweet treats! Throughout the month there are celebrations and events filled with the joy of treats and the anticipation of tricks. Halloween is probably the holiday that most indulges the imagination and encourages the outrageous in children and parents alike. It's also a time for costumes, trick-or-treating, and parties, so let's gather up our broomsticks and soar off into the October sky for some spine-tingling, masquerading, ghostly-good fun!

KEY OCTOBER CONCEPTS:

1. The colors black and orange are generally associated with Halloween.

2. Halloween is celebrated on October 31 throughout most of North America and some areas in Western Europe.

3. Spiders, pumpkins, and bats are some of the icons associated with Halloween.

4. Role-playing and playing "pretend" are creative ways to use your imagination and express yourself.

5. October is Fire Prevention and Safety Month.

6. Oktoberfest is a fall festival dedicated to eating, drinking, and merrymaking.

"To a child, love is a four-letter word spelled T-I-M-E."

—Dr. Cindy Nurik

ITSY BITSY SPIDER
Art Activity • 20 to 30 Minutes

Your Child Will Learn

About spiders

Black and orange

Fine motor skills

Creative expression

Halloween traditions

Mommy's Materials

Styrofoam balls

Black tempera paint

Paintbrush

Black pipe cleaners

Glue

Wiggly eyes

Black and orange yarn

*C*reepy crawlers are usually met with mixed reactions. Most little boys love them and plenty of girls find them fascinating, too. But bug-phobia is universal and it's important to teach children that spiders are part of nature and that we need to respect them. After all, what would Halloween—or life—be without spiders? Imagine no Itsy Bitsy Spider, no spider rings, no Spiderman, no spider webs! If you teach your child early that spiders are unique and amazing creatures, not ugly and creepy, he will see their beauty and learn to live with them in peace.

STEP BY STEP

1. Paint several small Styrofoam balls black and let dry. You can either leave them round or slice them in half so they lay flat.

2. Cut black pipe cleaners in half and insert eight pieces into the Styrofoam ball. (Remember, spiders have eight legs.)

3. Glue on two wiggly eyes.

4. Use the orange yarn to make a small nose by rolling up one strand and gluing it on.

5. Attach a piece of black yarn into the top of each spider with a brass fastener and hang from the ceiling or attach to a web made of black pipe cleaners.

MORE MOMMY AND ME FUN

Spider Prints: Paint the palm and fingers of your child's hand (except the thumb) with black paint. Press the hand on a piece of orange construction paper with the fingers pointing to the left side of the paper. Do the same print with the fingers pointing to the right and overlap the palms. Cut a circle about 1 inch in diameter out of black construction paper, draw a face on it with white chalk, and glue it over the prints to make a head. Cut out the spider, glue a piece of yarn to his head, and hang him for a Halloween decoration!

Spider Hat: Cut a wide strip of black construction paper and glue or staple to fit around your child's head. Cut a large circle to paste to the front for the spider's head and decorate with wiggly eyes and a pom-pom for the nose. Cut out eight strips of construction paper for legs, fold accordion style, and glue around the crown.

Hanging Spider: Cut eight long strips of black construction paper and a circle for the spider's head. Place the legs and head on top of one paper plate. (Make sure they hang over the sides.) Glue a second paper plate on top to secure the appendages. Paint the body black and glue a long piece of string onto its back so the spider can dangle from the ceiling.

Spider Stats

Spiders are small, eight-legged creatures best known for spinning silk webs.

Spiders are part of the arachnid family.

Baby spiders can make perfect webs shortly after hatching.

Spiders are helpful to people because they eat harmful insects.

There are more than 30,000 kinds of spiders.

Spiders live on land, but some have adapted to living in fresh water by trapping bubbles and carrying them underwater.

CREEPY CRAWLY PRETZELS
Creative Cooking • 2+ hours (including prep)

Your Child Will Learn

To follow directions

Fine motor skills

Number recognition

Measuring and counting

About insects

Mommy's Materials

Pretzel Dough:
2 packages active dry yeast
2 cups warm water
1 tbsp. sugar or honey
2 tsp. salt (preferably sea salt)

6 cups all-purpose or whole-wheat flour, or a combination

Egg Wash:
1 egg, beaten
¼ cup water

Coarse kosher salt

Decorations:
Chocolate chips, raisins, nuts, or small candies

Halloween treats should always elicit a shriek before they're gobbled up. Since everyone loves soft pretzels, here's a seasonal version that will definitely be an attention grabber. Baking these creepy crawlies helps children with a variety of math skills, from measuring ingredients to counting legs. Show your child how to measure and explain the importance of using the right amount of each ingredient. And if you want to get creative, you can roll and mold the pretzel dough into spiders, bats, snakes, scorpions, and other Halloween critters.

STEP BY STEP

1. Put the yeast in a bowl with the water (it should be luke-warm) and whisk with sugar or honey.

2. Mix in the salt and flour. Stir everything together. Start with a spoon and finish with your hands as the dough becomes stiff. It's ready when it's a little crumbly.

3. Turn the dough onto a lightly floured board and knead it until it is smooth and elastic (up to 10 minutes).

4. Place the dough in a lightly oiled bowl, cover and let rise in a warm place until it has doubled in size (1–2 hours).

5. Punch the dough down and knead it again to remove any air bubbles.

6. Divide the dough into ten equal sections.

7. For each pretzel, roll a section into a body. To make the legs, break small pieces off and use your hands to roll to about 2 inches in length.

8. Attach the legs to the body, cover with a damp cloth, and let rise for about 30 minutes.

9. Place creepy crawlies on baking sheet, brush on egg wash, and sprinkle with coarse salt.

10. Bake in an oven preheated to 400 degrees for 12–15 minutes or until lightly brown. While still warm, press in decorations for eyes. Makes about 10 pretzels.

MORE MOMMY AND ME FUN

Edible Eyeballs: Pick up some doughnut holes and decorate with a gummy lifesaver for the iris of the eye. Place a chocolate chip in the center for the pupil and glue it all in place with red gel icing that makes the eyeball look bloodshot. You can also make Rice Krispie treats and mold them into small eyeballs. Add a raisin or small round candy for the pupil and use frosting or gel for the iris.

Mommy's Memo

Explain that sugar helps yeast grow, causing it to smell. Let it sit for 5–10 minutes. When tiny bubbles appear and the mixture starts to expand, you're ready to move on.

Mom, Did You Know?

The word pretzel comes from the Latin word pretzola, or "little reward."

Selected Stories

Witches' Supermarket
by Susan Meddaugh

Bat Bones and Spider Stew
by Michelle Poploff

Miss Spider's Tea Party
by David Kirk

• O C T O B E R   A C T I V I T I E S •

• OCTOBER ACTIVITIES •

SING ALONG
Music, Fingerplays, and Action Rhymes

Your Child Will Learn

Counting

Shape concepts

Emotions

Halloween traditions

Fine motor skills

Selected Stories

Bean's Night
by Sarah Hines Stephens

Silly Spider!
by David Wood

Monster Faces
by Tom Brannon

Maisy Dresses Up
by Lucy Cousins

Patty's Pumpkin Patch
by Teri Sloat

The Pumpkin Fair
by Eve Bunting

"JACK-O-LANTERN"

(Sing to the tune of "Frere Jacques"/ "Are You Sleeping?")

Jack-o-lantern, Jack-o-lantern,
Halloween, Halloween.
See the witches flying,
Hear the wind a-sighing,
Woo-oo-o, Woo-oo-o.

"PUMPKIN SONG"

(Sing to the tune of "Mary Had a Little Lamb")

We are pumpkins, big and round,
Big and round, big and round.
We are pumpkins, big and round,
Sitting on the ground.
See our great big shiny eyes,
Shiny eyes, shiny eyes.
See out great big shiny eyes,
Looking all around.
See our great big laughing mouths,
Laughing mouths, laughing mouths,
See our great big laughing mouths,
Smiling right at you.

"LITTLE WITCHES"

One little, two little, three little witches,
(hold up three fingers)
Ride through the sky on a broom.
(ride fingers through the air)
One little, two little, three little witches,
(hold up three fingers)
Wink their eyes at the moon. (wink your eyes)

"EENSY, WEENSY SPIDER"

An eensy, weensy spider,
(opposite thumbs and pointer fingers)
Climbed up the water spout. (climb up each other)
Down came the rain,
And washed the spider out. (hands sweep down)
Out came the sun, (arms form circle overhead)
That dried up all the rain, (arms sweep upward)
And the eensy, weensy spider
Climbed up the spout again. (as above)

"FIVE LITTLE PUMPKINS"

Five little pumpkins sitting on a gate, (one hand up)
The first one said, "Oh my, it's getting late." (thumb)
The second one said, "There are witches in the air."
(pointer finger)
The third one said, "But we don't care." (middle finger)
The fourth one said, "I'm ready for some fun."
(fourth finger)
The fifth one said, "Let's run, and run, and run."
(little finger)
O-o-o-o-o went the wind. . . .
And, out went the light. . . . (close finger into fist)
And the five little pumpkins (open hand, fingers)
Rolled out of sight.

"PUMPKIN FACES"

Here is a pumpkin who's happy,
Here is a pumpkin who cries,
Here is a pumpkin who's sleepy,
Here is a pumpkin who sighs.
Here is a pumpkin who's angry,
Here is a pumpkin who's sad,
Here is a pumpkin who's noisy,
Here is a pumpkin who's glad.
(frame face with hands and it becomes a pumpkin)
Smile!!

Mommy's Memo

Have your child make faces displaying various emotions. If he is not sure how to do that, show him how. Encourage your child to talk about feelings and emotions. Check out <u>How Are You Peeling?</u> by Saxton Freymann and Joost Elffers.

Mom, Did You Know?

In the seventeenth century, Druids would go from house to house wearing masks to keep bad spirits away.

HALLOWEEN PARTY
Physical Fun

Your Child Will Learn

Creative expression

Halloween traditions

Language acquisition

Gross motor skills

Mommy's Materials

Costume

Trick-or-treat bag or bucket

Safe and Sound

Make sure costumes are nonflammable, and tell your child to stand well back from jack-o-lanterns with candles.

An alternative to trick-or-treating is a Halloween party or parade for the littlest spooks in the neighborhood. This is a great way to celebrate the holiday, allowing you to target activities to a specific age range. Decorate the house with black and orange crepe paper, pumpkins, fall leaves, dried corn, scarecrows, hanging bats, white balloons, and plastic spiders. For a nonscary party, have a costume contest with awards for the funniest, silliest, cutest, prettiest, and so on. You can also decorate pumpkins and tell Halloween stories. For some spooky fun, try some of the following games.

Halloween Stroll: It's fun to pretend on Halloween. For some extra giggles, have your child's playmates promenade about, crawling like a spider, rolling like a pumpkin, floating like a ghost, or flying like a bat. Add the dimension of sound by directing your child to purr like a cat, cackle like a witch, bark like a dog, or hoot like an owl. Play a guessing game if you like—make a sound, and ask the children to identify which creature you are.

Pumpkin Bowling: Stack four to six plastic pumpkin buckets in a pyramid and try to knock them down by bowling a small rubber or plastic ball.

Musical Monster Mash: Play a version of musical chairs with spooky music or a traditional Halloween song like "Monster Mash." Kids who like to dance can try dancing like a monster. If there is a group of kids, hold a dance contest to see who can dance the spookiest.

Trick or Treat: If you do go out trick-or-treating, review the following rules before the witching hour:

● Carry a flashlight (be sure to check batteries) and use it so drivers can see you and you can see hazards and other people.
● For greater visibility during dusk and darkness, wear light-colored costumes or trim your child's costume with reflective tape that glows in the beam of a car's headlights. You can also purchase glow sticks that can be hooked onto your child's clothes. ● Have your child wear well-fitting, comfortable shoes, even if they don't match her costume—your pumps may look cute with the hoop skirt but they can cause a spill that might ruin the entire evening. ● Use the sidewalk if there is one. If not, walk on the left side of the street facing traffic. Cross only at street corners, never between parked cars, and never diagonally across an intersection. Watch out for driveways, where cars may be entering or leaving. ● Only trick-or-treat at houses with outdoor lights on and do not go inside anyone's home alone. ● Discuss in advance whether you'll accompany your child to the door or wait on the sidewalk. Make a plan in case of accidental separation. ● Discard any homemade, questionable, or unwrapped treats.

Mummy's Memo

Explain that Halloween is a day to pretend. Encourage your child to dress up and use his imagination. And don't forget to take lots of pictures!

Mom, Did You Know?

Halloween is celebrated on October 31 throughout most of North America and a few areas in Western Europe. Also known as All Hallow's Eve, the holiday has its origins in ancient Celtic rituals that marked the beginning of winter with bonfires, masquerades, and the telling of ghost stories.

• OCTOBER ACTIVITIES •

PUMPKIN PICKING
Terrific Trips

Your Child Will Learn

Creative expression

Shape concepts

Color concepts

Body awareness

Seasonal traditions

Mommy's Materials

Pumpkins

Markers or paint for decorating

Halloween is getting closer and closer. Deciding on a costume is an important activity, but what else is there to do? The holiday would not be complete without a pumpkin to decorate for your very own. A visit to the local pumpkin patch is a mini-adventure for the whole family. You can pick out a nice large pumpkin to bring home, or you can choose several smaller ones. How about Mommy and Daddy pumpkins and smaller ones for each child in the family?

Pumpkin Decorating: Pick an assortment of different-size pumpkins. Spread out newspapers and guide your children to decorate them any way they want with markers or paint. Encourage them to use their imagination: draw an open mouth with just a few teeth, place some yarn on the top for hair, glue on some autumn leaves, and so forth. When your work is done, you can paint the pumpkins with gloss medium varnish to give them a finished look. Display them where guests will be sure to notice!

Toasted Pumpkin Seeds: Don't throw away those wet seeds from your pumpkin—they're a delicious treat. Wash the seeds and remove the strings as best you can. Let the seeds soak in salted water overnight (1½ teaspoons salt per ⅔ cup water). Then spread the seeds in a shallow baking pan or on a cookie sheet and bake in the oven at 300 degrees for approximately 20 minutes or until golden brown. Eat with or without removing the shell. This is a great treat for family and friends, but keep away from small children.

MORE MOMMY AND ME FUN

Oktoberfest: One of the most popular festivals of the fall is Oktoberfest, a communal feast of eating, drinking, and merrymaking that dates back to October 17, 1810, the day the future King Louis I of Bavaria got married. Oktoberfest is celebrated in many communities throughout the world and everyone, from children to grandparents, is welcome. For children, there are often pony rides, merry-go-rounds, pumpkin-carving contests, and other attractions to keep them fully entertained.

Fire Station: Fire Prevention and Safety Week is in the month of October. Why not call the local firehouse to see if you can organize a tour? Your child can get a glimpse of the hook-and-ladder truck or meet the department Dalmatian. If you're lucky, the firefighters may let you sit in the cab of the truck and run the lights and sirens. The thrill of an up-close look may only be surpassed by a chance to slide down the exit pole in the firehouse.

Mom, Did You Know?

Pumpkins, gourds, and squash are part of the family known as Cucurbita, and the species contains over 760 varieties. Believe it or not, the largest pumpkin on record is over 1000 pounds!

Safe and Sound

The United States Fire Administration (USFA) encourages parents to teach children at an early age about the dangers of playing with fire, and a trip to the fire station is a good start. (You can also check out the children's Web site www.sparky.org.)

MOMS ONLY
Advice, Tips, and Suggestions

Safe and Sound

October is Breast Cancer Awareness month. More than 175,000 cases of breast cancer are diagnosed each year and 43,000 women die. Even though the statistics are frightening, the key to living is early detection. Contact The American Cancer Society for more information about breast self-exams and mammograms, and give yourself some peace of mind.

DISCIPLINE DO

Candy Consumption: After you roam the neighborhood with your kids gathering tons of candy, the bargaining begins. How much candy should they be allowed to eat? What's fair and reasonable? Be sure your children are aware of your policy prior to trick-or-treating, and stick with it once it's been established. One option that might help you control the amount of candy consumed in your house is to allow your children to monitor their candy intake. Explain that you trust they can manage the amount they eat (while subtly suggesting that two to three pieces a day is more than enough). Or you can take away the candy bags when your kids return from trick-or-treating, and ration out a limited number of pieces daily. This takes work on your part (especially dealing with the begging and the whining), but at least you won't have to worry about your kids overdosing on sugar. Another option is to permit your children to keep a portion of their haul and give the rest away. Take the candy to a senior citizens' center, or charitable organization. Your children might complain, but with your steady guidance, they'll probably relinquish their stash without a scene.

RELAXATION Rx

Halloween Mask: While your kids are busy figuring out what mask to wear, take time to put on one of your own. An herbal face mask will perk up your pores and make you feel like a new person. Peel a cucumber and puree in a blender until smooth. Strain the puree through a sieve and reserve the juice. Take 2 ounces (¼ cup) each of freshly brewed chamomile and green tea and place in a pan. (You can sip the leftover tea while preparing the recipe!) Add a packet of unflavored gelatin and 1 ounce of aloe vera gel, heating until the gelatin is dissolved. Add cucumber juice to the mixture and set in the refrigerator for 30 minutes or so. Apply to the face and let dry. Peel off if your skin is normal or rinse off if your skin is extra sensitive. You'll feel instantly rejuvenated and ready to show your face to the world.

TODDLER TIDBIT

Making the Most of Halloween: Most parents have fond memories of scampering through their neighborhood on Halloween night dressed as a fairy princess or superhero. For a toddler experiencing Halloween for the first time, however, this magical holiday can provoke a range of emotions including fear, insecurity, and confusion. In your enthusiasm for the festivities, don't ignore their feelings. Take the time to be certain your child's first Halloween is a positive experience:

● Highlight the festive aspects of the holiday. Decorate your house in Halloween colors without emphasizing frightening images such as monsters, tombstones, or ghouls. ● A few days before Halloween, have a dress rehearsal. By putting on a costume, your toddler will better understand the holiday. If your child is not ready to put on a costume, don't pressure him. ● Children this age are unable to distinguish between fantasy and reality, so scary masks or costumes are not usually a good idea. ● Most toddlers are more comfortable celebrating Halloween during the daylight hours. If possible, organize a parade or party for the littlest spooks in the neighborhood. ● Be sure your child remembers to say "thank you" for his treats.

MEDICAL MESSAGE

Sweet Tooth: While it seems all children have a sweet tooth, research indicates that children who eat a lot of sugary foods early on develop a stronger taste for it later. These foods have little nutritional value, are one of the main causes of obesity, and the leading cause of tooth decay. Sugar is found in both likely and unlikely places including beverages, juices, pastries, cereal, cookies, cake, candy, and frozen desserts. If possible, limit your child's intake of refined (white granulated or powdered) sugars. It's okay to offer sugar-sweetened treats for special occasions, but it's better to encourage naturally sweetened ones instead. Most important, don't offer sweets as a reward. And remember, if you want your kids to develop healthy eating habits, you have to be a good role model. If they see you eating sugary junk food, they'll want it, too.

Mummy's Memo

To establish a sense of continuity, discuss Halloweens you remember as a child. Pull out the photo album and the home movies, if you have any.

Mom, Did You Know?

While many people worry about poisoning or other dangerous tampering with Halloween candy, the biggest danger for children is choking. Monitor what they eat, and do not give very small children hard candies.

• OCTOBER ACTIVITIES •

Brown and
Yellow are
the Colors of
the Month.

A Rectangle is
the Shape of
the Month.

NOVEMBER

It's November and that marks the unofficial beginning of the winter holiday season. This is one of the most colorful times of the year and Thanksgiving—which offers a time to reflect on all we have to be thankful for—is one of the highlights of the season. Turkey, sweet potatoes, cranberry sauce, stuffing, and pumpkin pie are all traditional foods of this festive holiday. It's also time for traveling, family gatherings, shopping, cooking, and, of course, eating. One of the easiest ways to make the holiday fun for children is to involve them in the preparations. Even a two-year-old can help cut out cookies or "supervise" the pie baking. This month offers a feast of interactive projects for you and your child to enjoy, so gobble, gobble, let's go!

KEY NOVEMBER CONCEPTS:

1. Thanksgiving, the fourth Thursday in November, is a time when Americans give thanks for what they have.

2. Native Americans and Pilgrims feasted together for the first time in 1621 to celebrate their friendship and the harvest.

3. Today people often celebrate Thanksgiving by having a big feast with relatives and friends.

4. Traditions—long-standing customs repeated over time—are important to family life.

5. Election Day, the second Tuesday in November, is when Americans have a chance to vote to express their opinion.

6. Veterans Day, November 11, honors all men and women who have served in America's armed forces.

"A mother never stands so tall as when she bends down to help her child."

— Unknown

THANKSGIVING TABLE TOPPERS
Art Activity • 15 to 30 Minutes

Your Child Will Learn

Fine motor skills

Creative expression

Thanksgiving traditions

How to set a table

Mommy's Materials

Safety scissors

Paper towel tubes

Craft glue

Black, white, and yellow construction paper

Markers

Yarn, feathers, etc. (optional)

Okay, little Pilgrims. It's time to prepare for your Thanksgiving celebrations. One of the first things you need to do is set the table for the fabulous meal. From special place mats and cards to centerpieces, it's easy to turn Thanksgiving dinner into a feast for the eyes as well as the tummy. Here are some seasonal table toppers that will help make your Thanksgiving dinner a festive spread. But you needn't preserve these decorations for Thanksgiving Day alone—give your child the pleasure of displaying them at other meals, too.

STEP BY STEP

1. Cut paper towel tubes in half and paint or cover with construction paper (if using paper, glue in place).

2. Draw faces on the tubes or cut 3-inch circles out of construction paper and glue them onto the tubes. For facial features, cut small circles for eyes and noses, mini-rectangles for eyebrows, and crescent shapes for mouths.

3. Add headbands and feathers for the Native Americans and construction paper collars and hats for the Pilgrims. (A ring of black construction paper slipped over the tube makes an authentic-looking hat brim).

4. You can also add arms, feet, hair, and aprons. Write the name of each dinner guest and set by his or her place setting.

MORE MOMMY AND ME FUN

Pilgrim Place Mats: For each place mat, draw the outline of a Pilgrim's hat on black paper and let your child cut out with safety scissors. Glue the hat onto a sheet of yellow construction paper. Cut out the shape of a square buckle using white construction paper, and glue buckle onto hat.

Colorful Cornucopia: To make a centerpiece for the Thanksgiving dinner table, buy some large, pointed sugar ice-cream cones to use as mini-cornucopias. Place a few of them on a large platter that has been lined with colorful leaves. Gather a variety of nuts, berries, dried fruit, raisins, and small apples or other fruits to fill the cones. Set the platter on the center of your Thanksgiving table.

Do-It-Yourself Thanksgiving Tablecloth: If you set a special child's table, cover it with white craft paper and supply markers and crayons for kids to use to decorate. Thanksgiving cookie cutters or stencils are fun, or you can have the kids write or draw pictures of all the things they're thankful for.

Mommy's Memo

Try laminating a set of place mats so they can be used throughout the month and again next Thanksgiving. Children feel proud when something that they've created is used year after year, becoming part of the family ritual.

Selected Stories

It's Thanksgiving
by Jack Prelutsky

The Pilgrims' First Thanksgiving
by Ann McGovern

Clifford's Thanksgiving Visit
by Norman Bridwell

PASTA NECKLACE
Art Activity • 15 to 30 Minutes

Your Child Will Learn

Fine motor skills

Creative expression

Color concepts

Sequencing

Patterns

Mommy's Materials

Assorted tubular pasta

Paintbrushes

Acrylic paints in assorted colors

Water

Colored dyes (optional)

Yarn or string, 30 inches long

Paper towels for the mess!

Native American culture is full of beautiful artifacts and legends that our children should be aware of in order to appreciate our country's heritage. The image of native dancers stepping to the rhythm of the drums, creating a colorful swirl of feathers, fringe, and beadwork, is endlessly fascinating to little ones. Native American jewelry is a unique and easily recognizable art form, and children love making this attractive necklace that they can wear to their Thanksgiving feast.

STEP BY STEP

1. Let your child paint the pasta tubes using different colors. Browns and yellows can be supplemented with other seasonal colors.

2. Alternatively, you can soak the pasta in a bowl of water tinted with food coloring. (You can also buy tinted pasta in some educational or school supply stores, or find tri-colored pasta in many supermarkets.)

3. Allow the paint or dye to dry.

4. String the pasta on the yarn in a pattern.

5. Tie ends together.

MORE MOMMY AND ME FUN

Hand Turkeys: Even little ones can make a beautiful turkey decoration by using just their hands. Paint the palm and thumb of your child's hand brown and paint each finger a different color. Have your child spread his fingers and press hand firmly in the middle of a white piece of paper to make a good print. When the paint is dry, let your child color in the eyes, wattle, and feet. Why not make a whole turkey family by adding Mommy's and Daddy's hands to the picture?

Thank-you Tree: Have your children make a tree out of brown construction paper. Cut it out and tape it to the refrigerator or a wall. Using autumn-colored construction paper (orange, red, yellow, and green), cut out different-size leaves. As the holiday week unfolds, have your child dictate thankful thoughts on the leaves and tape them to the tree for the whole family to see.

Thanksgiving Garland: A garland can easily be made by stringing dried cranberries, kernels of Indian corn (soaked to make them softer), popcorn, acorns, and miniature pine cones. Start with heavy-duty nylon thread and use a large tapestry needle (adult supervision, please) to alternately thread the seasonal items.

Mommy's Memo

Thanksgiving isn't the only time when you should encourage children to count their blessings. Try to foster appreciation of what they have regularly, so they'll be grateful for everyday things.

Mom, Did You Know?

The first Thanksgiving was three days long, and was shared by the Pilgrims and some of the Wampanoag tribe, who provided most of the food. The Wampanoag women ate with the men, but the Pilgrim women ate after the men, as was their custom.

TROPICAL FEAST
Creative Cooking • 2½ Hours (including prep)

Your Child Will Learn

Fine motor skills

Eye-hand coordination

To follow directions

Shapes and colors

Patterns

Mommy's Materials

Kabobs:

Turkey breast meat

Vegetables of choice (peppers, onions, cherry tomatoes, and zucchini work well)

Skewers

Marinade:

Teriyaki sauce

Lemon juice

Minced garlic

In 1621, Pilgrims and Native Americans enjoyed a harvest feast in Plymouth, Massachusetts, that may have become the model for today's American celebration. In addition to turkey, cranberries, pumpkin pie, and corn bread, they also ate venison, clams, oysters, and green vegetables. When you live in the tropics, as I do in south Florida, celebrating the traditional customs of Thanksgiving sometimes takes on a different tone. To celebrate in a tropical manner, why not have a luau and cook the turkey outdoors on the grill? Set a tropical table, make coconut drinks with tiny umbrellas, and be sure to give everyone a customary flower lei!

276

STEP BY STEP

1. Cut up the turkey breast and vegetables in 1½ inch pieces and mix with the marinade in a glass bowl for at least 2 hours.

2. Skewer the turkey and vegetables, alternating pieces. (Try not to pierce the meat too often, as the juices will be lost.)

3. Place the skewers on a hot outdoor grill. Brush with marinade and turn frequently.

4. Check for doneness after about 12 minutes. Serve while warm!

MORE MOMMY AND ME FUN

A Great Tropical Side Dish: Preheat oven to 350 degrees. Mix 2 cups crushed pineapple and 4 cups cooled mashed sweet potato in a baking dish (canned yams will also work). Spread 1 package of shredded coconut on top. Cover and heat for 30 minutes.

Thanksgiving Corn Cakes: Corn, also known as maize, was a food staple for Native Americans. To make Thanksgiving corn cakes, mix 1 cup of cornmeal, ½ cup of milk, and 1 teaspoon of oil together in a bowl. Heat up a frying pan or griddle on a medium setting and drop the mixture by teaspoonfuls onto the pan. Turn the cakes to cook on both sides. Let cool and enjoy. Cornmeal can also be used to make cornbread or corn pudding, or it can be mixed with beans to make succotash.

Cranberry Sauce: Wash 1 cup of fresh cranberries and remove the stems. Put berries and 1 cup of water in a large pot. Cook over medium heat until cranberries break open. Slowly add ½ cup of sugar and bring to a slow boil. Cook 5 minutes. Remove from heat. Let stand until cool.

Painted Cookies: Cut sugar cookies into holiday shapes. Combine evaporated milk and food coloring and paint before baking.

Mommy's Memo

If you have a picky eater, make him something he's sure to enjoy: a "turkey" peanut butter sandwich. Use a hand-shaped cookie cutter to cut one piece of bread, smear it with peanut butter and decorate to resemble a turkey using red jam for the wattle, raisins for eyes, and different colored jams or pieces of dried fruits to transform the fingers into feathers.

Mom, Did You Know?

The first meal eaten on the moon by astronauts Neil Armstrong and Buzz Aldrin was roasted turkey and all the trimmings!

• NOVEMBER ACTIVITIES •

SING ALONG
Music, Fingerplays, and Action Rhymes

Your Child Will Learn

Language acquisition

Auditory discrimination

Thanksgiving traditions

Rhythm

Selected Stories

Arthur's Thanksgiving
by Marc Brown

One Tough Turkey
by Steven Kroll

The Berenstain Bears'
Thanksgiving
by Stan & Jan Berenstain

The Best Thanksgiving Ever!
by Nancy Inteli

Clifford's Thanksgiving Visit
by Norman Bridwell

"OVER THE RIVER"

Over the river, and through the wood,
to Grandfather's house we go;
the horse knows the way to carry the sleigh,
through the white and drifted snow.
Over the river, and through the wood,
to Grandfather's house away!
We would not stop for doll or top,
for 'tis Thanksgiving Day.
Over the river, and through the wood,
when Grandmother sees us come,
She'll say, "O, dear, the kids are here,
pie for everyone."
Over the river, and through the wood,
now Grandmother's cap I spy!
Hurrah for the fun! Is the pudding done?
Hurrah for the pumpkin pie!

"WE ARE TURKEYS BIG AND FAT"
(Sing to the tune of "Mary Had a Little Lamb")

We are turkeys big and fat,
Big and fat, big and fat,
We are turkeys big and fat,
Strutting all around.

Here's the gobble sound we make,
Sound we make, sound we make,
Here's the gobble sound we make,
Gobble, gobble, gobble.

"TURKEY IS A FUNNY BIRD"

The turkey is a funny bird,
(put fingers behind you to make a tail)
His head goes bobble, bobble, bobble;
(wobble your head)
But all he knows is just one word:
(hold up one finger)
Gobble, gobble, gobble.

"THANKSGIVING DAY IS COMING"

Thanksgiving day is coming,
So Mister Turkey said,
And very careful I must be,
Or I will lose my head.
The pumpkin heard the turkey.
I'm worried, too, oh my!
They'll mix me up with sugar and spice,
And I'll be a pumpkin pie!

THE STORY OF THANKSGIVING

(act out story points)

A long time ago, people called Pilgrims left their home in England and sailed across the ocean in a boat called the *Mayflower*. When they arrived in America they made friends with the Native Americans, who taught them how to plant corn and hunt for animals they could eat. In the fall, when the corn was ready, the Pilgrims picked it. It was their first harvest and they had a party to celebrate and give thanks that they had enough food to last through the winter. Everyone came, including their Native American friends. Each November we celebrate Thanksgiving to remember the Pilgrims and to give thanks for all our blessings.

Mommy's Memo

In 2000, the Grammy Awards introduced a category for Best Native American Music. Check your local stores or online for a tape or CD of our country's first folk music! And try "Tales of Wonder, Native American Stories for Children," legends retold by Gregg Howard, a member of the Cherokee nation.

Mom, Did You Know?

Ben Franklin thought that the turkey should have been America's national bird instead of the eagle.

TOUCH FOOTBALL
Physical Fun

Your Child Will Learn

Gross motor skills

Language development

To follow directions

Teamwork

Mommy's Materials

Football (junior size if possible)

Family members

With everyone assembled for Thanksgiving, you've got more than a lot of mouths to feed—you've got a team. Why not drum up a healthy appetite for your holiday feast with some active, calorie-burning games? Or—when the turkey's no longer stuffed, but you are—work it off with some outdoor fun such as turkey tag or touch football. Watching the smile on your child's face as he plays with the "big kids" and has his parents' full attention is priceless. And once everyone has had plenty of fresh air, come back inside and follow up with second servings or dessert.

STEP BY STEP

1. Set up a goal line on each end of your playing field. Equally divide players into two teams, making sure the youngest have a parent or mentor to help them, and flip a coin to determine which team will kick off first.

2. After each team lines up across its goal line, one player begins the game by kicking (or throwing) the football as far down the field as possible. Someone on the receiving team must either catch or pick up the ball and then try to run it back to the opponent's goal line to score a touchdown.

3. If an opposing player touches the runner, the runner is "tackled" and must stop. After a tackle, the receiving team has four tries, or downs, to get the ball to the goal line. (Before each down, remember to huddle to discuss the next play—who will pass off, who will run, and so on.)

4. If a team fails to score a touchdown in four tries, it must turn the ball over to the other team, which begins play at the position where it gained possession of the ball. A team can also gain possession when the other team fumbles or if it intercepts a pass.

5. At a predetermined end, the team with the most points wins.

MORE MOMMY AND ME FUN

Turkey Hunt: On a dozen or so index cards, have children draw or paste pictures of turkeys. To play, everyone leaves the room while Mom hides the cards around the room. The hunters come back in to begin the hunt and the one with the most turkeys is the winner.

Turkey Tag: All the children are turkeys except one who is a Pilgrim. The Pilgrim chases the turkeys until he catches one. All the turkeys should gobble and strut around the room. The turkey who is caught becomes the next Pilgrim.

Mommy's Memo

To overcome differences in skill levels, you can make handicap rules—for instance, that the fastest runners run backward, or that no player may score twice. You can also rule that the youngest player must carry the ball at least once for a touchdown to count.

Mom, Did You Know?

The earliest record of a football-like game dates back 2000 years to the Chinese Han Dynasty! Historians believe that the Romans brought the game to Britain, where it developed into rugby.

SUPERMARKET FEAST
Terrific Trips

Your Child Will Learn

Shape concepts

Comparison

Language acquisition

To follow directions

Sensory discrimination

Counting

Selected Stories

What Is Thanksgiving?
by Harriet Ziefert

The Popcorn Book
by Tomie de Paola

Manners
by Aliki

Eating the Plates:
A Pilgrim Book of Food
and Manners
by Lucille Recht Penner

For adults, the word *supermarket* conjures up images of long lines, squeaky carts, and high prices. But to a young child, the supermarket is a delightful array of sounds, shapes, colors, and delicious smells. As you buy your holiday groceries, there are endless ways in which you can help your young child learn new words and concepts. So from now on, instead of dreading the supermarket, look at it as a veritable smorgasbord of learning activities.

Comparison Shop: Count the oranges as you put them in the bag or point out the shapes, textures, and colors of the vegetables in the produce department. Engage your child's attention and name items as you put them in your cart. Compare sizes as you make choices. "These apples are smaller than the watermelons," or "This big can is heavier than the little can." Let your child select one new fruit or vegetable to try on each shopping trip. Finally, give your child simple directions by asking them to "hold the bread" or "put the apples in the bag."

MORE MOMMY AND ME FUN

Memory Lane: When a few generations are gathered for the holidays, the family album can be the perfect inspiration for some lively stories about past events and a trip down memory lane. For fun, make a game of matching up childhood photos with more recent snapshots of different relatives. If possible, give Grandma or Grandpa the floor and let them tell about how things were when they were young. Though this may not be a physical trip, little ones will find it a most remarkable adventure. If you're visiting out-of-town relatives, go on a family tour of the town. Grandma can point out every place she's lived, from when she was born until the present day. You can even videotape the homes and her recollections, and have other relatives chime in when you get to places they remember growing up in. This makes a wonderful keepsake.

Volunteerism: November 20 is National Family Volunteer Day. What better time to teach your children about charity and volunteering? Spend some time volunteering at a food kitchen and let the kids help fix plates and clear the tables. Volunteer for Meals on Wheels and let kids come along to help with deliveries. Many shelters and food kitchens also need drivers to pick up donations at markets and restaurants each day, and you can have your child pitch in and help. Whatever the activity, volunteering introduces children to important values that will last a lifetime.

Mommy's Memo

To supplement your trip to the supermarket, make a recipe box together. Your child will learn about the alphabet, numbers, nutrition, and patience. And when he grows up, there will be a collection of family recipes to cherish.

Mom, Did You Know?

More turkeys are sold in November than any other time of the year. Most domesticated turkeys weigh between 14 to 45 pounds but the biggest recorded turkey weighed in at 86 pounds.

MOMS ONLY
Advice, Tips, and Suggestions

Safe and Sound

Motion sickness—a disturbance of the inner ear—is common in children. If your child gets dizzy and nauseated in the car, he is also likely to become sick on a boat, train, or plane as well. You may be able to prevent it by giving him an anti-motion-sickness pill such as Dramamine® about an hour before traveling. If he does get sick, have him lie down and sip only clear liquids.

DISCIPLINE DO

Routines: Thanksgiving is a hectic time of year, and it usually means a lot of company. Just when you think you've devised a perfect routine, relatives come for a visit and disrupt it. Having your home invaded by strangers (which relatives may be to your little ones) can be upsetting and can cause your child to react in some negative ways. They do this because your attention is being diverted and young children are typically self-centered. If you understand this, it may help you be more patient. Tell your child ahead of time that there will be company and that you need her to help out and be on her best behavior. Your child will react to all the excitement, so try not to have unrealistic expectations. Attempt to adhere to a normal schedule and maintain regular rules of discipline. If your child misbehaves, be sure to follow through with predetermined consequences. Children learn through consistency and they need to know you mean what you say.

RELAXATION Rx

Chill Out: After all the holiday cooking and preparation (not to mention stress and company), you'll really need to take a break. This may be the time to recruit Dad and have him take more parental responsibility. There are a lot of ways he can give you some relief, and taking the kids for an afternoon is one of them. Some health clubs offer child care—he could work out while Junior's there, then take him to the park. Or your husband could recruit a few friends who are also fathers and have a dads-and-kids get-together. Don't feel you need to be responsible for everything. Moms who control every moment of their child's life cut their partners out of the picture and set themselves up for burnout. If you can convince Dad to take the kids to the park or with him on errands, you'll get lots of little slices of relaxation during the week and everyone will benefit.

TODDLER TIDBIT

Holiday Travel: This month parents across the country board planes and trains and strap kids into car seats en route to Grandma's house. No matter how you choose to get where you're going, keeping your child entertained and your sanity intact is a top concern. Though traveling during the holidays (or any time of year) can be a nightmare, the best advice is to be prepared. The most important item for your trip is a well-stocked bag. Make sure it's filled with enough snacks, drinks, wipes, diapers, extra clothes, (for Mom, too), activities, and games for twenty-four hours, and be prepared for any disaster. If your toddler is still in diapers, make sure you have plenty on hand. Also be sure to bring a first-aid kit, including pediatric medicines like acetaminophen (Tylenol) so you won't have to search for an open drugstore. Include travel sickness medication, any necessary prescriptions, and your children's insurance cards. Don't forget the favorite doll or snuggly, and bring a new or surprise toy for variety. If you are traveling by air, arrive at the airport early.

MEDICAL MESSAGE

Food Poisoning: In the rush to prepare your Thanksgiving dinner, don't neglect to take a few important health precautions. Salmonella is bacteria that can be present on uncooked food and it can ruin a holiday feast. In addition to poultry, foods that may grow salmonella include pork, beef, unpasteurized dairy products, and eggshells. To prevent the spread of bacteria, be sure that all kitchen counters are clean and follow these simple rules:

• Prevent juices from dripping onto other foods in the refrigerator by placing wrapped turkey on a tray. • Cook fresh turkey within two days. Keep the turkey refrigerated prior to cooking. Thaw a frozen turkey in the refrigerator. • Place raw poultry on nonporous surfaces that are easy to clean. Avoid wooden cutting boards. • Use paper towels, not cloth, to dry off the turkey and wipe up juices. • Wash hands, work surfaces, and utensils touched by raw poultry and its juices with hot, soapy water. • When stuffing the turkey, use only cooked ingredients and pasteurized egg products.

Mommy's Memo

Planning holiday trips with your child helps keep him involved and gives everyone a chance to talk about their expectations.

Mom, Did You Know?

Most airlines offer a choice of special meals. Vegetarian, Kosher, low-fat, and children's selections are among those you can order. Call at least twenty-four hours before your flight to request a special meal and identify yourself to the flight attendant when you board. These meals are often better than the regular meals!

• NOVEMBER ACTIVITIES •

Red, Green,
Black, Blue,
and White are
the Colors of
the Month.

A Triangle and
a Star are the
Shapes of
the Month.

DECEMBER

Whether you celebrate Christmas, Chanukah, or Kwanzaa, December is filled with holiday festivities. This month brings shopping sprees, good food, time with friends and family, and most importantly, the gift of giving. Your child will undoubtedly be caught up in all the excitement of the season, but may still be too young to understand the abstract ideas of the holidays. Young children love rituals, though, and it's never too early to start your own traditions. Whether that means driving around the neighborhood to look at all the sparkling lights, lighting Chanukah or Kwanzaa candles, reading aloud from a favorite holiday book, or listening to Christmas carols, rituals and tradition provide a sense of security in a world that often moves too fast.

KEY DECEMBER CONCEPTS:

1. Red and green are familiar colors in the month of December.

2. Christmas (December 25) is the most widely celebrated holiday of the Christian year.

3. The Jewish holiday of Chanukah, usually celebrated in December, is known as the Festival of Lights and is symbolized by the colors blue and white.

4. Kwanzaa (beginning December 26) is a seven-day spiritual festival that celebrates African-American heritage and culture, and is symbolized by the colors black, red, and green.

5. The holidays provide opportunities to show kindness and charity.

"The best things you can give your child are good memories."

—*Unknown*

PICTURE FRAMES
Art Activity • 20 Minutes

Your Child Will Learn

Fine motor skills

The concept of giving

To follow directions

Creative expression

Holiday traditions

Mommy's Materials

Craft sticks

Safety scissors

Photographs

Crayons, paints, stickers
and ribbon (optional)

Glue or tape

'Tis the season for glue and glitter. There is nothing more wonderful during the holiday season than getting a handmade gift. Grandparents and other relatives treasure them more than they do expensive, store-bought items, and creating the gifts provides a meaningful way for your child to experience the pleasure that comes with giving. Friends and relatives will not only cherish the item itself but also the look of personal satisfaction on your child's face. Making handmade gifts can also become a family tradition. One day, when your child is grown, she will be able to pass on the secrets of handmade love to her own children.

STEP BY STEP

1. Glue craft sticks together to make a frame. Leave an opening in the center a bit smaller than your photograph.

2. Decorate the front of the picture frame in any way you like. You can customize it for Christmas, Chanukah, or Kwanzaa. For example, decorate with trees or candy canes for Christmas; blue and white six-pointed stars for Chanukah; or black, red, and green candles for Kwanzaa.

3. Paste a picture inside the frame and see a happy face smiling out.

MORE MOMMY AND ME FUN

Holiday Gift Wrapping: Just think of the fun your child will have wrapping holiday presents with his very own, very original gift wrap. Spread a roll of shelf-lining paper or butcher paper on a table and decorate with holiday stickers, crayons and markers, or paint. Alternatively, you can do sponge or potato prints on the gift paper as well. Or have your child dip Christmas cookie cutters into the paint and make prints on the paper. When dry, use to wrap all of your handmade gifts! You can also use the above technique to make gift bags out of brown paper lunch bags. Place gift inside, add tissue paper, and add a yarn handle.

To Walk in Your Shoes: In Germany and Holland, Christmas is called St. Nicholas Day, and is celebrated on December 6. The two countries share similar legends. If you leave your boots or shoes outside the night before, St. Nicholas fills them with treats! To share this custom with a needy child in your area, buy a new pair of shoes or find a pair that no longer fits your child. Take tissue paper and line the inside of the shoes. Gather up treats such as candy and cookies or small useful items and fill the shoes. Make a card and donate the shoes to a local children's charity. What better way to teach your child about giving and learning to appreciate the gifts he has in his life.

Mommy's Memo

Let your children help you write holiday cards and assist in wrapping the presents. Allow them to feel as if they are part of the holiday festivities and are really helping out!

Mom, Did You Know?

The seven symbols of Kwanzaa include:

1. Zawadi—handmade gifts

2. Kinara—a seven-branch candleholder

3. Muhindi—ears of corn symbolizing each child

4. Mishumaa Saba—the seven candles of Kwanzaa

5. Mkeka—a straw mat

6. Mazao—fruits and vegetables of the harvest

7. Kikombe—a large commemorative cup

GINGERBREAD HOUSE
Art Activity • 30 to 60 Minutes

Your Child Will Learn

Holiday traditions

Fine motor skills

Color concepts

Shape concepts

Creative expression

Mommy's Materials

Graham crackers

Empty milk carton

Frosting (homemade or mix)

Edible decorations:

  Small pretzels

  Jelly beans

  Gumdrops

  Candy canes

  Red hots

  Licorice (black and red)

Make your home merry and bright this season with an array of dazzling decorations. From Christmas ornaments and Chanukah menorahs to wreaths and Kwanzaa necklaces, your holiday celebrations will feel more festive with homemade curios in every room. For extra fun, invite some other moms and kids over and have a holiday decorating party. The supplies are minimal and everyone can join in on the fun. To really inspire a festive atmosphere, play holiday music and have plenty of apple cider and holiday cookies on hand.

STEP BY STEP

1. Prepare frosting. If making it yourself, cut down a bit on the amount of liquid. You want it to be stiff rather than runny.

2. Paste graham crackers to the outside of the milk carton using the frosting.

3. Let your child decorate with candies or pretzels.

MORE MOMMY AND ME FUN

Pinecone Christmas Trees: Collect (or buy) some pinecones—the bigger the better—and spray paint them green. Once dry, mix up some plaster of paris and fill a small single-serving apple sauce or pudding container. Next stand the pinecone in the plaster so it looks like a tree. Once it's set, have your child decorate the tree with glitter, sequins, and other ornaments. This is a keepsake you'll treasure for years.

Holiday Wreath: Bend a wire coat hanger into a circle. Tie clear plastic food-storage bags all around the wire and bunch together. When the wire is completely covered in puffy plastic, decorate with red and green ribbons and, voila—a wreath you can use for years to come!

Kwanzaa Necklace: Your child can show her pride in African-American history by wearing a handcrafted necklace made with traditional holiday colors—black to symbolize the people of Africa, red to recall struggles for freedom, and green for growth. Use beads or painted tube pasta to make this handsome piece of jewelry.

Magical Menorah: Chanukah is known as The Festival of Lights. This holiday commemorates the rededication of the Temple of Jerusalem where a one-day supply of holy oil miraculously burned for eight days. To make your own menorah, find a piece of scrap wood at least nine inches long. Create candle holders by gluing nine metal bolts to the wood. Why the ninth candle? The extra candle, called the *Shamash*, or helper candle, is used to light the ones surrounding it.

Mom, Did You Know?

Mexico celebrates Las Posadas the third week in December. During the nine-day festival, celebrations feature traditional Mexican foods and the breaking of a piñata! Feliz Navidad!

Safe and Sound

If you decorate a Christmas tree, make sure tree lights and fragile ornaments are hung out of reach of young children, and be certain to secure electrical cords so that children cannot pull at them.

MARSHMALLOW WREATH

Creative Cooking • 20 Minutes

Your Child Will Learn

Color and shapes

Sensory discrimination

Measuring

Fine motor skills

Mommy's Materials

4 cups miniature marshmallows

4 tbsp. butter or margarine

Green food coloring

1 tsp. vanilla

4 cups rice cereal

Waxed paper

Raisins, cherry candies, assorted edibles

*H*oliday cooking means forgetting about fat and calories and pulling out all the stops. Opportunities for cooking fun increase significantly this time of year and kids really do love the smells and energy that emanate from the kitchen. There's a certain fulfillment that comes from giving a toddler license to mix ingredients in a bowl and then carry the cooking process through to the triumphant and tasty conclusion. A great idea for celebrating peace, love, and friendship is to have your friends and family bring a special dish that represents the holiday they celebrate this time of year.

STEP BY STEP

1. Over a low heat, melt the marshmallows and butter.

2. Add a few drops of food coloring and vanilla to the mixture. Mix in the cereal.

3. Give your child a large spoonful of the cooked mixture and have him drop it on the waxed paper.

4. Shape into a wreath and decorate with raisins, cherry candies, and assorted edibles.

MORE MOMMY AND ME FUN

Stained Glass Cookies: Use your favorite sugar cookie recipe, then cut the center out of your cookies with a holiday shape and fill the center with crushed hard candy. Bake as called for in the recipe. The crushed candy will melt and fill in the cut-out shape.

Candy Cane Cookies: With peppermint extract and red food coloring, you can turn sugar cookie dough into edible ornaments. Divide the dough in half. Color one half with red food coloring and leave the other half plain. Roll out a tablespoon of red dough and a tablespoon of plain until they are each 6 to 8 inches long. Twist them into a candy cane, pinching the ends. Repeat. Bake on an ungreased cookie sheet for 8 to 10 minutes, or until set but not brown.

Kwanzaa Cookies: Frost rectangular-shaped sugar cookies with red, black, and green stripes to resemble the bendera, a flag created to honor African Americans.

Chanukah Latkes: Potato pancakes fried in oil are a Chanukah tradition. Fried foods at this time of year commemorate the miracle of a one-day supply of oil lasting eight days. Whether you make the pancakes from scratch (grating 2 potatoes and combining with 1 egg and a minced onion) or use a mix, your child will have fun dipping them in her choice of sour cream or applesauce.

Mommy's Memo

Parents of different faiths often find this time of year confusing. It's important to establish a religious foundation while introducing traditions that allow children to connect to others. In this case, exposure to two religious holiday traditions is better than no exposure at all.

Mom, Did You Know?

Other special events celebrated at this time of year include Ramadan, a month-long holy fast by Muslims, and Diwali, the four-day Hindu festival of lights.

• DECEMBER ACTIVITIES •

293

SING ALONG
Music, Fingerplays, and Action Rhymes

Your Child Will Learn

Holiday traditions

Counting

Rhythm

Language acquisition

Selected Stories

A Christmas Carol
by Charles Dickens

Kwanzaa
by Deborah M. Newton
Chocolate

Together for Kwanzaa
by Juwanda G. Ford

Seven Spools of Thread
by Angela Shelf Medearis

Hanukkah!
by Roni Schotter

Latkes and Applesauce
by Fran Manushkin

"JINGLE BELLS"

Jingle bells, jingle bells, jingle all the way,
Oh, what fun it is to ride in a one horse open sleigh.
Jingle bells, jingle bells, jingle all the way,
Oh, what fun it is to ride in a one horse open sleigh. Hey!
Dashing through the snow, in a one horse open sleigh,
O'er the fields we go, laughing all the way.
Bells on bobtails ring, making spirits bright,
What fun it is to ride and sing a sleighing song tonight.

"COME LIGHT THE MENORAH"

O Chanukah, O Chanukah, come light the menorah,
Let's have a party, we'll all dance the hora.
Gather 'round the table, we'll give you a treat;
Dreidels small to play with, latkes to eat!
And while we are playing,
The candles are burning low,
One for each night, they shed a sweet light,
To remind us of days long ago!

"KWANZAA'S HERE"
(Sing to the tune of "Three Blind Mice")

Red, black, green,
Red, black, green,
Kwanzaa's here, Kwanzaa's here.
The decorations are quite a sight,
We light a candle every night.
The festival is quite a delight.
Kwanzaa's here!

294

"WE WISH YOU A MERRY CHRISTMAS"

We wish you a merry Christmas,
We wish you a merry Christmas,
We wish you a merry Christmas, and a Happy New Year.
Good tidings we bring to you and your kin,
Good tidings for Christmas and a Happy New Year.

"FIVE LITTLE BELLS"

Five little bells hanging in a row, (hold up hand)
The first one said, "Ring me slow." (point to thumb)
The second one said, "Ring me fast." (pointer finger)
The third one said, "Ring me last." (middle finger)
The fourth one said, "I'm like a chime."
(ring finger)
The fifth one said, "Ring me at Christmastime."
(little finger)

"EIGHT REINDEER"

Eight little reindeer playing in the snow.
(hold up eight fingers)
Eight little reindeer at the North Pole.
All of them anxious for Christmas Day,
Waiting for Santa to say, "Up, up, and away!"
(place fingers up in the air)

"I HAVE A LITTLE DREIDEL"

I have a little dreidel,
I made it out of clay.
And when it's dry and ready,
Oh, dreidel I will play.

• D E C E M B E R   A C T I V I T I E S •

Mommy's Memo

Caroling is a great way for friends and family to get together, sing songs, and get into the spirit of the season.

Selected Songs

"Rudolph the Red-Nosed Reindeer"

"Here Comes Santa Claus"

"Winter Wonderland"

"Deck the Halls"

"Jingle Bell Rock"

Selected Videos

A Charlie Brown Christmas

How the Grinch Stole Christmas

Frosty the Snowman

295

HOLIDAY GAMES
Physical Fun

Your Child Will Learn

Fine motor skills

Gross motor skills

Holiday traditions

To follow directions

Counting

Mommy's Materials

Boxes
Wrapping paper
Soft ball

Jingle bells

Dreidel

In an era filled with electronic fun, playing games with actual people seems a tad old-fashioned. But games are still a delightful way to exercise the brain and form bonds with friends and family. Especially around the holidays, playing games together establishes traditions that can be handed down from generation to generation. There's generally a lot of joking, talking, and telling family stories while you're sitting around playing and this is something kids remember for a lifetime. From the Santa Snowball Toss to Spin the Dreidel, these games will make for hours of festive fun.

HOLIDAY GAMES

Bowling for Boxes: This activity is great fun and it doesn't cost a penny. Collect gift boxes of various sizes. Stacking helps develop problem-solving skills and is a great way for kids to learn about size and balance. Be sure to stack them up high. Take a big soft ball and roll it at the stack. You can encourage counting by setting up the boxes and counting the ones that are knocked over.

Santa Snowball Toss: Cover the bottom and sides of a rectangular cardboard box with wrapping paper or butcher paper. On a piece of white paper, draw a Santa face with a large mouth. Paint or color the face with markers. Glue the face to the box and cut out the large mouth. Cover six to ten large marshmallows (or cotton balls) with plastic wrap to make your snowball. To play, have your child try to throw the snowball into Santa's mouth. If you're playing with more than one child, see who feeds Santa the most.

Angelic Ankles: It's holiday time and the sounds of bells are in the air! Take jingle wrist bells (available in music or school supply stores) and place them around your child's ankles. Have him jump, hop, and skip all around the room. Be sure you both sing "Jingle Bells"—this adds to the fun. Have a jolly old time!

Spin the Dreidel: Young children love this game since spinning the four-sided top provides hours of fascination. To start, each player puts one candy, penny, or chocolate coin (gelt) in the pot. The first player spins the dreidel and when it stops spinning, the side facing up decides the player's fate. *Nun* means nothing. You win nothing, you lose nothing. *Gimel* means whole. You take the whole kitty, leaving one object. *Hay* means half. You win half of what's in the kitty, and everyone puts one more piece into the pot. *Shin* means pay. You lose, and must put one object into the kitty. Players take turns spinning the top and following directions. When a player has all the objects, that person wins.

Mommy's Memo

Boxing Day is celebrated in Britain, Australia, New Zealand, and Canada on December 26. No matter where you live, why not celebrate the Boxing Day tradition of giving charitable gifts by having your child box up books, toys, or clothes he has outgrown to donate?

Mom, Did You Know?

The North Pole, legendary home to Santa Claus and his merry elves, is in the Arctic Ocean, about 450 miles north of Greenland.

• DECEMBER ACTIVITIES •

THE NUTCRACKER
Terrific Trips

Whis the holiday season without going to see *The Nutcracker*? I can't imagine! As the holidays grow closer, Tchaikovsky's score fills my mind and I have to track down the closest performance. Waltzing flowers, dancing snowflakes, and a Christmas tree that grows and grows have become as much a part of my holiday celebration as eggnog, mistletoe, and lighting the menorah! I'm not alone. Even after 100 years, *The Nutcracker* is the most widely attended and performed ballet in the world. Its fairy-tale plot, familiar music, and special effects captivate audiences of all ages.

Local Holiday Performances: Even children sampling their first ballet find *The Nutcracker* spellbinding. The scores of young dancers who participate in the onstage productions may be what inspire many youngsters to dream of a life en pointe. I never did get to dance in *The Nutcracker* but my daughter did. She was the cutest little soldier I ever saw. Every town and city in the country presents a performance of *The Nutcracker* during the holiday season. Why not make it a family tradition? It's an event you will all look forward to. And if your child loves watching the story of a young girl transported to the kingdom of sweets by a handsome prince, try other popular ballets such as *Swan Lake* or *Sleeping Beauty*.

MORE MOMMY AND ME FUN

Holiday Shopping: On your mark, get set, go! It's time to start shopping. Get out your list and check it twice to see who has been naughty and nice. Pick a time to go shopping when you have some energy. Make sure the kids have napped and are rested and you're mentally prepared. Allow the children to be involved and help pick out presents for family members and friends. Let them use money they may have saved to help buy the gifts. This will give them a real sense of giving!

Tree Farm: Create some Christmas memories by visiting a local tree farm and letting your children pick their favorite. Christmas tree farms offer learning opportunities this month as well as year round. You'll discover the process for growing and harvesting real Christmas trees and you'll find out that in addition to providing traditions and memories, Christmas trees play a vital role in creating a healthy environment. For families who want to spend the day together, many farms also feature hayrides, Santa visits, and hiking trails. Check your local listings or the National Christmas Tree Association to find a farm near you. And after the holidays, don't just put your tree out in the garbage. Find a recycling center that accepts foliage.

Mom, Did You Know?

Originally, only men were allowed to perform in ballets. They played the part of women by dressing in masks and women's clothes.

Noteworthy Nutcrackers

Pacific Northwest Ballet

Ballet Met

New York City Ballet

Oregon Ballet Theatre

Houston Ballet

Milwaukee Ballet

Joffrey Ballet

• DECEMBER ACTIVITIES •

299

MOMS ONLY
Advice, Tips, and Suggestions

Safe and Sound

Poinsettias are beautiful holiday plants but they can cause serious poisoning if large quantities are ingested. Mistletoe is also potentially dangerous. Make sure to keep both out of your child's reach.

DISCIPLINE DO

Theater Etiquette: If you do go to the theater this holiday season, gently brief your children on theater etiquette. Talking about decorum a few days before you attend a performance can help ensure a smooth evening or afternoon for both you and the people around you. Here are a few tips to begin with:

- No talking during the performance. Tell your kids they should try to save their questions until intermission. If they must talk, they should whisper into a grown-up's ear so no one else can hear them.
- No eating during the performance. If you have purchased or brought hard candy or cough drops, unwrap them before the curtain rises, so the wrappers don't make noise.
- No running in the aisles. It's okay to clap or cheer for the dancers, but wait until they stop moving or until a dancer's music ends to give your applause.

RELAXATION Rx

A Gift Certificate for You!: Shopping during the holidays may be less than therapeutic. As a matter of fact, shopping can be a nightmare. So, why not request a gift certificate (from your husband or Santa) that you can use for yourself. That way you can take all the time you want, when you want, and with whom you want! (I suggest you go alone). Like riding a bike, you'll quickly remember what it was like to shop leisurely. You'll be able to try on outfits without worrying if your toddler is pulling down racks of clothes in the store, and talk to a salesperson without someone pulling on your pant leg begging to go home. You've shopped all month for everyone else, now it's time to buy something special for yourself.

TODDLER TIDBIT

The True Meaning of Giving: Whatever holiday you celebrate, your child may well be focused on only one thing—her gift list. For many of us, those longed-for gifts are either too expensive or hard to find. Even if we are able to find and afford the gifts, we would all like the experience to have deeper meaning. I believe that the best way to teach children to become more appreciative and grateful for the gifts that they receive is to help them to understand the true meaning of giving. Here are some simple suggestions to help:

● Read a great classic such as *The Gift of the Magi*. Storytelling is an effective way to teach children about important concepts. ● Instead of shopping, help your children create their own homemade gifts. ● Have your children go through their old clothes and toys and put a package together for less fortunate children. ● Try to give emotionally meaningful gifts, such as writing some poetry, or even gathering up Grandma's favorite recipes.

MEDICAL MESSAGE

Holiday Alcohol Poisoning: Holiday parties are fun for the entire family. However, many children are innocently poisoned by alcohol every year. Adults leave glasses of wine or cocktails on coffee tables, not realizing a little one may pick it up and drink it. Here are some signs of alcohol poisoning and what to do if you suspect it: A child who drinks alcohol may become lightheaded, confused, hyperactive, or lethargic. They may lose their coordination and their speech may become altered. In very little children, the reaction is heightened. If your child displays any of these symptoms seek medical help immediately. Your child will need to be observed closely because of the risk of dehydration. Be aware that alcohol is present in common household products such as mouthwash, vanilla extract, cosmetics, windshield-wiper fluid, some liquid medicines, cleaning fluids, and rubbing alcohol—all of which should be stored in childproof cabinets.

Mom, Did You Know?

Operation Santa Claus began in the New York Post Office nearly sixty-five years ago, when clerks dug into their pockets to buy food and toys for children who faced an empty Christmas. Today, everyone is invited to come in and read through letters to Santa from needy children all over the country, and pick some to respond to. Check to see if your local Post Office sponsors a similar program, then take your child shopping for something to send a child in need.

DECEMBER ACTIVITIES

301

MOMMY AND ME
PLAYGROUPS

4

MOMMY AND ME IN A GROUP SETTING

The world of *Mommy and Me* offers you and your child many wonderful opportunities. Not only can *Fun with Mommy and Me* be used on a one-to-one basis, but you can incorporate the activities in a group setting. If you want to join other moms and children on a regular basis, consider joining or starting a playgroup. Playgroups provide wonderful opportunities for children to play together and for their parents to socialize. Here are just some of the many benefits for using *Fun with Mommy and Me* in a group setting:

- Parent-child activity groups provide an opportunity for a parent to socialize with other parents while at the same time providing valuable experiences for the child.

- They offer a way to introduce your child to more formal social groups so that later on when they start preschool, they'll feel more comfortable.

- They can be your child's primary source of social interaction and one of the first places he makes friends.

- They can help your child develop relationships with other adults.

- They will provide healthy stimulation for your child to grow emotionally and intellectually.

- They can be a source of valuable information and emotional support for the parent through parent networking and communication.

- They provide the opportunity for busy parents to have a ready social activity for their child.

HOW TO FIND INTERESTED MOMS

The best part of a playgroup is meeting new people. You can try to find an existing playgroup in your area or decide to start your own. There are numerous ways to find interested mothers and children. Here are a few you can consider:

Mommy's Memo

Choose days and times convenient for all participants in the playgroup. You can decide to use one location or take turns hosting the group.

Daddy and Me

Playgroups don't have to be limited to moms only. Dads can participate, too. In fact, the guys can even organize a special father-child playgroup that meets weekly or monthly.

- Place an ad in your local newspaper.

- Place a notice in the newsletters of organizations such as: Girl Scouts, YMCA, a school, PTA, or childbirth classes.

- Post a bulletin board announcement at the market, gym, local school, your doctor's office, the library, nearby hospitals and birthing centers, your church or synagogue, or local rec centers.

- Invite your friends who have children to join you or try contacting friends of friends with children.

- Create a flyer, letter, or postcard and attach flyers to the outside of mailboxes in your neighborhood. You may want to target houses with toys in the yard, swings hanging from trees, or minivans in the driveway.

SAMPLE ANNOUNCEMENT

Mothers and Children Wanted for Fun and Learning!
Mommy and Me Activity Playgroup
Ages: Birth to 5 years of age
For more information contact: Robin at 888-8502

MOMS-ONLY MEETING

After you have had a response from your ads, you should plan a meeting where only the parents attend. This will allow everyone to discuss the purpose of the group, agree on the day and time of future meetings, and talk about other issues. You may want to provide name tags and offer some sort of refreshment to the other parents. During the meeting, distribute some handouts including a registration form (you can download from www.mommyandme.com). Introduce yourself, and allow everyone else to introduce themselves. Ask everyone to include the name and age of their child and their expectations for the group.

Mommy's Memo

Some playgroups offer organized parent-child activities and others provide less-structured time geared more to play and social interaction. Decide on the age-range for the children in the group and whether you want to target any special interests.

PLAYGROUP PARTICULARS

Location: Meetings should be held in a facility that is babyproof, quiet, cheerful, clean, and convenient for all participants involved. You can either meet in your own home or find a facility that has a meeting room open to the public. Some of the most common locations for a group setting include preschools and public schools, churches and synagogues, recreation centers, colleges and universities, hospitals, and malls. Wherever you choose to meet, make sure the following requirements for safety are met:

- The area is clean and well-maintained.
- All dangerous objects are removed.
- Electrical outlets have been childproofed and electrical wires are out of the way.
- Smoke detectors and a fire extinguisher are available.
- Any animals and pets are confined.
- Safe toys are provided.
- Poisonous substances are locked up.
- A fire escape route has been posted.

How Often Should You Meet?: *Fun with Mommy and Me* provides enough activities for a weekly meeting. However, you can add additional meetings at your own discretion or better yet, organize field trips or other outings that are outlined in the book.

How Long Is Each Meeting?: The meetings can be one to two hours depending on what the group's needs are. A time limit should be decided upon, then wait to see how it goes. You can then change it to a suitable length. After the group is formed, a monthly "Moms-Only Meeting" can be scheduled to discuss problems and evaluate how the class is progressing.

Safe and Sound

If you meet outdoors, it is important that a fence be provided around the play area to restrict the children from the dangerous possibility of wandering off. If there's a swimming pool or other body of water, a safety enclosure is a must. During the summer, watch out for insects and be sure to wear sunscreen. Make sure the gate to the yard is locked, the children are always supervised, and you regularly account for all participants.

Who Supervises?: Supervision is a group effort. Every parent needs to take an active role. Of course, each mommy needs to keep a constant watch on her child. However, you may decide to have one facilitator, if the group chooses.

What Are the Costs?: The costs vary from program to program across the country if the classes are held in a public building. However, if the classes are held in a home, there should be no charge to attend the class. The costs should be for the materials and for snacks. Each group should decide individually how these costs should be handled.

TROUBLESHOOTING

Problems will arise in every group setting. However, if the problem is handled with care, love, and understanding, the stormy seas will be calmed and there will be smooth sailing! Make sure that everyone receives group guidelines when they join the playgroup (available at www.mommyandme.com). Adults in the group should also follow these suggestions:

- Be prepared.

- Have realistic expectations. Realize things will not be perfect all the time.

- Discuss problems openly and as a group.

- Allow every member to voice an opinion.

- The majority rules on a vote.

- Try to behave politely: Your children are watching!

Collect all 3 Mommy & Me® Together-Time Videos

Each Mommy & Me video was created to enhance the parent-child bond through songs, activities, and together-time fun. The programs invite participation, encouraging moms and kids to join in and sing, dance, and play along as they enjoy special multi-sensory segments designed to stimulate young minds.

Look for new
Mommy & Me
Audio CDs and Cassettes
including "Lullaby &
Goodnight" – A gentle
mix of childhood
favorites and classic
lullabies.

Splish Splash

A fun-filled exploration of all things wet and wonderful, this program includes music ranging from the popular "Splish Splash," "Three Little Fishies," "Six Little Ducks," and "Singin' in the Rain," to Chopin's beautiful "Raindrop Prelude." The featured story is "The Frog Prince," and the fun includes bubbles and baths, fish and flowers, and sand and surf.

Fun & Friends

Join our cast in together-time fun as we sing old favorites like "Head, Shoulders, Knees and Toes," "Do Re Mi," "Wheels on the Bus," "Hokey Pokey," and "Bingo," and hear a delightful story about friendship. With circle games, fingerplays, nursery rhymes and wonderful activities for you and your child to share, this program offers a unique opportunity for family fun.

Lullaby & Goodnight

The perfect addition to your bedtime routine, this program takes you and your child from washing up and getting into PJs to wishing on a star and hearing the bedtime story "Wynken, Blynken and Nod." Featured songs include "Mister Sandman," "You Are So Beautiful," "Clair de Lune," and "Brahms' Lullaby."

To order, visit www.mommyandme.com or call Sound Distributing at (800)784-0991.

Manufactured and distributed by Madacy Kids, a division of Madacy Entertainment Group Inc.

Jane Mayer

DARK MONEY

Jane Mayer is a staff writer for *The New Yorker* and the author of three previous bestselling and critically acclaimed narrative nonfiction books. She coauthored *Landslide: The Unmaking of the President, 1984–1988*, with Doyle McManus, and *Strange Justice: The Selling of Clarence Thomas*, with Jill Abramson, which was a finalist for the National Book Award. Her book *The Dark Side: The Inside Story of How the War on Terror Turned into a War on American Ideals*, for which she was awarded a Guggenheim Fellowship, was named one of *The New York Times*'s Top 10 Books of the Year and was a finalist for the National Book Award and the National Book Critics Circle Award, among numerous other accolades. For her reporting at *The New Yorker*, Mayer has been awarded the John Chancellor Award, the George Polk Award, the Toner Prize for Excellence in Political Reporting, and the I. F. Stone Medal for Journalistic Independence presented by the Nieman Foundation at Harvard. Mayer lives in Washington, D.C.

www.jane-mayer.com

DARK MONEY

The Hidden History of the
Billionaires Behind the Rise of the
Radical Right

Jane Mayer

ANCHOR BOOKS

A DIVISION OF PENGUIN RANDOM HOUSE LLC

NEW YORK

FIRST ANCHOR BOOKS EDITION, JANUARY 2017

Copyright © 2016, 2017 by Jane Mayer

All rights reserved. Published in the United States by Anchor
Books, a division of Penguin Random House LLC, New York,
and distributed in Canada by Random House of Canada,
a division of Penguin Random House Canada Limited, Toronto.
Originally published in hardcover in the United States
by Doubleday, a division of Penguin Random House LLC,
New York, in 2016.

Anchor Books and colophon are registered trademarks
of Penguin Random House LLC.

The Cataloging-in-Publication Data for the Doubleday edition
is available from the Library of Congress.

Anchor Books Trade Paperback ISBN: 978-0-307-94790-1
eBook ISBN: 978-0-385-53560-1

Author photograph © Stephen Voss
Maps by Mapping Specialists, Ltd.
Book design by Maria Carella

www.anchorbooks.com

Printed in the United States of America
10

We must make our choice. We may have democracy,
or we may have wealth concentrated in the hands of a few,
but we can't have both.

—*Louis Brandeis*

CONTENTS

CONTENTS

PART THREE:
PRIVATIZING POLITICS: TOTAL COMBAT,
2011–2014

11 The Spoils: Plundering Congress   333

12 Mother of All Wars: The 2012 Setback   370

13 The States: Gaining Ground   410

14 Selling the New Koch: A Better Battle Plan   435

Author's Note   467

Notes   469

Index   523

PREFACE TO THE
ANCHOR BOOKS EDITION (2017)

ELECTION NIGHT 2016 WAS A STUNNING POLITICAL UPSET auguring a new political order in almost every respect. Donald Trump, a billionaire businessman with no experience in elected office, running on a promise to upend the status quo, defeated Hillary Clinton, the designated heir to Barack Obama's Democratic presidency. Trump's triumph defied the predictions of almost every pundit and pollster. It rocked the political establishments in both parties and sent shock waves around the globe. Markets trembled before recovering their equilibrium. The political world seemed to shift on its axis, spinning toward an unknown and unpredictable future. Although Trump ran as a self-proclaimed outsider against what he portrayed as entrenched and corrupt political elites, there was an unexpectedly familiar representative of this moneyed class at his victory party in Manhattan. Standing with a jubilant smile amid the throng of revelers at the Hilton hotel in midtown Manhattan was David Koch.

During the presidential primaries, Trump had mocked his Republican rivals as "puppets" for flocking to the secretive fund-raising sessions sponsored by David Koch and his brother Charles, co-owners of the second-largest private company in the United States, the Kansas-based energy and manufacturing conglomerate Koch Industries. Affronted, the Koch brothers, whose political spending had made their name almost shorthand for special-interest clout, withheld their financial support from Trump. As a result, the story line adopted by many in the media was that the Koch brothers in particular, and big political donors in general, were no longer a major factor in American politics. Trump had after all defeated far bigger-spending rivals, including Clinton.

It might be nice to think the era of big money in American politics is over, but a closer look reveals a far more complicated and far less reassuring reality.

Trump had indeed campaigned by attacking the big donors, corporate lobbyists, and political action committees that have come to dominate American politics as "very corrupt." In doing so, he fed into a national, bipartisan outpouring of disgust at the growing extent to which campaigns have become little more than relentless pursuits of obscene amounts of cash. To the surprise of many, Trump and Bernie Sanders, the left-wing insurgent who challenged Clinton in the Democratic primaries, seemed to transform big political money from an advantage into a liability. Trump nicknamed Clinton "Crooked Hillary," claiming that she was "100% owned by her donors." By Election Day, the public's trust in her was in tatters.

Improbably, Trump, a New York businessman who had global financial interests and who spent some $66 million of his own fortune to get elected, ran against Wall Street. He successfully positioned himself as pristine because he was a billionaire in his own right, rather than one beholden to other billionaires. In a tweet less than a month before the election, Trump promised, "I will Make Our Government Honest Again—believe me. But first I'm going to have to #DrainTheSwamp." His DrainTheSwamp hashtag became a rallying cry for supporters riled by the growing economic inequality in the country and intent on ending corruption in Washington, which they blamed for putting the interests of the rich and powerful over their own.

Yet as Ann Ravel, a Democratic member of the Federal Election Commission who had championed reform of political money for years, observed just days after Trump's election, instead "the alligators are multiplying."

Despite having been elected as a populist outsider, Trump

put together a transition team that was crawling with the kinds of corporate insiders he vowed to disempower. Especially prominent among them were lobbyists and political operatives who had financial ties to the Kochs. This was perhaps unexpected, because the Kochs had continued to express their distaste for Trump throughout the campaign. Charles Koch called himself a libertarian. He supported open immigration and free trade, both of which benefited his vast multinational corporation. He had denounced Trump's plans to bar Muslim immigrants as "monstrous" and "frightening."

Yet there were signs of a rapprochement. The chair of Trump's transition team, Vice President elect Mike Pence, had been Charles Koch's first choice for the presidency in 2012 and a major recipient of Koch campaign contributions. David Koch had personally donated $300,000 to Pence's campaigns in the four years before Trump chose Pence as his running mate. Pence, who in the past had shared the Kochs' enthusiasm for privatizing Social Security and denying the reality of climate change, had been a featured guest at a fund-raiser that David Koch hosted for about seventy of the Republican Party's biggest political donors at his Palm Beach, Florida, mansion in the spring of 2016. He had also been slated to speak at the Kochs' donor summit in August 2016 but canceled after joining the Republican ticket. Meanwhile, Pence's senior adviser in the sensitive task of managing Trump's transition to power was Marc Short, who just a few months earlier had actually run the Kochs' secretive donor club, Freedom Partners. This was the same elite group whose meetings Trump had ridiculed during the campaign.

The Kochs' influence was also evident in the transition team members that Trump picked in the areas of energy and the environment, which were crucial to Koch Industries' bottom line. For policy and personnel advice regarding the Department of Energy, an early chart of the transition team showed that Trump chose Michael McKenna, the president of the lobbying firm MWR Strategies, whose clients included Koch Industries. McKenna also had ties to the American Energy Alliance, a tax-exempt nonprofit that advocated for corporate-friendly energy policies, to which the Kochs' donor group, Freedom Partners, had given $1.5 million in 2012. The group, which didn't disclose its revenue sources, was a textbook example of the way secret spending by billion-dollar private interests aimed to manipulate public opinion.

Another lobbyist for Koch Industries, Michael Catanzaro, a partner at the lobbying firm CGCN Group, headed "energy independence" for Trump's transition team and was mentioned as a possible White House energy czar. Meanwhile, Harold Hamm, a charter member of the Kochs' donor circle, who became a billionaire by founding Continental Resources, an Oklahoma-based shale-oil company known for its enormously lucrative "fracking" operation, was reportedly advising Trump on energy issues and under consideration for a cabinet post, possibly energy secretary.

To the alarm of the scientific community, Trump chose Myron Ebell, an outspoken climate change skeptic, to head his transition team for the Environmental Protection Agency (EPA). Ebell too had Koch money ties. He worked at a Washington think tank, the Competitive Enterprise Institute. It didn't disclose its funding sources, but in the past, it had been bankrolled by fossil fuel interests, including the Kochs. His stridently antiregulatory views meshed perfectly with theirs. The Kochs had long been at war with the EPA, which had ranked Koch Industries one of only three companies in America that was simultaneously a top ten polluter of air, water, and climate. Joining Ebell on the transition team was David Schnare, a self-described "free-market environmentalist" who had accused the EPA of having "blood on its hands." Schnare worked for a think tank affiliated with the State Policy Network, which was also funded in part by the Kochs. He was reviled in environmental circles for hounding the climate scientist Michael

Mann with onerous public records requests until the Virginia Supreme Court ordered him to desist in 2014. The Union of Concerned Scientists had described these actions against climate scientists as "harassment."

Thus, less than a week after having been elected on a wave of populist anger, Trump appeared set to fulfill many of the special interests' fondest dreams, including the deregulatory schemes of the Kochs. He promised to "get rid of" the EPA in "almost every form" and to withdraw from the 2015 international climate accord in Paris, and against the overwhelming scientific evidence to the contrary, he called climate change "a hoax." The Trump transition had a self-imposed ethics code barring lobbyists from shaping the rules and staffing the departments in which they had financial interests, but in the early stages, at least, these commonsense strictures appeared to have been sidestepped.

Experts in government ethics were aghast. "If you have people on the transition team with deep financial ties to the industries to be regulated, it raises questions about whether they are serving the public interest or their own interests," warned Norman Eisen, who devised the Obama administration's conflict-of-interest rules. "Let's face it, in the Beltway nexus of corporations and dark money, lobbyists are the delivery mechanism for special-interest influence." Peter Wehner, who served in the administrations of Ronald Reagan and both presidents Bush, told the *New York Times*, "This whole idea that he was an outsider and going to destroy the political establishment and drain the swamp were the lines of a con man, and guess what—he is being exposed as just that."

The Kochs' influence reached greater heights with Trump's nomination of Mike Pompeo, a Republican congressman from Kansas, to direct the CIA. Pompeo was the single largest recipient of Koch campaign funds in Congress. The Kochs had also been investors, and partners, in Pompeo's business ventures prior to his entry into politics. In fact, as Burdett Loomis, a University of Kansas professor of political science, noted, the future CIA director's nickname was "the congressman from Koch." Helping to guide the transition team in these fateful choices was Rebekah Mercer, the daughter of Robert Mercer, the wealthy New York hedge fund manager who "out-Koched the Kochs" in 2014, as Bloomberg News put it, giving more money to their political club than even they had.

Clearly the reports of the Kochs' political death in 2016 were exaggerated. While they had refrained from backing a presidential candidate, the tentacles of the "Kochtopus," as their sprawling political machine was known, were already encircling the Trump administration before it had even officially taken power.

Many had counted the Kochs out after their refusal to back a presidential candidate. Their initial 2015 plan called for their donor group to spend an astounding budget of $889 million in order to purchase the presidency. But they sat out the primaries, as they had in the past, and then found their plan rudely upended when Trump emerged as the nominee. He was the only major Republican presidential candidate whom they opposed. Sidelined, they continued to withhold their support.

But while the media fixated on the extraordinary presidential race, the Kochs and their network of right-wing political patrons quietly spent more money than ever on the three-pronged influence-buying approach they had mastered during the previous forty years. They combined corporate lobbying, politically tinged nonprofit spending, and "down ballot" campaign contributions in state and local races, where their money bought a bigger bang for the buck.

Far from shutting their wallets, they simply downgraded their budget to $750 million and directed several hundred million dollars of it to races beneath the presidential level. Few noticed, but in 2016 Koch Industries and Freedom Partners poured huge sums into at least nineteen Senate, forty-two House, and four gubernatorial races as well as countless lesser ones all over the country.

They also mobilized what a 2016 study by two Harvard University scholars, Theda Skocpol and Alexander Hertel-Fernandez, described as an unprecedented and unparalleled permanent, private political machine. In fact, amazingly, in 2016 the Kochs' private network of political groups had a bigger payroll than the Republican National Committee. The Koch network had 1,600 paid staffers in thirty-five states and boasted that its operation covered 80 percent of the population. This marked a huge escalation from just a few years earlier. As recently as 2012, the Kochs' primary political advocacy group, Americans for Prosperity, had a paid staff of only 450.

The Kochs ran their political operation centrally like a private business, with divisions devoted to various constituency groups, such as Hispanics, veterans, and young voters. One of their top people explained that their aim during the 2016 election had been to target five million voters in eight states with key Senate races. In the past, labor unions probably provided the closest parallel to this kind of private political organizing, but they of course represented the dues of millions of members. In comparison, the Koch network was sponsored by just four hundred or so of the richest people in the country. It was for this reason that the Harvard scholars who studied it said that the Koch network was "like nothing we've ever seen."

Irrespective of Trump, the Kochs and their fellow mega-donors succeeded in their chief political objective in 2016, which was to keep both houses of Congress under conservative Republican control, ensuring that they could continue to advance their corporate agenda. They succeeded in their secondary goal too, which was to further crush the Democratic Party by continuing the nationwide sweep of state legislatures and local offices that they had begun in 2010. By controlling statehouses, they could dominate not just legislation but also the gerrymandering of congressional districts, in hopes of securing their grip on the House of Representatives for years to come.

Many of the races they backed were too minor to merit press attention. In Texas alone, they supported candidates in seventy-four different races, reaching all the way down to a county court commissioner. Thanks in no small part to huge quantities of targeted money spent by the Kochs and their allied donors, the Democratic Party lost both houses of Congress, fourteen governorships, and thirty state legislatures, comprising more than nine hundred seats, during Obama's presidency. By the time the votes were tallied in the 2016 election, Republicans controlled thirty-two state legislatures, while Democrats controlled only thirteen. Five others were split. This imbalance posed a huge problem for Democrats not only in the present but for the future, because state legislatures serve as incubators for rising leaders.

The Kochs might have disavowed Trump, but in several important respects he was their natural heir and the unintended consequence of the extraordinary political movement they had underwritten since the 1970s. For forty years, they had vilified the very idea of government. They had propagated that message through the countless think tanks, academic programs, front groups, ad campaigns, legal organizations, lobbyists, and candidates they supported. It was hard not to believe that this had helped set the table for the takeover of the world's most powerful country by a man who made his inexperience and antipathy toward governing among his top selling points.

Charles Koch's mentor, the quasi-anarchist Robert LeFevre, had taught the Kochs that "government is a disease masquerading as its own cure." Their extreme opposition to the expansions of the federal government that had taken place during the Progressive Era, the New Deal era, the Great Society, and Obama's presidency had helped to convince voters that Washington was corrupt and broken and that, when it came to governing, knowing nothing was preferable to expertise. Charles Koch had referred to himself as a "radical," and in Trump he got the radical solution he had helped to spawn.

The Kochs had also primed America for Trump by pouring gasoline on the fires lit by the antitax Tea Party movement starting in 2009. Charles Koch decried Trump's toxic rhetoric in 2016, and David Koch complained to the *Financial Times* that "you'd think we could have more influence" after spending hundreds of millions of dollars on American politics. But in fact, the influence of the Kochs and their fellow big donors was manifest in Trump's use of incendiary and irresponsibly divisive rhetoric. Only a few years ago, it was they who were sponsoring the hate.

In the 1960s, Charles Koch had funded the all-white private Freedom School in Colorado, whose head had told the *New York Times* that the admittance of black students might present housing problems because some students were segregationists. That was long ago, and his views, like those of many others, could well have changed. But in a 2011 interview with the *Weekly Standard*, David Koch echoed specious claims, made by the conservative gadfly Dinesh D'Souza, that Obama was somehow African rather than American in his outlook. He claimed that Obama, who was born in America and abandoned by his Kenyan father as a toddler, nonetheless derived his "radical" views from his African heritage.

The effort to attack Obama, not as a legitimate and democratically elected American political opponent, but as an alien threat to the country's survival, was very much in evidence at a summit that the Kochs' political organization Americans for Prosperity hosted in Austin, Texas, during the summer of 2010. Between Tea Party training sessions, operatives working for the Kochs gave an award to a blogger who had described Obama as the "cokehead-in-chief" and asserted that he suffered from "demonic possession (aka schizophrenia, etc.)." The Kochs and other members of the Republican donor class might have disowned the vile language of the 2016 campaign, but six years earlier they were honoring it with trophies.

The same incendiary style characterized the big donors' fight against the Affordable Care Act. Rather than respectfully debating Obama's health-care plan as a policy issue, the Kochs and their allied donors poured cash into a dark-money group called the Center to Protect Patient Rights, which mounted a guerrilla war of fearmongering and vitriol. Television ads sponsored by the group featured the false claim that Obama's plan was "a government takeover" of health care, which Politi-Fact named "the Lie of the Year" in 2010. Meanwhile, a spin-off of Americans for Prosperity organized anti-Obamacare rallies at which protesters unfurled banners depicting corpses from Dachau, implying that Obama's policies would result in mass murder. Koch operatives also purposefully sabotaged the democratic process by planting screaming protesters in town hall meetings at which congressmen met with constituents that year. In short, during the Obama years, the Kochs radicalized and organized an unruly movement of malcontents, over which by 2016 they had lost control. "We are partly responsible," one former employee in the Kochs' political operation admitted to *Politico* a month before Trump was elected. "We invested a lot in training and arming a grassroots army that was not controllable."

In other ways too, the Kochs and their allied big donors became victims of their own success in 2016. They inadvertently laid the groundwork for Trump's rise by too thoroughly capturing the Republican Party with their cash. Their narrowly self-serving policy priorities were at odds with those of the vast majority of voters. Yet virtually every Republican presidential candidate other than Trump pledged fealty to the donors' wish lists as they jockeyed for their support. The candidates promised to cut taxes for those in the highest brackets, preserve Wall Street loopholes, tolerate the off-shoring of manufacturing jobs and profits, and downgrade or privatize middle-class entitlement programs, including Social Security. Free trade was barely debated. These positions faithfully reflected the agenda of the wealthy donors, but studies showed that they were increasingly out of step with the broad base of not just Democratic but also Republican voters, many of whom had been left behind economically and socially for decades, particularly acutely since the 2008 financial crash. Trump, who could afford to forgo the billionaires' backing and ignore their policy priorities, saw the opening and seized it.

Whether Trump would fulfill his supporters' hopes and break free from the self-serving elites whose money had captured the Republican Party prior to his unorthodox election remained to be seen. The early signs were not promising. Not only was Trump's early transition team swarming with corporate lobbyists, including those who had worked for the Kochs, but Trump's inaugural committee featured several members of the Kochs' billion-dollar donor club, too. Neither Diane Hendricks, a building supply company owner whose $3.6 billion fortune made her the wealthiest woman in Wisconsin, nor billionaire Sheldon Adelson, founding chairman and chief executive of the Las Vegas Sands Corporation casino empire, signaled a break from politics as usual.

Inaugurals had long been underwritten by rich donors, so perhaps reading too much into this was unfair. But Trump's tax proposals, to the extent that they could be gleaned, were if anything even more of a bait and switch. While he had garnered blue-collar support by promising to stick it to the elites who "are getting away with murder," his proposals, according to economic experts, threatened instead to enshrine a permanent aristocracy in America. He appeared poised to repeal the estate tax, presenting a windfall to heirs of estates worth $10.9 million or more. There had been fewer than five thousand estates of this size in 2015. He also had plans to abolish the gift tax, which put the brakes on inherited wealth. Capital gains taxes and income taxes for top earners were headed toward the chopping block, too. Charles and David Koch, who together were worth some $84.5 billion, stood to benefit to an extent that dwarfed earlier administrations, as did many other billionaires. As the headline on Yahoo Finance proclaimed on the day after the election, "Trump's Win Is a 'Grand Slam' for Wall Street Banks."

The fact of the matter was that while Trump might have been elected by those he described as "the forgotten" men, he would have to deal with a Republican Party that had been shaped substantially by the billionaires of the radical Right. He would have to work with a vice president once funded by the Kochs and a Congress dominated by members who owed their political careers to the Kochs. Further, he would have to face a private political machine organized in practically every state, ready to attack any deviation from their agenda. No one could predict what Trump would do. Nor could they predict how much longer the Kochs, by then in their eighties, would stay active. But one thing was certain. The Kochs' dark money, which they had directed their successors to keep spending long after they had passed away, would continue to exert disproportionate influence over American politics for years to come.

November 2016
Washington, D.C.

Dark Money

The Investors

ON JANUARY 20, 2009, THE EYES OF THE COUNTRY WERE ON Washington, where over a million cheering celebrants crowded the National Mall to witness the inauguration of the first African-American president. So many supporters streamed in from all across the nation that for twenty-four hours they nearly doubled Washington's population. Inaugurations are always moving celebrations of the most basic democratic process, the peaceful transfer of power, but this one was especially euphoric. The country's most famous and iconic musicians, from the Queen of Soul, Aretha Franklin, to the cellist Yo-Yo Ma, gave soaring performances to mark the occasion. Celebrities and dignitaries pulled strings to get seats. Excitement was so feverish that the Democratic political consultant James Carville was predicting a long-term political realignment in which the Democrats "will remain in power for the next forty years."

But on the other side of the country during the last weekend in January 2009, another kind of gathering was under way, of a group of activists who aimed to do all they could to nullify the results of the recent election. In Indian Wells, a California desert town on the outskirts of Palm Springs, one polished sports utility vehicle after the next cruised down the long, palm-lined drive of the Renaissance Esmeralda Resort and Spa. Stepping out onto the curb, as bellboys darted for the luggage, were some of America's most ardent conservatives, many of whom represented the nation's most powerfully entrenched business interests. It would be hard to conjure a richer tableau of the good life than the one greeting them. Overhead, the sky was a brilliant azure. In the distance, the foothills of the Santa Rosa Mountains rose steeply from the Coachella Valley, creating a stunning backdrop of ever-changing hues. Velvety green lawns stretched as far as the eye could see, meandering toward a neighboring thirty-six-hole golf course. Swimming pools, one with a man-made sandy beach, were surrounded by chaises and intimate, curtained pavilions. As dusk fell, countless tea lights and tiki torches magically lit the walkways and flower beds.

But inside the hotel's dining room, the mood was grim, as if these luxuries merely highlighted how much the group gathered there had to lose. The guests meeting at the resort that weekend included many of the biggest winners during the eight years of George W. Bush's presidency. There were billionaire businessmen, heirs to some of America's greatest dynastic fortunes, right-wing media moguls, conservative elected officials, and savvy political operatives who had made handsome livings helping their patrons win and hold power. There were also eloquent writers and publicists, whose work at think tanks, advocacy groups, and countless publications was quietly subsidized by corporate interests. The guests of honor, though, were the potential political donors—or "investors," as they referred to themselves—whose checkbooks would be sorely needed for the project at hand.

The group had been summoned that weekend not by the leader of a recognized opposition party but rather by a private citizen, Charles Koch. In his seventies, he was white-haired but youthfully fit and very much in charge of Koch Industries, a conglomerate headquartered in Wichita, Kansas. The company had grown spectacularly since its founder, Charles's father, Fred, had died in 1967, and he and his brother David took charge, buying out their two other brothers. Charles and David—often referred to as the Koch brothers—owned virtually all of what had become under their leadership the second-largest private company in America. They owned four thousand miles of pipelines, oil refineries in Alaska, Texas, and Minnesota, the Georgia-Pacific lumber and paper company, coal, and chemicals, and they were huge traders in commodity futures, among other businesses. The company's consistent profitability had made the two brothers the sixth- and seventh-wealthiest men in the world. Each was worth an estimated $14 billion in 2009. Charles, the elder brother, was a man of unusual drive, accustomed to getting his way. What he wanted that weekend was to enlist his fellow conservatives in a daunting task: stopping the Obama administration from implementing Democratic policies that the American public had voted for but that he regarded as catastrophic.

Given the size of their fortunes, Charles and David Koch automatically had extraordinary influence. But for many years, they had magnified their reach further by joining forces with a small and intensely ideological group of like-minded political allies, many of whose personal fortunes were also unfathomably large. This faction hoped to use their wealth to advance a strain of conservative libertarian politics that was so far out on the political fringe as recently as 1980, when David Koch ran for vice president of the United States on the Libertarian Party ticket, it received only 1 percent of the American vote. At the time, the conservative icon William F. Buckley Jr. dismissed their views as "Anarcho-Totalitarianism."

The Kochs failed at the ballot box in 1980, but instead of accepting America's verdict, they set out to change how it voted. They used their fortune to impose their minority views on the majority by other means. In the years since they were trounced at the polls, they poured hundreds of millions of dollars into a stealthy effort to move their political views from the fringe to the center of American political life. With the same foresight and perseverance with which they invested in their businesses, they funded and built a daunting national political machine. As far back as 1976, Charles Koch, who was trained as an engineer, began planning a movement that could sweep the country. As a former member of the John Birch Society, he had a radical goal. In 1978, he declared, "Our *movement* must destroy the prevalent statist paradigm."

To this end, the Kochs waged a long and remarkable battle of ideas. They subsidized networks of seemingly unconnected think tanks and academic programs and spawned advocacy groups to make their arguments in the national political debate. They hired lobbyists to push their interests in Congress and operatives to create synthetic grassroots groups to give their movement political momentum on the ground. In addition, they financed legal groups and judicial junkets to press their cases in the courts. Eventually, they added to this a private political machine that rivaled, and threatened to subsume, the Republican Party. Much of this activism was cloaked in secrecy and presented as philanthropy, leaving almost no money trail that the public could trace. But cumulatively it formed, as one of their operatives boasted in 2015, a "*fully integrated network.*"

The Kochs were unusually single-minded, but they were not alone. They were among a small, rarefied group of hugely wealthy, archconservative families that for decades poured money, often with little public disclosure, into influencing how Americans thought and voted. Their efforts began in earnest during the second half of the twentieth century. In addition to the Kochs, this group included Richard Mellon Scaife, an heir to the Mellon banking and Gulf Oil fortunes; Harry and Lynde Bradley, midwesterners enriched by defense contracts; John M. Olin, a chemical and munitions company titan; the Coors brewing family of Colorado; and the DeVos family of Michigan, founders of the Amway marketing empire. Each was different, but together they formed a new generation of philanthropists, bent on using billions of dollars from their private foundations to alter the direction of American politics.

When these donors began their quest to remake America along the lines of their beliefs, their ideas were, if anything, considered marginal. They challenged the widely accepted post–World War II consensus that an activist government was a force for public good. Instead, they argued for "limited government," drastically lower personal and corporate taxes, minimal social services for the needy, and much less oversight of industry, particularly in the environmental arena. They said they were driven by principle, but their positions dovetailed seamlessly with their personal financial interests.

By Ronald Reagan's presidency, their views had begun to gain more traction. For the most part, they were still seen as defining the extreme edge of the right wing, but both the Republican Party and much of the country were trending their way. Conventional wisdom often attributed the rightward march to a public backlash against liberal spending programs. But an additional explanation, less examined, was the impact of this small circle of billionaire donors.

Of course rich patrons on both sides of the ideological spectrum had long wielded disproportionate power in American politics. George Soros, a billionaire investor who underwrote liberal organizations and candidates, was often singled out for criticism by conservatives. But the Kochs in particular set a new standard. As Charles Lewis, the founder of the Center for Public Integrity, a nonpartisan watchdog group, put it, "The Kochs are on a whole different level. There's no one else who has spent this much money. The sheer dimension of it is what sets them apart. They have a pattern of lawbreaking, political manipulation, and obfuscation. I've been in Washington since

Watergate, and I've never seen anything like it. They are the Standard Oil of our times."

By the time Barack Obama was elected president, the billionaire brothers' operation had become more sophisticated. By persuading an expanding, handpicked list of other wealthy conservatives to "invest" with them, they had in effect created a private political bank. It was this group of donors that gathered at the Renaissance. Most, like the Kochs, were businessmen with vast personal fortunes that placed them not just in the top 1 percent of the nation's wealthiest citizens but in a more rarefied group, the top 0.1 percent or higher. By most standards, they were extraordinarily successful. But for this cohort, Obama's election represented a galling setback.

During the previous eight years of Republican rule, this conservative corporate elite had consolidated its power, amassing enormous sway over the U.S. government's regulatory and tax laws. Some in this group faulted President Bush for not having been conservative enough. But having molded policy to serve their interests during the Bush years, many members of this caste had accumulated phenomenal wealth and regarded the newly elected Democratic president as a direct threat to all they had gained. Participants feared they were seeing not just the passing of eight years of Republican dominance but the end of a political order, one that they believed had immeasurably benefited both the country and themselves.

In the 2008 election, Republicans had been defeated up and down the ballot. Democrats had not only recaptured the White House but held majorities in both houses of Congress. The 2008 election hadn't just been a disappointment. It was a complete rout. "They'd just gotten blown out. The question was whether they could survive at all," recalled Bill Burton, former deputy press secretary to President Obama. John Podesta, the liberal political activist who later became Obama's senior adviser, recalled that in the early days after the election "there was a sense of triumphalism, that Bush had crapped out, that he'd be Hoover and Obama would be Franklin Roosevelt and dominate. There was a feeling that the pendulum had swung and a new progressive era had begun. Bush's poll ratings were below those of Nixon! There had been a complete failure of his economic and foreign policy ideas. There was a sense of 'How can we blow it?'"

Exacerbating conservatives' sense of political peril, the economy was in the most vertiginous free fall since the Great Depression of the 1930s. The day that Obama was inaugurated, the stock market had plummeted on fresh doubts about the viability of the nation's banks, with the Standard & Poor's 500 stock index shedding more than 5 percent of its value and the Dow Jones Industrial Average plunging by 4 percent. The continuing economic collapse had laid waste not just to some conservatives' portfolios but also to their belief system. The notion that markets are infallible, a fundamental tenet of libertarian conservatism, looked like a folly. Free-market advocates saw their entire ideological movement in peril. Even some Republicans had become doubters. The retired general Colin Powell, for instance, a veteran of both Bush administrations, argued that "Americans are looking for more government in their life, not less." *Time* magazine captured the zeitgeist by emblazoning a Republican elephant on its cover under the headline "Endangered Species."

Charles Koch himself described Obama's election in almost apocalyptic terms, sending an impassioned newsletter to his company's seventy thousand employees earlier that January declaring that America faced "the greatest loss of liberty and prosperity since the 1930s." Fearing a liberal resurgence of federal spending, he told his employees that more government programs and regulation were exactly the wrong approach to the deepening recession. "It is markets, not government, that can provide the strongest engine for growth, lifting us out of these troubling times," he insisted.

Obama's inaugural address lived up to his worst dreams. The freshly sworn-in president all but declared war on the notion that markets work best when government regulates them least. "Without a watchful eye, the market can spin out of control," Obama warned. Then, sounding almost as if he were taking aim directly at corporate plutocrats like those gathered in Indian Wells, Obama declared that "the nation cannot prosper long when it favors only the prosperous."

It was against this threatening political backdrop that Charles Koch mustered what a fellow conservative, Craig Shirley, described as "the mercantile Right" to take back, and if possible take over, American politics. Obama's election added urgency to the mission, but the gathering in Indian Wells was not a first for the Kochs. Charles and his brother David had been quietly sponsoring similar sessions for conservative donors twice a year since 2003. The enterprise started small but exploded as antagonism toward Obama built among the 0.01 percent on the right.

While they largely hid their ambitious enterprise from the public, avoiding all but the minimum legally required financial disclosures, the Kochs portrayed their political philanthropy inside their circle as a matter of noblesse oblige. "If not us, who? If not now, when?" Charles Koch asked in the invitation to one such donor summit, paraphrasing the call to arms of the ancient Hebrew scholar Rabbi Hillel. "It was obvious we were headed for disaster," Koch later told the conservative writer Matthew Continetti, explaining his plan. The idea was to gather other free-market enthusiasts and organize them as a pressure group. The first seminar in 2003 attracted only fifteen people.

One former insider in the Kochs' realm, who declined to be named because he feared retribution, described the early donor summits as a clever means devised by Charles Koch to enlist others to pay for political fights that helped his company's bottom line. The seminars were, in essence, an extension of the company's corporate lobbying. They were staffed and organized by Koch employees and largely treated as a corporate project. Of particular importance to the Kochs, he said, was drumming up support from other business leaders for their environmental fights. The Kochs vehemently opposed the government taking any action on climate change that would hurt their fossil fuel profits. But suddenly in January 2009, these narrow concerns were overshadowed. Obama's election stirred such deep and widespread fear among the conservative business elite that the conference was swarmed, becoming a hub of political resistance. The planners were all but overwhelmed. "Suddenly they were leading the parade!" he said. "No one anticipated that."

By 2009, the Kochs had indeed succeeded in expanding their political conference from a wonky free-market swap fest to the point where it was beginning to attract an impressive array of influential figures. Wealthy businessmen thronged to rub shoulders with famous and powerful speakers, like the Supreme Court justices Antonin Scalia and Clarence Thomas. Congressmen, senators, governors, and media celebrities came too. "Getting an invitation means you've arrived," one operative who still works for the Kochs explained. "People want to be in the room."

The amount of money raised at the summits was also increasingly eye-catching. Earlier businessmen had certainly spent outsized sums in hopes of manipulating American politics, but the numbers at the Koch seminars far outstripped those in the past. As *The Washington Post*'s Dan Balz observed,

"When W. Clement Stone, an insurance magnate and philanthropist, gave $2 million to Richard M. Nixon's 1972 campaign, it caused public outrage and contributed to a movement that produced the post-Watergate reforms in campaign financing." Accounting for inflation, Balz estimated that Stone's $2 million might be worth about $11 million in today's dollars. In contrast, for the 2016 election, the political war chest accumulated by the Kochs and their small circle of friends was projected to be $889 million, completely dwarfing the scale of money that was considered deeply corrupt during the Watergate days.

The clout of the participants at the retreats served to burnish the Kochs' reputations, conferring a new aura of respectability on their extreme libertarian political views, which many had dismissed in the past as far outside the mainstream. "We're not a bunch of radicals running around and saying strange things," David Koch proudly told Continetti. "Many of these people are very successful, and occupy very important, respected positions in their communities!"

Exactly who attended the January 2009 summit, the first of the Obama era, and what transpired inside the resort can only be partly pieced together because the guest list, like many other aspects of the Kochs' political and business affairs, was shrouded in secrecy. As one Republican campaign consultant who has worked for the Kochs in the past said of the family's political activities, "To call them under the radar is an understatement. They are underground!"

Participants at the summits, for instance, were routinely admonished to destroy all copies of any paperwork. "Be mindful of the security and confidentiality of your meeting notes and materials," the invitation to one such gathering warned. Guests were told to say nothing to the news media and to post nothing about the meetings online. Elaborate security steps were taken to keep both the names of the participants and the meetings' agendas from public scrutiny. When signing up to attend the conferences, participants were warned to make all arrangements through the Kochs' staff, rather than trusting the employees at the resort, whose backgrounds were nonetheless investigated by the Kochs' security detail. In an effort to detect intruders and impostors, name tags were required at all functions, and smartphones, iPads, cameras, and other recording gear were confiscated prior to sessions. In order to foil eavesdroppers 'during one such gathering, audio technicians planted white-noise-emitting loudspeakers around the perimeters, aimed outward toward any uninvited press and public. It went without saying that breaches of this secrecy would result in excommunication from future meetings. When a breach did occur, the Kochs launched an intense weeklong internal investigation to identify and plug the leak. The donations raised at the summits were not publicly disclosed, nor were the names of the donors, although the planners' hope was that the money would have a decisive impact on the nation's affairs. "There is anonymity that we can protect," Kevin Gentry, vice president for special projects at Koch Industries and vice president of the Charles G. Koch Charitable Foundation, reassured the donors at one summit while soliciting their cash, according to a recording that later leaked out.

In case anyone misunderstood the seriousness of the enterprise, Charles Koch emphasized in one invitation that "fun in the sun" was not "our ultimate goal." Golf games and gondola rides were fine for after hours, but breakfast discussions would start bright and early. He reminded the invitees, "This is a gathering of *doers*."

No fewer than eighteen billionaires would be among the "doers" joining the Kochs' clandestine opposition movement during the first term of Obama's presidency. Ignoring the mere millionaires in attendance, many of whose fortunes were estimated to be worth hundreds of millions of dollars, the combined fortunes of the eighteen known billionaire participants alone as of 2015 topped $214 billion. In fact more billionaires participated anonymously in the Koch planning sessions during the first term of the Obama presidency than existed in 1982, when *Forbes* began listing the four hundred richest Americans.

The participants at the Koch seminars reflected the broader growth in economic inequality in the country, which had reached the level of the Gilded Age in the 1890s. The gap between the top 1 percent of earners in America and everyone else had grown so wide by 2007 that the top 1 percent of the population owned 35 percent of the nation's private assets and was pocketing almost a quarter of all earnings, up from just 9 percent twenty-five years earlier. Liberal critics, like the *New York Times* columnist Paul Krugman, a Nobel Prize–winning economist, worried that the country was in danger of being transformed from a democracy into a plutocracy, or worse, an oligarchy like Russia, where a handful of extraordinarily powerful businessmen bent the government into catering to them at the expense of everyone else. "We are on the road not just to a highly unequal society, but to a society of an oligarchy. A society of inherited wealth," Krugman warned. "When you have a few people who are so wealthy that they can effectively buy the political system, the political system is going to tend to serve their interests."

The term "oligarchy" was provocative and might have seemed an exaggeration to those accustomed to thinking of oligarchs as despotic rulers who were incompatible with democracies like the United States. But Jeffrey Winters, a professor at Northwestern University specializing in the comparative study of oligarchies, was one of a growing number of voices who were beginning to argue that America was a "civil oligarchy" in which a tiny and extremely wealthy slice of the population was able to use its vastly superior economic position to promote a brand of politics that served first and foremost itself. The oligarchs in America didn't rule directly, he argued, but instead used their fortunes to produce political results that favored their interests. As the left-leaning Columbia University professor Joseph Stiglitz, a Nobel Prize–winning economist, put it, "Wealth begets power, which begets more wealth."

For years, American economists had tended to downplay the importance of economic inequality in the country, arguing that its growth was simply the inevitable result of huge and unavoidable shifts in the global economy. Over time, they suggested, extreme inequality would naturally stabilize, and a rising tide would lift all boats. What mattered most, free-market advocates argued, was not equality of results but rather equality of opportunity. As the conservative Nobel Prize–winning economist Milton Friedman wrote, "A society that puts equality—in the sense of equality of outcome—ahead of freedom will end up with neither equality nor freedom . . . On the other hand, a society that puts freedom first will, as a happy by-product, end up with both greater freedom and greater equality."

In the new millennium, however, this consensus was beginning to fray. A growing number of academics studying the nexus of politics and wealth regarded the accelerating inequality in America as a threat not only to the economy but to democracy. Thomas Piketty, an economist at the Paris School of Economics, warned in his zeitgeist-shifting book, *Capital in the Twenty-First Century*, that without aggressive government intervention economic inequality in the United States and elsewhere was likely to rise inexorably, to the point where the small portion of the population that currently held a growing slice of the world's wealth would in the foreseeable future own not just a quarter, or a third, but perhaps half of the globe's wealth, or more. He predicted that the fortunes of those with great wealth, and their inheritors, would increase at a faster rate of return than the rate at which wages would grow, creating what he called "patrimonial capitalism." This dynamic, he predicted, would widen the growing chasm between the haves and the have-nots to levels mimicking the aristocracies of old Europe and banana republics.

Some argued that an elite minority was also driving extreme political partisanship as its interests and agenda lost touch with the economic realities faced by the rest of the population. Mike Lofgren, a Republican who spent thirty years observing how wealthy interests gamed the policy-making apparatus in Washington, where he was a staff member on the Senate Budget Committee, decried what he called the "secession" of the rich in which they "disconnect themselves from the civic life of the nation and from any concern about its well-being except as a place to extract loot." America, as Jacob Hacker and Paul Pierson described it, had become a "winner-take-all" country in which economic inequality perpetuated itself by pressing its political advantage. If so, the Koch seminars provided a group portrait of the winners' circle.

Only one full guest list of attendants at any of the Koch summits has surfaced publicly. It was for a session in June 2010. Like Mrs. Astor's famous 400, which defined the top bracket of New York society in the late nineteenth century on the basis of those who could fit into the Astors' ballroom, the Kochs' donor list provides another portrait of a fortunate social subset. They were mostly businessmen; very few were women. Fewer still were nonwhite. And while some had made their own fortunes, many others were intent on preserving vast legacies they had inherited. While those attracted to the Kochs' meetings were uniformly conservative, they were not the predictable cartoon villains of conspiracy theories but spanned a wide range of views and often disagreed among themselves about social and international issues. The glue that bound them together, however, was antipathy toward government regulation and taxation, particularly as it impinged on their own accumulation of wealth. Unsurprisingly, given the shift in the way great fortunes were made by the end of the twentieth century, instead of railroad magnates and steel barons who had ruled in the Astors' day, the largest number of participants came from the finance sector.

Among the better-known financiers who participated or sent representatives to Koch donor summits during Obama's first term were Steven A. Cohen, Paul Singer, and Stephen Schwarzman. All might have been principled philosophical conservatives, with no ulterior motives, but all also had personal reasons to fear a more assertive federal government, as was expected from Obama.

Cohen's spectacularly successful hedge fund, SAC Capital Advisors, was at the time the focus of an intense criminal investigation into insider trading. Prosecutors described his firm, which was based in Stamford, Connecticut, as "a veritable magnet of market cheaters." *Forbes* valued Cohen's fortune at one point at $10.3 billion, making his checkbook a formidable political weapon.

Paul Singer, whose fortune *Forbes* estimated at $1.9 billion, ran the hugely lucrative hedge fund Elliott Management. Dubbed a vulture fund by critics, it was controversial for buying distressed debt in economically failing countries at a discount and then taking aggressive legal action to force the strapped nations, which had expected their loans to be forgiven, to instead pay him back at a profit. Although Singer insisted that he didn't buy debt from the poorest of the poor nations, his methods, while highly lucrative, brought public scorn and government scrutiny. Even New York's tabloid newspapers chimed in. After Singer supported the campaign of the former New York mayor Rudolph Giuliani, a July 2007 *New York Post* story was headlined "Rudy's 'Vulture' $$ Man" with the subhead "Profits Off Poor." Singer described himself as a Goldwater free-enterprise conservative, and he contributed gene~ to promoting free-market ideology, but at the same ti firm reportedly sought unusual government help in squ several desperately impoverished governments, a contradiction that applied to many participants in the Koch donor network.

Stephen Schwarzman, who was in general less of a political activist than Singer, might have first become involved in the Kochs' political enterprise out of happenstance. In 2000, he paid $37 million for the palatial triplex that had previously belonged to John D. Rockefeller Jr. at 740 Park Avenue, the same Manhattan co-op building in which David Koch bought an apartment three years later. By the time Obama was elected, Schwarzman had become something of a poster boy for Wall Street excess. As Chrystia Freeland writes in her book *Plutocrats*, the June 21, 2007, initial public offering of stock in Blackstone, his phenomenally successful private equity company, "marked the date when America's plutocracy had its coming-out party." By the end of the day, Schwarzman had made $677 million from selling shares, and he retained additional shares then valued at $7.8 billion.

Schwarzman's stunning payday made a huge and not entirely favorable impression in Washington. Soon after, Democrats began criticizing the carried-interest tax loophole and other accounting gimmicks that helped financiers amass so much wealth. In the wake of the 2008 market crash, as Obama and the Democrats began talking increasingly about Wall Street reforms, financiers like Schwarzman, Cohen, and Singer who flocked to the Koch seminars had much to lose.

The hedge fund run by another of the Kochs' major investors, Robert Mercer, an eccentric computer scientist who made a fortune using sophisticated mathematical algorithms to trade stocks, also seemed a possible government target. Democrats in Congress were considering imposing a tax on stock trading, which the firm he co-chaired, Renaissance Technologies, did in massive quantities. Although those familiar with his thinking maintained that his political activism was separate from his pecuniary interests, Mercer had additional business reasons to be antigovernment. The IRS was investigating whether his firm improperly avoided paying billions of dollars in taxes, a charge the firm denied. Employment laws, too, would prove an embarrassing headache to him; three domestic servants soon sued him for refusing to pay overtime and maintained that he had docked their wages unfairly for infractions such as failing to replace shampoo bottles from his bathrooms when they were less than one-third full. The tabloid news stories about the case invariably mentioned that Mercer had previously brought a suit of his own, suing a toy-train manufacturer for overbilling him by $2 million for an elaborate electric train set he had installed in his Long Island, New York, mansion. With a pay package of $125 million in 2011, Mercer was ranked by *Forbes* as the sixteenth-highest-paid hedge fund manager that year.

Other financiers active in the Koch group had additional legal problems. Ken Langone, the billionaire co-founder of Home Depot, was enmeshed in a prolonged legal fight over his decision as chairman of the compensation committee of the New York Stock Exchange to pay his friend Dick Grasso, the head of the exchange, $139.5 million. The sum was so scandalously large that it forced Grasso to resign. Angry at his critics, Langone reportedly felt that "if it wasn't for us fat cats and the endowments we fund, every university in the country would be fucked."

Another Koch seminar goer from the financial sector, Richard Strong, founder of the mutual fund Strong Capital Management, was banned from the financial industry for life in a settlement following an investigation by the former New York attorney general Eliot Spitzer into his improperly timing trades to benefit his friends and family. Strong paid a $60 million fine and publicly apologized. His company paid an additional $115 million in related penalties. But after Strong sold his company's assets to Wells Fargo, the Associated Press reported that he would be "an even wealthier man."

Many participants in the Koch summits were brilliant leaders not only in business but also in tax avoidance. For

instance, the Colorado oil and entertainment billionaire Philip
Anschutz, a founder of Qwest Communications, whom *Fortune* magazine dubbed America's "greediest executive" in 2002,
was fighting an uphill battle on a tax matter that practically
required an accounting degree to explain. Anschutz, a conservative Christian who bankrolled movies with biblical themes,
had attempted to avoid paying capital gains taxes in a 2000–
2001 transaction by using what are called prepaid variable
forward contracts. These contracts allow wealthy shareholders such as Anschutz, whose fortune *Forbes* estimated at $11.8
billion as of 2015, to promise to give shares to investment firms
at a later date, in exchange for cash up front. Because the stock
does not immediately change hands, capital gains taxes are
not paid. According to *The New York Times,* Anschutz raised
$375 million in 2000–2001 by promising shares in his oil and
natural gas companies through the firm Donaldson, Lufkin &
Jenrette.

Eventually, the court sided against Anschutz on something
of a technicality. The former *Times* reporter David Cay Johnston wrote that in essence the court had ruled that "prepaids
done slightly differently than the Anschutz transactions will
survive. But why should they?" he asked. "Why should anyone get to enjoy cash from gains now without paying taxes?"
Johnston concluded, "The awful truth is that America has two
income tax systems, separate and unequal. One system is for
the superrich, like Anschutz and his wife, Nancy, who are
allowed to delay and avoid taxes on investment gains, among
other tax tricks. The other system is for the less than fabulously
wealthy."

Some donor families had clearly committed tax crimes.
Richard DeVos, co-founder of Amway, the Michigan-based
worldwide multilevel marketing empire, had pleaded guilty to
a criminal scheme in which he had defrauded the Canadian
government of $22 million in customs duties in 1982. DeVos
later claimed it had been a misunderstanding, but the record

showed the company had engaged in an elaborate, deliberate hoax in an effort to hoodwink Canadian authorities. He and his co-founder, Jay Van Andel, were forced to pay a $20 million fine. The fine didn't make much of a dent in DeVos's fortune, which *Forbes* estimated at $5.7 billion. By 2009, DeVos's son Dick and daughter-in-law Betsy were major donors on the Koch list and facing a record $5.2 million civil fine of their own for violatihg Ohio's campaign-finance laws.

Energy magnates were also heavily represented in the Koch network. Many of this group too had significant government regulatory and environmental issues. The "extractive" industries, oil, gas, and mining, tend to be run by some of the most outspoken opponents of government regulation in the country, yet all rely considerably on government permits, regulations, and tax laws to aid their profits and frequently to give them access to public lands. Executives from at least twelve oil and gas companies, in addition to the Kochs, were participants in the group. Collectively, they had a huge interest in staving off any government action on climate change and weakening environmental safeguards. One prominent member of this group was Corbin Robertson Jr., whose family had built a billion-dollar oil company, Quintana Resources Capital. Robertson had bet big on coal—so big he reportedly owned what *Forbes* called the "largest private hoard in the nation—21 billion tons of reserves." Investigative reports linked Robertson to several political front groups fighting efforts by the Environmental Protection Agency (EPA) to control pollution emitted by coal-burning utilities. Almost comically, one such front group was called Plants Need CO_2.

Another coal magnate active in the Kochs' donor network was Richard Gilliam, head of the Virginia mining concern Cumberland Resources. The dire stakes surrounding the sinking coal industry's regulatory fights were evident in the 2010 sale of Cumberland for nearly $1 billion to Massey Energy, just weeks before a tragic explosion in Massey's Upper Big Branch mine killed twenty-nine miners, becoming the worst coal mine disaster in forty years. A government investigation into Massey found it negligent on multiple safety fronts, and a federal grand jury indicted its CEO, Don Blankenship, for conspiring to violate and impede federal mine safety standards, making him the first coal baron to face criminal charges. Later, Massey was bought for $7.1 billion by Alpha Natural Resources, whose CEO, Kevin Crutchfield, was yet another member of the Koch network.

Several spectacularly successful leaders of hydraulic fracturing, who had their own set of government grievances, were also on the Kochs' list. The revolutionary method of extracting gas from shale revived the American energy business but alarmed environmentalists. Among the "frackers" in the group were J. Larry Nichols, co-founder of the huge Oklahoma-based concern Devon Energy, and Harold Hamm, whose company, Continental Resources, was the biggest operator in North Dakota's booming Bakken Shale. As Hamm, a sharecropper's son, took his place as the thirty-seventh-richest person in America with a fortune that *Forbes* estimated at $8.2 billion as of 2015, and campaigned to preserve tax loopholes for oil producers, his company gained notoriety for a growing record of environmental and workplace safety violations.

One shared characteristic of many of the donors in the Kochs' network was private ownership of their businesses, placing them in a low-profile category that *Fortune* once dubbed "the invisible rich." Private ownership gave these magnates far more managerial latitude and limited public disclosures, shielding them from stockholder scrutiny. Many of the donors had nonetheless attracted unwanted legal scrutiny by the government.

It was, in fact, striking how many members of the Koch network had serious past or ongoing legal problems. Sheldon Adelson, founding chairman and chief executive of the Las

Vegas Sands Corporation, the world's largest gambling company, whose fortune *Forbes* estimated at $31.4 billion, was
facing a bribery investigation by the Justice Department into
whether his company had violated the Foreign Corrupt Practices Act in securing licenses to operate casinos in Macao.

The Kochs had looming worries about the Foreign Corrupt Practices Act, too. As Bloomberg News later revealed,
the company's record of illicit payments in Algeria, Egypt,
India, Morocco, Nigeria, and Saudi Arabia was spilling out
in a French court. Further, in the summer of 2008, just a few
months before Obama was elected, federal officials had questioned the company about sales to Iran, in violation of the U.S.
trade ban against the state for sponsoring terrorism.

Meanwhile, another donor, Oliver Grace Jr., a relation of
the family that founded the William R. Grace Company, was
at the center of a stock-backdating scandal that resulted in his
being ousted from the board of Take-Two, the company behind
the ultraviolent *Grand Theft Auto* video games.

The legal problems of Richard Farmer, the chairman of
the Cincinnati-based Cintas Corporation, the nation's largest
uniform supply company, included an employee's gruesome
death. Just before the new and presumably less business-
friendly Obama administration took office, Cintas reached a
record $2.76 million settlement with the Occupational Safety
and Health Administration (OSHA) in six safety citations
including one involving a worker who had burned to death
in an industrial dryer. The employee, a Hispanic immigrant,
had become caught on a conveyor belt leading into the heat
source. Prior to the fatal accident, OSHA had cited Cintas for
over 170 safety violations since 2003, including 70 that regulators warned could cause "death or serious physical harm." As
Obama took office, the company was still fighting against paying a damage claim to the employee's widow and arguing that
his death had been his own fault. Farmer, too, ranked among

the Koch group's billionaire donors, with a fortune that *Forbes* estimated at $2 billion.

Given the participants' unanimous espousal of antigovernment, free-market self-reliance, the network also included a surprising number of major government contractors, such as Stephen Bechtel Jr., whose personal fortune *Forbes* estimated at $2.8 billion. Bechtel was a director and retired chairman of the huge and internationally powerful engineering firm Bechtel Corporation, founded by his grandfather, run by his father, and, after he retired, by his son and grandson. Paternalistic and family-owned, Bechtel was the sixth-largest private company in the country, and it owed almost its entire existence to government patronage. It had built the Hoover Dam, among other spectacular public projects, and had storied access to the innermost national security circles. Between 2000 and 2009 alone, it had received $39.2 billion in U.S. government contracts. This included $680 million to rebuild Iraq following the U.S. invasion.

Like so many of the other companies owned by the Koch donors, Bechtel had government legal problems. In 2007, a report by the special inspector general for Iraq reconstruction accused Bechtel of shoddy work. And in 2008, the company paid a $352 million fine to settle unrelated charges of substandard work in Boston's notorious "Big Dig" tunnel project. The company was facing congressional reproach too for cost overruns in the multibillion-dollar cleanup of the Hanford nuclear facility in Washington State.

Antagonism toward the government ran so high within the Koch network that one donor angrily objected to federal interference not just in his business but on behalf of his own safety as well. Thomas Stewart, who built his father's Seattle-based food business into the behemoth Services Group of America, reportedly loved flying in his helicopter and corporate jet. But when a former company pilot refused to take his

aeronautic advice because it violated Federal Aviation Administration regulations, according to an interview with the pilot
in the *Seattle Post-Intelligencer,* Stewart "rose out of his chair,
and screamed, 'I can do any fucking thing I want!'"

The highlight of the Koch summit in 2009 was an unin-
hibited debate about what conservatives should do next in
the face of their electoral defeat. As the donors and other
guests dined in the hotel's banquet room, like Roman senators attending a gladiator duel in the Forum, they watched a
passionate argument unfold that encapsulated the stark choice
ahead. Sitting on one side of a stage, facing the participants,
was the Texas senator John Cornyn, the head of the National
Republican Senatorial Committee and a former justice on the
Texas Supreme Court. Tall, with a high pink forehead, puffy
cotton-white hair, and a taste for dark pin-striped suits, his
image conveyed his role as a pillar of the establishment wing
of the Republican Party. Cornyn was rated as the second-most
conservative Republican in the Senate, according to the nonpartisan *National Journal.* But he also was, as one former aide
put it, "very much a constitutionalist" who believed it was occasionally necessary in politics to compromise.

Poised on the other side of the moderator was the South
Carolina senator Jim DeMint, a conservative provocateur who
defined the outermost antiestablishment fringe of the Republican Party and who in the words of one admirer was "the leader
of the Huns." Fifty-seven at the time, he was five months older
than Cornyn, but his dark hair, lean build, and more casual,
aw-shucks style made him appear years younger. Before his
election to Congress, DeMint had run an advertising agency
in South Carolina. He understood how to sell, and what he was
pitching that night was an approach to politics that according
to the historian Sean Wilentz would have been recognizable

to DeMint's forebears from the Palmetto State as akin to the radical nullification of federal power advocated in the 1820s by the slavery defender John C. Calhoun.

The two Republican senators had been at loggerheads for some time. That night they gave opposing opening statements. Cornyn spoke in favor of the Republican Party fighting its way back to victory by broadening its appeal to a wider swath of voters, including moderates. "He understands that Republicans in Texas and in Maine aren't necessarily exactly alike," the former aide explained. "He believes in making the party a big tent. You can't win unless you get more votes."

In contrast, DeMint portrayed compromise as surrender. He had little patience for the slow-moving process of constitutional government. He regarded many of his Senate colleagues as timid and self-serving. The federal government posed such a dire threat to the dynamism of the American economy, in his view, that anything less than all-out war on regulations and spending was a cop-out. DeMint was the face of a new kind of extremism, and he spoke that evening in favor of purifying, rather than diluting, the Republican Party. He argued that he would rather have "thirty Republicans who believed in something than a majority who believed in nothing," a line that was a mantra for him and that brought cheers and applause from the gathered onlookers. Rather than compromising their principles and working with the new administration, DeMint argued, Republicans needed to take a firm stand against Obama, waging a campaign of massive resistance and obstruction, regardless of the 2008 election outcome.

As the participants continued to cheer him on, in his folksy, southern way, DeMint tore into Cornyn over one issue in particular. He accused Cornyn of turning his back on conservative free-market principles and capitulating to the worst kind of big government spending, with his vote earlier that fall in favor of the Treasury Department's massive bailout of failing banks. The September 15, 2008, failure of Lehman Brothers, one of the nation's largest investment banks, had triggered a stunning run on financial institutions and the beginning of a generalized panic. The Federal Reserve chairman, Ben Bernanke, warned congressional leaders that "it is a matter of days before there is a meltdown in the global financial system." In hopes of staving off economic disaster, Bush's Treasury Department begged Congress to approve the massive $700 billion emergency bailout known as the Troubled Asset Relief Program, or TARP.

Both Obama and the Republican presidential nominee, John McCain, supported the emergency measure in the run-up to the 2008 election. But ever since, outraged opposition to the bailouts had built both from the public and from antigovernment, free-market conservatives like DeMint. Having expected a gentlemanly debate over the future of the Republican Party, Cornyn suddenly found himself on the defensive as the donors jeered and the moderator, Stephen Moore, a free-market gadfly and contributor to *The Wall Street Journal*'s editorial page, egged them on. The room started to explode. Rebuking Cornyn, one donor, Randy Kendrick, said, "You just keep electing RINOs!"—invoking the slur that Moore was said to have coined for squishy moderates who were, in his phrase, "Republicans in Name Only."

Sitting silently at a table in the front row through all of this were Charles Koch and his wife, Liz. No one came to Cornyn's defense. It was widely assumed that the Kochs, as hard-core free-market enthusiasts, had opposed the huge government bailouts of the private sector. Later, many reporters assumed this too, ascribing the Kochs' opposition to Obama as stemming from their principled disagreement over issues such as the TARP bailouts. But none of this was true. Had people checked the record carefully, they would have found it quite revealing. At first, the Kochs' political organization, Americans for Prosperity (AFP), had in fact taken what appeared to be a principled libertarian position against the bailouts. But the organization quickly and quietly reversed sides when the bottom began to fall out of the stock market, threatening the Kochs' vast investment portfolio. The market began to collapse on Monday, September 29, when, in the face of heavy opposition from conservatives, the House unexpectedly failed to pass the federal rescue plan. By the end of the day, the Dow Jones Industrial Average had fallen 777 points, losing 6.98 percent of its value. It was the stock market's largest one-day point drop ever.

Although some conservative groups and politicians such as DeMint still opposed the bailout, the market panic was enough to change many minds. Among those who flipped during the next forty-eight hours were the Kochs. Two days after the unexpected House vote, as the measure was about to be considered by the Senate, a list of conservative groups now supporting the bailouts was circulated behind the scenes to Republican legislators, in hopes of persuading them to vote for the bailouts. Among the groups now listed as supporters was Americans for Prosperity. Soon after, the Senate passed TARP with overwhelming bipartisan support, including that of John Cornyn. A source familiar with the Kochs' thinking says that Americans for Prosperity's flip-flop mirrored their own.

But if the Kochs' personal interest in protecting their portfolio had trumped their free-market principles, they weren't about to mention it in front of a roomful of fired-up libertarians whose cash they wanted to combat Obama. So, although they could have changed the dynamic in the room instantly by speaking up, no one defended Cornyn or the idea of acting responsibly within the bounds of traditional, reasonable political opposition.

Instead, the sentiment among the donors as the first Koch seminar of the Obama era came to an end was, as one witness put it, "like a bunch of gorillas beating their chests." After hearing both sides out, the assembled guests chose the path of extremism.

The Kochs had already concluded that they would need

to resort to extraordinary political measures to achieve their goals. A few days before the January 2009 donor seminar, Charles and David Koch had privately weighed their options with their longtime political strategist in a meeting inside the black-glass fortress that served as Koch Industries' corporate headquarters in Wichita, Kansas.

As they later revealed in an interview with Bill Wilson and Roy Wenzl in *The Wichita Eagle,* after hearing Obama's inauguration address, they agreed with their political adviser, Richard Fink, that America was on the road to ruin. Fink reportedly told the billionaire brothers, whose wealth, when combined, put at their disposal the single largest fortune in the world, that if they wanted to beat back the progressive tide that Obama's election represented, it would take "the fight of their lives."

"If we're going to do this, we should do it right, or not at all," Fink said, according to the Wichita newspaper account. "But if we don't do it right, or we don't do it at all, we will be insignificant and we will just waste a lot of time, and I would rather play golf."

If the Kochs decided that they did want "to do it right," however, as Fink put it, they should be prepared, he warned, because "it is going to get very, very ugly."

Advisers to Obama later acknowledged that he had no inkling of what he was up against. He had campaigned as a post-partisan politician who had idealistically taken issue with those who he said "like to slice and dice our country into red states and blue states." He insisted, "We are one people," the United States of America. His vision, like his own blended racial and geographic heredity, was of reconciliation, not division. Echoing these themes in his first inaugural address, Obama had chided "cynics," who, he said, "fail to understand . . . that the ground has shifted beneath them—that the stale political arguments that have consumed us for so long no longer apply."

The sentiment was laudable but, alas, wishful thinking.

Had the newly sworn-in president looked down at the ground directly beneath his polished shoes as he delivered these optimistic words, he might have been wise to take note. The red-and-blue carpet on which he was standing, which had been custom made in accordance with a government contract, had been manufactured by Invista, a subsidiary of Koch Industries. In American politics, the Kochs and all they stood for were not so easy to escape.

Part One

Weaponizing
Philanthropy

The War of Ideas, 1970–2008

CHAPTER ONE

Radicals: A Koch Family History

ODDLY ENOUGH, THE FIERCELY LIBERTARIAN KOCH FAMILY owed part of its fortune to two of history's most infamous dictators, Joseph Stalin and Adolf Hitler. The family patriarch, Fred Chase Koch, founder of the family oil business, developed lucrative business relationships with both of their regimes in the 1930s.

According to family lore, Fred Koch was the son of a Dutch printer and publisher who settled in the small town of Quanah, Texas, just south of the Oklahoma border, where he owned a weekly newspaper and print shop. Quanah, which was named for the last American Comanche chief, Quanah Parker, still retained its frontier aura when Fred was born there in 1900. Bright and eager to get out from under his overbearing old-world father, Fred once ran away to live with the Comanches as a boy. Later, he crossed the country for college, transferring from Rice in Texas to attend the Massachusetts Institute of Technology. There, he earned a degree in chemical engineering and joined the boxing team. Early photographs show him as a tall, formally dressed young man with glasses, a tuft of unruly curls, and a self-confident, defiant expression.

In 1927, Fred, who was an inveterate tinkerer, invented an improved process for extracting gasoline from crude oil. But as he would later tell his sons bitterly and often, America's major oil companies regarded him as a business threat and shut him out of the industry, suing him and his customers in 1929 for patent infringement. Koch regarded the monopolistic patents invoked by the major oil companies as anticompetitive and unfair. The fight appears to be an early version of the Kochs' later opposition to "corporate cronyism" in which they contend that the government and big business collaborate unfairly. In Fred Koch's eye, he was an outsider fighting a corrupt system.

Koch fought back in the courts for more than fifteen years, finally winning a $1.5 million settlement. He correctly suspected that his opponents bribed at least one presiding judge, an incompetent lush who left the case in the hands of a crooked clerk. "The fact that the judge was bribed completely altered their view of justice," one longtime family employee suggests. "They believe justice can be bought, and the rules are for chumps." Meanwhile, crippled by lawsuits in America during this period, Koch took his innovative refining method abroad.

He had already helped build a refinery in Great Britain after World War I with Charles de Ganahl, a mentor. At the time, the Russians supplied England with fuel, which led to the Russians seeking his expertise as they set up their own oil refineries after the Bolshevik Revolution.

At first, according to family lore, Koch tore up the telegram from the Soviet Union asking for his help. He said he didn't want to work for Communists and didn't trust them to pay him. But after securing an agreement to get paid in advance, he overcame his philosophical reservations. In 1930, his company, then called Winkler-Koch, began training Russian engineers and helping Stalin's regime set up fifteen modern oil refineries under the first of Stalin's five-year plans. The program was a success, forming the backbone of the future Russian petroleum industry. The oil trade brought crucial hard currency into the Soviet Union, enabling it to modernize other industries. Koch was reportedly paid $500,000, a princely sum during America's Great Depression. But by 1932, facing growing domestic demand, Soviet officials decided it would be more advantageous to copy the technology and build future refineries themselves. Fred Koch continued to provide technical assistance to the Soviets as they constructed one hundred plants, according to one report, but the advisory work was less profitable.

What happened next has been excised from the official corporate history of Koch Industries. After mentioning the company's work in the Soviet Union, the bulk of which ended in 1932, the corporate history skips ahead to 1940, when it says Fred Koch decided to found a new company, Wood River Oil & Refining. Charles Koch is equally vague in his book *The Science of Success*. He notes only that his father's company "enjoyed its first real financial success during the early years of the Great Depression" by "building plants abroad, especially in the Soviet Union."

A controversial chapter is missing. After leaving the U.S.S.R., Fred Koch turned to Adolf Hitler's Third Reich. Hitler became chancellor in 1933, and soon after, his government oversaw and funded massive industrial expansion, including the buildup of Germany's capacity to manufacture fuel for its growing military ambitions. During the 1930s, Fred Koch traveled frequently to Germany on oil business. Archival records document that in 1934 Winkler-Koch Engineering of Wichita, Kansas, as Fred's firm was then known, provided the engineering plans and began overseeing the construction of a massive oil refinery owned by a company on the Elbe River in Hamburg.

The refinery was a highly unusual venture for Koch to get involved with at that moment in Germany. Its top executive was a notorious American Nazi sympathizer named William Rhodes Davis whose extensive business dealings with Hitler would eventually end in accusations by a federal prosecutor that he was an "agent of influence" for the Nazi regime. In 1933, Davis proposed the purchase and conversion of an existing German oil storage facility in Hamburg, owned by a company called Europäische Tanklager A.G., or Eurotank, into a massive refinery. At the time, Hitler's military aims, and his need for more fuel, were already well-known. Davis's plan was to ship crude petroleum to Germany, refine it, and then sell it to the German military. The president of the American bank

with which Davis dealt refused to have anything to do with
the deal, because it was seen as supporting the Nazi military
buildup, but others extended the credit. After lining up the
American financing, Davis needed the Third Reich's backing.
To gain it, he first had to convince German industrialists of
his support for Hitler. In his effort to ingratiate himself, Davis
opened an early meeting with Hermann Schmitz, the chairman of I.G. Farben—the powerful and well-connected chemical company that soon after produced the lethal gas for the
concentration camps' death chambers—by saluting him with
a Nazi "Heil Hitler." When these efforts didn't produce the
green light he sought, Davis sent messages directly to Hitler,
eventually securing a meeting in which the führer walked in
and ordered his henchmen to approve the deal. On Hitler's
orders, the Third Reich's economic ministers supported Davis's
construction of the refinery. In his biography of Davis, Dale
Harrington draws on eyewitness accounts to describe Hitler
as declaring to his skeptical henchmen, "Gentlemen, I have
reviewed Mr. Davis's proposition and it sounds feasible, and I
want the bank to finance it." Harrington writes that during the
next few years Davis met at least half a dozen more times with
Hitler and on one occasion asked him to personally autograph
a copy of *Mein Kampf* for his wife. According to Harrington,
by the end of 1933 Davis was "deeply committed to Nazism"
and exhibited a noticeable "dislike for Jews."

In 1934, Davis turned to Fred Koch's company, Winkler-
Koch, for help in executing his German business plan. Under
Fred Koch's direction, the refinery was finished by 1935. With
the capacity to process a thousand tons of crude oil a day, the
third-largest refinery in the Third Reich was created by the
collaboration between Davis and Koch. Significantly, it was
also one of the few refineries in Germany, according to Harrington, that could "produce the high-octane gasoline needed
to fuel fighter planes. Naturally," he writes, "Eurotank would
do most of its business with the German military." Thus, he

concludes, the American venture became "a key component of the Nazi war machine."

Historians expert in German industrial history concur. The development of the German fuel industry "was hugely, hugely important" to Hitler's military ambitions, according to the Northwestern University professor Peter Hayes. "Hitler set out to create 'autarchy,' or economic self-sufficiency," he explained. "Gottfried Feder, the German official in charge of the program, reasoned that even though Germany would have to import crude oil, it would be able to save foreign exchange by refining the products itself."

In the run-up to the war, Davis profited richly from the arrangement, engaging in elaborate scams to keep the crude oil imports flowing into Germany despite Britain's blockade. When World War II began, the high-octane fuel was used in bombing raids by German pilots. Like Davis, the Koch family benefited from the venture. Raymond Stokes, director of the Centre for Business History at the University of Glasgow in Scotland and co-author of a history of the German oil industry during the Nazi years, *Faktor Öl* (The oil factor), which documents the company's role, says, "Winkler-Koch benefited directly from this project, which was designed to help enable the fuel policy of the Third Reich."

Fred Koch often traveled to Germany during these years, and according to family lore he was supposed to have been on the fatal May 1937 transatlantic flight of the *Hindenburg*, but at the last minute he got delayed. In late 1938, as World War II approached and Hitler's aims were unmistakable, he wrote admiringly about fascism in Germany, and elsewhere, drawing an invidious comparison with America under Franklin Roosevelt's New Deal. "Although nobody agrees with me, I am of the opinion that the only sound countries in the world are Germany, Italy, and Japan, simply because they are all working and working hard," he wrote in a letter to a friend. Koch added, "The laboring people in those countries are proportion-ately much better off than they are any place else in the world. When you contrast the state of mind of Germany today with what it was in 1925 you begin to think that perhaps this course of idleness, feeding at the public trough, dependence on government, etc., with which we are afflicted is not permanent and can be overcome."

When the United States entered World War II in 1941, family members say that Fred Koch tried to enlist in the U.S. military. Instead, the government directed him to use his chemical engineering prowess to help refine high-octane fuel for the American warplanes. Meanwhile, in an ironic turn, the Hamburg refinery that Winkler-Koch built became an important target of Allied bombing raids. On June 18, 1944, American B-17s finally destroyed it. The human toll of the bombing raids on Hamburg was almost unimaginable. In all, some forty-two thousand civilians were killed during the long and intense Allied campaign against Hamburg's crucial industrial targets.

Fred Koch's willingness to work with the Soviets and the Nazis was a major factor in creating the Koch family's early fortune. By the time he met his future wife, Mary Robinson, at a polo match in 1932, the oilman's work for Stalin had put him well on his way to becoming exceedingly wealthy.

Robinson, a twenty-four-year-old graduate of Wellesley College, was tall, slender, and beautiful, with blond hair, blue eyes, and an expression of amusement often captured in family photographs. The daughter of a prominent physician from Kansas City, Missouri, she had grown up in a more cosmopolitan milieu. Koch, who was seven years older than she, was so smitten he married her a month after they met.

Soon, the couple commissioned the most fashionable architect in the area to build an imposing Gothic-style stone mansion on a large compound on the outskirts of Wichita, Kansas, where Winkler-Koch was based. Reflecting their rising social status, the estate was baronial despite the flat and empty prairie surrounding it, with stables, a polo ring, a kennel for hunting dogs, a swimming pool and wading pool, a circular drive, and stone-terraced gardens. Some of the best craftsmen in the country created decorative flourishes such as wrought-iron railings and a stone fireplace carved with a whimsical snowflake motif. Within a few years, the Kochs also purchased the sprawling Spring Creek Ranch near Reece, Kansas, where Fred, who loved science and genetics, bred and raised cattle. Family photographs show the couple looking glamorous and patrician, hosting picnics and pool parties, and riding on horseback, dressed in jodhpurs and polo gear, surrounded by packs of jolly friends.

In the first eight years of their marriage, the couple had four sons: Frederick, known by the family as Freddie, was born in 1933, Charles was born in 1935, and twins, David and William, were born in 1940. With their father frequently traveling and their mother preoccupied with social and cultural pursuits, the boys were largely entrusted to a series of nannies and housekeepers.

It is unclear what Fred Koch's views of Hitler were during the 1930s, beyond his preference for the country's work ethic in comparison with the nascent welfare state in America. But he was enamored enough of the German way of life and thinking that he employed a German governess for his first two sons, Freddie and Charles. At the time, Freddie was a small boy, and Charles still in diapers. The nanny's iron rule terrified the little boys, according to a family acquaintance. In addition to being overbearing, she was a fervent Nazi sympathizer, who frequently touted Hitler's virtues. Dressed in a starched white uniform and pointed nurse's hat, she arrived with a stash of gruesome German children's books, including the Victorian classic *Der Struwwelpeter,* that featured sadistic consequences for misbehavior ranging from cutting off one child's thumbs to burning another to death. The acquaintance recalled that the nurse had a commensurately harsh and dictatorial approach to child rearing. She enforced a rigid toilet-training regimen requiring the boys to produce morning bowel movements precisely on schedule or be force-fed castor oil and subjected to enemas.

The despised governess ruled the nursery largely unchallenged for several years. In 1938, the two boys were left for months while their parents toured Japan, Burma, India, and the Philippines. Even when she was home, Mary Koch characteristically deferred to her husband, declining to intervene. "My father was fairly tough with my mother," Bill Koch later told *Vanity Fair*. "My mother was afraid of my father." Meanwhile, Fred Koch was often gone for months at a time, in Germany and elsewhere.

It wasn't until 1940, the year the twins were born, when Freddie was seven and Charles five, that back in Wichita the German governess finally left the Koch family, apparently at her own initiative. Her reason for giving notice was that she was so overcome with joy when Hitler invaded France she felt she had to go back to the fatherland in order to join the führer in celebration. What if any effect this early experience with authority had on Charles is impossible to know, but it's interesting that his lifetime preoccupation would become crusading against authoritarianism while running a business over which he exerted absolute control.

Fred Koch was himself a tough and demanding disciplinarian. John Damgard, David's childhood friend, who became president of the Futures Industry Association, recalled that he was "a real John Wayne type." Koch emphasized rugged pursuits, taking his sons big-game hunting in Africa and filling the basement billiard room with what one cousin remembered as a frightening collection of exotic stuffed animal heads, including lions and bears and others with horns and tusks, glinting glassy-eyed from the walls. In the summer, the boys could hear their friends splashing in the pool at the country club across the street, but instead of allowing the boys to join them, their father required them to dig up dandelions by the time they were five, and later to dig ditches and shovel manure at the family ranch. Fred Koch cared about his boys but was determined to keep them from becoming what he called "country-club bums," like some of the other offspring of the oil moguls with whom he was acquainted. "By instilling a work ethic in me at an early age, my father did me a big favor, although it didn't seem like a favor back then," Charles has written. "By the time I was eight, he made sure work occupied most of my spare time."

All four sons later professed admiration and affection for their father, but their fond recollections gloss over a dark streak. Fred Koch's rule was absolute, and his idea of punishment was corporal. He did not just spank the boys for their transgressions. Sometimes he hit them with a belt or worse. One family member remembers seeing him take a tree branch, strip it down, and "whip the twins like dogs." They had marred the stone patio in some way that enraged him. "He was a hard man to love," adds the family member, who declines to be identified. A second family member too remembers the belt beatings. Fred Koch "wasn't around much," he said, but when his sons misbehaved, they "really got it."

Sibling rivalry in the family, which reached epic levels in adulthood, was always intense. Family photographs and films show the brothers fenced in outdoor playpens, grabbing each other's toys, making each other cry, and boxing at early ages with gloves almost as big as their heads. Before long, Charles, the second born, emerged as the domineering leader of the pack. Fiercely competitive, driven, and self-confident, he appeared a paragon of handsome, blond athleticism. One family member recalls that Charles's favorite game was king of the hill. "It hasn't changed," another family member said.

Charles rarely lost, but when he did, he took it badly. When his younger brother Bill defeated him once in a boxing match, according to family lore, Charles refused to ever box again.

It became clear early that Freddie was different from the others, and not of his rough-hewn father's type. He was bookish and oriented toward his artistic mother, preferring to disappear into his room to read while the twins played ball with Charles, who liked to give commands. (Freddie did, however, hold his own against Charles on at least one occasion, punching him so hard in the face he broke his brother's nose.) Charles later told *Fame* magazine, "Father wanted to make all his boys into men and Freddie couldn't relate to that regime." Charles added, "Dad didn't understand and so he was hard on Freddie. He didn't understand that Freddie wasn't a lazy kid—he was just different."

The father was hard on the other boys too. David liked reading and became obsessed for a while with the Wizard of Oz books, which of course are set in Kansas, but his father preferred that he do chores. Increasingly, David attached himself to his elder brother Charles, becoming his sidekick and accomplice, willing to drop everything at his brother's command. "I was closer to David because he was better at everything [than the others]," Charles told *Fame*, bluntly.

Mary Koch recalled that as a result, "Billy always felt that Charles and David were leaving him out." She said that he "had no confidence or self-esteem." The only redhead among the pack, Bill had an explosive temper that resulted in memorable tantrums, including one in which he picked up a priceless antique vase and hurled it to the floor, shattering it. Fred Koch's response was more spanking.

Clayton Coppin, a former associate professor and research historian based at George Mason University, was one of the rare outsiders to the Koch family with firsthand knowledge of its inner workings. In 1993, Koch Industries commissioned him to write a confidential corporate history. For the next six years, Coppin had nearly unlimited access to the private archives in the company's headquarters in Wichita, along with the private papers of Fred and Mary Koch. He also had carte blanche to interview their business associates. After he completed the history in 1999, the company laid Coppin off. Subsequently, in 2002, Bill Koch hired him for a second confidential research project, this time on his brother Charles's political activities. In interviews, Coppin described what he learned about the family while researching the first report and shared a copy of the second report, a lengthy three-part 2003 study titled "Stealth: The History of Charles Koch's Political Activities."

According to Coppin, who read many of Fred Koch's private letters, in 1946, when Freddie was thirteen, his father confided to a family friend that there was a child-rearing crisis at home with which he needed help. Freddie had undergone some kind of emotional turmoil while being forced to labor at the family ranch that summer. The family friend recommended a consultation with Portia Hamilton, a clinical psychologist in New York who specialized in child development, with whom Fred began to correspond. Hamilton met with the family and wrote up an evaluation. The psychologist recommended that the boys be separated and that Mary Koch, who was already busy with social life and travel, further distance herself from them in order to make them more "manly." Psychological theories during that period attributed homosexuality to "over mothering."

As a result, Freddie was sent to Hackley, a prep school in Tarrytown, New York, where he could follow his cultural interests, attending the opera in Manhattan and acting in school productions. Later, he came to feel that Hackley rescued him.

In order to keep him from picking on his brothers, the Kochs sent Charles away to school as well, in his case, at the age of eleven. The school they chose for him was the Southern Arizona School for Boys, renowned for its strictness. His mother made clear that it was done for his younger brother Billy's sake, which only heightened resentments between the boys.

"I pleaded with them not to send me away," Charles told *Fortune* in 1997. Charles did poorly at the boarding school, but instead of yielding to his pleas to come home, the Kochs sent him to an even more rigid boarding school, the Fountain Valley School in Colorado. "I hated all that," Charles recalled. At one point, his parents finally "took pity" on him, he said, and let him attend public high school in Wichita, which he loved, but "I got into trouble," he recalled, so they packed him off to the Culver Military Academy in Indiana, which also emphasized discipline. There, Charles did better academically but repeatedly got into trouble. Eventually, Culver expelled him for drinking on a train (although he was eventually readmitted, enabling him to earn his diploma). "I have a little bit of a rebel, and free spirit in me," Charles later acknowledged. As punishment, Charles's father banished him to live with his relatives in Texas. "Father put the fear of God in him," David later recalled. "He said, 'If you don't make it, you'll be worthless. You've disappointed me.' Father was a severe taskmaster."

In his confidential report for Bill Koch, Coppin wrote, "Charles spent little of the next fifteen years at home, only coming there for an occasional holiday." After he was exiled by the family, "the first thing Charles did when he came home on vacation was to beat up" his younger brother Bill.

Young Bill grew alarmingly depressed. He was socially withdrawn and preoccupied with his sense of inferiority to his twin, David, and his older brother Charles. Soon the twins too were sent to boarding school. Bill, interestingly, chose to follow Charles's footsteps to Culver Military Academy, while David chose the eastern prep school Deerfield Academy. "There was a lot of strife between the boys. Charles was in constant rebellion against authority. It was a miserable childhood," Coppin said in an interview.

Yet later, as a parent, Charles partially repeated the pattern. When his own son, Chase, then thirteen, played a half-hearted tennis match, Charles had an employee pick him up and deliver him to a baking, reeking feedlot on one of the family ranches where he was forced to work seven days a week, twelve hours a day. Charles proudly recounted the story with a grin, telling *The Wichita Eagle*, "I think he thought he'd have a job here in Wichita and could go out with his friends at night." Chase became an exceptionally good tennis player but later had another, more serious problem. While driving as a high school student in Wichita, he ran a red light and fatally injured a twelve-year-old boy. He pleaded guilty to a misdemeanor charge of vehicular manslaughter and was sentenced to eighteen months of probation and a hundred hours of community service and was required to pay for the boy's funeral. After college, Chase, like his father, joined the family company.

Meanwhile, in an online blog, Charles's other child, Elizabeth, a Princeton graduate, described her own efforts to prove herself to her father. Of a visit home, she wrote, "As soon as we arrived I felt an overwhelming urge to prostrate myself on the floor and eat dirt in order to illustrate how grateful I am for everything they've done for me, that I'm not the spoiled monster they warned me I'd become if I wasn't careful." She described "chasing" her father around the house, trying to impress him with her interest in economics, and "staring down that dark well of nothing you do will ever be good enough you privileged waste of flesh."

A generation before, stern admonitions against becoming spoiled had emanated from Fred Koch to his offspring as well. Even as he laid plans to leave huge inheritances to his sons, he wrote a prophetic letter to them in 1936. In it, he warned,

> When you are 21, you will receive what now seems like a large sum of money. It will be yours to do what you will. It may be a blessing or a curse. You can use it as

a valuable tool for accomplishment or you can squander it foolishly. If you choose to let this money destroy your initiative and independence, then it will be a curse to you and my action in giving it to you will have been a mistake. I should regret very much to have you miss the glorious feeling of accomplishment and I know you are not going to let me down. Remember that often adversity is a blessing in disguise and certainly the greatest character builder. Be kind and generous to one another and to your mother.

Charles Koch keeps a framed copy of this letter in his office, but as *Fortune* observed, given the brothers' future protracted legal fights against each other, "Never did such good advice fall on such deaf ears."

David Koch recalled that his father tried to indoctrinate the boys politically, too. "He was constantly speaking to us children about what was wrong with government," he told Brian Doherty, an editor of the Koch-funded libertarian magazine *Reason* and the author of *Radicals for Capitalism*, a 2007 history of the libertarian movement with which the Kochs cooperated. "It's something I grew up with—a fundamental point of view that big government was bad, and imposition of government controls on our lives and economic fortunes was not good."

Fred Koch's political views were apparently shaped by his traumatic exposure to the Soviet Union. Over time, Stalin brutally purged several of Koch's Soviet acquaintances, giving him a firsthand glimpse into the murderous nature of the Communist regime. Koch was also apparently shaken by a steely government minder assigned to him while he worked in the Soviet Union, who threatened that the Communists would soon conquer the United States. Koch was deeply affected by the experience and later, after his business deals were completed, said he regretted his collaboration. He kept photographs in the company headquarters in Wichita aimed at documenting how the refineries he had built had later been destroyed. "As the Soviets became a stronger military power, Fred felt a certain amount of guilt at having helped build them up. I think it bothered him a lot," suggests Gus diZerega, a Wichita acquaintance of the family's.

In 1958, Fred Koch became one of eleven original members of the John Birch Society, the archconservative group best known for spreading far-fetched conspiracy theories about secret Communist plots to subvert America. He attended the founding meeting held by the candy manufacturer Robert Welch in Indianapolis. The organization drew like-minded businessmen from all over the country, including Harry Bradley, the chairman of the Allen-Bradley company in Milwaukee, who later financed the right-wing Bradley Foundation. Members considered many prominent Americans, including President Dwight D. Eisenhower, Communist agents. (The conservative historian Russell Kirk, part of an effort to purge the lunatic fringe from the movement, famously retorted, "Ike isn't a Communist; he's a golfer.")

In a 1960 self-published broadside, *A Business Man Looks at Communism*, Koch claimed that "the Communists have infiltrated both the Democrat [*sic*] and Republican Parties." Protestant churches, public schools, universities, labor unions, the armed services, the State Department, the World Bank, the United Nations, and modern art, in his view, were all Communist tools. He wrote admiringly of Benito Mussolini's suppression of Communists in Italy and disparagingly of the American civil rights movement. The Birchers agitated to impeach Chief Justice Earl Warren after the Supreme Court voted to desegregate the public schools in the case *Brown v. Board of Education*, which had originated in Topeka, in the Kochs' home state of Kansas. "The colored man looms large in the Communist plan to take over America," Fred Koch claimed in his pamphlet.

Welfare in his view was a secret plot to attract rural blacks to cities, where he predicted that they would foment "a vicious race war." In a 1963 speech, Koch claimed that Communists would "infiltrate the highest offices of government in the U.S. until the President is a Communist, unknown to the rest of us."

Blazing a trail that would later be followed by his sons, Koch tapped his fortune to subsidize his political activism. He underwrote the distribution of what he claimed were, over two and a half million copies of his book, as well as a speaking tour. According to the Associated Press, during one speech in 1961 he told the members of a Kansas Women's Republican club that if they were afraid of becoming too "controversial" by joining his fight against Communism, they should remember that "you won't be very controversial lying in a ditch with a bullet in your brain." Such rants brought Koch to the attention of the FBI, which filed a report describing his rhetoric as "utterly absurd."

The John Birch Society's views were primitive, but its marketing was quite sophisticated. Welch, the candy manufacturer who founded the group, urged organizers to implement a modern sales plan, advertising heavily and pushing pamphlets door-to-door. The movement flourished in Wichita, where Fred Koch frequently attended local John Birch Society meetings and was a generous benefactor.

Ironically, the organization modeled itself on the Communist Party. Stealth and subterfuge were endemic. Membership was kept secret. Fighting "dirty" was justified internally, as necessary to combat the imputed treacherousness of the enemy. Welch "explicitly sought to use the same methods" he attributed to the Communists, "manipulation, deceit, and even dishonesty," recalled diZerega, who attended Birch Society meetings in Wichita in his youth. One ploy the group used, he said, was to set up phony front groups "pretending to be other than what they were." An alphabet soup of secretly connected organizations sprang up, with acronyms like TRAIN

(To Restore American Independence Now) and TACT (Truth About Civil Turmoil). Another tactic was to wrap the group's radical vision in mundane and unthreatening slogans that sound familiar today, such as "less government, more responsibility." One of Welch's favorite tropes, decrying "collectivism," would cause some head-scratching more than fifty years later when it was echoed by Charles Koch in a 2014 diatribe in *The Wall Street Journal* denouncing his Democratic critics as "collectivists."

Welch was "a very intelligent, sharp man, quite an intellectual," Fred Koch's wife, Mary, later told her hometown newspaper *The Wichita Eagle*. The family's admiration for the John Birch Society, however, proved somewhat embarrassing on November 22, 1963, when President John F. Kennedy was assassinated. As Lee Fang recounts in his book, *The Machine: A Field Guide to the Resurgent Right*, when President Kennedy arrived in Dallas that morning, he was confronted by a hate-stoked, full-page newspaper ad paid for by several Texas members of the John Birch Society, accusing him of treasonously promoting "the spirit of Moscow." At the time, Kennedy had moved from trying to ignore the Birchers to realizing he needed to confront their increasingly pernicious fearmongering, which he denounced as "crusades of suspicion" and "extremism."

In a hasty turnabout, soon after the assassination Fred Koch took out full-page ads in *The New York Times* and *The Washington Post* mourning JFK. The ads advanced the conspiracy theory that JFK's assassin, Lee Harvey Oswald, had acted as part of a Communist plot. The Communists wouldn't "rest on this success," the ads warned. In the corner was a tear-out order form, directing the public to sign up for John Birch Society mailings. In response, the columnist Drew Pearson slammed Koch's "gimmick" and exposed him as a hypocrite for having profited himself from Soviet Communism by building up the U.S.S.R.'s oil industry.

Fred Koch continued to be active in extremist politics.

He provided substantial support for Barry Goldwater's right-wing bid for the Republican nomination in 1964. Goldwater, too, opposed the Civil Rights Act and the Supreme Court's landmark desegregation decision, *Brown v. Board of Education*. Instead of winning, the Far Right helped ensure the Republican Party's humiliating defeat by Lyndon Johnson that year. In 1968, Fred Koch went further right still. Before the emergence of George Wallace, he called for the Birch Society member Ezra Taft Benson to run for the presidency with the South Carolina senator Strom Thurmond on a platform calling for racial segregation and the abolition of all income taxes.

David and Charles absorbed their father's conservative politics and joined the John Birch Society too, but they did not share all of his views. According to diZerega, who befriended Charles in the mid-1960s after meeting him while browsing in a John Birch Society bookstore in Wichita, Charles didn't accept all of the group's conspiracy theories. He recalls that Charles, who was several years older, steered him away from the Communist conspiracy books and toward the collection of antigovernment economic writers whose work he found especially exciting. "This is the good stuff," he recalls Charles telling him. The founder of the John Birch Society, Welch, was a board member of the Foundation for Economic Education, which spread a version of laissez-faire economics so extreme "it bordered on anarchism," as Rick Perlstein writes in his history of Goldwater's ascent, *Before the Storm*. Unlike his father's conspiracies, these were the theories that captivated Charles.

The postcollege years were a restless period in Charles's life. In 1961, when he was twenty-six, his father, whose health was failing, persuaded him despite his doubts to return to Wichita to help run the family business. After graduating with a bachelor of science in engineering and master's degrees in nuclear and chemical engineering from MIT, where his father was on the board of trustees, Charles had been enjoying his freedom working in Boston as a business consultant. Convinced that his father would sell the company otherwise, Charles reluctantly returned to Wichita to help but found himself intellectually hungry back in his hometown. In his telling, he was almost feverishly bent on finding some overarching system of political theory to bridge his father's emotional anti-Communism with his own more analytical approach to the world. He also wanted to merge his thinking about business and his interests in engineering and mathematics. "I spent the next two years almost like a hermit, surrounded by books," he told *The Wall Street Journal* in 1997. Visitors to his apartment recall him littering almost every surface with abstruse economic and political texts. He later explained that having learned that "there are certain laws that govern the natural world," he was trying to discover "if the same isn't true for the societal world."

Contributing to Charles's intellectual ferment at this time were his father's dinner table diatribes against taxation. Fred saw taxes in America darkly, as incipient socialism. Early on, the Internal Revenue Service had sued his company for underpayment of taxes, requiring a large additional payment as well as penalties and legal fees. He remained vehemently opposed to estate taxes, and told Charles that he feared the U.S. government would tax him so heavily it might force him to sell the family business, diminishing his sons' inheritances. To minimize future taxes, Fred Koch took advantage of elaborate estate planning. Among other strategies, he set up a "charitable lead trust" that enabled him to pass on his estate to his sons without inheritance taxes, so long as the sons donated the accruing interest on the principal to charity for twenty years. To maximize their self-interest, in other words, the Koch boys were compelled to be charitable. Tax avoidance was thus the original impetus for the Koch brothers' extraordinary philanthropy. As David Koch later explained, "So for 20 years, I had to give away all that income, and I sort of got into it."

Fred Koch's estate plan treated each son equally, but according to Coppin, to ensure that his offspring would continue to obey him, he arranged to pass his fortune on to them in two stages, with the second half passing on only after his death. The first distribution gave all four boys equal owner-ship of Koch Engineering, the smaller of his two companies. The later distribution thus hung over his sons' heads, subject to their father's whim.

Charles's embrace of the John Birch Society, according to Coppin, was in part designed to please the old man. Accord-ing to diZerega, whom Charles invited to participate in an informal discussion group at the Koch mansion during this period, "It was pretty clear that Charles thought some of the Birch Society was bullshit." He recalls that "Charles was bright as hell." And in fact, in 1968, the year after his father died, Charles resigned from the organization over its support for the Vietnam War, which he opposed.

A related fringe group, though, became seminal to Charles Koch's political evolution during this period, the Freedom School, which was led by a radical thinker with a checkered past named Robert LeFevre. LeFevre opened the Freedom School in Colorado Springs in 1957 and from the start there were close ties to the John Birch Society. In 1964, Robert Love, a major figure in the Wichita branch of the John Birch Society, introduced Charles to the school, which offered one- and two-week immersion courses in "the philosophy of freedom and free enterprise." Robert Welch, the John Birch Society's founder, also visited. But LeFevre's preoccupations were slightly differ-ent. He was almost as adamantly opposed to America's govern-ment as he was to Communism.

LeFevre favored the abolition of the state but didn't like the label "anarchist," so he called himself instead an "autarchist." LeFevre liked to say that "government is a disease masquerad-ing as its own cure." Doherty, the historian of the libertarian movement, related that "LeFevre was an anarchist figure who won Charles's heart" and that the school was "a tiny world of people who thought the New Deal was a horrible mistake." An FBI file on the Freedom School shows that by 1966 Charles Koch was not only a major financial supporter of the school but also an executive and trustee.

LeFevre, who looked like a jolly, white-haired Santa, had reportedly been indicted earlier for mail fraud in connection with his role in a cultlike right-wing self-actualization movement called the Mighty "I AM" that worked audiences into frenzies as they chanted in response to Franklin and Eleanor Roosevelt's names, "Annihilate them!" As the journalist Mark Ames recounts, LeFevre escaped prosecution by becoming a witness for the state, but he continued on a wayward path, claiming to have supernatural powers and struggling through bankruptcy and an infatuation with a fourteen-year-old girl. Later, at the height of Senator Joe McCarthy's anti-Communist crusades, LeFevre became an FBI informant, accusing Hollywood figures of Communist sympathies and leading a drive to purge the Girl Scouts of Reds. A stint writing editorials for the archconservative *Gazette-Telegraph* in Colorado Springs enabled him to drum up funds to launch the Freedom School on a rustic, five-hundred-acre campus nearby. There, he assumed the title of dean.

The school taught a revisionist version of American history in which the robber barons were heroes, not villains, and the Gilded Age was the country's golden era. Taxes were denigrated as a form of theft, and the Progressive movement, Roosevelt's New Deal, and Lyndon Johnson's War on Poverty, in the school's view, were ruinous turns toward socialism. The weak and poor, the school taught, should be cared for by private charity, not government. The school had a revisionist position on the Civil War, too. It shouldn't have been fought; instead, the South should have been allowed to secede. Slavery was a lesser evil than military conscription, the school argued, because human beings should be allowed to sell themselves into slavery if they wished. Like Charles Koch during this period, the school tried to meld its version of history, economics, and philosophy into one theoretical framework, which it called "Phronhistery."

A group of Illinois teachers sent to a session at the school in 1959 by a local chamber of commerce returned so shocked that they notified the FBI and published a letter denouncing the school for advocating "no government, nó police department, no fire department, no public schools, no health or zoning laws, not even national defense." They noted that "this of course is anarchy." They also described the school as proposing that the Bill of Rights be reduced to "just a single one: the right to own property."

In 1965, *The New York Times* ran a feature describing the school as a bastion of "ultraconservatism" and mentioning that among the prized alumni whose lives had been transformed by its teachings was Charles Koch. He had obtained a second graduate degree from MIT in chemical engineering, the *Times* reported, after realizing that his previous degree in nuclear engineering would have required him to work closely with the government. At the time, according to the paper, the school was so implacably opposed to the U.S. government it was proposing that the Constitution be scrapped in favor of one that limited the government's authority to impose "compulsory taxation." The *Times* described LeFevre as also opposing Medicare and antipoverty programs and hinted that the school opposed government-sponsored integration, too. LeFevre told the paper that black students, of which the school had none, might pose a problem because, the *Times* wrote, "some of his students are segregationists."

Charles Koch was so enthusiastic about the Freedom School he talked his three brothers into attending sessions. But Freddie, the outlier in the family, who had spent more time than the others studying history and literature, disparaged the curriculum as bilge. He said that LeFevre reminded him of the con artists in Sinclair Lewis's novels. Charles was so incensed by his brother's apostasy, Frederick told people later, he threatened to "deck" him if he didn't toe the line.

DiZerega says that Charles arranged for him to attend a session at the school, too, and, he believes, paid his tuition. At the time, the only other faculty member he recalls besides LeFevre was James J. Martin, an anarchist historian who later won a reputation as a notorious Holocaust denier for his "revisionist" work with the Institute for Historical Review, in which he described claims of Nazi genocide in World War II as "invented." "It was a stew pot of ideas," recalled diZerega, who later became a liberal academic, "but if you grew up with more money than God, and felt weird about it, this version of history, where the robber barons were heroes, would certainly make you feel a lot better about it."

At the Freedom School, Charles became particularly enamored of the work of two laissez-faire economists, the Austrian theorist Ludwig von Mises and his star pupil, Friedrich Hayek, an Austrian exile, who visited the Freedom School. Hayek's book *The Road to Serfdom* had become an improbable best seller in 1944, after *Reader's Digest* published a condensed version. It offered a withering critique of "collectivism" and argued that centralized government planning, in which liberals were then engaged, would lead, inexorably, to dictatorship. In many respects, Hayek was a throwback, romanticizing a lost golden age of idealized unfettered capitalism that arguably never existed for much of the population. But Hayek's views were more nuanced than many American adherents understood. As Angus Burgin describes in *The Great Persuasion*, many reactionary Americans knew only the distorted translation of Hayek's work that had appeared in *Reader's Digest*. The conservative publication omitted Hayek's politically inconvenient support for a minimum standard of living for the poor, environmental and workplace safety regulations, and price controls to prevent monopolies from taking undue profits.

Hayek's ideas arrived in America during the post-Depression years, when conservative businessmen were scrambling to salvage the credibility of the laissez-faire ideology that had been popular before the 1929 market crash. Since then, Keynesian economics had taken its place. Hayek's genius was to recast the discredited ideology in an appealing new way. As Kim Phillips-Fein writes in her book *Invisible Hands: The Making of the Conservative Movement from the New Deal to Reagan*, rather than describing the free market as just an economic model, Hayek touted it as the key to all human freedom. He vilified government as coercive, and glorified capitalists as standard-bearers for liberty. Naturally, his ideas appealed to American businessmen like Charles Koch and the other backers of the Freedom School, whose self-interest Hayek now cast as beneficial to all of society.

Charles's funding of the Freedom School was his first step toward what would become a lifelong, tax-deductible sponsorship of libertarianism in America. His hope was to use his wealth to inject his fringe views into the mainstream by turning the Freedom School into an accredited graduate school and then a four-year undergraduate program specializing in libertarian philosophy, to be called Rampart College. A 1966 brochure features a photograph of LeFevre with Charles, shovel in hand, breaking ground for the new institution. Martin was hired to head Rampart's history department. But, as Ames recounts, the venture soon fell victim to mismanagement, leaving a trail of disgruntled backers. Eventually, the school moved to the South, where for a number of years it was sustained by the anti-union textile tycoon Roger Milliken. By the time LeFevre died in 1986, the Kochs had largely distanced themselves from him, perhaps sensing that he was a political liability. But Charles wrote a warm letter to LeFevre in 1973. He also gave a speech in the 1990s crediting the Freedom School with profoundly influencing him. It was, he said, "where I began developing a passionate commitment to liberty as the form of social organization most in harmony with reality and man's nature, because it's where I was first exposed in-depth to thinkers such as Mises and Hayek." He added, "In short, market principles have changed my life and guide everything I do."

As Charles grew increasingly ideologically driven, his brothers David and Bill, as he had, earned engineering degrees at their father's alma mater, MIT. In contrast, Frederick, who no longer went by the name Freddie, attended Harvard and later, after serving in the U.S. Navy, studied playwriting at the Yale School of Drama. He evinced no interest in joining the family company, preferring to write and produce plays and to collect art, antiques, antiquarian books, and spectacularly lavish historic houses.

The private life of the younger Frederick, who remained single, became the focus of a vicious blackmail attempt by the other brothers, according to a sworn deposition given by Bill Koch in 1982. In his deposition, Bill described an emotionally wrenching confrontation in the mid-1960s in which he, Charles, and David tried to force their older brother Frederick, who they believed was gay, to relinquish his claim to a share of the family company, or else they threatened to expose his private life to their father.

According to Bill's account, the brothers' blackmail scheme began after Charles and a friend talked the manager of the Greenwich Village building in which Frederick lived into letting them into his apartment without his permission when he was not home. Evidently, once inside, they snooped around and discovered personal information that they regarded as compromising. Frederick returned to find the uninvited twosome in his apartment. Soon after, according to Bill's deposition, Charles called his younger brothers to discuss whether Frederick should be allowed to continue as an officer of the family company. Bill admitted in cross-examination that he,

along with his brothers, had regarded the situation as potentially embarrassing to the family enterprise, and so they had
entrusted Charles to work out a plan to confront Frederick.
According to the deposition, Charles then arranged a meeting in Boston of the directors of Koch Engineering, the part
of the enterprise that the four boys had inherited together by
this point and whose board they formed. In reality, as Bill
described it, the meeting was a trap. Instead of addressing
corporate business, it was a kangaroo court aimed at putting
Frederick's personal life on trial. Chairs were arranged so that
Frederick was on one side, facing his three brothers. According
to the deposition, Charles then led an inquisition in which he
accused Frederick of being gay and argued that his behavior
was inappropriate for the family company. If Frederick refused
to turn over his shares to his brothers, he was told, they would
expose him to their father. If their father learned, they warned,
it would likely impair his fragile health and also result in Frederick's disinheritance.

The subject of Frederick's private life had never been openly
discussed in the family. Mary Koch referred to her eldest son,
with whom she was close, as "artistic," and the senior Fred
Koch evidently avoided the subject. One family member says
homosexuality was so taboo in the family during those years,
"it would have meant excommunication."

According to Bill's deposition, Frederick tried to defend
himself in the face of his brothers' accusations, arguing that
he had a right to speak. But Charles cut him off, telling him
to "shut up," insisting that he had no say in the matter. At that
point, Frederick stood up, said he wanted no more of the discussion, and walked out. Bill swore that he had tried to intercede
on Frederick's behalf in the end, feeling bad for him. Because
of this, he claimed, Charles had angrily reprimanded him after
Frederick left, saying the three brothers had to stand together.
Under cross-examination Bill recounted that afterward he had
apologized to Frederick, who had thanked him for trying to

defend him, however belatedly. The subject, though, remained almost too painful to talk about.

The full story of this confrontation never surfaced because Bill's deposition is sealed. But in 1997 *Fortune* carried a fleeting reference to "a homosexual blackmail attempt by Charles against Freddie to get his stock at a cheap price." The magazine noted that Charles "vigorously denied" it. Years later, Frederick also briefly alluded to it, telling the biographer Daniel Schulman that "Charles' 'homosexual blackmail' to get control of my shares did not succeed for the simple reason that I am not homosexual." For reasons that remain disputed, Frederick's inheritance was nonetheless handled differently than that of the other boys. He took more money up front, and was left out of a final distribution.

In the midst of this filial rancor, in 1967, Fred Koch died of a heart attack. Charles, then thirty-two years old, became chairman and CEO of the family business, which the sons renamed Koch Industries, in honor of their father. At the time, the company's principal business was refining oil, operating pipelines, and cattle ranching. Its annual revenues were estimated at $177 million, making it a substantial company but slight in comparison with the behemoth it would become.

Fred Koch's fears of confiscatory taxes turned out to be overblown. When he died, he was described as the wealthiest man in Kansas, and his will made his sons extraordinarily rich. Charles Koch has often lauded the virtuous habits it takes to succeed, publishing a book on the subject in 2007 called *The Science of Success*. He has been less forthcoming about his inheritance. His brother David, in contrast, has made less pretense of being self-made. He joked about his good fortune in a 2003 speech to alumni at Deerfield Academy, the Massachusetts prep school from which he graduated and where, after pledging $25 million, he was made the school's sole "lifetime trustee." He said, "You might ask: How does David Koch happen to have the wealth to be so generous? Well, let me tell you a story. It all started when I was a little boy. One day, my father gave me an apple. I soon sold it for five dollars and bought two apples and sold them for ten. Then I bought four apples and sold them for twenty. Well, this went on day after day, week after week, month after month, year after year, until my father died and left me three hundred million dollars!"

Fred Koch also left his sons the building blocks with which they could construct one of the most lucrative corporate empires in the world. The crown jewel, according to one former Koch Industries insider, was the Pine Bend Refinery, then called the Great Northern Oil Company, in Rosemount, Minnesota, not far from Minneapolis. In 1959, Fred Koch bought a one-third interest in the concern.

In 1969, two years after Charles Koch took the company's helm, Koch Industries acquired the majority share in the refinery. Charles later described the purchase as "one of the most significant events in the evolution of our company."

Pine Bend was a gold mine because it was uniquely well situated geographically to buy inexpensive, heavy, "garbage" crude oil from Canada. After refining the cheap muck, the company could sell it at the same price as other gasoline. Because the heavy crude oil was so cheap, Pine Bend's profit margin was superior to that of most other refineries. And because of a host of environmental regulations, it became increasingly difficult for rivals to build new refineries in the area to compete.

By 2015, Pine Bend was processing some 350,000 barrels of Canadian crude a day, and according to David Sassoon of the Reuters-affiliated *InsideClimate News*, Koch Industries was the world's largest exporter of oil out of Canada. In 2012, he wrote, "This single Koch refinery is now responsible for an estimated 25 percent of the 1.2 million barrels of oil the U.S. imports each day from Canada's tar sands territories." The Kochs' good fortune, however, was the globe's misfortune, because crude oil derived from Canada's dirty tar sands requires far greater amounts of energy to produce and so is especially harmful to the environment.

In 1970, a year after Koch Industries completed the Pine Bend deal, the twins joined their elder brother at Koch Industries, with David working out of New York and Bill near Boston. Charles characteristically assumed control, and it was not long before the long-standing sibling rivalries flared anew. Bill, according to court records, felt slighted and resented Charles's insistence on plowing almost all of the earnings back into the company, skimping on pay for his brothers. "Here I am one of the wealthiest men in America and I had to borrow money to buy a house," he complained. A political independent, Bill also complained that "Charles was giving as much to the Libertarians as he was paying out in dividends. Pretty soon we would get the reputation that the company and the Kochs were crazy."

In 1980, Bill, with assistance from Fred, attempted to wrest control of the company from Charles, who ran it with "an iron hand," according to Bruce Bartlett, a former associate. The attempted coup fizzled when Charles and David caught on and swung the board their way and, in retaliation, fired Bill.

Lawsuits were filed, with Bill and Frederick on one side and Charles and David on the other, re-creating the sibling rivalries of their childhood. In 1983, Charles and David bought out their brothers' shares in the company for about $1.1 billion. The settlement reportedly left Charles and David owning over 80 percent of Koch Industries' stock, evenly split between the two of them. But the fraternal litigation continued for seventeen more years. Among other accusations, Bill and Frederick alleged that Charles and David had cheated them by undervaluing the company. The Pine Bend Refinery in particular became the focus of contention, with Bill and Frederick arguing that Charles and David had hidden its true worth from them—an accusation Charles and David denied. As the acrimony built, the brothers hired rival legal teams and rival private investigators, who reportedly literally rummaged through the family garbage of the opposing brothers.

In 1990, the brothers walked past one another with stony expressions at their mother's funeral. Frederick, however, was absent. A confidant claimed later that Charles, who lived in Wichita, where their mother had died, hadn't given him early enough notice about the funeral arrangements for him to be able to attend. There had been an ice storm in Chicago, which complicated his travel arrangements. In the end, Frederick was only able to arrive in Kansas in time to attend a reception after the service. "He was heartbroken," the confidant said.

Bill, too, nearly missed the funeral. He was given such short notice he had to charter a private plane to make it in time and then was seated not with the immediate family but with cousins. In addition, both he and Frederick believed they were excluded from a private memorial at their father's ranch, arranged and attended by Charles and David.

Then, when Mary Koch's will was opened, it included a provision denying any inheritance from her $10 million estate to any son who was engaged in litigation against any other within six weeks of her death. Frederick and Bill, who were in the midst of suing their other two brothers, suspected their mother, who had suffered from dementia, had been unduly influenced during her fading days into adding this provision to her will. Again they sued, but lost, appealed, and lost again.

Eventually, Frederick, who lived alone, spent much of his life abroad, buying and restoring spectacular historic estates in France, Austria, England, New York, and Pennsylvania and filling them with art, antiques, and literary manuscripts, many of which he donated to museums and rare book libraries. Unlike his brothers, Frederick preferred to keep most of his donations anonymous, explaining to friends that his father had taught them to be modest and that taking credit for charity was vulgar. He refused to speak to Charles for the rest of his life.

Bill founded his own carbon-heavy energy company,

Oxbow, becoming a billionaire in his own right, according to *Forbes*. He lived lavishly, spending an estimated $65 million to win yachting's America's Cup in 1992. Like his brothers, he was a major Republican donor and became embroiled in tumultuous legal fights against environmentalists, opposing a proposed wind farm in the waters off his Cape Cod summer compound, because it would interfere with his view. He, too, barely spoke to Charles for decades but gradually underwent a rapprochement with his twin, David.

With Charles as the undisputed chairman and CEO, Koch Industries expanded rapidly. Roger Altman, who heads the investment-banking firm Evercore, described the company's performance as "beyond phenomenal." He added, "I'd love to know how they do it." Much of the credit went to Charles, who won a reputation as a brilliant, detail-oriented, metrics-driven manager. He was such a tough negotiator, one associate joked, that "in a fifty-fifty deal, he takes the hyphen."

As the company grew, Charles remained in Wichita, working ten-hour days, six days a week. When he proposed to his future wife, Liz, he did so reportedly over the phone, and she could hear him flipping through his busy date book in search of an open day for the wedding. In preparation, he required her to study free-market economics.

David, meanwhile, resided in New York City, where he became an executive vice president of the company and the CEO of its Chemical Technology Group. A financial expert who knows Koch Industries confided, "Charles *is* the company. Charles runs it." David, described by associates as "affable" and "a bit of a lunk," enjoyed for years the life of a wealthy bachelor. He rented a yacht in the South of France and bought a waterfront home in Southampton, where he threw parties that the Web site New York Social Diary likened to an "East Coast version of Hugh Hefner's soirées." David was known for his laugh, which has been described as a "window-shattering honk." To one longtime family insider, however, he often seemed "a bit lost" and "socially awkward. People don't really register with him that much," she said. In 1991, he was badly injured in a plane crash in Los Angeles. He was the sole passenger in first class to survive. As he was recovering, a routine physical exam led to the discovery of prostate cancer. He received treatment and reconsidered his life. He got married, settled down, and started a family. As he told *Upstart Business Journal,* "When you're the only one who survived in the front of the plane and everyone else died—yeah, you think, 'My God, the good Lord spared me for some greater purpose.' My joke is that I've been busy ever since, doing all the good work I can think of, so He can have confidence in me."

When they are not at their vacation houses in Southampton, Palm Beach, and Aspen, he and his wife, Julia Flesher, a former fashion assistant, live in a nine-thousand-square-foot duplex at 740 Park Avenue with their three children. The wealthiest resident of New York, David has become a huge benefactor of the arts and medicine, donating millions of dollars to Lincoln Center, the Metropolitan Museum of Art, and the American Museum of Natural History, among other institutions. But according to *Park Avenue,* a documentary by the Academy Award winner Alex Gibney, he has been less generous with the household help. A former doorman described Koch as "the cheapest person" in the building. "We would load up his trucks—two vans usually—every weekend for the Hamptons. In and out, in and out, heavy bags. We would never get a tip from Mr. Koch. We would never get a smile from Mr. Koch." For Christmas, which the doorman had anticipated would make up for the year's travails, Koch merely gave him a $50 check. When the documentary aired on the Public Broadcasting Service in 2012, David Koch was so incensed he resigned from the board of New York's public television station, WNET, reneging on a promise to make a major donation. A spokeswoman at Koch Industries declined to comment on whether the documentary was his reason for punishing the station, but Koch bluntly told one friend about the film, "It's going to cost them $10 million."

"They live, and always have, in a rarefied bubble," said the longtime family insider, explaining the Kochs' outrage at being subjected to critical scrutiny. "They move in a world with people like them, or who want to be. They know no poor people at all. They're not the kind of people who feel obligated to get to know the help."

As their fortunes grew, Charles and David Koch became the primary underwriters of hard-line libertarian politics in America. Though David's manner is more cosmopolitan, and more sociable, than that of Charles, Doherty, the libertarian chronicler who has interviewed both brothers, couldn't think of a single issue on which the brothers disagreed. Charles's aim, he said, was to tear the government out "at the root."

Having read the family's private letters and conducted interviews with the Kochs and their intimates as few other outsiders could, Clayton Coppin, the researcher hired first by the company and later by Bill Koch, saw Charles Koch's strong political views in the context of his family upbringing. In "Stealth," his unpublished 2003 report on Charles's political development, Coppin suggests that Charles harbored a hatred of the government so intense it could only be truly understood as an extension of his childhood conflicts with authority.

From his earliest years, he writes, Charles's goal was to achieve total control. "He did not escape his father's authority until his father died," he notes. After that, Charles went to great lengths to ensure that neither his brothers nor anyone else could challenge his personal control of the family company. Later clashes with unionized workers at the Pine Bend Refinery and with the expanding regulatory state strengthened his resolve. "Only the governments and the courts remained as sources of authority," Coppin writes, and if enacted, Charles's "libertarian policies would eliminate these."

Had Charles wanted merely to promote free-market economic theories, he could have supported several established organizations, but instead he was attracted to fringe groups that bordered on anarchism. Coppin suggests, "He was driven by some deeper urge to smash the one thing left in the world that could discipline him: the government."

Drawing on a cache of private documents, some of which remain in the possession of Bill Koch, Coppin was able to trace Charles's political evolution as he moved away from the intellectual fringe of his old mentor, LeFevre, in favor of gaining hands-on power. In response to libertarian thinkers who argued that ideas, not practical politics, were the best instruments of change, Charles wrote a revealing 1978 article in the *Libertarian Review,* arguing that outsiders like themselves needed to organize. "Ideas do not spread by themselves; they spread only through people. Which means we need a *movement,*" he wrote. His language was militant, demanding that "our movement must destroy the prevalent statist paradigm."

In Coppin's view, it was already clear by this point, at the end of the 1970s, that Charles "was not going to be satisfied with being the Engels or even the Marx of the libertarian revolution. He wanted to be the Lenin."

Around the same time, an obscure conference subsidized by Charles Koch laid out much of the road map for the Kochs' future attempted takeover of American politics. In 1976, with a contribution of some $65,000 from Charles Koch, the Center for Libertarian Studies in New York City was launched and soon held a conference featuring several leading lights of the libertarian movement. Among those delivering papers on how the fringe movement could obtain genuine power was Charles Koch. The papers are striking in their radicalism, their disdain for the public, and their belief in the necessity of political subterfuge. Speakers proposed that libertarians hide their true antigovernment extremism by banishing the word "anarchism," because it reminded too many people of "terrorists." To attract a bigger following, some suggested, they needed to organize synthetic "grassroots" groups and issue meaningless titles to volunteers, without yielding any real control.

Charles Koch's contribution was a paper that methodically analyzed the strengths and weaknesses of a group he knew intimately, the John Birch Society, as a model for their future enterprise. His assessment was clear-eyed and businesslike. He pointed out that despite the fringe group's shortcomings, it boasted 90,000 members, 240 paid staffers, and a $7 million annual budget. While these numbers were impressive, he faulted the John Birch Society's obsession with conspiracies, as well as the unchecked cult of personality that Welch had built up. He noted that Welch's ownership of the organization's stock had centralized control in his hands, making him impervious to constructive criticism. (Interestingly, Charles would go on to issue stock in his own nonprofit think tank, the Cato Institute, in much the same way.) But he also found much to admire. In particular, he argued in favor of copying the John Birch Society's secrecy.

"In order to avoid undesirable criticism, how the organization is controlled and directed should not be widely advertised," Charles wrote, arguing for stealth in his future plans to influence American politics.

He also wrote that to fund their future political enterprise, they should, like the John Birch Society, make use of "all modern sales and motivational techniques to raise money and attract donors . . . including meeting in a home or other place the prospect enjoys being." The Kochs' donor summits would follow this marketing approach, transforming fund-raising into exclusive, invitation-only social events held in luxurious settings.

Charles cautioned his fellow radicals that to win, they

would need to cultivate credible leaders and a positive image, unlike the John Birch Society, requiring them to "work with, rather than combat, the people in the media and arts." The brothers followed this plan too. David became a lavish supporter of the arts in New York and appeared regularly in the society pages. Charles, meanwhile, kept a lower profile but assiduously invited sympathetic members of the media to his donor summits, such as the talk radio host Glenn Beck, the *Washington Post* columnist Charles Krauthammer, and the *National Review* columnist Ramesh Ponnuru. Two of the top donors in the Koch network owned their own news outlets. The oil tycoon Philip Anschutz owned the *Washington Examiner* and *The Weekly Standard,* and the mutual fund magnate Foster Friess was the largest shareholder of *The Daily Caller.* The Kochs seriously considered buying the Tribune Company in 2013, too.

As for gaining adherents, Charles suggested, their best bet was to focus on "attracting youth" because "this is the only group that is open to a radically different social philosophy." He would act on this belief in years to come by funneling millions of dollars into educational indoctrination, with free-market curricula and even video games promoting his ideology pitched to prospects as young as grade school.

In support of building their own youth movement, another speaker, the libertarian historian Leonard Liggio, cited the success of the Nazi model. In his paper titled "National Socialist Political Strategy: Social Change in a Modern Industrial Society with an Authoritarian Tradition," Liggio, who was affiliated with the Koch-funded Institute for Humane Studies (IHS) from 1974 until 1998, described the Nazis' successful creation of a youth movement as key to their capture of the state. Like the Nazis, he suggested, libertarians should organize university students to create group identity.

George Pearson, a former member of the John Birch Society in Wichita, who served as Charles Koch's political lieuten-

ant during these years, expanded on this strategy in his own
eye-opening paper. He suggested that libertarians needed to
mobilize youthful cadres by influencing academia in new ways.
Traditional gifts to universities, he warned, didn't guarantee
enough ideological control. Instead, he advocated funding
private institutes within prestigious universities, where influence over hiring decisions and other forms of control could be
exerted by donors while hiding the radicalism of their aims.

As Coppin summarized Pearson's arguments, "It would
be necessary to use ambiguous and misleading names, obscure
the true agenda, and conceal the means of control. This is the
method that Charles Koch would soon practice in his charitable giving, and later in his political actions."

So on after the 1976 conference, Charles plunged into Libertarian Party politics. He became not just the group's financial
angel but also the author of its plank on energy policy, which
called for the abolition of all government controls. The brothers took an even more audacious step into electoral politics
in 1979, when Charles, who preferred to operate behind the
scenes, persuaded David, then thirty-nine, to run for public
office. The brothers were by then backing the Libertarian Party's presidential candidate, Ed Clark, who was running against
Ronald Reagan from the right. They opposed all limits on
campaign donations, so they found a legal way around them.
They contrived to make David the vice presidential running
mate, and thus according to campaign-finance law he could
lavish as much of his personal fortune as he wished on the campaign rather than being limited by the $1,000 donation cap.

"David Koch ran in '80 to go against the campaign-
finance rules. By being a candidate, he could give as much as
he wanted," the conservative activist Grover Norquist later
acknowledged. "It was a trick," suggests Bartlett, the economist who formerly worked at a Koch-funded think tank. David

Koch had no political experience and was little known, which initially caused consternation. But at the Libertarian Party convention, when he pledged to spend half a million dollars on his campaign, whoops of joy reportedly rose from stunned party members. The ticket's slogan was "The Libertarian Party has only one source of funds: You." The populist language was misleading. In fact, its primary source of funds was David Koch, who spent more than $2 million on the effort, just short of 60 percent of the campaign's entire budget.

In hindsight, it seems that David Koch's 1980 campaign served as a bridge between LeFevre's radical pedagogy and the Tea Party movement. Indeed the Libertarian Party's standard-bearer that year, Clark, told *The Nation* that libertarians were getting ready to stage "a very big tea party," because people were "sick to death" of taxes. The party's platform, meanwhile, was almost an exact replica of the Freedom School's radical curriculum. It called for the repeal of all campaign-finance laws and the abolition of the Federal Election Commission (FEC). It also favored the abolition of all government health-care programs, including Medicaid and Medicare. It attacked Social Security as "virtually bankrupt" and called for its abolition, too. The Libertarians also opposed all income and corporate taxes, including capital gains taxes, and called for an end to the prosecution of tax evaders. Their platform called for the abolition too of the Securities and Exchange Commission, the Environmental Protection Agency, the FBI, and the CIA, among other government agencies. It demanded the abolition of "any laws" impeding employment—by which it meant minimum wage and child labor laws. And it targeted public schools for abolition too, along with what it termed the "compulsory" education of children. The Libertarians also wanted to get rid of the Food and Drug Administration, the Occupational Safety and Health Administration, seat belt laws, and all forms of welfare for the poor. The platform was, in short, an effort to repeal virtually every major political reform passed during the twentieth century. In the view of the Kochs and other members of the Libertarian Party, government should be reduced to a skeletal function: the protection of individual and property rights.

That November, the Libertarian ticket received only 1 percent of the vote. Its stance against war and the military draft, and in favor of legalizing drugs and prostitution, won it some support among young rebels. But as a market experiment, libertarianism proved a massive flop. The brothers realized that their brand of politics didn't sell at the ballot box. Charles Koch became openly scornful of conventional politics. "It tends to be a nasty, corrupting business," he told a reporter at the time. "I'm interested in advancing libertarian ideas."

According to Doherty's history, the Kochs came to regard elected politicians as merely "actors playing out a script." Instead of wasting more time, a confidant of the Kochs' told Doherty, the brothers now wanted to "supply the themes and words for the scripts." In order to alter the direction of America, they realized they would have to "influence the areas where policy ideas percolate from: academia and think tanks."

After the 1980 election, Charles and David Koch receded from the public arena. "They weren't really on my radar," recalls Richard Viguerie, whose hugely successful right-wing direct-mail company won him the nickname the "Founding Funder of the Right." But during the next three decades, they contributed well over $100 million, much of it undisclosed, to dozens of seemingly independent organizations aimed at advancing their radical ideas. Their front groups demonized the American government, casting it as the enemy rather than the democratic representative of its citizens. They defined liberty as its absence, and the unfettered accumulation of enormous private wealth as America's purpose. Cumulatively, the many-tentacled ideological machine they built came to be known as the Kochtopus.

The Kochs were not alone. As they sought ways to steer

American politics hard to the right without having to win the popular vote, they got valuable reinforcement from a small cadre of like-minded wealthy conservative families who were harnessing their own corporate fortunes toward the same end. Philanthropy, with its guarantees of anonymity, became their chosen instrument. But their goal was patently political: to undo not just Lyndon Johnson's Great Society and Franklin Roosevelt's New Deal but Teddy Roosevelt's Progressive Era, too.

In taking on this daunting task, they were in many cases refighting battles that had been lost by their fathers. Complacent liberals, and many Republicans also, assumed by the 1970s that the political pendulum in America had shifted permanently away from archconservative groups like the John Birch Society. Robust government was almost universally accepted as a necessary instrument for social and economic betterment. Redistributive taxes and spending were largely uncontroversial. Even Richard Nixon had proclaimed in 1971, "I am now a Keynesian in economics."

Not everyone in the Grand Old Party, however, agreed. A small but deep-pocketed reactionary rear guard was already hard at work, devising plans to fight moderation and win the battle for the radical Right in an ingenious new way.

CHAPTER TWO

The Hidden Hand:
Richard Mellon Scaife

FOR MANY YEARS, IN THE FOYER OF RICHARD MELLON SCAIFE'S Pittsburgh mansion stood a prized possession, a brass elephant on a mahogany stand. Visitors could be forgiven for mistaking it for the usual Republican mascot, because Scaife's forebears, who founded the Mellon banking, Alcoa aluminum, and Gulf Oil empire, were a financial mainstay of the Republican Party in Pennsylvania for more than a century. But the elephant in question was instead an homage to Hannibal, the fabled military strategist who daringly scaled the Alps on elephant back to launch a surprise attack on the Roman Empire. It served as the inspiration for a private organization that Scaife founded in 1964. This little-heralded group was just the first small step in what would become an improbably successful effort by one of the richest men in the country, along with a few other extraordinarily wealthy conservative benefactors, to cast themselves as field generals, in Hannibal's mold, in a strategic war of ideas aimed at sacking American politics.

For decades, Scaife was described as a recluse, mysterious even to the recipients of his largesse. Over a fifty-year period, he personally spent what he estimated to be upward of $1 billion from his family fortune on philanthropy, once the sum was adjusted for inflation. Most of it, some $620 million, he reckoned, was aimed at influencing American public affairs. In 1999, *The Washington Post* called him "the leading financial supporter of the movement that reshaped American politics in the last quarter of the 20th century." When he died on July 4, 2014, *The New York Times* carried a lengthy obituary, along with his photograph. Yet he gave almost no interviews or speeches on his motives and aims. He rarely spoke with those who ran the institutions he funded and was estranged from many former friends and family members, including two former wives and his two grown children. When Karen Rothmyer, a reporter for the *Columbia Journalism Review*, tried to ambush him into an interview in 1981, he warned her, "You fucking Communist cunt, get out of here!" In 2009, however, five years before he was diagnosed with inoperable cancer, Scaife penned a previously private, still-unpublished memoir, "A Richly Conservative Life," that serves as a secret tell-all about the building of the modern conservative movement.

In his memoir, Scaife describes how he and a handful of other influential conservatives who shared the view that American civilization faced an existential threat from progressivism began meeting during the Cold War years, at first informally, to plot against the country's liberal drift. At one such session, someone suggested that the threadbare cliché comparing America's ostensible downfall to that of ancient Rome was inadequate. The group decided that a better analogy was to the fall of Carthage, in North Africa. Carthage ostensibly fell when its wealthy elites failed to adequately back their military leader, Hannibal, as he reached the gates of Rome. The passivity of the ruling class allowed the enemy to triumph, burying the noble Carthaginian culture forever. Out of this discussion was born the League to Save Carthage, an informal network of influential, die-hard American conservatives determined, as Scaife writes, "that America must not go the way of Carthage, that we must win the struggles of our time."

In 1964, when this group incorporated itself formally as the Carthage Foundation, many conservatives felt like the remnants of a lost civilization. Their standard-bearer, the Republican presidential nominee, Barry Goldwater, had been badly defeated at the polls. The Democratic victor, Lyndon Johnson, meanwhile, was forging ahead with liberal civil rights legislation and ambitious Great Society antipoverty programs, radically expanding the reach of government and challenging the old order. Liberal dominance over arts and letters was so uniform during these postwar years that the cultural critic Lionel Trilling had declared with self-satisfaction, "Nowadays there are no conservative or reactionary ideas in general circulation." M. Stanton Evans, a leading intellectual on the right, captured conservatives' sense of marginalization in his 1965 book, *The Liberal Establishment: Who Runs America . . . and How*. He declared that "the chief point about the Liberal Establishment is that it is in control." In response, right-wing activists like Evans, who had studied with Ludwig von Mises, militated for a "counter-establishment." Yet they lacked the wherewithal with which to build it.

Stepping into this void and up to this challenge was, as the engraved brass plate beneath his elephant proclaimed, "Field Marshall Richard Mellon Scaife, the Carthaginian hero of the half century, 1950–2000." The plaque praised Scaife's "Audacity, Fidelity and Persistence." Christopher Ruddy, a conservative reporter and publisher who worked closely with Scaife for many years, sharing some of his political adventures, believes that Scaife was the progenitor of a new form of hard-hitting political philanthropy. "He's the originator" of the current model, says Ruddy. "I don't know anyone who did what he did before. He's a bit like Santa Claus."

In his early years, few would have expected Scaife to exert major influence on politics, or much else. Certainly he was born into extraordinary wealth. In 1957, *Fortune* ranked his mother, Sarah Mellon Scaife, and three other members of the Mellon family among the eight wealthiest people in America. But Scaife wasn't notably distinguished in any other way. Until his mid-thirties, he had no real career or accomplishments. Even by his own estimation, his life was dissolute. In his memoir, he writes that one of his favorite authors was John O'Hara because no one has better captured the decadence and the disappointment that were rife in his own upper-crust circle. "How beautifully he summed up Pennsylvanians of a certain class," Scaife writes, "their country club values, the wrecks they made of their lives on too much money and alcohol."

Scaife's great-grandfather Judge Thomas Mellon, the founder of the family fortune, had worried about the corrupting influence that inherited wealth might have on future heirs. The son of an Irish farmer who settled in Pennsylvania during the first half of the nineteenth century, Mellon proved an uncannily good businessman. He leveraged real estate investments into a thriving loan business that became Pittsburgh's stately Mellon Bank. During the Gilded Age, the family acquired huge stakes in a number of burgeoning industrial corporations, including Gulf Oil and Alcoa. Surveying his great fortune, however, in 1885, Mellon fretted that "the normal condition of man is hard work, self-denial, acquisition and accumulation; as soon as his descendants are freed from the necessity of exertion they begin to degenerate sooner or later in body and mind."

By the time his great-grandson Richard Mellon Scaife was born in Pittsburgh in 1932, some of the patriarch's darkest fears had been realized. Sarah Mellon Scaife, the mother of the boy who was known to his family as Dickie, by all accounts struggled to fight a losing battle with alcoholism. She was "a gutter drunk," according to her daughter, the late Cordelia Scaife May. "So was Dick," Cordelia said of her brother. "So was I."

If they were born with silver spoons, they were also born with chips on their shoulders. In his memoir, Scaife describes himself as fundamentally "anti-establishment," which may seem puzzling given his heritage, but his place within the Mellon dynasty was tinged with resentment. His mother had married a handsome and well-connected local patrician, Alan Scaife, who rode well to the hounds and had attended all the most elite schools but whose forebears had run the family metalworking company into the ground. As a result, Richard

Scaife's uncle R. K. Mellon, who like his mother had inherited a large part of the vast Mellon fortune, treated the Scaife family with scorn. "My father—he was suckin' hind tit," Scaife told Burton Hersh, who wrote a biography of the family in 1978. In his memoir, Scaife writes that his uncle, who was his closest Mellon relative and whom he and his sister dubbed Uncle Piggy, "treated my father like an errand-boy." Alan Scaife was given ceremonial titles in the various Mellon business concerns but no real power, other than to oversee his wife's enormous inheritance.

Alan Scaife briefly cut a dashing figure during World War II, when he enlisted in the Office of Strategic Services (OSS), the forerunner of the Central Intelligence Agency (CIA), as an army major. But while his tailor-made uniforms made a memorable impression, this was less true of his job performance. Richard Helms, who later became director of the CIA, recalled Scaife, who had been a colleague, as "a lightweight."

The family brush with the spy service, however, ignited Richard Scaife's lifelong infatuation with intelligence intrigue, conspiracy theories, and international affairs. Scaife writes that it also gave rise to his strongly anti-Communist views. In his memoir, he recalls his father admonishing the family while on furlough from the war that the scourge of Communism loomed large, not just abroad, but at home in America. "My political conservatism which eventually unmasked me as the villain behind the 'vast right-wing conspiracy' of Hillary Clinton's imagination—but only her imagination," he writes, began "before I had reached my twelfth birthday" over a lunch with his father at New York's Colony Club in 1944. Alan Scaife warned the family that wealthy capitalists like themselves were under attack. He invoked images of labor riots and class warfare. "He was concerned for the security of the country and gave us the feeling around the table that our entire future was at stake," Scaife writes. A local newspaper editor, William

Block of the *Pittsburgh Post-Gazette*, had similar recollections. He remembered Alan Scaife as overwrought during the 1940s about what he regarded as the growing threat that leftists posed to the rich. "Alan Scaife was terribly worried about inherited wealth," he later recalled.

The family's preoccupation with preserving its wealth was shared by previous generations. Scaife was heir not just to one of the country's greatest industrial fortunes but also to a distinctly reactionary political outlook rooted in the age of the robber barons. His great-uncle the Pittsburgh banker Andrew Mellon, who served as Treasury secretary under Presidents Warren Harding, Calvin Coolidge, and Herbert Hoover, was a leading figure in the counterrevolution against the Progressive movement, and in particular he was an implacable foe of the income tax.

Before Congress instituted the federal income tax in 1913, following the passage of the Sixteenth Amendment to the Constitution, America's tax burden fell disproportionately on the poor. High taxes were levied on widely consumed products such as alcohol and tobacco. Urban property was taxed at a higher rate than farms and estates. "From top to bottom, American society before the income tax was a picture of inequality, and taxes made it worse," writes Isaac William Martin, a professor of sociology at the University of California in San Diego.

In his history, *Rich People's Movements: Grassroots Campaigns to Untax the One Percent*, Martin notes that the passage of the income tax in 1913 was regarded as calamitous by many wealthy citizens, setting off a century-long tug-of-war in which they fought repeatedly to repeal or roll back progressive forms of taxation. Over the next century, wealthy conservatives developed many sophisticated and appealing ways to wrap their antitax views in public-spirited rationales. As they waged this battle, they rarely mentioned self-interest, but they consistently opposed high taxes that fell most heavily on themselves. And no figure was more instrumental in leading the early opposition than Andrew Mellon.

When Congress instituted the federal income tax, Mellon was one of the wealthiest men in America, with interests in dozens of monopolistic conglomerates then called "trusts." His Union Trust bank reportedly financed almost half the investments in Pittsburgh. In his view, the economic inequality that such arrangements produced was not only inevitable; it was the just reward for excellence and virtue. In an effort to win popular support for this outlook, he wrote a mass-market book called *Taxation: The People's Business,* in which he argued counterintuitively that cutting taxes on the rich would boost tax payments, not lower them, and so was a matter of broad public interest, not narrow private gain. Sixty years later, Jude Wanniski, the father of "supply-side economics," would pay homage to Mellon as his inspiration. At the time, though, Mellon's antitax book sold poorly, despite bulk purchases by business leaders.

Once in public office, Mellon helped define the 1920s as an era during which business succeeded in rolling back many of the Progressive Era's reforms. In 1921, capital gains taxes were cut, and the stock market boomed. After repeated efforts during his dozen-year tenure at Treasury, in 1926 Mellon finally succeeded in getting a bill passed that "cut the tax rates on the richest Americans more deeply than any other tax law in history," according to Martin. Mellon promised greater growth and prosperity. When instead the stock market crashed in 1929 after a frenzy of speculation, his legacy was tarnished. Not only did his economic theories look self-serving and irresponsible, but it surfaced that Mellon himself had been secretly providing tax credits and subsidies to some of the country's biggest businesses, including many in which the Mellon family had major investments. Eventually, Mellon was charged and acquitted of income tax fraud. He was required, though, to pay back taxes, which was a humiliation and indignity for the patrician family.

Three years after the 1929 stock market crash, against this backdrop of class conflict and financial chicanery, Richard Mellon Scaife was born. His family, and later he himself, would continue to portray their embrace of low taxes and limited government as matters of high principle, as Andrew Mellon had. But his parents' elaborate estate planning in order to minimize their own tax bills suggests that they had more than an abstract interest in the subject.

Scaife's parents created the largest of the family's tax-exempt, charitable foundations, the Sarah Scaife Foundation, in December 1941, days after the Japanese attack on Pearl Harbor. It appears to have been timed to shelter the family's wealth from anticipated tax increases. Scaife writes, "I don't know what my parents' specific motives were," but he notes that because of the impending war "there was talk . . . of a top income tax rate of above 90 percent." Roosevelt and the labor unions argued that the wealthy should shoulder a greater share of the cost of the war buildup, to provide an "equality of sacrifice." Despite their hawkish views on national defense, the family nonetheless took steps to avoid paying its share for the military buildup. As Scaife writes matter-of-factly in his memoir, "The rich inevitably are going to organize their wealth to avoid government confiscation. They'll do whatever the law allows to use their money as they see fit, out of reach of the tax collector."

Meanwhile, the Scaifes lived large. They commissioned a hulking Cotswold-style stone country house on 725 acres in Ligonier, Pennsylvania, next to Rolling Rock Farms, the Mellon family's 9,000-acre ancestral estate. They called their place Penguin Court, for the pet penguins that Sarah Scaife found amusing to let waddle the grounds. (Rookeries were built in the shape of igloos and filled daily with slabs of ice.) The weekend house was so vast that by Scaife's reckoning he had four rooms to himself as a boy. Rather than counting sheep, like less well-off insomniacs, he writes, "When I can't sleep, I try to recount the rooms, which numbered fifty or sixty."

The lavish lifestyle didn't protect Scaife, however, from suffering a terrible head injury in a riding accident at the age of nine. The fall fractured his skull, knocking him unconscious for eight to ten hours and requiring metal clips to be implanted in his head. As a result, he had to be tutored at home for more than a year and avoid vigorous athletics all his life. The injury also barred him from military service. But as he lay at home in his sickbed, he followed current events closely, mapping the troop movements during World War II and developing a life-long passion for newspapers, which he read avidly as a boy and later would own.

The family's insulation from workaday life also couldn't protect the Scaife children from being jeered during the Depression and war years by passersby who catcalled at the sight of them being chauffeured, by themselves in the backs of limousines, as gas was rationed for others. Scaife recalls that by the time he was about ten, he realized that "compared to most people, the Scaifes were different. We were very wealthy." He says that in his youth he feared people would dislike him because of it. But he writes that unlike most liberals, as he grew older, he came to feel entitled to his good fortune. "Some of my friends—most I'd say—feel a sense of guilt about having money. I do not, and never have." As he describes it, "An inheritance comes to the person but also to his community and country. It can do powerful good." He notes, "I've felt good about being able to put dollars to work in the battle of ideas."

Scaife recalled his childhood as happy. He liked the governess who raised him, admired his father, and adored his mother. But his sister, Cordelia, who was four years older, saw their upbringing differently. She described the family as excelling principally in "making each other totally miserable." The only substance that appears to have been in nearly as great supply as money in the Scaife household was alcohol. By the time he was sent off to Deerfield Academy at the age of fourteen (the same prep school attended eight years later by David Koch), Scaife was already a drinker. Caught drinking off campus with some local girls in his senior year, in violation of Deerfield's rules, he almost didn't graduate. Scaife recalls that his parents hastily donated funds for a new dormitory for the school in order to assure his diploma. Years later, he would nonetheless help fund the social critic Charles Murray, a leading proponent of the theory that a superior work ethic and moral codes account for much of the success among the affluent.

Despite having barely squeaked through prep school, Scaife was accepted at his father's college, Yale, from which he was soon expelled following several drunken benders. A reputation as a frat boy bully was cemented by an episode in which an empty beer keg was rolled down a flight of stairs, injuring a classmate. (Scaife writes that he was falsely accused of launching the keg, which was actually jettisoned by his friends.) After getting arrested off campus in another drunken escapade, he belittled the dean who was adjudicating his case, hastening his expulsion. Nonetheless, the following year, Scaife was given the chance to repeat his freshman year at Yale. But after spending time at the movies rather than in class, he soon flunked out, this time for good. Yet with the help of his father, who was chairman of the board, he graduated from the University of Pittsburgh and soon went on to enter the family business, Gulf Oil.

His behavior, however, didn't much improve. At the age of twenty-three, after drinking and in a hurry to visit his fiancée, Frances Gilmore, on a rainy night, he caused a near-fatal car accident that left him with a shattered knee and an expensive legal settlement with the family whose car he had rear-ended. Alcoholism and freakish tragedy continued to dog his adult life. One friend committed suicide in front of him. Another, his sister's husband, died of a gunshot wound under mysterious circumstances. His brother-in-law's death was ruled an accident or suicide but caused a scandal and a lasting rift between the siblings because Cordelia suspected that somehow her brother had been involved. In 2005, facing fatal illness, Cordelia, too, took her own life, asphyxiating herself with a plastic bag. She left an estate valued at $825 million.

Before these later tragedies unfolded, though, in 1958, Scaife's father died suddenly. Scaife was only twenty-six. He recalled that it "was a watershed year for me." His father bequeathed him the failing family metal company, which he soon sold for a dollar, and a powerless seat on the Mellon Bank board, which his disdainful uncle chaired. More important, Scaife was put in charge of his mother's finances, giving him responsibility for investing hundreds of millions of dollars. "The first priority had to be to look after Mother's affairs, as Dad had done," he writes. "At the age of fifty-four Sarah Scaife was a woman of wealth, but no experience managing it . . . so an unavoidable role for me became simply that of investor. Just taking care of it all."

Soon after his father died, his mother set up two charitable trusts of $50 million each. The beneficiaries were Scaife and his sister. Like the Koch family, the Scaifes designed the trusts so that all net income had to be donated to nonprofit charities for the next twenty years. After that, the $50 million principal could pass to each of the Scaife offspring free from inheritance taxes. In other words, two decades of philanthropy was the price for a tax-free inheritance. As Scaife wrote of the setup, "Isn't it grand how tax law gets written?"

Scaife notes that his mother thought it a good deal because in 1961 she created a second pair of similar trusts for her children, this time with $25 million for each beneficiary. This time the terms of the trust required Scaife and his sister to donate the net interest to charity over just ten years. And in 1963, his mother set aside another $100 million more in trusts, this time for her grandchildren, called the Sarah Scaife Grandchildren's

Trust. The net interest, again, had to be donated, this time over twenty-one years. Because Cordelia had no children, control of the entire $100 million in the Grandchildren's Trust reverted to Scaife, who by then had a small son and a daughter. So for the next twenty-one years, until 1984, he thus directed virtually all of the charitable donations stemming from the interest on all three trusts, which cumulatively held assets of $250 million. Both the assets and the amount of annual interest they spun off were remarkably large sums in those years.

Scaife, in his memoir, describes the method by which his mother was able to pass on her fortune to him tax-free as "a socially useful tax shelter." He writes, "It enabled a donor to set aside a lump sum for heirs free of inheritance tax or gift tax, but only after an interval of public benefit. To me, that's a good deal for both sides."

A consequence, however, was that the tax code turned many extraordinarily wealthy families, intent upon preserving their fortunes, into major forces in America's civic sector. In order to shelter themselves from taxes, they were required to invent a public philanthropic role. In the instance of both the Kochs and the Scaifes, the tax law ended up spurring the funding of the modern conservative movement.

Motivated in part by tax concerns, Scaife's role as a philanthropist grew. An immediate question, however, was how to disperse the constantly accumulating piles of interest from the trusts, which needed to be distributed to charity in order to satisfy the tax laws. One attractive solution for enormously wealthy families like the Scaifes and the Kochs was to donate to their own private philanthropic foundations. By doing so, they could get the tax deductions and still keep control of how the charitable funds were spent.

Private foundations have very few legal restrictions. They are required to donate at least 5 percent of their assets every year to public charities—referred to as "nonprofit" organizations. In exchange, the donors are granted deductions, enabling them to reduce their income taxes dramatically. This arrangement enables the wealthy to simultaneously receive generous tax subsidies and use their foundations to impact society as they please. In addition, the process often confers an aura of generosity and public-spiritedness on the donors, acting as a salve against class resentment.

Because of all these advantages, private philanthropic foundations proliferated among the ultra-wealthy during the last century. Today, they are commonplace, and rarely controversial, but Americans across the political spectrum once regarded the whole idea of private foundations with enormous suspicion. These aggregations of private wealth, intruding into the public arena, were seen as a form of unelected and unaccountable plutocratic power.

The practice began in the Gilded Age with John D. Rockefeller, whose philanthropic adviser Rev. Frederick Gates warned him with alarm, "Your fortune is rolling up, rolling up like an avalanche! You must keep up with it! You must distribute it faster than it grows!" In response, in 1909 Rockefeller sought legal permission from Congress to obtain a federal charter to set up a general-purpose private foundation whose broad mission was to prevent and relieve suffering and promote knowledge and progress. Critics, including the former president Theodore Roosevelt, assailed the idea, declaring, "No amount of charity in spending such fortunes can compensate in any way for the misconduct in acquiring them." At the time, a parade of notable Americans testified in Congress against the creation of private foundations, including the Reverend John Haynes Holmes, who denounced them as "repugnant to the whole idea of a democratic society." Frank Walsh, chairman of the U.S. Commission on Industrial Relations, in 1915, suggested that "huge philanthropic trusts, known as foundations, appear to be a menace to the welfare of society." Rob

Reich, a professor of political science at Stanford University and co-director of the Stanford Center for Philanthropy and Civil Society, explains that private foundations, which "represent virtually by definition plutocratic voices," were "troubling because they were considered deeply and fundamentally anti-democratic . . . an entity that would undermine political equality, affect public policies, and could exist in perpetuity."

Unable to gain congressional approval, Rockefeller got the New York state legislature to approve his plan. Legally, however, the Rockefeller Foundation, the granddaddy of all private foundations, was at first limited to promoting only education, science, and religion. Over time, however, the number of private foundations grew along with the kaleidoscope of issues into which they delved. By 1930, there were approximately two hundred private foundations, according to Reich. By 1950, the number had grown to two thousand, and by 1985 there were thirty thousand. In 2013, there were over a hundred thousand private foundations in the United States with assets of over $800 billion. These peculiarly American organizations, run with little transparency or accountability to either voters or consumers yet publicly subsidized by tax breaks, have grown into 800-billion-pound Goliaths in the public policy realm. Richard Posner, the iconoclastic libertarian legal scholar, has called perpetual charitable foundations a "completely irresponsible institution, answerable to nobody," and suggested that "the puzzle in economics is why these foundations are not total scandals."

When the robber barons first began donating to charities, their gifts were not tax deductible. With the implementation of the federal income tax in 1913, however, the wealthy soon convinced Congress that unless they were granted a special tax break, philanthropists might no longer donate their fortunes for public purposes. So in 1917 donors were granted unlimited charitable deductions. The rationale was that despite their wealth they deserved the public subsidy, so long as their gifts profited the public, rather than their own private interests. Conservatives who opposed the use of the tax code for all kinds of other social engineering nonetheless fully embraced the loophole in this instance.

Scaife had already set up his own small foundation by the time his father died in 1958. A family lawyer had explained to him when he turned twenty-one and received the first "booster shot," as he put it, of his inheritance that charitable foundations provided good tax shelters. Called the Allegheny Foundation, his early foundation was focused on local community improvement projects. In 1964, he added the Carthage Foundation, named for his political club. It focused on national security issues at first.

After his mother died in 1965, he and his sister shared control of the much larger Sarah Scaife Foundation. But their different priorities soon created irreconcilable fights. Before long, the siblings were at such odds they ceased speaking to each other for most of the rest of their lives. Cordelia Scaife's priorities, like their mother's, were art, conservation, education, science, and population control (Sarah Scaife had been a friend of Margaret Sanger's and was a staunch supporter of Planned Parenthood). Scaife too was a supporter of Planned Parenthood over the years, but his interests tilted more toward what he terms in his memoir "public affairs." By 1973, he had succeeded in reorienting the Sarah Scaife Foundation's grant making almost entirely to his own causes. "The result," he writes, "was very considerable grant-making power," enabling him to "advance ideas that I believe are good for America." Spurred by tax avoidance, Scaife became not only one of the country's richest citizens but also one of its biggest philanthropists. "This was the beginning of the legend of Richard Mellon Scaife as the dark spirit behind right-wing causes," he writes archly in his memoir.

The looming question, though, was how all this money could best be spent. Scaife, who was an early admirer of William F. Buckley Jr.'s, came into his full inheritance just as intellectuals on the right were incubating the idea that they needed to build their own establishment to counter that of the liberals. A leading voice of this cause was a member of Scaife's League to Save Carthage—Lewis Powell, the future Supreme Court justice who was then an eminent corporate lawyer from Richmond, Virginia. And at just that moment, Powell was in search of deep-pocketed donors to bankroll the project.

Powell was the author of a brilliant battle plan detailing how conservative business interests could reclaim American politics. In the spirit of Hannibal, it called for a devastating surprise attack on the bloated and self-satisfied establishment, which regarded itself as nonpartisan but which the conservatives regarded as liberal. Carrying out this attack would be an alternative opinion elite that would look like the existing one, except that it would be privately funded by avowedly partisan donors intent on implementing a pro-business—and, critics would say, self-serving—political agenda.

Powell's ties to corporate conservatives were manifold. In addition to a thriving corporate law practice, he held seats on the boards of over a dozen of the largest companies in the country, including the cigarette maker Philip Morris. So in the spring of 1971, Powell, who was then sixty-three, had watched with growing agitation as student radicals, antiwar demonstrators, black power militants, and much of the liberal intellectual elite turned against what they saw as the depravity of corporate America. Powell believed American capitalism was facing a crisis. All summer long, he clipped magazine and newspaper articles documenting the political threat. He was particularly preoccupied with Ralph Nader, the young Harvard Law School graduate whom Daniel Patrick Moynihan, then assistant secretary of labor, had hired to investigate auto safety hazards. Nader's 1965 exposé on General Motors, *Unsafe at Any Speed,* accused the auto industry of putting profits ahead of safety, triggering the American consumer movement and undermining Americans' faith in business. Powell was a personal friend of General Motors' corporate counsel and regarded this and other anticorporate developments with almost apocalyptic alarm.

That summer, two months before Powell was nominated by Richard Nixon to the Supreme Court, his neighbor Eugene Sydnor Jr., a close friend and director of the U.S. Chamber of Commerce, who shared Powell's political upset, commissioned Powell to write a special memorandum for the business league. In August, Powell delivered a seething memo that was nothing less than a counterrevolutionary call to arms for corporate America, warning the business community that its very survival was at stake if it didn't get politically organized and fight back. The five-thousand-word memo was marked "confidential" and titled "Attack on American Free Enterprise System." A virtual anti–*Communist Manifesto,* it laid out a blueprint for a conservative takeover. As Kim Phillips-Fein describes it in her history, *Invisible Hands,* Powell's memo transformed corporate America into a "vanguard."

Also heeding the battle cry were the heirs to some of America's greatest corporate fortunes, including Scaife, who were poised to enlist their private foundations as the conservative movement's banks. Foundations had several advantages for both the donors and the recipients of this largesse. Unlike most businesses, few people controlled them, so they could move quickly on controversial projects. And they provided the donors with tax breaks while conferring the aura of a high-minded cause. Reflecting on this period, James Piereson, a scholar at the Manhattan Institute who became a crucial figure in several conservative foundations, said, "We didn't have anything when we started in the late 1970s. We had no institutions at all in the mainstream of American political life." He debunked what he called the liberal misconception that corporations directly funded most of the far-right movement, arguing, "What we did was way too controversial for corporations." Instead, he said, in the beginning "there were only a small number of foundations," including the Earhart Foundation, based on an oil fortune, the Smith Richardson Foundation, derived from the cough and cold medicine dynasty, and, most importantly, the various Scaife family foundations.

The late 1960s and the early 1970s were in fact a daunting time for corporate America and for those living off great corporate fortunes. The business community was reeling from the birth of the environmental and consumer movements, which spawned a host of tough new government regulations. Following the 1962 publication of Rachel Carson's *Silent Spring*, exposing the devastating environmental fallout from irresponsible chemical practices, Congress passed the Clean Air Act, the Clean Water Act, the Toxic Substances Control Act, and other laws creating the modern regulatory state. In 1970, with strong bipartisan support, President Nixon signed legislation creating both the Environmental Protection Agency and the Occupational Safety and Health Administration, giving the government new powers with which to police business. The standards decreed by the Clean Air Act were notably tough. In developing regulations, the EPA was directed to weigh only one concern—public health. Costs to industry were explicitly deemed irrelevant. Meanwhile, as opposition grew to the Vietnam War, protesters turned angrily against companies they accused of fueling the conflict, such as Dow Chemical, the producer of napalm, which became the target of more than two hundred demonstrations in the 1970s. New Left leaders, like Staughton Lynd, urged the antiwar movement not to waste time on Washington but instead, as he wrote in 1969, to "lay siege to corporations." Polls showed that Americans' respect for business was plummeting.

As scientists linked smoking to cancer, the tobacco industry was under particularly pointed attack, which might have heightened Powell's alarmism. As a director at Philip Morris from 1964 until he joined the Supreme Court, Powell was an unabashed defender of tobacco, signing off on a series of annual reports lashing out at critics. The company's 1967 annual report, for instance, declared, "We deplore the lack of objectivity in so important a controversy . . . Unfortunately the positive benefits of smoking which are so widely acknowledged are largely ignored by many reports linking cigarettes and health, and little attention is paid to the scientific reports which are favorable to smoking." Powell took umbrage at the refusal by the Federal Communications Commission to grant the tobacco companies "equal time" to respond to their critics on television and argued that the companies' First Amendment rights were being infringed. Powell's legal argument failed in the courts, increasing his sense of corporate embattlement. Jeffrey Clements, in *Corporations Are Not People*, suggests Powell's defense of the tobacco companies was a harbinger of the corporate rights movement and a big part of what led him to push in his memo for conservatives to empower more pro-business courts.

Exacerbating corporate America's woes, the economy was buckling from "stagflation," the unusual combination of high inflation and high unemployment. There were oil shocks and gas lines as well. And after generations of redistributive progressive income and inheritance taxes, the economic elite was losing its lead. Income in America during the mid-1970s was as equally distributed as at any time in the country's history.

"No thoughtful person can question that the American economic system is under broad attack," Powell declared in his memo. What distinguished his jeremiad from many other conservative screeds was his argument that the greatest threat was posed not by a few "extremists of the left," but rather by "perfectly respectable elements of society." The real enemies, he suggested, were "the college campus, the pulpit, the media, the intellectual and literary journals, the arts and sciences," and "politicians."

Powell called on corporate America to fight back. He urged America's capitalists to wage "guerilla warfare" against those seeking to "insidiously" undermine them. Conservatives must capture public opinion, he argued, by exerting influence over the institutions that shape it, which he identified as academia, the media, the churches, and the courts. He argued that conservatives should control the political debate at its source by demanding "balance" in textbooks, television shows, and news coverage. Donors, he argued, should demand a say in university hiring and curriculum and "press vigorously in all political arenas." The key to victory, he predicted, was "careful long-range planning and implementation," backed by a "scale of financing available only through joint effort."

Powell was not alone. A number of activists on the right issued similar calls to arms, including Irving Kristol, the godfather of neoconservatism. A former Trotskyite, Kristol had become a columnist on the conservative editorial page of *The Wall Street Journal,* where he counseled business leaders to be more wily about public relations, arguing that they needed to downplay their "single-minded pursuit of self-interest" and instead tout moral values like family and faith. The Nixon White House aide Patrick Buchanan similarly argued in 1973 that in order to become a permanent political majority, conservatives needed to persuade corporate America and pro-Republican foundations to fund a think tank that would act as a "tax-exempt refuge," a "talent bank," and a "communications center." But it was Powell's memo that electrified the Right, prompting a new breed of wealthy ultraconservatives to weaponize their philanthropic giving in order to fight a multifront war of influence over American political thought.

———

During this period, Scaife, like many conservatives, was growing disillusioned with more conventional political spending. Goldwater's defeat was a huge personal disappointment. Afterward, Scaife got involved in one more campaign in a big way, donating almost $1 million in $3,000 checks to 330 different front groups associated with Nixon's 1972 reelection campaign. The small increments of cash were designed to evade federal contribution limits.

But when Nixon was implicated in the Watergate scandal, Scaife turned against him and against the idea of funding candidates. Scaife, who by then had bought a local newspaper, the *Tribune-Review*, in Greensburg, outside Pittsburgh, published a scalding editorial demanding Nixon's impeachment in 1974. Soon after, he refused to even take the president's phone calls. "He was never a big candidate person since," says Christopher Ruddy.

Frustrated by the electoral process, Scaife, like Charles and David Koch, sought to finance political victory through more indirect means. Though he continued to donate money to political campaigns and action committees, he began to invest far more in conservative institutions and ideas. His private foundations emerged as a leading source of funds for political and policy entrepreneurship. Think tanks, in particular, became what Pierson called "the artillery" in the conservative movement's war of ideas. In his memoir, Scaife estimates that he helped bankroll at least 133 of the conservative movement's 300 most important institutions.

In 1975, the Scaife Family Charitable Trust donated $195,000 to a new conservative think tank in Washington, the Heritage Foundation. For the next ten years, Scaife became its largest backer, donating $10 million more. By 1998, these donations had reached a total of some $23 million, which meant that Scaife accounted for a vastly disproportionate share of the think tank's overall funding. Previously, Scaife had been the largest donor to the American Enterprise Institute (AEI), the older, rival conservative think tank in Washington, but Heritage had a new model that won him over. In contrast to the research centers of the past, it was purposefully political, priding itself on creating, selling, and injecting deeply conservative ideas into the American mainstream.

In fact, the Heritage Foundation was born out of two congressional aides' frustration with the more conventional think tank model. One of them, Edwin Feulner Jr., was a Wharton School graduate and Hayek acolyte, with a flair for fund-raising. The other, Paul Weyrich, was a brilliant and fiercely conservative working-class Catholic press aide from Wisconsin, who described himself openly as a "radical" who was "working to overturn the present power structure." The duo had become exasperated by AEI's refusal to weigh in on legislative fights until after they were settled, a cautious approach reflecting the older think tank's fear of losing its nonprofit status. Instead, they wanted to create a new sort of action-oriented think tank that would actively lobby members of Congress before decisions were made, take sides in fights, and in every way not just "think" but "do."

Lewis Powell's memo awoke the financial angels their project needed. The first of these was Joseph Coors, a scion of the archconservative Colorado-based Coors brewery family. After reading Powell's memo, he was so "stirred" up he sent a letter to his senator the Colorado Republican Gordon Allott, offering "to invest in conservative causes." Weyrich, who worked for Allott, saw Coors's letter and pounced. He urged the magnate, who seemed to be offering unlimited funds with no strings attached, to come to Washington immediately. "I do believe I've never met a man as politically naive as Joe Coors," he reportedly said with a chuckle afterward. But Coors was enthralled. Weyrich had talked of being "engaged in a war to preserve the freedom this country was built on. Think of what we need as combat intelligence," he told Coors.

Coors immediately enlisted. Like the Kochs and Scaife, he and his brothers had inherited a lucrative private family business along with their parents' reactionary views. A supporter of the John Birch Society, Joe Coors regarded organized labor, the civil rights movement, federal social programs, and the counterculture of the 1960s as existential threats to the way of life that had enabled him and his forebears to succeed. The Coors Brewing Company, founded in 1873 by Adolph Coors, a Prussian immigrant, was famously hostile to unions and had repeated run-ins with the Colorado Civil Rights Commission, which accused the company of discriminating against minority employees. Convinced that radical leftists had overrun the country, Joe Coors, the youngest grandson of the founder, became the center of controversy when as a regent at the University of Colorado he had tried to bar left-wing speakers, faculty, and students on campus. His attempt to require faculty to take a pro-American loyalty oath was defeated by the other regents. Enraged that his own son had become a hippie at the school, he railed during a commencement address against "pleasure-minded parasites . . . living off the state dole." By the time he connected with Weyrich, he already believed that the Right needed new and more militant national institutions of the kind Weyrich described.

Before long, Coors became the first donor to the fledgling conservative think tank that Weyrich and Feulner were launching, the forerunner of the Heritage Foundation, then called the Analysis and Research Association. On top of his initial contribution of $250,000, Coors promised $300,000 more for a headquarters building. Soon he was reveling in his new status as a national figure and jetting back and forth from Golden, Colorado, to Washington. Backed by the first of many multimillionaire political ideologues, the Heritage Foundation opened for business in 1973.

Scaife's money soon followed, on an even bigger scale. A popular saying at the time was "Coors gives six-packs; Scaife gives cases."

Independent research institutes had existed since at least the turn of the century in the United States, but as John Judis writes in *The Paradox of American Democracy,* 'the earlier think tanks strove to promote the general public interest, not narrow private or partisan ones. In the tradition of the Progressive movement, they professed to be driven by social science, not ideology. Among the best known was the Brookings Institution, founded in 1916 by the St. Louis businessman Robert Brookings, who defined its mission as "free from any political or pecuniary interest." To assure an ethic of "disinterestedness," Brookings, who was himself a Republican, mandated that scholars of many viewpoints populate its board.

The same ideals animated the Rockefeller, Ford, and Russell Sage Foundations, as well as most of academia and the elite news organizations of the era, like *The New York Times,* which strove to deliver the facts free from partisan bias. Because the self-perception of these institutions was that they were engaged in a modern, even scientific pursuit of the truth, they did not regard themselves as liberal, although frequently the answers they brought to social problems involved government solutions.

In the 1970s, with funding from a handful of hugely wealthy donors like Scaife, as well as some major corporate support, a whole new form of "think tank" emerged that was more engaged in selling predetermined ideology to politicians and the public than undertaking scholarly research. Eric Wanner, the former president of the Russell Sage Foundation, summed it up, saying, "The AEIs and the Heritages of the world represent the inversion of the progressive faith that social science should shape social policy."

According to one account, it was Hayek who spawned

the idea of the think tank as disguised political weapon. As Adam Curtis, a documentary filmmaker with the BBC, tells the story, around 1950, after reading the *Reader's Digest* version of Hayek's *Road to Serfdom,* an eccentric British libertarian named Antony Fisher, an Eton and Cambridge graduate who believed socialism and Communism were overtaking the democratic West, sought Hayek's advice about what could be done. Should he run for office? Hayek, who was then teaching at the London School of Economics, told him that for people of their beliefs getting into politics was futile. Politicians were prisoners of conventional wisdom, in Hayek's view. They would have to change how politicians thought if they wanted to implement what were then considered outlandish free-market ideas. To do that would require an ambitious and somewhat disingenuous public relations campaign. The best way to do this, Hayek told Fisher, who took notes, was to start "a scholarly institute" that would wage a "battle of ideas." If Fisher succeeded, Hayek told him, he would change the course of history.

To succeed, however, required some deception about the think tank's true aims. Fisher's partner in the venture, Oliver Smedley, wrote to Fisher saying that they needed to be "cagey" and disguise their organization as neutral and nonpartisan. Choosing a suitably anodyne name, they founded the grandfather of libertarian think tanks in London, calling it the Institute of Economic Affairs. Smedley wrote that it was "imperative that we should give no indication in our literature that we are working to educate the public along certain lines which might be interpreted as having a political bias. In other words, if we said openly that we were re-teaching the economics of the free market, it might enable our enemies to question the charitableness of our motives."

Fisher would go on to found another 150 or so free-market think tanks around the world, including the Manhattan Institute in New York, to which both Scaife and other conservative philanthropists would become major contributors. The Sarah

Scaife Foundation in fact for many years was the Manhattan Institute's single largest contributor. The donations paid off, from Scaife's viewpoint, when they helped launch the careers of the conservative social critic Murray and the supply-side economics guru George Gilder, whose arguments against welfare programs and taxes had huge impacts on ordinary Americans.

Fisher's early collaborator in founding the Manhattan Institute was William Casey, the Wall Street financier and future director of the CIA. The early think tank was not a spy operation, but it was funded by wealthy men who had no objections to using pretexts and disinformation in the service of what they regarded as a noble cause. In fact, Scaife during this period was simultaneously funding a CIA front group. In his memoir, he acknowledges that in the early 1970s he owned a London-based news organization called Forum World Features that was in reality a CIA-run propaganda operation. He had taken it over from Jock Whitney, the publisher of the *New York Herald Tribune*, who was a friend of his father's in the OSS.

An element of subterfuge was also discernible in Weyrich's early planning. His papers include correspondence that make his political organizations sound like clandestine corporate front groups. One associate writes, "As you well know, business people have been notoriously apathetic in the political field. This is primarily, I feel, due to the businessman's fear of his involvement with respect to his business and possible repercussions from the federal government. The organization we propose would screen him and provide him a vehicle which would in effect do his political work for him at a price."

Earlier attempts by American tycoons to hide behind nonprofit front groups had proven both legally and politically toxic. In the 1930s, Democrats gleefully unmasked the Du Pont family's funding for the American Liberty League, an ostensibly independent organization that opposed FDR's

New Deal, ridiculing it as the "American Cellophane League" because "it's a DuPont product and you can see right through it." In 1950, Congress investigated the group that became AEI, denouncing it as a "'big business' pressure organization" that should register as a lobbying shop and get barred from offering its donors tax deductions. In 1964, top AEI personnel took leaves of absence to form the brain trust for Goldwater's 1964 presidential campaign. The Internal Revenue Service nonetheless threatened the think tank's tax-exempt status. It was this searing experience that prompted AEI and other conservative groups of this period to avoid the appearance of being too partisan or of acting as corporate shills.

But in the 1970s, such concerns became outmoded. Powell and others in the newly aggressive corporate vanguard inverted from a negative into a positive the accusation that conservative organizations were slanted by successfully redefining existing establishment organizations like Brookings and *The New York Times* as equally biased but on the liberal side. They argued that a "market" of ideas was necessary that would give equal balance to all views. In effect, they reduced the older organizations that prided themselves on their above-the-fray public-service-oriented neutrality to mere combatants in a polarized war.

Disoriented, Brookings and the *Times* rushed to add conservatives to their ranks in hopes of demonstrating their nonpartisanship. Brookings hurriedly made a Republican its president, while the *Times* in 1973 added Nixon's former speechwriter Bill Safire to its op-ed page as a columnist. In 1976, after the Scaife-funded Institute for Contemporary Studies issued a report accusing the media of liberal bias, the *Times* forced out the editorial page editor John Oakes for having an antibusiness tone. The Ford Foundation, meanwhile, which had funded much of the early bipartisan environmental movement, as well as the public interest law movement, donated the first installment of $300,000 in grants to AEI in 1972 in an attempt to fight criticism that it was liberal. "That was quite the heist you pulled on the Ford Foundation, congratulations!" a friend exclaimed in a note to a top AEI official.

The upshot was that by the end of the 1970s conservative nonprofits had achieved power that was almost unthinkable when the League to Save Carthage first formed. Enormously wealthy right-wing donors had transformed themselves from the ridiculed, self-serving "economic royalists" of FDR's day into the respected "other side" of a two-sided debate.

The new, hyper-partisan think tanks had impact far beyond Washington. They introduced doubt into areas of settled academic and scientific scholarship, undermined genuinely unbiased experts, and gave politicians a menu of conflicting statistics and arguments from which to choose. The benefit was a far more pluralistic intellectual climate, beyond liberal orthodoxy. The hazard, however, was that partisan shills would create "balance" based on fraudulent research and deceive the public about pressing issues in which their sponsors had financial interests.

Some insiders, like Steve Clemons, a political analyst who worked for the Nixon Center among other think tanks, described the new think tanks as "a Faustian bargain." He worried that the money corrupted the research. "Funders increasingly expect policy achievements that contribute to their bottom line," he admitted in a confessional essay. "We've become money launderers for monies that have real specific policy agendas behind them. No one is willing to say anything about it; it's one of the big taboo subjects."

In an effort to prove their intellectual integrity, all of the new think tanks could cite occasional instances where they parted positions with some of their donors, but far more typical was the example of John M. Olin, a chemical and munitions company magnate whose foundation was a top sponsor of the American Enterprise Institute. Letters from Olin show that he grew increasingly agitated over what he regarded as the think tank's lassitude after he had earmarked a donation demanding that AEI militate against raising the estate tax during the Nixon years. In a note to the think tank's president, Olin railed about the tax as "socialism out and out" and complained that if the think tank didn't speak out soon, "my estate would be practically liquidated upon my death."

David Brock, a conservative apostate who became a liberal activist, described the Heritage Foundation, where he was a young fellow, as almost completely under the thumb of its wealthy sponsors. In his tell-all book *Blinded by the Right,* he writes, "I saw how right-wing ideology was manufactured and controlled by a small group of powerful foundations" like Smith Richardson, Adolph Coors, Lynde and Harry Bradley, and John M. Olin. Scaife in his estimation was "by far the most important"; indeed, Brock describes him as "the most important single figure in building the modern conservative movement and spreading its ideas into the political realm."

How intellectually engaged Scaife personally was—rather than delegating authority to key advisers such as his longtime aides, Richard Larry and Larry's fellow ex-marine R. Daniel McMichael—remains something of a mystery. The recipients of Scaife's largesse, such as David Abshire, head of the Center for Strategic and International Studies, and Edwin Meese III, Reagan's former attorney general and a fellow at the Heritage Foundation, invariably praised his acumen. It was Meese who described Scaife as "the unseen hand" who brought "balance and sound principles back to the public arena" and "quietly helped to lay the brick and mortar for an entire movement." Yet one former aide to Scaife, James Shuman, told *The Washington Post* that had Scaife not inherited a huge fortune, "I don't think he had the intellectual capacity to do very much."

In his memoir, Scaife recounts his life story with some wit and charm, suggesting he could be quick and entertaining, if lacking in self-awareness. Yet one of the few public speeches he gave, at a Heritage Foundation rally celebrating Republicans' takeover of the House and Senate in 1994, was less than reassuring about his clarity of mind. Scaife meandered somewhat incoherently as he declared, "With political victory, the ideological conflicts that have swirled about this nation for half a century now show clear signs of breaking into naked ideological warfare in which the very foundations of our republic are threatened and that we had better take heed."

Scaife's rambling remarks were made in the same year that he returned to drinking after a life in and out of rehab programs. In 1987, his second wife, Margaret "Ritchie" Battle, took him with her to the Betty Ford Center. He stayed sober, associates said, for several years. His life, however, remained flamboyantly turbulent. After he met Ritchie—who was married, as was he—in 1979, the couple carried on a soap-opera-worthy affair. Scaife claimed he consummated it after Ritchie, a glamorous and memorably feisty southerner, appeared in his office in an irresistible white angora sweater. "We did what comes naturally," he told *Vanity Fair.* She retorted, "Never owned an angora sweater. I'm allergic to things like that!" While they were courting, Ritchie reportedly kicked Scaife in the testicles so hard he had to be taken to a hospital emergency room. Meanwhile, he and his first wife wrangled for almost ten years over the divorce settlement as he fought to keep her from taking a share of some Gulf Oil stock he'd belatedly come into. At one point, in order to evade a subpoena, Ritchie was carried out of Scaife's house rolled in a carpet, like Cleopatra, by his servants.

His family life was in tatters. According to Scaife's son, David, Ritchie and Scaife visited him during this period at prep school—Deerfield again—bringing alcohol and marijuana, which Scaife smoked with his son. In 1991, he married Ritchie, who continued to live in her own house around the corner. Their wedding reception scandalized Pittsburgh's upper crust with its blazing double-entendre lawn sign spelling out "Ritchie loves Dick."

That scandal paled, however, in comparison with the couple's spectacular breakup. After hiring a private detective who trailed Scaife to a roadside motel where rooms rented by the hour, and after documenting trysts between Scaife and a tall, blond woman named Tammy Vasco who had an arrest record for prostitution, Ritchie herself was arrested for "defiant trespass" at her husband's house, for peeping into his windows and crawling in after spying servants setting a romantic, candlelit dinner table for two. The charges were dismissed, but the scorned wife soon came to blows with Scaife's housekeeper over custody of the couple's yellow Labrador retriever, Beauregard. After Ritchie succeeded in absconding with the dog, Scaife posted a sign in his front yard reading, "Wife and dog missing—reward for dog."

These skirmishes were a minor prelude to the epic fight over their divorce settlement. Over the advice of his lawyer, Scaife had declined to insist upon a prenuptial agreement with Ritchie, a mistake he regretted bitterly in his memoir. Scaife maintained he hadn't meant to humiliate his former wife, explaining that he just believed in having "an open marriage." It was an issue, he joked, "that Bill Clinton and I have in common." Tammy Vasco, meanwhile, stayed in Scaife's life through his final days, accompanying him on trips to his houses in Nantucket and Pebble Beach, California, to the chagrin of his household staff and the disdain of Pittsburgh society. A friend of Scaife's said that despite her arrest record for prostitution, he kept a photograph of Vasco by his bedside as he lay dying of cancer.

All of which calls into question how in 1990 the Scaife Foundation could justify pressing the Heritage Foundation, of which it was the largest funder, to focus more on conservative social and moral issues and in particular family values. Heritage's president, Ed Feulner, quickly complied with his donor's request, hiring William J. Bennett. Soon after, Bennett, an outspoken social conservative who had been the secretary of education under Ronald Reagan and the director of National Drug Control Policy under George H. W. Bush, was appointed Heritage's new distinguished fellow in cultural policy studies. Lee Edwards, who wrote Heritage's official history, confirms that the Scaife Foundation "had particularly in mind the disintegration of the family, an issue which became a major Heritage concern." Bennett also served as a Scaife Foundation director.

Equally hard to fathom is how Scaife rationalized his foundations' funding of an obsessive investigation of President Clinton's marital infidelities during the 1990s that came to be known as the Arkansas Project. Hiring private detectives to dig up dirt from anti-Clinton sources, the project funneled smutty half-truths to *The American Spectator* magazine, which was also funded by Scaife's family foundations. Scaife's foundations also poured money into lawsuits against Clinton, all of which helped whip up the political frenzy that led to the Clinton impeachment hearings.

Scaife, meanwhile, succumbed to a far-fetched conspiracy theory positing that the death of the Clinton White House aide Vincent Foster, which police had ruled a suicide, was actually a murder and, as he put it at one point, "the Rosetta Stone to the Clinton Administration." Scaife even insisted in an interview that Clinton "can order people done away with at will . . . God there must be 60 people [associated with Clinton] who have died mysteriously."

Scaife's extraordinary self-financed and largely tax-deductible vendetta against Clinton demonstrated the impact that a single wealthy extremist could have on national affairs, and served as something of a dress rehearsal for the Kochs' later war against Obama. Presidents might surround themselves with Secret Service agents and phalanxes of lawyers and operatives, but Scaife proved how hard it was to defend against unlimited, untraceable spending by an opponent hiding behind nonprofit front groups.

Eventually, however, the Arkansas Project got so out of hand that Scaife found himself ensnared in a serious legal mess, subpoenaed to testify before a grand jury about possible charges of tampering with a federal witness. One of the two pilots he kept on his staff flew him down to Arkansas in his private DC-9 to testify. No charges were brought. Enraged, however, Scaife cut off *The American Spectator* from his foundation's funding and turned against his longtime aide Richard Larry, who had led the anti-Clinton charge. Soon after, Larry resigned.

Then, in a stunning turnaround in 2008, Scaife met with Hillary Clinton, who had fingered him as the ringleader of what she called a "vast right-wing conspiracy" to torment the Clintons. Conservative political pundit Byron York declared, "Hell has officially frozen over." After a pleasant editorial board chat, Scaife came out and wrote an opinion piece in his own paper declaring that his view of her as a Democratic presidential contender had changed and was now "very favorable indeed." The rapprochement testified both to Hillary Clinton's political skills and to Scaife's almost childlike impressionability. Repeatedly in his memoir, he changes his political views after meeting antagonists in person, whether the liberal Kennedy family member Sargent Shriver or the Democratic congressman Jack Murtha. "Like many billionaires, he lived in a bubble," concluded his friend Ruddy (whose relations with the Clintons also thawed). Contrary information rarely penetrated it. Instead, Scaife's family fortune enabled him to build a political bulwark reinforcing his ideology and imposing it on the rest of the country.

In Wichita, meanwhile, where he was rapidly expanding his family's company and searching for more effective means than electoral politics with which he could spread libertarianism, Charles Koch, too, was galvanized by Lewis Powell. In

1974, Charles gave a speech to a group of businessmen gathered at a hotel in Dallas, quoting Powell. "As the Powell Memorandum points out," Koch warned the group, "business and the enterprise system are in trouble, and the hour is late."

Koch urged his fellow business leaders to "undertake radical new efforts to overcome the prevalent anti-capitalist mentality." He declared that "the development of a well-financed cadre of sound proponents of the free enterprise philosophy is the most critical need facing us today." Opponents of "socialistic" regulations, he said, should "leverage" their power by investing in "pro-capitalist research and educational programs." That way, he argued, their efforts would have a "multiplier effect."

Charles's anger at the government by this point was more than merely philosophical. Koch Industries had just become the target of federal regulators. One month earlier, the government had charged the company with violating federal oil price controls. By 1975, the government had also cited a subsidiary of Koch Industries for overcharging $10 million for propane gas. More serious government allegations against the company were to come.

Not long after echoing Powell's call to arms, Charles too set up a think tank, transforming his private foundation into the Cato Institute. The name paid homage to the nom de plume used by the authors of a series of pro-liberty letters during the American Colonial period. Its start-up funding, according to one account, dwarfed even Scaife's early contributions to the Heritage Foundation, with Charles giving an estimated $10 to $20 million of tax-deductible donations to the nation's first libertarian think tank during its first three years.

According to Ed Crane, a young, rakish California financier who shared Koch's enthusiasm for libertarianism but lacked his checkbook, the idea for the think tank was his. After the Libertarian Party candidate was predictably crushed in his 1976 presidential quest, Crane, who had been instrumental in the campaign, was ready to go back to the private sector.

Instead, Charles, whom he'd met during the campaign, took him aside and asked what it would take to keep him in the libertarian movement. "I said my bank account is empty," Crane later recalled. "He said, 'How much do you need?'" "A libertarian think tank along the model of Brookings or AEI might be nice," Crane answered. To which, he said, Charles instantly replied, "I'll give it to you."

Crane became Cato's president, but early employees at Cato described Charles as single-handedly exerting absolute iron control. David Gordon, a libertarian activist who worked at Cato in the early days, told *Washingtonian* magazine, "Ed Crane would always call Wichita and run everything by Charles. It was quite clear that Koch was in charge." Another early Cato employee, Ronald Hamowy, added, "Whatever Charles said, went." Despite Crane's antipathy toward government, by 1977 Cato was based in Washington, D.C. It soon hired a slew of scholars whom the mainstream media respectfully quoted as nonpartisan experts.

Fundamentally, though, Cato was devoted to espousing Charles Koch's vision: that government's only legitimate role was to "serve as a night watchman, to protect individuals and property from outside threat, including fraud. That is the maximum," as he told the Wichita Rotary Club in the 1970s. The Kochs consistently depicted Cato and other ideological projects their philanthropy supported as nonpartisan and disinterested. But from the start, the Kochs' ideology and business interests dovetailed so seamlessly it was difficult to distinguish one from the other. Lower taxes, looser regulations, and fewer government programs for the poor and the middle class all corresponded to the Kochs' accumulation of wealth and power.

It's impossible to know exactly how much money private foundations and trusts, funded by a handful of extraordinarily wealthy families, poured into the right-wing think tanks begin-

ning in the 1970s or how effective it was. Their grants were
soon mixed with those from corporate donors, who cautiously
followed the families' bold lead. Unlike other forms of paid
political influence, much of this money was never revealed.
Gifts to nonprofit groups could be concealed from the public. The new think tanks thus became fast-growing, sub-rosa
corporate arsenals. In fact, after Watergate the conservative
think tanks pitched themselves to businesses as the safest way
to influence policy without scandal. By the early 1980s, a list of
the Heritage Foundation's sponsors found in the private papers
of one of its early supporters, Clare Boothe Luce, is crammed
with Fortune 500 companies. Amoco, Amway, Boeing, Chase
Manhattan Bank, Chevron, Dow Chemical, Exxon, General
Electric, General Motors, Mesa Petroleum, Mobil Oil, Pfizer,
Philip Morris, Procter & Gamble, R. J. Reynolds, Searle,
Sears, Roebuck, SmithKline Beckman, Union Carbide, and
Union Pacific were all by then paying the think tank's bills—
while the think tank was promoting their agendas.

James Piereson, the scholar and key figure in conservative philanthropy, has suggested at a minimum "that the think
tanks and conservative foundations made conservative ideas
respectable." Before the surge in spending, he said, conservatives were seen as "cranks" on America's political fringe.

One measure of the movement's impact was that starting in
1973, and for successive decades afterward, the public's trust in
government continually sank. If there was a single unified message pushed by those financing the conservative movement, it
was that government rather than business was America's problem. By the early 1980s, the reversal in public opinion was so
significant that Americans' distrust of government for the first
time surpassed their distrust of business.

Another early sign that the investment was yielding real
results on the national scale was the Republican wave that
swept the 1978 midterm elections. That year, Republicans
gained three Senate seats, fifteen House seats, and six gov-

ernorships. In Georgia, in a development that would have unforeseen future repercussions, Newt Gingrich was elected to Congress. External events such as the energy crisis and "stag-flation" of course played into the election results, too. But the new conservative think tanks and other right-wing political organizations fanned the discontent and shaped the dominant narrative.

Aiding the conservative resurgence was a newly organized and shockingly aggressive independent campaign offensive funded by donors on the right, run by the National Conservative Political Action Committee, or NCPAC, which introduced a whole new level of privately financed attack ads to American campaigns.

Growing conservative clout was apparent in Congress, too. The labor movement, which had expected ambitious gains under Jimmy Carter's presidency, instead soon suffered a series of devastating setbacks dealt by the ascendant business caucus backed by the expanding network of think tanks and outside lobby groups. Weyrich's hand was key here, too. He cemented the movement's influence in Congress by creating the Republican Study Committee, a caucus that united outside activists and conservative elected officials. For years, Heritage Foundation personnel were the only outsiders allowed to regularly caucus with Republican members of Congress because of this hybrid organization. "We are basically a conduit to and from the Heritage Foundation to and from conservative members of the House," its director, Don Eberly, said in 1983.

Weyrich, with Scaife's financial backing, launched several other ingenious political organizations during this period. One was the American Legislative Exchange Council (ALEC), a group aimed at waging conservative fights in every state legislature in the country. From 1973 until 1983, the Scaife and Mellon family trusts donated half a million dollars to ALEC, constituting most of its budget. "ALEC is well on its way to fulfilling the dream of those who started the organization," a Weyrich aide wrote to Scaife's top adviser in 1976, "thanks wholly to your confidence and the tremendous generosity of the Scaife Family Charitable Trusts." When one ALEC administrator complained that Scaife's foundation had too much influence over the organization's agenda, a Scaife employee retorted that they operated on "the Golden Rule—whoever has the gold rules."

Weyrich, meanwhile, dramatically enlarged the conservative groundswell by co-founding with Jerry Falwell the Moral Majority, which brought social and religious conservatives into the pro-corporate fold. Weyrich was particularly adept at capitalizing on white anger over desegregation.

The results of these efforts became visible in 1980. At the top of the ticket, Reagan, a movement conservative, overwhelmingly defeated Carter. Conservatives, whose obituaries had been written by the liberal elite just a few years before, were stunningly resurgent. The upset reverberated at every level, including the Senate, where four liberal marquee names, George McGovern, Frank Church, John Culver, and Birch Bayh, were all defeated.

Scaife, like the Kochs, hadn't initially backed Reagan's candidacy in 1980. In the primary, Scaife preferred John Connally. It barely mattered, though. By creating their own private idea factory, extreme donors had found a way to dominate American politics outside the parties. Once elected, Reagan embraced the Heritage Foundation's phone-book-sized policy playbook, *Mandate for Leadership*, and distributed a copy of it to every member of Congress. His administration soon delivered an impressive number of items on its wish list. Heritage had laid out 1,270 specific policy proposals. According to Feulner, the Reagan administration adopted 61 percent of them.

Andrew Mellon himself would have been pleased with the succession of hefty tax cuts that Reagan pushed through Congress. He slashed corporate and individual tax rates, particularly helping the wealthy. Between 1981 and 1986, the top income tax rate was cut from 70 percent to 28 percent. Meanwhile, taxes on the bottom four-fifths of earners rose. Economic inequality, which had flatlined, began to climb.

The fossil fuel industry's fondest wishes were also fulfilled. Following proposals set forth by the Heritage Foundation, as soon as Reagan entered the White House, he abolished the economic controls on oil and gas that Nixon had imposed in order to address the energy crisis. These were among the regulations that Charles Koch had so bitterly opposed. He also cut taxes on oil profits. Koch Industries' profits, predictably, skyrocketed. *Forbes* noted that Koch, though little known, "may well be the most profitable private business in the U.S."

The new conservative nonprofits were thriving, too. By 1985, the Heritage Foundation's budget equaled that of Brookings and AEI combined. Scaife, who by then had donated $10 million to the think tank, was contributing at a rate of $1 million a year. He had gone far to turn Lewis Powell's dream into a reality. But one key part of Powell's agenda remained unfinished. Conservative foundations might have financed a parallel intellectual establishment of their own, but the League to Save Carthage still hadn't conquered America's colleges and universities. The Ivy League was no more hospitable to Scaife and his ilk than it had been the day he was expelled. Scaife claimed he was thankful to have been spared the liberal indoctrination. "I was lucky. Higher education did not push me left, and I've never regretted it," he wrote in his memoir. "I'd say the main reason that rich people feel guilty is that the schools *teach* them they should."

That was about to change.

CHAPTER THREE

Beachheads: John M. Olin
and the Bradley Brothers

IF THERE WAS A SINGLE EVENT THAT GALVANIZED CONSER-
vative donors to try to wrest control of higher education in
America, it might have been the uprising at Cornell University
on April 20, 1969. That afternoon, during parents' weekend
at the Ithaca, New York, campus, some eighty black students
marched in formation out of the student union, which they
had seized, with their clenched fists held high in black power
salutes. To the shock of the genteel Ivy League community,
several were brandishing guns. At the head of the formation
was a student who called himself the "Minister of Defense" for
Cornell's Afro-American Society. Strapped across his chest,
Pancho Villa–style, was a sash-like bandolier studded with
bullet cartridges. Gripped nonchalantly in his right hand, with
its butt resting on his hip, was a glistening rifle. Chin held
high and sporting an Afro, goatee, and eyeglasses reminiscent
of Malcolm X, he was the face of a drama so infamous it was
regarded for years by conservatives such as the journalist David
Horowitz as "the most disgraceful occurrence in the history of
American higher education."

John M. Olin, a multimillionaire industrialist, wasn't there
at Cornell, which was his alma mater, that weekend. He was
traveling abroad. But as a former Cornell trustee, he could not
have gone long without seeing the iconic photograph of the
armed protesters. What came to be known as "the Picture"
quickly ricocheted around the world, eventually going on to
win that year's Pulitzer Prize.

Traveling almost as fast was the news that Cornell's
administrators had quickly capitulated to the demands of the

black militants, rather than risk a bloody confrontation. Under duress, the university's president had promised to accelerate plans to establish an independent black studies program at Cornell, as well as to investigate the burning of a cross outside a building in which several black female students lived. And to the deep consternation of many conservative faculty members and students on campus, the president also agreed to grant full amnesty to the protesters, some of whom were facing previous disciplinary proceedings following an earlier uprising in which they had reportedly flung books from the shelves of Cornell's libraries, denouncing the works as "not relevant" to the black experience.

By all accounts, the confrontation was especially distressing to Olin. Cornell's library was one of four buildings on the Cornell campus bearing his family's name. Both he and his father had graduated from the school and had been proud and generous donors. Almost worse than the behavior of the protesters, from his standpoint, was the behavior of Cornell's president, James Perkins, a committed liberal who had gone out of his way to open the university's doors to inner-city minority students and now seemed to be bending the curriculum and lowering disciplinary standards to placate them.

"The catastrophe at Cornell inspired Olin to take his philanthropy in a bold, new direction," according to John J. Miller, whose authorized biography, *A Gift of Freedom*, provides a treasure trove of original research on Olin's life and legacy. Olin "saw very clearly that students at Cornell, like those at most major universities, were hostile to businessmen and to business enterprise, and indeed had begun to question the ideals of the nation itself," an Olin Foundation memo recounts.

As a result, according to Miller, instead of continuing to direct the bulk of his charitable contributions to hospitals, museums, and other standard patrician causes, as he had in the early years after he set up the John M. Olin Foundation in 1953, Olin embarked on a radical new course. He began to fund an ambitious offensive to reorient the political slant of American higher education to the right. His foundation aimed at the country's most elite schools, the Ivy League and its peers, cognizant that these schools were the incubators of those who would hold future power. If these young cadres could be trained to think more like him, then he and other donors could help secure the country's political future. It was an attempted takeover, but instead of waging it with bandoliers and rifles, he chose money as his weapon.

By the time the John M. Olin Foundation spent itself out of existence in 2005, as called for in its founder's will, it had spent about half of its total assets of $370 million bankrolling the promotion of free-market ideology and other conservative ideas on the country's campuses. In doing so, it molded and credentialed a whole new generation of conservative graduates and professors. "These efforts have been instrumental in challenging the campus left—or more specifically, the problem of radical activists' gaining control of America's colleges and universities," Miller concluded in a 2003 pamphlet published by the Philanthropy Roundtable, an organization run for conservative philanthropists.

"These guys, individually and collectively, created a new philanthropic form, which was movement philanthropy," said Rob Stein, a progressive political strategist, speaking of the Olin Foundation and a handful of other private foundations that funded the creation of a conservative counter-intelligentsia during this period. "What they started is the most potent machinery ever assembled in a democracy to promote a set of beliefs and to control the reins of government." Stein was so impressed that he went on to try to build a liberal version of the model. Each side would argue that the other had more money and more influence, depending on how broadly they defined the rival camp. But beginning in the 1970s, the Left felt hardpressed to match the far-ranging propagation of ideology pioneered by a few enterprising donors on the right.

There is little doubt that the Cornell uprising radicalized Olin's philanthropy, but the official account citing this as the key to his thinking is incomplete. The protest took place in 1969, and Olin didn't begin to transform his foundation into an ideological instrument aimed at "saving the free enterprise system," as his lawyer put it, until four years later, in the spring of 1973. On closer inspection, it appears that there were additional factors involved that shed less flattering light on his motivations.

By 1973, the Olin Corporation was embroiled in multiple, serious controversies over its environmental practices, undermining its reputation, threatening its revenues, and ensnarling the company in expensive litigation. Founded by Olin's father, Franklin, in 1892, the company had begun in East Alton, Illinois, as a manufacturer of blasting powder for coal miners but expanded into making small arms and ammunition. Like the Koch sons, Olin followed closely in his father's path. After attending prep school, he entered his father's alma mater, Cornell, where he struggled until he was allowed to conduct chemical research relating to his family's company. He graduated in 1913 with a degree in chemistry. He then returned to Illinois to join the family business.

Although Olin regarded himself as self-made and disapproved of the New Deal–era government social programs, beliefs that fueled his later financing of free-market ideology, the federal government was one of the greatest contributors to his company's growth and his personal wealth. As Miller's biography details, the firm's huge government arms contracts in World Wars I and II dramatically improved its bottom line. Revenues quintupled during World War I and exploded during World War II. Olin complained about the government's interference and inefficiency, but his company reaped $40 million in profits during World War II alone. By 1953, it was being celebrated by *Fortune* as one of the few great family-owned corporations.

In 1954, the company went public and merged with the Mathieson Chemical Corporation, doubling in size, diversifying its operations, and eventually changing its name to the Olin Corporation. The conglomeration, whose revenues were half a billion dollars a year by then, made everything from pharmaceuticals in its Squibb division to cigarette paper. It manufactured Winchester rifles and, later, the hydrazine rocket fuel that powered Neil Armstrong's 1969 lunar landing. Meanwhile, Olin's national profile was growing. By 1957, *Fortune* ranked John M. Olin and his brother Spencer, who had taken over the company from their father, as the thirty-first wealthiest Americans, with fortunes estimated at over $75 million. Honors proliferated along with Olin's great wealth. Following his retirement as the company's executive committee chairman in 1963, he devoted himself to serving on the boards of several prestigious universities, including Cornell, and to his passion for the outdoors. He had appeared on the cover of *Sports Illustrated* with his wife in 1958, carrying shotguns and dressed in natty tweeds amid picturesque tall grass, for a profile highlighting his role as a hunter, and a breeder of champion dogs. Known as a conservationist, he was a director of the World Wildlife Fund.

So it must have been a rude blow to him personally, as well as to the prestige and bottom line of his company, when in 1973 the Environmental Protection Agency singled out the Olin Corporation as one of its first targets, soon after Richard Nixon signed the agency into existence. Suddenly under tougher scrutiny, the company that Olin had built was an outlaw, facing charges of egregious pollution practices in several states at once.

In Alabama, the Olin Corporation became embroiled over its production of DDT. Rachel Carson, in her book *Silent Spring*, had identified the pesticide as a deadly contaminant to the biological food chain. The Olin Corporation had been producing 20 percent of the DDT used in the United States. Soon it was fighting a vigorous but losing battle with federal officials against new pollution standards tightening the chemical's production and use, which the company said would make it impossible to keep its plant open. In addition, three conservation groups, the Environmental Defense Fund, the National Audubon Society, and the National Wildlife Federation, were all suing the company to enjoin it from releasing effluents laced with DDT into a national wildlife preserve near Olin's Alabama plant. In 1972, the federal government banned the use of DDT altogether, forcing Olin to shut its production down.

The company's extensive use of mercury in its production of chlorine and other products had also become a huge problem. In the summer of 1970, according to a front-page story in *The New York Times,* the U.S. Interior Department charged the Olin Corporation with dumping 26.6 pounds of mercury a day into the Niagara River in upstate New York. Mercury was by then a known human health hazard. Scientists had documented its damage to the human brain and reproductive and nervous systems. Subsequently, the Justice Department also charged the Olin Corporation with falsifying records, showing that the company had dumped sixty-six thousand tons of chemical waste, including mercury, into a landfill in Niagara Falls, New York. The Hooker Chemicals and Plastics Corporation was simultaneously charged with dumping toxic chemicals at the same site, as well as the nearby "Love Canal," which became an international symbol of toxic pollution. Eventually, the Olin Corporation and three of its former corporate officers were convicted of falsifying records in the dumping case, after which the presiding judge imposed the maximum available fine of $70,000 on the company.

In the tiny Appalachian town of Saltville, Virginia, meanwhile, in the far southwestern corner of the state, the Olin Corporation was facing an environmental crisis of such major proportions that it threatened to end not only Olin's industrial operations there but also the entire town's way of life for years to come. The Olin Corporation's pollution was so extensive and intractable that the company faced the prospect of tens if not hundreds of millions of dollars in cleanup costs, with no end in sight.

For decades, Saltville had been a prototypical company town, owned and run in an almost feudal fashion, by its only large employer, the Olin Corporation. The company owned ten thousand acres in the ruggedly beautiful mountainous gap, as well as 450 modest clapboard houses that it rented to the town's 2,199 residents. It also owned the local grocery stores, the water system, the sewerage system, and the only school, which many workers left after no more than sixth or seventh grade. The company prided itself on paternalistic flourishes like a swimming pool and a small stadium for residents. When employees got sick, the company paid for the doctors. The mayor and virtually everyone else in Saltville worked in the chemical plant, which Olin acquired in its merger with the Mathieson Chemical Corporation in 1954. The town's vast natural salt deposits made it a perfect place to produce chlorine and salt ash, and for years it was the picture of American industrial prosperity, at least for its owners. But for the employees, there was an ominous, unaddressed issue. Olin's chlorine production process used huge quantities of mercury, which the plant leaked into the public waterways on a daily basis. From 1951 to 1970, the company estimated its factory spilled about a hundred pounds of mercury every day. Most of it emptied directly into the North Fork of the Holston River, which ran picturesquely along the town's edge. An open sediment pond, meanwhile, into which the company dumped its mercury waste, contained an astounding fifty-three thousand pounds of the toxic substance.

"They all knew the dangers back then. They had some

really good scientists and chemists. But you didn't have the regulations," says Harry Haynes, who runs a small history museum in Saltville and whose father used to work at the Olin plant. "We all played with the mercury as children," he recalls. "Daddy brought it home from the chemical plant. You'd drop it on the floor, and it would explode into a zillion little bits, and then sweep it together and it would clump back together again." The company issued gas masks to workers because of the pervasive chemical vapors, but, another resident recalled, "no one wore them."

In 1972, however, the world recoiled at photographs of birth defects resulting from severe mercury contamination at Minamata Bay in Japan. Scientists definitively linked the birth defects—as well as other health horrors including cerebral palsy, mental retardation, blindness, deafness, coma, and death—to consumption of seafood that had been contaminated by mercury waste in local fishing areas. After having been dumped in the water, the mercury had broken down into a soluble form toxic to aquatic life and to those ingesting it. The nightmare at Minamata drew concern about the effects of mercury pollution elsewhere, including at the Olin plant in Saltville. Testing conducted by the state soon revealed high levels of mercury in the sediment in the North Fork of the Holston River, which ran from Saltville on down to Tennessee, where it flowed into the Cherokee Lake recreation area, a favorite fishing destination. Dangerous levels of mercury were discovered in the fish for eighty miles south of the Olin plant, according to one report.

In response to the rising concerns in Saltville, in 1970 Virginia passed strict new standards that the company said it couldn't meet. As a result, Olin said, it would cease operations in Saltville by the end of 1972. The company actually had several other reasons for shutting the plant. It was unable to compete with more efficient western salt ash manufacturers. Also, it was under pressure from the United Mine Workers union, which had succeeded after bitter battles in representing the employees. In all likelihood, the factory was doomed not just for environmental reasons.

Yet the story line blaming environmental activists for its problems proved irresistible. *Life* magazine produced an elegiac photo essay called "End of a Company Town," and *The Wall Street Journal* lamented the crushing new regulatory burden on corporate America. The Olin Corporation, meanwhile, demolished its factory and sold most of its Saltville real estate back to local residents but found no takers for its mercury waste "muck" pond. It tried removing a foot or so of topsoil around it, and it tried building a ditch along the river to divert the toxic runoff, but these efforts were hopelessly deficient. Soon after, the EPA designated Saltville one of the country's first "Superfund" sites.

"It's a ghost town. It was extremely polluted and still is," says Shirley "Sissy" Bailey, who grew up near Saltville and still lives there. "To this day, that muck pond is still there, and you can still see clumps of mercury along the river. The drinking water is so full of lead and mercury it isn't fit for a dog to drink." She says she "lived" the history, ran as a kid on riverbanks so poisoned no grass grew. The air often smelled of chlorine and other chemicals. "The Olin Company was dirty and treated the people bad, not like people," she says. "Most of the workers were poorly educated, and they led them around like sheep. A lot of people got sick, and there were more birth defects in Saltville than in other parts of the state," she asserts, although there has been no study proving this or establishing any causal correlation.

"Common sense should have made companies take responsibility, but until the 1970s there were no regulations on this. The EPA became a form of accountability," says Stephen Lester, the Harvard-educated science director for the Center for Health, Environment, and Justice in Falls Church, Virginia, a nonprofit environmental group that provided technical assis-

tance to Bailey in a later mercury contamination fight in Saltville. "Of course that imposes costs and affects the bottom line,
so it wasn't popular with the company." The cost of cleaning
up Saltville, in fact, was projected to be upward of $35 million.

Former officials at the Olin Foundation, when asked about
the company's ignominious environmental record, downplay
any link to the nonprofit's pro-corporate, antiregulatory ideology. "It is possible that Mr. Olin was influenced to some degree
by litigation and regulations against the company," says James
Piereson, the conservative scholar, who was executive director and trustee of the Olin Foundation from 1985 to 2005.
"But that would be one factor among many others; and he was
no longer running the company on a day to day basis by this
time." He added, "There were a lot of cross currents in the air:
the Cold War, détente, Watergate, inflation, a stock market
crash, war in the Middle East, Vietnam, environmentalism,
feminism." William Voegeli, who was program officer at the
Olin Foundation from 1988 to 2003, says, "The Olin family
had very little to do during these years with either the John
Olin Foundation or the Olin Corporation." He added, "I never
heard one word, during my years at the foundation, about how
its grants might affect the Olin Company (whose stock constituted less than one percent of our endowment), or the finances
of the Olin family. Whatever else can be said of our conservative agenda, it was disinterested."

It was, however, against a backdrop of serious clashes with
the increasingly robust regulatory state that John Olin directed
his lawyer to enlist his fortune in the battle to defend corporate America. As he put it, "My greatest ambition now is to
see free enterprise re-established in this country. Business and
the public must be awakened to the creeping stranglehold that
socialism has gained here since World War II."

At first, the foundation funneled money into the same conservative think tanks that Scaife and Coors were supporting, the Heritage Foundation, the American Enterprise Institute, and the Hoover Institution, the conservative think tank located on Stanford University's campus. But soon John Olin's focus diverged. Perhaps because of his upset over Cornell, his foundation became uniquely centered on transforming academia. As he wrote in a private letter to the president of Cornell, he regarded the campus as overrun by scholars "with definite left-wing attitudes and convictions." Olin noted, "It matters little to me whether the economic development is classified as Marxism, Keynesianism, or whatnot." He said he regarded "liberalism" and "socialism" as "synonymous." All of these academic trends, he asserted, needed "very serious study and correction."

To get his bearings, Olin's labor lawyer, Frank O'Connell, contacted a handful of other private conservative foundations. He sought advice from colleagues at the Koch and Scaife Foundations, as well as a few others on the right such as the Earhart Foundation and the Smith Richardson Foundation, which was funded by the Vicks VapoRub fortune. George Pearson, who was running the Charles G. Koch Foundation at that point, guided O'Connell, assigning him a free-market reading list that included Hayek's essay "The Intellectuals and Socialism." Hayek's point was emphatic: to conquer politics, one must first conquer the intellectuals. O'Connell recalled, "It was like a home-study course."

The fledgling right-wing foundations were also studying their establishment counterparts during this period, particularly the giant Ford Foundation. By the late 1960s, Ford was pioneering what its head, McGeorge Bundy, a former dean at Harvard and national security adviser to the Kennedy and Johnson administrations, called "advocacy philanthropy." Ford was, for instance, pouring money into the environmental movement, funding the Environmental Defense Fund and the Natural Resources Defense Council. By supporting public interest litigation, it showed conservatives how philanthropy could achieve large-scale change through the courts while bypassing the democratic electoral process, just as the early critics of private foundations had feared.

In 1977, Olin raised his foundation's stature by choosing William Simon as its president. Simon was a social acquaintance of Olin's from East Hampton, Long Island, where they both had beach houses, and Olin described Simon's thinking as "almost identical with mine." While Olin kept a low profile, however, Simon loved the spotlight, the hotter the better. As Voegeli recalled, Simon was like Alice Longworth's description of her father, Theodore Roosevelt. "He wanted to be the bride at every wedding, and the corpse at every funeral."

Simon had been energy czar and later Treasury secretary under Presidents Nixon and Ford and was a famously intemperate critic of those he considered "stupid." This large category included liberals, radicals, and moderate members of his own Republican Party. Like Olin, he was incensed by the expansion of the regulatory state. He especially detested environmentalists and other self-appointed guardians of the public interest, describing them as the "New Despots." In his 1978 manifesto, *A Time for Truth,* he wrote, "Since the 60's, the vast bulk of regulatory legislation passed by congress . . . [has] been largely initiated by a powerful new lobby that goes by the name of the Public Interest movement." Simon disparaged these "college-educated idealists" who claimed to be working for "the well being of 'consumers,' the 'environment,' 'minorities,'" and other nonmaterial causes, accusing them of wanting to "expand the police powers of the state over American producers." He challenged their purity. Noting that they claimed to care little for money, he accused them of being driven by another kind of self-interest. Quoting his colleague Irving Kristol, the neoconservative intellectual, he charged that these usurpers wanted "the power to shape our civilization." That power, he argued, should belong exclusively to "the free market."

Simon's hatred and suspicion of the liberal elite approached Nixonian levels in his 1980 sequel manifesto, *A Time for Action*. He claimed that a "secret system" of academics, media figures, bureaucrats, and public interest advocates ran the country. Picking up where Lewis Powell had left off in his memo nine years earlier, Simon warned that unless businessmen fought back, "Our freedom is in dire peril."

Simon's foreboding, like that of Olin, is somewhat hard to fathom given that both men had reached pinnacles of American power and wealth. They were both millionaires many times over, with more properties, possessions, titles, honors, and accomplishments than they could easily count. Both men were born into privilege. Like Scaife, Simon was chauffeured to grade school, and his family was so wealthy he likened his parents to the carefree and careless characters in F. Scott Fitzgerald's fiction. Nonetheless, he regarded himself proudly as self-made. His father evidently lost his mother's fortune, motivating Simon to make his own. On Wall Street, he became a hugely successful partner at Salomon Brothers, where he was an early leader in the lucrative new craze for leveraged buyouts. But what neither Olin nor Simon had was influence over the next generation. "We are careening with frightening speed towards collectivism," Simon warned.

Only an ideological battle could save the country, in Simon's view. "What we need is a counter-intelligentsia . . . [It] can be organized to challenge our ruling 'new class'— opinion makers," Simon wrote. "Ideas are weapons—indeed the only weapons with which other ideas can be fought." He argued, "Capitalism has no duty to subsidize its enemies." Private and corporate foundations, he said, must cease "the mindless subsidizing of colleges and universities whose departments of politics, economics and history are hostile to capitalism."

Instead, they "must take pains to funnel desperately needed funds to scholars, social scientists and writers who understand the relationship between political and economic liberty," as he put it. "They must be given grants, grants, and more grants in exchange for books, books, and more books."

Under Simon's guidance, the Olin Foundation tried to fund the new "counter-intelligentsia." At first, it tried supporting little-known colleges where conservative ideas—and money—were welcome. But Simon and his associates soon realized that this was a losing strategy. If the Olin Foundation wanted impact, it needed to infiltrate prestigious schools, especially the Ivy League.

The man who put his mark on the Olin Foundation more than its namesake, or even Simon, was its executive director, Michael Joyce, a fierce former liberal who had become a neoconservative acolyte of Kristol's. A friend of Joyce's said that he believed philanthropy was about power and that those with great fortunes needed political capos like him to tell them how to wield it. Joyce was a brawler who wanted to take on America's liberal establishment, not just supplement it in some milquetoast way. In the words of Ralph Benko, a libertarian blogger for *Forbes*, "Joyce was a true radical. He was inspired by Antonio Gramsci. He wanted to effect radical transformation." In Miller's view, Joyce was "an intellectual among activists, and an activist among intellectuals. He understood how the world of ideas influenced the real world." Joyce was characteristically more blunt. "My style," he said, "was the style of the toddler and the adolescent: fight, fight, fight, rest, get up, fight, fight, fight. No one ever accused me of being pleasant. I made a difference. It was acknowledged by friend and foe."

Joining Joyce was Piereson, a thoughtful, soft-spoken neoconservative whose path to the Olin Foundation had also run through Irving Kristol. Piereson had befriended the Kristol family at the University of Pennsylvania, where he taught government and political theory alongside Irving's son, Bill.

Both had felt marginalized by their more liberal peers. Having closely observed America's academic intelligentsia, Pierson concluded that the foundation needed to "penetrate" the most elite institutions, "because they were emulated by other colleges and universities of lesser stature." As Hillel Fradkin, who also worked at the Olin Foundation, put it, "The only way you're going to change the debate in this country is by looking to those schools. Giving money to conservative outposts won't get much done."

What emerged was a strategy they called the "beachhead" theory. The aim, as Pierson later described it in an essay offering advice to fellow conservative philanthropists, was to establish conservative cells, or "beachheads," at "the most influential schools in order to gain the greatest leverage." The formula required subtlety, indirection, and perhaps even some misdirection.

The key, Pierson explained, was to fund the conservative intelligentsia in such a way that it would not "raise questions about academic integrity." Instead of trying to earmark a chair or dictate a faculty appointment, both of which he noted were bound to "generate fierce controversy," he suggested that conservative donors look for like-minded faculty members whose influence could be enlarged by outside funding. In time, such a professor could administer an expanded program. But Pierson warned that it was "essential for the integrity and reputation of the programs that they be defined not by ideological points of view." To overtly acknowledge "pre-ordained conclusions" would doom a program. Instead of saying the program was designed to "demonstrate the falsity of Marxism" or to promote "free-enterprise," he advised that it was better to "define programs in terms of fields of study, [like the] John M. Olin Fellowships in Military History." He wrote, "Often a program can be given a philosophical or principled identity by giving it the name of an important historical figure, such as the James

Madison Program [in] American Ideals and Institutions at Princeton University."

(Indeed, after years of trial and error, the Olin Foundation funded Princeton's Madison Program with $525,000 in start-up grants in 2000. Run by Robert George, an outspoken social and religious conservative, the program serves as the beau ideal of the "beachhead" theory. As a friend of George's described him to *The Nation* in 2006, he is "a savvy right-wing operative, boring from within the liberal infrastructure.")

Piereson warned conservative philanthropists that taking the liberal out of liberal arts education would require patience and cunning. As a former academic himself, he knew how politically charged a frontal assault would be. Rather than openly trying to overhaul academia overnight, he suggested, "perhaps we should think instead about challenging it by adding new voices." As he put it, "This may well be the best means of changing the college culture, for a few powerful voices of criticism may at some point bring the entire ideological house of cards crashing down upon itself."

If the Olin Foundation was less than transparent about its mission, it was not for the first time. Between 1958 and 1966, it secretly served as a bank for the Central Intelligence Agency. During these eight years, the CIA laundered $1.95 million through the foundation. Olin, according to Miller, regarded his undercover role as just part of his patriotic duty. Many of the government funds went to anti-Communist intellectuals and publications. But in 1967, the press exposed the covert propaganda operation, triggering a political furor and causing the CIA to fold the program. The CIA money at the Olin Foundation, which was not publicized at the time, disappeared as quietly as it had arrived. The idea of using the private foundation to fund ideologically aligned intellectuals, however, persisted.

Soon the Olin Foundation was investing in William F. Buckley Jr., whose television show, *Firing Line*, the foundation supported. It was also funding Allan Bloom, author of the best-selling slam from the right at American higher education, *The Closing of the American Mind* (in which Bloom also lashed out at rock music as a "nonstop, commercially prepackaged masturbation fantasy"). The foundation also supported Dinesh D'Souza, author of *Illiberal Education*, which blasted "political correctness," castigating rules requiring sensitivity to women and minorities as the overreaching of liberal thought police. In addition, the Olin Foundation funded professors at leading schools all over the country, including Harvard's Harvey C. Mansfield and Samuel P. Huntington. It donated $3.3 million to Mansfield's Program on Constitutional Government at Harvard, which emphasized a conservative interpretation of American government, and the foundation donated $8.4 million to Huntington's John M. Olin Institute for Strategic Studies, which inculcated a hawkish approach to foreign policy and national security.

Through these carefully curated programs, the foundation trained the next generation of conservatives, whom Joyce likened to "a wine collection" that would grow more valuable as its members aged, increasing in stature and power. The foundation kept track of those who passed through Huntington's Olin program, proudly noting that many went into public service and academia. Between 1990 and 2001, fifty-six of the eighty-eight Olin fellows at the Harvard program continued on to teach at the University of Chicago, Cornell, Dartmouth, Georgetown, Harvard, MIT, Penn, and Yale. Many others became public figures in government, think tanks, and the media. In all, by the time it closed its doors in 2005, the Olin Foundation had supported eleven separate programs at Harvard, burnishing the foundation's name and ideas and proving that even the best-endowed American university would allow an outside, ideological group to build "beachheads," so long as the project was properly packaged and funded.

On top of these programs, the foundation doled out $8 million to more than a hundred John M. Olin faculty fellows. These funds enabled scores of young academics to take the time needed to research and write in order to further their careers. The roster of recipients includes John Yoo, the legal scholar who went on to become the author of the George W. Bush administration's controversial "torture memo" legalizing the American government's brutalization of terror suspects.

Without the rigorous peer-reviewed standards required by prestigious academic publications, the Olin Foundation was able to inject into the mainstream a number of works whose scholarship was debatable at best. For example, Olin Foundation funds enabled John R. Lott Jr., then an Olin fellow at the University of Chicago, to write his influential book *More Guns, Less Crime*. In the work, Lott argued that more guns actually reduce crime and that the legalization of concealed weapons would make citizens safer. Politicians advocating weaker gun control laws frequently cited Lott's findings. But according to Adam Winkler, the author of *Gunfight*, Lott's scholarship was suspect. Winkler wrote that "Lott's claimed source for this information was 'national surveys,'" which under questioning he revised to just one survey that he and research assistants had conducted. When asked to provide the data, Winkler recounts, Lott said he had lost it in a computer crash. Asked for any evidence of the survey, writes Winkler, "Lott said he had no such evidence." (Proving that the recipients of Olin funds weren't ideologically monolithic, Winkler, too, had received funds from the foundation.)

Another Olin-funded book that made headlines and ended in accusations of intellectual dishonesty was David Brock's *Real Anita Hill*, to which the foundation gave a small research stipend. In the book, Brock defended the Supreme Court justice Clarence Thomas by accusing Hill of fabricating her sworn testimony against him during his Senate confirmation hearings. Later, though, Brock recanted, admitting that he had been wrong. He apologized for the book and said that he had been deceived by conservative sources who had misled him.

Still, the combined impact of the Olin grantees was "a triumph," according to Miller. Writing as a conservative in 2003, he enthused that "a small handful of foundations have essentially provided the conservative movement with its venture capital." He noted that in contrast to the days when Lionel Trilling had declared conservatism over, "conservative ideas are in broad circulation, and many believe they are now ascendant." He added, "If the conservative intellectual movement were a NASCAR race, and if the scholars and organizations who compose it were drivers zipping around a race track, virtually all of their vehicles would sport an Olin bumper sticker."

In time, the Olin Foundation's success in minting right-leaning thinkers drew the envy of the Left. "On the right, they understood that books matter," says Steve Wasserman, now the editor at large at Yale University Press, who was dismayed by the failure of wealthy liberal donors to match the intellectual investments being made by conservatives. "I remember meeting at a restaurant in California with some of the most savvy Democratic supporters, Margery Tabankin, Stanley Sheinbaum and Danny Goldberg. We wanted to figure out how to fund books on the Left. But they said that for most donors books weren't sexy, preferring to give money to candidates and causes. The Democrats were hostage to star personalities and electoral politics."

The Olin Foundation's most significant beachheads, however, were established in America's law schools, where it bankrolled a new approach to jurisprudence known as Law and Economics. Powell, in his memo, had argued that "the judi-

ciary may be the most important instrument for social, economic and political change." The Olin Foundation agreed. As
the courts expanded consumer, labor, and environmental rights
and demanded racial and sexual equality and greater workplace
safety, conservatives in business were desperate to find more
legal leverage. Law and Economics became their tool.

As a discipline, Law and Economics was seen at first as
a fringe theory[1] embraced largely by libertarian mavericks
until the Olin Foundation spent $68 million underwriting its
growth. Like an academic Johnny Appleseed, the Olin Foundation underwrote 83 percent of the costs for all Law and Economics programs in American law schools between the years of
1985 and 1989. Overall, it scattered more than $10 million to
Harvard, $7 million to Yale and Chicago, and over $2 million
to Columbia, Cornell, Georgetown, and the University of Virginia. Miller writes, "John Olin, in fact, was prouder of Law
and Economics than any other program he supported."

Following Piereson's cautious playbook, the program's title
conveyed no ideology. Law and Economics stresses the need
to analyze laws, including government regulations, not just for
their fairness but also for their economic impact. Its proponents
describe it in apolitical terms as bringing "efficiency" and "clarity" to the law, rather than relying on fuzzy, hard-to-quantify
concepts like social justice.

Piereson, however, admitted that the beauty of the program was that it was a stealth political attack and that the
country's best law schools didn't grasp this and therefore didn't
block the ideological punch it packed. "I saw it as a way into
the law schools—I probably shouldn't confess that," he told
The New York Times in 2005. "Economic analysis tends to have
conservatizing effects." In a later interview with the political
scientist Steven M. Teles, he added that he would have preferred to fund a conservative constitutional law program, but
had the foundation tried such a direct political challenge, it
probably would have been barred entry to America's best law

schools. "If you said to a dean that you wanted to fund conservative constitutional law, he would reject the idea out of hand. But if you said you wanted to support Law and Economics, he would be much more open to the idea," he confided. "Law and Economics is neutral, but it has a philosophical thrust in the direction of free markets and limited government. That is, like many disciplines, it seems neutral, but it isn't in fact."

The Olin Foundation's route into the country's best law schools was circuitous. The foundation began by financially supporting an early leading figure in Law and Economics, the libertarian Henry Manne, an acolyte of the Chicago school of free-market economics. Brilliant, impolitic, and an ideological purist, Manne "was considered a marginal, even eccentric character in the legal academy," according to Teles, when the Olin Foundation first started funding him in the early 1970s. To the frustration of the foundation, though, he didn't teach at high-prestige schools. In 1985, however, the foundation seized a golden opportunity to establish a beachhead at the pinnacle of legal prestige. That year, Harvard Law School was riven by controversy. Leftist professors were urging students to "sabotage" corporate law firms from within. Conservative professors and alumni were scandalized. The ruckus attracted national press coverage in *The New Yorker* and elsewhere. Among the many outraged Harvard Law School alumni was one of the Olin Foundation's trustees, George Gillespie. Sensing an opening, he contacted a conservative Harvard Law School professor, Phil Areeda, whom he had been in school with, and offered the foundation's help. The Olin Foundation took the initiative, and Harvard took the cash. Out of this ideological pact came the John M. Olin Center for Law, Economics, and Business at Harvard Law School, on which the foundation ultimately spent $18 million. The donation was the biggest in Olin's history. Harvard's president at the time, Derek Bok, was reportedly delighted at the new source of funding and the opportunity to soothe the disgruntled alumni.

After Harvard approved Law and Economics, other schools soon followed. By 1990, nearly eighty law schools taught the subject. Olin fellows in Law and Economics, meanwhile, began to beat a path to the top of the legal profession, winning Supreme Court clerkships at a rate of approximately one each year, starting in 1985. Many of the adherents were outstanding lawyers and not all were conservative, but they were changing the prevailing legal culture. By 1986, Bruce Ackerman, then a professor at Columbia Law School, called Law and Economics "the most important thing in legal education since the birth of Harvard Law School." Teles, in his 2008 book, *The Rise of the Conservative Legal Movement,* described Law and Economics as "the most successful intellectual movement in the law of the past thirty years, having rapidly moved from insurgency to hegemony."

As Law and Economics spread, underwritten at each step by the Olin Foundation and other conservative backers including the Kochs and Scaife, liberal critics grew alarmed. The Alliance for Justice, a liberal nonprofit in Washington, published a critical report in 1993 warning that "a small wealthy group" was trying to "fundamentally alter the way that justice is dispensed in our society." It revealed that the Olin Foundation was paying students thousands of dollars to take classes in Law and Economics at Georgetown Law School and to attend workshops on the subject at Columbia Law School. Despite this ethically dubious situation, only one law school, at the University of California in Los Angeles, turned the Olin funds away, arguing that by plying students with grant money, the foundation was "taking advantage of students' financial need to indoctrinate them with a particular ideology."

More controversial still were Law and Economics seminars that the Olin Foundation funded for judges. The seminars were initiated by Henry Manne, who had become dean of the George Mason University School of Law in Virginia, which he was trying to transform into a hub of libertarian jurisprudence.

The seminars treated judges to two-week-long, all-expenses-paid immersion training in Law and Economics usually in luxurious settings like the Ocean Reef Club in Key Largo, Florida. They soon became popular free vacations for the judges, a cross between Maoist cultural reeducation camps and Club Med. After a few hours of learning why environmental and labor laws were anathema, or why, as Manne argued, insider-trading laws did more harm than good, the judges broke for golf, swimming, and delightful dinners with their hosts. Within a few years, 660 judges had gone on these junkets, some, like the U.S. Court of Appeals judge and unconfirmed Supreme Court nominee Douglas Ginsburg, many times. By one count, 40 percent of the federal judiciary participated, including the future Supreme Court justices Ruth Bader Ginsburg and Clarence Thomas.

A variety of major corporations eagerly joined Olin and other conservative foundations in footing the bills. A study by the nonpartisan Center for Public Integrity found that between 2008 and 2012 close to 185 federal judges attended judicial seminars sponsored by conservative interests, several of which had cases before the courts. The lead underwriters were the Charles Koch Foundation, the Searle Freedom Trust, Exxon-Mobil, Shell Oil, the pharmaceutical giant Pfizer, and State Farm, the insurance company. Topics ranged from "The Moral Foundations of Capitalism" to "Terrorism, Climate, and Central Planning: Challenges to Liberty and the Rule of Law."

Simultaneously, the Olin Foundation provided crucial start-up funds for the Federalist Society, a powerful organization for conservative law students founded in 1982. With $5.5 million from the Olin Foundation, as well as large donations from foundations tied to Scaife, the Kochs, and other conservative legacies, the Federalist Society grew from a pipe dream shared by three ragtag law students into a powerful professional network of forty-two thousand right-leaning lawyers, with 150 law school campus chapters and about seventy-five lawyers' groups nationally. All of the conservative justices on the Supreme Court are members, as are the former vice president Dick Cheney, the former attorneys general Edwin Meese and John Ashcroft, and numerous members of the federal bench. Its executive director, Eugene B. Meyer, son of a founding editor of *National Review,* acknowledged that without Olin funding "it possibly wouldn't exist at all." Looking back, the Olin Foundation's staff described it as "one of the best investments" the foundation ever made.

John M. Olin died in 1982 at the age of eighty-nine, but after his death his foundation became even more robust. He left it about $50 million in his estate and another $50 million in a trust for his widow, which came to the foundation in 1993 after she died. The funds were well invested, growing to some $370 million in all before the foundation spent it down and closed its doors in 2005. Olin had directed his foundation to shut down during the lifetime of the trustees for fear that it would fall into the hands of liberals, as he believed the Ford Foundation had tragically done.

William Simon remained the head of the Olin Foundation until his own death in 2000. He also continued to amass a stupendous fortune of his own during the 1980s, using controversial financial maneuvers. By the late 1980s, *Forbes* estimated Simon's wealth at $300 million.

Around the same time, the Olin Foundation made a key $25,000 investment of its own in an unknown writer named Charles Murray, funding a grant at the Manhattan Institute that would support a book he was writing that attacked liberal welfare policies. The backstory to *Losing Ground,* Murray's book, was a primer on the growing and interlocking influence of conservative nonprofits. At thirty-nine, Murray was an unknown academic, toiling thanklessly at a Washington Beltway firm evaluating U.S. government social programs.

Frustrated and just scraping by, he was about to try writing a thriller novel in order to make ends meet when his application for a job at the Heritage Foundation caught the eye of the conservative philanthropy world. Soon, he was the beneficiary of its growing network. Heritage placed an antiwelfare piece by Murray on the op-ed page of *The Wall Street Journal.* This sparked a grant from the Olin Foundation that enabled him to work full-time on what became his pathbreaking 1984 book, *Losing Ground,* even though he hadn't previously considered turning his research into a book. "It was a classic case of philanthropic entrepreneurship," Murray says. The hidden force behind Murray was Joyce, the Olin Foundation's enfant terrible. "Mike Joyce was one of the most influential obscure people of the last century," says Murray.

Losing Ground, which was written in a tone of sorrow rather than anger, blamed government programs for creating a culture of dependence among the poor. Critics said it overlooked macroeconomic issues over which the poor had no control, and academics and journalists were split, with several challenging Murray's scholarship. Nonetheless, with ample funding from Olin and other conservative foundations, Murray succeeded in shifting the debate over America's poor from society's shortcomings to their own.

Despite Reagan's professed antipathy toward big government, his administration steered cautiously away from Murray's controversial libertarianism, preferring to criticize welfare cheaters rather than the whole idea of government-run antipoverty programs. But to the dismay of liberals, Bill Clinton, a "New Democrat," later embraced his ideas, calling Murray's analysis "essentially right" and incorporating many of his prescriptions, including work requirements and the end to aid as an entitlement, in his 1996 welfare reform bill. "It took ten years," Murray has said, "for *Losing Ground* to go from being controversial to conventional wisdom."

The Olin Foundation also backed what came to be known

as the Collegiate Network, privately financing a string of right-wing newspapers on America's college campuses. Among them was *The Dartmouth Review,* which infamously published an editorial in Ebonics proclaiming, "Now we be comin' to Dartmut' and be up over our 'fros in studies, but we still be not graduatin' Phi Beta Kappa." The paper hosted a feast of lobster and champagne to mock a student fast against global hunger, sledgehammered¹ shantytowns erected by students protesting apartheid in South Africa, and published a transcript of a secretly taped meeting of students belonging to Dartmouth's gay student association. *The Dartmouth Review* became an incubator for right-wing media figures like D'Souza and the future conservative radio host Laura Ingraham. Its counterpart at Vassar, meanwhile, gave starts in journalism to the ABC correspondent Jonathan Karl and Marc Thiessen, an online columnist at *The Washington Post* best known for his defense of the Bush administration's use of torture.

As the Olin Foundation spent itself out of existence, Michael Joyce jumped to a new and far more powerful private foundation, started by another conservative family. In 1985, a corporate merger in Milwaukee created a spectacular windfall, boosting a previously sleepy local charity, the Lynde and Harry Bradley Foundation, overnight into a nonprofit juggernaut. Its assets rocketed from $14 million to over $290 million, making it one of the twenty largest foundations in the country. Swimming in cash, the foundation's small, unpaid staff, which had mostly focused on conventional local do-gooding until then, sought out Joyce, telling him, "We've got money, and we want to do what you did at Olin. We want to become Olin West." Almost on the spot, Joyce moved to Milwaukee to run the Bradley Foundation himself. He left Pierson behind to cope with Simon's famously short temper and the twenty-year plan to spend the Olin Foundation out of business.

At the Bradley Foundation, Joyce had a freer hand. "He basically invented the field of modern conservative philanthropy," according to Piereson. During the next fifteen years, the Bradley Foundation would give away $280 million to his favorite conservative causes. It was small in comparison with older research foundations like the Ford Foundation, but unlike Ford, under Joyce's direction Bradley regarded itself as a righteous combatant in an ideological war, giving it a single-minded focus. At least two-thirds of its grants, according to one analysis, financed conservative intellectual activity. It paid for some six hundred graduate and postgraduate fellowships, right-wing think tanks, conservative journals, activists fighting Communism abroad, and its own publishing house, Encounter Books. Continuing the strategic emphasis on prestigious schools, the foundation gave both Harvard and Yale $5.5 million during its first decade under Joyce's management. It was an activist force on the secondary-school level, too. The Bradley Foundation virtually drove the early national "school choice" movement, waging an all-out assault on teachers' unions and traditional public schools. In an effort to "wean" Americans from government, the foundation militated for parents to be able to use public funds to send their children to private and parochial schools.

When Joyce took over the Bradley Foundation, he continued to fund many of the same academic organizations he had at Olin, including half of the same colleges and universities. "Typically, it was not just the same university but the same department, and in some cases, the same scholar," Bruce Murphy wrote in *Milwaukee Magazine,* charging that this led to a kind of "intellectual cronyism." The anointed scholars were good ideological warriors but "rarely great scholars," he wrote. For instance, Joyce stuck with Murray in the face of growing controversy over his 1994 book, *The Bell Curve,* which correlated race and low IQ scores to argue that blacks were less likely than whites to join the "cognitive elite," and was loudly and convincingly discredited. The Manhattan Institute fired Murray over the controversial project. "They didn't want the grief," says Murray. But Joyce reportedly kept an estimated $1 million in grants flowing to Murray, who decamped to the American Enterprise Institute. "I knew from Mike Joyce my fellowship was portable," Murray says. But the controversy stirred by the book clouded the Bradley Foundation's reputation. Joyce, who was accused of racism, said he received death threats. He felt so threatened he demanded enhanced security. The book, he acknowledged, left "an indelible imprint on us."

Joyce stepped down from Bradley in 2001 amid rumors of alcoholism and erratic and self-destructive behavior. "Demons were rumored," recalls a friend. According to one well-informed source, Joyce's drinking, which had escalated from three-beer lunches to complete benders, reached a crisis when he presided as the master of ceremonies at a formal Washington event in a state of scandalous, public inebriation. Afterward, the Bradley Foundation's board gave Joyce the choice of going into a rehab program or resigning. Realizing he had lost the board's respect, he resigned. After that, the few remaining years of his life were a lonely, powerless downward spiral.

Nonetheless, Joyce's achievements transcended his personal problems. When he retired, Joyce was showered with accolades from the Right. *National Review* described him as "the chief operating officer of the conservative movement." It added, "Wherever you looked in the battle of ideas, a light dusting would have turned up his fingerprints." The tribute concluded, "Over the period of his Bradley service, it's difficult to recall a single, serious thrust against incumbent liberalism that did not begin or end with Mike Joyce."

What received no attention, however, was that the small-government conservatism that the Bradley Foundation promoted was fueled by federal funds. The Bradley Foundation very deliberately cast itself as a foe of big government. In 1999, Joyce wrote a confidential memo to the foundation's board arguing that to win, conservatives needed to "package for public consumption . . . dramatic stories" depicting citizens as "plucky Davids fighting gallantly against the massive, statist, bureaucratic Goliath." But the foundation owed much of its existence to that Goliath—in the form of taxpayer-funded defense spending.

The event that multiplied the Bradley Foundation's assets by a factor of twenty almost overnight, transforming it into a major political force, was the 1985 business takeover in which Rockwell International, then America's largest defense contractor, bought the Allen-Bradley company, a Milwaukee electronics manufacturer, for $1.65 billion in cash. The deal created an instant windfall for the Bradley family's private foundation, which held a stake in the company. Its assets leaped from $14 million to some $290 million.

When it bought the Allen-Bradley company, two-thirds of Rockwell's revenues, and half of its profits, came from U.S. government contracts. Rockwell had become, in fact, a poster child for wasteful government spending. The *Los Angeles Times* called it a "symbol of a military industrial complex gone berserk." Rockwell's coffers were bulging with cash, but its reputation had taken a hit from its role as the main contractor producing the B-1 bomber, an aircraft so maligned it earned the nickname the Flying Edsel. President Carter had canceled the program as a waste of money, but after Rockwell waged a strenuous lobbying campaign, President Reagan had brought it back to life. As part of his administration's huge defense buildup, Reagan also authorized the manufacture of the MX missile system, another multibillion-dollar defense program that was widely criticized as unnecessary, for which Rockwell was the largest contractor. Thus, by 1984, thanks to profligate government spending, Rockwell had one of the strongest balance sheets in the business, with $1.3 billion in cash piling up on its ledgers. Business analysts warned that the company needed to diversify in order to become less reliant on federal contracts. It was this dubious set of circumstances that sent the company on the shopping spree that ended in its purchase of Allen-Bradley and the phenomenal enrichment of the Bradley Foundation.

In its early days especially, Allen-Bradley had relied heavily on government defense contracts, too, to pull it through. Founded in 1903 by two enterprising high school dropouts, brothers Lynde and Harry Bradley, along with investor Stanton Allen, it grew from making rheostats to many other kinds of industrial controls, particularly for the radio, machine tool, and auto industries. The business had "teetered on the edge of solvency" until the United States entered World War I, according to a history by the Milwaukee historian John Gurda that was commissioned and published by the Bradley Foundation. But thanks to government defense contracts, which accounted for 70 percent of the company's business, orders increased tenfold over six years, and the company was, according to Gurda, "launched." World War II proved even more of a boon. Gurda describes its impact on the company as "staggering." By 1944, government war work accounted for nearly 80 percent of the company's orders. Its business volume more than tripled during World War II.

Even more than the Olin Corporation, Allen-Bradley sponsored an amazing array of generous if paternalistic fringe benefits for its workers, including its own jazz orchestra, led by a full-time music director, which serenaded lunch crowds. There were badminton courts on its roof deck, overseen by an athletic director, and an employee reading room, too. The Bradley brothers, who erected an iconic four-faced, Florentine-style clock tower that soared seventeen stories above the plant on the South Side of Milwaukee, regarded themselves as benevolent civic leaders, overseeing a family of employees. They were therefore bitterly wounded when their employees, who saw the situation differently, unionized and then went out on strike in 1939.

The elder brother, Lynde, died not long after, but the younger brother, Harry, who lived until 1965, became avidly right-wing. Like Fred Koch, he was a vigorous supporter of the John Birch Society, frequently hosting its founder, Robert Welch, as a speaker at company sales meetings. Bradley also was a devoted follower of Dr. Frederick Schwarz, a melodramatically anti-Communist physician from Australia who had converted to Christianity from Judaism, and who stumped across the heartland for his Christian Anti-Communism Crusade preaching that "Karl Marx was a Jew," and "like most Jews he was short and ugly and lazy and slovenly and had no desire to go out and work for a living" but also possessed "a superior, evil intelligence like most Jews." Schwarz, too, was a regular visitor to the company and a favorite among Bradley's causes. Bradley was also a keen supporter of the Manion Forum, whose followers believed that social spending in America was part of a secret Russian plot to bankrupt the United States. Despite the lifesaving financial boost that federal spending had provided to his own company, Bradley reportedly regarded the growing federal government in America and world Communism as "the two major threats" to human "freedom."

The company's embrace of the free market, however, didn't preclude price-fixing. In 1961, Harry Bradley's successor and confidant of many years, Fred Loock, was convicted of price-fixing with twenty-nine other electrical equipment firms. He narrowly escaped incarceration, according to the authorized history. Both the company and its chief executive paid substantial fines.

The company's relations with federal authorities worsened further in the 1960s as the Allen-Bradley company, not unlike the Olin Corporation, found itself in the crosshairs of new laws driven by more demanding societal expectations. In 1966, a federal judge sided with a group of female employees who sued the company for paying them lower wages than male employees operating the same machinery. Then, in 1968, federal

authorities targeted the company for racially discriminatory
hiring policies. In response, the company agreed to institute
an affirmative action plan. Meanwhile, unionized employees at
the plant went on strike, causing an eleven-day work stoppage.
The combination of antitrust, race, gender, and labor disputes
at the company provided fertile ground for the politics of backlash building in the executive suite.

The Bradley Foundation, meanwhile, also became increasingly politicized. Originally, the foundation's purpose was to
help aid needy employees and the residents of Milwaukee, as
well as prevent cruelty to animals. Harry Bradley and his wife
were animal lovers, doting on a pet poodle, Dufy, who was
named for the modern artist and who had a penthouse dog
run. After Joyce took over the foundation in 1985, however, a
new mission statement was drafted, directing its grants to the
support of "limited, competent government," "a dynamic marketplace," and "vigorous defense."

The Bradley brothers had hoped to keep the company in
the private hands of the family, and the jobs in the community,
in perpetuity. Their will was explicit about this. Their heirs,
however, with the help of the Milwaukee law firm Foley &
Lardner, managed to sell the company to Rockwell nonetheless, cashing in handsomely. One of the law firm's partners,
Michael Grebe, subsequently became chairman and CEO of
the newly enriched foundation.

What remained of Allen-Bradley, however, did less well.
Its sad slide traced the fall of American manufacturing during the end of the twentieth century and the hollowing out
of decent blue-collar jobs. In 2010, Rockwell Automation,
which is what was left of the company in Milwaukee twenty-
five years after it was sold, outsourced the last of the plant's
remaining manufacturing jobs to low-wage areas, largely in
Latin America and Asia. Robert Granum, president of Local

1111 of the United Electrical, Radio, and Machine Workers of America, the union that represented the last laid-off workers, told the *Milwaukee Business Journal* that Rockwell's decision would "deprive future generations of working people of the opportunity to have decent family-supporting jobs."

Allen-Bradley's distinctive Florentine clock tower still rose above Milwaukee's South Side. But by then Milwaukee was described as "the most polarized part of the most polarized state in a polarized nation." The industrial base had collapsed, the manufacturing jobs disappeared, and many of the white immigrants who had worked at Allen-Bradley had long since moved to the suburbs, leaving Milwaukee close to 40 percent black, with the second-highest black poverty rate in the country and with an unemployment rate that was nearly four times higher for blacks than for whites.

The Bradley Foundation, meanwhile, had become central to the conservative movement. Thanks to smart investments, its assets ballooned, enabling it to finance a movement that ascribed poverty to dependency on government handouts, not to the trade, labor, and industrial policies that had resulted in American jobs, such as those at Allen-Bradley, getting shipped overseas. By 2012, the Bradley Foundation's assets had reached more than $630 million, enabling it to dole out more than $32 million in grants during that year alone. The funds continued to finance welfare reform initiatives that required the poor to find jobs, as well as attacks on public schools. The foundation also continued to support conservative beachheads in thirty-five different elite colleges and universities including Harvard, Princeton, and Stanford.

The foundation's annual Bradley Prizes had by then become the glittering Academy Awards ceremony for conservatives, a night at Washington's Kennedy Center on the banks of the Potomac filled with evening gowns, tuxedos, overlong acceptance speeches, live musical fanfares, and up to four annual $250,000 prizes given to a Who's Who of the movement.

Over the years, winners have included the newspaper columnist George Will, who subsequently became a trustee of the
foundation. Also honored with the award were the founders
of the Federalist Society as well as Princeton's Robert George;
Bill Kristol, the neoconservative editor of *The Weekly Standard;*
the Harvard professor Harvey Mansfield; the Fox News president, Roger Ailes; and the Heritage Foundation's stalwarts Ed
Meese and Ed Feulner. Almost all of the recipients had played
major roles in tugging the American political debate to the
right. And almost all had also been supported over the years
by a tiny constellation of private foundations filled with tax-
deductible gifts from a handful of wealthy reactionaries whose
identities and stories very few Americans knew but whose
"overarching purpose," as Joyce said, "was to use philanthropy
to support a war of ideas."

CHAPTER FOUR

The Koch Method:
Free-Market Mayhem

FOR TWENTY-ONE YEARS, WHILE THE KOCHS WERE FINANCING an ideological war aimed at freeing American business from the grip of government, Donald Carlson was cleaning up the dregs their industry left behind. Stitched to the jacket he wore to work at Koch Refining Company, the booming Pine Bend Refinery in Rosemount, Minnesota, was the name Bull. His colleagues called him this because of his brawn and his willingness to shoulder the tasks no one else wanted to touch. "He wasn't always the greatest guy or dad, but he got up every morning and went to work. He stepped up to the plate every day," recalls his widow, Doreen Carlson. "If a job was too hard, they gave it to him."

Beginning in 1974, when he was hired, Carlson worked twelve- and sometimes sixteen-hour shifts at the refinery. Its profitability had proven the Kochs' purchase of Pine Bend prophetic. It had become the largest refinery north of Louisiana with the capacity to process 330,000 barrels of crude a day, a quarter of what Canada exported to the United States. It provided over half of the gas used in Minnesota and 40 percent of that used by Wisconsin. Carlson's job was demanding, but he enjoyed it. He cleaned out huge tanks that contained leaded gasoline, scraping them down by hand. He took samples from storage tanks whose vapors escaped with such force they sometimes blew his helmet off. He hoisted heavy loads and vacuumed up fuel spills deep enough to cause burns to his legs. Like many of the one thousand employees at the refinery, Carlson was often exposed to toxic substances. "He was practically swimming in those tanks," his wife recalled. But Carlson never thought twice about the hazards. "I was a young guy," he explained later. "They didn't tell me anything, I didn't know anything."

In particular, Carlson said, no one warned him about benzene, a colorless liquid chemical compound refined from crude oil. In 1928, two Italian doctors first detected a connection between it and cancer. Afterward, numerous scientific studies linked chronic benzene exposure to greatly increased risks of leukemia. Four federal agencies—the National Institutes of Health (NIH), the Food and Drug Administration, the Environmental Protection Agency, and the Centers for Disease Control—have all declared benzene a human carcinogen. Asked under oath if he'd been warned about the harm it posed to his hemoglobin, Carlson replied, "I didn't even know what hemoglobin was."

In 1995, Carlson became too sick to work any longer at the refinery. When he obtained his company medical records, he and his wife were shocked by what they read. In the late 1970s, OSHA had issued regulations requiring companies whose workers were exposed to benzene to offer annual blood tests, and to retest, and notify workers if any abnormalities were found. Companies were also required to refer employees with abnormal results to medical specialists. Koch Refining Company had offered the annual blood tests as legally required, and Carlson had dutifully taken advantage of the regular screening. But what he discovered was that even though his tests had shown increasingly serious, abnormal blood cell counts beginning in 1990, as well as in 1992 and 1993, the company had not mentioned it to him until 1994.

Charles Koch had disparaged government regulations as "socialistic." From his standpoint, the regulatory state that had grown out of the Progressive Era was an illegitimate encroachment on free enterprise and a roadblock to initiative and profitability. But while such theories might appeal to the company's owners, the reality was quite different for many of their tens of thousands of employees.

Carlson continued working for another year but grew weaker, needing transfusions of three to five pints of blood a week. Finally, in the summer of 1995, he grew too sick to work at all. At that point, his wife recalls, "they let him go. Six-months' pay is what they gave him. It was basically his accumulated sick pay." Carlson argued that his illness was job related, but Koch Refining denied this claim, refusing to pay him workers' compensation, which would have covered his medical bills and continued dependency benefits for his wife and their teenage daughter. "The doctor couldn't believe he was never put on workmen's comp," she added. "We were just naive. We didn't think people would let you die. We thought, 'They help you, don't they?'"

In February 1997, twenty-three years after he joined Koch Industries, Donald Carlson died of leukemia. He was fifty-three. He and his wife had been married thirty-one years. "Almost the worst part," she said, was that "he died thinking he'd let us down financially." She added, "My husband was the sort of man who truly believed that if you worked hard and did a good job, you would be rewarded."

Furious at the company, Doreen waged a one-woman battle to get Koch Industries to acknowledge some responsibility for her husband's death and apologize. "I'm looking for some accountability," she told Tom Meersman, a reporter for the Minneapolis *Star Tribune*. For three years, Carlson pressed her legal claim. The company offered her some money but refused to call it compensation for a work-related death. It resisted until minutes before the case was about to be heard by a judge. And when it did finally agree to her terms, it did so only if there was no written agreement. "They never admitted it. They avoided court. There was no written record. They just gave me those little crumbs," she recalled.

More than a dozen years later, Carlson took the opportunity to speak out. "I don't think you could write what I think of Koch. You're just collateral damage. It's just money for them, and they never have enough." Pressed about whether it was fair to pin the blame on the Kochs themselves, rather than on lower-level executives she dealt with, she retorted, "Charles Koch owns the refinery." She went on, "And they want less regulations? Can you imagine? What they want is things that benefit them. They never cut into their profits. I hear they're backing a lot of people politically, and I bet it's all about getting rid of regulations," she said. "But those regulations are for safety. It's not to make your workers rich; it's so they don't die."

Carlson's case was just one of many targeting Koch Industries' corporate conduct in the decades after Charles took over the company. The company was expanding at a breathtaking rate into a global conglomerate with vast chemical, manufacturing, energy, trading, and refining interests. But growing at an equally astonishing pace were its legal conflicts. Rather than making peace with the government overseers who frustrated his libertarian ideals, Charles declared war. As he portrayed it, his defiance was a stand for high principle. In 1978, for instance, he wrote an impassioned call to arms to other businessmen in the *Libertarian Review,* arguing, "We should *not* cave in the moment a regulator sets foot on our doorstep . . . Do not cooperate voluntarily; instead, resist wherever and to whatever extent you legally can. And do so in the name of *justice.*"

It's difficult to disentangle Charles's philosophical opposition to regulations from his financial interest in avoiding them. As he described it, he was trying to "unceasingly advance the cause of liberty" in the face of "arrogant, intrusive, totalitarian laws." Critics such as Thomas Frank, the author of *What's the Matter with Kansas?* who grew up in Kansas watching the

Kochs, saw it quite differently. "Libertarianism is supposed to be all about principles, but what it's really about is political expedience. It's basically a corporate front, masked as a philosophy." What is indisputable is that whatever the motivations were, in the quarter century between 1980 and 2005, under Charles Koch's leadership, his company developed a stunning record of corporate malfeasance.

In April 1996, for instance, as Bull Carlson was dying of leukemia in Minnesota, Sally Barnes-Soliz, a Koch Industries environmental technician, knocked on the door of government regulators in Corpus Christi, Texas, where the Kochs owned and operated another refinery, and blew the whistle on the company for lying about illegal quantities of benzene that it was leaking into the air. Environmental regulations, even more than those dealing with workplace safety, proved to be constant obstacles for Koch Industries, as the problems at the refinery in Corpus Christi exemplified.

Barnes-Soliz later told *Bloomberg Markets* magazine, "The refinery was just hemorrhaging benzene into the atmosphere." Rather than comply with a new 1995 federal regulation requiring reductions in such emissions, Koch Industries had tried to conceal its output in a report that it was required to file with the Texas Natural Resource Conservation Commission. Internally, a Koch lawyer conceded that the company's self-reporting was "misleading and inaccurate," so the company had then called in Barnes-Soliz to provide a more accurate account.

She had been working with Koch Industries for five years and loved the job because she felt she was contributing directly to the health and safety of employees and the public. As directed, she carefully re-tabulated the refinery's benzene emissions and found the company had released fifteen times more than the legal limit. Her bosses were unhappy with her findings. She had a bachelor's degree in science and environmental health and a master's of science in industrial hygiene, so she knew what she was doing, but nonetheless she redid the math many times. But she kept getting the same unwelcome results. "There were a lot of meetings to try and get me to change the number. It was hard, but I held firm to my convictions," she recounted to *Bloomberg Markets*. She was thus shaken when she saw the subsequent report submitted by Koch to the Texas authorities. It falsified the benzene emissions to 1/149th of the amount she had calculated.

"When I saw they had actually falsified that document, I had no recourse but to notify the authorities," she told *Bloomberg Markets,* which described the episode as part of a pattern of outlaw behavior by Koch Industries. On her lunch break, she drove to the state regulators' office and reported the fraud.

Defenders of Koch Industries have suggested that the whistle-blower was merely a disgruntled employee, looking for a pretext to save her job. But Koch Industries in Corpus Christi was hit with a ninety-seven-count indictment on September 28, 2000, charging it with covering up the discharge of ninety-one metric tons of benzene. The company faced the potential of $352 million in fines, and four Koch employees faced potentially long prison sentences and fines of $1.75 million each. The company fought back hard in the courts, trying to withhold hundreds of internal e-mails about its emissions, but the presiding judge rejected its argument that these were trade secrets, castigating its lawyer as a "front man" who was trying to "impede" regulators from discovering the "extent of its noncompliance." During the course of the wrangling, the company revealed that it would have cost $7 million to comply with the emission standards. High though the cost might seem, it was dwarfed by the refinery's profits. Prosecutors testified that the Kochs' Corpus Christi refinery earned $176 million in profits during 1995 alone.

Eventually, Koch Industries pleaded guilty to one felony charge of "concealment of information" about its benzene emissions and paid $10 million in fines, and made another $10 million payment for projects to improve the environment in Corpus Christi. A spokeswoman for the company stressed afterward that the charges against the individual Koch managers had been dropped, and she argued, "The government's case ultimately collapsed." David Uhlmann, the career prosecutor who headed the environmental crimes section of the Justice Department at the time, however, said that to the contrary Koch Industries pleaded guilty to "an orchestrated scheme to conceal benzene emissions—a known carcinogen"—from regulators and the community. He calls the suit "one of the most significant cases ever brought under the Clean Air Act." He notes, "Environmental crimes are almost always motivated by economics and arrogance, and in the Koch case there was a healthy dose of both."

An eye-opening sideline was the company's treatment of Barnes-Soliz. For her whistle-blowing, she said she was quarantined to an empty office with no responsibilities and no e-mail access. Eventually, she quit and sued the company for harassment, and in 1999 Koch paid her an undisclosed amount in a sealed settlement.

Around the same time, another would-be whistle-blower, Carnell Green, who was a low-level employee at Koch Industries in Louisiana, said that the company threatened to arrest him if he didn't recant. According to two statements that Green gave in 1998 and 1999 to a private investigator who was working for Bill Koch, Green was a pipeline technician and gas meter serviceman for Koch Industries when he ran afoul of the management. He had worked for the company from 1976 until 1996, during which time he said that he was told to sweep mercury spills from the thirty-six gas meters that he monitored out the door and onto the ground. He said that he was also told to dispose of the old meters, which contained about a quart of mercury each, in dumpsters and to pour additional containers of mercury down the sink, as he witnessed his supervisor doing. Green said the mercury was so pervasive that when he got home, balls of it would roll off his clothes and out of his shoes.

After attending a class on hazardous materials in 1996, though, Green said that he sent a report to his supervisors alerting them that mercury posed a serious health hazard and should be disposed of more carefully. Green said his supervisors told him not to talk about it. Soon after, Green said, a man who identified himself as "FBI Special Agent Moorman" came to interrogate him and accused him of lying about the mercury. He said the official threatened to arrest him and put him in jail if he did not retract his allegations against the company and also warned him that if he told anyone else, including outside authorities, about the mercury, he would be fired. Green said his immediate supervisor then presented him with a prepared statement to sign, saying there was no mercury at the Koch facilities. Fearing that he would otherwise be imprisoned, Green signed it.

Worried about his health, Green said that he nonetheless filed a complaint with OSHA. Koch Industries subsequently fired him, he said, for "making false statements."

In his statement, Green added that he later learned that Special Agent Moorman worked not for the FBI but "for Koch Security in Wichita Kansas." At the time, Larry M. Moorman was an investigator in Koch Industries' legal department. Moorman later became the director of corporate security for Koch Industries.

According to the private investigator, Richard "Jim" Elroy, soil samples were later taken from one of the locations that Green identified as having been polluted with mercury by Koch Industries and sent to an independent laboratory for testing. The soil samples, according to Elroy's report, were so highly contaminated with mercury that the lab refused to send them back through the U.S. mail and demanded payment for specialized disposal of hazmat substances. But by then, Green had lost his job. "Green was just a nice, working-class black guy from Louisiana, trying the best he could to make a living," said Elroy, who took Green's statement while working on behalf of Bill Koch in his litigation against his brothers Charles and David at the time. "Koch just runs over these people and then discards them as trash," Elroy said. Asked about Green's allegations, neither Moorman nor the spokesman for Koch Industries responded.

But as allegations concerning pollution mounted nationally, federal prosecutors began to piece together an enormous case against the company for violating the Clean Water Act. In 1995, the Justice Department sued Koch for lying about leaking millions of gallons of oil from its pipelines and storage facilities in six different states. Federal investigators documented over three hundred oil spills during the previous five years, including one 100,000-gallon crude oil spill that left a twelve-mile-long slick in the bay off Corpus Christi, not far from where the Koch refinery was located.

Angela O'Connell, the lead federal prosecutor in the case against Koch Industries, later described it as unlike any other oil company she had ever dealt with, noting that over her twenty-five-year career at the Justice Department she dealt with most of them. "They're always operating outside of the system," she told Daniel Schulman, who provides a vivid account of the company's serial lawbreaking in *Sons of Wichita*. Leaks and spills, she noted, are endemic in the oil business, but she maintained that while other companies would sit down with regulators and admit their failings, Koch Industries "repeatedly lied . . . to avoid penalties."

As O'Connell compiled the massive multistate case against Koch Industries, she developed an uneasy sense that she was being spied on. She thought her trash was being searched, and her phone bugged, but she could never prove it. She was rattled badly enough by the situation that from that point on she monitored everything she said and did, to make sure it couldn't be used against her.

Documents show that beginning in 1983 Koch Industries hired a former employee of the U.S. Secret Service, David Nicastro, to assist its security operations. By 1994, Nicastro had his own small investigative firm in Texas, Secure Source, and "for the next four or five years," he confirmed, "I worked on different projects" for the Kochs, including the litigation between the brothers. In court papers, he described his role as conducting "numerous investigations" for Koch Industries and what he called its "entities." Joining Nicastro was Charles Dickey, a former FBI agent.

In looking back many years later, O'Connell said she regarded the Kochs as "dangerous" and still felt uncomfortable talking about them. Dropping her voice, as if they might be listening, she recalled, "They tried to attack my reputation." She recounted that as she was working on the case against the company, it obtained a meeting with the head of the Environmental Protection Agency at the time, Carol Browner, at which company representatives accused O'Connell of acting overzealously, in an unsuccessful effort to have her removed from the case. "They lie about everything, and they get away with it because they're a private company," she says. "They obstructed every step of discovery. It was always, 'I didn't do it,' 'It's not our oil,' 'It's not our pipes.' You can't believe anything they say. They definitely don't play the game the way other companies do," she says.

On January 13, 2000, O'Connell's division at the Justice Department prevailed. Koch Industries agreed to pay a $30 million fine, which was the biggest in history at that point, for violations of the Clean Water Act. The EPA issued a press release accusing Koch Industries of "egregious violations" and trumpeting that the huge fine proved that "those who try to profit from polluting our environment will pay the price." But

O'Connell, who retired from the Justice Department in 2004, was still haunted by the damage from the oil leaks a decade later. "The thing is, oil sinks to the bottom and poisons the fish. If people eat it, they get really, really sick," she said. "People die."

While a few legal violations could be understood as misfortunate accidents, Koch Industries' pattern of pollution was striking not just for its egregiousness but also for its willfulness. As the company was settling the oil spill case that O'Connell brought, its Pine Bend Refinery in Rosemount, Minnesota, pleaded guilty to still more violations of the Clean Water Act. The refinery paid an $8 million fine for dumping a million gallons of ammonia-contaminated wastewater onto the ground, along with negligently spilling some 600,000 gallons of fuel into a protected natural wetland and the nearby Mississippi River. Earlier the refinery had already paid a $6.9 million fine to the Minnesota Pollution Control Agency to settle charges stemming from the same violations. In this pollution case, like that in Corpus Christi, government authorities accused Koch of trying to cover up its offenses, in this instance by surreptitiously dumping extra pollutants on weekends and late at night in order to evade monitoring, and later falsifying the records. A former employee, Thomas Holton, who had worked at the Pine Bend Refinery, told the Minnesota *Star Tribune*, "There were times when . . . yeah, we lied. We did do that. And I won't cover that up."

These misdeeds paled, however, in comparison with what befell two teenagers in the rural town of Lively, Texas, some fifty miles southeast of Dallas, on August 24, 1996. That afternoon, Danielle Smalley, a newly minted high school graduate, was at home in the family trailer, packing her things for college. A friend, Jason Stone, was over, to talk about the farewell party they were planning for her that night. Smalley's father, Danny, a mechanic, was home too, watching sports on television. A faint but increasingly nauseating gassy smell was the only sign that something was amiss. After they could find no source, Danielle and Jason decided to drive to a neighbor's house to report a possible gas leak. The family had no phone of their own. Borrowing Danny Smalley's truck, they set out, but the truck stalled a few hundred yards away. When Danielle, who was at the wheel, tried to restart it, the ignition lit an invisible cloud of butane gas that was leaking from a corroded, underground Koch pipeline that ran not far from the house, setting off a monstrous blast. A towering fireball utterly consumed the truck. Danielle and Jason burned to death.

Koch Industries offered Danny Smalley, Danielle's father, money to drop the wrongful death lawsuit he subsequently brought against the company. Like Doreen Carlson, however, the surviving family member wanted more than cash.

The pretrial maneuvering was fierce, with Koch Industries reportedly hiring a fleet of top-flight lawyers and a private investigator to tail Smalley. Smalley's lead lawyer, Ted Lyon, meanwhile, suspected his law office was being bugged. He hired a security firm to inspect, which discovered that tiny transmitters had been planted in his office. "I'm not saying the Kochs did it," the lawyer later said. "I just thought it was very interesting that it happened during the period we were litigating the case."

As the two sides prepared for trial, a chilling picture of corporate negligence emerged. An investigation by the National Transportation Safety Board found that Koch Pipeline Company, the unit in charge, knew that the pipeline was corroded and had neither made all of the necessary repairs nor told the forty or so families living near the explosion site how to handle an emergency. An expert witness for the Smalleys described the pipeline as "Swiss cheese." The explosion, according to the witness, Edward Ziegler, a certified oil industry safety expert, resulted from "a total failure of a company to follow the regulations, keep their pipeline safe and operate it as the regulations require."

For three years, the company had in fact stopped using the old pipeline in favor of a newer one. But the company decided to revive the older pipeline when it realized it could make an additional $7 million annually by patching it and using it to carry liquid butane. Bill Caffey, an executive vice president at Koch Industries, admitted in a deposition, "Koch Industries is definitely responsible for the death of Danielle Smalley," but he stressed that he had believed that the pipeline was safe when he authorized its use. He praised Charles Koch as admirably focused on complying with safety and other regulations but acknowledged there were financial pressures. "We were to work on reducing wasteful spending," he explained. A former employee, Kenoth Whitstine, testified in a deposition that when he brought concerns to his boss at the company about another corroding pipeline, which he feared could cause a fatal accident if ruptured, he was told that it would be cheaper to pay off damages from a lawsuit than make the repairs.

Finally getting the chance he had waited for, Danny Smalley took the stand as the last witness in the trial and delivered an enraged soliloquy denouncing the Kochs as caring only about money. As he later told *60 Minutes*, "They said, 'We're sorry, Mr. Smalley, that your child lost her life and Jason lost his life.' Sorry doesn't get it. They're not sorry. The only thing they looked at was the bottom dollar. How much money would they lose if they shut the pipeline down. They didn't care, all they wanted was the money."

If the Kochs' cavalier safety practices were a gamble, they lost when the jury rendered its verdict. On October 21, 1999, it found Koch Industries guilty not just of negligence but of malice, too, because it had known about the extreme hazard its decaying pipeline had posed. In his suit, Danny Smalley had asked for $100 million in damages from the company, a staggering sum. The jury, however, imposed a fine almost three times larger, demanding Koch Industries pay him $296 million. At the time, it was the largest wrongful death award on record.

As they reeled from the verdict, the brothers also faced a growing political crisis. The U.S. Senate had opened an investigation into allegations that the company stole tens of millions of dollars' worth of oil from wells on Native Americans' tribal land. After a yearlong investigation in 1989, it released a scathing report accusing Koch Oil of "a widespread and sophisticated scheme to steal crude oil from Indians and others through fraudulent mis-measuring."

The Senate investigation had penetrated Koch Industries' well-guarded secrecy, compelling Charles Koch to be deposed at the company headquarters in Wichita. One committee official recalled him as "quietly enraged" by the government intrusion. Under oath, Charles admitted that the company had improperly taken approximately $31 million worth of crude oil over a three-year period from Indian lands but argued that it had been accidental. He told investigators that oil measurement is "a very uncertain art." The committee, however, produced evidence showing that none of the other companies buying oil from Indian land at the time had substantial problems with measurements. In fact, the other companies, most of which were far better known, had secretly turned Koch in, because they regarded it as cheating.

The Senate investigation was marked by what was becoming a familiar pattern: those challenging the Kochs began to feel that someone was trying to watch and possibly intimidate them. Richard "Jim" Elroy, who later became a private eye himself, was at the time an FBI agent detailed to the Senate investigation. His specialty had been investigating corruption in Oklahoma, and he had handled a number of tough cases, including some involving organized crime. But he soon faced a situation that he said he had never before encountered even when investigating the Mafia: he became certain that he was being followed.

One day, Elroy stopped his car, jumped out, and confronted the driver who had been tailing him, dragging him out of his car at gunpoint, flashing his FBI identification, and warning him, "Tell your boss the next time he tries this, you'll be in a body bag." Elroy recounted that the driver explained, "I'm a private investigator who works with Koch Industries." The company's legal affairs head reportedly denied hiring private investigators to spy on Elroy. But other Senate investigators had unsettling experiences as well. According to the Senate report, another investigator discovered that a Koch employee tried to get dirt on him from his former wife.

The committee's chief counsel, Kenneth Ballen, who had previously worked as a prosecutor against organized crime in New Jersey, believed that one of his assistants was paid to get dirt on him. Luckily, Ballen said, there wasn't any. "It wasn't like politics; it was like investigating organized crime," Ballen recalled. Charles Koch, he maintains, "is a scary guy to take on. Most people back off, rather than tangling with them," Ballen observed. "These people have amassed an amazing amount of unaccountable power."

Another young lawyer working on the Senate investigation, Wick Sollers, who later became a managing partner at the blue-chip law firm King & Spalding, also found the experience disturbing. Sollers was an assistant U.S. attorney in Baltimore when the Senate committee recruited him. "The company was unhappy with the investigation," he noted. "They sent various people to try to stop us—emissaries, lawyers—as well as a senator to try to stop the investigation." The senator in question was the Oklahoma Republican Don Nickles, a social and fiscal conservative who received many campaign contributions from Koch Industries over the years and whose lobbying firm was later hired by the company.

Sollers said that several staff members believed that someone was going through their garbage. "We don't know who
sent them," Sollers said carefully, "but someone hired private
investigators to dig up anything they could." Later, after he left
the Senate for King & Spalding, he recalled that an anonymous package was sent to his mentor at the firm, filled with
news clippings and court documents meant to sully his reputation. Some of the documents trumpeted the Kochs' innocence.
"I've not experienced anything like this in any other part of
my practice," he said. "Someone was trying to intimidate and
silence the Kochs' critics. I'm not political, but it was troubling."

Christopher Tucker, a witness against the Kochs who testified to committee investigators, also experienced unusual
harassment. After accusing Koch Industries of cheating in its
oil measurements, he was smeared in newspaper stories as a
perjurer, denounced in a letter by four senators, and tipped off
by his landlady's daughter that men in business suits had taken
away his garbage. The basis of the complaint against him was
that a professional credential he had cited on his résumé wasn't
finalized until shortly after he testified. In this instance, when
pressed, the company acknowledged initiating the senators'
letter against him. "It's very intimidating," Tucker told the reporter Robert Parry. "You have a company with lots of money.
They've got more money than many small countries do."

The Senate Select Committee on Indian Affairs nonetheless released a remarkably damning report on Koch Industries.
Afterward, Elroy, who was still an FBI agent, wrote a memo
to the U.S. attorney in Oklahoma City referring a potential
criminal case against the company, alleging that it stole oil.
Before sending the memo, however, Elroy warned Bill Koch
that these developments could result in his brothers going to
jail. "Then lock 'em up!" Elroy recalled Bill saying. "I did not
want my family, my legacy, my father's legacy, to be based on
organized crime," Bill told one news outlet.

The level of enmity between the brothers had only grown.

Soon after Charles and David bought the other two brothers out in 1983 for a total of some $800 million, Bill became convinced that he had been cheated out of his fair share of the family fortune, because he thought his brothers had deliberately undervalued the company. In retaliation, Bill had launched a barrage of litigation against Charles and David, and even at one point against their mother. But soon Bill Koch again felt outmaneuvered.

After weighing the committee's charges against Koch Industries for eighteen months, the Oklahoma City grand jury cleared the company in a decision that was clouded by the kind of intrigue that would characterize the Kochs' later political involvement. *The Nation* obtained internal company records showing that in the face of potential criminal charges the Kochs had launched an emergency strategy aimed at buying political leverage. In Oklahoma, where the grand jury was meeting, they made donations to key politicians, including Senator Nickles. Around the same time, Nickles recommended the appointment of a new U.S. attorney in Oklahoma City to oversee the grand jury investigation. In making his recommendation, Senator Nickles passed over the head of the criminal division in the office and chose a protégé, Timothy Leonard, a former Republican state senator with no experience in criminal law whose family had financial interests in oil wells receiving Koch royalties. There were calls for his recusal, but President George H. W. Bush's Justice Department granted his request for a waiver.

Nancy Jones, the assistant U.S. attorney in the office who was handling the Oklahoma grand jury investigation of Koch Industries, parsed her words carefully when asked later if political pressure had ended the probe. "You can say this," she said, after a notably long pause. "The man who was passed over to be U.S. attorney was a liberal Democrat from out of state, and the one they appointed was a Republican with no federal, criminal, or trial experience." Elroy, the former FBI agent, was less circumspect. In his opinion, "Nickles put the kibosh on the prosecution there. He got involved in the appointment of the U.S. attorney. He was getting a tremendous amount of support from Koch. He was their man. He was the best senator money could buy."

Nickles summarily dismissed allegations of political interference, saying he was "not even aware that the U.S. Attorney's office was involved in a criminal investigation of Koch." He added that he had "never had a conversation" with Leonard, the U.S. attorney, "about it." Leonard also denied any impropriety.

But Arizona's Democratic senator, Dennis DeConcini, a former prosecutor who had chaired the Select Committee on Indian Affairs, said at the time, "I was surprised and disappointed. Our evidence was so strong. Our investigation was some of the finest work the Senate has ever done. There was an overwhelming case against Koch."

The federal criminal investigation had also been stymied by the mysterious disappearance of key Koch Industries documents. Jones had tried to assemble the record corroborating the Senate testimony so that it wasn't reliant on witnesses whose testimony might be dismissed as the word of disgruntled employees. But when she subpoenaed documents from the company, she was told that many had simply vanished. Discouraged, she eventually gave up and resigned. Elroy also departed. He retired from the FBI and went to work for Bill Koch as a full-time private investigator, ensuring that both sides of the family had their own personal detectives. Bill Koch also retained the services of a former Israeli intelligence officer. "You have to have intelligence," Bill explained when asked about this. "But there are legal ways, and illegal ways to do it."

With his hopes fading of seeing his brothers criminally prosecuted, Bill Koch pressed an alternative legal strategy that stirred even greater problems for Koch Industries. In his own display of the family's relentlessness, he filed a whistle-blower lawsuit against Koch Industries under the False Claims Act, accusing the company of stealing oil from government lands. A Civil War–era statute allows citizens to bring such *qui tam* suits in instances where they can prove that private contractors have defrauded the government. It was essentially the same case as the one that the Oklahoma grand jury had rejected, but the level of proof required in civil cases is lower.

As the civil case wended its way forward, Elroy went to work, gathering more evidence against Koch Industries. He crisscrossed the country, interviewing five hundred potential witnesses. In a fraternal version of the comic *Spy vs. Spy*, Bill Koch's investigators became convinced that Charles and David had private eyes intercepting their communications. Bill's team resorted to buying a $5,000 secure phone. Suspecting that Bill's lawyer's office had been infiltrated, his team also planted a salacious fake memo on a desk as bait, which his investigator, Elroy, claims the other side soon asked about. "They had a mole who was getting into the lawyer's office," maintains Elroy. "He worked on another floor in the same building, and they were paying him to get into the legal department."

Elroy's suspicions were not baseless. A Republican political operative who signed a confidentiality agreement, and so asked not to have his name disclosed, admits that Charles and David Koch hired him, through a law firm, to trek across the country for months, scouring for anything he could find in the way of damaging personal, business, or legal information on their brother Bill. He recalled, "It was to find anything that would cause trouble, that could be used like a sharp stick to poke in his eye."

The results of one such espionage operation still reside in a padlocked rental storage locker just off a busy highway on the Eastern Shore of Maryland. Inside the locker, boxes of old files document a remarkable effort by private investigators to compile dirt on Bill Koch. The files contain the confidential work records of a now-defunct private investigative firm called Beckett Brown International. Handwritten notes scrawled on the documents reveal that in 1998 the detective firm was hired to find out if Bill Koch was behind a spate of anti-Koch television advertisements that had begun airing. The ads, which were made by a group calling itself Citizens for a Clean America, showed the Koch brothers stuffing money into their pockets while they polluted the environment. The investigation did in fact point to Bill Koch being behind the group. But it appears that the methods used to unmask him were easily as questionable as his ploy.

The files show that the detective firm set up "D lines," which is slang for an operation that digs through garbage containers. They also surreptitiously obtained private telephone records, including those belonging to the advertising executive in Richmond, Virginia, whose small firm had produced one of the anti-Koch commercials. The executive, Barbara Fultz, says that she had no idea any of the Kochs were involved. She thought that she was making an ad for a good-government group. When she heard fifteen years later that investigators had somehow obtained her personal phone records, which still sat in a pile of old files in a locked storage unit on Maryland's Eastern Shore, many with handwritten notes scrawled about whom she was calling, Fultz said, "That blows my mind."

"I definitely did not give my phone records to anyone," said Fultz, a grandmother who is now retired. Fultz remembered that many years earlier the Richmond police had called her at two in the morning to tell her that the door to her office suite was ajar, which struck her as strange. She wondered if this is how her phone records were obtained. "It's frightening that someone would go into my space looking through my records without me knowing. I'm not political," she said, "but it makes me sad that the awesome freedom we have in the U.S.A. can be undermined by sneaky, power-hungry, unethical people."

In late 1999, at the same moment that Danny Smalley's wrongful death case went to trial in Texas, Bill Koch's whistle-blowing lawsuit alleging that Koch Industries engaged in a "deliberate pattern of fraud" simultaneously went on trial in Tulsa, Oklahoma. Elroy and other investigators working for Bill Koch had produced a devastating list of witnesses. Under oath, one former Koch employee after the next described stealing oil for the company. "I had to do what they said to do or I wouldn't have a job," one former employee, L. B. Perry, told the jury. In rebuttal, Koch Industries produced its own witnesses, who defended the company's practices as commonplace and legal and debunked its accusers as liars and disgruntled employees. But the turning point in the trial was reached when Phil Dubose, a Louisianan who had worked for Koch Industries for twenty-seven years before being laid off in 1994, took the stand.

Dubose had started as a "gauger," one of the grunts who measure crude oil as it's bought from suppliers, and had worked his way up to a senior management post supervising the company's transport of oil up and down the Eastern Seaboard. He oversaw four thousand miles of pipeline, 186 trucks, and a full marine division of barges. Dubose took the stand and testified about what he and other employees called "the Koch Method." As he later described it, "They were just mis-measuring crude oil from the Indian reservations as they did all over the U.S. If you bought crude, you'd shorten the gauge. They'd show you how. They had meters in the field. They'd recalibrate them, so if it showed a barrel, they'd say it was just three-quarters of a barrel when they were buying it. You did it in different ways. You cheated. If we sold a barge with fifteen hundred barrels, you'd say it was two thousand. It all involved weights and measurements, and they had their thumb on the scale. That was the Koch Method."

Bill Koch's investigators said they had stumbled across Dubose blindly, going down a list of former Koch employees. Not long before they knocked on Dubose's door, he had suffered a family tragedy and become more religious. When they arrived to ask him questions about Koch Industries, Dubose said he'd try to answer as best he could. As he began talking, in his Louisiana drawl, they knew they had struck another kind of gusher—an invaluable witness.

Dubose contended, "The Kochs never did play by the rules. They had their own playing field. They just didn't abide by anything. Not the EPA or anything else. They constantly polluted. If they got fined, it didn't matter, because they made so much money doing it. We never reported things like busted pipeline out in the field. Otherwise, we'd get fined. When we spilled oil, we never reported the real amount. We were told to do that, to keep our costs down. The Kochs expected us to lie and try to cover it up," he said.

Dubose maintained that the pressure to keep costs low was intense and, he believed, sprang from the top, infusing every level of the company. "If your books were short for more than a month or two, you'd be looking for a job," he said. Perhaps because he had been laid off without explanation, he was bitter, but he made an indelible impression. "They got that money dishonestly," he asserted. "They made it off the girls and the boys in the trenches, through their deceit. You don't have to be a genius like Bill Gates to make money the way they did," he concluded. "They just did it by breaking the rules all over the country."

Before the trial ended, Charles Koch himself took the stand, while his wife as well as David and David's wife, Julia, all watched. He denied defrauding the government and argued that if oil producers believed his company cheated, they would have sold their oil to the Kochs' competitors instead.

Evidently, the jury wasn't convinced. On December 23, 1999, it found Koch Industries guilty of making 24,587 false claims to the government. The company faced a potential fine of more than $200 million. As an additional insult, it would have to pay up to a quarter of the penalty to Bill Koch, who triumphantly declared to the press, "This shows they are the biggest crooks in the oil industry."

"It was the first time they were defeated," said Dubose, looking back. "We won because they didn't have a weapon as big as the one we used." Asked to what he was referring, he answered, "The truth."

In the end, Koch Industries settled Bill Koch's whistle-blower suit for $25 million. While most of the fines went to the federal government, the company paid over $7 million to Bill, along with his legal fees. As part of what came to be known in the family as the "global settlement," by mid-2001 the warring brothers finally also agreed to a cease-fire. Charles, David, and Bill signed a pact promising no further litigation and agreeing to a binding non-disparagement clause that imposed hefty escalating financial penalties for violations. On at least one occasion when Bill spoke too freely about his brothers, the general counsel for Koch Industries warned him that he was risking a fine. The pact bought an uneasy peace. But the damage to the company's image, and to the family's reputation, was already profound.

The Koch Industries' spokeswoman Melissa Cohlmia has said that the Kochs' serious legal losses were a learning experience and that as a result the company stepped up its corporate compliance efforts. After the 1990s, the company's overall environmental record did improve some, although in 2010 the company was still rated as one of the top ten air polluters in the United States by the Political Economy Research Institute at the University of Massachusetts Amherst. In 2012, the Environmental Protection Agency's database revealed Koch Industries to be the number one producer of toxic waste in the country. Producing 950 million pounds of toxic waste, it topped the list of 8,000 companies required by law to account for their handling of 650 toxic and carcinogenic chemicals spun off by industrial processes.

Charles Koch has acknowledged that he miscalculated earlier, writing in his 2007 book, *The Science of Success,* "We were caught unprepared by the rapid increase in regulation." As he explained it, "While business was becoming increasingly regulated, we kept thinking and acting as if we lived in a pure market economy."

From Charles's standpoint, the problem wasn't so much Koch Industries' conduct as the legal regime in which it operated. He seemed to be arguing that in the "pure market economy" that he favored, no such regulations would exist. As the Kochs took stock, it was clear that America was far from the laissez-faire utopia they idealized in the Freedom School. Having had their company fined hundreds of millions of dollars, labeled crooked by the U.S. Senate, and barely escaping federal criminal prosecution, the Kochs retooled. They sold off many of their most troublesome pipelines, paring their holdings down to four thousand miles, and they moved heavily into the finance sector, trading commodities and derivatives, where regulations and oversight were weaker. They diversified rapidly, acquiring DuPont's synthetic textile division, Invista, for $4.1 billion in 2004, which made them the world's producers of Lycra and other well-known brands such as StainMaster carpet. A year later, in 2005, they bought out Georgia-Pacific, the huge wood-products company, for $21 billion, which made them among the world's biggest manufacturers of plywood, laminates, and ubiquitous paper products like Dixie cups, Brawny paper towels, and Quilted Northern toilet paper. It also made them a major producer of formaldehyde, whose classification as a human carcinogen Koch Industries quietly fought, despite David Koch's public philanthropic support for cancer research.

The clash between Koch Industries' corporate interests

and David Koch's philanthropic work surfaced publicly in
2009. While David Koch sat on the advisory board of the
National Cancer Institute (NCI), and the National Institutes
of Health was concluding that formaldehyde should be treated
as a "known human carcinogen," a top executive at Georgia-
Pacific protested the government's findings. Traylor Champion, the company's vice president of environmental affairs,
sent a formal letter of protest to federal health authorities
stating that the company "strongly disagrees" with the NIH's
conclusion that formaldehyde should be treated as "a known
human carcinogen." David Koch neither recused himself from
the NCI's advisory board nor divested himself of his company's
stock while the carcinogenic properties of formaldehyde were
evaluated.

When questions were raised, Koch, who had undergone
rounds of advanced treatment for prostate cancer, was incensed
that anyone could question his integrity. But James Huff, deputy director at the National Institute of Environmental Health
Sciences, a division of the NIH, said it was "disgusting" for
Koch to be serving on the advisory board. "It's just not good
public health," he said. "Vested interests should not be on the
board. Those boards are very important. They're very influential as to whether NCI goes into formaldehyde or not. Billions
and billions are involved in formaldehyde." Harold Varmus, a
former director of the National Cancer Institute, who knew
Koch as a donor to scientific institutions, noted that many philanthropists had large business interests but admitted that he
was "surprised" to learn of the company's stance on formaldehyde.

The Kochs' corporate interests clashed with their philosophical positions on other issues as well, including their opposition to government-supported "crony capitalism." Koch
Industries took full advantage of a panoply of federal subsidies,
ranging from artificially low grazing fees on the 40 percent of
their 500,000 acres of cattle ranches that used federal lands, to

a deal with the Bush administration in 2002 to sell eight million barrels of crude oil to fill the Strategic Petroleum Reserve, a federal supply set aside as a hedge against market disruptions. "Can you think of any more anti-free-market tool than the Strategic Petroleum Reserve?" asked a former Koch executive. "Energy doesn't operate in a free market," he pointed out.

Koch Industries' practices belied its owners' virtuous talk in other ways, too. According to an investigative report by *Bloomberg Markets*, Koch Industries was "involved in improper payments to win business in Africa, India and the Middle East" and had "sold millions of dollars of petrochemical equipment to Iran, a country the U.S. identifies as a sponsor of global terrorism." The report suggested that the Kochs' Iranian deals flouted a trade ban put in place against the outlaw state by President Clinton in 1995. Koch Industries acknowledged that it had helped Iran build what became the largest methanol plant in the world in the midst of the trade embargo but insisted that the deal had been structured in a strictly legal way, by relying on foreign subsidiaries. The company subsequently fired the employee who exposed the controversial practices.

Yet as Charles and David continued to plow 90 percent of their company's profits back into their business—a strategy they often noted would be impossible if they were required to pay quarterly dividends to public shareholders—its revenues grew phenomenally. In 1960, it grossed a healthy $70 million, but by 2006 it was grossing an astounding $90 billion. "It is beyond spectacular," one Wall Street investment banker, Roger Altman of Evercore, observed. "It's just gigantically successful. It is in *everything*."

CHAPTER FIVE

The Kochtopus:
Free-Market Machine

AFTER SUFFERING HUMILIATING LOSSES IN THE COURTS AND Congress, the Kochs began to retool their approach not just to business but also to politics. They began to engage far more strategically, funneling money into the pursuit of power in a whole new way. More than anyone else, the man behind the Kochs' political transformation was Richard Fink, nicknamed the Pirate by detractors within their sphere for the handsome living he made on their payroll.

Fink was famous for flying to Wichita in the late 1970s as a twenty-seven-year-old graduate student, wearing a garish blue tie, a checkered shirt, and a brand-new white-piped black polyester suit, to beg for money from Charles. "What a jackass I looked like," he later admitted. After growing up in Maplewood, New Jersey, in a family that he joked made *The Sopranos* look like a home movie, Fink had become a devotee of Austrian free-market theory. He hoped Charles would fund a program in it at Rutgers in New Jersey, where he was teaching part-time while pursuing a graduate degree at NYU. Courses in Austrian economics were as rare as Viennese waltzes in most colleges at that time. But soon after Fink made the pitch, Charles pledged $150,000 for the program. When Fink later asked Charles why he'd thrown so much money at a long-haired, bearded graduate student in a shiny disco suit, Charles had supposedly quipped, "I like polyester. It's petroleum based."

By the late 1980s, Fink had supplanted Cato's Ed Crane as Charles Koch's main political lieutenant. Unlike Crane, who was interested in libertarian ideas but regarded it as "creepy when you have to deal with politicians," Fink was fascinated by the nuts and bolts of power. After studying the Kochs' political problems for six months, he drew up a practical blueprint, ostensibly inspired by Hayek's model of production, that impressed Charles by going beyond where his own 1976 paper on the subject had left off. Called "The Structure of Social Change," it approached the manufacture of political change like any other product. As Fink later described it in a talk, it laid out a three-phase takeover of American politics. The first phase required an "investment" in intellectuals whose ideas would serve as the "raw products." The second required an investment in think tanks that would turn the ideas into marketable policies. And the third phase required the subsidization of "citizens" groups that would, along with "special interests," pressure elected officials to implement the policies. It was in essence a libertarian production line, waiting only to be bought, assembled, and switched on.

Fink's plan was tailor-made for Charles Koch, who deeply admired Hayek and approached both business and politics with the systematic mind-set of an engineer. While some might find it disturbing to regard the democratic process as a factory, Charles soon adopted the approach as his own. As he told Brian Doherty, the libertarian writer, "To bring about social change requires a strategy that is vertically and horizontally integrated." It must span, he said, from "idea creation to policy development to education to grassroots organizations to lobbying to political action." Before long, libertarian wags had dubbed the Kochs' publicity-shy, multiarmed assembly line the Kochtopus, a name that stuck.

In contrast to their idealistic but amateurish approach during the old Libertarian Party days, with Fink's help the Kochs' methods became decidedly more pragmatic. Facing serious threats to their business, they began playing the Washington political game as aggressively as any other corporation, if not more so. After the public relations fiasco of the Senate hearings into Indian oil theft, for instance, Koch Industries crossed ideological lines to hire Robert Strauss, the former chairman of the Democratic National Committee, who was by then Washington's premier lobbyist. The company soon opened an office in the capital, which grew into a formidable in-house lobbying operation. Fink explained that it had been necessary for the company to establish a presence in Washington because it had felt "so brutalized by the process" and lacked "corporate defense" capabilities.

The Kochs had previously disdained conventional politics, but now they became major Republican donors. "It was the investigation that got them to the Republican Party," notes Kenneth Ballen, the former counsel to the Senate's investigative committee. Before that, he points out, "Charles had been so far right he was off in the ether. They thought Reagan was a sellout. But they were worried about their business. It was about power." Doherty saw the Kochs' embrace of the Republican Party in much the same way. He credits the Kochs with being by far the largest funders of libertarian ideas but notes they also became "direct funders of Republican politicians for all the same reasons other businesses are. It confuses a lot of people in the libertarian world, who think of them as sellouts," he conceded.

Their investment quickly transformed the brothers' political status. By 1996, they had grown into major players in the Republican Party. David Koch went from dismissing Bob Dole, the senator from Kansas, the home of Koch Industries, as just another "Establishment" politician "with no moral principles," in the early 1980s, to becoming the vice-chair of Dole's 1996 presidential campaign against Bill Clinton. No longer an outsider, the Koch family became Dole's third-largest financial backer. David Koch in fact hosted a birthday party for Dole, at which the candidate raised $150,000.

Dole reportedly helped the Kochs, too. Critics said he

did them a legislative favor designed to indemnify companies like theirs that had been charged with regulatory violations from having to pay huge federal legal fines. But the proposed legislative fix died when a sudden outbreak of salmonella in hamburgers scared Congress from weakening such penalties. Had it passed, though, it would have nullified tens of millions of dollars in fines that had been levied on Koch Industries. According to *The Washington Post*, Koch Industries did succeed in getting Dole's help on another matter, an exemption from a new real estate depreciation schedule, a favor that saved the company millions of dollars. As Dole conceded decades later, after he retired from politics, "I've always believed when people give big money, they—maybe silently—expect something in return."

The Kochs' affinity for hardball in politics, as in business, soon stirred controversy. In 1997, they became the focus of yet another Senate investigation. That year, the Clintons were in the headlines for campaign-finance scandals ranging from virtually renting the Lincoln Bedroom to big donors to taking contributions from a dubious Democratic bundler who later pleaded guilty to raising some of the money from China. The bundler, Johnny Chung, had infamously said, "I see the White House is like a subway. You have to put in coins to open the gates." In retaliation, the Democrats in the Senate, who were in the minority, conducted their own much less noticed probe, which soon led to the two little-known brothers from Wichita.

The Democrats produced a scathing report exposing what they called an "audacious" scheme by undisclosed big donors to illegally buy elections in the final moments of the 1996 campaign. It was undertaken by a suspicious shell corporation called Triad Management Services that had paid more than $3 million for unusually harsh attack ads against Democratic candidates in twenty-nine races. More than half of the advertising money came from an obscure nonprofit group whose real source of funds was a mystery, the Economic Education

Trust. The Senate committee's investigators believed that "the 'trust' was in fact financed in whole or in part by Charles and David Koch of Wichita, Kansas." The trust was a front group, according to the Senate report, designed to conceal the real donors' identities, in violation of campaign-finance laws.

The brothers, who had long opposed restrictions on their political spending, were suspected of having secretly paid for the attack ads, most of which aired in states where Koch Industries did business. In Kansas, where Triad Management was especially active, the funds were suspected of having tipped the outcome in four close races. The conservative Republican Sam Brownback's race for the U.S. Senate received a special boost, which included a barrage of phone calls informing voters that his opponent, Jill Docking, was a Jew. The shady victories in Kansas had national impact, helping Republicans retain control of the House of Representatives, despite President Clinton's reelection.

The Kochs, when asked by reporters if they had given the money, refused to comment. Charles Koch also failed to respond to an inquiry from the Senate investigators. In 1998, however, *The Wall Street Journal* finally confirmed a link, noting that a consultant on the Kochs' payroll had been involved in the scheme. Republicans argued that they were simply trying to balance the score against spending by labor unions, but in 1998 business outspent labor by a ratio of twelve to one. In the end, the Federal Election Commission ruled that the Triad scheme was illegal and fined its president and founder, Carolyn Malenick. Other participants, however, were never identified.

Charles Lewis, who heads the Investigative Reporting Workshop at American University and who founded the Center for Public Integrity, a nonpartisan watchdog group, describes the Triad scandal of 1996 as a "historic" moment in American politics. There had of course been many bigger campaign scandals before then. But Triad was a new model. He said it was the first time a major corporation used a tax-exempt nonprofit as a front group or, as he put it, "a cutout to secretly influence elections in a threatening way." He said the Kochs showed that "you could dump a million dollars on someone's head by using cutouts." After reporting on political corruption in Washington for years, Lewis concluded that "Koch Industries was the poster child of a company run amok."

What made the Koch family's growing financial role in American politics extraordinary was not just its willingness to flout the rules but also the way that in accordance with Fink's plan it merged all forms of political spending—campaign, lobbying, and philanthropic—into one investment aimed at paying huge future dividends to the donors. Lewis's Investigative Reporting Workshop spent a year in 2013 culling through the Kochs' financial records and concluded that their operation was "unprecedented in size, scope, and funding" and also in the way that it was "mutually reinforcing to the direct financial and political interests" of Koch Industries.

In 1992, David Koch likened the brothers' multipronged political strategy to that of venture capitalists with diversified portfolios. "My overall concept is to minimize the role of government and to maximize the role of the private economy and to maximize personal freedoms," he told the *National Journal.* "By supporting all of these different [nonprofit] organizations I am trying to support different approaches to achieve those objectives. It's almost like an investor investing in a whole variety of companies. He achieves diversity and balance. And he hedges his bets."

What resulted from this approach was a complicated flow-chart enabling the Kochs to use their fortune to influence public policy from an astounding number of different directions at once. At the top, the funds all came from the same source—the Kochs. And in the end, the contributions all served the same pro-business, limited-government goals. But they funneled the money simultaneously through three different kinds of channels. They made political contributions to party committees and candidates, such as Dole. Their business made contributions through its political action committee and exerted influence by lobbying. And they founded numerous nonprofit groups, which they filled with tax-deductible contributions from their private foundations. Other wealthy activists made political contributions, and other companies lobbied. But the Kochs' strategic and largely covert philanthropic spending became their great force magnifier.

By 1990, enterprising conservative and libertarian activists were wearing a path to Wichita, where they, like Fink before them, would pitch their proposals to Charles Koch in hopes of his patronage. Typical was the experience in 1991 of two former Reagan administration lawyers, Clint Bolick, a former aide to Clarence Thomas, and William "Chip" Mellor III, in search of seed money for a new kind of aggressive, right-wing public interest law firm that would litigate against government regulations in favor of "economic liberty." Mellor recalled thinking, "Who else would give us enough money to be serious?" According to Mellor, after lower-level aides initially turned down the proposal, Charles Koch himself committed $1.5 million on the spot, but with strings attached, keeping him in control. As Mellor recalled, "He said, 'Here's what I'm going to do. I'll give you up to $500,000 a year for three years, each year, but you have to come back each year and demonstrate that you've met these milestones that you've set out to accomplish and I will evaluate it on a yearly basis, and there's no guarantees.'" The legal group, the Institute for Justice, went on to bring numerous successful cases against government regulations, including campaign-finance laws, several of which reached the Supreme Court.

"In recent years," a prescient news story noted in 1992, "money from Wichita has gushed into the coffers of virtually every Washington think tank and public interest group dedicated to free-market economics and the libertarian credo of minuscule government regulation." In 1990 alone, the article noted, the three main private foundations controlled by Charles and David Koch disbursed $4 million to such ostensibly nonpartisan but politically motivated groups.

Few outside the rarefied world of far-right, laissez-faire economics noticed, but the Kochs' multidimensional political spending kept growing. Between 1998 and 2008, for instance, Charles Koch's private fund, the Charles G. Koch Charitable Foundation, made more than $48 million in tax-deductible grants, primarily to groups promoting his political views. The Claude R. Lambe Charitable Foundation, which was controlled by Charles and his wife, Liz, along with two company employees and an accountant, similarly made more than $28 million in tax-deductible grants. David Koch's fund, the David H. Koch Charitable Foundation, made more than $120 million in tax-deductible grants—many to cultural and scientific projects rather than political. Meanwhile, during those years Koch Industries spent more than $50 million on lobbying. Separately, the company's political action committee, Koch-PAC, donated some $8 million to political campaigns, more than 80 percent of it to Republicans. In addition, the Kochs and other family members spent millions more on personal campaign contributions.

Only the Kochs know precisely how much they spent on this sprawling political enterprise, because the public record remains incomplete. By dispersing much of the money through a labyrinth of nonprofit groups, the Kochs made the full extent of their political "investment" difficult if not impossible for the public to detect. In 2008 alone, public tax records indicate that the three main Koch family foundations gave money to thirty-four different political and policy organizations, three of which they founded and several of which they directed.

There were some legal boundaries. By law, tax-exempt charities, which the IRS designates as 501(c)(3)s, must refrain from involvement in lobbying and electoral politics and serve the public rather than their donors' interests. But such laws are rarely enforced and are subject to flexible interpretation.

Critics began to complain that the Kochs' approach to philanthropy subverted the purpose of tax-exempt charitable giving. A 2004 report by the National Committee for Responsive Philanthropy, a watchdog group, found the Kochs' philanthropy self-serving. "These foundations give money to nonprofit organizations that do research and advocacy on issues that impact the profit margin of Koch Industries," it charged.

But the Kochs defended the millions they gave to groups fighting environmental regulations and supporting lower taxes on industry and the rich as public-spirited. Several longtime associates questioned this. Gus diZerega, the former family friend, suggested that the Kochs' youthful ardor for libertarianism had largely devolved into a rationale for corporate self-interest. "Perhaps he has confused making money with freedom," he said of Charles. One conservative who worked closely with the Kochs but declined to be identified in order not to inflame the relationship went so far as to call their tax-exempt giving "a shell game." He contended they merely saw philanthropy as preferable to paying taxes. "People say, 'Wow—they're so generous!'" he marveled. "It's just the best available option for them. If they didn't give it to their causes, they would have to give it to the government. At least this way they control how it's spent." He noted that by blending their corporate and charitable work, "they draw some pretty fine lines. It's really another form of lobbying." But he conceded, "They've built a pretty amazing machine."

From the start, the Kochs exerted unusually tight personal control over their philanthropic endeavors. "If we're going to give a lot of money, we'll make darn sure they spend it in a way that goes along with our intent," David Koch has acknowledged. "And if they make a wrong turn and start doing things we don't agree with," he told Doherty, "we withdraw funding."

An early example of Charles Koch flexing his muscles took place at the Cato Institute in 1981, when he fired one of the think tank's five original stockholders. Ironically, although Charles had criticized Robert Welch for turning the John Birch Society into a cult of personality by flaunting his owner- ship of the organization's stock, Charles had set Cato up in the same way, as a nonprofit with stockholders, who picked the board of directors. The arrangement was rare in the nonprofit world. But as Charles had observed of the John Birch Society, it guaranteed the directors an unusual measure of continuing control.

The director whom Charles fired at Cato was a major fig- ure in libertarian circles, Murray Rothbard, a radical Upper West Side Jewish intellectual whose work Charles had subsi- dized in happier days. Rothbard called the putsch "iniquitous," "high-handed," and "illegal." He went on to claim that Charles had "confiscated the shares which I had naively left in Koch's Wichita office for 'safekeeping,' an act clearly in violation of our agreement as well as contrary to every tenet of libertarian principle."

Some suspected that Rothbard, an Austrian economic school purist, was fired for criticizing Koch, whom he had accused of watering down unpopular libertarian positions in order to get more votes for his brother's 1980 candidacy. The platform, for instance, had pulled back from advocating the complete abolition of all income taxes. It also called for shrink- ing rather than abolishing the military. The controversy set off alarms in the hothouse libertarian community, marking Charles in the eyes of those who took Rothbard's side as ruth- less and rapacious, more interested in power than in principle.

Charles's drive for control was the focus later of testimony that Rothbard gave in one of the many rounds of fights between the four Koch brothers over their patrimony. A memo sum- marizing Rothbard's prospective testimony quoted him saying that Charles "cannot tolerate dissent" and will "go to any end to acquire/retain control over the nonprofit foundations with which he is associated." Rothbard accused Charles of dictating everything from the office decor to the design of Cato's stationery. Further, he alleged that while Charles wanted "absolute control" of the nonprofits with which he was associated, he was intent on "being able to spend other people's money." This criticism would later be reprised in connection with the Koch seminars, which some saw as Charles's means of creating a political slush fund filled with other people's money but under his own control. Rothbard also accused Charles of using nonprofit organizations to "acquire access to, and respect from, influential people in government."

In the mid-1980s, as called for in the first phase of Fink's plan, the Kochs also began to establish an academic beachhead of their own. Their particular focus was on George Mason University, a little-known campus of Virginia's prestigious higher-education system, located in the Washington suburbs. In 1977, *The Washington Post* described the school as toiling in "the wilderness of obscurity." By 1981, Fink had moved his Austrian economics program there from Rutgers, eventually naming it the Mercatus Center. The think tank was entirely funded by outside donations, largely from the Kochs, but it was located in the midst of the public university's campus, so it touted itself, somewhat misleadingly, as "the world's premier university source for market-oriented ideas—bridging the gap between academic ideas and real-world problems."

Financial records show that the Koch family foundations donated some $30 million to the school, much of it going to the Mercatus Center. *The Washington Post* described Mercatus as a "staunchly anti-regulatory center funded largely by Koch Industries Inc." This, however, raised questions about whether the Mercatus Center was in fact an independent intellectual center or an extension of the Kochs' lobbying operation. Clayton Coppin, who taught history at George Mason and compiled the confidential study of Charles's political activities for

Bill Koch, describes Mercatus outright in his report as "a lobbying group disguised as a disinterested academic program."
The arrangement, he points out, had financial advantages for
the Kochs, because it enabled Charles "to have a tax deduction
for financing a group, which for all practical purposes is a lobbying group for his corporate interest."

Sharing a building with the Mercatus Center was the
heavily Koch-funded Institute for Humane Studies, chaired by
Charles Koch. The IHS was founded by F. A. "Baldy" Harper,
a free-market fundamentalist who had been a trustee at the
Freedom School, where he had written essays for *The Freeman*, calling taxes "theft," welfare "immoral," and labor unions
"slavery" and opposing court-ordered remedies to racial segregation. Charles Koch had eulogized Harper glowingly, saying, "Of all the teachers of liberty, none was as well-beloved as
Baldy, for it was he who taught the teachers and, in teaching,
taught them humility and gentleness."

The aim of the IHS was to cultivate and subsidize a farm
team of the next generation's libertarian scholars. Anxious
at one point that the war of ideas was proceeding too slowly,
Charles reportedly demanded better metrics with which to
monitor students' political views. To the dismay of some faculty
members, applicants' essays had to be run through computers
in order to count the number of times they mentioned the free-
market icons Ayn Rand and Milton Friedman. Students were
tested at the beginning and the end of each week for ideological
improvement. The institute also housed the Charles G. Koch
summer internship program, a paid fellowship placing students
who shared the Kochs' views in like-minded nonprofit groups,
where they could join the libertarian network.

George Mason's economics department, meanwhile,
became a hotbed of controversial theories that began to transform Americans' tax bills, serving as an incubator for the
supply-side tax cuts in the Reagan administration that hugely
advantaged the rich. Paul Craig Roberts, an adjunct professor at

GMU, drafted a precursor to the first supply-side tax cut bill of the Reagan era, which was introduced by his former boss Congressman Jack Kemp. While these tax cuts starved the government, George Mason also belittled its role philosophically. A star on its faculty was James Buchanan, the founder of "public choice" theory, who often described his approach as "politics without romance" because he categorized elected officials and public servants as just another greedy, self-aggrandizing private interest group, a view popular with antigovernment libertarians. In 1986, Buchanan was awarded a Nobel Prize in economics. Liberal economists were aghast. Robert Lekachman, for instance, lambasted Buchanan for reducing "all human behavior to simple self-interest." The prize nonetheless was an indisputable achievement, helping to put the school, and libertarianism, on the map.

Julian Sanchez, a fellow at the Cato Institute, soon exalted George Mason as a "libertarian mecca," saying, "It may well be the most heavily libertarian-staffed institution of higher education in the country." Liberals, however, regarded the Kochs' singular influence over the school with suspicion. "It's ground zero for deregulation policy in Washington," said Rob Stein, the Democratic political strategist who studied how the right wing spent money. Noting the Kochs' unusually large role, he said, "George Mason is a public university and receives public funds. Virginia is hosting an institution that the Kochs practically control."

The many hats that Rich Fink wore only underscored critics' concerns. As he grew in importance to Charles Koch, Fink relinquished his formal role at the Mercatus Center, handing its stewardship off to a protégé, and joined Koch Industries as its head of lobbying but remained on the university's prestigious Board of Visitors. He also was at one point the president of the Charles G. Koch Charitable Foundation, the president of the Claude R. Lambe Charitable Foundation, a director of the Fred C. and Mary R. Koch Foundation, and an integral member of several of the Kochs' political groups. The fungibility of his roles hinted at the fine line between nonprofit and for-profit pursuits within the Kochs' enterprise.

As Fink's star rose, Crane's fell. Crane still ran the Cato Institute, but in 1992 Charles Koch resigned from the libertarian think tank's board, although David remained a trustee. Associates suspected that Crane, who didn't take orders gladly, had not demonstrated sufficient fealty to his patron. Crane had privately ridiculed Charles's management philosophy, which Charles trademarked under the name Market-Based Management, or MBM, and later distilled into his book *The Science of Success*. In essence, Charles believed that businesses' corporate culture should replicate the competitiveness of the free market. Employees at almost every level of his company were compensated on the basis of the value they created, competing with each other for bonuses, which constituted large portions of their annual pay. Charles described MBM as a "holistic system" containing "five dimensions: vision, virtue and talents, knowledge processes, decision rights and incentives." Some company employees privately mocked the cutthroat culture that MBM fostered as "Making the Brothers Money." *Forbes*, too, lampooned Charles a bit, in its review of his book, describing him as an "autodidact" who had "almost a Marxist faith in 'fixed laws' that 'govern human well-being'" and whose "system for grading employees" was "especially obtuse."

Despite the mixed reviews, Charles insisted that personnel in all corners of his enterprise adhere to his system, setting aside regular time to practice and review the techniques. "It became exactly the kind of bureaucracy that libertarians detest," noted one former employee, before adding, "He's the billionaire, not me, so who knows?" Market-Based Management embraced the notion that employees at every level, even the bottom, might have superior ideas to those at the top. Theoretically, it was an egalitarian approach, yet how open Charles really was to those like Crane who challenged his top-down authority is debatable. Many found him remarkably humble for one of the wealthiest men in the world, noting that he lunched regularly in the company cafeteria alongside his employees. But in a 1999 speech, Charles likened his fixed beliefs to those of Martin Luther, the founder of Protestantism. "In that, I echo Martin Luther," he said of his own free-market views. "Here I stand. I can do no other." The comparison was revealing.

In any case, Crane was less than reverent when Charles tried to impose his management system on the Cato Institute. From his large office in Cato's strikingly modern, light-filled Washington headquarters, Crane later made clear that he regarded Charles as a serious thinker and an exemplary businessman, but he couldn't help but poke fun at MBM. "He thinks he's a genius. He's the emperor, and he's convinced he's wearing clothes," Crane said with a snicker. Fink, by contrast, was much more solicitous of Charles's ideas. "Richie exploited MBM to the hilt," a Cato official said of Fink. "He took over with a shiv" in Crane's back. "He's well named."

With Cato and the Institute for Humane Studies, the Kochs checked off the first item on Fink's shopping list for social change—institutions that could hatch scholarly ideas in line with their own thinking. The Mercatus Center checked off the second item, a more practical organization aimed at promoting these ideas into action. Its location, just across the Potomac from the Capitol, was a bonus, enabling its fellows to testify regularly as independent experts at congressional hearings. By 2004, *The Wall Street Journal* dubbed it "the most important think tank you've never heard of" and noted that fourteen of the twenty-three regulations that President George W. Bush placed on a "hit list" had been suggested by Mercatus scholars. Eight of those were environmental protections. Fink told the paper that the Kochs have "other means of fighting [their] battles" and that the Mercatus Center does not actively promote the company's private interests. But Thomas McGarity, a law professor at the University of Texas who specialized in environmental issues, argued that "Koch has been constantly in trouble with the EPA, and Mercatus has constantly hammered on the agency." One environmental lawyer who clashed repeatedly with the Mercatus Center dismissed it as a lobbying shop dressed up as a nonprofit, calling it "a means of laundering economic aims." The lawyer explained the strategy: "You take corporate money and give it to a neutral-sounding think tank," which "hires people with pedigrees and academic degrees who put out credible-seeming studies. But they all coincide perfectly with the economic interests of their funders."

In 1997, for instance, the EPA moved to reduce surface ozone, a form of air pollution caused, in part, by emissions from oil refineries. Susan Dudley, an economist who became a top official at the Mercatus Center, came up with a novel criticism of the proposed rule. The EPA, she argued, had not taken into account that by blocking the sun, smog cut down on cases of skin cancer. She claimed that if pollution were controlled, it would cause up to eleven thousand additional cases of skin cancer each year.

In 1999, the District of Columbia Circuit Court embraced Dudley's pro-smog argument. Evaluating the EPA rule, the court found that the EPA had "explicitly disregarded" the "possible health benefits of ozone." In another part of the opinion, the court also ruled, 2–1, that the EPA had overstepped its authority.

Afterward, the Constitutional Accountability Center, a watchdog group, revealed that the judges in the majority had previously attended one of the all-expenses-paid legal seminars for judges that were heavily funded by the Kochs' foundations. This one had taken place on a Montana ranch run by a group that the Kochs helped subsidize called the Foundation for Research on Economics and the Environment. The judges claimed that their decision was unaffected by the junket. Their embrace of the Mercatus Center's novel argument, however, soon proved embarrassing. The Supreme Court overruled their position unanimously, noting that the Clean Air Act's standards are absolute and not subject to cost-benefit analysis. Although their side lost in the end, the case illustrated that the Kochs' ideological pipeline was humming.

The most fateful Mercatus Center hire might have been Wendy Gramm, an economist and director at the giant Texas energy company Enron who was the wife of Senator Phil Gramm, the powerful Texas Republican. In the mid-1990s, she became the head of Mercatus's Regulatory Studies Program. There, she pushed Congress to support what came to be known as the Enron Loophole, exempting the type of energy derivatives from which Enron profited from regulatory oversight. Both Enron and Koch Industries, which also was a major trader of derivatives, lobbied desperately for the loophole. Koch claimed there was no need for government policing because corporations' concern for their reputations would cause them to self-regulate.

Some experts foresaw danger. In 1998, Brooksley Born, chair of the Commodity Futures Trading Commission, warned that the lucrative but risky derivatives market needed more government oversight. But Senator Gramm, who chaired the Senate Banking Committee, ignored such warnings, crafting a deregulatory bill made to order for Enron and Koch, called the Commodity Futures Modernization Act. Despite Born's warning, the Clinton administration embraced the exemptions too, swayed by Wall Street pressure.

In 2001, Enron collapsed in a heap of bogus financial statements and fraudulent accounting practices. But Wendy Gramm had pocketed up to $1.8 million from Enron the year after arguing for the loophole. And it emerged that before going under, Enron had made substantial campaign contributions to Senator Gramm, while its chairman, Kenneth Lay, had given money to the Mercatus Center.

By the end of 2002, the Gramms had gone into semire-
tirement, but at the Mercatus Center the zeal to exempt enormously risky markets, including energy derivatives favored by
Koch Industries, lived on. The consequences wouldn't become
fully visible until the economic crash of 2008. By then, George
Mason University was both the largest single recipient of Koch
funds for higher education and the largest research university
in Virginia.

George Mason was the Kochs' largest libertarian academic project but far from the only one. By 2015, according
to an internal list, the Charles Koch Foundation was subsidizing pro-business, antiregulatory, and antitax programs in 307
different institutions of higher education in America and had
plans to expand into 18 more. The schools ranged from cash-
hungry West Virginia University to Brown University, where
the Kochs, in the tradition of the Olin Foundation, established
an Ivy League "beachhead."

At Brown, which is often thought of as the most liberal
of the Ivy schools, Charles Koch's foundation gave $147,154
in 2009 to the Political Theory Project, a freshman seminar
in free-market classics taught by a libertarian, Professor John
Tomasi. "After a whole semester of Hayek, it's hard to shake
them off that perspective over the next four years," Tomasi confided "slyly," according to a conservative publication. Charles
Koch's foundation gave additional funds to Brown to support
faculty research and postdoctoral candidates in such topics as
why bank deregulation is good for the poor.

At West Virginia University, the Charles Koch Foundation's donation of $965,000 to create the Center for Free
Enterprise came with some strings attached. The foundation
required the school to give it a say over the professors it funded,
in violation of traditional standards of academic independence.
The Kochs' investment had an outsized impact in the small,
poor state where coal, in which the Kochs had a financial interest, ruled. One of the WVU professors approved for funding,

Russell Sobel, edited a 2007 book called *Unleashing Capitalism: Why Prosperity Stops at the West Virginia Border and How to Fix It*, arguing that mine safety and clean water regulations only hurt workers. "Are workers really better off being safer but making less income?" it asked. Soon, Sobel was briefing West Virginia's governor and cabinet, as well as a joint session of the Senate and the House Finance Committees. The state Republican Party chairman declared Sobel's antiregulatory book the blueprint for its party platform.

In 2014, a sparsely regulated West Virginia company, Freedom Industries, spilled ten thousand gallons of a mysterious, foul-smelling chemical into the drinking water of Charleston, the state's largest city, triggering panic in 300,000 residents, whom authorities ordered away from their taps. It was just another in a seemingly endless history of tragic industrial disasters afflicting West Virginia. By then, though, Sobel was long gone. He was listed as a visiting scholar at the Citadel in South Carolina, and an expert at the Mercatus Center at George Mason University.

Defenders of the Kochs' growing academic influence, like John Hardin, director of university relations at the Charles Koch Foundation, argued that their grants were bringing ideological diversity and debate to campuses. "We support professors who add to the variety of ideas available on college campuses. And in every case the school maintains control over its staffing and teaching decisions," he wrote in *The Wall Street Journal*.

But in the eyes of critics, the Kochs had not so much enriched as corrupted academia, sponsoring courses that would otherwise fail to meet the standards of legitimate scholarship. John David, an economics professor at West Virginia University Tech who witnessed the school's transformation, wrote in a scathing newspaper column that it had become clear that "entire academic areas at universities can be bought just like politicians. The difference is that universities are supposed to permit open dialogue and exchange of ideas and not be places for the indoctrination of innocent students with dictated propaganda prescribed by outside special interests."

The first two steps of Fink's plan were now complete. Yet the Koch brothers concluded that these steps were still not enough to effect change. Free-market absolutism was still a sideshow in American politics. They needed the third and final phase of Fink's plan—a mechanism to deliver their ideas to the street and to mobilize the public's support behind them. "Even great ideas are useless if they remain trapped in the ivory tower," Charles noted in a 1999 speech. David put it differently. "What we needed was a sales force."

Part Two

Secret Sponsors

Covert Operations, 2009–2010

Total liberty for wolves is death to the lambs.

—*Isaiah Berlin*

CHAPTER SIX

Boots on the Ground

IN HIS 1976 BLUEPRINT FOR THE CREATION OF A LIBERTARIAN
movement, Charles Koch had emphasized the need to use
"all modern sales and motivational techniques." Less than a
decade later, in 1984, he set out to launch a private political
sales force. On paper, it was yet another Koch-funded conservative nonprofit group fighting for less government. It called
itself Citizens for a Sound Economy (CSE). From the outside,
it looked like an authentic political group, created by a groundswell of concerned citizens, much like Ralph Nader's Public
Interest Research Groups, which had sprung up all over the
country.

According to the nonpartisan Center for Public Integrity,
however, it was in fact a new kind of weapon in the arsenal
of several of America's biggest businesses—a fake populist
movement secretly manufactured by corporate sponsors—not
grass roots, but "Astroturf," as such synthetic groups came
to be known. Unlike corporate lobbying or campaign spending, contributions to Citizens for a Sound Economy could be
kept hidden because it classified itself as a nonprofit "educational" group (as well as having its own charitable foundation
and political action committee). By far the largest of the new
group's shadowy sponsors were the Kochs, who provided it
with at least $7.9 million between 1986 and 1993.

The idea of employing a deceptive front group to mask corporate self-interest was not original, even within the Koch family. The same ruse had been used not just by the du Pont family
and others during the New Deal years but also by a group to
which Fred Koch belonged in the 1950s. He was an early and

active member of the Wichita-based DeMille Foundation for Political Freedom, an antilabor union group that was a forerunner of the National Right to Work Legal Defense Foundation. In a revealing private letter, one of its staff members explained the group's "Astroturf" strategy. In reality, he said, big-business industrialists would run the group, serving as its "anonymous quarterbacks," and "call the turns." But he said they needed to sell the "yarn" that the group was "composed of housewives, farmers, small businessmen, professional people, wage earners—not big business industrialists." Otherwise, he admitted, the movement was "almost certainly doomed to failure."

Fred Koch's sons used the same playbook at Citizens for a Sound Economy. Libertarianism remained a lonely crusade, but CSE used corporate treasuries to market its spread and give it the aura of a mass movement. Its mission, according to one early participant, Matt Kibbe, "was to take these heavy ideas and translate them for mass America." Kibbe explained, "We read the same literature Obama did about nonviolent revolutions—Saul Alinsky, Gandhi, Martin Luther King. We studied the idea of the Boston Tea Party as an example of nonviolent social change. We learned we needed boots on the ground to sell ideas, not candidates."

Within a few years, the group had mobilized fifty paid field workers, in twenty-six states, to rally voters behind the Kochs' agenda of lower taxes, less regulation, and less government spending. CSE, for instance, pushed to abolish progressive taxes in favor of a flat tax and to "privatize" many government programs, including Social Security. "Ideas don't happen on their own," noted Kibbe. "Throughout history, ideas need patrons."

Although the Kochs were the founders and early funders of the group, it soon served as a front for dozens of the country's largest corporations. Its head denied that it was a rent-a-movement. But private records obtained by *The Washington*

Post showed that a procession of large companies ranging from Exxon to Microsoft had made contributions to the organization after which it had mobilized public support for their agendas. Many of the companies were embroiled in fights against the government. Microsoft, for instance, was trying to stave off an antitrust suit. It reportedly made a contribution to the foundation set up by Citizens for a Sound Economy that was aimed at reducing the Justice Department's antitrust work.

The group's unorthodox practices occasionally stirred controversy. In 1990, the organization created a spin-off, Citizens for the Environment, which called acid rain and other environmental problems "myths." When the *Pittsburgh Post-Gazette* investigated the matter, it discovered that the spin-off group had "no citizen membership of its own."

One insider said the main organization's membership claims were deceptive as well. "They always said they had 250,000 members," he later recalled, but when he asked if that meant they carried cards or paid dues, he was told no, it just meant they'd contributed money at one point, no matter how long ago or how small an amount. "It was intellectually dishonest," he maintains.

By the time Bill Clinton became president, Citizens for a Sound Economy had become a prototype for the kinds of corporate-backed opposition campaigns that would proliferate after Obama was elected. In 1993, it waged a successful assault on Clinton's proposed tax on energy, which would have taxed fossil fuel use but exempted renewable energy sources. In a show of force, without revealing its corporate sponsors, CSE ran advertisements, staged media events, and targeted political opponents. It also mobilized noisy, grassroots-seeming antitax rallies outside the Capitol—which NPR described as "designed to strike fear into the hearts of wavering Democrats."

Dan Glickman, one of the Democrats who supported the energy tax and who formerly represented the Kochs' hometown of Wichita, believes that secret money they funneled against him ended his eighteen-year congressional career. "I can't prove it, but I think I was probably their victim," he said. Having come from Wichita, he had friends in common with the Kochs who vouched for their ideological sincerity, yet to him it seemed obvious that sincere though they may be, "Their political theory is nothing more than a rationalization for self-interest."

Fink later gave credence to Glickman's suspicions. After the election, he admitted that their campaign to defeat the energy tax had been motivated by their bottom line. "Our belief is that the tax, over time, may have destroyed our business," he told *The Wichita Eagle*.

CSE's success in helping to kill Clinton's energy tax emboldened the group. Next, it went after his proposed tax increase on high earners. According to *The Wall Street Journal*, however, CSE's ads were deeply misleading, focusing on owners of car washes and other mom-and-pop small businesses, implying that the tax was aimed at the middle class when in fact it would affect only the wealthiest 4 percent. It was the kind of exaggerated scare tactic that would become a Koch trademark during the Obama years. The secret corporate donors, though, were ecstatic about Citizens for a Sound Economy. "They can fly under the radar screen . . . There are no limits, no restrictions and no disclosure," one exulted.

But at the end of 2003, internal rivalries caused Citizens for a Sound Economy to split apart. "The split was about control," recalled Dick Armey, the former Republican House majority leader from Texas who chaired the organization after leaving Congress. "I never totally understood it, and I'm not sure I understand it now." He believed the Kochs wanted to use the group "to push their business interests; they wanted CSE to lobby on those issues," he said. Others have suggested it was Armey who was pushing the interests of his law firm's clients, a charge Armey denies. There was another factor, too, behind the split, Armey suggested. "I saw it as a power grab by Richard Fink. He was trying to get a greater place in the sun to maintain his standing and his good living with the Koch family."

Armey didn't know the Kochs well, but he had talked with Charles before joining the organization and found him "a little peculiar. Charles seemed half-mysterious," he said. "He was half-secretive. He'd speak in cryptic tones. You'd have to think, 'What does he mean?' He'd talk about this business of trying to 'save the country' and all that." It seemed to Armey that Charles had conflicting aims. "Charles wanted to be more in control, but he also wanted to be more behind the scenes. I don't get it." Another veteran of Citizens for a Sound Economy concluded that while the Kochs loved liberty as an abstraction, "they were very controlling, very top-down. You can't build an organization *with* them. *They* run it."

Armey went on to start another conservative free-market group, FreedomWorks, with a few other renegades from the organization. It was at this moment, in 2003, that the Kochs inaugurated the first of their twice-a-year donor summits, which, according to one insider, were originally designed as a means of off-loading the costs of Koch Industries' environmental and regulatory fights onto others. The first conference was a fairly dismal affair, with fewer than twenty participants, mostly from Charles's social circle. The lectures were painfully dull, according to one insider.

Meanwhile, David Koch and Richard Fink created a new nonprofit advocacy group out of the remaining shards of Citizens for a Sound Economy. They called their new organization Americans for Prosperity. Like CSE, it would be accused by critics of using the guise of nonprofit status to work, behind a screen of anonymity, on behalf of the Kochs' corporate and political interests. Like Citizens for a Sound Economy, the new group had several different divisions, with different tax statuses. One wing of the new organization was the Americans for Prosperity Foundation, whose board members included both David Koch and Richard Fink. The foundation was a 501(c)(3) educational organization, so donations to it could be written off as tax-deductible charitable gifts. But while it could "educate" the public, it could not participate in electoral politics. The other division was an advocacy organization, just called Americans for Prosperity. Under the tax code, it was a 501(c)(4) "social welfare" group, which meant that it could participate in electoral politics so long as this was not its "primary" activity. Donations to this side of the organization could also be made in secret but were not tax deductible.

To run this more political side of the operation, the Kochs hired Tim Phillips, a political veteran who had worked with Ralph Reed, the former head of the Christian Coalition. Reed was regarded as the religious Right's savviest political operative. He and Phillips had co-founded Century Strategies, a dynamo of a campaign-consulting firm that became notorious for its close and lucrative business ties to Jack Abramoff, a lobbyist who went to prison for defrauding millions of dollars from Native American casino owners, among other clients. Phillips was not charged in connection with the scandal but had helped create a religious-sounding organization that in fact handled casino cash for Abramoff.

Phillips was part of a tough, hardball-playing group, far from the wonky, intellectual mists of Charles Koch's early libertarian musings. Both Reed and Abramoff were early protégés of Grover Norquist, the influential Washington-based antitax activist famous for proclaiming his hope of shrinking government to the size where he could "drown it in the bathtub." Norquist had confided once that he regarded Reed and Abramoff as his two greatest students. "Grover told me Ralph was his Trotsky, and Abramoff was his Stalin," recalls Bruce Bartlett, the conservative economist.

Phillips had grown up poor in South Carolina in a family of Democrats so ardent that his father, who worked in the textile mills before becoming a bus driver, was named Franklin Delano Roosevelt and his grandfather had worked in Roosevelt's WPA. But in what Phillips recalled as one of the most "traumatic" moments of his adolescence, he was mesmerized one evening in 1980 by Ronald Reagan while watching the television news. He told his father, "I'm gonna be for that guy." Shocked, his father turned off the television, called his mother into the room, and warned him sternly that the Republicans "are for the rich man, Son. Come on, are you kidding me?"

Phillips retorted, "Well maybe I want to be rich one day." His parents were so dismayed, he recalled, "You'd have thought I'd said, you know, I'm moving to the Soviet Union, I'm gonna become, you know, a Godless communist atheist or whatever."

A Southern Baptist, Phillips enrolled in Liberty University, Jerry Falwell's evangelical school in Lynchburg, Virginia. But after one semester, he ran out of money and dropped out. From that point on, he was helped by one conservative group after the next, taking internships with free housing until he was hired as an operative on a Republican congressional campaign in Virginia. By 1997, he had founded Century Strategies with Reed. Together, they helped turn out evangelical voters in 2004 to reelect George Bush. The Christian Right drew criticism that year for motivating social conservatives by fanning fears about gay rights. In 2005, David Koch and Art Pope, the North Carolina dime store magnate and regular at the Koch seminars, drafted him to run Americans for Prosperity. "I was intrigued by the idea of being able to build a movement based on economic issues, the way that Christian Right folks had built a movement based on social issues," he recalled, explaining why he took the job.

Phillips's online biography described him as an expert in "grasstops" and "grassroots" political organizing. The Kochs' choice of Phillips, a hardened professional, signaled a tough new phase for the Kochtopus. Norquist, famous for praising "throat slitters" in politics, approvingly called Phillips "a grownup who can make things happen."

Phase three of Fink's plan could now begin in earnest.

CHAPTER SEVEN

Tea Time

ACCORDING TO MOST CONVENTIONAL WISDOM, THE TEA PARTY movement sprang to life in America spontaneously, unsullied by vested financial interests. As with most creation myths, however, the reality is quite another story.

The often-told tale was that the remarkable awakening of antigovernment rage that spread across the country in 2009 was triggered by an unplanned outburst on live television from Rick Santelli, a former futures trader, who was a regular on-air contributor to the CNBC business news network. The date of Santelli's tirade was notably early in Obama's presidency, February 19, 2009, less than one month after Obama was sworn in as president. At the time, Obama enjoyed approval ratings of over 60 percent. A year later, a congressman championing Obama's health-care proposal would be spat on, and two years later his party would lose control of the House of Representatives, effectively ending his ability to enact "change you can believe in," as promised in his campaign. Arguably, the precipitous downhill slide began that day.

Pundits, opponents, and disillusioned supporters would blame Obama for squandering the promise of his administration. Certainly he and his administration made their share of mistakes. But it is hard to think of another president who had to face the kind of guerrilla warfare waged against him almost as soon as he took office. A small number of people with massive resources orchestrated, manipulated, and exploited the economic unrest for their own purposes. They used tax-deductible donations to fund a movement to slash taxes on the rich and cut regulations on their own businesses. While they paid focus groups and seasoned operatives to frame these self-serving policies as matters of dire public interest, they hid their roles behind laws meant to protect the anonymity of philanthropists, leaving more folksy figures like Santelli to carry the message.

What came to be known as Santelli's "rant" started slowly and built as he held forth from the floor of the Chicago Mercantile Exchange. The immediate provocation was the previous guest. Minutes before Santelli appeared, Wilbur Ross Jr. had denounced a proposal Obama had floated the previous day to provide emergency help in restructuring mortgages for millions of homeowners facing foreclosure. Ross, a personal friend of David Koch's, wasn't a disinterested policy analyst. His private equity company, WL Ross & Co., a so-called vulture fund, was heavily involved in servicing mortgages.

Santelli, who tended in general toward tough-guy, free-market pronouncements, excitedly agreed with Ross that the government shouldn't help. "Mr. Ross has nailed it!" he began. He denounced Obama's plan as Cuban-style statism. Stressed homeowners in his view were "losers" who deserved their fate. He objected to the government playing a redistributive role, casting his argument in moral terms. By helping to bail out homeowners who made bad financial bets, he argued, the government was "promoting bad behavior." Critics would later point out that his indignation had not been similarly stirred by the Bush administration's bailouts of the country's largest banks, about which he had grumblingly conceded, "I agree, something needs to be done." Yet when Obama proposed help for the overextended underclasses, Santelli looked into the camera and shrieked, "This is America! How many of you people want to pay your neighbor's mortgage that has an extra bathroom, and can't pay their bills? Raise their hand. President Obama, are you listening?"

As his fellow traders whistled and cheered, he went on to say, "We're thinking of having a Chicago Tea Party in July. All you capitalists that want to show up to Lake Michigan, I'm gonna start organizing." From the start, the analogy was inapt. As Michael Grunwald, author of *The New New Deal*, a richly reported book about Obama's stimulus plan, observed, "The Boston Tea Party was a protest against an unelected leader who raised taxes, while Obama was an elected leader who had just cut them."

Nonetheless, Santelli's spontaneous invocation of the Boston Tea Party, according to most accounts, was what launched the movement. For instance, the Kochs' political adviser, Richard Fink, said, "It was the guy in Chicago, yelling on the stock exchange floor," that started it. He added, "Our programs had nothing to do with it."

In April 2009, as the Tea Party movement was gathering force, Melissa Cohlmia, a spokesperson for Koch Industries, also denied that the Kochs had any direct links to the unrest, issuing a statement saying, "No funding has been provided by Koch companies, the Koch foundations, or Charles Koch or David Koch specifically to support the tea parties." A year later, David Koch continued to insist in *New York* magazine, "I've never been to a tea-party event. No one representing the tea party has ever even approached me." When asked by a sympathetic interviewer for *The Daily Beast*, Elaine Lafferty, if *The New Yorker*'s report on the Kochs' involvement was true, he responded, "Oh, *please*."

Such denials helped shape the early narrative of the Tea Party movement as an amateur uprising by ordinary citizens, "a new strain of populism metastasizing before our eyes," as Mark Lilla wrote in *The New York Review of Books*. Its members were described as nonpartisan everymen, incensed by the "Democrats and Republicans, national debt and other assorted peeves," as National Public Radio reported.

These reports of spontaneous political combustion weren't entirely wrong. But they were far from the whole story. To begin with, the Tea Party was not "a new strain" in American politics. The scale was unusual, but history had shown that similar reactionary forces had attacked virtually every Democratic president since Franklin Roosevelt. Earlier business-funded right-wing movements, from the Liberty League to the John Birch Society to Scaife's Arkansas Project, all had cast Democratic presidents as traitors, usurpers, and threats to the Constitution. The undeniable element of racial resentment that tinged many Tea Party rallies was also an old and disgracefully enduring story in American politics. Nor could the Tea Party accurately be described as nonpartisan. As a *New York Times* poll later showed, over three-quarters of its supporters identified as Republican. The bulk of the remainder felt the Republican Party was not Republican *enough*. Finally, although many of its supporters were likely political neophytes, from the start the ostensibly anti-elitist rebellion was funded, stirred, and organized by experienced political elites. On closer inspection, as the Harvard political scientist Theda Skocpol and the Ph.D. student Vanessa Williamson observed in their 2012 book, *The Tea Party and the Remaking of Republican Conservatism*, the Tea Party movement was a "mass rebellion . . . funded by corporate billionaires, like the Koch brothers, led by over-the-hill former GOP kingpins like Dick Armey, and ceaselessly promoted by millionaire media celebrities like Glenn Beck and Sean Hannity."

Behind the street theater were some of the country's wealthiest businessmen who had painstakingly been trying to build up the "counter-establishment" since the 1970s and now saw the public's unrest as an amazing opportunity to at long last mobilize popular support for their own agendas. As Bruce Bartlett, the economist, put it, "The problem with the whole libertarian movement is that it's been all chiefs and no Indians. There weren't any actual people, like voters, who gave a crap about it. So the problem for the Kochs has been trying to create an actual movement." With the emergence of the Tea Party, he said, "everyone suddenly sees that for the first time there are Indians out there—people who can provide real ideological power." The Kochs, he said, immediately began "trying to shape and control and channel the populist uprising into their own policies."

In fact they and a handful of other wealthy allies had made repeated efforts to foment antigovernment rebellions well before Santelli's rant, often invoking the image of the Boston Tea Party. The history stretched back decades, to Charles Koch's blueprint for a libertarian revolution in the late 1970s and Richard Fink's three-part plan, "The Structure of Social Change," in the 1980s. By the 1990s, nonprofit "grassroots" advocacy groups funded by the Kochs and a few close associates had begun explicitly pushing the antitax Tea Party theme. But the early efforts, as Bartlett suggested, got little traction.

In 1991, Citizens for a Sound Economy promoted what was advertised as a massive "re-enactment of the Boston Tea Party" in Raleigh, North Carolina, to protest tax increases. Among those present, the press corps nearly outnumbered the clutch of protesters in Revolutionary War, Uncle Sam, and Santa Claus costumes. The following year, Citizens for a Sound Economy was involved in another plan to stage a Tea Party protest. This one was secretly funded by tobacco companies to fight cigarette taxes and was canceled after its covert funding was exposed. By 2007, Citizens for a Sound Economy had split up. The Kochs' new organization, Americans for Prosperity, tried to stage another Tea Party protest against taxes, this time in Texas. It too was a dud. Nonetheless, by the time Obama was elected and the economy was melting down, the rudiments of a political machine were in place, along with a network of paid operatives expert in creating colonially garbed "Astroturf" groups to fake the appearance of public support.

What Obama was up against was a new form of permanent campaign. It was waged not by politicians but by people whose wealth gave them the ability to fund their own private field operations with which they could undermine the outcome of the election. So-called outside money—that spent by individuals and groups outside of the campaigns themselves—exploded during the Obama years. Much attention was paid to the portion of this spending that was directed at elections. Less attention was paid to the equally unrivaled role that outside money played in influencing the way the country was governed. Most of this spending was never disclosed. But as the Kochs' political lieutenant, Fink, boasted to *The Wichita Eagle* in 2012, "I think that's actually one of the things that happened at the Obama administration, is that every rock they overturned, they saw people who were against it, and it turned out to be us."

A trial run of this non-electoral outside spending actually began in the summer of 2008. Karl Rove, the operative whom George W. Bush called "the architect" of his 2004 reelection, had long dreamed of creating a conservative political machine outside the traditional political parties' control that could be funded by virtually unlimited private fortunes. His hope was to draft conservative donors of all stripes into creating a self-financed militia that could be called into action without the transparency, legal restrictions, or accountability that circumscribed conventional campaigns. And that summer, the Kochs had participated briefly in a version of this project, according to the *Politico* reporter Kenneth Vogel. Their representatives met clandestinely with political operatives working for other hugely wealthy donors, such as the Las Vegas casino magnate Sheldon Adelson. The ideal, one participant said, was "a never-ending campaign." After the disappointment of Obama's victory, though, the group disbanded. The Kochs, among others, regrouped.

The lesson learned, as one donor, the late Texas billionaire Harold Simmons, put it, was that next time they needed to spend even more. Simmons, who made a fortune in leveraged buyouts, had put almost $3 million into a group running television ads trying to tie Obama to the 1960s radical Bill Ayers during the 2008 campaign. "If we had run more ads, we could have killed Obama," he lamented.

When Obama took office, the stock market was down nearly six thousand points, and unemployment was shooting up toward 7 percent. As the former senator Tom Daschle later recalled, "There was a growing sense of calamity." Obama expected bipartisan support at a moment that seemed like an economic version of the September 11, 2001, crisis. He had proclaimed in his 2004 keynote address to the Democratic National Convention, "There is not a liberal America and a conservative America. There is the United States of America!" Or so he thought.

Obama's billionaire opponents wasted no time indulging him in a honeymoon. Forty-eight hours after Obama was sworn in, Americans for Prosperity started attacking his first major piece of legislation, a massive $800 billion Keynesian-inspired boost in public spending and tax cuts meant to stimulate the economy, the American Recovery and Reinvestment Act. The Kochs' advocacy group began organizing "Porkulus" rallies around the country, deriding public spending as corrupt "pork." The term was coined by Rush Limbaugh. It's reasonable to assume that the Kochs were too busy to follow such minutiae, but a former member of their inner circle asserts that Americans for Prosperity did "nothing more, and nothing less than they wanted it to do." Poorly attended at first, the "Porkulus" rallies became dress rehearsals for the Tea Party.

Americans for Prosperity soon launched a "No Stimulus" effort that sponsored anti-Obama media events featuring the star of the Koch seminar that January, South Carolina's senator Jim DeMint. The group also hosted a Web site, aired television advertisements, and pushed a petition that it claimed collected 500,000 signatures aimed at stopping Congress from passing Obama's stimulus bill. "We cannot spend our way to prosperity," it proclaimed. As the bill took shape, the group sent a sharply worded letter to Republicans in Congress, demanding that they vote no on the spending bill, regardless of any compromises or modifications that the new administration might offer.

The attacks reflected Charles Koch's revisionist belief that government interference in the economy was what had caused the last Great Depression. "Bankers, brokers and businessmen," he argued, had been falsely blamed. The true culprits were Herbert Hoover and Franklin Roosevelt, both of whom he regarded as dangerous liberals. In his view, the economic policies of Warren Harding and Calvin Coolidge—the latter had famously declared, "The chief business of the American people is business"—had been unfairly maligned. Charles argued that the New Deal only "prolonged and deepened the decline." Shortly after Obama was elected, Charles sent out a newsletter with this "History Lesson" to his seventy thousand or so employees, essentially reprising the robber barons' revisionism that he had been taught at the Freedom School. He also mobilized the Kochtopus, the sprawling network of some thirty-four public policy and political organizations his fortune supported by 2008. During the Bush years, it had been relatively quiescent.

Think tanks funded by the Kochs and their allied network of donors, such as the Cato Institute, the Heritage Foundation, and the Hoover Institution at Stanford University—where six attendees at the Kochs' annual seminars served in official capacities—began cranking out research papers, press releases, and op-ed columns opposing Obama's stimulus plan. Much of the research was later challenged by less biased experts. The Mercatus Center at George Mason University, for instance, released a report claiming that stimulus funds were directed disproportionately at Democratic districts. Eventually, the author was forced to correct the report but not before Rush Limbaugh, citing the paper, had labeled Obama's program "a slush fund" and Fox News and other conservative outlets had echoed the sentiment.

The paid advocates formed a national echo chamber. Phil Kerpen, the vice president for policy at Americans for Prosperity, was a contributor to the Fox News Web site. Another officer at Americans for Prosperity, Walter Williams, the John M. Olin Distinguished Professor of Economics at George Mason University, was a frequent guest host on Limbaugh's radio show, which claimed to have an audience of twenty million listeners.

Some conservatives have insisted that the Tea Party movement owed nothing to wealthy donors, citing the example of Keli Carender, an ostensibly lone Seattle activist whose "Porkulus" protest preceded Santelli's rant by a week. Carender, however, borrowed the term "porkulus" from Limbaugh. The company that syndicated Limbaugh's show, Premiere Networks, meanwhile, was getting paid a handsome $2 million or so a year by the Heritage Foundation to push the think tank's line on issues, tying the message back to the same ultra-rich funding pool.

The steady stream of exposés accusing the fledgling Obama administration of malfeasance fanned public anger and provided useful ammunition for congressional Republicans, who in truth needed all the help they could get. The conventional wisdom at the beginning of the Obama presidency was that the 2008 election had been such a wipeout for Republicans that their only hope of staying relevant was to cut deals with Obama, who was seen as far too popular to oppose. But those who expected compromise—which included the president and his top aides—hadn't noticed the growing extremism in the Grand Old Party.

Even before the new congressional session began, Eric Cantor, a lawyer from Richmond, Virginia, who was about to become the new minority whip in the House, told a handful of trusted allies in a private planning meeting in his Washington condo, "We're not here to cut deals and get crumbs and stay in the minority for another forty years." Instead, he argued, the

Republicans needed to fight. They needed to unite in opposition to virtually anything Obama proposed in order to deny him a single bipartisan victory. The group, which included his deputy, Kevin McCarthy, called itself the Young Guns. The strategy of obstruction that they adopted won the Republicans the nickname the Party of No.

At their first official leadership retreat in January 2009, the model that the House Republicans chose to emulate was the Taliban. The Texas congressman Pete Sessions, the new leader of the Republican House campaign committee, held up Afghanistan's infamous Islamic extremists as providing an example of how they could wage "asymmetric warfare." The country might be in an economic crisis, but governing, he told his colleagues, was not the reason they had been elected. As he flashed through a slide presentation at the Annapolis Inn, he asked his colleagues, "If the Purpose of the Majority is to Govern . . . What is Our Purpose?" His answer was simple: "The Purpose of the Minority is to become the Majority." That one goal, he said, was "the entire Conference's mission."

John Boehner, the new minority leader, wasn't himself part of the Young Guns, but it was increasingly clear that if he didn't yield to them, they might depose him. As power shifted from the parties to outside money, much of which came from donors more extreme than the electorate at large, moderates had to fear primary challenges and internal coups from their right flank.

Steve LaTourette, a longtime Republican moderate congressman from Ohio who was a close friend of Boehner's, explained, "In the past, it was rare that someone would run against an incumbent in their own party. But the money that these outside groups have is what gives these people liquid courage to run against an incumbent." He described the outside donors as "a bunch of rich people who you can count on maybe two hands who have an inordinate impact. One or two might have been the guy in high school with the pocket protector picking his nose, but now he's inherited $40 million and has his chance to be a player. Once they were able to infuse massive amounts of money, they got a disproportionate amount of influence. It's not one man one vote anymore," he said with a sigh. "It's all about the money. It's not a function of anything else."

LaTourette was astonished, he said, when he went to the first meeting of the Republican caucus after Obama was elected. "When the question came up, about why we lost, these folks were saying, 'It's because we weren't conservative enough.' Well, I looked at the numbers, and we lost 58 percent of the independents!" Yet moderates like himself were getting frozen out. He became so frustrated he eventually retired, becoming a lobbyist and starting an organization aimed at battling the forces of extremism in his party. "I left," he said, "because I was sick of it. I couldn't take it anymore. I was there eighteen years. I understood it was a contact sport, but whether it was transportation or student loans, there were things you'd do without thinking. Now you can't get anything done. Some people don't want the government to do anything," he concluded.

The Republican leadership, according to an anecdote related by Grunwald, told GOP members of the House that as one of them, Jerry Lewis, a member of the House Appropriations Committee, put it, "We can't play." David Obey, the Democratic chairman of the House Appropriations Committee, was incensed at the lack of cooperation. "What they said right from the get-go," he said, was that "it doesn't matter what the hell you do, we ain't going to help you. We're going to stand on the sidelines and bitch."

The Republicans of course saw it differently. They accused Obama of being too partisan and took umbrage when he flaunted his election mandate and reminded Cantor during one tense session, "I won." In Lewis's view, the Democrats were arrogant, intolerant, and overbearing.

Obama nonetheless continued to seek bipartisan support.

His experience with what Hillary Clinton labeled the "vast right-wing conspiracy" was limited. He had vaulted in only five years from the Illinois State Senate to the White House. He turned out to be unrealistically confident that he could transcend partisan rancor as he had while editing the *Harvard Law Review.* So when he received an invitation from Boehner and the others in the House Republican caucus to come up to Capitol Hill to consult with them about the stimulus package, Obama accepted, with much fanfare.

On January 27, he climbed into his armored limousine for his first presidential motorcade to the Hill. Meeting exclusively with Republicans was unusual, as was a president coming to their turf to lobby. But the administration had promised to discard narrow partisan division. In fact Obama's economic advisers thought they had tailored the stimulus plan for Republican support by deriving one-third of it from tax cuts. Liberals were dismayed by the compromise, warning that government spending would do more to revive the economy than tax cuts and that the overall stimulus spending numbers were too small to really jump-start the economy. Despite these concessions, Obama's meeting on the Hill nonetheless turned out to be a demeaning disaster. Shortly before he arrived to pitch his plan, news leaked that the Republican leadership in the House was already instructing its caucus to vote against it. Obama was left to speak to a roomful of firmly closed minds. Afterward, he was left facing the gathered press corps looking lame and empty-handed.

"It was stunning," David Axelrod, Obama's longtime political adviser, later admitted. "Our feeling was, we were dealing with a potential disaster of epic proportions that demanded cooperation. If anything was a signal of what the next two years would be like, it was that."

The next morning, readers of *The New York Times* and *The Wall Street Journal* opened their papers to see a full-page ad paid for by the Cato Institute, the think tank that Charles

Koch had founded and on whose board David Koch sat. The ad directly challenged Obama's credibility. It quoted Obama saying, "There is no disagreement that we need action by our government, a recovery plan that will help jump start the economy." In large, boldface letters, the ad copy retorted, "With all due respect, Mr. President, that is not true." The statement was signed by 203 individuals, many of whose careers had been subsidized by the largesse of the Kochs, the Bradley Foundation, the John M. Olin Foundation, and other right-wing family fortunes.

Bill Burton, the deputy press secretary for Obama in the White House, looks back at the level of obstruction in the administration's first month as a complete shock. "They turned on Obama so early," he later recalled ruefully. "Not only did we not have the answers yet, we barely knew where to sit down. The chairs in the White House were still spinning from the people who had left them." Looking back, Burton shook his head at the administration's naïveté. "No one at the time saw it coming."

Specifically, he said, "We didn't really see the force, the outside money, until after he was elected. Then the first thing he had to do, the only thing he could do, was spend trillions and trillions of dollars, passing the stimulus bill first, and that led to Stimulus Two, and TARP, and the auto bailouts. The right-wing plutocrats really fed off of that. They tapped into this anger about spending." He admits, "No one saw the Kochs or the Dick Armeys out there."

Within two months of Obama taking office, he recalled, the political environment had been transformed. "In January, we were working with the Republicans on an economic recovery package grounded firmly in centrist thinking," he recalls. "The mainstream economic view was that the size of the calamity required massive economic spending. We asked the Republicans for their ideas. We were getting cooperation. Letters from all sorts of members of Congress were coming in with their heartfelt ideas. One high-ranking member of the House Republicans even suggested high-speed rail! But by early February, it started to shift. They were no longer sending letters. They were all expressing doubt about any kind of spending at all." Senator DeMint, who was headlining the Kochs' No Stimulus campaign, began a floor speech by proclaiming, "I like President Obama very much." He then went on to call the stimulus bill "a trillion-dollar socialist experiment" that was "the worst piece of economic legislation Congress has considered in a hundred years." As Burton put it, "DeMint was saying 'One-Term President' within six weeks of Obama taking office."

On February 17, Obama signed the Recovery Act into law. It had squeaked through Congress with only three Republican votes in the Senate and none in the House. Five years later, a survey of leading American economists chosen for their ideological diversity and eminence in the field, taken by the Initiative on Global Markets, a project run by the University of Chicago, found nearly unanimous consensus that the Recovery Act had achieved its goal of reducing unemployment. Only one of the thirty-seven economists surveyed disagreed. The free-market orthodoxy that dominated the Republican Party in Washington had completely veered from rational, professional expertise, yet the extremists nearly prevailed. As it was, Obama's opponents forced the administration to adopt a smaller stimulus package than many economists thought necessary, undercutting the recovery. One month into his presidency, extreme opponents, fueled by outside money, had already wounded Obama. The day after signing the stimulus bill, Obama announced the $75 billion homeowner rescue plan.

The next morning, Santelli delivered his rant, and within moments it went viral. Matt Drudge, the conservative news aggregator, linked to it under one of his Web site's rotating red siren emblems, promoting it to the site's three million daily readers as a pulsating political emergency.

Within hours, another Web site called TaxDayTeaParty .com appeared on the Internet, spreading the rebellion under the Tea Party label. Its domain name was registered by Eric Odom, a young member of the Libertarian Party of Illinois who lived in Chicago. Odom had been working until recently for an organization called the Sam Adams Alliance, whose chief executive had long and close ties to the Kochs. The strange story of the Sam Adams Alliance was yet another demonstration of the way that years of private funding by a few wealthy ideologues had created an underground political infrastructure.

The Chicago-based tax-exempt organization was named for the original 1773 Boston Tea Party activist Sam Adams. While the group's title evoked the Founding Fathers, its chief executive officer was a Wisconsin investor named Eric O'Keefe who had been involved with the Kochs since his days as a young volunteer in David Koch's Libertarian Party campaign for vice president. O'Keefe eventually became the national director of the Libertarian Party. By 1983, however, like the Kochs, he had moved on to promoting free-market fundamentalism through other means, often joining forces with the brothers through their donor seminars and other ventures. Influenced as a child by *The Wall Street Journal* and the Conservative Book Club, O'Keefe, as *The Washington Post* wrote, "had money. He grew up with some and made a lot more as an investor, allowing him to devote decades to a series of ambitious political crusades, nearly all of them failures."

The founder of the Sam Adams Alliance, according to one account, was a balding, publicity-shy Brooklyn-born real estate tycoon named Howard Rich. Known to friend and foe as Howie, Rich had also been involved in numerous far-flung political ventures with the Kochs. Impressed early by the writings of Hayek and Milton Friedman, he became a tireless supporter of long-shot libertarian causes while amassing a fortune buying apartment buildings in Manhattan, Texas, and North Carolina. Both O'Keefe and Rich served on the Cato Institute's board of directors with David Koch. They had years' worth of ties, as well as ups and downs, with Charles Koch as well. Relations were good enough that the Institute for Humane Studies at George Mason University, whose board Charles Koch chaired, placed some of its thirty or so chosen Charles G. Koch fellows in summer internships with the Sam Adams Alliance.

For decades this small, wealthy, and intense circle had been trying to advance their fervently held libertarian ideas, almost always working in secret, cloaked behind layers of shell groups, so that their role couldn't be detected. Rich in particular rivaled Houdini for sleights of hand, having obscured his role behind a positively dizzying number of name-changing, shape-shifting, interlocking organizations. He almost invariably declined to talk to the press or debate opponents. Until the Tea Party, however, the results had been disappointing. "My 32 years of engagement has been a long and expensive lesson in frustration," his frequent political partner, O'Keefe, admitted.

Among this group's earlier political efforts was a stealth attempt in the early 1990s to get voters to approve ballot measures imposing congressional term limits. Experts suggested that term limits would hurt Democrats, who had more congressional incumbents at the time, and also strengthen the power of outsiders with money, like themselves. As was true of the later Tea Party movement, the supporters of term limits described their movement as a grassroots outpouring fueled by populist outrage at entrenched power. In California, the Kochs were rumored to be behind a 1992 referendum on whether to impose them, but a spokesman denied they had any direct role. But after the referendum succeeded, the *Los Angeles Times* discovered that the true organizers and much of its funding traced back to a secretive group run by Howie Rich and Eric

O'Keefe, U.S. Term Limits. There were ties to the Kochs, too. Fink admitted when confronted by the paper that they had in fact provided "seed money."

Similarly, in Washington State a congressional term-limits ballot initiative nearly passed in 1991 until *The New York Times* exposed what Murray Rothbard, the irreverent libertarian theorist who had split with the Kochs, called "the Kochian deep pockets behind the 'grassroots' movement." The paper discovered that what supporters billed as "a prairie fire of populism" was in fact the product of a Washington-based group calling itself Citizens for Congressional Reform, which was started with hundreds of thousands of dollars from David Koch. "I ignited the spark, and the fire is raging on its own," he claimed once his role was exposed. Fanning the flames, however, was his checkbook. His group contributed nearly three-quarters of the campaign's budget, paying for professional signature gatherers to collect enough names to get the issue on the ballot.

Eventually, the Supreme Court ruled that federal term limits were unconstitutional. This finished off the movement at the congressional level for good, though not its backers' penchant for ersatz populism.

The patrons of libertarianism kept on trying to buy at least the aura of public support. In 2004, one of the first ventures of the Kochs' newly formed advocacy group, Americans for Prosperity, was a radical antitax measure called the Taxpayer Bill of Rights. The measure placed drastic restrictions on state legislators, requiring all tax increases to first be approved by public referenda. The group chose Kansas as its first battleground for the Taxpayers Bill of Rights just as the Kochs were fighting a proposed tax increase in their home state. Despite an outcry about shadowy spending, AFP spent a record amount of money on television ads, and the tax increase was defeated.

Two years later, in 2006, a group created and run by Rich

called Americans for Limited Government spent some $8 million promoting a variety of other ballot drives, including one that demanded that owners get compensated for the impact of land-use laws on their property. Supporters again claimed to have widespread grassroots support. But an investigation by the Center for Public Integrity revealed that in fact just three donors, none of them disclosed, accounted for 99 percent of the organization's funding. Despite the heavy spending, the fringe antigovernment measures were voted down almost everywhere.

Soon afterward, the State of Illinois suspended Rich's group of its charitable license after it failed to supply required financial statements, and in 2006 the group shut down its Chicago headquarters. At this point, Americans for Limited Government moved to Fairfax, Virginia, where several other nonprofit organizations run by Rich were based. Back in Chicago, meanwhile, a new tax-exempt group sprang up at its former address, calling itself the Sam Adams Alliance.

Eric O'Keefe, who had served on the board of Americans for Limited Government, was now the chairman and chief executive officer of the new organization. "We're not going to be shut up," he had vowed when previously investigated in Wisconsin for campaign-finance violations. Tax records showed that some 88 percent of the Sam Adams Alliance's funding that year came from a single gift of $3.7 million from a mysterious undisclosed donor.

In the summer of 2008, as Barack Obama grew closer to capturing the presidency, Eric Odom at the Sam Adams Alliance started experimenting with some of the online communications methods that would later help to organize the Tea Party movement. He tested out the use of Twitter to trigger a right-wing flash mob in the House of Representatives in Washington. He and a friend, Rob Bluey, a twenty-eight-year-old blogger who described himself as "a card-carrying member of the vast right-wing conspiracy," created something they called the DontGo movement. They sent out Twitter messages demanding that the Democratic leadership in the House schedule a vote on legalizing offshore oil and gas drilling, or else Republicans would refuse to go home for the summer recess.

The Twitter experiment worked remarkably well. That August, conservative congressmen, oil lobbyists, and other supporters of offshore drilling poured into the House, creating a wild and seemingly spontaneous protest. They chanted, "Don't go!" and "Drill here! Drill now!" They didn't succeed in lifting the restriction on offshore drilling, but one leader of the revolt, the Arizona congressman John Shadegg, a conservative Republican, exulted that the protest was "the 2008 version of the Boston Tea Party."

Six months later, immediately after Santelli's rant, Eric Odom reactivated the "DontGo" list. He fired off a call to action to the same ten thousand hard-core conservative insiders whose contact information he and Bluey had compiled. Odom also formed what he called the Nationwide Tea Party Coalition with other activists, including operatives from Dick Armey's group, FreedomWorks, and the Kochs' group, Americans for Prosperity. AFP quickly registered a Web site called TaxPayerTeaParty.com and used its network of fifty-some staffers to plan rallies across the country.

As the operatives linked forces online, they set a date for the first national Tea Party protests, February 27. That day, more than a dozen protests were held in cities across the country. The organizers claimed 30,000 participants, but the crowds in many places were still sparse. But on April 15, when there was a second series of "Tax Day" Tea Party rallies across the country, the numbers had increased tenfold, to 300,000.

The Heritage Foundation, the Cato Institute, and Americans for Prosperity provided speakers, talking points, press releases, transportation, and other logistical support. Lee Fang, a blogger for the progressive Web site *ThinkProgress*, was among the first to question whether the movement was organic or synthetic "Astroturf." He noted that Americans for Prosperity was suddenly planning protests "coast to coast," while FreedomWorks seemed to have taken over a local rally in Florida. Not everyone liked the top-down control of the protests. "Americans for Prosperity annoyed some of the Tea Partiers," recalls the libertarian blogger Ralph Benko. "These people drove up, opened the door, put T-shirts on them, then took pictures and sent them to Charles [Koch] saying, 'See? We're doing great things with your money.'"

Thomas Frank, author of *What's the Matter with Kansas?*, had stopped by to see an early Tea Party rally in Lafayette Square, across from the White House, in February 2009. "It was very much a put-up job," he concluded. "All the usual suspects were there, like FreedomWorks, 'Joe the Plumber,' and *The American Spectator* magazine. There were also some people who had Revolutionary War costumes and 'Don't Tread on Me' flags, actual activists, and a few ordinary people," he said. "But it was very well organized by the conservative groups. Back then, it was really obvious that it was put on, and they'd set it up. But then it caught on." Frank argues that "the Tea Party wasn't subverted," as some have suggested. "It was *born* subverted." Still, he said, "it's a major accomplishment for sponsors like the Kochs that they've turned corporate self-interest into a movement among people on the streets."

While the Kochs were continuing to profess no involvement, Peggy Venable, a spunky veteran of the Reagan administration who had been on their payroll as a political operative in Texas since 1994, becoming the head of the Texas chapter of Americans for Prosperity, gushed about her role in the movement. "I was a member of the Tea Party before it was cool!" she said during a conversation at a Koch-sponsored political event called Defending the American Dream, in Austin. As the Tea Party movement took off, she described how Americans for Prosperity had helped to "educate" the activists on policy details. She said they had given the supporters what she called "next-step training" after their rallies so that their political energy could be channeled "more effectively." The organization also supplied the angry protesters with lists of elected officials to target. Venable, who spoke without first checking with the Kochs' public relations representatives, happily said of the brothers, "They're certainly our people. David's the chairman of our board. I've certainly met with them, and I'm very appreciative of what they do." She added, "We love what the Tea Parties are doing, because that's how we're going to take back America!"

Venable honored several Tea Party "citizen leaders" at the summit. The Texas branch of Americans for Prosperity gave its Blogger of the Year Award to a young woman named Sibyl West. Writing on her Web site, West described Obama as the "cokehead in chief" and speculated that the president was exhibiting symptoms of "demonic possession (aka schizophrenia, etc.)."

During a catered lunch at the summit, Venable introduced Ted Cruz, a former solicitor general of Texas and future senator, who told the crowd that Obama was "the most radical president ever to occupy the Oval Office" and had hidden from voters a secret agenda—"the government taking over our economy and our lives." Countering Obama, Cruz proclaimed, was "the epic fight of our generation!" As the crowd rose to its feet and cheered, he quoted the defiant words of a Texan at the Alamo: "Victory, or death!"

No organization played a bigger early role than Freedom-Works, the estranged sibling of Americans for Prosperity, which was funded by donations from companies like Philip Morris and from billionaires like Richard Mellon Scaife. "I'd argue that when the Tea Party took off, FreedomWorks had as much to do with making it an effective movement as anyone," said Armey.

In looking back, Armey gave particular credit to a young aide named Brendan Steinhauser, the group's director of state and federal campaigns, who created a Web site immediately after Santelli's rant that provided all kinds of practical advice to supporters. It counseled them on how to plan rallies and what issues to protest, with Obama's stimulus spending high on the target list. He also suggested slogans and signs and sponsored a daily conference call with over fifty Tea Party activists around the country to coordinate their efforts. Soon FreedomWorks was providing a professional support team of nine for the operation. Armey recalled that Steinhauser "spent hours and hours on the phone with people who'd found the FreedomWorks Web site. The other guys at FreedomWorks were laughing at him" in the beginning, he said. But Armey described how Steinhauser organized the inchoate anger into a mass political movement. "He told them what to do. He gave them training. If it hadn't been for FreedomWorks, the Tea Party movement would never have taken off," Armey later said.

The fact that Armey was himself a Washington insider belied the notion that the Tea Party movement was anti-elitist. Armey had spent eighteen years in Congress and was reportedly paid $750,000 a year as a lobbyist at the law firm DLA Piper, which represented corporate clients such as the pharmaceutical giant Bristol-Myers Squibb. But billionaire backers were useful. They gave the nascent Tea Party movement organization and political direction, without which it might have frittered away like the Occupy movement. The protesters in turn gave the billionaire donors something they'd had trouble buying— the numbers needed to lend their agenda the air of legitimacy. As Armey put it, "We'd been doing this lonely work for years. From our point of view, it was like the cavalry coming."

FreedomWorks, it was later revealed, also had some hired help. The tax-exempt organization quietly cemented a deal with Glenn Beck, the incendiary right-wing Fox News television host who at the time was a Tea Party superstar. For an annual payment that eventually topped $1 million, Beck read "embedded content" written by the FreedomWorks staff. They told him what to say on the air, and he blended the promotional material seamlessly into his monologue, making it sound as if it were his own opinion. The arrangement was described on FreedomWorks' tax disclosures as "advertising services."

"We thought it would be a useful tool if it was done in moderation, but then they started doing it by leaps and bounds," Armey recalled about the arrangement. "They were keeping it secret from their activists and supporters," he alleged. "They were creating an illusion that they were so important this icon, this hero of the movement, was bragging about them. Instead of earning the media, they were paying for it."

Beck, whose views were shaped by W. Cleon Skousen, the fringe theorist whose political paranoia had inspired the John Birch Society, reached a daily audience of some two million, disseminating the ideas of early conservative extremists like Fred Koch on a whole new scale. Frank Luntz describes the impact as historic. "That rant from Santelli woke up the upper middle class and the investor class, and then Glenn Beck woke up everyone else. Glenn Beck's show is what created the Tea Party movement," he said, adding, "It started on Tax Day 2009, and it exploded at town hall meetings in July. You can create a mass movement within three months."

Another factor was Obama's aversion to confrontation and hot rhetoric, which resulted in largely milquetoast messaging about Wall Street. Unlike Franklin Roosevelt, who blamed the "money changers" for the Great Depression in his first inaugural address, Obama's public utterances were muted. In a matter of weeks, critics argued that he had ceded the mantle of populism to his Tea Party opponents. "In an atmosphere primed for a populist backlash, he allowed the right wing to define the terms," John Judis observed in the liberal *New Republic* magazine.

Despite Steinhauser's efforts to police the Tea Party's signs for racism and other expressions of hate, within two months of Obama taking office, the streets and parks were filling with rallies at which white protesters carried placards reading, "Impeach Now!" and "Obama Bin Lyin'." Obama's face was plastered on posters making him look like the Joker from the Dark Knight films, his skin turned chalk white, his mouth stretched almost to his ears, and his eye sockets blackened, with a zombielike dead gaze, over the word "Socialism." A for-profit Internet activism company, ResistNet, featured a video titled "Obama = Hitler" on its Web site. One protester at a February 27 rally, who said he was with the group, carried a sign calling Congress slave owners and taxpayers "the Nigger." Obama's image was also photoshopped to look like a primitive African witch doctor, with a bone stuck through his nose.

Fink, the Kochs' political lieutenant, professed to be discomfited by the racism. But David Koch echoed the specious claims that Obama was somehow African in his outlook, even though he was born in America, abandoned by his Kenyan father as a toddler, raised mainly in Hawaii by his American mother, and had never set foot on the African continent until he was an adult. In a revealing later interview with the conservative pundit Matthew Continetti, David nonetheless disparaged Obama as "the most radical president we've ever had as a nation" and opined that the president's radicalism derived from his African heritage. "His father was a hard core economic socialist in Kenya," he said. "Obama didn't really interact with his father face-to-face very much, but was apparently from what I read a great admirer of his father's points of view. So he had sort of antibusiness, anti–free enterprise influences affecting him almost all his life. It just shows you what a person with a silver tongue can achieve."

Bill Burton, who is biracial himself, believes that "you can't understand Obama's relationship with the right wing without taking into account his race. It's something no one wants to talk about, but really you can't deny the racial factor. They treated him in a way they never would have if he'd been white. The level of disrespect was just dialed up to eleven."

By the end of Obama's second month in office, *Newsweek* ran a tongue-in-cheek cover story asserting, "We are all socialists now," and even the lofty *New York Times* picked up the right wing's framing of Obama as outside the American mainstream. In a presidential interview, the paper asked whether he was a socialist. Obama was apparently so stunned he had to contact the *Times* afterward to fully answer. "It was hard for me to believe that you were entirely serious about that socialist question," he said, noting that it was under his predecessor, George Bush, a Republican, not "under me that we began buying a bunch of shares of banks. And it wasn't on my watch that we passed a massive new entitlement, prescription drug plan, without a source of funding."

As Obama was put on the defensive about the economy, another line of attack was stealthily attracting the attention of many of the same wealthy financial backers. At the Kochs' secretive January summit in Palm Springs, one of the group's largest donors, Randy Kendrick, posed a question. Her shoulder-length cascades of frosted hair and flashy jewelry made her an unlikely-looking rabble-rouser, but Kendrick was an outspoken lawyer who had abandoned the women's movement decades earlier for the Goldwater Institute, a far-right libertarian think tank in Phoenix, where she was on the board of directors. She and her husband, Ken, the co-owner and managing general partner of the Arizona Diamondbacks baseball team, had the kind of fortune that made people take note.

Earl "Ken" Kendrick, who hailed from West Virginia, had made many millions on Datatel, a company he founded that provided computer software to colleges and universities. He

subsequently bought into the Woodforest National Bank in
Texas, a private bank that was in 2010 forced to refund $32 mil-
lion and pay a $1 million civil fine to settle charges of usurious
overdraft fees. Hard-core economic and social conservatives—
except for the state subsidies that paid for the Diamondbacks
stadium and brought public transit to the field—the Kendricks
were horrified by the election of Obama. They were charter
members of the Kochs' donor network, having written at least
one seven-figure check. Their generosity had been a two-way
street. They had supported institutions that the Kochs favored,
such as the Institute for Humane Studies and the Mercatus
Center at George Mason University. The Kochs had meanwhile supported the "Freedom Center" at the University of
Arizona that they founded, where the Kendrick Professor of
Philosophy taught "freedom" to college students.

Now Randy Kendrick wanted to know what the group
planned to do to stop Obama from overhauling America's
health-care system. She had read the former Democratic senator Tom Daschle's 2008 book, *Critical: What We Can Do About
the Health-Care Crisis,* and was alarmed. She warned that
Daschle, who favored universal health-care coverage, likely
reflected Obama's thinking. Daschle was expected to become
Obama's secretary of health and human services. If the new
administration adopted a plan of the kind Daschle was floating, she said it would kill business, hurt patients, and lead to
the biggest socialist government takeover in their lifetimes. She
was adamant. Obama had to be stopped. What was the plan?

Kendrick spoke with passion. Her interest in the issue was
both political and personal. She argued that the choice of private health care had saved her from spending the rest of her
life confined to a wheelchair after a leg injury. She had initially
been told that because she suffered from a rare disorder, she
couldn't risk surgery. But a specialist at the renowned Cleveland Clinic had found a successful treatment. She survived
the surgery and was now an active mother of teenage twins.

"Randy was convinced that if America had government health care like Canada or Great Britain, she would be dead," a friend who asked not to be identified confided.

It was a powerful testimonial, and the donors at the Koch seminar were deeply moved. But the Obama administration had never proposed government health care like that in Canada or Great Britain. Reached later, after the implementation of Obama's Affordable Care Act, Donald Jacobsen, professor of molecular medicine at the Cleveland Clinic Lerner College of Medicine, who cared for Kendrick, recalled her as a generous donor but dismissed as nonsense her argument that Obama's health-care plan ever threatened treatment of the kind that she received. "I can assure you that 'Obamacare' did not diminish our research efforts in any way," he said. "However, the sequestration efforts of the right-wing conservatives and their Tea Party colleagues have hampered progress in medical research. The National Institutes of Health is suffering greatly, and it is very difficult for all investigators to obtain funding. You can't blame the Affordable Care Act, but you certainly can blame the Republicans."

Nonetheless, when Kendrick finished her emotional pitch, there was an awkward silence from the Kochs, according to two sources familiar with the meeting. The Kochs of course opposed the expansion of any government social program, including any potential universal health-care plan. But the sources said they hadn't focused much on the issue. They had assumed the health-care industry would fight its own battles, in its own interest, so they hadn't thought they'd need to step in. Instead, the Obama administration had cut deals with much of the health-care industry, winning much of its support. "They were unprepared on the issue," said one of the sources.

Despite their later reputation for orchestrating opposition to Obamacare, it was actually Kendrick, not the Kochs, who first led the way. She and a handful of other multimillionaires had recently helped fund an unsuccessful effort to prevent Ari-

zona from "coercing" citizens into buying government-run, or
any other kind of, health-care coverage. But Kendrick was not
giving up. She was strong-minded and accustomed to getting
her way. When she appeared every few weeks at the think tank,
a former colleague recalled, "they would often line up and hand
her a bouquet of flowers, like a queen."

After the defeat in Arizona, Kendrick vowed to take her
fight national. "Who do I have to give money to?" she asked
Sean Noble, a Republican political operative in Arizona who
had become her de facto personal political consultant. Kendrick demanded to know, "What organizations are doing
this?" according to an account written by Eliana Johnson for
National Review.

At Kendrick's request, Noble surveyed the field and found
virtually no organization set up in early 2009 to take aim at
Obama on the issue. Or at least none that was a 501(c)(4), the
IRS code for a tax-exempt "social welfare" group that can participate in politics so long as it's not the group's primary focus.
Unlike conventional political organizations, such nonprofits
can hide the identities of their donors from the public, reporting them only to the IRS. Noble knew these so-called dark-
money groups were especially appealing to wealthy individuals
who wanted to influence politics without public attention, like
the members of the Koch network.

Noble had attended Koch seminars with his former boss,
John Shadegg, a staunchly conservative Republican congressman from Arizona whose father, Stephen, had been Barry
Goldwater's campaign manager and alter ego. For over a
decade, Noble had worked for Shadegg, eventually becoming
chief of staff of the congressman's Arizona office. In 2008,
however, Noble decided to go out on his own, opening a political consulting firm, Noble Associates, at his home in Phoenix.
Kendrick, who had been a major supporter of Shadegg, was a
prized client. She and Noble had worked closely for years. He
hadn't been invited to the January Koch meeting where she

held forth, but she called him afterward for help. As he set up his business, her interest in launching a crusade against health-care reform, and her entrée into the Koch network, presented a lucrative opportunity.

Noble wasn't a first-string player in Washington's political big league, but he was respected and had a superabundance of charm. Fit and blond, with just enough gray around his temples to add gravitas to his cherubic features, he was unassuming and fun; even his political opponents found him hard to dislike. Noble described himself as a "Reagan Baby" who was raised in the tiny town of Show Low, Arizona—named by cardplayers—where as a boy he started the day listening to the national anthem on the radio with a hand over his heart. His mother, a homemaker, and father, a dentist, were Mormons and believed America was the promised land. In their household, Barry Goldwater was a hero, and Jimmy Carter a villain. When Carter was elected in 1976, Noble's mother warned that the Soviet Union would take over the world. By the time he was in college, Noble was working for conservative candidates, eventually connecting with Shadegg. Along the way, he got married, had five children, and became a Mormon bishop in his Phoenix ward. Antiabortion and libertarian, he voted for Ron Paul in 1988. In many ways, he was a perfect fit for the Koch network, except for one thing. Noble, who contributed almost compulsively to a personal online blog called *Noble Thinking*, was chatty. Taking on Obama's health-care plan with private money would require stealth.

On April 16, 2009, Noble and Kendrick began putting their plan in place when the Center to Protect Patient Rights (CPPR) was incorporated in Maryland. Physically, the organization existed only as a locked, metal mailbox, number 72465, inside the Boulder Hills post office at the edge of a desert road north of Phoenix. Later records would show Noble was its executive director. The effort was surrounded in such secrecy that when Noble was asked in a 2013 deposition who hired him, he declined to answer, citing confidentiality agreements, as ProPublica, the nonprofit investigative reporting concern, later reported.

Responding to the lawyer's question, he said, "I can't tell you who I do work for."

"Wait a minute," the lawyer interjected. "I asked how your salary got set, and you're telling me that you had a discussion with some people in 2009 and you're refusing to tell me who?"

"I am," Noble answered.

The identities of the donors remained opaque, but one thing clear from tax records was that Noble's sponsors had an astounding amount of money. By June, the Center to Protect Patient Rights had accumulated some $3 million in donations. By the end of 2009, the sum reached $13 million. More than $10 million of that was quickly passed on to other tax-exempt groups, including Americans for Prosperity, which soon took a lead in attacking Obama's health-care plan. By the end of 2010, the sum sloshing through the post office box belonging to the Center to Protect Patient Rights would reach nearly $62 million, much of it raised through the Kochs' donor network.

The first tangible sign of this underground funding stream was a television ad called "Survivor." It featured a Canadian woman named Shona Holmes who said, "I survived a brain tumor," but claimed that if she had been forced to wait for treatment from Canada's government health service, "I'd be dead." Instead, she said, she had received lifesaving treatment in Arizona. Fact-checkers later revealed that her dramatic story was highly dubious and that in fact the reason the Canadian health authorities hadn't expedited her treatment was that she actually had a benign cyst on her pituitary gland. Nonetheless, the Americans for Prosperity Foundation, the charitable wing of the tax-exempt organization chaired by David Koch, spent $1 million airing the ad in the summer of 2009.

The message was made by Larry McCarthy, a veteran Washington media consultant best known for creating the racially charged Willie Horton ad, which featured the crimes of a convicted African-American murderer on a weekend furlough from prison in Massachusetts. It helped sink the presidential campaign of Michael Dukakis in 1988 by making him look soft on crime. McCarthy was infamous for using manipulative emotional messages, especially fear. As Peter Hart, the Democratic pollster, said of McCarthy, whom he had worked against, and occasionally with, over the years, "If you want an assassination, you hire one of the best marksmen in history." That spring, flush with cash, Noble signed McCarthy up.

The Center to Protect Patient Rights wasn't flying blind. At Noble's instigation, that spring the organization had also quietly paid Frank Luntz, the Republican pollster and pitchman, to conduct market testing on the best ways to attack Obama's health-care proposal. Luntz's political science professor at Penn had been James Piereson, who later ran the Olin Foundation. Luntz had studied the building of the conservative movement and become something like a translator, interpreting elite opinion for the masses. "The think tanks became the creators of the ideas, and I became the explainer of the thoughts," he said. "Mostly what I do is listen and I process." He admitted that as communicators "these guys were impossible." In playing this role, Luntz was one of a long succession of "policy entrepreneurs" who served to popularize the agenda of wealthy backers by "framing" their issues in more broadly appealing language.

Luntz used polls, focus groups, and "instant response dial sessions" to perfect the language of health-care attacks and then tested the lines on average Americans in St. Louis, Missouri. Out of these sessions, Luntz compiled a seminal twenty-eight-page confidential memo in April warning that there was no groundswell of public opposition to Obama's health-care plan at that point; in fact, there was a groundswell of public support. By far the most effective approach to turning the public against the program, Luntz advised, was to label it a "government takeover." He wrote, "Takeovers are like coups. They both lead to dictators and a loss of freedom."

"I did create the phrase 'government takeover' of health care. And I believe it," Luntz maintained, noting too that "it gave the Republicans the weapon they needed to defeat Obama in 2010." But most experts found the pitch patently misleading because the Obama administration was proposing that Americans buy private health insurance from for-profit companies, not the government. In fact, progressives were incensed that rather than backing a "public option" for those who preferred a government insurance program, the Obama plan included a government mandate that individuals purchase health-care coverage, a conservative idea hatched by the Heritage Foundation to stave off nationalized health care. Luntz's phrase was so false that it was chosen as "the Lie of the Year" by the nonpartisan fact-checking group PolitiFact. Yet while a rear guard of administration officials tried lamely to correct the record, Luntz's deceptive message stuck, agitating increasingly fearful and angry voters, many of whom flocked to Tea Party protests.

Noble's strategy was carefully targeted. He aimed the attack ads especially at the states of members of the Senate Finance Committee, which was writing the health-care bill and whose support would be needed to vote it out of the committee. The Obama White House had delegated a tremendous amount of authority to the committee's chairman, the Montana Democrat Max Baucus, whom it was entrusting to win bipartisan support. Baucus, in turn, was trying fitfully to win the support of the committee's leading Republican, the Iowa senator Chuck Grassley. Noble studied the committee and singled out members who might be especially susceptible to pressure, along with a few other key swing votes, narrowing his list down to those from Louisiana, Nebraska, Maine, Iowa, and

Montana. With enough pressure, he believed he could even unnerve both Grassley and Baucus.

At the time, few thought that Obama's health-care plan could be derailed. Conservative opposition was focused more on other issues. Noble needed to generate "grassroots" pressure on the potentially persuadable senators, but constituents weren't yet engaged. The stakes grew as the Senate approached its summer recess. "We knew we had to make that summer absolute hell," he told *National Review*. For help, he turned to an old friend in Arizona, Doug Goodyear, whose controversial public relations firm, DCI Group, had truly professionalized the modern use of phony "Astroturf" campaigns on behalf of big-money interests, starting with the industry that really set the standard for deceptive advertising, tobacco.

Goodyear, the firm's managing partner and chief executive, had founded DCI Group in 1996 with two Republican campaign operatives while he was handling outside public relations for the huge tobacco company R. J. Reynolds. The work had shown the trio that ordinary campaign tools could succeed at marketing even the most toxic products. The key, according to an internal 1990 memo the tobacco industry was forced to disclose in a later legal settlement, was to disguise the company's financial interest as a matter of great principle. Instead of pitching cigarette sales, it would create fake "smokers' rights" groups who would agitate against smoking restrictions as a fundamental matter of liberty. Or, as the memo written by Tim Hyde—one of the three founding partners of DCI Group and at the time R. J. Reynolds's director of national field operations—put it, the company needed to "create a movement" that would "build broad coalitions around the issue-cluster of freedom, choice, and privacy." The company, Hyde wrote, "should proceed along two tracks." One was the "intellectual track within the DC–New York corridor," which could influence elite opinion with op-ed pieces, lawsuits, and expert think tank studies. The other was "a grassroots organizational and largely local track," which would use front groups to simulate the appearance of popular political support.

Noble knew that by 2009 DCI Group was unsurpassed at these dark arts. The firm had deep ties to the Republican Party and had worked for powerful interests ranging from Exxon-Mobil and the Teamsters to the military junta in Myanmar. Goodyear was especially versed in corporate lobbying disguised as hidden-hand "Astroturf" campaigns. But the firm had numerous other talents. While working for ExxonMobil, it had mocked Al Gore's environmental jeremiad, *An Inconvenient Truth,* by secretly launching a cartoon spoof that went viral called "Al Gore's Penguin Army." Only later were DCI's fingerprints discovered on the fake indie film. Unlike lobbying firms, which have to disclose some information, public relations firms exerting political pressure can hide the money trail.

Soon Noble's Center to Protect Patient Rights was dispersing millions of dollars to other nonprofit groups, some of which appeared to be shell organizations fronting for DCI Group. In June, the Center to Protect Patient Rights sent $1.8 million to a confusingly similar-sounding organization called the Coalition to Protect Patient Rights, which was set up that month in Virginia by an accountant who worked for DCI Group. The Virginia organization soon passed most of the funds on to DCI Group. Pretty soon, a former head of the American Medical Association named Donald Palmisano appeared on the national media circuit to take swipes at Obama's health-care proposal on behalf of the newly created coalition. He admitted that donors, whom he declined to name and who were not in the medical field, had recruited him to speak for the group, which called itself a "doctor-led coalition."

The same DCI Group accountant's name appeared on paperwork filed by another Washington-area nonprofit, a tiny organization calling itself the Institute for Liberty. It soon received a $1.5 million grant from Noble's Center to Protect

Patient Rights. Four hundred thousand dollars of these funds were channeled back to DCI Group for "consulting." The previous year, the Institute for Liberty's entire budget had been $52,000. Suddenly it was so awash in cash that the group's president, Andrew Langer, told *The Washington Post,* "This year has been really serendipitous for us." He said a donor, whom he declined to name, had earmarked the funds for a five-state advertising blitz targeting Obama's health-care plan. Although *The Washington Post* wrote about the surprisingly large ad campaign, it failed to trace the money back to its true source. On air, the ads' only sponsorship information was completely misleading. There was a line that said, "Paid for by Keeping Small Business Healthy."

Americans for Prosperity, meanwhile, threw itself headlong into the fight, spinning off a group called Patients United Now, which, according to Tim Phillips, organized more than three hundred rallies against the health-care legislation. At one rally, an effigy of a Democratic congressman was hanged; at another, protesters unfurled a banner depicting corpses from Dachau, implying that Obama's health-care plan was akin to the Nazis' state-ordered murders.

The Bradley Foundation also pitched in. While the tax-exempt foundation did not directly support Tea Party groups, its president, Michael Grebe, said the foundation supported "public education programs run by Americans for Prosperity and FreedomWorks, both of which are very active in the Tea Party."

Although Grebe openly described the Kochs' group, Americans for Prosperity, as "very active" in the Tea Party, Fink was still claiming otherwise. "We never funded the tea party," he still maintained. "We met for 20 or 30 years advancing free-market ideas in universities, think tanks and citizen groups. I am hopeful those ideas filtered down and were a part of the cause of the Tea Party taking off."

By the time of the Kochs' second donor summit of 2009,

titled "Understanding and Addressing Threats to American Free Enterprise and Prosperity," which took place in Aspen, Colorado, at the end of June, Noble had earned his place as an insider. Not only had he been invited; he had been officially put on contract as a Koch political consultant. The Kochs felt they needed extra help, a former insider said, because Obama's election had sparked such vitriol on the right that they were almost overwhelmed by the number of wealthy donors eager to join them. "Suddenly they were raising big money! They were in a hot spot. They were almost hyperventilating," he said.

This time, instead of having to interrupt the proceedings, Randy Kendrick was a scheduled speaker on a health-care panel. And this time, the pitch she made to the others, according to one eyewitness, "set the place on fire." Before the donors dispersed, many more millions were pledged to stop Obama's top legislative priority.

That summer, traditional town hall meetings held by Democratic congressmen and senators returning to their districts and states exploded in acrimony. The anger appeared entirely spontaneous. But the investigative reporter Lee Fang discovered that a volunteer with FreedomWorks was circulating a memo instructing Tea Partiers on how to disrupt the meetings. Bob MacGuffie, who ran a Web site called Right Principles.com, advised opponents of Obama's policies to "pack the hall . . . spread out" to make their numbers seem more significant, and to "rock-the-boat early in the Rep's presentation . . . to yell out and challenge the Rep's statements early . . . to rattle him, get him off his prepared script and agenda . . . stand up and shout and sit right back down." While MacGuffie was quickly dismissed as a lone amateur, some of the outside agitation was professional, paid for by the Koch network. Noble later admitted, "We packed these town halls with people who were just screaming about this thing."

After a military veteran assailed the Washington Democratic congressman Brian Baird for ostensibly defiling the

Constitution by supporting Obama's universal health-care plan, Baird decided to retire from politics, citing the intolerably toxic atmosphere. In Philadelphia, Senator Arlen Specter, a moderate Republican, and the secretary of health and human services, Kathleen Sebelius, were drowned out by hundreds of booing detractors at an event as they tried to explain the health-care legislation. Members of Congress all over the country, in districts as far apart as Tampa, Florida, and Long Island, New York, found themselves ambushed by screaming citizens, some mistakenly believing specious rumors about Obama's plans to create government "death panels" to euthanize senior citizens.

The raucous rallies proved pivotal in eroding Obama's agenda. Grover Norquist, the antitax activist who held a weekly meeting for conservative leaders in Washington, including representatives from Americans for Prosperity, described the summer's pandemonium as a turning point. The Republican leadership in Congress, he said, "couldn't have done it without August, when people went out on the streets. It discouraged deal makers, like Grassley"—Republicans who might otherwise have worked constructively with Obama. Moreover, the appearance of growing public opposition to Obama affected corporate donors on K Street, the center of Washington's lobbying industry. "K Street is a $3 billion weather vane," Norquist said. "When Obama was strong, the Chamber of Commerce said, 'We can work with the Obama administration.' But that changed when thousands of people went into the street and 'terrorized' congressmen. August is what changed it."

As Obama and his family vacationed in Martha's Vineyard during the congressional recess that month, Grassley, who was under bombardment from anti-health-care ads paid for by the Koch network, made clear he would not provide bipartisan support. Baucus, whose state Noble's campaign was also heavily targeting, dithered and delayed. The death of Senator Edward Kennedy, the liberal Democratic senator who had been the greatest champion of universal health care, cast health-care reform under a further cloud. A special election was set for January to fill what was assumed to be his reliably Democratic Senate seat.

Jim Margolis, the Democratic political consultant and advertising expert who had created many of Obama's 2008 campaign spots, watched with growing dismay. He had been advising both the White House and Democrats in Congress on the health-care issue and had begun with high hopes. "I thought on health care you'd get a modest amount of support from thoughtful Republicans," he said. "In March and April, Max Baucus was reaching out to Olympia Snowe and Chuck Grassley. The moderate Republicans were making some of the right sounds. But the progress was slow. Then, over the August recess, it really explodes. It would be interesting to know what the funding streams were like," he mused. "My suspicion is that the outside forces were kicking into high gear as we moved into the summer." Axelrod later acknowledged that he "wasn't really tracking" the right-wing money during this period and only belatedly came to realize that there was a set of "right-wing oligarchs" that "found Obama threatening," because he "believes in using government to solve problems. It was the Gilded Age all over again."

The press, ever alert to a colorful political drama, exaggerated the size of the grassroots groundswell. When fewer than sixty-five thousand Tea Party supporters flocked to the National Mall in Washington on September 12 for Glenn Beck and FreedomWorks' "9/12" rally, carrying signs like one reading, "Bury Obamacare with Kennedy," it was treated as if the entire center of gravity in American politics had shifted.

To be sure, the numbers on the far right had grown. Membership in the Liberty League, the anti–New Deal corollary to the Tea Party during the 1930s, has been estimated at 75,000, while membership in the John Birch Society in the 1960s has been estimated at 100,000 core members. Overall, at its height, 5 percent of Americans approved of the John Birch

Society. The Tea Party movement, in contrast, was estimated by *The New York Times* to have won the support of 18 percent of the population at its zenith, but at its core, according to the researcher Devin Burghart, were some 330,000 activists who had signed up with six national organizational networks. If the estimates were correct, the actual number of hard-core Tea Party activists was not, by historical standards, all that large. But the professionalization of the underground infrastructure, the growth of sympathetic and in some cases subsidized media outlets, and the concentrated money pushing the message from the fringe to center stage were truly consequential.

On October 3, as the first anniversary of Obama's election approached, David Koch came to the Washington area to attend a triumphant Defending the American Dream Summit, sponsored by Americans for Prosperity. Obama's poll numbers were falling fast. Only one Republican senator, Olympia Snowe of Maine, was working with the administration on health care, and she would eventually peel off. Aides said Obama was deeply disappointed. By obstructing every initiative, including his most ambitious domestic program, the Republicans had undermined his greatest appeal, his promise to be a bridge builder beyond old partisan divisions.

Mitch McConnell, the Republican minority leader in the Senate, held the Republican caucus in line partly by noting that Tea Party forces were ready and waiting to launch primary challenges against any who strayed. The outside groups funded by outside money thus provided crucial leverage. The plan worked so well that by the fall pundits who had fallen over themselves to praise Obama a year before were writing about his political ineptitude.

In a speech to a filled ballroom at the Crystal Gateway Marriott in Arlington, Virginia, on that October day, Koch said, "Five years ago, my brother Charles and I provided the funds to start the Americans for Prosperity, and it's beyond my wildest dreams how AFP has grown into this enormous organization." He went on, "Days like today bring to reality the vision of our board of directors when we founded this organization, five years ago." Rubbing his hands together somewhat awkwardly, he added, "We envisioned a mass movement, a state-based one, but national in scope, of hundreds of thousands of American citizens from all walks of life standing up and fighting for the economic freedoms that made our nation the most prosperous society in history . . . Thankfully, the stirrings from California to Virginia, and from Texas to Michigan, show that more and more of our fellow-citizens are beginning to see the same truths as we do."

As he stood at the lectern beaming, delegates from the various chapters of Americans for Prosperity reported in, one by one, describing how they had organized "dozens of tea parties" in their regions as they stood beside oversized vertical signs marking their states. Strobe lights crisscrossed the auditorium as excitement surged. It was hard not to notice that twenty-nine years after David Koch left the national political stage in utter defeat, he had succeeded in financing something that looked a lot like a presidential nominating convention, with himself as the winner.

CHAPTER EIGHT

The Fossils

IN THE FINAL MONTHS BEFORE THE 2008 PRESIDENTIAL ELEC-
tion, Michael Mann, a tenured meteorology and geosciences
professor at Penn State University who had become a leading figure in climate change research, told his wife that he
would be happy whichever candidate won. Both the Republican and the Democratic presidential nominees had spoken
about the importance of addressing global warming, which
Mann regarded as the paramount issue of the day. But what
he didn't fully foresee was that the same forces stirring the Tea
Party would expertly channel the public outrage at government
against scientific experts like himself.

Mann had started out unconvinced by the science of climate change, but in 1999 he and two co-authors had published
a study tracking the previous thousand years of temperatures in
the Northern Hemisphere. It included a simple, easy-to-grasp
graph showing that the earth's temperature had hovered in a
more or less straight line for nine hundred years but then shot
sharply upward, like the blade of a hockey stick, in the twentieth century. What came to be known as the hockey stick graph
was so powerfully persuasive it gained iconic status within the
climate debate. By 2008, Mann, like most experts, had long
since concluded that the scientific evidence was overwhelming that human beings were endangering the earth's climate by
burning too much oil, gas, and coal. The carbon dioxide and
other gases these fuels released were trapping the earth's heat,
with devastating effects.

As even the Pentagon, a cautious bastion of technological

nonpartisanship, concluded, "the danger from climate change is real, urgent, and severe." An official U.S. National Security Strategy report declared the situation a growing national security threat, arguing, "The change wrought by a warming planet will lead to new conflicts over refugees and resources; new suffering from drought and famine; catastrophic natural disasters; and the degradation of land across the globe." The report unambiguously predicted that if nothing were done, "climate change and pandemic disease" would directly threaten "the health and safety of the American people."

The American Association for the Advancement of Science, the world's largest and most prestigious scientific society, was equally if not more adamant. It warned that "we face risks of abrupt, unpredictable and potentially irreversible changes" with potentially "massively disruptive consequences."

Mann wasn't particularly political. Middle-aged, friendly, and balding, with a dark goatee shadowing his round face, he was a quintessential science nerd who had majored in applied math and physics at the University of California, Berkeley, got advanced degrees in geology and geophysics at Yale, and for many years didn't think scientists had much of a role to play in public policy. When Obama won, he recalls, "I shared the widespread view that we would see some action on the climate front."

Certainly this assumption seemed reasonable. On the night that Obama clinched the Democratic nomination, he spoke passionately about climate change, vowing that Americans would look back knowing that "this was the moment when the rise of the oceans began to slow and our planet began to heal." Once in office, he pledged to pass a "cap and trade" bill forcing the fossil fuel industry to pay for its pollution, as other industries did, rather than treating it as someone else's problem. Cap and trade was a market-based solution, originally backed by Republicans, requiring permits for carbon emissions. The theory was that it would give the industry a financial incentive to stop polluting. It had worked surprisingly well in previous years to reduce industrial emissions that caused acid rain. By choosing a tested, moderate, bipartisan approach, the Obama administration and many environmentalists assumed a deal would be winnable.

"What we didn't take into account," Mann later noted, "was the ferociousness of the moneyed interests and the politicians doing their bidding. We are talking about a direct challenge to the most powerful industry that has ever existed on the face of the earth. There's no depth to which they're unwilling to sink to challenge anything threatening their interests even if it's science and the scientists involved in it."

Mann contended that "the fossil fuel industry is an oligarchy." Some might dispute that American oil, gas, and coal magnates met the dictionary definition of a small, privileged group that effectively rules over the majority. But it was indisputable that they funded and helped orchestrate a series of vitriolic personal attacks that would threaten Mann's livelihood, derail climate legislation, and alter the course of the Obama presidency.

If there was a single ultra-wealthy interest group that hoped to see Obama fail as he took office, it was the fossil fuel industry. And if there was one test of its members' concentrated financial power over the machinery of American democracy, it was this minority's ability to stave off government action on climate change as science and the rest of the world were moving in the opposite direction. While Obama's health-care bill was useful in riling up Tea Party protesters, his environmental and energy policies were the real target of many of the multimillionaires and billionaires in the Koch circle. For most of the world's population the costs of inaction on climate change were far greater than those of action. But for the fossil fuel industry, as Mann put it, "it's like the switch from whale oil in the nineteenth century. They're fighting to maintain the status quo, no matter how dumb."

Coal, oil, and gas magnates formed the nucleus of the Koch donor network. Guest lists for the summits read like a Who's Who of America's most successful and most conservative fossil fuel barons, the majority of whom were private, independent operators of privately owned companies. They were men who had either made or inherited enormous fortunes in "extractive" energy without having to answer to public shareholders or much of anyone else. Among the group, for instance, was Corbin "Corby" Robertson Jr., the grandson of one of Texas's most legendary oil barons, Hugh Roy Cullen. Robertson, a former captain of the football team at the University of Texas, from which he graduated in 1969, had taken a bold, unorthodox risk with his inherited oil fortune. He had bet almost all of it on coal, reportedly accumulating by 2003 the single largest private cache of coal reserves in America. He owned, by one count, twenty-one billion tons of coal reserves—enough to fuel the entire country for twenty years. Only the U.S. government reportedly owned more coal than his private, Houston-based company, Quintana Resources Capital.

Other donors in the network included Harold Hamm and Larry Nichols, two of the most successful pioneers in "fracking," the environmentally controversial process by which water and chemicals are injected underground into rock formations to extract oil and natural gas. Hamm, the founder of Continental Resources, was a self-made billionaire wildcatter whom the *National Journal* likened to John D. Rockefeller. While his nearly billion-dollar divorce settlement and amazing rise from being born the youngest of thirteen children in a family of sharecroppers made tabloid history, business journals were more focused on his company, which almost overnight had become the face of fracking in North Dakota's Bakken Shale.

Joining him in the network, on the opposite end of the

social scale, was Larry Nichols, head of Devon Energy and later chairman of the American Petroleum Institute, the foremost trade association for the oil industry. A graduate of Princeton and a former Supreme Court clerk, Nichols had urged his family's Oklahoma energy company to buy Mitchell Energy after he noticed that its natural gas output was climbing because of fracking. Nichols combined the process with his own company's expertise in horizontal drilling to "unleash what became known as the unconventional gas revolution," as the energy industry historian Daniel Yergin wrote in *The Quest*. The Kochs, too, had investments in the chemicals, pipelines, and other aspects of fracking.

The donor network also boasted spectacularly successful oilmen like Philip Anschutz, heir to a western oil-drilling fortune, who himself discovered a fabled oil field on the Wyoming-Utah border in the 1980s, after which he diversified into ranches, railroads, and communications. The network included many smaller operators too. There were oilmen from Wyoming, Oklahoma, Texas, and Colorado and coal magnates from Virginia, West Virginia, Kentucky, and Ohio. The largest distributor of propane canisters in the country was also involved. Participating, too, were many of those whose businesses provided ancillary support to America's energy sector. In addition to the Kochs there were numerous other owners of pipelines, drilling equipment, and oil service companies, including the legendary Bechtel family, which made billions building refineries and pipelines in Saudi Arabia, Venezuela, and elsewhere.

Most of the actual donors in this group preferred to keep low profiles, letting the politicians speak for them. They were expert in casting the group's reservations about government regulation in lofty philosophical terms. The politicians called them "job creators" and patriots, responsible for American energy independence. Clearly, though, there were few Americans for whom government caps on carbon posed a more direct financial threat.

The problem for this group was that by 2008 the arithmetic of climate change presented an almost unimaginable challenge. If the world were to stay within the range of carbon emissions that scientists deemed reasonable in order for atmospheric temperatures to remain tolerable through the mid-century, 80 percent of the fossil fuel industry's reserves would have to stay unused in the ground. In other words, scientists estimated that the fossil fuel industry owned roughly five times more oil, gas, and coal than the planet could safely burn. If the government interfered with the "free market" in order to protect the planet, the potential losses for these companies were catastrophic. If, however, the carbon from these reserves were burned wantonly without the government applying any brakes, scientists predicted an intolerable rise in atmospheric temperatures, triggering potentially irreversible global damage to life on earth.

As early as 1997, one member of the Koch group sounded the alarm about the coming regulatory threat. That year Lew Ward, the retiring chairman of the Independent Petroleum Association of America, the trade group of independent oil and gas producers, delivered a jeremiad as his swan song. Ward, who was himself an Oklahoma oilman, began by proudly ticking off the various tax loopholes he helped pass during his tenure. "We've been fortunate the past couple of years to have a Republican Congress," he noted. But he warned that the various policy "skirmishes" the industry had survived recently were nothing but "a dress rehearsal for the real show . . . the possible 'Carbon Tax' that could help pay the costs of reducing greenhouse gas emissions." Ward perceived accurately that the climate change issue was coming and argued that if the "radical environmentalist 'off-oil' agenda" succeeded, "we can look down the road a little way and see an industry under siege." He vowed, "We are not going to let that happen. You can take that to the bank!"

Ward's swagger was well-grounded. The oil industry had held parochial but powerful sway over American politics for years. As early as 1913, the oil industry used its clout to win a special tax loophole, the "oil depletion allowance." On the theory that oil exploration was risky and costly, it enabled the industry to deduct so much income when it hit gushers that many oil companies evaded income taxes altogether. After the loophole was scandalously enlarged in 1926, liberals, stymied by the oil patch's defenders in Congress, tried unsuccessfully for five decades before they were finally able to close it.

No American politician's rise to power in the last century was more fueled by oil than that of Lyndon Johnson. As Robert Caro recounts in *The Path to Power*, starting in 1940 Johnson rose from a neophyte congressman to the Democratic Party's consummate power broker by handing out campaign contributions from his enormously wealthy backers in the Texas oil fields and defending their interests.

Although the oil industry benefited enormously from the federal government in the form of favorable tax treatment, huge government contracts, and aid in building pipelines, as well as other handouts, it became a bastion of antigovernment conservatism. In fact, as its wealth grew, the Texas oil patch was the source not only of an astounding amount of campaign lucre but also of a particularly extreme strain of right-wing politics. In his book about the state's oil fortunes, *The Big Rich*, Bryan Burrough speculates that what animated many of the magnates was "the deep-tissue insecurity of the nouveau riche" who were hell-bent on keeping all they had just gained.

If there was a progenitor of Texas's modern-day ultraconservative oil faction, it was Corby Robertson's grandfather Hugh Roy Cullen, who helped make Quintana a billion-dollar enterprise. With roots in the fallen gentry of the Confederacy, he belonged to a band of oilmen that loathed northern liberals, denigrated FDR's administration as the "Jew Deal," and formed a third party whose plank called for "the restoration of the supremacy of the white race." Cullen's political ambitions expanded with his fortune, and in 1952—half a century before the Kochs became giant political spenders—he was the single biggest donor in American politics and a key supporter of Senator Joseph McCarthy's anti-Communist crusade. But at the time, his brand of radically right-wing, oil-fueled politics was doomed to be marginalized. Burrough explains that "to succeed in politics Cullen needed a support organization of some kind, but building one was something he was unwilling or incapable of doing." Half a century later, however, with the "Kochtopus" in place, Cullen's grandson and fellow oilmen would fare far better.

Opposition to curbs on carbon had long been building in the industry. The concept that the earth was warming, and mankind was causing it, first broke into the mainstream media in 1988 when the climate modeler James Hansen, director of NASA's Goddard Institute for Space Studies, testified before a Senate committee about it, amid a nationwide heat wave. *The New York Times* played his dramatic findings on its front page. During his presidency, George H. W. Bush, like most political leaders of both parties at the time, accepted the science without dispute. He vowed to protect the environment, promising to fight "the Greenhouse Effect with the White House Effect" and sending his secretary of state, James Baker, to the first international summit of climate scientists, the Intergovernmental Panel on Climate Change. Although Bush was a Republican, he was not an outlier in his party. For decades, the environmental movement had enjoyed bipartisan support.

As public opinion mounted in favor of climate action, however, the fossil fuel industry organized and financed a stealthy state-of-the-art counteroffensive. Despite the agreement of both parties' presidential candidates in 2008 that something

needed to be done to stave off climate change, powerful outside interests had been working overtime to erode that consensus. The conservative infrastructure necessary to wage a war
of ideas was already in place. All it took to focus the attack on
climate science was money. And beneath the surface, it was
pouring in.

Kert Davies, the director of research at Greenpeace, the
liberal environmental group, spent months trying to trace the
funds flowing into a web of nonprofit organizations and talking
heads, all denying the reality of global warming as if working
from the same script. What he discovered was that from 2005
to 2008, a single source, the Kochs, poured almost $25 million
into dozens of different organizations fighting climate reform.
The sum was staggering. His research showed that Charles and
David had outspent what was then the world's largest public oil
company, ExxonMobil, by a factor of three. In a 2010 report,
Greenpeace crowned Koch Industries, a company few had ever
heard of at the time, the "kingpin of climate science denial."

The first peer-reviewed academic study on the topic added
further detail. Robert Brulle, a Drexel University professor of
sociology and environmental science, discovered that between
2003 and 2010 over half a billion dollars was spent on what
he described as a massive "campaign to manipulate and mislead the public about the threat posed by climate change."
The study examined the tax records of more than a hundred
nonprofit organizations engaged in challenging the prevailing
science on global warming. What it found was, in essence, a
corporate lobbying campaign disguised as a tax-exempt, philanthropic endeavor. Some 140 conservative foundations funded
the campaign, Brulle found. During the seven-year period he
studied, these foundations distributed $558 million in the form
of 5,299 grants to ninety-one different nonprofit organizations.
The money went to think tanks, advocacy groups, trade associations, other foundations, and academic and legal programs.
Cumulatively, this private network waged a permanent cam-

paign to undermine Americans' faith in climate science and to defeat any effort to regulate carbon emissions.

The cast of conservative organizations identified by Brulle was familiar to anyone who had followed the funding of the modern conservative movement. Among those he pinpointed as the largest bankrollers of climate change denial were foundations affiliated with the Koch and Scaife families, both of whose fortunes derived partly from oil. Also heavily involved were the Bradley Foundation and several others associated with hugely wealthy families participating in the Koch donor summits, such as foundations run by the DeVos family, Art Pope, the retail magnate from North Carolina, and John Templeton Jr., a doctor and heir to the fortune of his father, John Templeton Sr., an American mutual fund pioneer who eventually renounced his U.S. citizenship in favor of living in the Bahamas, reportedly saving $100 million on taxes. Brulle found that as the money was dispersed, three-quarters of the funds from these and other sources financing what he called the "climate change counter-movement" were untraceable.

"Powerful funders are supporting the campaign to deny scientific findings about global warming and raise public doubts about the roots and remedies of this massive global threat. At the very least," he argued, "American voters deserve to know who is behind these efforts."

Instead, by the time Obama took office some of the biggest bankrollers of the war against climate science had, if anything, gone further underground. Rather than funding the campaign directly, a growing number of private conservative foundations and donors had begun directing their contributions through an organization called DonorsTrust that in essence became a screen for the right wing, behind which fingerprints disappeared from the cash. Housed in a humdrum brick building in Alexandria, Virginia, DonorsTrust and its affiliate, Donors Capital Fund, were memorably described by *Mother Jones*'s

Andy Kroll as "the dark-money ATM of the conservative movement."

Founded in 1999 by Whitney Ball, an ardent libertarian from West Virginia who had overseen development of the Koch-founded Cato Institute, DonorsTrust boasted one key advantage for wealthy conservatives. It made their contributions appear to be going to Ball's bland-sounding "donor-advised fund," rather than to the far more controversial conservative groups she distributed it to afterward. The mechanism thus erased the donors' names from the money trail. Meanwhile, the donors retained the same if not bigger charitable tax deductions. As the DonorsTrust Web site advertised, "You wish to keep your charitable giving private, especially gifts funding sensitive or controversial issues. Set up a DonorsTrust account and ask that your gifts remain anonymous. Know that any contributions to your DonorsTrust account that have to be reported to the IRS will not become public information. Unlike with private foundations, gifts from your account will remain as anonymous as you request."

Between 1999 and 2015, DonorsTrust redistributed some $750 million from the pooled contributions to myriad conservative causes under its own name. Ordinarily, under the law, in exchange for their tax breaks, private foundations such as the Charles G. Koch Foundation were required to publicly disclose the charitable groups to whom they made their grants. It was one way to assure that these public service organizations were in fact serving the public. But donor-advised funds defeated this minimum transparency. Ball argued that the mechanism wasn't suspicious, or even unusual, and that liberals too had their own donor-advised fund, the Tides Foundation. DonorsTrust, the conservative answer to the Tides Foundation, however, soon had four times the funds and a far more strategic board. Its directors consisted of top officials of several of the most important institutions in the conservative movement, including the

American Enterprise Institute, the Heritage Foundation, and the Institute for Justice, the libertarian legal center whose start-up funds had been supplied by Charles Koch. They functioned as a central committee, coordinating grant making.

What Brulle noticed as he studied the money behind climate change denial was that as criticism of those blocking reform increased around 2007, tens of millions of dollars of contributions from fossil fuel interests like Koch and Exxon-Mobil seemed to have disappeared from the public fight. Meanwhile, a growing and commensurate amount of anonymous money from DonorsTrust started funding the climate change countermovement. In 2003, for instance, Brulle found that DonorsTrust money was the source of only 3 percent of the 140 groups whose financial records he studied. By 2010, it had grown to 24 percent. The circumstantial evidence suggested that the fossil fuel interests bankrolling climate change denial were deliberately hiding their hands, but Brulle couldn't prove it. "We just have this great big unknown out there about where all the money is coming from," he said.

Relations between the Kochs and DonorsTrust were close. Disclosures showed that the Kochs' foundations made sizable gifts to DonorsTrust, which in turn dispersed large amounts of cash to their favorite nonprofit groups. In 2010, for instance, the single largest grant that it made to any organization was a $7.4 million gift to the Americans for Prosperity Foundation, whose chairman was David Koch. These funds accounted for about 40 percent of the AFP Foundation's funding that year, belying the notion that it was a genuine grassroots organization. AFP, meanwhile, not only took a lead role in organizing the Tea Party rebellion but also spearheaded a national drive to block action on climate change, aiming in every way possible to merge the two movements.

What much of the stealth funding bought was the dissemination of scientific doubt. The fossil fuel industry thus followed the same deceptive playbook that had been devel-

oped by the public relations firm Hill & Knowlton on behalf
of the tobacco companies in the 1960s, in order to fabricate
uncertainty about the science linking smoking to cancer. As
the firm's memo had notoriously put it, "Doubt is our product."
To add credibility to their side, the tobacco companies funded
a network of official-sounding institutes and smokers' rights
groups. This strategy soon characterized the global warming
denial movement, too.

There was in fact some uncertainty about global warming,
as there is about virtually every scientific hypothesis. Probabil-
ity, rather than absolute certainty, is the nature of the scientific
method. But as Dr. James Baker, former head of the National
Oceanic and Atmospheric Administration, said in 2005,
"There's a better scientific consensus on this than on any issue
I know—except maybe Newton's second law of dynamics."

Nonetheless, in 1998, the American Petroleum Institute,
along with several top oil industry executives and conservative think tank officials, colluded on a secret plan to spend $2
million to confuse the press and the public about this growing scientific consensus. The plan called for recruiting skeptical scientists and training them in public relations so that they
could act as spokesmen, thereby adding legitimacy and cover to
the industry's agenda.

According to *The Republican War on Science,* the plan was
the brainchild of William O'Keefe, a former chief operating
officer at the American Petroleum Institute and a lobbyist for
ExxonMobil who became president of the George C. Marshall
Institute, a conservative think tank in Virginia. O'Keefe continued to lobby for ExxonMobil while heading the research
center. Described by *Newsweek* as a "central cog in the denial
machine," the think tank specialized in providing contrarian
scientific defenses for dubious clients. Funded by the Scaife,
Olin, and Bradley Foundations, among others, it had begun as
a center for Cold War hawks vouching for President Reagan's
"Star Wars" missile shield, but expanded into debunking other

scientific findings that could be construed as liberal or anti-corporate. Money from threatened corporate interests, meanwhile, frequently funded the research.

Leading the charge against climate science were two elderly, retired physicists affiliated with the George C. Marshall Institute who had previously defended the tobacco industry, Fred Seitz and Fred Singer. As Naomi Oreskes and Erik Conway write in *Merchants of Doubt*, the two Freds had been eminent physicists in their day, but neither had any expertise in either the environment or health, "yet, for years the press quoted these men as experts." What they were in fact expert in was converting a torrent of unseen funding into "fighting facts, and merchandising doubt," according to Oreskes and Conway.

But for the fossil fuel industry, winning over public opinion was no easy feat. As the new millennium dawned, the general public was broadly in favor of environmental regulations. As late as 2003, over 75 percent of *Republicans* supported strict environmental regulations, according to polls. For help on their public relations campaign, in 2002 the opponents of carbon regulations hired Frank Luntz, who warned that "the environment is probably the issue on which Republicans in general—and President Bush in particular—is most vulnerable." To win, he argued, global warming deniers had to portray themselves as "preserving and protecting" the environment. In his confidential memo "Winning the Global Warming Debate," which eventually leaked to the public, Luntz stressed as his number one point that opponents of carbon regulations "absolutely" must "not raise economic arguments first." In other words, telling the truth about their financial interests was a recipe for losing.

The key, he went on, was to question the science. "You need to continue to make the lack of scientific certainty a primary issue in the debate," he advised. So long as "voters believe there is no consensus about global warming within the scientific community," he said, regulations could be forestalled.

The Koch family poses for a Christmas card, circa 1950s. Left to right: Charles, David, Fred, Mary, Bill, Frederick. (Wichita State University Libraries, Special Collections and University Archives)

The Winkler-Koch unit at the Eurotank oil refinery in Hamburg was completed in 1935. (The United States Strategic Bombing Survey)

David Koch, left, the running mate of Libertarian presidential candidate Ed Clark, center, with Clark's wife, Alicia Garcia Cobos de Clark, at a fund-raising rally and telethon in Los Angeles in 1980 (Randy Rasmussen / Associated Press)

Charles Koch with Liz Koch, his wife, at Koch Headquarters in Wichita in 2012 (Bo Rader / *The Wichita Eagle* / Associated Press)

Richard Mellon Scaife, age twenty-three, at a cocktail party in 1955
(Margaret Bourke-White / The LIFE Picture Collection / Getty Images)

John M. Olin, left, presents the 1957 Outdoorsman of the Year award to
General Curtis E. LeMay. (*The Denver Post* / Getty Images)

Michael Mann in Iceland in 2016 (Courtesy of Michael Mann)

Sheldon Adelson, chairman and CEO of the Las Vegas Sands Corporation, at the opening of his casino resort in Macau in 2012 (Kin Cheung / Associated Press)

Robert Mercer at the World Science Festival Gala in New York City in 2014 (Andrew Toth / Getty Images Entertainment / Getty Images)

James Arthur "Art" Pope, then budget director for North Carolina governor Pat McCrory, in his office in Raleigh in 2014 (Ted Richardson / *The Washington Post* / Getty Images)

Philip Anschutz, co-founder of Qwest Communications and founder of The Anschutz Corporation, in 2008 (Lucy Nicholson / Reuters)

Corbin Robertson Jr., owner of the country's largest private cache of coal (Steve Campbell / *Houston Chronicle*)

Language that "worked," he advised, included phrases like "we must not rush to judgment" and "we should not commit America to any international document that handcuffs us." Later, Luntz would switch sides and publicly admit that global warming was a real peril. But in the view of Michael Mann, whose scientific work soon became the target of climate change deniers, Luntz's 2002 memo served as a virtual hunting license. "It basically said you have to discredit the scientists and create fake groups. It doesn't say 'engage in character assassination,' but it was leaning in that direction."

On cue, organizations funded and directed by the Kochs tore into global warming science and the experts behind it. The Cato Institute, the libertarian think tank that Charles Koch founded, put out a steady stream of reports like *Apocalypse Not: Science, Economics, and Environmentalism* and *Climate of Fear: Why We Shouldn't Worry About Global Warming*. A grant from the Charles G. Koch Charitable Foundation, along with funds from ExxonMobil and the American Petroleum Institute, also helped pay for a non-peer-reviewed study claiming that polar bears, who were mascots of the global warming debate, were not endangered by climate change. It quickly drew criticism from experts in the field like the National Wildlife Federation, which predicted that by 2050 two-thirds of the polar bear population would disappear because their habitat was melting. Nonetheless, the conclusions of the oil-financed study were echoed throughout the network of Koch-funded groups. "There are more polar bears today than there have ever been," Ed Crane, the head of Cato, insisted. He argued that "global warming theories just give the government more control of the economy."

It was the authors of the revisionist polar bear study who also took one of the first shots at Michael Mann's iconic hockey stick study, publishing a takedown in 2003. The credentials of the critics, Sallie Baliunas and Wei-Hock "Willie" Soon, looked impressive. Soon was identified as a scientist at the Harvard–Smithsonian Center for Astrophysics. But it later emerged that he had a doctoral degree in aerospace engineering, not climate science, and had only a part-time, unpaid affiliation with the Smithsonian Institution. Without disclosing it, he had accepted more than $1.2 million from the fossil fuel industry from 2005 to 2015, including at least $230,000 from the Charles G. Koch Charitable Foundation. It was later revealed that some of the payments for his papers were marked as "deliverables" by the fossil fuel companies.

Soon's attack on Mann was so controversial that the editor and several other staffers sympathetic to Mann resigned in protest against *Climate Research,* the small journal that published it. Yet from that moment on, Mann, who was at the time an assistant professor in the Department of Environmental Sciences at the University of Virginia, had a target on his back.

As the scientific consensus grew in support of global warming, the industry's efforts to fight it became increasingly aggressive. The presidential candidacy of the environmental activist Al Gore in 2000 posed an obvious threat to the fossil fuel industry. That election cycle, Koch Industries and its employees disbursed over $800,000 in support of his opponent George W. Bush and other Republicans. Koch Industries' political action committee was spending more on federal campaigns than any other oil and gas company, including Exxon-Mobil. The company's expenditures on Washington lobbying expanded more than twenty-fold from 2004 to 2008, reaching $20 million. The Kochs' corporate self-interest had by then thoroughly trumped their youthful disdain for engaging in conventional politics.

Political contributions from oil, gas, and coal companies became increasingly polarized during this period. In 1990, the oil and gas industry's political giving was skewed 60 percent in favor of Republicans and 40 percent in favor of Democrats. By the middle of the Bush years, 80 percent of the industry's giving went to Republicans. Giving from coal-mining firms was even more lopsided, with 90 percent going to Republicans, according to the Center for Responsive Politics.

The investment soon paid off. As the Harvard political scientist Theda Skocpol writes in a study of climate change denial, the Republican Party, particularly in the U.S. Congress, soon swung sharply to the right on climate issues. Partisan differences remained small among the general public but grew into a gaping chasm among elected officials.

Conservative opponents of carbon regulations, like James Inhofe, a Republican senator from Oklahoma who received serial campaign donations from Koch Industries PAC, turned the rhetoric up to a boiling point. Global warming, he proclaimed, was "the greatest hoax ever perpetrated on the American people." Inhofe's spokesman, Marc Morano, had a reputation as a professional "pit bull," as Mann later put it, derived from his earlier role promoting the claims of the Swift Boat Veterans for Truth, a group that had smeared John Kerry's military record during his 2004 presidential campaign. At the time, Morano was working for a conservative news outlet that was funded in part by the Scaife, Bradley, and Olin Foundations.

By 2006, Morano had moved on to "swiftboating" scientists. "You've got to name names and you've got to go after individuals," he explained in an interview with the documentary filmmaker Robert Kenner. He seemed to relish making political disagreements personal, taunting and inflaming opponents with a grin in televised showdowns. Morano denounced James Hansen as a "wannabe Unabomber" and Mann as a "charlatan." He said of the scapegoating, "We had a lot of fun with it."

Morano charged that Mann was part of what he called "the 'climate con,'" which he described as "a lavishly funded climate

machine that is lobbying for laws and uses every bit of data or
new study to proclaim 'it's worse than we thought' or 'we must
act now.'" Morano's background was in political science, which
he studied at George Mason University, not climate science.
"I'm not a scientist but I play one on TV," he joked. Nonetheless, he asserted authoritatively that "man-made global warming fears are a grand political narrative, not science."

The George W. Bush years, meanwhile, proved a bonanza
for the fossil fuel industry, which had thrown its weight behind
his election. The coal industry in particular had played a major
role in delivering West Virginia's five electoral votes to Bush in
2000, sealing a victory that would have gone to Al Gore had he
carried the formerly Democratic state instead. "State political
veterans and top White House staffers concur that it was basically a coal-fired victory," *The Wall Street Journal* wrote. The
industry was lavishly rewarded. Vice President Dick Cheney, a
former CEO of the oil-field equipment and services company
Halliburton, personally took charge of energy policy. Bush had
vowed during the campaign to act on climate change by limiting greenhouse gas emissions, but once in office Cheney coun-
termanded him. In what Cheney's biographer Barton Gellman
describes as a "case study in managing an errant boss," Cheney
shifted the administration's position to arguing that the science on global warming was "inconclusive," requiring "more
scientific inquiry."

The 2005 energy bill, which Hillary Clinton dubbed at the
time the "Dick Cheney Lobbyist Energy Bill," offered enormous subsidies and tax breaks for fossil-fuel-intensive companies. The Bush administration weakened regulations, for
instance, on coal-fired power plants. Taking a position that was
eventually overturned by the courts, it exempted mercury emissions from regulation under the Clean Air Act, reversing the
position taken by the Clinton administration. Fracking got a
boost too. Cheney used his influence to exempt it from regula-

tion under the Safe Drinking Water Act, over objections from the Environmental Protection Agency. The fracking industry boomed. Within five years, Devon Energy, Larry Nichols's company, would rank as the fourth-largest producer of natural gas in the United States. Harold Hamm would become a multibillionaire. Cheney's former company Halliburton also became a major player in the fracking industry, illustrating that free-market advocates greatly benefited from government favors.

In all, the Bush energy act contained some $6 billion in oil and gas subsidies and $9 billion in coal subsidies. The Kochs routinely cast themselves as libertarians who deplored government taxes, regulations, and subsidies, but records show they took full advantage of the special tax credits and subsidies available to the oil, ethanol, and pipeline business, among other areas of commerce in which they were engaged. In many cases, their lobbyists fought hard to protect these perks. In addition, their companies benefited from nearly $100 million in government contracts in the decade after 2000, according to a study by Media Matters, a liberal watchdog group.

When Barack Obama took office, the fossil fuel industry was not only eager to preserve its perks but also more militant in its opposition to climate change science than ever. Skocpol notes that 2007 had been a turning point in the fight. That year, Al Gore was awarded both a Nobel Peace Prize and featured in an Academy Award–winning documentary film, *An Inconvenient Truth*. The film featured Mann's hockey stick graph. Gore's acclaim and Mann's simple chart helped raise concern about global warming to a new peak, with 41 percent of the American public saying it worried them "a great deal."

"At this critical juncture—when Americans in general might have been persuaded of the urgency of dealing with global warming," Skocpol notes, opponents fought back with new vigor. The whole ideological assembly line that Richard

Fink and Charles Koch had envisioned decades earlier, including the entire conservative media sphere, was enlisted in the fight. Fox Television and conservative talk radio hosts gave saturation coverage to the issue, portraying climate scientists as swindlers pushing a radical, partisan, and anti-American agenda. Allied think tanks pumped out books and position papers, whose authors testified in Congress and appeared on a whirlwind tour of talk shows. "Climate denial got disseminated deliberately and rapidly from think tank tomes to the daily media fare of about thirty to forty percent of the U.S. populace," Skocpol estimates.

Climate contrarians also recruited conservative evangelical Christian leaders, who distrusted government in general and had impressive political and communications clout. One by-product of this pact was an organization in the Washington suburbs called the Cornwall Alliance, which released a hit film in evangelical circles called *Resisting the Green Dragon* that equated environmentalism with worship of a false god. It described global warming as "one of the greatest deceptions of our day." Climate change became such a hot-button issue for Christian fundamentalists that Richard Cizik, a vice president of the National Association of Evangelicals, who was considered among the most powerful leaders in the movement, was forced to resign in late 2008 after publicly endorsing climate change science.

Before long, public opinion polls showed that concern about climate change among all but hard-core liberals had collapsed. As the 2008 presidential campaign played out, the issue grew increasingly polarized. Just before the election, with the economy in tumult, John McCain, the Republican presidential candidate, reiterated that the climate problem was real. He also said that green jobs would lead the way to economic recovery. But his choice of Sarah Palin as his running mate, one of whose mantras was "Drill, Baby, Drill," indicated just how influential the voice of climate extremism was becoming within the Republican Party.

As Obama took office, America derived over 85 percent of its total energy from oil, gas, and coal. The business was enormous, with profits and influence to match.

Conventional wisdom nonetheless held that Obama's election portended well for environmentalists. Mann, too, was optimistic, but he worried about what he regarded as a "troubling complacency" among his colleagues. He knew that the Obama administration posed two huge threats to the fossil fuel industry, and he doubted the industry would just roll over. The first threat was Obama's Environmental Protection Agency. Lisa Jackson, the EPA administrator, announced that she intended to treat greenhouse gas emissions as hazardous pollutants, regulating them for the first time under the Clean Air Act. It was an authority that the Supreme Court had upheld in 2007. But no previous administration had tried to take on the industry so frontally. The second was the Democrats' plan to introduce the long-incubating cap-and-trade bill to limit greenhouse gas emissions.

Even before Obama was inaugurated, Americans for Prosperity had begun taking aim at the cap-and-trade idea, circulating a pledge requiring elected officials to oppose new spending to fight climate change. Koch Industries, meanwhile, began lobbying against government mandates to reduce carbon emissions. Then, soon after Obama was inaugurated, an odd television ad popped up around the country that seemed strangely off message. While most Americans were transfixed by the unfolding economic disaster that was preoccupying the Obama administration in its first few months, out of nowhere, it seemed, was a discordant television spot about a spoiled slacker named Carlton.

"Hey there," said a louche-looking young man, plucking away at a plate of canapés. "I'm Carlton, the wealthy eco-hypocrite. I inherited my money and attended fancy schools. I own three homes and five cars, but always talk with my rich friends about saving the planet. And I want Congress to spend billions on programs in the name of global warming and green energy, even if it causes massive unemployment, higher energy bills, and digs people like you even deeper into the recession. Who knows? Maybe I'll even make money off of it!"

"Carlton" was, in fact, the creation of Americans for Prosperity, the nonprofit "social welfare" group founded and heavily funded by David Koch, who of course had inherited hundreds of millions of dollars, attended Deerfield Academy, owned *four* homes (a ski lodge in Aspen; a Belle Epoque mansion, Villa el Sarmiento, in Palm Beach; a sprawling beach house in the Hamptons; and an eighteen-room duplex at 740 Park Avenue in Manhattan), and drove, among other cars, a Land Rover and a Ferrari.

By creating "Carlton" as a decoy, the Kochs and their allies evidently hoped to convince the public that government action on climate change posed a threat to "people like you" or ordinary Americans' pocketbooks. But it of course posed a far greater threat to their own. With ownership of refineries, pipelines, a coal subsidiary (the C. Reiss Coal Company), coal-fired power plants, fertilizer, petroleum coke manufacturing, timber, and leases on over a million acres of untapped Canadian oil sands, Koch Industries alone routinely released some 24 million tons of carbon dioxide into the atmosphere a year. Any financial penalty that the government placed on carbon pollution would threaten both their immediate profit margins and the long-term value of the enormous investments they had in still-untapped fossil fuel reserves.

The Kochs themselves said little about their views on climate change at the time.

But in one interview, David Koch suggested that if real,

it would prove a boon. "The Earth will be able to support enormously more people because a far greater land area will be available to produce food," he argued. Charles's thinking was reflected in the company's in-house newsletter, which featured an article titled "Blowing Smoke." "Why are such unproven or false claims promoted?" it asked. Rather than fighting global warming, the newsletter suggested, mankind would be better off adapting to it. "Since we can't control Mother Nature, let's figure out how to get along with her changes," it advised. A similar line was subtly argued in the David H. Koch Hall of Human Origins at the Smithsonian's National Museum of Natural History in Washington, which opened in March 2010. The message of the exhibition, funded by his fortune, was that the human race had evolved for the better in response to previous environmental challenges and would adapt in the face of climate change, too. An interactive game suggested that if the climate on earth became intolerable, people might build "underground cities" and develop "short, compact bodies" or "curved spines" so that "moving around in tight spaces will be no problem."

Soon the climate issue was creeping into Tea Party rallies, too. As protesters erupted in generalized rage in the spring and summer of 2009, Americans for Prosperity, FreedomWorks, and the other secretly funded Tea Party groups succeeded to a remarkable extent in channeling the populist anger into the climate fight. At the first big "Tax Day" Tea Party rallies on April 15, 2009, while most protesters were flaying Obama's bank bailouts and stimulus plan, the staff of Americans for Prosperity handed out free T-shirts and signs protesting what would ordinarily seem to be an arcane issue for most people in the streets, the cap-and-trade bill. "The Obama budget proposes the largest excise tax in history," the advocacy group's talking points stressed.

To dramatize the issue, offshoots of Americans for Prosperity sent "Carbon Cops," who pranced into Tea Party rallies pretending to be overreaching emissaries from the EPA, warning that backyard barbecues, churches, and lawn mowers were about to be shut down because of new, stricter interpretations of the Clean Air Act. The advocacy group also launched what it called the Cost of Hot Air Tour to mock the cap-and-trade proposal. It featured a seventy-foot-tall bright red hot-air balloon on whose side was emblazoned a slogan reducing the argument against the cap-and-trade proposal to six scary words. Cap and trade, it said, means "higher taxes, lost jobs, less freedom." Americans for Prosperity sent the balloon to so many states in 2009 that the group's president, Tim Phillips, later admitted, "I rode more hot-air balloons in that year-and-a-half period than I ever want to ride again. I do not like hot-air balloons."

The public campaign was accompanied by a darker covert one. Tom Perriello, a freshman Democratic congressman from Charlottesville, Virginia, who favored the cap-and-trade bill, discovered this in the summer of 2009 when constituents started bombarding his office with angry missives. Reams of faxes arrived from voters, many representing local chapters of ordinarily supportive liberal groups like the NAACP and the American Association of University Women. Under official letterheads, they argued passionately that the cap-and-trade legislation would raise electric bills, hurting the poor. But an effort by the congressman's staff to reach the angry constituents revealed that the letters were forgeries, sent on behalf of a coal industry trade group by Bonner and Associates, a Washington-based public relations firm.

After the fraud was exposed, the firm fired an employee. But it wasn't an isolated incident. Perriello, like many other elected officials that summer, also found himself heckled during town hall meetings. One such heckler called him a "traitor" for supporting the cap-and-trade bill, while another videotaped the showdown. Later one of the disruptive members of the audience admitted to the investigative reporter Lee Fang that he had been put up to it by the Virginia director of Americans for Prosperity. Similar outbursts took place all over the country that summer. Mike Castle, a moderate Republican congressman from Delaware, was accosted by voters demanding to know how he could even consider voting for such a "hoax," according to Eric Pooley's account in *The Climate War*. The U.S. Chamber of Commerce, the American Petroleum Institute, and other industry representatives, it turned out, had created a "grassroots" group called Energy Citizens that joined Tea Party organizations in packing the town halls with protesters.

Fanning the flames were the right-wing radio hosts. "It's not about saving the planet," Rush Limbaugh told his audience. "It's not about anything, folks, other than raising taxes and redistributing wealth." Glenn Beck warned listeners it would lead to water rationing. "This is about controlling every part of your life, even taking a shower!" Torquing up the fear, Republicans in Congress quoted from a study by the Heritage Foundation that predicted it would add thousands of dollars to Americans' energy bills and lead to devastating unemployment. The nonpartisan Congressional Budget Office put out an authoritative study contradicting this, demonstrating that the average cost to Americans would be the same as buying a postage stamp a day. But John Boehner, the Republican minority leader in the House, dismissed the real numbers, suggesting anyone who believed them could "go ask the unicorns."

Despite the inflammatory atmosphere, the House passed a bill to cap and trade carbon dioxide emissions on June 26, 2009. The process wasn't pretty. It took an extraordinary push from its sponsors, Congressmen Henry Waxman of California and Ed Markey of Massachusetts, and an epic amount of horse-trading between environmentalists and the affected industries. Many environmentalists thought the final product was so flawed that it wasn't worth the trouble. But for those looking for Congress to reach the kind of moderate compromises Obama had been elected to deliver, it was a first step.

Rather than causing elation, though, the victory was clouded by trepidation. Supporters, particularly Democrats from conservative, fossil-fuel-heavy states like Perriello and Rick Boucher of Virginia, feared there would be a steep price to pay. As the threat to the industry grew, so would its determination to stop them.

That fall, television ads began appearing in states like Montana, where the Democratic senator Max Baucus was already under attack from members of the Koch network on the health-care issue. "There is no scientific evidence that CO_2 is a pollutant. In fact higher CO_2 levels than we have today would help the Earth's ecosystems," the ads said, urging viewers to tell Baucus not to vote for the cap-and-trade bill, which would "cost us jobs." The sponsor for the ad was a group curiously called CO_2 Is Green. Quietly funding it, according to Steven Mufson, the energy reporter for *The Washington Post*, was Corbin Robertson, owner of the country's largest private cache of coal.

Robertson's fingerprints were detectable behind another anti-climate-change front group, too, the Coalition for Responsible Regulation. As soon as Obama's EPA took steps to regulate greenhouse gases, the previously unknown group took legal action to stop it. The group's private e-mails surfaced later, revealing how it successfully egged on Texas's bureaucrats to join the lawsuit, despite the state's own climatologist's belief that man-made global warming posed a real danger and that the EPA's scientific findings were solid. Neither Robertson's name nor that of his company appeared in the papers incorporating the organization. But its address and its top officers were the same as those of Robertson's company, Quintana.

Following hard on the summer's raucous Tea Party protests, things got uglier in Washington as well. As Obama addressed a joint session of Congress laying out his health-care proposal in September 2009, his speech was interrupted by Joe Wilson, a Republican congressman from South Carolina, shouting, "You lie!" from the well of the House. Congress rebuked Wilson for his extraordinary breach of decorum, but within a month, climate skeptics were echoing Wilson's belligerence. One posted a report titled "UN Climate Reports: They Lie!"

The opposition grew as the Obama administration got ready to head to Copenhagen in December 2009 for its first international climate summit. World leaders expected the United States would finally commit to serious reform. Previously, the United States had declined to join other developed nations in agreeing to limit greenhouse gas emissions under the Kyoto Protocol. Given Obama's position, time seemed to be running out for the fossil fuel forces and their free-market allies. Then, on November 17, 2009, an anonymous commenter on a contrarian Web site declared, "A miracle has happened."

With lethal timing, an unidentified saboteur had hacked expertly into the University of East Anglia's Web site and uploaded thousands of internal e-mails detailing the private communications of the scientists working in its famed Climatic Research Unit. The climatologists at the British university had been in constant communication with those in America, and now all of their unguarded professional doubts, along with their unguarded and sometimes contemptuous asides about their opponents, stretching all the way back to 1996, were visible for the entire world to read.

Chris Horner, a conservative climate contrarian working at the Competitive Enterprise Institute, another pro-corporate think tank subsidized by oil and other fossil fuel fortunes, including the Kochs', declared, "The blue dress moment may have arrived." But instead of using Monica Lewinsky's telltale garment to impeach Bill Clinton, they would use the words of the world's leading climate scientists to impeach the climate change movement. If edited down and taken out of context, their exchanges could be made to appear to suggest a willingness to falsify data in order to buttress the idea that global warming was real.

Dubbing the alleged scandal Climategate, they went into overdrive. The web of organizations, funded in part by the Kochs, pounced on the hacked e-mails. Cato scholars were particularly energetic in promoting the story. In the two weeks after the e-mails went public, one Cato scholar alone gave more than twenty media interviews trumpeting the alleged scandal. The story soon spread from obviously slanted venues to the pages of *The New York Times* and *The Washington Post*, adding mainstream credence. Tim Phillips, the president of Americans for Prosperity, jumped on the hacked e-mails, describing them to a gathering of conservative bloggers at the Heritage Foundation as "a crucial tipping point" and adding, "If we win the science argument, I think it's game, set, and match for them."

Eventually, seven independent inquiries exonerated the climate scientists, finding nothing in the e-mails to discredit their work or the larger consensus on global warming. In the meantime, though, Michael Mann's life, along with the environmental movement, was plunged into turmoil.

Mann was among the scientists most roiled by the mysterious hacking incident. Four words in the purloined e-mails were seized upon as evidence that he was a fraud. In describing his research, his colleagues had praised his use of a "trick" that had helped him "hide the decline." Mann's detractors leaped to the conclusion that these words proved that his research was just a "trick" to fool the public and that he had deliberately hidden an actual "decline" in twentieth-century temperatures in order to fake evidence of global warming.

The facts, when fully understood, were very different. It was a British colleague, not Mann, who had written the ostensibly damning words, and when examined in context, they were utterly mundane. The "trick" referred to was just a clever technique Mann had devised in order to provide a backup data set. The "decline" in question was a reference to a decline in available information from certain kinds of tree rings after 1961, which had made it hard to have a consistent set of data. Another scientist, not Mann, had found an alternative source of data to compensate for this problem, which was what was meant by "hide the decline." The only genuinely negative disclosure from the e-mails was that Mann and the other climatologists had agreed among themselves to withhold, rather than share, their research with some of their critics, whom they disparaged. Given the harassment they had been subjected to, their reasoning was understandable, but it violated the customary transparency expected within the scientific community. Other than that, the "Climategate" scandal was, in other words, not one.

It took no time, nevertheless, for the hacked e-mails to spur a witch hunt. Within days, Inhofe and other Republicans in Congress who were recipients of Koch campaign donations demanded an investigation into Mann. They sent threatening letters to Penn State, where he was by then a tenured professor. Later, Virginia's attorney general, Ken Cuccinelli, a graduate of the George Mason School of Law, would also subpoena Mann's former employer, the University of Virginia, demanding all records relating to his decade-old academic research, regardless of libertarians' professed concerns about government intrusion. Eventually, Virginia's Supreme Court dismissed its own attorney general's case "with prejudice," finding he had misread the law.

By New Year's Eve 2009, Mann was feeling under attack from all sides. Conservative talk radio hosts lambasted him regularly. Contrarian Web sites were lit up with blog posts detailing his iniquity. A self-described former CIA officer contacted colleagues in Mann's department offering a $10,000 reward to any who would provide dirt on him, "confidentiality assured." Soon after, Mann asserts, a think tank called the

National Center for Public Policy Research led a campaign to get Mann's National Science Foundation grants revoked. As Mann recounts in his book *The Hockey Stick and the Climate Wars,* two conservative nonprofit law firms, the Southeastern Legal Foundation and the Landmark Legal Foundation, brought legal actions aimed at him. The think tank and the two law firms were funded by combinations of the same small constellation of family fortunes through their private charitable foundations. Omnipresent were Bradley, Olin, and Scaife.

Charles Koch's foundation also was engaged in piling on. It helped subsidize the Landmark Legal Foundation. The Kochs evidently admired Landmark's president, Mark Levin, a longtime associate of the former attorney general Edwin Meese III. In 2010, Americans for Prosperity hired Levin to promote it on his nationally syndicated talk radio show, thereby copying the deal that FreedomWorks had struck with Glenn Beck. Levin was a curious choice of spokesman for the buttoned-down, erudite Koch brothers. His style was incendiary, even rude. He later called Kenneth Vogel, the *Politico* reporter who broke the news of the deal with Americans for Prosperity, "a vicious S.O.B." and told a female caller, "I don't know why your husband doesn't put a gun to his temple. Get the Hell out of here!" His attacks on Obama's policies were similarly heated, particularly regarding climate change. He said Mann "and the other advocates of man-made global warming" did not "know how to conduct a correct statistical analysis" and accused "envirostatists" of inventing global warming in order to justify a tyrannical government takeover. Their "pursuit," he claimed, "after all, is power, not truth."

An especially grave attack on Mann's livelihood was launched, meanwhile, by yet another group, the Commonwealth Foundation for Public Policy Alternatives in Harrisburg, Pennsylvania. The self-described think tank belonged to a national web of similar conservative organizations known as the State Policy Network. Much of Commonwealth's financial support came through DonorsTrust and Donors Capital Fund, making it impossible to identify the individual backers. But because it was based in Scaife's home state, Commonwealth had particularly deep ties to his family foundations. Michael Gleba, the chair of Commonwealth's board of directors, was also the president of the Sarah Scaife Foundation and treasurer of Scaife's Carthage Foundation and a trustee of both. This arrangement gave Commonwealth unusual clout, particularly over Pennsylvania's state legislature.

The Pennsylvania think tank waged a campaign to get Mann fired and successfully lobbied Republican allies in the legislature to threaten to withhold Penn State's funding until the university took "appropriate action" against Mann. With the public university's finances held hostage, it agreed to investigate Mann. Meanwhile, the think tank ran a campaign of attack ads against him in the university's daily newspaper, as well as helping to organize an anti-Mann campus protest.

"It was nerve-racking to be under that pressure at Penn State," recalls Mann. "There were these nebulous accusations based on stolen e-mails. Ordinarily, it would have been clear there were no grounds for investigation. But it was promoted by the Commonwealth Foundation, which seems to almost have a stranglehold on Republicans in the state legislature. I knew I had done nothing wrong, but there was this uncertain future hanging over me. There was so much political pressure being brought to bear on Penn State I wasn't sure if they'd cave."

In the meantime, death threats began appearing in Mann's in-box. "I tried to shield my family as much as I could," he says. But this became impossible when one day he opened a suspicious-looking letter without thinking, only to have it release a cloud of white powder into his office. Fearing anthrax, he called the campus police. Soon the FBI quarantined his office behind crime tape, disrupting the whole department.

The powder turned out to be harmless, but, Mann recalls, "it was a spectacle. There was a point where I had the hotline number for the chief of police on our fridge, in case my wife saw anything unusual. It felt like there was a very calibrated campaign of vilification to the extent where the crazies might go after us."

It was particularly disturbing to Mann that there appeared to be overlap between hard-core climate change deniers and Second Amendment enthusiasts, whipped up, he came to believe, by "cynical special interests." Mann says, "The disaffected, the people who have trouble putting dinner on the table, were being misled into believing that action on climate change meant that 'They' want to take away your freedom and probably your guns, too. There was a very skillful campaign to indoctrinate them," he said. "We've seen Second Amendment enthusiasts take action against abortion doctors. There's an attempt to paint us as villains in the same way."

He was not alone in receiving death threats. Several climatologists, he said, including Phil Jones, director of the hacked Climatic Research Unit in Great Britain, felt compelled to hire personal bodyguards. "Luckily," Mann relates, both the Penn State investigations—which the legislature required to be done a second time in greater depth—and another one by the inspector general of the National Science Foundation, essentially the highest scientific body in the United States, exonerated Mann. "It lasted two years. It came out well. But two years is a long time," he says. "I never imagined I'd be at the center of some contentious debate. It's not why you study what I did. What worries me," he adds, "is that this circus-like atmosphere may have scared off many young scientists. It actually has a chilling effect. It prevents scientists from participating in the public discourse, because they fear they, or their department head, will be threatened."

By the time Mann's scientific research was upheld, underscoring his integrity as well as the genuine danger posed by climate change, it hardly mattered. By then, the percentage of Americans who believed the world was warming had dropped a precipitous fourteen points from 2008. Almost half of those polled by Gallup in 2010—48 percent—believed that fears of global warming were "generally exaggerated," the highest numbers since the polling firm first posed the question more than a decade before. Watching from afar, Mann could see no cause for the United States to move in the opposite direction from science other than money. "In the scientific community, the degree of confidence in climate change is rising," he said. "In the public, it's either steady or falling. There's a divergence. That wedge is what the industry has bought."

Although the cap-and-trade bill moved to the Senate, it was already dead. At first, Lindsey Graham, the independent-minded Republican from South Carolina, took a courageous leadership role in the fight, offering to co-sponsor the legislation with the Democrat John Kerry and the Independent Joe Lieberman after declaring, to the surprise and delight of environmentalists, "I have come to conclude that greenhouse gases and carbon pollution" are "not a good thing."

Graham, however, feared pressure from his right flank. He warned the Democrats that they had to move fast, before Fox News caught wind of the process. As he feared, in April 2010, Fox News attacked him for backing a "gas tax." A vitriolic Tea Party activist immediately held a press conference in his home state denouncing him as "gay," and a political front group called American Solutions launched a negative campaign against him for his climate stance in South Carolina. American Solutions, it later turned out, was funded by huge fossil fuel and other corporate interests, many of whom were in the Koch fold. Among them were Larry Nichols of Devon Energy,

Dick Farmer of Cintas, Stan Hubbard of Hubbard Broadcasting, and Sheldon Adelson, chairman of the Las Vegas Sands Corporation. Within days of the drubbing, Graham withdrew from the process. Harry Reid, the Democratic majority leader from Nevada, dealt the final blow to the cap-and-trade bill. Facing a tough reelection himself and worried about making Democrats walk the plank for the bill, he refused after Graham backed out to bring the legislation to the Senate floor for a vote.

Opponents of climate change reform got their wish. "Gridlock is the greatest friend a global warming skeptic has, because that's all you really want," Morano later acknowledged. "There's no legislation we're championing. We're the negative force. We are just trying to stop stuff."

Asked why the climate legislation failed, Al Gore told *The New Yorker*'s Ryan Lizza, "The influence of special interests is now at an extremely unhealthy level. It's at a point," he said, "where it's virtually impossible for participants in the current political system to enact any significant change without first seeking and gaining permission from the largest commercial interests who are most affected by the proposed change."

As the first legislation aimed at addressing climate change sputtered out, the Massey mine in West Virginia collapsed in a methane explosion, killing twenty-nine miners. Soon after, a leak from the Deepwater Horizon oil rig in the Gulf of Mexico triggered the largest accidental oil spill in history, killing and causing birth defects in record numbers of marine animals. A grand jury would charge the owner of the Upper Big Branch mine with criminally conspiring to evade safety regulations, while a federal judge would find the oil rig's principal owner, British Petroleum, guilty of gross negligence and reckless conduct.

Meanwhile, the amount of carbon dioxide in the atmosphere was already above the level that scientists said risked causing runaway global warming. Obama acknowledged at this point that he knew "the votes may not be there right now," but, he vowed, "I intend to find them in the coming months." The conservative money machine, however, was already far ahead of him on an audacious new plan to try to ensure that he would never succeed.

CHAPTER NINE

Money Is Speech:
The Long Road to *Citizens United*

ON MAY 17, 2010, A BLACK-TIE AUDIENCE AT THE METROPOLITAN Opera House in New York City applauded as a tall, jovial-looking billionaire loped to the stage. It was the seventieth annual spring gala of American Ballet Theatre, and David Koch was being honored for his generosity as a member of the board of trustees. A longtime admirer of classical ballet, he had recently donated $2.5 million toward the company's upcoming season and had given many millions before that. As Koch received a token award, he was flanked by two of the gala's co-chairs, the socialite Blaine Trump, in a peach-colored gown, and the political scion Caroline Kennedy Schlossberg, in emerald green. Kennedy's mother, Jacqueline Kennedy Onassis, had been a patron of the ballet and, coincidentally, the previous owner of a Fifth Avenue apartment that Koch had bought in 1995 and then sold eleven years later for $32 million, having found it too small.

The gala marked the official arrival of Koch as one of New York's most prominent philanthropists. At the age of seventy, he was recognized for an impressive history of giving. In 2008, he donated $100 million to modernize Lincoln Center's New York State Theatre building, which now bore his name. He had given $20 million to the American Museum of Natural History, whose dinosaur wing was named for him. That spring, after noticing the decrepit state of the fountains outside the Metropolitan Museum of Art, he pledged at least $10 million for their renovation. He was a trustee of the museum, perhaps the most coveted social prize in the city, and served on the board of Memorial Sloan Kettering Cancer Center, where, after he donated more than $40 million, an endowed chair and a research center were named for him.

One dignitary was conspicuously absent from the gala: the event's third honorary co-chair, Michelle Obama. Her office said that a scheduling conflict had prevented her from attending. In New York philanthropic circles, though, David Koch was a celebrity in his own right. With the help of a bevy of public relations advisers, he had sculpted an impressive public image. One associate said Koch had confided that he gave away approximately 40 percent of his income each year, which he estimated at about $1 billion. This of course left him with an annual income of some $600 million and considerably helped ease his tax burden, but he enjoyed the role, a family member said, in part because it bought him respectability. There was another side to his spending, however, that was then still largely secret. While David was happy to put his name on some of the country's most esteemed and beloved cultural and scientific institutions and to take a public bow at the ballet, his family's prodigious political spending was a much more private affair.

It would in fact take years before the faint outlines of the Kochs' massive political machinations began to surface through required public tax filings, and the full story may never be known. But a decision by the Supreme Court four months earlier in a case that began over a dispute about a right-wing attack on Hillary Clinton had already launched the family's covert spending into a new, more electorally ambitious phase. At the moment that David Koch took the stage in New York, operatives working for his brother and himself were quietly converting thirty years' worth of ideological institution building into a machine that would resemble, and rival, those of the two major political parties. Rather than representing broad-based support, however, theirs was financed by a tiny fraction of the wealthiest families in America, who could now, should they wish, spend their entire fortunes influencing the country's politics.

On January 21, 2010, the Court announced its 5–4 decision in the *Citizens United* case, overturning a century of
restrictions banning corporations and unions from spending all
they wanted to elect candidates. The Court held that so long
as businesses and unions didn't just hand their money to the
candidates, which could be corrupt, but instead gave it to outside groups that were supporting or opposing the candidates
and were technically independent of the campaigns, they could
spend unlimited amounts to promote whatever candidates they
chose. To reach the verdict, the Court accepted the argument
that corporations had the same rights to free speech as citizens.

The ruling paved the way for a related decision by an
appeals court in a case called *SpeechNow,* which soon after
overturned limits on how much money individuals could give
to outside groups too. Previously, contributions to political
action committees, or PACs, had been capped at $5,000 per
person per year. But now the court found that there could be
no donation limits so long as there was no coordination with
the candidates' campaigns. Soon, the groups set up to take the
unlimited contributions were dubbed super PACs for their
augmented new powers.

In both cases, the courts embraced the argument that independent spending, as opposed to direct contributions to the
candidates, wouldn't result in corruption. From the start, critics like Richard Posner, a brilliant and iconoclastic conservative federal judge, declared the Court had reasoned "naively,"
pointing out that it was "difficult to see what practical difference there is between super PAC donations and direct campaign donations, from a corruption standpoint." The immediate
impact, as the *New Yorker* writer Jeffrey Toobin summarized it,
was that "it gave rich people more or less free rein to spend as
much as they want in support of their favored candidates."

Among the few remaining restraints that the majority of

the Court endorsed was the long-standing expectation that any spending in a political campaign should be visible to the public. Justice Anthony Kennedy, who wrote the majority opinion, predicted that "with the advent of the Internet, prompt disclosure of expenditures" would be easier than ever. This, he suggested, would prevent corruption because "citizens can see whether elected officials are 'in the pocket' of so-called moneyed interests."

The assumption soon proved wrong. Instead, as critics had warned, more and more of the money flooding into elections was spent by secretive nonprofit organizations that claimed the right to conceal their donors' identities. Rich activists such as Scaife and the Kochs had already paved the way to weaponize philanthropy. Now they and other allied donors gave what came to be called dark money to nonprofit "social welfare" groups that claimed the right to spend on elections without disclosing their donors. As a result, the American political system became awash in unlimited, untraceable cash.

In striking down the existing campaign-finance laws, the courts eviscerated a century of reform. After a series of campaign scandals involving secret donations from the newly rich industrial barons in the late nineteenth and early twentieth centuries, Progressives had passed laws limiting spending in order to protect the democratic process from corruption. The laws were meant to safeguard political equality at a time of growing economic inequality. Reformers had seen the concentration of wealth in the hands of oil, steel, finance, and railroad magnates as threatening the democratic equilibrium. The Republican William McKinley's elections in 1896 and 1900, for instance, were infamously lubricated by donations raised by the political organizer Mark Hanna from big corporations like Rockefeller's Standard Oil. In a growing backlash to the corruption, at President Theodore Roosevelt's behest, Congress passed the Tillman Act in 1907, which banned corporate contributions to federal candidates and political committees. Later scandals resulted in further restrictions limiting spending by unions and the size of individual contributions, and requiring public disclosure. By overturning many of these restrictions, the *Citizens United* decision was in many respects a return to the Gilded Age.

Justice John Paul Stevens, a moderate Republican when first appointed but long part of the court's liberal wing, described the decision as "a radical departure from what has been settled First Amendment law." In a lengthy dissent, he argued that the Constitution's framers had enshrined the right of free speech for "individual Americans, not corporations," and that to act otherwise was "a rejection of the common sense of the American people who have recognized the need to prevent corporations from undermining self-government since the founding, and who have fought against the distinctive corrupting potential of corporate electioneering since the days of Theodore Roosevelt." Memorably, Stevens added, "While American democracy is imperfect, few outside the majority of this Court would have thought its flaws included a dearth of corporate money in politics."

Most analyses attributed the about-face on these vital rules guaranteeing fair elections to the increasingly assertive conservatism of Chief Justice John Roberts's Court. Clearly, this was the decisive factor. But there was a backstory, too.

For almost four decades, a tiny coterie of ultrarich activists who wished to influence American politics by spending more than the laws would allow had been chafing at the legal restraints. One family had been particularly tireless in the struggle, the DeVos clan of Michigan. The family, whose members became stalwarts in the Kochs' donor network, had made a multibillion-dollar fortune from a remarkable American business success, the Amway direct-marketing empire.

Founded in 1959 by two boyhood friends, Richard DeVos Sr. and Jay Van Andel, in Ada, Michigan, a suburb of Grand Rapids, it sold household products door-to-door while preaching the gospel of wealth with cultlike fervor. Over time, the private company grew into a marketing behemoth, generating revenues of nearly $11 billion a year by 2011.

The DeVoses were devout members of the Dutch Reformed Church, a renegade branch of Calvinism brought to America by Dutch immigrants, many of whom settled around Lake Michigan. By the 1970s, the church had become a vibrant and, some would say, vitriolic center of the Christian Right. Members crusaded against abortion, homosexuality, feminism, and modern science that conflicted with their teachings. Extreme free-market economic theories rejecting government intervention and venerating hard work and success in the Calvinist tradition were also embraced by many followers. Within this community of extreme views, no family was more extreme or more active than the DeVoses. They were less well-known outside Michigan than some of the other founding families of the conservative movement, but few played a bigger role as its bankrollers. Among the many causes they supported was the Koch donor network. Although their views on social issues were considerably more reactionary than those of the Kochs, they ardently shared the brothers' antipathy toward regulations and taxes.

Amway in fact was structured to avoid federal taxes. DeVos and Van Andel achieved this by defining the door-to-door salesmen who sold their beauty, cleaning, and dietary products as "independent business owners" rather than employees. This enabled the company's owners to skip Social Security contributions and other employee benefits, greatly enhancing their bottom line. It resulted, however, in numerous legal skirmishes with the Internal Revenue Service and the Federal Trade Commission (FTC). In a charge that was later dropped,

the government alleged that the company was little more than
a pyramid scheme built upon misleading promises of riches to
prospective distributors, many of whom bought its products in
bulk, found themselves unable to sell them, and so were forced
to cover their debts by recruiting additional distributors.

The gray zone in which the company operated made its cul-
tivation of political influence important. In 1975, after Grand
Rapids's Republican congressman Gerald R. Ford became
president, the usefulness of political clout became particularly
apparent. While the Federal Trade Commission investigation
was ongoing, DeVos and Van Andel obtained a lengthy meeting with Ford in the Oval Office. Two of Ford's top aides, soon
after, became investors in a new venture founded by DeVos
and Van Andel. After news of their involvement surfaced, the
White House aides dropped out, but Amway later hired one
of them as a Washington lobbyist. Meanwhile, perhaps coincidentally, the FTC investigation into whether Amway was an
illegal pyramid scheme fizzled, resulting only in the company
having its knuckles rapped for misleading advertising about
how much its distributors could earn.

The company's political activism was so unusually intense
that one FTC attorney at the time told *Forbes,* "They're not a
business, but some sort of quasi-religious sociopolitical organization." Indeed as Kim Phillips-Fein writes in *Invisible Hands,*
"Amway was much more than a simple direct-marketing firm.
It was an organization devoted with missionary zeal to the very
idea of free enterprise."

There were legal limits, however, to how much the DeVoses
could spend on elections. In 1974, after the Watergate scandal,
Congress set new contribution limits and established the public financing of presidential campaigns. Opponents struggled
to find ways around the new rules. In 1976, they partly succeeded when the Supreme Court, judging a case brought by a
Republican Senate candidate, William F. Buckley Jr.'s brother
James, struck down limits on "independent expenditures."

This opened what became an ever-expanding opportunity for big donors.

In 1980, Richard DeVos and Jay Van Andel led the way in "independent expenditures," becoming the top spenders on behalf of Ronald Reagan's presidential candidacy. By 1981, their titles reflected their growing clout. Richard DeVos was the finance chair of the Republican National Committee (RNC), while Jay Van Andel headed the U.S. Chamber of Commerce. In Washington, the pair cut a swath, hosting lavish parties on the Amway yacht, which was docked on the Potomac River, attended by Republican big shots and dignitaries from the dozen countries in which Amway operated. DeVos, the son of a poor Dutch immigrant, appeared as if dressed by a Hollywood costume department, flashing a pinkie ring and driving a Rolls-Royce.

The flood of money from Amway's founders failed, though, to quash an investigation by the Canadian government into a tax-fraud scheme in which both DeVos and Van Andel were criminally charged in 1982. The scandal exploded when Kitty McKinsey and Paul Magnusson, then reporters for the *Detroit Free Press*, shocked readers accustomed to DeVos and Van Andel's professions of patriotism and religiosity with an exposé tracing an elaborate, thirteen-year-long tax scam directly to the bosses' offices. At its highest levels, they revealed, Amway had secretly authorized a scheme creating dummy invoices to deceive Canadian customs officials into accepting falsely low valuations on products the company imported into Canada. Amway had thus fraudulently lowered its tax bills by $26.4 million from 1965 until 1978.

Amway denounced the news reports and threatened to file a $500 million libel suit against the *Free Press*. But the next year, the company released a terse statement announcing that it had pleaded guilty to defrauding the Canadian government and would pay a $20 million fine. In exchange, the plea agreement called for criminal charges to be dropped against four of the company's top executives, including DeVos and Van Andel. In 1989, Amway paid an additional $38 million to settle a related civil suit.

DeVos was soon dethroned as the RNC's finance chair. His standing hadn't been helped by his reference to the brutal 1982 economic recession as a welcome "cleansing process" or by his insistence that he'd never seen an unemployed person who wanted to work. Top donors were also put off by his attempts to transform RNC meetings into patriotic pep rallies akin to those run for Amway salesmen. DeVos would call wealthy contributors to the stage and ask, "Why are you proud to be an American?" A longtime Republican activist told *The Washington Post*, "We were losing contributions and that was the last straw."

The DeVos family nonetheless remained huge financiers of the Republican Party and the growing conservative movement, as well as sponsoring efforts to undo campaign-finance laws. Starting in 1970, they began to direct at least $200 million into virtually every branch of the New Right's infrastructure, from think tanks like the Heritage Foundation to academic organizations such as the Intercollegiate Studies Institute, which funded conservative publications on college campuses. "There's not a Republican president or presidential candidate in the last fifty years who hasn't known the DeVoses," Saul Anuzis, a former chairman of the Michigan Republican Party, said.

The DeVoses were also deeply involved in the secretive Council for National Policy, described by *The New York Times* as "a little-known club of a few hundred of the most powerful conservatives in the country," which it said "met behind closed doors in undisclosed locations for a confidential conference" three times a year. Membership lists were secret, but among the names tied to the organization were Jerry Falwell, Phyllis Schlafly, Pat Robertson, and Wayne LaPierre of the National Rifle Association (NRA). There was overlap with a number of other participants in the Koch seminars, too, including Foster Friess, the multimillionaire founder of a Wyoming mutual fund, Friess Associates, who had collaborated politically with the Kochs at least since the 1996 election, when they both channeled money into Triad Management to surreptitiously fund attack ads. Charles Koch accepted an award from the Council for National Policy but was not a member of the group. It was, in Richard DeVos's phrase, a place that brought together "the doers with the donors."

If anything, the DeVos family's brushes with the law merely emboldened them. During the 1994 midterm elections, Amway gave $2.5 million to the Republican Party, which was the largest known soft money donation from a corporation in the country's history. In 1996, clean-government groups criticized the family for skirting campaign contribution limits by also donating $1.3 million to the San Diego tourist bureau to help air the Republican National Convention there that year.

By then, Richard DeVos Sr. had bought the NBA's Orlando Magic and had passed the management of Amway on to his son Richard junior, who was known as Dick. The younger DeVos shared his father's political and religious views. But he was a pragmatist when it came to business, expanding the zealously free-market company deeply into China. By 2006, fully a third of Amway's revenue came from the Communist state.

The DeVos family's stature and wealth were magnified by Dick's marriage to the other royal family of Michigan's Dutch Reformed community, Betsy Prince. Her father, Edgar Prince, had founded an auto parts manufacturing company that sold for $1.35 billion in cash in 1996. Her brother Erik Prince, meanwhile, founded the global security firm Blackwater, which the reporter Jeremy Scahill described as "the world's most powerful mercenary army."

Betsy DeVos, who eventually became the chairwoman of Michigan's Republican Party, was said to be every bit as politically ambitious as her husband, if not more so. With her support, in 2002 Dick DeVos ceased managing Amway in order to devote more time to his political career. The results, though, were dismal. The DeVos family spent over $2 million in 2000 on a Michigan school voucher referendum that was defeated by 68 percent of the voters. The family then spent $35 million in 2006 on Dick DeVos's unsuccessful bid to become the state's governor.

In their zeal to implement their conservative vision, few issues were more central to the DeVos family's mission than eradicating restraints on political spending. For years, the family funded legal challenges to various campaign-finance laws. Ground zero in this fight was the James Madison Center for Free Speech, of which Betsy DeVos became a founding board member in 1997. The nonprofit organization's sole goal was to end all legal restrictions on money in politics. Its honorary chairman was Senator Mitch McConnell, a savvy and prodigious fund-raiser.

Conservatives cast their opposition to campaign-finance restrictions as a principled defense of free speech, but McConnell, who was one of the cause's biggest champions, had occasionally revealed a more partisan motive. As a Republican running for office in Kentucky in the 1970s, when it was almost solidly Democratic, he once admitted "a spending edge is the only thing that gives a Republican a chance to compete." He had once opened a college class by writing on the blackboard the three ingredients that he felt were necessary to build a political party: "Money, money, money." In a Senate debate on proposed campaign-finance restrictions, McConnell reportedly told colleagues, "If we stop this thing, we can control the institution for the next twenty years."

The James Madison Center aimed to make this dream a reality by taking the fight to the courts. In addition to the DeVos family, early donors included several of the most powerful groups on the right, such as the Christian Coalition and the NRA. But the driving force behind the organization was a single-minded lawyer from Terre Haute, Indiana, James

Bopp Jr., who was general counsel to the anti-abortion National Right to Life Committee. Bopp also became the Madison Center's general counsel.

In fact, Bopp's law firm and the James Madison Center had the same office address and phone number, and although Bopp listed himself as an outside contractor to the center, virtually every dollar from donors went to his firm. By designating itself a nonprofit charitable group, though, the Madison Center enabled the DeVos Family Foundation and other supporters to take tax deductions for subsidizing long-shot lawsuits that might never have been attempted otherwise. "The relationship between this organization and Bopp's law firm is such that there really is no charity," observed Marcus Owens, a Washington lawyer who formerly oversaw tax-exempt groups for the Internal Revenue Service. "I've never heard of this sort of captive charity/foundation funding of a particular law firm before."

In 1997, the same year that she helped found the Madison Center, Betsy DeVos explained her opposition to campaign-finance restrictions. At the time, there was a national outcry against the way both the Democratic and the Republican Parties had evaded contribution limits in the 1996 presidential campaign by paying for what they claimed were "issue" ads rather than campaign ads, with unlimited funds that came to be known as soft money. There was a bipartisan Senate push for reform. But in a guest column in the Capitol Hill newspaper *Roll Call,* DeVos defended the unlimited contributions.

"Soft money," she wrote, was just "hard-earned American dollars that Big Brother has yet to find a way to control. That is all it is, nothing more." She added, "I know a little something about soft money, as my family is the largest single contributor of soft money to the national Republican Party." She said, "I have decided, however, to stop taking offense at the suggestion that we are buying influence. Now I simply concede the point. They are right. We do expect some things in return. We

expect to foster a conservative governing philosophy consist-
ing of limited government and respect for traditional American virtues. We expect a return on our investment; we expect
a good and honest government. Furthermore, we expect the
Republican Party to use the money to promote these policies,
and yes, to win elections. People like us," she concluded archly,
"must surely be stopped."

Most of the big donors fighting the campaign-finance
restrictions were conservatives, but a few extraordinarily rich
liberal Democrats belonged to this rarefied club, too. In 2004,
Democratic-aligned outside groups spent $185 million—more
than twice what the Republican outside groups spent—in a
failed effort to defeat George W. Bush's reelection. Of this,
$85 million came from just fourteen Democratic donors. Lead-
ing the pack was the New York hedge fund magnate George
Soros, an opponent of the U.S. invasion of Iraq who regarded
President Bush as such a scourge that he vowed he would spend
his entire $7 billion fortune to defeat him, if the result could
be guaranteed. With the help of Democratic operatives, Soros
funneled more than $27 million into the outside spending vehi-
cle of choice that year, known as 527 groups. It was the same
year that Republicans used the same mechanism to fund the
"Swift Boat" attacks on John Kerry. Prior to *Citizens United,*
such schemes were legally dubious at best. The Federal Election Commission ruled that the gargantuan outside spending
schemes violated campaign-finance laws and imposed hefty
fines on both the Democratic and the Republican perpetrators.
Afterward, Soros remained active in ideological philanthropy,
spending hundreds of millions to support a network of human
rights and civil liberties groups, but he largely withdrew from
spectacular campaign contributions.

If the DeVoses expected a "return on our investment" in
the Madison Center, as Betsy had put it, they got one in the
Supreme Court's *Citizens United* decision. It "was really Jim

[Bopp]'s brainchild," Richard L. Hasen, an expert on election law at Loyola Law School in Los Angeles told *The New York Times*. "He has manufactured these cases to present certain questions to the Supreme Court in a certain order and achieve a certain result," said Hasen. "He is a litigation machine."

Bopp agreed. "We had a 10-year plan to take all this down," he told the *Times*. "And if we do it right, I think we can pretty well dismantle the entire regulatory regime that is called campaign finance law."

Such a statement would have seemed ludicrous just a few years earlier, and in fact, in the beginning, no one took Bopp seriously. With his shaggy gray Beatles haircut and his dogmatic legal style, not to mention his extreme views, he was literally laughed at by one federal judge. At the time, he was arguing that a hyperbolic film attacking Hillary Clinton, who was running for president, deserved the same First Amendment protection as newscasts aired by CBS's *60 Minutes*. The film, a screed called *Hillary: The Movie*, had been produced by Citizens United, an old right-wing group with a history of making vicious campaign ads. The question, as the Supreme Court interpreted it, was whether *Hillary: The Movie* was a protected form of speech or a corporate political donation by its backers, which could be regulated as a campaign donation.

Case by case, financed by wealthy donors who treated the cause as a tax-deductible charity, Bopp had battered away at the foundation of modern campaign-finance law. He had succeeded in part by using the liberals' language of civil rights and free speech against their own practices. The tactic was intentional. Clint Bolick, a pioneer in the conservative legal movement whose group, the Institute for Justice, had received start-up funds from Charles Koch, had argued that the Right needed to combat the Left by asserting appealing "counter-rights" of its own. Thus *Citizens United* was cast as the right of corporations to exercise their free speech. As conservatives had hoped, the argument disarmed and divided the Left, even attracting the support of traditionally liberal champions of the First Amendment.

While polls consistently showed that large majorities of the American public—both Republicans and Democrats— favored strict spending limits, the key challenges that led to dismantling the laws were initiated by an extraordinarily rich minority: the Kochs and their clique of ultra-wealthy conservative activists.

A close look at the *SpeechNow* case, for instance, the lower-court decision following quickly on the heels of *Citizens United,* leads right back to the same people. There was no organization called SpeechNow until several libertarian activists invented it solely for the purpose of challenging the spending limits. The suit was the brainchild of Eric O'Keefe, among others, the Wisconsin investor who had been a libertarian ally of the Kochs since working in David's 1980 vice presidential campaign, which called for the end of campaign spending limits.

Leading the suit was Bradley Smith, a bright and radically antiregulatory lawyer who co-founded the conservative Center for Competitive Politics. He was a proponent of zero public disclosure of political spending and didn't disclose his funders, but IRS records showed that in 2009 his center enjoyed support from several conservative foundations, including the Bradley Foundation. Smith's career illustrated the way that the fortunes of conservative philanthropists cultivated and nurtured talent like his. He had been a scholar at Charles Koch's Institute for Humane Studies before becoming the most outspoken foe of finance restrictions ever to chair the Federal Election Commission, the federal agency charged with policing campaign spending. His patrons for this key post were Mitch McConnell and the Cato Institute. As he acknowledged, "I would not have been an FEC commissioner if not for Cato's efforts to promote me on the Hill."

Also essential to the *SpeechNow* suit was the Institute for

Justice, the group founded with Charles Koch's seed money. The litigation, meanwhile, was underwritten heavily by Fred Young, a libertarian retiree in Wisconsin who made tens of millions of dollars by selling his father's firm, Young Radiator Company, after outsourcing the jobs of unionized workers to non-union states. Young served on the boards of the Koch-backed Reason Foundation and Cato Institute and was yet another regular attendee at the Kochs' donor summits.

In 2010, Young took full advantage of the newfound freedom to spend. He contributed 80 percent of the money spent that year by SpeechNow.org's super PAC, all of which paid for television ads targeting Wisconsin's Democratic senator Russ Feingold. Feingold was a particularly symbolic target. He had been the Senate's premier supporter of strict campaign spending laws. Standing on principle, he urged outside groups not to spend on his behalf. That fall, he went down to defeat.

In the view of defenders, *Citizens United* and its progeny did not represent the black-and-white contrast of progressives' nightmares so much as it clarified gray areas. But this alone was extremely important. By flashing a bright green light, the Supreme Court sent a message to the wealthy and their political operatives that when it came to raising and spending money, they now could act with impunity. Both the legal fog and the political stigma lifted.

Soon, the sums pledged at the Koch donor summits began to soar from the $13 million that Sean Noble raised in June 2009 to nearly $900 million at a single fund-raising session in the years that followed. "This Supreme Court decision essentially gave a Good Housekeeping seal of approval," acknowledged Steven Law, president of American Crossroads, the conservative super PAC formed by the Republican political operative Karl Rove soon after the *Citizens United* decision.

Critics, though, including Obama, saw the change as far more consequential. In his 2010 State of the Union address, Obama made headlines by denouncing the Court's decision, saying that it "reversed a century of law that I believe will open the floodgates for special interests—including foreign corporations—to spend without limit in our elections." In response, the associate Supreme Court justice Samuel Alito Jr., who attended the address, was seen shaking his head and mouthing the words "not true."

Another consequence was that the *Citizens United* decision shifted the balance of power from parties built on broad consensus to individuals who were wealthy and zealous enough to spend millions of dollars from their own funds. By definition, this empowered a tiny, atypical minority of the population.

"It unshackled the big money," David Axelrod contends. "*Citizens United* unleashed constant negativity, not just toward the president, but toward government generally. Presidents before have been under siege, but now there is no longer the presumption that they are acting in the public interest. There's a pernicious drumbeat." After the ruling, he said, "we felt under siege."

CHAPTER TEN

The Shellacking:
Dark Money's Midterm Debut, 2010

AS DONORS GATHERED IN PALM SPRINGS AT THE END OF JANU-
ary for the first Koch summit of 2010, the desert air was full
of optimism. "It was just a week or two after the special election in Boston," one participant recalled. "Feeling was running
pretty high."

A torrent of contributions from undisclosed donors had
helped deliver the surprise election of Scott Brown in Massachusetts earlier that month, making him the first Republican
elected to the Senate from the liberal state in thirty-eight years.
Organizing much of the cash from behind the scenes had been
Sean Noble, who was by then on the payroll of the Kochs.
Early on, when many others dismissed Brown as a hopeless
long shot, Noble had decided that the payoff would be so rich
that backing him was worth the gamble. Brown's victory was
calamitous for Obama. By filling the seat that had long been
held by Ted Kennedy, the legendary Democrat who had died
in August, Brown transformed the balance of power in Congress. The Democrats still held the majority in the Senate, but
their loss of one seat crippled their power in one key way. Just
as Obama was desperately trying to pass a final version of his
health-care bill, it deprived the Democrats of the sixty-vote
minimum necessary to overcome a Republican filibuster. The
Democrats were left without the numbers necessary to bring
the bill to a new vote. Brown's triumph appeared to be the
Affordable Care Act's downfall.

Brown hadn't won without a lot of help. The numbers told
part of the story. Although Brown was a low-profile Republican state senator best known for posing nude for *Cosmopoli-*

tan magazine, he had unexpectedly outspent his Democratic opponent, Martha Coakley, by roughly $8.7 million to $5.1 million during the six weeks after the primaries. An unusual amount of this, almost $3 million, had come from shadowy out-of-state nonprofit groups funded by undisclosed donors. Two of the most active of these dark-money groups, the American Future Fund and Americans for Job Security, had received large infusions of cash from the mysterious "social welfare" group that Noble had registered the spring before, based at an Arizona post office box. For months, the post office box otherwise known as the Center to Protect Patient Rights had been filling with fistfuls of secret cash from Randy Kendrick and other members of the Koch network in an uphill battle to stop the passage of the Affordable Care Act. Noble had redirected much of this money into the front groups spending against Coakley in the Massachusetts special election. The hope was that if Republicans could turn one Senate seat, they could block the health-care bill and mortally wound Obama. So when the plan worked, Brown's win electrified the donors. Many felt that they had personally turned the tide on Obamacare. "We thought we had it won!" the seminar participant recalled.

Obama had been so flummoxed by Brown's election that at a White House senior staff meeting the next morning he had beseeched his staff accusingly, demanding to know, "What's my narrative? I don't have a narrative!" His administration's momentum had been buried in outside money.

Lifting the donors' spirits further was the Supreme Court's *Citizens United* ruling, which had been handed down on January 21, two days after Scott Brown's victory in Massachusetts, and shortly before the Kochs' summit. Brown's race now seemed a promising dress rehearsal for even more outside money, which the Court had ennobled as free speech. So as the self-described "investors" came together to plan for the 2010 midterm elections, they were in a buoyant mood.

Sean Noble, looking dashing with a tan, had been elevated by then from merely moderating a panel at the June 2009 summit six months earlier to now speaking on one. His congressional staff job and unpaid student loans were remnants of the past. As the Web site of his political consulting firm proclaimed ebulliently, "It's not what you know but who you know."

The panel discussion was titled "The Opportunity of 2010: Understanding Voter Attitudes and the Electoral Map." Noble spoke optimistically about the health-care fight, which he believed had awakened a national rebellion. Joining him on the dais were three other men, each representing aspects of the underground political operation that would rout the Democrats in the year ahead.

The best known of the panelists was Ed Gillespie, a top national political tactician who had become the chairman of the Republican National Committee in 2003 at the age of forty-one. Gillespie had made a fortune in lobbying, estimated at as much as $19 million. He was a former Democrat, and the firm he co-founded, Quinn Gillespie & Associates, was bipartisan, more concerned with making deals than political purity. Its clients ranged from Enron, the huge energy company that went scandalously bust, to a health-care group promoting individual insurance mandates akin to those that Obama's opponents called treasonous. The son of an Irish immigrant, Gillespie, according to Capitol lore, had started out parking cars and worked his way up to the top of Washington's booming influence-peddling industry by dint of his easy affability and quick political instincts.

As soon as the Court handed down its *Citizens United* decision, Gillespie grasped its promise. Within weeks, he set out to Texas with his fellow Bush White House alumnus Karl Rove to pitch deep-pocketed oilmen at the Dallas Petroleum Club on a plan to fund a new kind of shadow political machine. Instead of giving just to the Republican Party or its candidates and having the size of their donations limited, the high rollers could now legally funnel limitless amounts of cash to "outside" organizations that Rove and Gillespie were about to create, the two operatives explained. These new groups would act as the privatized auxiliary force Rove had been dreaming of for years. Rove told the moneymen, "People call us a vast right-wing conspiracy, but we're really a half-assed right-wing conspiracy. Now," he emphasized, "it's time to get serious."

Even before the *Citizens United* decision, Gillespie had been busy. While many other conservatives were despondent during the early months of the Obama administration, when the president's approval ratings were stratospherically high, Gillespie had come up with an ingenious plan to exploit the only opening he could see. With Obama dominating Washington, Gillespie looked to the states. He knew that 2011 was a year in which many state legislatures would redraw the boundaries of their congressional districts based on a new census, a process that only took place once a decade. So he put together an ambitious strategy aimed at a Republican takeover of governorships and legislatures all across the country. Capturing them would enable Republicans to redraw their states' congressional districts in order to favor their candidates. While the mechanics of state legislative races were abstruse and deadly dull to most people, to Gillespie they were the key to a Republican comeback.

"It was all conceived sitting in Ed's office in Alexandria, Virginia . . . it was entirely his vision," Gillespie's associate Chris Jankowski later told *Politico*. "It seems like an obvious strategy now, but you have to turn back the clock to realize how demoralized we all were . . . He was saying, 'Here's something smart we can do.'"

Gillespie called the plan "REDMAP," an acronym for the Redistricting Majority Project. To implement it, he took over the Republican State Leadership Committee (RSLC), a nonprofit group that had previously functioned as a catchall bank account for corporations interested in influencing state laws. All he needed was enough money to put REDMAP into action. By the end of 2010, with the help of million-dollar donations from the tobacco companies Altria and Reynolds, as well as huge donations from Walmart, the pharmaceutical industry, and rich private donors like those at the Koch summit, the RSLC would have $30 million, three times its Democratic counterpart. "It was three yards and a cloud of dust," Gillespie later recalled of his scramble for money. "It was a constant working, and working, and working," especially at honeypots like the Koch summit.

Joining the panel with Noble and Gillespie was a short, balding figure with a seemingly inexhaustible command of political minutiae. With his North Carolina drawl and his glasses slipping down his nose, he might be mistaken for a southern shop clerk. But James Arthur "Art" Pope was actually a shop *owner*, in fact the multimillionaire chairman and CEO of Variety Wholesalers, a family-owned discount-store conglomerate with hundreds of outlets stretching up and down the mid-Atlantic and the South. Pope was also a charter member of the Koch network. A longtime friend and ally, he shared Charles's passion for free-market philosophy and credited a summer program he attended at the Cato Institute with exposing him to conservative icons like Hayek and Ayn Rand. After graduating from the Duke School of Law in 1981 and taking over his family's private company, he began to transform the Pope family foundation, which had assets of nearly $150 million, into a remarkable political force.

In the previous decade, Pope and his family and the family foundation had spent more than $40 million in efforts to push American politics to the right. In addition to regularly attending the Kochs' secret planning summits, he served on the board of the Kochs' main public advocacy group, Americans for Prosperity, as he had on its predecessor, Citizens for a Sound Economy, and had joined forces with the brothers on numerous other political enterprises. Tax records showed that Pope had given money to at least twenty-seven of the groups supported by the Kochs, including organizations opposing environmental regulations, tax increases, unions, and campaign spending limits. Pope, like the DeVos family, was a supporter of the James Madison Center for Free Speech. Indeed, Pope's role in his home state of North Carolina was in many respects a state-sized version of the Kochs' role nationally. While he wasn't well-known outside the state, his growing influence at home had led the Raleigh *News & Observer* to begin calling him "the Knight of the Right."

What Pope brought to the panel that weekend was the chance for donors to help him turn North Carolina into a laboratory for REDMAP. Historically, North Carolina had been a pivotal swing state. It was both the face of the New South and the stomping ground of Jesse Helms's race-baiting National Congressional Club. But Obama had carried it narrowly in 2008 and remained popular in 2010. Democrats also dominated the state legislature; the Republicans hadn't controlled both houses of the North Carolina General Assembly for more than a hundred years. "Not since General Sherman," the joke went. Winning a legislative majority in 2010 wouldn't be easy. But no one was better situated than Pope to make it happen. He both was a master of arcane election law and had a fortune that few individuals could match. But like the Kochs and the DeVoses, he had had little luck over the years persuading voters to follow his lead. While he had served in the state legislature in North Carolina, he had been soundly defeated when he ran for lieutenant governor in 1992, his one bid for statewide office. "He was a terrible candidate," recalled Bob Geary, a political reporter for the *Indy Week,* an alternative newspaper in Durham, who covered the race. "I've never seen him smile. He was very introverted and pedantic." With the precision he was known for, Pope admitted, "I'm not a charismatic stump speaker."

Flipping the state would require political artistry and some guile. For this, the panel turned to its fourth member, Jim Ellis. The Kochs were notoriously picky about who received coveted invitations to their summits but didn't seem to mind that he was under indictment at the time for violating campaign-finance regulations. Ellis, an old friend of Noble's, was there to make predictions about the outcome of the 2010 races, but he had other specialties too.

Ellis had a history of creating fake movements in support of unpopular corporations and causes. In the 1990s, he had headed a company called Ramhurst, which documents revealed to be a covert public relations arm of R. J. Reynolds, the giant tobacco company. Under his guidance, Ramhurst organized deceptively homegrown-looking "smokers' rights" protests against proposed regulations and taxes on tobacco. In 1994 alone, R. J. Reynolds funneled $2.6 million to Ramhurst to deploy operatives who mobilized what they called "partisans" to stage protests against the Clinton health-care proposal, which would have imposed a stiff tax on cigarette sales. Anti-health-care rallies that year echoed with cries of "Go back to Russia!"

If the outbursts bore a striking resemblance to those against Obama's health-care proposal fifteen years later, it may be because the same political operatives were involved in both. Two of Ellis's former top aides at Ramhurst, Doug Goodyear and Tom Synhorst, went on in 1996 to form DCI Group, the public relations firm that was helping Noble foment Tea Party protests against the Affordable Care Act.

Ellis, meanwhile, had moved into the heart of Washington's Republican money stream. He became what some news reports described as the "right-hand man" to Tom DeLay, the powerful House Republican leader from Texas who was infamous for his "K Street operation," which serviced corporate lobbyists while shaking them down for campaign contributions. DeLay made him executive director of his political action committee. The duo's high-handed approach resulted in both men getting indicted for campaign-finance violations in 2005. In time, DeLay's conviction was overturned, but Ellis was less lucky. In 2012, he pleaded guilty to a single felony count and paid a fine. Undaunted, he airbrushed DeLay's name from his corporate résumé and kept on. Asked about his career in manufacturing protests for pay, Ellis sounded untroubled. "The grass roots was designed to give people the right to exercise their voice," he said with a shrug. As he addressed the big donors on the "opportunity of 2010," Ellis's legal status was uncertain, but his acquaintance with politics' seamier side was beyond doubt.

The donors left Palm Springs optimistic about 2010, inspired by Noble and the other members of his panel, but their elation over killing Obamacare soon proved premature. "The assumption in Washington and everywhere else was that when they got Scott Brown, it was the death knell for health care," Axelrod recalled. "The guy who wouldn't accept that was Obama. He said, 'We're going to do this underground and find a path.'"

The Democrats eventually came up with a plan to get the bill through. The House would approve the version that had already passed the Senate with sixty votes in December. Then the Senate would use a parliamentary maneuver that would require only fifty-one votes to add modifications—circumventing the threat of a Republican filibuster. Despite widespread skepticism, by mid-March the tenacious House Speaker, Nancy Pelosi, was on the verge of success.

As passage looked increasingly likely, Tea Party protests grew ever more ugly. Behind them, invisible to the public, was the Kochs' money. Tim Phillips, the head of Americans for Prosperity, popped up as the organizer of a March 16 "Kill the Bill" protest on Capitol Hill, at which he accused the Democrats of "trying to cram this 2,000-page bill down the throat of the American people!" At a second Capitol Hill rally a few

days later, protesters spat on a passing Democratic congressman; mocked Barney Frank, a gay representative from Massachusetts, in lisping catcalls as a "faggot"; and shouted racist
epithets at three black congressmen, John Lewis, Emanuel
Cleaver, and Jim Clyburn.

Nonetheless, on March 21, amid mounting excitement, the
House's scoreboard registered 216 votes for Obama's Affordable Care Act, the exact number needed to pass the legislation. Spontaneous chants of "Yes we can!" and "Yes we did!"
on the House floor evoked election-night euphoria. That night,
Obama and his staff held a rare celebration on the Truman Bal-
cony of the White House, but the president suspected political
payback wasn't going to wait long. As he raised a champagne
flute to his political director, Patrick Gaspard, he cracked, "You
know they're gonna kick our asses over this."

Downtown, in the Washington office space that Sean
Noble shared with several other Koch operatives, Obama's
premonitions proved correct. Shortly after the House passed
the Affordable Care Act, Noble and his partners studied the
vote numbers closely. The glimmer of a new plan formed. They
agreed that what they had to do now was to take the political organization they had built to fight the health-care plan
and use it to take over the legislative body that had just given
Obama his greatest victory.

"We made a deliberate recommendation that you gotta
focus on the House," Noble later told *National Review.* "That's
where this bill passed. Pelosi broke so many arms of Democrats
that had no business voting for that bill. Obamacare clearly was
the watershed moment that provided the juice to deliver the
majority back to the Republicans in the House."

Few knew it, but for all intents and purposes a midterm
election like no other had begun. Noble spent most of April on
the road, talking with Charles Koch, Rich Fink, Randy Kendrick, and others in the network to plan the operational details.

David Koch was more of an afterthought, or as one participant put it, he was very much the younger brother. Charles, who was methodical and deliberate, pressed the planners closely. The Koch network had grown so big that it took weeks just to touch base with its many donors. All across the country, millionaire by millionaire, Noble made his pitch. They've had their vote, the argument went. Now it's time for some accountability.

Fund-raising for Noble's group, the Center to Protect Patient Rights, quadrupled by the end of 2010, to $61.8 million. As with all such "social welfare" groups, under the tax code the sources of its funding didn't have to be publicly disclosed. The same held true for another mysterious Koch-tied group, something called the TC4 Trust, which raised an additional $42.7 million that year. About a third of this was steered back into the Center to Protect Patient Rights through a method disguised on disclosure forms. This brought Sean Noble's kitty up to almost $75 million. Flush with cash, the Kochs finally had a political operation commensurate with their wealth.

Previously, they had given relatively small amounts to 501(c)(4) "social welfare" groups. Before *Citizens United*, these nonprofit corporations, like for-profit corporations, had been restricted from spending money for or against candidates in elections. Some skirted the law by running what they claimed were issue ads. But legal danger hovered. After *Citizens United*, though, the Kochtopus essentially sprouted a second set of tentacles. The first cluster was the think tanks, academic programs, legal centers, and issue advocacy organizations that Fink had described as the ideological production line. These ventures were defined for legal purposes as charities and were still prohibited from participating in politics. Donations to them were tax deductible. Added to this in 2010 was a second cluster, a dizzying maze of "social welfare" groups that disbursed hidden money into the midterm elections.

When Congress created the legal framework for "social welfare" groups almost a century earlier, it never anticipated that they would become a means by which the rich would hide their political spending. In fact, to qualify as tax-exempt, such groups had to certify that they would be "operated exclusively for the promotion of social welfare." The IRS later loosened the guidelines, though, allowing them to engage marginally in politics, so long as this wasn't their "primary" purpose. Lawyers soon stretched the loophole to absurd lengths. They argued, for instance, that if a group spent 49 percent of its funds on politics, it complied with the law because it still wasn't "primarily" engaged in politics. They also argued that one such group could claim no political spending if it gave to another such group, even if the latter spent the funds on politics. Experts likened the setup to Russian nesting dolls. For example, at the end of 2010, the Center to Protect Patient Rights reported on its tax return that it spent no money on politics. Yet it granted $103 million to other conservative groups, most of which were actively engaged in the midterm elections.

The Kochs were part of a national explosion of dark money. In 2006, only 2 percent of "outside" political spending came from "social welfare" groups that hid their donors. In 2010, this number rose to 40 percent, masking hundreds of millions of dollars. Campaign-finance reformers were apoplectic but powerless. "The political players who are soliciting these funds and are benefiting from the expenditure of these funds will know where the money came from," argued Paul S. Ryan, senior counsel at the liberal Campaign Legal Center. "The only ones in the dark will be American voters."

Managing all of this new, dark money was a challenge. In April, as campaign professionals were trying to figure out how to take maximum advantage of the *Citizens United* decision, Gillespie invited Republican operatives to what he described in an e-mail as "an informal discussion of the 2010 landscape." The unusual meeting was to take place in Karl Rove's living room on Weaver Terrace, a well-off enclave of Northwest Washington. Some joked that they attended the first meeting of what came to be known as the Weaver Terrace Group simply so they could tell friends they had been inside the home of the storied political guru. What transpired was a war council in which the twenty assembled chieftains coordinated their plans of action and divided up their territory. Kenneth Vogel, in *Big Money*, describes it as "the birthplace of a new Republican Party—one steered by just a handful of unelected operatives who answered only to the richest activists who funded them."

Two organizations soon emerged as virtual private banks run by these operatives. The first, American Crossroads and its 501(c)(4) wing, Crossroads GPS, was initiated by Rove. For funds, it drew heavily on his network of Texas tycoons. The second was Noble's Center to Protect Patient Rights, which began to fill with donations from the Koch donor summits. Working closely with both was the U.S. Chamber of Commerce, which spent millions of dollars more in undisclosed contributions from businesses, much of it aimed at defeating Obama's health-care act. The chamber sent top officials to both the Weaver Terrace meetings and the Koch donor summits.

Each of the players' roles was carefully differentiated. Noble focused on House races, leaving the Senate to Rove's group. In accordance with his REDMAP strategy, Gillespie continued to concentrate on governorships and state legislatures. To hide their hands, the operatives steered the funds to a plethora of obscure, smaller groups. This also helped satisfy the legal requirement that no single public welfare group spend more than half of its funds on elections. Soon, to the unschooled eye, a rash of spontaneous attacks on Democrats appeared to be breaking out all across the country. In reality, the effort was so centrally coordinated, as one participant put it, "there wasn't one race in which there were multiple groups airing ads at the same time."

As Noble explained his methodology later to Eliana Johnson, Washington editor for the conservative publication *National Review,* he started by producing an Excel spreadsheet. It listed 64 Democratic congressmen "in order of the likelihood of their defeat." By the end of June, he said, the list of targets grew to 88, and by August, 105. He assigned each congressional district a "win potential" of between 1 and 5, and each candidate a score of 1 to 40, "based on the voting record of each member and the composition of the district, among other things." Eventually, he said, he sorted the 105 targeted candidates into "three tiers, based on the likelihood of a GOP victory."

He then disbursed the Koch network's money in accordance with what he regarded as each candidate's odds of winning. Rather than disclose that his organization was paying for the ads, he directed the money through an array of different front groups. For instance, Noble explained to *National Review* that he chose a group called the 60 Plus Association, which was a right-wing version of the senior citizens' lobby AARP, to air attack ads on Democrats in "Arizona's First Congressional District, Florida's Second and Twenty-Fourth, Indiana's Second, Minnesota's Eighth, New York's Twentieth, Ohio's Sixteenth, Pennsylvania's Third, and Wisconsin's Third and Eighth Congressional Districts." Meanwhile, he said, he used another group, Americans for Job Security, the same "business league" he had deployed in the Scott Brown race, to air ads in "New York's Twenty-Fourth, North Carolina's Second and Eighth, Ohio's Eighteenth, and Virginia's Ninth Congressional Districts." He chose the other shadow group that he had used in the Brown race, the Iowa-based American Future Fund, to air attack ads in Alabama's Second, Colorado's Seventh, New Mexico's First, and Washington's Second Congressional Districts.

The American Future Fund, like Noble's own nonprofit group, was a 501(c)(4) "social welfare" group, meaning it could hide the identity of its donors and was not supposed to be primarily engaged in electoral politics. Its stated mission was "to provide Americans with a conservative and free market viewpoint." In reality, though, it appeared to be little more than a front group acting as a screen for conservative political money. Efforts to track down its office led only to a post office box in Iowa. Founded in 2008 by a Republican operative in the state, it received seed money from one of the country's largest ethanol producers, Bruce Rastetter, but tax records showed that 87 percent of its funds in 2009 and approximately half its funds in 2010 came from just one source: Sean Noble's Center to Protect Patient Rights.

Similarly, Americans for Job Security, a 501(c)(6) "business league," or "trade association," was also entitled under the tax code to hide its funders, who were classified as "members." The organization had a physical office in Alexandria, Virginia, but the premises were almost empty. It had only one employee, a twenty-five-year-old Republican campaign aide who was acquainted with Sean Noble. Founded in 1997 with a million-dollar donation from the insurance industry, the organization had been accused of being nothing more than "a sham front group" by Public Citizen, a liberal group that favored tighter campaign-finance regulations. State officials in Alaska, where Americans for Job Security had waged an earlier campaign, concluded that the group "has no purpose other than to cover various money trails all over the country." The state charged the organization with violating Alaska's fair election rules. The group paid a $20,000 settlement but admitted no guilt. But in 2010, with Noble's help, its business was booming. Noble's center would steer this group $4.8 million that year.

In addition, Noble directed millions of dollars into other races through those and other groups, including the antitax activist Grover Norquist's organization, Americans for Tax Reform; Howard Rich's group, Americans for Limited Government; and the Kochs' flagship organization, Americans for

Prosperity. The budget for Americans for Prosperity soared accordingly. In 2004, the budget for the Kochs' flagship group and its foundation was $2 million. By 2008, it had grown to $15.2 million. And in 2010, it reached $40 million, engorged with funds from the Center to Protect Patient Rights.

In June, Noble tested out the system, using Americans for Prosperity to launch an assault on Tom Perriello, the freshman Democratic congressman from Charlottesville, Virginia, who had defied the fossil fuel interests over the cap-and-trade bill. Noble wanted to start unusually early in order to widen the field of Democrats he could weaken. In an exuberant moment, Perriello had called the climate change fight "a gift," proclaiming, "For the first time in a generation, we have the chance to redefine our energy economy." Instead, it was he who got redefined that summer by a barrage of negative ads paid for not by his opponent but by unrecognizable outsiders.

Perriello was an outspoken liberal in a swing district, so an obvious target. But soon mystery money was tarring Rick Boucher, too, a conservative Democratic congressman whose rural Virginia district encompassed Saltville, the factory town that the Olin Corporation had turned into a toxic waste dump. Boucher had represented the district for twenty-eight years in the House and eight more before that in the state senate. A Virginia lawyer and strong ally of business interests, he had been crucial to passage of the cap-and-trade bill in the House, drafting much of the measure and then winning support for it from a number of huge energy firms, including Duke Energy. He had given away so many goodies to the coal industry while negotiating the bill that many environmentalists had been disgusted. Nonetheless, the fact that he had supported the bill at all had angered conservative extremists, including several Virginia coal barons active in funding the Koch network. He was exactly the kind of centrist that big, polarized political money was rendering extinct.

"The Koch brothers went after me literally 24-7," recalled

Boucher, who after his defeat that November became a partner at the law firm Sidley Austin. By Election Day, he recalled, he was reeling from $2 million spent against him by Americans for Prosperity and other conservative outside groups. "This is Appalachia!" he said. "It's a cheap media market. That would have been like $10 million most other places." He said his Republican opponent, Morgan Griffith, "actually didn't raise and spend much, but he didn't have to, because the Koch groups carried his water."

Griffith's only issue was his opposition to addressing climate change and other environmental problems, according to Boucher. Griffith's victory left Saltville—where the EPA had forced the Olin Corporation to take responsibility for remediating a river that was still too toxic to fish—represented by a congressman who painted the EPA as the district's greatest foe.

In Boucher's view, the polluters had triumphed by overturning the campaign-finance laws. "There was a huge change after *Citizens United*," he contends. "When anyone could spend any amount of money without revealing who they were, by hiding behind amorphous-named organizations, the floodgates opened. The Supreme Court made a huge mistake. There is no accountability. Zero."

To shape the midterm message, Noble turned back to the pollster Frank Luntz for market testing. The Center to Protect Patient Rights paid for polls in a hundred congressional districts, often multiple times. The help did not come cheap. Records later showed that CPPR spent over $10 million in 2010 on "communications and surveys."

After conducting focus groups, Luntz suggested that opponents needed to avoid direct attacks on Obama, who was still popular, and instead tie Democratic candidates to Nancy Pelosi, the Speaker of the House. "She was totally toxic," one insider on the project said. "People saw her as so San Francisco, so out of touch. Their verbatims"—unedited comments— "about her were hilarious."

To make the anticipated attack ads, Noble again chose Larry McCarthy, the veteran media consultant who was known for his ability to distill a complicated subject into a simple, potent, and usually negative symbol. McCarthy had a reputation for being a particularly shrewd consumer of *O,* or opposition research on the rival candidates he was targeting. He often honed his ads using polls, focus groups, micro-targeting data, and "perception analyzers"—meters that evaluated viewers' split-second reactions to demo tapes.

McCarthy was an old hand at making disreputable ads for "outside" groups that wanted to be seen as unrelated to the candidates for reasons of legal and political hygiene. By saying the ads were "independent expenditures," candidates got deniability. The Willie Horton ad, for instance, had been paid for by an "outside" group run by the right-wing operative who founded Citizens United, Floyd Brown. It was the same group that later made the film attacking Hillary Clinton and that gave its name to the corporate speech test case. "Larry is not just one of the best ad-makers these days," Brown attested. "He's one of the best advertising minds this *century.* You go into a studio with Larry, and you're watching art. It's beautiful," he said, laughing. "From *my* standpoint, it's beautiful."

Geoff Garin, a Democratic pollster who had occasionally worked in the past with McCarthy but who was far more accustomed to being on the other side, was less effusive. He described McCarthy as a "serial offender" who had played "a pretty big part in lowering the bar on what is acceptable in American politics."

Shortly before the Kochs held their second summit of the year, a June get-together at the St. Regis Resort in Aspen, they got a break that enormously increased their network's financial clout when House Democrats passed a bill, backed by President Obama, to eliminate the so-called carried-interest loophole. The idea of eliminating the special tax break enjoyed by private equity and hedge fund managers struck fear in the finance industry. Obama had won the support of a surprisingly large share of New York's finance titans in 2008, but his stance on the tax—which would never make it through the Senate—enraged many of its heaviest hitters. Stephen Schwarzman, the chairman and CEO of the enormously lucrative private equity firm the Blackstone Group, whose personal fortune *Forbes* then estimated at $6.5 billion, would call the administration's efforts to close the loophole "a war," claiming it was "like when Hitler invaded Poland in 1939."

Schwarzman later apologized for the remark, but in truth the relationship between Obama and Wall Street had begun deteriorating almost as soon as he took office. Financiers resented being blamed for the collapse of the economy in 2008, they took extreme umbrage when Obama had chastised them as "fat cats," and they claimed that his administration was run by college professors who knew nothing about business. But Schwarzman and a number of other financiers regarded this as a new level of affront and flocked to the June Koch summit with their checkbooks in hand, determined to prevent his reelection.

Ironically, it was probably Schwarzman's own excesses that had brought the carried-interest loophole to critics' attention. In 2006, when he decided to transform Blackstone from a private partnership into a public company, he had been required to disclose his earnings for the first time. The numbers stunned both Wall Street and Washington. He made $398.3 million in 2006, which was nine times more than the CEO of Goldman Sachs. On top of this, his shares in Blackstone were valued at more than $7 billion. A 2008 *New Yorker* profile by James B. Stewart quotes a friend of Schwarzman's saying, "You have no idea what an impression this made on Wall Street. You have all these guys who have spent their entire lives working just as hard to make twenty million. Sure, that's a lot of money, but then Schwarzman turns around and, seemingly overnight, has eight billion."

Beyond this, Stewart wrote, Schwarzman "made himself an easy target for critics of Wall Street greed and conspicuous consumption" with "an expanding collection of trophy residences that are lavish even by the current standards of Wall Street." A 2007 *Wall Street Journal* profile also described how, at one of Schwarzman's five houses, an "11,000-square-foot home in Palm Beach, Fla., he complained to Jean-Pierre Zeugin, his executive chef and estate manager, that an employee wasn't wearing the proper black shoes with his uniform . . . [H]e found the squeak of the rubber soles distracting." His own mother told the paper that money is "what drives him. Money is the measuring stick."

Schwarzman's most serious self-inflicted wound, though, was the $3 million sixtieth birthday party he threw for himself in February 2007, at which he paid pop stars Rod Stewart and Patti LaBelle to serenade him. The media sensation stirred by the billionaire bacchanal led directly to congressional calls to close the carried-interest loophole.

The loophole was in essence an accounting trick that enabled hedge fund and private equity managers to categorize huge portions of their income as "interest," which was taxed at the 15 percent rate then applied to long-term capital gains. This was less than half the income tax rate paid by other top-bracket wage earners. Critics called the loophole a gigantic subsidy to millionaires and billionaires at the expense of ordinary taxpayers. The Economic Policy Institute, a progressive think tank, estimated that the hedge fund loophole cost the government over $6 billion a year—the cost of providing health care to three million children. Of that total, it said, almost $2 billion a year from the tax break went to just twenty-five individuals.

Congressional critics had been trying to close the loophole

since at least 2007, but while the Democratic House had passed reform bills three times, the measures always died in the Senate, the victim of both Republican and Democratic protectors, beholden to Wall Street.

With the issue back in play in the summer of 2010, the financiers were again mobilizing. As Clifford Asness, who ran a hedge fund in Greenwich, Connecticut, had declared in a call to arms when Obama first started speaking critically of hedge fund "speculators" and "fat cats," "Hedge funds really need a community organizer."

Organizers were waiting for Schwarzman and others at the June Koch summit, the theme of which was "Understanding and Addressing Threats to American Free Enterprise and Prosperity." The financiers represented a different strain of the Republican Party from the Kochs. Few were fanatically ideological. Most were simply concerned with protecting their continued accumulation of wealth. But when their resources were combined with the idea machinery built by the conservative movement's early funders, along with the ideological zealotry of the Kochs and other antigovernment radicals, the result was a raging river of cash capable of carrying the whole Republican Party to the right.

Another hedge fund manager who attended the Aspen session was the former Obama bundler Ken Griffin, founder and CEO of the Chicago-based hedge fund Citadel, whose shift from a Democratic bundler for Obama to the Republican side was part of what came to be known as the "Hedge Fund Switch." Other billionaire financiers at the event included the Home Depot founder turned investment banker Ken Langone and the Massachusetts-based private equity investor John Childs. Childs was the second-in-command at Thomas H. Lee Partners when it made $900 million in two years in a leveraged buyout deal for the beverage company Snapple. His own company, J. W. Childs Associates, had ups and downs, but he had been a consistently huge investor in conservative politics, once described as "the closest thing the Republican Party has to an automatic teller machine in Massachusetts." In the 2010 election cycle, Childs would go on to spend $907,000 on federal elections.

The hedge fund manager Paul Singer, chairman of the Manhattan Institute and a major contributor to the Republican Party, didn't attend, but his close aide Annie Dickerson appeared on his behalf. Singer's company, Elliott Management, had a unique niche in the financial world. It bought the distressed debt of bankrupt companies and countries and then demanded to be paid in full or, if necessary, took them to court. Critics had called the tactic immoral particularly when applied to impoverished countries, castigating him as a "vulture capitalist" who profited off poverty, but Singer had accumulated a fortune estimated at $900 million from the practice. Singer, who described himself as a Goldwater free-enterprise conservative, was a supporter of gay rights but a harsh critic of the Obama administration's proposed financial regulatory reforms. Furious with the Democrats, he hosted his own fund-raiser in Manhattan for Republican candidates opposing Dodd-Frank and other financial reforms that summer. He also attended a similar meeting at the $14 million home of another disgruntled hedge fund donor, Steve Cohen of SAC Capital. According to later reports, this small and intensely wealthy circle of billionaire moguls soon "pumped at least $10 million" into groups boosting Republicans in the midterms, often without any public trace.

The concentration of wealth at the Koch summit by this point was extraordinary. Of the two hundred or so participants meeting secretly with the Kochs in Aspen that June, at least eleven were on *Forbes*'s list of the four hundred wealthiest Americans. The combined assets of this group alone, assessed in accordance with the magazine's estimates of their wealth at the time, amounted to $129.1 billion.

Hoping to inspire their generosity, Noble previewed a

sample television ad for the donors, slamming Obamacare, as well as touting the Republicans' chances of winning, on a panel titled "Mobilizing Citizens for November." "Is there a chance this fall to elect leaders who are more strongly committed to freedom and prosperity?" the brochure for the discussion asked. "This session will further assess the landscape and offer a plan to educate voters on the importance of economic freedom."

Joining Noble on the panel was Tim Phillips, the president of Americans for Prosperity, who unveiled his group's plan to spend an unheard-of $45 million on a few targeted midterm races.

In the evening, conference goers were treated to a rousing dinner speech from the Fox News host Glenn Beck titled, in homage to Hayek, "Is America on the Road to Serfdom?" Finally, topping off the night was a "cocktails and dessert reception," hosted by DonorsTrust. Whitney Ball, the head of the organization that offered donors a politically safe way to give big and anonymously, later explained her attendance at the event succinctly: It's a "target-rich environment."

On the final day, the donors engaged in auction-like bids over lunch, one-upping each other with their seven-figure pledges amid laughter and applause. Charles and David Koch themselves reportedly pledged $12 million. By the end of the meal, the Koch-backed nonprofits could count on $25 million more in the kitty.

By July, Democratic strategists began to feel a strange undertow, as if an offshore tsunami were gathering force. One operative put together a chart compiling the pledged midterm expenditures by ten Republican-aligned independent groups and was appalled to discover that this slice of the total spending alone would likely reach at least $200 million. Americans for Prosperity had pledged to spend $45 million. Karl Rove's group American Crossroads had pledged $52 million. The

U.S. Chamber of Commerce had committed to spend $75 million. Countless other groups, including an unknown number of dark-money organizations loaded with secret funds, were lined up to spend millions and millions more. A Democratic operative who saw the chart, which was passed around like samizdat within the party, admitted that it was "one hell of a wake-up call."

The numbers caught the Obama administration off guard. The former White House aide Anita Dunn admits, "It was clear that *Citizens United* was going to open the floodgates and it would be bad for the Democrats. But it exploded in 2010. The amount spent in those midterms probably surprised everyone."

As late as May, Axelrod had barely known who the Kochs were. When a reporter asked what he knew about them, he seemed unsure. Later, the Koch public relations team would suggest that press coverage of them was initiated by the White House. In truth, Obama's political team was almost clueless. Only after Noble's team, working undercover, began launching attacks on Democrats all across the country did some in the White House start to sense something odd. As Axelrod recalls, "We began to wonder, where is all this money coming from?"

In Iowa, the American Future Fund began airing an ad created by Larry McCarthy that Geoff Garin, the Democratic pollster, described as perhaps "the most egregious of the year." The ad accused the then congressman Bruce Braley, an Iowa Democrat and a lawyer, of supporting a proposed Islamic community center in lower Manhattan, which it misleadingly called a "mosque at Ground Zero." As footage of the destroyed World Trade Center rolled, a narrator said, "For centuries, Muslims built mosques where they won military victories." Now it said a mosque celebrating 9/11 was to be built on the very spot "where Islamic terrorists killed three thousand Americans"; it was, the narrator suggested, as if the Japanese were to build a triumphal monument at Pearl Harbor. The ad then accused Braley of supporting the mosque.

In fact, Braley had taken no position on the issue. No surprise for a congressman from Iowa. But an unidentified video cameraman had ambushed him at the Iowa State Fair and asked him about it.

Braley replied that he regarded the matter as a local zoning issue for New Yorkers to decide. Soon afterward, he says, the attack ad "dropped on me like the house in 'The Wizard of Oz.'" Braley, who won his seat by a margin of 30 percent in 2008, barely held on in 2010. The American Future Fund's effort against Braley was the most expensive campaign that year by an independent group.

After the election, Braley accused McCarthy, the ad maker, of "profiting from Citizens United in the lowest way." As for those who hired McCarthy, he said, they "are laughing all the way to the bank. It's a good investment for them . . . They're the winners. The losers are the American people, and the truth."

In North Carolina, Congressman Bob Etheridge, a seven-term Democrat, fared worse. He was the target of ads made by McCarthy for another of Noble's front groups, Americans for Job Security. That summer, Etheridge was walking on Capitol Hill when he too found himself the victim of a video ambush. Two young men in suits approached him. One thrust a video camera in his face while the other demanded to know, "Do you fully support the Obama agenda?" Taken aback, Etheridge asked, "Who are you?" When he got no answer, he asked again. Growing irate, he repeated the question five times, until finally he pushed the camera away and gripped his inquisitor.

"Please let go of my arm, Congressman," the inquisitor pleaded as the camera kept recording.

"Who are you?" Etheridge repeated.

Finally, the interviewer stammered, "I'm just a student, sir."

"From?" Etheridge asked.

"The Streets," came the answer.

Within days, a video of the confrontation, edited to make Etheridge seem unhinged, was posted on the conservative Web site *Big Government* under the headline "Congressman Attacks Student." It went viral. Soon afterward, McCarthy inserted the video into an attack ad titled "Who Are You?" in which people purporting to be from Etheridge's district answered, "We're your constituents," and then accused Etheridge—inaccurately—of wanting to cut Medicare. As per Luntz's instructions, Nancy Pelosi figured prominently in the ads as well. The spot that dealt the deathblow to Etheridge, finally, was one that accused him, like Braley, of supporting the "Ground Zero Mosque."

The local television station WRAL-TV in Raleigh, which covered the campaign, noted that Americans for Job Security had spent $360,000 on media against Etheridge, but at the time no one was able to figure out who was behind the group.

After a seventeen-day recount, Etheridge lost in November in a stunning upset to a Tea Party sympathizer, Renee Ellmers, who was a nurse running with the support of Sarah Palin. The next day, the National Republican Congressional Committee (NRCC), which had previously denied any role, acknowledged that it had been behind the ambush video. How the video made its way into the "independent" ad was never revealed, but the NRCC, too, was one of McCarthy's clients.

It was not a coincidence that Braley, Etheridge, Perriello, and other Democrats were all ambushed that year by unidentified videographers. In 2010, Americans for Prosperity and several other conservative groups encouraged members to provoke Democratic candidates into on-camera outbursts. Some gave instructions on how to do it. In time, the practice spread to liberal groups too. The Internet had exponentially increased the power of viral videos, particularly those capturing compromising behavior.

Aiding the effort, several of the wealthiest members of the Koch network launched media ventures during this period, widening the exposure for partisan attacks. Foster Friess, the Wyoming mutual fund magnate, for instance, committed to spend $3 million to found *The Daily Caller* in 2010 after a single luncheon conversation about it with Tucker Carlson, its prospective editor in chief. The online news venture described itself as a conservative version of *The Huffington Post*. In fact, it functioned more as an outlet for opposition research paid for by the donor class. Charles Koch's foundation would later also back the news site. (After *The New Yorker* published my investigative article on the Kochs, "Covert Operations," that August, *The Daily Caller* was the chosen receptacle for the retaliatory opposition research on me, although, after it proved false, the Web site decided not to run it.)

Only in 2011 did it surface that in New York, at least, the "Ground Zero mosque" controversy had been stirred up for political gain in part by money from Robert Mercer, the co-CEO of the $15 billion Long Island hedge fund Renaissance Technologies. To aid a conservative candidate in New York, Mercer gave $1 million. It helped pay for ads attacking supporters of the "Ground Zero mosque." A former computer programmer who had a reputation as a brilliant mathematician and an eccentric loner, Mercer was a relative newcomer to the Koch summits. But he was immediately impressed by the organization. He had long held the government in low regard and shared the Kochs' antipathy toward government regulations. In addition to fanning flames around the "mosque" issue, in 2010 Mercer reportedly gave over $300,000 to a super PAC trying to defeat a Democratic congressman from Oregon, Pete DeFazio, who had proposed taxing stock trades. Renaissance, a so-called quant fund, traded stocks in accordance with computer algorithms at enormously high volumes, so the proposed tax would have bitten into the firm's legendary profits.

Someone familiar with Mercer's thinking maintained that the proposed tax on stock trades was not behind his involvement in the race; rather, Mercer shared deep skepticism about global warming with the Republican candidate, Arthur Robinson. Instead of openly debating these issues, though, Mercer, who declined to speak about his motivations, paid for ads that manipulated voters' fears about terrorism and Medicare.

As the congressional races grew nasty, Gillespie's Republican State Leadership Committee began to channel dark money into one local state legislature race after another. There were furtive, well-coordinated projects to take over the statehouses in Wisconsin, Michigan, Ohio, and elsewhere. North Carolina in particular was living up to its promise as a perfect testing ground for the REDMAP strategy. Art Pope's outsized role there, meanwhile, was also providing an instructive demonstration of how much influence one extraordinarily wealthy activist could have over a single state in the post–*Citizens United* era.

Many of the details remained shrouded from public view. But that fall, in the remote western corner of North Carolina, John Snow, a retired Democratic judge who had represented the district in the state senate for three terms, found himself subjected to one political attack after another. Snow, who often voted with the Republicans, was considered one of the most conservative Democrats in the general assembly, and his record reflected the views of his constituents. His Republican opponent, Jim Davis—an orthodontist loosely allied with the Tea Party—had minimal political experience, and Snow, a former college football star, was expected to be reelected easily. Yet somehow Davis seemed to have almost unlimited money with which to assail Snow.

Snow recalls, "I voted to help build a pier with an aquarium on the coast, as did every other member of the North Carolina House and Senate who voted." But a television attack ad presented the "luxury pier" as Snow's wasteful scheme. "We've lost jobs," an actress said in the ad. "John Snow's solution for our economy? 'Go fish!'" A mass mailing, decorated with a cartoon pig, denounced the pier as one of Snow's "pork projects."

In all, Snow says, he was the target of two dozen mass mailings, one of them reminiscent of the Willie Horton ad. It featured a photograph of a menacing-looking African-American convict who, it said, "thanks to arrogant state senator John Snow," could "soon be let off death row." Snow, in fact, supported the death penalty and had prosecuted murder cases. But in 2009, Snow had helped pass a new state law, the Racial Justice Act, that enabled judges to reconsider a death sentence if a convict could prove that the jury's verdict had been tainted by racism. The law was an attempt to address the overwhelming racial disparity in capital sentences.

"The attacks just went on and on," Snow later recalled. "My opponents used fear tactics. I'm a moderate, but they tried to make me look liberal." On election night, he lost by an agonizingly slim margin—fewer than two hundred votes.

After the election, the North Carolina Free Enterprise Foundation, a nonpartisan, pro-business organization, revealed that two seemingly independent outside political groups had spent several hundred thousand dollars on ads against Snow—a huge amount for a local race in a poor, backwoods district. Pope was instrumental in funding both groups, Civitas Action and Real Jobs NC. In fact, Pope gave $200,000 in seed money in 2010 to start Real Jobs NC, which was responsible for the "Go fish!" ad and the mass mailing that attacked Snow's "pork projects."

Real Jobs NC was also the recipient of a whopping $1.25 million from Ed Gillespie's Republican State Leadership Committee. But as the investigative news outfit ProPublica explained, Gillespie's group distributed its contributions in a way designed to hide its involvement from voters. Instead of putting its own name on the ads, it created new, local-sounding nonprofit groups that lacked the word "Republican." As a social welfare organization, it claimed to be nonpolitical, yet its funds were used to attack twenty different Democrats around the state and no Republicans.

Bob Phillips, the head of the North Carolina chapter of Common Cause, an organization that promotes stricter controls on political money, watched the unfolding drama closely and concluded that the *Citizens United* decision was an even bigger "game changer" at the local level than at the national. He said it enabled a single donor, particularly one with access to major corporate funds like Pope or the Kochs, to play a significant and even decisive role. "We didn't have that before 2010," Phillips says. "*Citizens United* opened up the door. Now a candidate can literally be outspent by independent groups. We saw it in North Carolina, and a lot of the money was traced back to Art Pope."

In fact, misleading attack ads sponsored by the same unknown outside groups popped up in local races all over the state. In Fayetteville, Margaret Dickson, a sixty-one-year-old pro-business Democrat who was seeking reelection to the North Carolina state senate, was depicted as a clone of Nancy Pelosi, even though her record was considerably more conservative. Another ad, funded by her opponent, made her look like "a hooker," she said, showing a doppelgänger applying lipstick and taking piles of greenbacks and suggesting she was prostituting her state job for money. Pope later said he was appalled by the ad, but Americans for Prosperity, on whose board he sat, promoted her opponent. "Those ads hurt me," she said later. "I've been through this four times before, but the tone of this campaign was much uglier, and much more personal, than anything I've seen." On election night, Dickson fell about a thousand votes short of victory in her district, which has a population of more than 150,000.

Chris Heagarty, a Democratic lawyer who ran for a legislative seat that fall in Raleigh, had previously directed an election-reform group and was not naive about political money.

Yet even he was caught off guard by the intensity of the effort marshaled against him. Real Jobs NC and Civitas Action spent some $70,000 on ads portraying him as fiscally profligate, while Americans for Prosperity spent heavily on behalf of his opponent. One ad accused him of having voted "to raise taxes over a billion dollars," even though he had not yet served in the legislature. He said, "If you put all of the Pope groups together, they and the North Carolina GOP spent more to defeat me than the guy who actually won." He fell silent, then added, "For an individual to have so much power is frightening. The government of North Carolina is for sale."

Pope, who regarded himself as an underdog in a historically Democratic state and an honest reformer, took umbrage at such talk. "People throw around terms like 'so-and-so tried to buy the election,'" he said in an interview. But in his view, that evoked bribery, and "that's illegal, corrupt, and something I've fought hard against in North Carolina." He said the money he spent simply helped "educate" citizens so that they could "make informed decisions. It's the core of the First Amendment!" Asked whether those with more cash might drown out less wealthy voices, he said, "I really have more faith in North Carolina voters than that." Martin Nesbitt Jr., the Democratic leader in the North Carolina Senate, wasn't convinced. Of Pope's 2010 spending, he said, "It wasn't an education; it was an onslaught. What he's doing is buying elections."

Other critics accused Pope of using tax-deductible philanthropic pursuits to promote aggressively pro-business, anti-tax policies that helped his company. Scholars who worked at a think tank funded by his family foundations, for instance, opposed any raise in the minimum wage, and in fact any minimum wage laws at all. At the same time, many employees at Pope's discount stores were paid the minimum wage. "I am careful to comply with the law," Pope argued, "and I keep my personal activities separate from my philanthropic, public-policy, grassroots and independent expenditure efforts."

He protested caricatures that portrayed him as greedy and self-serving, saying he deeply cared about the people of North Carolina but believed they were better served by private enterprise than government social programs. He therefore believed in cutting personal and corporate income taxes, abolishing estate taxes, and cutting state spending. Friends explained that Pope believed it was the role of charities, to which he contributed, not the government, to look after the poor and disadvantaged.

The Pope fortune was highly dependent on low-income patrons. In 1930, Pope's grandfather established five small dime stores in North Carolina that he sold to the next generation. Pope's father was a tough and thrifty merchant who expanded the family business into an empire spanning thirteen states. Pope then worked his way up in the company, becoming CEO. Variety Wholesalers owned several chains, including Roses, Maxway, Super 10, and Bargain Town. The company favored a specific demographic: neighborhoods with median incomes of less than $40,000 a year, and populations that were at least 25 percent African-American.

Despite the controversy it stirred, the triumph of Pope and "outside" money in North Carolina in 2010 was sweeping. Of twenty-two local legislative races targeted by Pope, his family, and their organizations, the Republicans won eighteen. As Gillespie and he had hoped, this placed both chambers of the general assembly firmly under Republican majorities for the first time since 1870.

According to the Institute for Southern Studies, three-quarters of the spending by independent groups in North Carolina's 2010 state races came from accounts linked to Pope. The total amount that Pope and his family and groups backed by him spent—$2.2 million—was not that much by national standards but was enough to exert crucial influence within the confines of one state.

The pattern did in fact repeat itself all across the nation.

"The Obama team has done some amazing things, those guys are really something, but the Democrats plain got skunked on the state houses," the former Republican congressman Tom Reynolds, the chairman of REDMAP, later told *Politico*. Gillespie's deputy, Chris Jankowski, later admitted, "At first I was a little panicked, they weren't out there really competing. I thought I was going to get hit by a sucker punch." But then, he said, "I realized what was happening and it was like, how much can we run up the score?"

In the final month before the midterm elections, Obama's political advisers realized there was almost nothing they could do to prevent disaster. "We lost all hope in October," one White House aide later admitted. "We didn't feel much of anything. We just had to let the ship hit the iceberg."

In a last-ditch effort, Obama tried to warn voters that Republicans were trying to steal the elections with secret, special-interest cash. He began speaking out on the campaign about how *Citizens United* had allowed "a flood of deceptive attack ads sponsored by special interests using front groups with misleading names." He even made a barely veiled reference to the Kochs, suggesting that big companies were hiding behind "groups with harmless-sounding names like Americans for Prosperity." Obama said, "They don't have to say who, exactly, Americans for Prosperity are. You don't know if it's a foreign-controlled corporation"—or even, he added, "a big oil company."

In the final days before the election, the Democratic Party aired a national ad accusing "Bush cronies," Ed Gillespie and Karl Rove, and "shills for big business" of "stealing our democracy." The spot depicted an old woman getting mugged. The image, though, was hackneyed, and the message simplistic. It was almost impossible to explain to the public in sound bites the connections between the sea of dark money, the donors' financial interests, the assault on Obama's policies, and their lives. The conventional wisdom among professional political consultants was that Americans either didn't get it or just didn't care.

It's likely given historical trends and an unemployment rate topping 9.5 percent that a Republican wave in 2010 was inevitable, but the unmatched money from a handful of ultrarich conservatives helped turn the likely win into a rout. Noble had made so much progress that by the final weeks in the campaign he was aiming beyond his third-tier candidates at congressmen no one had ever believed were vulnerable. After noticing how little money Jim Oberstar, a Democratic congressman from Duluth, Minnesota, had raised, Noble bought local television time and aired an ad thrown together by McCarthy casting Oberstar as a disco-era relic who cared more about himself than about his constituents. Oberstar, to almost everyone's surprise, became another notch on Noble's belt.

On November 2, 2010, the Democrats suffered massive defeats, losing control of the House of Representatives. Just two short years after he soared to power amid predictions of a lasting realignment, Obama's party, and his hopes of prevailing on any ambitious legislation, were crushed. Republicans gained sixty-three seats in the House, putting them firmly in control of the lower body. It was the largest such turnover since 1948. Pelosi, the first female Speaker and Luntz's favorite target, was exiled to minority status after only four years. The Ohio Republican John Boehner, the new Speaker, now had a caucus bursting with Tea Party enthusiasts who had ridden to power by attacking government in general and Obama in particular. Several had won primaries against moderates. Many owed their victories to donors expecting radically conservative change. Compromise wasn't in their interest.

The Democrats' setbacks were huge at almost every level. Republicans picked up half a dozen Senate seats. At the state level, the Democratic losses were even more staggering. Across the country, Republicans gained 675 legislative seats. They won control of both the legislature and the governor's office in twenty-one states; the Democrats had similar one-party rule in only eleven. The map looked red, with small islands of blue.

As a consequence of their gains, Republicans now had four times as many districts to gerrymander as the Democrats. By creating reliably safe seats, they could build a firewall protecting the Republican control of Congress for the next decade.

Clearly, REDMAP's payoff for a relatively modest investment was impressive. For the Republicans, as Glenn Thrush of *Politico* observed, it became "the gift that keeps on giving." Newly Republican states like Michigan, Wisconsin, Ohio, and North Carolina soon became breeding grounds for attacks on Obama's core agenda. They undermined his policies on health care, abortion, gay rights, voting rights, immigration, the environment, guns, and labor.

"It feels bad," Obama admitted at a press conference the day after the election. What hurt especially, he said, was having to make condolence calls to Democrats who had gone out on a limb to defend him and his policies, such as Ohio's governor, Ted Strickland. "The toughest thing in the last couple of days is seeing really terrific public servants not being able to serve more," he said. "There's not only sadness about seeing them go, but there's also a lot of questioning on my part in terms of could I have done something differently, or something more."

Waxing professorial, he suggested, "This is something that I think every president needs to go through," but then he paused and joked wanly, "Now, I'm not suggesting for every future president that they take a shellacking like I did last night."

One of the biggest, though least-known, winners of the evening was Sean Noble. When he had worked as a congressional aide on Capitol Hill, he had earned a salary of $87,000 a year. In contrast, by 2011 he was wealthy enough to make two major real estate purchases in addition to the two houses that he and his wife owned in Phoenix. He spent $665,000 on a Capitol Hill row house and an undisclosed amount on "a 5,700-square-foot, eight-bedroom house in Hurricane, Utah," Bloomberg News reported. And best of all, the record spending on the 2012 election was just around the corner.

Part Three

Privatizing Politics

Total Combat, 2011–2014

There's class warfare all right.
But it's my class, the rich class, that's making war,
and we're winning.

—*Warren Buffett*

CHAPTER ELEVEN

The Spoils: Plundering Congress

THE OFFICIAL OPENING OF THE 112TH CONGRESS TOOK PLACE on January 5, 2011, when Nancy Pelosi, the Speaker of the House, handed off an oversized ceremonial gavel to her successor, John Boehner. But a new era of ultraconservative billionaire influence had already begun. Before the public swearing-in ceremony got under way, David Koch, whose donor network had spent at least $130.7 million on winning a Republican majority, was in the new Speaker-to-be's ornate office, chatting amiably with his staff. "The People's House" was under new management and, critics would suggest, new ownership.

While Koch was a very public presence in the Capitol, his political adjutant, Tim Phillips, the president of Americans for Prosperity, was deep in the inner sanctum of the congressional committee that mattered most to the bottom line of Koch Industries. Phillips's most important destination that day was the House Energy and Commerce Committee, which under the new Republican majority had now increased its power to block President Obama's environmental agenda in Congress. The committee could bury progress on climate change and harass the Environmental Protection Agency for the foreseeable future.

David Koch's public appearance that day signified a remarkable transformation. The Kochs had come far from their days as Libertarian losers. As the *Los Angeles Times* noted a month later, "Charles and David Koch no longer sit outside Washington's political establishment, isolated by uncompromising conservatism." Instead, their "uncompromising conservatism" now dominated one of Congress's two legislative chambers, as well as one of the country's two major political parties. As the paper's headline put it, "Koch Brothers Now at Heart of GOP Power."

That afternoon, after Boehner was sworn in, Koch donned a herringbone tweed overcoat and a camel-colored cashmere muffler and strode out across the Capitol grounds toward Independence Avenue to celebrate. Before he could get far, though, he was stopped by Lee Fang, the dogged liberal blogger for *ThinkProgress* who had been chronicling the Kochs' rise to power for months. After Fang introduced himself, he and a videographer stuck a microphone in the billionaire's face and asked, "Mr. Koch, are you proud of the Tea Party movement, and what they've achieved in the past few years?"

"Yeah," Koch said, looking a little befuddled. Phillips, who was at his side, tried to cut the questioning off. "Hey, David, Lee here is a good blogger on the LEFT," he warned his boss with a nervous smile. But Koch, who had impaired hearing in his left ear, either didn't grasp the warning or didn't care, because he kept talking. "There are some extremists there," he acknowledged, "but the rank and file are just normal people like us. And I admire them. It's probably the best grassroots uprising since 1776 in my opinion!"

Phillips by this point was trying to drown out the interview without appearing rude on camera, insistently repeating, "Lee—Lee—I'm very disappointed in you—Lee—you're better than this—Lee, *LEE*—THE INTERVIEW IS OVER!"

Fang soldiered on nonetheless, asking Koch what he wanted from the new Congress under Speaker Boehner. "Well," Koch answered, with growing animation, licking his lips as he habitually did, "cut the hell out of spending, balance the budget, reduce regulations, and uh, support business!"

Later, in a round of image-repairing interviews, the Kochs would portray themselves as disinterested do-gooders and misunderstood social liberals who championed bipartisan issues such as criminal justice reform. But when put on the spot and stripped of public relations help, David Koch made his priorities clear. He regarded his self-interest and the public interest as synonymous.

In *Plutocrats: The Rise of the New Global Super Rich and the Fall of Everyone Else,* the journalist Chrystia Freeland describes how those with massive financial resources almost universally use them to secure policies beneficial to their interests, often at the expense of the less well-off. In the United States, a number of studies have shown that in recent years this tendency has distorted politics in very specific ways. In a study he conducted for the nonpartisan Sunlight Foundation, the political scientist Lee Drutman found that increasingly concentrated wealth in America resulted in more polarization and extremism, especially on the right. Very rich benefactors in the Republican Party were far more opposed to taxes and regulations than the rest of the country. "The more Republicans depend upon 1% of the 1% donors, the more conservative they tend to be," he discovered.

The 112th Congress soon unfolded as a case study of what David Frum, an adviser to the former president George W. Bush, described as the growing and in his view destructive influence of the Republican Party's "radical rich." The "radicalization of the party's donor base," he observed, "propelled the party to advocate policies that were more extreme than anything seen since Barry Goldwater's 1964 presidential campaign." It also "led Republicans in Congress to try tactics they would never have dared use before."

Hard data supported this. Harvard's Theda Skocpol found that the House "took the biggest leap to the far right" since political scientists began recording quantitative measurements of legislators' positions. There was no better example than the Kochs' newly won influence over the House Energy and Commerce Committee.

In the previous Congress, the panel had been chaired by Henry Waxman, the liberal Democrat from California who had quarterbacked the House's successful passage of the cap-and-trade bill, only to see it die in the Senate. Now the new Republican leadership stocked the committee with oil industry advocates, many of whom owed huge campaign debts to the Kochs. Koch Industries PAC was the single largest oil and gas industry donor to members of the panel, outspending even ExxonMobil. It had donated to twenty-two of the committee's thirty-one Republican members and five of its Democratic members, too. In addition, five out of the six Republican freshmen on the committee had received "outside" support from Americans for Prosperity.

Meanwhile, many of the new committee members had signed an unusual pledge swearing fealty to the Kochs' agenda. They promised to vote against any kind of carbon tax unless it was offset by comparable spending cuts—an unlikely scenario. The "No Climate Tax" pledge was invented by Americans for Prosperity in 2008 when the Supreme Court cleared the way for the EPA to regulate greenhouse gases, as it did other pollutants. The Kochs' pledge was modeled on the enormously successful one that the antitax crusader Grover Norquist had used to intimidate Republican lawmakers from raising taxes, but in this instance it served not a cause so much as a company.

By the start of the legislative session in 2011, fully 156 members of Congress had signed the Kochs' "No Climate Tax" pledge. Many returning members of the House Energy and Commerce Committee had already taken the pledge, and of the twelve new Republicans on the panel nine were signatories, including five of the six freshmen.

A prime example of the symbiotic relationship between the Kochs and the committee was Morgan Griffith, who had defeated Rick Boucher in the district that represented Saltville, Virginia, and was among the wave of new appointees to the

Energy and Commerce Committee who were openly indebted to the Kochs for their seats. Americans for Prosperity's operatives were guests of honor at a victory rally soon after the election, at which Griffith gushed, "I'm just thankful that you all helped me in so many ways."

The Kochs' investment soon paid off. Once in office, Griffith became an outspoken skeptic of mainstream climate science, drawing national ridicule for lecturing scientific experts, as they testified in Congress, that they needed to consider the possibility that Mesopotamia and the Vikings owed their success to global warming and that melting ice caps on Mars showed that humans were not its cause on Earth.

Congressman Griffith also became a lead player in the House Republicans' "war on the EPA," demanding that the agency be "reined in." Within a month after he took office, he and other House Republicans gutted the EPA's budget by a punishing 27 percent. The Senate objected but eventually agreed to cut 16 percent from the agency that had halted the flow of mercury into Saltville's streams. By then, the 1980 Superfund law that had charged polluters like the Olin Corporation for the cleanup costs had expired, and the $3.8 billion that had accumulated in the fund had run out. Nearly half of America's population lived within ten miles of a toxic waste site, according to one study, but in towns like Saltville, taxpayers rather than corporations were left to clean up the mess.

Koch Industries could breathe a bit freer, but the same couldn't be said of those living near its plants. On just one short street, South Penn Road in the blue-collar town of Crossett, Arkansas, eleven of the fifteen households had been stricken with cancer. Many residents were convinced their plight was caused by chemical waste dumped by the nearby Georgia-Pacific paper mill, owned by Koch Industries. The air stank so badly that young and old residents stayed indoors, breathing from respirators. The company denied responsibility and

pointed out that the cancer claims had earlier been "rejected in
a class action suit." But David Bouie, a black minister who lived
on the street, was trying desperately to get the EPA involved.
"All along our street here we have case after case of cancer,"
he told the liberal investigative filmmaker Robert Greenwald.
"We have a problem in this community, for this many people
to be sick or dead. Why is the cancer rate so high? Does the
paper mill have anything to do with it?" Two years earlier, *USA
Today* had published a devastating investigative report based on
EPA air pollution data that pinpointed a school in Crossett as
among the most toxic 1 percent in the country and identified
the Georgia-Pacific plant as a major cause. Lisa Jackson, the
EPA's administrator, vowed action, but the congressional budget cuts were huge constraints on doing anything.

The numbers regarding Koch Industries' pollution were
incontrovertible. In 2012, according to the EPA's Toxic Release
Inventory database, which documents the toxic and carcinogenic output of eight thousand American companies, Koch
Industries was the number one producer of toxic waste in the
United States. It generated 950 million pounds of hazardous
materials that year. Of this total output, it released 56.8 million pounds into the air, water, and soil, making it the country's
fifth-largest polluter. The company was also among the largest
emitters of greenhouse gases in America, spewing over twenty-
four million tons of carbon dioxide a year into the atmosphere
by 2011, according to the EPA, as much as is typically emitted
by five million cars.

Company officials didn't dispute the statistics but argued
that they merely reflected the size of its operations and the
kinds of products it made. They stressed that they had achieved
a record of compliance that compared favorably with other
manufacturers of their ilk. As Steve Tatum, president of Koch
Minerals, put it, "The investment banks, they don't pollute
very much, because they don't make anything. We make stuff."

Another defender on the committee was Mike Pompeo,

a freshman Republican from Koch Industries' hometown of Wichita, Kansas, who was so closely entwined with the billionaire brothers that he became known as the "congressman from Koch." The Kochs had once invested an undisclosed amount of money in an aerospace company that Pompeo founded. By the time he ran for office, the Kochs were no longer investors in his business but had become major backers of his candidacy. Their corporate PAC and Americans for Prosperity also weighed in on his behalf. After his election, Pompeo turned to the company for his chief of staff, choosing Mark Chenoweth, a lawyer who had worked for Koch Industries' lobbying team. Within weeks, Pompeo was championing two of Koch Industries' legislative priorities—opposition to Obama's plans to create a public EPA registry of greenhouse gas polluters and a digital database of consumer complaints about unsafe products. Without publicly accessible data, of course, it would be extremely difficult to track any company's toxic output. (Ultimately, the Kochs lost the battle, and the database was created.)

Koch Industries' lobbying disclosures showed that the company spent over $8 million lobbying Congress in 2011, much of it on environmental issues. The best measure of its new congressional clout might have been the "naked belly crawl," as the political reporter Robert Draper termed it, performed by the Michigan congressman Fred Upton in hopes of snaring the Energy and Commerce Committee's chairmanship. Prior to 2010, Upton had been known as an environmental moderate. In fact, in 2009, before the Tea Partiers and their patrons took charge, he had said, "Climate change is a serious problem that necessitates serious solutions," adding, "I strongly believe that everything must be on the table as we seek to reduce carbon emissions." In 2010, however, Upton, like many Republican moderates, faced a potentially career-killing primary challenge from the right. Upton survived, but others who accepted the growing scientific consensus on climate change, such as Robert Inglis of South Carolina, were defeated, serving as cautionary warnings to the rest. Inglis became convinced of the reality of global warming on a congressional trip to Antarctica during which scientists showed him polar ice samples containing rising amounts of carbon dioxide following the Industrial Revolution. He was a Christian conservative, but he couldn't in good conscience deny the reality. In the deep red state of South Carolina, his scientific awakening proved his political downfall. "It hurts to be tossed out," he conceded afterward. "But I violated the Republican orthodoxy."

In contrast, Upton became a born-again doubter. By 2010, he had renounced his previous climate apostasy and co-authored an op-ed piece in *The Wall Street Journal* with Tim Phillips, the president of Americans for Prosperity, in which they called the EPA's plans to regulate carbon emissions "an unconstitutional power grab that will kill millions of jobs unless Congress steps in." Upton also joined lawsuits ginned up by Americans for Prosperity aimed at stopping the EPA. The belly crawl paid off. As the new session of Congress began, Upton secured the chairmanship, promising to drag the EPA administrator, Lisa Jackson, to testify before his committee so often, he bragged, that she would need her own congressional parking space.

Soon after, Republicans in the House were proposing measures that Representative Norm Dicks, a Democrat from Washington, called "a wish list for polluters." In addition to halting action on global warming, they tried to prevent the protection of any new endangered species, permit uranium mining adjacent to the Grand Canyon, deregulate mountaintop mining, and prevent coal ash from being designated a form of air pollution. In an effort to subvert the EPA's core mission, they also proposed legislation requiring it to consider the costs of its regulations, without regard to the scientific and health benefits, which the editorial page of the *Los Angeles Times* said "rips the heart out of the 40-year-old Clean Air Act."

Two months into their tenure, Republicans on the House Energy and Commerce Committee also led a crusade against alternative, renewable energy programs. They successfully branded the government's stimulus support for Solyndra, a California manufacturer of solar panels, and other clean energy firms an Obama scandal. In fact, the loan guarantee program in the Energy Department that extended the controversial financing to the company began under the Bush administration. Contrary to the partisan hype, it actually returned a profit to taxpayers. Moreover, while Solyndra's investors were portrayed as Obama supporters, among its biggest backers were members of the conservative Walton family, the founders of Walmart. A huge investor in another solar company that went bust after taking the same Energy Department loans was the venture capitalist Dixon Doll, a major contributor to the Kochs' donor network. But as the House held hearings and various conservative front groups whipped up outrage about "crony capitalism," the facts were buried in favor of a narrative that helped the fossil fuel industry.

Congressman Upton insisted that he hadn't changed his position on environmental issues. But Jeremy Symons, then a senior vice president of the nonpartisan National Wildlife Federation, said that the transformation was "like night and day." He continued, "In the past the committee majority viewed the Clean Air Act as an effective way to protect the public. Now the committee treats the Clean Air Act and the EPA as if they are the enemy. Voters didn't ask for this pro-polluter agenda, but the Koch brothers spent their money well and their presence can be felt."

At the end of 2011, only twenty of the sixty-five Republican members of Congress who responded to a survey were willing to say that they believed climate change was causing the planet to warm. Tim Phillips gladly took credit for the dramatic spike in expressed skepticism. "If you look at where the situation was three years ago and where it is today, there's been a dramatic turnaround," he told the *National Journal*. "Most of these candidates have figured out that the science has become political," he said. "We've made great headway. What it means for candidates on the Republican side is, if you . . . buy into green energy or you play footsie on this issue, you do so at your political peril. The vast majority of people who are involved in the [Republican] nominating process—the conventions and the primaries—are suspect of the science. And that's our influence. Groups like Americans for Prosperity have done it."

Fred Koch, the family patriarch, had a saying, according to a former associate, which was that "the whale that spouts is the one that gets harpooned." As he had warned, the downside to the brothers' increasing visibility was growing public scrutiny. As the donors gathered for their January summit outside Palm Springs at the beginning of 2011, protesters swarmed the hitherto-secret meeting for the first time. Greenpeace, the theatrical environmental group, flew its 135-foot-long "airship" over the resort. Its Day-Glo green blimp was emblazoned with huge blowups of Charles and David's faces along with the words "Koch Brothers: Dirty Money."

The Koch network was no longer a secret. A squadron of local police in riot gear cordoned off the long, winding driveway to the Rancho Mirage resort, which was in virtual lockdown, while a ragtag assortment of protesters out front waved signs proclaiming, "Koch Kills!" and "Uncloak the Kochs!" Some twenty-five arrests were made, and the Kochs' private security guards, wearing gold-colored *K*s in their lapels, threatened to add one more when they caught the *Politico* reporter Kenneth Vogel in the resort's café. Unless he left the premises immediately, they warned, they would make a "citizen's arrest," forcing him to spend "a night in the Riverside County Jail."

Inside the fortified resort, some of America's most celebrated corporate chieftains huddled with Charles Koch, including the DeVos family of Amway, Ken Langone of Home Depot, and Tully Friedman, the private equity tycoon who was also chairman of the American Enterprise Institute. Like besieged royalty, David Koch and his wife, Julia, in dark sunglasses, made a brief appearance from one of the hotel's balconies, from which they grimly surveyed the street theater below.

The heavy-handed security reflected a more combative stance on the part of the Kochs toward the backlash that their outsized role in the public arena was stirring. Confidants described the brothers as obsessed with leaks and stung by the critical press coverage. They seemed surprised and resentful that their growing political influence had resulted in heightened scrutiny. They were accustomed to thinking of themselves as private citizens, and public-spirited ones at that. A golf partner said David "spumed and sputtered" about *The New Yorker* and other publications that had scrutinized the brothers, blaming the media for spurring death threats and forcing his family to hire personal bodyguards.

The Kochs also spoke darkly and inaccurately about the Obama White House conspiring with reporters to smear them. "They somehow thought that they could run tens of millions of dollars in ads, but fly under the radar screen, and that nobody was going to find out," a conservative source familiar with the Kochs told *Politico*. "So they're scrambling now because they weren't nearly as prepared as they should have been."

To handle the growing number of critics, particularly in the press, they brought in a new team of public relations advisers specializing in aggressive tactics. Michael Goldfarb, for instance, a Republican political operative whom the company hired at this point to improve its image, was described by *The New York Times* as "a conservative provocateur" who used "a blowtorch as his pen." Goldfarb had worked for Sarah Palin's vice presidential campaign, where he described his job as "attack the press." Later, he founded an online publication called *The Washington Free Beacon* that practiced what its editor called "combat journalism" against "liberal gasbags." Its motto was "Do unto them." In a profile, one conservative journalist told *The New Republic,* "I mean no disrespect, and I like him personally, but he is the single shadiest person on the right."

Joining Goldfarb was Philip Ellender, co-president of Koch Companies Public Sector, who oversaw the company's lobbying and public relations operations in Washington and who had a reputation, as *Politico* described it, for using "tactics that have helped cement the view that the Kochs play rough." Ellender oversaw a crisis communication project that included frequent polling to assess damage to the company's public image. To fight back, he launched a pugnacious corporate Web site called KochFacts that waged ad hominem attacks, questioning the professionalism and integrity of reporters whose work the company found unflattering, ranging from *The New York Times* to *Politico*. Brass-knuckle tactics were nothing new for the Koch brothers, but they were now deploying them against legitimate news reporters.

I got a taste of these tactics on the afternoon of January 3, 2011, when an e-mail popped onto my screen from David Remnick, the editor of *The New Yorker,* where I had been a staff writer since 1994. Remnick is a brilliant and busy editor who doesn't bother his writers unnecessarily. When he gets in touch, there's usually a good reason.

In his e-mail, Remnick explained that ten minutes earlier he'd received a baffling inquiry about me from Keith Kelly, the reporter who covered the media industry for the *New York Post*. Unsure how to respond, Remnick forwarded it and asked, "Can you help me out on this stuff?" He added courteously, "Sorry to bother you with this."

"Hi," Kelly's inquiry began, breezily. "We're hearing that a right-wing blogger may be preparing to let fly some pretty serious claims against Jane Mayer. On the one hand, it may be seen as payback for her bringdown of the Koch Brothers in August 2010."

His reference was to a ten-thousand-word article I had

written for *The New Yorker* five months earlier, titled "Covert Operations," with the reading line "The billionaire brothers who are waging a war against Obama." The story revealed in depth for the first time how the publicity-shy Koch brothers had stealthily leveraged their vast fortune to exert outsized influence over American politics. It also showed that their environmental and safety record was woefully at odds with their burnished public images as selfless philanthropists.

I had previously devoted the same amount of space in *The New Yorker* to profiling another such plutocratic donor, George Soros, a billionaire investor who spent a fortune underwriting liberal organizations and candidates. Soros hadn't liked the story, but he'd accepted that tough questions were to be expected from the press in a democracy. In contrast, when the *New Yorker* story on the Kochs came out, the brothers were enraged. Their company's general counsel, Mark Holden, later described the story as "a wake-up call," admitting, "We didn't have a response that was ready to go." Spearheading an aggressive damage-control effort, he soon sent a letter of complaint to the magazine. He was unable to identify any factual errors but argued that contrary to the article's title, "Covert Operations," there was nothing secretive or "covert" about them. Yet the Kochs, unlike Soros, had declined to grant *The New Yorker* an interview. Instead, after our story ran, David Koch denounced it in *The Daily Beast* as "hateful," "ludicrous," and "plain wrong." But his complaints lacked specificity, requiring no corrections, and so the magazine stood by the story, and we moved on. The calm, however, was deceptive.

In a squat Washington office building three blocks from the White House, a boiler room operation formed. Beginning in the summer of 2010, as the Kochs were ramping up spending on the midterm elections, half a dozen or so highly paid operatives labored secretly in borrowed office space in the back of the lobbying firm run by the former congressman J. C.

Watts. Their aim, according to a well-informed source, was to counteract *The New Yorker*'s story on the Koch brothers by undermining me. "Dirt, dirt, dirt" is what the source later told me they were digging for in my life. "If they couldn't find it, they'd create it."

Reprising the intimidating tactics that critics of Koch Industries had complained of for years, a private investigative firm with powerful political and law enforcement connections was retained. The firm, it appears, was Vigilant Resources International, whose founder and chairman, Howard Safir, had been New York City's police commissioner under the former mayor Rudolph Giuliani. The firm advertised itself as upholding "the highest standards of confidentiality and discretion."

It's uncommon for a private detective to be hired to conduct a retaliatory investigation into a reporter's character. It is after all the job of the press to cover politics. How much, if at all, the Kochs were personally involved in these activities remains unclear. Often private investigators are hired indirectly, working for law firms retained by the principals, so that they can claim attorney-client privilege, preserve deniability, and erase fingerprints. Asked whether he had investigated me, Howard Safir said only, "I don't comment. I don't confirm or deny it." His son, Adam Safir, who worked with him in the firm, also declined to comment. An effort to interview Charles and David Koch resulted in an e-mail from their company's spokesman, Steve Lombardo, saying simply, "We will have to decline." Asked in a follow-up e-mail whether the company had mounted a private investigation into me, he declined to respond.

However, clues leading back to the Kochs were everywhere. Sources described Goldfarb, Ellender, and other Koch Industries personnel as deeply involved in the project. Leading it, one source said, was Nancy Pfotenhauer, a longtime member of the Kochs' inner circle who has served as a Koch Industries spokesperson, as the head of its Washington office, and as the president of Americans for Prosperity.

I had no inkling about this until that fall, when, a few months after my story ran, a blogger called me to ask if I had heard the rumor that I was the target of some sort of cloak-and-dagger private detective's investigation. I laughed it off. At a Christmas party that winter, I was equally nonchalant when a former reporter pulled me aside with an odd warning. "This may be nothing," she said, but a private investigator she knew had mentioned there were a couple of conservative billionaires who wanted help digging up dirt on a Washington reporter. The reporter had written a story they disliked. "It occurred to me afterward that the reporter they wanted to investigate might be you."

These warnings flashed through my mind as I read the e-mail that Remnick forwarded from the *New York Post* reporter that afternoon in January. Kelly, the *Post* reporter, was hoping to get comment on "allegations" that he said were about to be published against me, claiming that I had "borrowed heavily" from other reporters' work. Before I had the chance to respond, though, a second set of e-mails reached both Remnick and me. This time the sender was Jonathan Strong, then a reporter at the online conservative news site *The Daily Caller,* whose editor, Tucker Carlson, was a senior fellow at the Cato Institute. Strong, too, it appeared, was about to publish a hit piece on me. His e-mails were ominous, asking Remnick outright whether my work fell "within the realm of plagiarism." He provided several samples of my writing and demanded an answer by ten o'clock the next morning.

Plagiarism ranks pretty high up on the list of crimes of moral turpitude in journalism. In a business where your name and credibility are everything, allegations like these could prove ruinous. Upon close inspection, though, it became clear that the allegations were inane and easily refutable. Someone, probably using a computer program, had mechanically sifted through almost a decade of my work and isolated quotations from officials, and other widely repeated phrases, to argue that "the structure and wording" were "quite close" to four other reporters' news stories. None of the supposedly purloined sentences were of any particular significance. This wasn't the sort of material anyone who actually knew anything about journalism would pay any attention to. Even sillier, in two of the four stories I was alleged to have "plagiarized," I had specifically given credit to the authors whose work *The Daily Caller* was claiming I'd stolen.

In twenty-five years of journalism, I'd made my share of spectacular mistakes, but no one had ever accused me of misappropriating their work. In fact, I'd always gone out of my way to credit others. But I also knew that if these charges weren't answered immediately, the truth would scarcely matter. Once the smear got into print, people would assume that there must have been *something* to it.

I was later told that by cooking up these charges, the boiler room operatives felt close to victory. "They thought they had you. They thought they were going to be knighted by the Kochs," said one source. Their search for dirt had started with my personal life, I was told, but when that turned up nothing truly incriminating, they moved on to plagiarism.

With only a few hours before these allegations were set to go online, all I could do was to try to get out the truth before the lies were spread. By midnight, I had reached three of the four authors from whom I was alleged to have plagiarized. All offered to make public statements supporting me and denying I had misappropriated their work. *The Daily Caller's* reporter hadn't even interviewed them.

Lee Fang, a blogger for the liberal Web site *ThinkProgress* whose pathbreaking work on the Kochs I had cited in my story, issued a statement saying, "These accusations are without merit." He went on, "Ms. Mayer properly credited me in her story, and clearly did a ton of her own research. I have nothing but admiration for her integrity as a journalist."

Paul Kane, a reporter at *The Washington Post,* quickly looked up the story in question and sent me an e-mail saying, "Not only did you not steal from me, you Frickin' credited me in the VERY NEXT line." *The New Yorker* had even linked to his story online. And, I later learned, my husband, who was then an editor at *The Washington Post,* had edited the story that I supposedly stole. The allegations were becoming comical. The third reporter I reached also gave a statement saying she had no complaints. Later, the fourth did as well. If this was the best opposition research money could buy, it was pretty shoddy.

I sent the facts to *The Daily Caller,* which, after confirming them, dropped the story.

But Keith Kelly, to his credit, kept reporting. He tried to press the Koch spokesmen on whether they were behind the smear but, interestingly, got no response. He wrote a follow-up called "Smear Disappears," asking, "Who is behind the apparently concerted campaign to smear the New Yorker's Jane Mayer?" He noted, "The story is dead but the person or persons behind the allegations remains a shadowy mystery." He asked *The Daily Caller*'s editor, Carlson, who its source was, but Carlson claimed, "I have no clue where we got it."

There actually was a big clue. The plagiarism ploy had been timed to try to stop *The New Yorker* from nominating the Koch story for a National Magazine Award, according to the *New York Post.* And when *The New Yorker* went ahead and nominated the story anyway, the Kochs tried to stand in the way. Koch Industries' general counsel, Holden, sent a highly unusual letter to the board of the American Society of Magazine Editors, trying to stop it from picking my story for the prize. (The story didn't win anyway. *Que sera.*)

By then, as David Remnick told the *New York Post,* the

whole opposition research campaign seemed "pathetic." He added derisively, "I'm a little surprised to see a big-time operation behave like a bunch of Inspector Clouseaus."

The Kochs also went after Ed Crane, the Cato Institute head, who admitted to having been behind an unattributed quotation in my *New Yorker* story making light of Charles's "Market-Based Management" system. In response, shortly before the January 2011 summit, Charles invoked his ownership of Cato shares to force a management change, insisting that two longtime company loyalists, Nancy Pfotenhauer and Kevin Gentry, neither of whom was known as a deep libertarian thinker, join the think tank's board. Crane, who had co-founded Cato, was furious, but it was prelude to the final shake-up later that year in which Charles and David forced him out completely. David reportedly told Cato's chairman of the board, Robert Levy, that instead of producing esoteric intellectual theories, the ostensibly nonpartisan think tank should provide "intellectual ammunition that we can then use at Americans for Prosperity and our allied organizations" to influence elections.

If anything, the Kochs' ham-fisted reaction to criticism, and sense of aggrieved embattlement, seem to have only spurred their backers on, because by the time they left the guarded enclave near Palm Springs on February 1, 2011, the Koch coffers had $49 million more to spend. The bidding during the final fund-raising spree was so exuberant that one hotel staffer claimed he heard donors making pledges in increments of $5 million. With the House of Representatives safely delivered, the group was now on a roll, looking ahead to finishing off Obama once and for all in 2012.

First, though, there was a lot of discussion about how they could help the Republicans in the House, now that the GOP had the majority. Sean Noble, who continued as a contract political consultant to the Kochs, was pushing hard for them to start by helping Paul Ryan, the Wisconsin congressman who was the incoming chairman of the House Budget Committee.

For the big donors, Ryan was a superstar, a square-jawed, blue-eyed, earnest young Ayn Rand disciple described as "wonky" so often it seemed affixed to his title. His problem, though, was that his budget-slashing ideas scared the public, horrified liberals, and worried many Republicans, too. As he put it himself, "There's a lot of sharp knives in my drawer."

In the coming congressional session, Ryan planned to introduce a budget proposal that would serve as a blueprint for hard-line fiscal conservatives. No one expected it to pass in 2011, because the Democrats still held the Senate and the White House. But if Ryan gathered enough support, he could push the party hard to the right, tie Obama in knots, and provide a first draft for the GOP's 2012 platform. Tactically, a lot was riding on his success.

For several years, Ryan had been advocating radically deep cuts in government spending, including to Medicare and Medicaid, the two main government health programs for the elderly and the poor. He had also floated the idea of partially privatizing Social Security by introducing alternative private retirement accounts. He argued that the bloodletting was necessary for the country's fiscal health. The deficit, in his view, was reaching a crisis level, and these programs were unsustainable. His ideas were wildly popular with most of the wealthy donors. As the country's highest taxpayers, they would be the biggest beneficiaries of the tax savings produced by spending cuts. Moreover, none of them needed to rely on government social services for their health or welfare.

But many of Ryan's ideas were anathema to much of the middle class. When President George W. Bush had tried to privatize Social Security, a plan pushed by the Cato Institute, he had been forced to retreat in the face of overwhelming public opposition. The reality was that despite mobilizing the Tea

Party, the big conservative donors had a number of different priorities from the less affluent followers. Tea Party leaders had deliberately "fudged" their agenda on Social Security in order not to alienate the followers, according to one study. They talked in vague terms about keeping America from "going broke" but avoided specifics. Meanwhile, not one grassroots Tea Party supporter encountered by the study's authors argued for privatizing Social Security. Entitlement programs aiding the middle class were in fact so popular with most Americans that they were virtually sacrosanct. While rich free-market enthusiasts often favored replacing these programs with market-oriented alternatives, polls showed that virtually everyone else was adamantly opposed to the kinds of changes that Newt Gingrich candidly called "right-wing social engineering."

To popularize his radical budget plan, Ryan would need help, and Noble soon came up with a way for the donors to deliver it. He suggested they pay for expensive private polling and market testing to help Ryan fine-tune his pitch, as well as a campaign by "Astroturf" groups to create a drumbeat of public support. It was an intriguing idea, but it teetered on the edge of impropriety. Drafting the government's annual budget was a core congressional function.

At first, in the beginning of 2011, the donors were unenthused about the idea. Having already paid for an expensive election, they didn't understand why they now also needed to pay for polling and focus groups about government policy. But in the following months, this changed, and mysterious money from the Koch network started flowing. Much of it moved from the donors to a 501(c)(4) "social welfare" group cryptically called the TC4 Trust, working closely with a subgroup focused on budget issues called Public Notice. The TC4 Trust was little more than a UPS box in Alexandria, Virginia, but between 2009 and 2011 it reported revenue to the IRS of approximately $46 million and gave away some $37 million to other conservative nonprofit groups. It defined itself as a free-market advocacy group and filed papers with the IRS proclaiming that "the grant funds shall not be used for political activity." But it soon was paying for polling and a public advocacy campaign aimed at shaping and selling the Republican budget.

Ed Goeas, the president of the Tarrance Group, a Republican polling company that worked on the budget project, said that the challenge was to minimize political damage from cuts to entitlement spending. "It wasn't about developing policy," Goeas said, "it was about selling it." The solution, it appears, was to avoid the frank use of the word "cut" when talking about Medicare or Social Security. "There was discussion that you could deal with it as 'getting your money's worth out of the government,'" said Goeas. "You could talk about it as 'more effective'—but not as cutting it. It had to be more about 'efficiencies.' That was a large part of it," he said. Public Notice, which paid for the research, also mounted a public advocacy campaign describing the deficit as a looming catastrophe. "Public Notice was one of the Koch Brothers' groups," Goeas confirmed, adding that his firm worked "for it for three or four years" while simultaneously advising Ryan.

Ryan evidently proved eminently teachable. He was expert in the fine print of the budget but less certain about the public relations. So long as what emerged from these sessions was in line with his values, he was described as grateful for the help. Moreover, unlike most such advice, it came prepaid. As President Obama worked up his own budget proposal that spring, a process at the heart of governing, he had no idea that some of the richest people in the country, with huge stakes in the outcome, were partly paying to shape and sell the Republican alternative.

As the attention lavished on Ryan suggested, tax issues loomed large on the victorious donors' agenda. Dull though the mechanics can be, as Neera Tanden, the president of the liberal Center for American Progress, puts it, "When oligarchs control the levers of government, they get the spoils. It's litigated through tax policy."

Even before the Republicans formally took control of the House, the president felt forced into making concessions on tax issues vital to the donor class. In December 2010, he reached a deal that temporarily extended unemployment benefits to the millions of Americans still out of work, along with reducing payroll taxes and providing other help for the middle class. In exchange, Obama gave Republicans what they most wanted—an extension of the Bush-era income tax cuts that had disproportionately benefited the wealthy, which were slated to automatically expire.

Those cuts had lowered the top income tax rate from 39.6 percent to 35 percent. With bipartisan support, Bush had also slashed taxes on unearned income, most of which went to the rich. Taxes on dividends, for instance, were reduced dramatically from 39.6 percent to 15 percent. Taxes on capital gains, the overwhelming bulk of which were reaped by the wealthy, fell from 20 percent to 15 percent. As a result, many of the richest Americans were taxed at lower rates than middle- and working-class wage earners.

A 2008 study of the wealthiest four hundred taxpayers, for instance, showed that they earned an average of $202 million and paid an effective income tax rate of less than 20 percent. Fully 60 percent of their declared income derived from capital gains. In other words, the effective tax rate on earning $202 million was lower than the rate paid by Americans earning $34,501 a year.

The tax code hadn't always been so lopsided. As income grew increasingly concentrated at the top during the twentieth century, the tax code grew more generous to those with extreme wealth in response to the political pressure they put on lawmakers. The first peacetime income tax was enacted in 1894 as the result of William Jennings Bryan's Populist movement and

applied to only the richest eighty-five thousand Americans out
of a population of sixty-five million, or the top 0.1 percent. But
the Supreme Court struck it down after the robber barons waged
a proxy legal battle. Eighteen years later, the Sixteenth Amendment to the Constitution legalized the income tax, which in the
beginning was only levied on the very rich. Rates were especially high in wartimes, when the taxes were seen as part of
the patriotic duty of the privileged. During World War I, top
earners paid a rate of 77 percent, and during World War II they
paid a rate of 94 percent. (It was this tax that the Scaife family
had avoided with its elaborate trusts and foundations.)

Soon, though, those at the very top succeeded in shifting
the burden to those beneath them, so that by 1942 nearly two-
thirds of the population paid income taxes. The rates remained
relatively progressive for decades, with the top bracket paying
a 50 percent rate in 1981. But the 1970s kicked off a three-
decade-long "tax-cutting spree" during which the wealthiest
1 percent succeeded in getting their average effective federal
tax rate slashed by a third, and the very, very richest, the 0.01
percent of the population, did even better, getting its effective
federal tax rate cut in half. Unsurprisingly, the distribution of
wealth in America grew increasingly skewed.

Critics argued that the extraordinarily rich had managed
to shirk their fair share. But this was not how Charles Koch
looked at it. He argued that "there is no 'fair share'" of the tax
burden. The notion that cutting taxes on the wealthy shifted
the burden to others, he said, was a false premise. Everyone's
taxes should be cut, he argued. The aim, he said, was to shrink
the government. "Our goal," he wrote in an impassioned essay
in 1978, is "not to *reallocate* the burden of government; our goal
is to *roll back* government."

From the standpoint of a radically antigovernment libertarian, paying lower taxes wasn't a matter of greed; it was a
matter of principle. Libertarianism elevated tax avoidance into
a principled crusade. Indeed, Koch argued that it was a moral

act for the wealthy to cut their own taxes. As he put it in the same essay, "Morally, lowering taxes is simply *defending* property rights." It was, as the Libertarian Party platform put it in 1980, the responsibility of citizens to "challenge the cult of the omnipotent state."

Foster Friess, the Wyoming mutual fund manager who had joined political forces with the Kochs since the 1980s, depicted opposition to taxes as selfless too, but from a slightly different angle. He argued that the public benefited more when the wealthy paid less because the rich could do more good with their money than the government. "Wealthy people self-tax," he argued, by contributing to charities. "It's a question—do you believe the government should be taking your money and spending it for you, or do you want to spend it for you?" He argued, "It's that top 1 percent that probably contributes more to making the world a better place than the 99 percent."

Charles Koch, however, favored neither taxes nor charity. As he explained in a speech in 1999, "I agree with the 12th century philosopher, Maimonides, who defined the highest form of charity as dispensing with charity altogether, by enabling your fellow humans to have the wherewithal to earn their own living."

But according to the cultural critic and Jewish scholar Leon Wieseltier, who has taught several university courses on Maimonides, "This is false and tendentious and idiotic." He explains, "Maimonides did indeed prize the sort of charity that made its recipient more self-reliant, but he believed that the duty of charity is permanent" and that the responsibility to help the poor was "unequivocal and absolute." In fact, he points out, Maimonides declared that "he who averts his eyes from the obligation of charity is regarded as a villain."

While Koch and others in his group described their opposition to taxes as matters of pure principle, they put the Obama administration under constant pressure to accept tax cuts that directly increased their own wealth at the expense of everyone else. To reach the deal in December 2010, for instance, Republican negotiators insisted on cuts in estate taxes that would cost the Treasury $23 billion and save some sixty-six hundred of the wealthiest taxpayers an average of $1.5 million each.

The demand didn't materialize out of thin air. For years, some of the Republican Party's wealthiest backers, including the Kochs and the DeVoses, had been agitating to abolish what were cleverly dubbed "death taxes." The Kochs joined with sixteen of the other richest families in the country, including the Waltons of Walmart and the Mars candy clan, in financing and coordinating a massive, multiyear campaign to reduce and eventually repeal inheritance taxes. According to one 2006 report, these seventeen families stood to save $71 billion from the tax change, explaining why they willingly spent almost half a billion collectively, lobbying for it, beginning in 1998.

They were represented by a handful of front groups, including the American Family Business Institute, which strove to cast the tax break as necessary to preserve family farms. Unfortunately, in 2001, the group couldn't find a single family farm put out of business by the estate tax. After Hurricane Katrina, the same group scoured the country to find a storm victim whose heirs were hurt by the estate tax, in order to create some sympathy for its cause, but again failed to find a single one. In truth, only 0.27 percent of all estates were wealthy enough to be affected by estate taxes.

The lengths that some members of the Kochs' donor circle went to, hoping to ensure the biggest possible share of their family's fortunes, were impressive. The Koch brothers were far from alone in having litigated aggressively against their relatives. One member of their network during this period, Susan Gore, heiress to a piece of the Gore-Tex fabric fortune and founder of a conservative think tank called the Wyoming Liberty Group, was so intent on increasing her personal inheritance that she tried to legally adopt her ex-husband in order to claim that she had as many children as her siblings and thereby enlarge her portion of the family trust. But in late 2011, a judge rejected the seventy-two-year-old heiress's scheme, ruling that she could not count her former husband as her "son."

Although it enraged progressives, President Obama reluctantly consented to many of the Republicans' demands, including the enlarged exemptions from the estate tax. He had campaigned against extending the Bush tax cuts for those earning over $250,000 a year, but in December 2010, with the Republicans poised to take over the House, he tried to convince his disappointed supporters that this was the best deal they were likely to get for some time. "It used to be that you could govern by peeling off a couple of Republicans to do the right thing," he said, "but now, Glenn Beck and Sarah Palin are the center of the Republican Party—and there is no possibility of cooperation."

December's machinations were just the opening act, it turned out, in an unfolding drama in which Republicans in the House would eventually threaten to default on paying America's debts, potentially pitching the fragile U.S. economy into a calamitous free fall, in order to extort further tax and spending concessions favored by wealthy donors. All of this played out against a backdrop of growing economic inequality and stagnating social mobility. The United States, which idealized itself as a classless society in which everyone had the opportunity to get ahead, had in fact fallen behind many other rich nations in terms of intergenerational economic mobility, including such old-world, class-bound countries as France, Germany, and Spain.

Advancing the agenda of America's wealthiest winners under such circumstances would ordinarily be a hard sell. After all, in 2011, twenty-four million Americans were still out of work. The Great Recession had wiped out some $9 trillion in household wealth. But after forty years, the conservative nonprofit ecosystem had grown quite adept at waging battles of ideas. The think tanks, advocacy groups, and talking heads on the right sprang into action, shaping a political narrative that staved off the kind of course correction that might otherwise have been expected.

A key skirmish in this battle was the reframing of the history of the 2008 economic crash. From an empirical standpoint, it was hard to see it as anything other than a wipeout for the proponents of free-market fundamentalism and an argument for stronger government regulations. Like the Great Depression, it might have been expected to produce a backlash against those seen as irresponsible profiteers, resulting in more government intervention and a fairer tax system.

Joseph Stiglitz, the liberal economist, described the 2008 financial meltdown as the equivalent for free-market advocates to the fall of the Berlin Wall for Communists. Even the former Federal Reserve chairman Alan Greenspan, Washington's free-market wise man nonpareil, admitted that he'd been wrong in thinking Adam Smith's invisible hand would save business from its own self-destruction. Potentially, the disaster was a "teachable moment" from which the country's economic conservatives could learn. This is not what happened, however. They instead started with their preferred conclusion and worked backward to reach it.

In what the economic writer and asset manager Barry Ritholtz labeled Wall Street's "big lie," scholars at conservative think tanks argued that the problem had been too much government, not too little. The lead role in the revisionism was played by the American Enterprise Institute, whose board was stocked with financial industry titans, many of whom were free-market zealots and regulars at the Koch donor seminars.

Specifically, AEI argued that government programs that helped low-income home buyers get mortgages caused the collapse. Ritholtz noted that these theories "failed to withstand even casual scrutiny." There was plenty wrong with the government's quasi-private mortgage lenders, Fannie Mae and Freddie Mac, but numerous nonpartisan studies ranging from Harvard University's Joint Center for Housing Studies to the Government Accountability Office proved they were not a major cause of the 2008 crash. Yet by shifting the blame, Ritholtz noted, those "whose bad judgment and failed philosophy helped cause the crisis" could continue to champion the "false narrative" that free markets "require no adult supervision."

Self-serving research from corporate-backed conservative think tanks wasn't exactly news by 2011, but what was surprising, Ritholtz contended, was that "they are winning. Thanks to the endless repetition of the big lie." Phil Angelides, the chairman of the bipartisan commission that Congress set up to investigate the causes of the crash, was also taken aback by the revisionism. In an op-ed column, he tried to remind the public that it had been "the recklessness of the financial industry and the abject failures of policymakers and regulators that brought the economy to its knees." Instead, though, he said, "those at the top of the economic heap" were peddling "shopworn data" that had been "analyzed and debunked by the committee." He conceded that history was written by the winners and that by 2011, while much of the country lagged behind, most of the financial sector had bounced back and "the historical rewrite is in full swing."

Soon politicians backed by the same conservative donors who funded the think tanks were echoing the "big lie." Marco Rubio, a rising Republican star from Florida, for instance, who had defeated a moderate in the 2010 Republican Senate primary with the help of forty-nine donors from the June 2010 Koch seminar, soon proclaimed, "This idea—that our problems were caused by a government that was too small—it's just not true. In fact, a major cause of our recent downturn was a housing crisis created by reckless government policies."

Against this backdrop, on April 15, 2011, Ryan's budget

plan, now packaged as "The Path to Prosperity," came up for a vote in the House of Representatives. In the past, its prospects had been uncertain at best. Not just Democrats but many Republicans had deemed previous versions too harsh. A year earlier, Speaker of the House John Boehner had given it only lukewarm support. But by then the Republican caucus had moved far to the right, and the proposal had been repackaged. It now passed easily in the House 235–193, losing only four Republican votes but not attracting a single Democrat.

In the name of fixing Medicare, it shrank it to voucher-like "premium supports," with which senior citizens could buy private medical insurance. It also transformed Medicaid into a tattered patchwork of state-run block grants while cutting overall funding. Further, it repealed the Medicaid expansion that was a part of Obama's Affordable Care Act. At the same time, it reduced income taxes into two rates, cutting the top rate down to 25 percent—half of what it was when Ronald Reagan was elected. Theoretically, any losses were to be made up by eliminating deductions, but these were not specified. As the *New York Times* reporter Noam Scheiber summarizes it in *The Escape Artists: How Obama's Team Fumbled the Recovery*, Ryan's plan cut taxes for the wealthy by $2.4 trillion in comparison with Obama's proposed budget and then cut spending by $6.2 trillion. He describes it in short as "right-wing lunacy."

The most shocking aspect was its radical rewrite of America's social contract. To reduce the deficit, Ryan prescribed massive cuts in government spending, 62 percent of which would come from programs for the poor, even though these programs accounted for only about a fifth of the federal budget. According to a *New York Times* analysis of a similar, later version of Ryan's budget, 1.8 million people would be cut off food stamps, 280,000 children would lose their school lunch subsidies, and 300,000 children would lose medical coverage. Robert Greenstein of the liberal Center on Budget and Policy

Priorities called the plan "Robin Hood in reverse," arguing, "It would likely produce the largest redistribution of income from the bottom to the top in modern U.S. history."

The plan was successfully sold, nonetheless, winning a chorus of acclaim from conservative pundits and think tank scholars, whom the Republican leadership had treated to high-level policy briefings. Singing the plan's praise were the Cato Institute, the Heritage Foundation, and Grover Norquist's powerful antitax group, Americans for Tax Reform, which declared, "Paul Ryan's budget is what a REAL conservative budget looks like!" Many other nonprofit advocacy groups, like Public Notice, the 60 Plus Association, the Independent Women's Forum, and American Commitment, also chimed in for the drastic spending cuts. The clamor seemed multitudinous, but beneath the surface each of these groups shared a common aquifer—the pool of cash contributed by the Koch donor network.

A number of opinion writers also embraced Ryan as oracular. David Brooks, a moderately conservative *New York Times* columnist whose opinion Obama valued, declared Ryan's plan "the most courageous budget reform proposal any of us have seen in our lifetimes . . . His proposal will set the standard of seriousness for anybody who wants to play in this discussion. It will become the 2012 Republican platform, no matter who is the nominee."

The broader news media also echoed Ryan's claim that the federal deficit was the most pressing economic issue facing the country. As Freeland noted in *Plutocrats,* in April and May the five largest papers in the country published over three times more stories about the deficit than they did about jobs, even though unemployment was at 9 percent. "The right had succeeded in setting the terms of the economic debate. A good outcome for the 1 percent," she writes.

Ryan's success in convincing much of the Washington

media establishment that he was tackling hard problems, showing leadership, and bravely putting forth a plan to rescue entitlement programs while also fixing the country's daunting deficit threw the White House into a tailspin. It scrambled to put forth its own new alternative plan, which to the dismay of liberals called for additional cuts in spending beyond those the administration had already offered. Top political advisers to the president, like David Plouffe and Bill Daley, had long been preoccupied with looking centrist and winning independent voters, rather than catering to their liberal base, whom Plouffe had memorably dismissed as "bedwetters."

President Obama now proposed $4 trillion in spending cuts over the next twelve years, not all that far from the $4.4 trillion that Ryan had proposed. The proposal so distressed Hillary Clinton, then secretary of state, a colleague said, she had to go outside to get some air.

Then, in what came to be known as "the ambush," the White House invited Ryan to Obama's speech unveiling his counterproposal. With the congressman sitting in front of him, Obama lambasted Ryan's plan as "a vision that says we can't afford to keep the promises we made to our seniors . . . Put simply, it ends Medicare as we know it." Obama accused the Republicans of giving "more than $1 trillion in new tax breaks to the wealthy" and argued that it was "less about reducing the deficit than it's about changing the basic social compact in America."

Ryan was affronted at being attacked so publicly and personally. The breach of decorum became a mini-flap in Washington. Obama later told Bob Woodward that he hadn't known Ryan was there in the auditorium when he delivered his pointed speech. "We made a mistake," he confessed.

Out in the country, where people were less concerned with political etiquette than whether their benefits were about to be slashed, Ryan's proposed Medicare makeover proved immediately toxic. A Democratic underdog in a special congressional election in upstate New York clobbered the expected Republican winner by campaigning against Ryan's Medicare plan.

But the House Republicans were jubilant anyway. They had forced Obama to play their budget game. Instead of talking about jobs and spending, he was talking about the deficit and bargaining with them over how many trillions to cut. "*We* led. *They* reacted to *us*," exulted Kevin McCarthy, the House Republican whip. The donors were excited, too. Just the fact that Obama had been thrown on the defensive convinced those whose fortunes had helped pay for the Ryan plan that their investment was worth it.

———

By the late spring, the House Republicans had Obama in a bind on another issue as well. No sooner had the president reached a temporary budget agreement with the Republicans— one that included large Democratic concessions—than the self-styled "Young Guns," backed by the Tea Party faction in the House, forced a fight over raising the debt ceiling, a pro forma measure long used to authorize payment of the country's financial obligations. It looked as if the Tea Party radicals were protesting profligate spending, but in fact all they were doing was refusing to formally authorize payment of funds that Congress had already appropriated, in essence refusing to pay Congress's credit card bill after the previous year's shopping spree. In the end, their self-destructive fight hurt themselves more than anyone else, but meanwhile the radicals' willingness to pitch the U.S. government into default created a national crisis. The increasingly desperate standoff might produce chaos and dysfunction, but that prospect merely served the conservatives' antigovernment agenda. In the words of Mike Lofgren, a longtime Republican congressional aide, his party was becoming like "an apocalyptic cult."

If Congress failed to pay its bills, the country's AAA credit rating would be downgraded, potentially rocking markets, shaking business confidence, and worsening the painful recession. No one knew exactly how bad the consequences of default would be. Ordinarily, it would be unthinkable. Boehner had warned the insurgents in his caucus that they needed to "deal with it as adults." But Eric Cantor, the House majority leader and a founder of the Young Guns, seized on the debt ceiling vote as what he called "a leverage moment."

By 2011, the extremist upstarts had formed a powerful clique within the party's leadership and appeared itching to challenge Boehner's authority. Many owed more to the Kochs and other radical rich backers than they did to the party. The White House was under the misimpression that stolid business forces within the Republican Party would see the threat to the economy and force the radicals back from the edge. But while more traditional business interests, as represented by the U.S. Chamber of Commerce, took this stance, the right flank of the donor base was urging the Young Guns on to a showdown. In *The Wall Street Journal*, Stanley Druckenmiller, a billionaire hedge fund manager, described government default as less "catastrophic" than "if we don't solve the real problem," by which he meant government spending. And Charles Koch made clear in a March 2011 op-ed piece in *The Wall Street Journal* that he regarded any raise of the debt ceiling as simply a way to "delay tough decisions."

Pushing the Young Guns forward toward the financial cliff was Americans for Prosperity, the Kochs' political arm. Some forty other Tea Party and antitax groups also clamored for all-out war. Among the most vociferous was the Club for Growth, a small, single-minded, Wall Street–founded group powerful for one reason: it had the cash to mount primary challenges against Republicans who didn't hew to its uncompromising line. The club had developed the use of fratricide as a tactic to keep officeholders in line after becoming frustrated that many candidates it backed became more moderate in office. It discovered that all it had to do was threaten a primary challenge, and "they start wetting their pants," one founder joked. Its top funders included many in the Koch network, including the hedge fund managers Robert Mercer and Paul Singer and the private equity tycoon John Childs.

The Young Guns portrayed their opposition to compromise as a matter of pure principle, but beneath the surface huge vested interests were at play. The president and Boehner were close to negotiating what they called a "grand bargain" that anticipated closing some tax loopholes. The Young Guns were categorically opposed to reforms that might cut into the profits of hedge funds and private equity firms.

Cantor was especially protective of the carried-interest tax loophole. For him, the happiness of hedge fund and private equity titans was personal. He was among the House's top recipients of contributions from securities and investment firms. Three of the largest contributors to Cantor's two campaign funds in 2010 were financiers affiliated with the Koch network: Steven Cohen, the billionaire founder of the hugely lucrative hedge fund SAC Capital; Paul Singer, the multimillionaire head of the so-called vulture fund Elliott Management; and Stephen Schwarzman, the billionaire co-founder of the Blackstone Group. So although one study showed that the top twenty-five hedge fund managers earned an average of nearly $600 million a year and that closing this one loophole would raise $20 billion over the next decade, Cantor and the other rebels in the House who professed concern over the deficit "crisis" refused to back Boehner's proposed "grand bargain."

As tensions built in the increasingly calamitous debt ceiling stalemate, two sources say, Boehner traveled to New York to personally beseech David Koch's help. One former adviser to the Koch family says that "Boehner begged David to 'call off the dogs!' He pointed out that if the country defaulted, David's own investments would tank." A spokeswoman for

Boehner, Emily Schillinger, confirmed the visit but insisted, "Anyone who knows Speaker Boehner knows he doesn't 'beg.'" But the spectacle of the Speaker of the House, who was among the most powerful elected officials in the country, third in line in the order of presidential succession, traveling to the Manhattan office of a billionaire businessman to ask for his help in an internecine congressional fight captures just how far the Republican Party's fulcrum of power had shifted toward the outside donors by 2011.

In the final days of July, with default looming, Obama thought he was close to reaching a deal with Boehner. It was an abomination in the eyes of many Democrats because, among other features, it included cuts in projected Medicare and Medicaid spending. Obama had bought into the idea that cutting the deficit was of paramount importance and believed that the deal was necessary to stabilize the economy. He started preparing Democrats on the Hill for the painful news. Yet when the president called Boehner to formalize the agreement the night of July 21, to Obama's growing fury, with the clock ticking dangerously toward default, the Speaker didn't call him back. The president made multiple calls. He left messages. Almost an entire day passed. Finally, when Boehner called, it was to break off the talks, walk away, and then denounce Obama publicly.

"With no basis in fact," according to Thomas Mann and Norman Ornstein's study of congressional dysfunction, *It's Even Worse Than It Looks*, Boehner claimed that the president had reneged on the terms of their agreement. "I gave it my all," Boehner proclaimed. "Unfortunately, the president would not take yes for an answer."

Cantor later told the real story to Ryan Lizza of *The New Yorker*. Blowing up the grand bargain had been his idea. He said it was a "fair assessment" to say that in the critical final moments he had talked Boehner out of accepting the deal for purely political reasons. Cantor had argued, why give Obama a win? Why aid his reelection campaign by helping him look competent? It would be more advantageous for the Republicans to sabotage the talks, regardless of the mess it left the country in, and wait to see if the next year's presidential election brought them a Republican president who would give them a better deal.

The eventual result was what Lizza described as a "byzantine" arrangement in which in order to forestall default, both parties agreed to automatic spending cuts, imposed indiscriminately across the whole budget. No one believed the mindless cuts, which were called a "sequester," would ever get enacted. But in fact, when no other resolution could be reached, they were. The mechanism placed Obama in a fiscal straitjacket indefinitely. The chairman of the Congressional Black Caucus, Emanuel Cleaver, denounced the deal as "a sugar-coated Satan sandwich," which the House minority leader, Pelosi, amended to "a Satan sandwich with Satan fries on the side."

The political damage stretched far and wide. The nonpartisan Congressional Budget Office estimated that the sequester would cost the economy 750,000 jobs a year and hurt millions of Americans who were reliant on public services. Standard & Poor's downgraded America's credit rating for the first time in the country's history. The stock market plummeted, falling 635 points on the spot. The public, meanwhile, was so disgusted with Congress that polls registered the lowest approval rating in the history of such measurements. Obama's popularity also took a hit, dropping below the all-important 50 percent threshold for the first time. He was derided and belittled by both the Left and the Right. Internal polls called him "weak."

A political minority, responding to the interests of its extreme sponsors, had succeeded in rendering the most powerful democracy in the world dysfunctional. Thirty years after the Libertarian Party platform called for the "abolition of Medicare and Medicaid," the "repeal . . . of the increasingly oppressive Social Security System," and "the eventual repeal of all taxation," its billionaire backers had the upper hand.

At this point, Neera Tanden believes, the president finally understood what he was up against. "I think he came in truly trying to be post-partisan," she said. "I think it took the debt ceiling fight to make him see that they hated him more than they wanted to succeed. It was an irrational deal, driven by their funders." Two and a half years into his presidency, she said, "he finally realized they would rather kill him than save themselves."

CHAPTER TWELVE

Mother of All Wars:
The 2012 Setback

ON A SOFT, SUMMERY NIGHT IN BEAVER CREEK, COLORADO, AT
the end of June 2011, the Kochs mustered their troops once
again for what Charles described as "the Mother of All Wars."
The phrase, borrowed from the Iraqi dictator Saddam Hussein,
hinted at the level of martial ferocity with which the billionaire brothers planned to approach the coming 2012 presidential campaign.

It would be the first presidential race after the Supreme
Court's *Citizens United* decision. For those with the requisite
financial resources, political spending was now as limitless as
the open sky above the Bachelor Gulch Ritz-Carlton. Three
hundred or so participants were there for the semiannual seminar, whose theme was "Understanding and Addressing Threats
to American Free Enterprise and Prosperity." This time, the
planners took extra precautions to keep the proceedings secret.
A series of loudspeakers formed a fence around an outdoor
pavilion in which the donors met, emitting static toward the
outside world, to prevent eavesdropping. Or so they thought
until a reporter for *Mother Jones,* Brad Friedman, obtained an
audio recording of the weekend's highlights and published a

As they gathered in the foothills of the Rockies, the donors
had ample reason for optimism. *The New York Times*'s resident
number cruncher, Nate Silver, who handicapped political odds
with the unsentimental eye of a racetrack bookie, was openly
asking, "Is Obama toast?" After analyzing Obama's sagging
approval rating and the economy's lagging indicators, he concluded that Obama had gone from "a modest favorite to win

re-election to, probably, a slight underdog." If the Republicans chose a weak candidate or the economy miraculously revived, he noted, this could change. But if the challengers played it right, he predicted, Obama would go the way of the recent reelection losers Jimmy Carter and George H. W. Bush.

The choice of a strong Republican candidate, however, fifteen months before the next presidential election, was far from assured. Behind the scenes, Sean Noble, with the assent of the Kochs, had been furtively trying for months to persuade Paul Ryan to run for the White House. The billionaire backers were eager for him to apply his "sharp knives" to the federal budget. But Ryan had demurred. Neither he nor his wife relished a presidential marathon. "Wouldn't it be easier just to be picked as vice president?" he asked an emissary from the Kochs, in a meeting in the congressman's Washington office. "Because then it's only, like, two months."

With Ryan declining to run, the Kochs and their operatives searched anxiously for an alternative. Mitt Romney was obviously a serious contender, but they worried that he couldn't relate well enough to ordinary people to get elected. Polls showed that Romney, who had made a fortune in finance before his stint as governor of Massachusetts, fared dismally when voters were asked if he "cares about people like you." The search for a more promising candidate set off a torrid courtship of Chris Christie, the tough-guy governor of New Jersey. David Koch invited Christie to his Manhattan office, where the two spent almost two hours bonding over Christie's brawls with the unions and other liberal forces. The governor's scrappy blue-collar style, combined with his plutocrat-friendly economic policies, made him an almost irresistible prospect. By June, the Kochs had given Christie the keynote speaker slot at their seminar, where he could audition for his party's leading role in front of the people who could pay his way.

Rick Perry, the governor of Texas, who preceded Christie as a speaker, provided a perfect foil. In a prelude to Perry's later "oops" moment during the Republican debates, the governor made a poor impression on the numerically minded business-men in the audience by displaying five fingers to illustrate a four-point plan, only to be left with one digit still waving in the air, programmatically unaccounted for.

In comparison, Christie was the political equivalent of his idol, Bruce Springsteen. David Koch personally introduced him, showering him with praise as not just a "true political hero" who "tells it like it is" but also "my kind of guy." Koch was especially effusive about the "courage and leadership" Chris-tie showed in forging a bipartisan deal to cut future pension and benefit payments to New Jersey's unionized public sector employees. In exchange for these concessions, the Democrats and their union allies had obtained a promise from Christie to increase payments into the ailing funds. This tough-minded seeming "fix" vaulted Christie to national prominence. Four years later, a judge would rule that it was more like a bait and switch. The workers' benefits were cut, but the state, which was in an economic slump, reneged on its end of the bargain. In 2011, however, for the Kochs and their assembled allies, Christie was the cherished face of the future. "Who knows?" Koch teased, as the donors cheered, whistled, and hooted their approval during his introduction. "With his enormous suc-cess in reforming New Jersey, some day we might see him on a larger stage where, God knows, he is desperately needed!"

Christie soon brought the well-heeled crowd to its feet by casting low taxes on high-income earners as a populist cause. In a bravura performance, he described going to battle against what he called a "Millionaires Tax"—a 1 percent income tax increase on the state's top earners. "Take this back where it came from, 'cuz I ain't signin' it," he recounted telling the Democrats as the donors cheered. Christie had campaigned on making his state a superpower in wind energy, but his reversal and withdrawal from a regional program to reduce greenhouse

gas emissions also drew cheers. When it came time for questions from the audience, the first speaker voiced the excitement in the room, saying, "You're the first guy I've seen who I
know could beat Barack Obama," and then, amid laughter and
applause, begged Christie to run.

But the dinner's main course was the fund-raising session
led by Charles Koch. In a folksy midwestern voice, he appealed
for contributions as if America's survival depended on it. After
invoking Saddam Hussein's famous battle cry from the first
Gulf War, Koch struck a more alarmist note. The stakes in the
coming presidential campaign, he warned, were nothing short
of "the life or death of this country." Not, he added with good
humor, that he was trying to "put any pressure on anyone here,
mind you. This is not pressure. But if this makes your heart
feel glad and you want to be more forthcoming, so be it." Then,
in a move guaranteed to put the squeeze on everyone else, he
publicly identified and commended the largest donors to date.
"What I want to do is recognize not all our great partners, but
those partners who have given more than a billion—a mill—no,
billion," at which point he caught and corrected himself. As the
wealthy crowd knowingly guffawed at the easy confusion over
a few extra zeros, Charles ad-libbed, "Well, I was thinking of
Obama and his billion dollar campaign, so I thought we gotta
do better than that." He went on, "If you want to kick in a billion, believe me, we'll have a special seminar just for you."

Charles then ticked off the names of the thirty-two donors
who had contributed a million dollars or more during the previous twelve months. Nine were billionaires whose fortunes
had landed them on *Forbes*'s list of the four hundred wealthiest
Americans. Some, like the finance stars Charles Schwab, Ken
Griffin, and Paul Singer, as well as Amway's Richard DeVos
and the natural gas entrepreneur Harold Hamm, were fairly
well-known. Many others, though, were members of the invisible rich—owners of enormously profitable private enterprises

that rarely drew public attention. Two among the nine billionaires, for instance, John Menard Jr., whose fortune *Forbes* estimated at $6 billion, and Diane Hendricks, whose fortune the magazine valued at $2.9 billion, owned private building and home supply companies in Wisconsin and were not well-known outside the state, let alone in it. Many of the nonbillionaires whom Charles recognized were familiar faces in the Kochs' circle. There were the Popes from North Carolina, the Friess family from Wyoming, and the Robertsons of the Texas oil clan, as well as coal barons like Joe Craft and the Gilliams and members of the Marshall family, the only significant outside owners of Koch Industries' stock.

Charles then added, "Ten more will remain anonymous, including David and me. So we're very humble in that," he joked. More seriously, though, he declared that "the plan is, the next seminar, I'm going to read the names of the *ten* million"—not mere one million—dollar donors.

As he read the names of the generous, he made clear what he expected their money to buy. He promised those he referred to as his "partners" that "we are absolutely going to do our utmost to invest this money wisely and get the best possible payoff for you in the future of the country."

None of these thoughts were shared with the rest of the country. Far from the Supreme Court majority's assumption in the *Citizens United* case that political spending would be transparent, the Kochs and their partners took great pains to hide what they were up to. Indeed this was a selling point. Kevin Gentry, vice president of Koch Industries for special projects, who had overseen fund-raising for the brothers for years and who played the role of master of ceremonies at the seminars, assured the donors that weekend, "There is anonymity we can protect."

The Kochs had recently come up with a new and even cleverer way of masking the money. Rather than simply directing the funds through the maze of secretive nonprofit charities and social welfare groups that they had used during the 2010 campaign, they now established a more efficient method. They pooled much of the cash first in a form of nonprofit corporation that the tax code defined as a 501(c)(6), or a "business league." The advantage of this umbrella organization, which they named the Association for American Innovation (AAI), was that donations to it could be classified as "membership dues" and to some extent get deducted as business expenses. As with contributions to a 501(c)(4), the law protected the donors' anonymity. But as a business league, it fell outside the charitable trust purview of state attorneys general, further safeguarding the secrecy.

By the time the Beaver Creek seminar adjourned, the Kochs had collected some $70 million in new pledges. There is no public record showing specifically how these new funds were spent, but it appears that much of the money was directed into the new "business league," the Association for American Innovation. During 2011 alone, tax records show, the AAI, which soon changed its name to Freedom Partners, accumulated over a quarter of a billion dollars.

The new business league, which was at first run by Wayne Gable, the head of lobbying for Koch Industries, was less than candid with the Internal Revenue Service about its intentions. According to its founding documents, it told the IRS it "does not currently plan to attempt to influence any election" and in the future might do so but only to "an insubstantial" extent. From the start, however, the organization financed many of the same political front groups that the Kochs had mobilized in the 2010 midterms. This time, though, their underground guerrilla war against Obama was waged by a "business league" and treated as a partially tax-deductible business expense. From November 2011 to October 2012, the Kochs' new "business league" transferred $115 million to Sean Noble's Center to Protect Patient Rights and $32.3 million to David Koch's group, Americans for Prosperity.

In October 2011, Christie announced definitively that 2012 was not his year. The truism about the two parties was that when it came to choosing candidates, "Democrats fall in love, while Republicans fall in line." But 2012 was shaping up to be the exception. With power shifting from the centralized party professionals to rogue billionaires, top-down consensus was giving way to warring factions. Even within the Koch camp, there were divergent opinions. After the infatuation with Ryan, David Koch liked Christie. Charles Koch admired Mike Pence, then a congressman and later governor of Indiana. When Pence declined to get in the race, the Kochs hired his former chief of staff, Marc Short, as yet another political adviser. The donors, meanwhile, were all over the Republican lot. Noble was trying hard to herd everyone in one direction but failing.

Unsure what else to do, in late 2011 the Koch operatives made one of the first attack ads of the general election season. Sponsored by Americans for Prosperity, it slammed Obama as corruptly showering his friends with "green giveaways" such as Solyndra. AFP spent $2.4 million running the ad thousands of times in the key states of Florida, Michigan, Nevada, and Virginia. Sean Noble had sold the idea as a clean shot. But it caused a little problem. One of the Koch donors turned out to have invested in Solyndra and was not happy.

A subsequent Koch-created ad, aired by the American Future Fund, also proved problematic. The mysterious Iowa-based front group was a favorite choice for messages from which the Koch camp preferred to distance itself. Shot as populist rage against the "1 percent" was coalescing in the Occupy movement and protesters were marching on David Koch's apartment, the ad slyly attacked Obama for being too cozy with Wall Street. After quoting Obama calling Wall Street bankers "fat cats," it asked, "Guess who voted for the Wall Street bailout? His White House is full of Wall Street executives," it went on, as mug shots of Obama's advisers flashed by. The Kochs' political operatives tested the ad in fifteen separate focus groups. Once aired, it seemed to be a great success, getting over five million hits on YouTube. But some of the finance industry executives in the donor group were not amused by the political misdirection. "Why attack Wall Street?" they asked.

One donor, Peter Schiff, an attendee at the June Koch seminar, evidently didn't receive the new, populist talking points. A Connecticut financial analyst and broker, he barged into the midst of the Occupy movement's Manhattan encampment in October with a sign proclaiming, "I am the 1%. Let's talk." Subsequent video footage of him arguing in favor of eliminating the minimum wage and paying "mentally retarded" people $2 an hour made him a laughingstock on Jon Stewart's *Daily Show*. The Kochs' "Mother of All Wars" wasn't starting out all that much better than Saddam Hussein's.

The picture was far brighter in the key presidential battleground state of Wisconsin. There, the first-term governor, Scott Walker, had vaulted to national stardom by enacting unexpectedly bold anti-union policies. Walker exemplified the new generation of Republicans who had coasted to victory in 2010 on a wave of dark money, ready to implement policies their backers had painstakingly incubated in conservative nonprofits for decades.

For the Koch network, Walker's improbable rise was a triumph. Koch Industries PAC was the second-largest contributor to Walker's campaign. More important, the Kochs were an important source of funds to the Republican Governors Association, which Republicans used in Wisconsin and elsewhere in 2010 to work around strict state contribution limits. The Kochs' PAC had also contributed to sixteen state legislative candidates in Wisconsin, who all won their races, helping conservatives take control of both houses of the legislature and setting the stage for Wisconsin's dramatic turn to the right.

Walker had also benefited enormously from the philanthropy of two other archconservative brothers, the late Lynde and Harry Bradley, whose foundation had grown into an ideological behemoth in Milwaukee. Walker's campaign manager, Michael Grebe, was the Bradley Foundation's president. Think tanks had long supplied policy ideas to those in power. Some, like the liberal Center for American Progress, were led by well-known partisans who moved in and out of government. It was rare, though, to wear both hats simultaneously. But Grebe's dual role would have made his predecessor at the Bradley Foundation, Michael Joyce, proud. It was exactly the kind of hands-on political impact Joyce had sought when he set out to weaponize conservative philanthropy.

The Bradley Foundation's close ties to Walker were evident on his social calendar. Among his first private engagements after the election was a celebratory dinner with the foundation's board and senior staff at Bacchus, a stylish Milwaukee restaurant overlooking Lake Michigan. By then, Lynde and Harry Bradley's foundation had assets of over $612 million and had provided the playbook for many of Walker's policies.

Grebe denied his foundation had hatched the initiative that made Walker famous, his crackdown on the state employees' unions. But he applauded the move and had personally sent out fund-raising letters asking supporters to help Walker fight "the big government union bosses." The Bradley Foundation, meanwhile, in 2009, gave huge grants to two conservative Wisconsin think tanks developing plans to break the power of the state's public employee unions. As the *Milwaukee Journal Sentinel* noted in 2011, the Bradley Foundation was "one of the most powerful philanthropic forces behind America's conservative movement" and "the financial backer behind public policy experiments that started in the state and spread across the nation—including welfare reform, public vouchers for private schools and, this year, cutbacks in public employee benefits and collective bargaining." As Grebe later acknowledged about Walker's meteoric rise to *The New York Times*, "At the risk of being immodest, I probably lent some credibility to his campaign early on."

As a college dropout with no exceptional charisma or charm, Walker might not ordinarily have been marked for high office, but Americans for Prosperity, which had a large chapter in Wisconsin, had provided him with a field operation and speaking platform at its Tea Party rallies when he was still just the Milwaukee county executive. The Kochs' political organization had been fighting the state's powerful public employee unions there since 2007. The fight was freighted with larger significance. In 1959, Wisconsin had become the first state to allow its public employees to form unions and engage in collective bargaining, which conservatives detested in part because the unions provided a big chunk of muscle to the Democratic Party. "We go back a long way on this in Wisconsin, and in other states," Tim Phillips, the head of Americans for Prosperity, acknowledged to *Politico*. In the past, Phillips had spoken enviously of the unions as the Left's "army on the ground."

Walker's anti-union, antitax, and small-government message harmonized perfectly with the Kochs' philosophy and also served their business interests. Koch Industries had two Georgia-Pacific paper mills in the state, as well as interests in lumber mills, coal, and pipelines employing some three thousand workers.

Soon, a handful of Wisconsin's wealthiest magnates, who were part of the Koch donor network, started writing checks, too. John Menard Jr., for instance, the richest man in Wisconsin, was both a million-dollar donor at the Kochs' June 2011 summit and a million-and-a-half-dollar donor to the Wisconsin Club for Growth, an outside dark-money group boosting Walker. Like many of Menard's investments, the political contributions more than paid off. Once in office, Walker chaired a state economic development corporation that bestowed $1.8

million in special tax credits on Menard's business. Walker's administration also eased up on enforcement actions against polluters.

Seventy years old at the time Walker was elected, Menard had made a fortune, estimated at about $6 billion in 2010, from a chain of home improvement stores bearing his name, but until Walker entered the statehouse, his relationship with the government had been contentious, to say the least. According to a 2007 profile in *Milwaukee Magazine,* his company had more clashes with the state's Department of Natural Resources than any other firm in Wisconsin. Ultimately, his company and Menard personally paid $1.7 million in fines for illegally disposing of hazardous waste. In one memorable instance, his company reportedly labeled arsenic-tainted mulch as "ideal for playgrounds."

Menard's hostility to organized labor was pronounced. He imposed an absolute ban on hiring anyone who had ever belonged to a union. One employee described having to fire two promising management prospects because they had worked in high school as baggers for a unionized supermarket. Managers, meanwhile, were subject to 60 percent pay cuts if their stores became unionized. They also had to agree to pay fines of $100 per minute for infractions such as opening late and to submit any disputes to management-friendly arbitration rather than the courts. Menard also forbade employees to build their own houses, for fear they would pilfer supplies. When one employee got special permission to build a ramp-equipped home in order to accommodate a wheelchair-bound daughter (in exchange for a demotion and a large salary cut), he was fired. His offense was that his contractor was using building materials from a competitor.

Menard had a disputatious record on compensation and taxes as well. The IRS ordered him to pay $6 million in back taxes after he allegedly mischaracterized $20 million as salary, not dividends, deducting it as a business expense. In a separate case, the Wisconsin Supreme Court forced Menard to pay $1.6 million to a former legal counsel, a woman who was the sister of his girlfriend at the time, to compensate for gender discrimination and gross underpayment. The woman's lawyer described Menard as "a man without parameters, no limits, no respect for the law, and obviously no self-discipline."

That case was followed by another in which the wife of a former business associate whom Menard fired in 2011 accused him of retaliating against her husband because of her refusal to engage in a sexual threesome with the billionaire and his wife. A spokesman for Menard denied the allegation. Meanwhile, a second woman, the wife of a former Indianapolis Colts quarterback, claimed Menard fired her for rebuffing his sexual advances. The company spokesman denied this as well. All in all, Menard seemed an unlikely patron for Walker, who emphasized his Christian conservatism as the son of a Baptist preacher, but on economic policies there was a meeting of the minds. Moreover, Menard was famously press shy, and little of his involvement with Walker surfaced until years later.

Diane Hendricks, the richest woman in Wisconsin and another of the Kochs' million-dollar donors, might also have stayed beneath the radar except for a documentary filmmaker who fortuitously caught her on camera. Fifteen days after Walker was inaugurated, in January 2011, Hendricks was captured in what she thought was a private chat, urging the governor to go after the unions. Looking glamorous but impatient, the sixty-something widow pressed Walker to turn Wisconsin into a "completely red" "right-to-work" state. Walker assured her that he had a plan. He had kept voters in the dark about it during his campaign, but he confided to Hendricks that his first step was to "deal with collective bargaining for all public employees' unions." This, he assured her, would "divide and conquer" the labor movement. Evidently, this was what Hendricks wanted to hear. She had amassed a fortune estimated at $3.6 billion from ABC Supply, the nation's largest wholesale distributor of roofing, windows, and siding, which she and her late husband, Ken, founded in 1982. Despite her phenomenal success, Hendricks said she was worried that America was becoming "a socialist ideological nation." Soon after the governor reassured her that he shared her concern, Hendricks and her company began a series of record-setting contributions that would reportedly make her Walker's biggest financial backer.

When Walker "dropped the bomb" on the unions, as he put it, he effectively stripped most state employees of the right to bargain collectively on their pay packages. He singled out the public employees, and particularly teachers, whose average salary was $51,264, as causes of the state's deficit. Amid the doomsday talk about overindulged and under-contributing public workers who were bankrupting the state, one awkward fact went unmentioned. Thanks to complicated accounting maneuvers, Diane Hendricks, according to state records, did not pay a dime in personal state income taxes in 2010.

Lines were drawn in Madison. In a desperate attempt to deprive Republicans of the quorum necessary to pass Walker's anti-union bill, Democratic legislators fled the state. Angry activists stormed the legislature, thronged the streets, and lambasted Walker as the Kochs' anti-union stooge. Walker unwittingly lent credence to the caricature less than a month into his tenure by carrying on a long, cringe-worthy phone conversation with a prankster pretending to be David Koch, the contents of which were soon made public. In a phrase that said all too much, Walker enthusiastically signed off with the impostor by saying, "Thanks a million!"

As the furious backlash against Walker evolved into a prolonged and ultimately unsuccessful effort by his critics to recall him from office, the Kochs, who by then had become the face of the opposition, mounted a fierce counterattack. They used Americans for Prosperity and other vehicles to mobilize pro-Walker rallies and air thousands of "Stand with Walker" and "It's Working!" television and radio ads. They also utilized

Themis, a high-tech data bank they had developed, to help get out the vote.

After Walker triumphed in the recall fight, putting him in line for his ill-fated run for the White House in 2016, an independent counsel's investigation into possible campaign-finance violations disgorged a trove of e-mails revealing just how many hugely wealthy, out-of-state hidden hands were involved in his campaign to stay in office. The e-mails revealed advisers to Walker scheming to get the Kochs and allied donors to help him by donating to what purported to be an independent group, the Wisconsin Club for Growth. One e-mail suggested, "Take Koch's money." Another insisted that the governor should "get on a plane to Vegas and sit down with Sheldon Adelson." It went on, "Ask for $1m now." A third advised Walker that Paul Singer, the hedge fund mogul, would be at the same resort as he and insisted, "Grab him." Soon after, the Wisconsin Club for Growth received $250,000 from Singer.

At the helm of the Wisconsin Club for Growth, and thus at the center of the web, was an old ally of the Kochs', Eric O'Keefe. He was the same Wisconsin investor who had volunteered in David Koch's ill-fated Libertarian campaign for vice president, before going on to run the Sam Adams Alliance, which had played a seminal role in launching the Tea Party movement, and join the Cato Institute's board. Over the years, O'Keefe's various political gambits had also been greatly aided by the Bradley Foundation. According to one tally, it contributed over $3 million to groups directed or founded by O'Keefe between 1998 and 2012. The Bradley Foundation, meanwhile, tightened its ties to several members of the Kochs' circle. It soon added to its board both Diane Hendricks and Art Pope, the Kochs' longtime North Carolina ally, who also was on the board of Americans for Prosperity. The club that O'Keefe and the others belonged to was ingrown and small, but its reach was growing.

Richard Fink made clear what the stakes were for both

himself and his benefactors after the embarrassment of the trick phone call. "We will not step back at all," he proclaimed. "With the Left trying to intimidate the Koch brothers to back off of their support for freedom and signaling to others that this is what happens if you oppose the administration and its allies, we have no choice but to continue the fight." Fink defiantly claimed, "This is a big part of our life's work. We are not going to stop."

Buoyed by their success in Wisconsin, the Kochs began to focus in earnest on the presidential race. It had taken years, but by 2012 they were becoming a rival center of power to the Republican establishment. Political insiders who had once scoffed at them now marveled at the breadth of their political operation.

While amassing one of the most lucrative fortunes in the world, the Kochs had also created an ideological assembly line justifying it. Now they had added a powerful political machine to protect it. They had hired top-level operatives, financed their own voter data bank, commissioned state-of-the-art polling, and created a fund-raising operation that enlisted hundreds of other wealthy Americans to help pay for it. They had also forged a coalition of some seventeen allied conservative groups with niche constituencies who would mask their centralized source of funding and carry their message. To mobilize Latino voters, they formed a group called the Libre Initiative. To reach conservative women, they funded Concerned Women for America. For millennials, they formed Generation Opportunity. To cover up fingerprints on television attack ads, they hid behind the American Future Fund and other front groups. Their network's money also flowed to gun groups, retirees, veterans, antilabor groups, antitax groups, evangelical Christian groups, and even $4.5 million for something called the Center for Shared Services, which coordinated administrative tasks such as office space rentals and paperwork for the others. Americans for Prosperity, meanwhile, organized chapters all across the country. The Kochs had established what was in effect their own private political party.

Secrecy permeated every level of the operation. One former Koch executive, Ben Pratt, who became the chief operating officer of the voter data bank, Themis, used a quotation from Salvador Dalí on his personal blog that could have served as the enterprise's motto: "The secret of my influence is that it has always remained secret."

Robert Tappan, a spokesman for Koch Industries, defended the secrecy as a matter of security, because "Koch has been targeted repeatedly in the past by the Administration and its allies because of our real (or, in some cases, perceived) beliefs and activities concerning public policy and political issues," overlooking decades of secrecy from the John Birch Society onward.

This consolidation of power reflected the overall national trend of increasingly large and concentrated campaign spending by the ultra-wealthy in the post–*Citizens United* era. The spending, in turn, was a reflection of the growing concentration of wealth more generally in America. As a result, the 2012 election was a tipping point of sorts. Not only was it by far the most expensive election in the country's history; it was also the first time since the advent of modern campaign-finance laws when outside spending groups, including super PACs and tax-exempt nonprofit groups, flush with unlimited contributions from the country's richest donors, spent more than $1 billion to influence federal elections. And when the spending on attack ads run by nonprofits was factored in, outside spending groups might well have outspent the campaigns and the political parties for the first time.

The Koch network loomed as a colossus over this new political landscape. On the right, there were other formidable donor networks, including the one assembled by Karl Rove, but no single outside group spent as much. On its own, in 2012 the Kochs' network of a few hundred individuals spent at least $407 million, almost all of it anonymously. This was more than John McCain spent on his entire 2008 presidential bid. And it was more than the combined contributions to the two presidential campaigns made by 5,667,658 Americans, whose donations were legally capped at $5,000. *Politico*'s Kenneth Vogel crunched the numbers and discovered that in the presidential race the top 0.04 percent of donors contributed about the same amount as the bottom 68 percent. No previous year for which there were data had shown more spending by fewer people. The staggeringly lopsided situation made 2012 the starkest test yet of Louis Brandeis's dictum that the country could have either "democracy, or we may have wealth concentrated in the hands of a few," but not both.

The Kochs' growing clout was evident in a confidential internal Romney campaign memo dated October 4, 2011. Romney, like virtually every ambitious Republican in the country, was angling for David Koch's support. The memo described him plainly as "the financial engine of the Tea Party," although it noted that he "denies being directly involved."

Romney, it revealed, had hoped to woo Koch in a private tête-à-tête at the billionaire's beachfront mansion in Southampton, New York, over the summer. But to the campaign's dismay, Hurricane Irene had washed the meeting out. With the Iowa caucuses looming, and Chris Christie out of the race, Romney tried again in the fall.

Shortly after the memo was written, Romney took two controversial campaign stances that were guaranteed to please the billionaire brothers. First, he reversed his earlier position on climate change. In his 2010 book, *No Apology,* Romney had written, "I believe that climate change is occurring—the reduction in the size of global ice caps is hard to ignore. I also believe that human activity is a contributing factor." When he hit the campaign trail in June of 2011, Romney reiterated this view and stressed that it was "important for us to reduce our emissions of pollutants and greenhouse gases that may well be significant contributors to the climate change and the global warming that you're seeing." But at a rally in Manchester, New Hampshire, in late October, he suddenly declared himself a climate change skeptic. "My view is that we don't know what's causing climate change on this planet," he said. "And the idea of spending trillions and trillions of dollars to try to reduce CO_2 emissions is not the right course for us," he declared. By the time he accepted the Republican nomination in Tampa the following summer, Romney treated the notion of acting on climate change as a joke. "President Obama promised to begin to slow the rise of the oceans. And to heal the planet," he mocked. "My promise is to help you and your family."

A week after first reversing himself on climate change, Romney skipped a campaign event attended by every other Republican presidential candidate in Iowa in order to speak at Americans for Prosperity's annual Defending the American Dream summit in Washington. There he delivered a keynote address that could have passed as an audition for David Koch, who was in the audience. Romney had governed Massachusetts as a northeastern moderate, but now he unveiled a budget plan reminiscent of Paul Ryan's.

Soon afterward, Romney proposed to cut all income tax rates by one-fifth. According to the nonpartisan Tax Policy Center, Romney's proposal would save those in the top 0.1 percent an average of $264,000 a year, and the poorest 20 percent of taxpayers an average of $78. The middle class would get on average $791. Romney also proposed other items high on his donors' wish lists, including eliminating estate taxes, lowering the corporate tax rate, and ending taxes owed by companies that had shipped operations overseas. Taken as a whole, the Tax Policy Center said the proposal would add $5 trillion to the deficit over the next decade. Romney said he would make up the difference by closing unspecified tax loopholes.

Charles Koch often described his support for slashing taxes

as motivated by a concern for the poor. "They're the ones that suffer" from "bigger government," he argued in an interview with his hometown paper. Yet there was no getting around the fact that the numbers added up to a disproportionately huge gift to the already rich. "These guys all talk about the deficit, but there's not a single tax benefit for the wealthy they'll get rid of," Dan Pfeiffer, Obama's former communications adviser, later pointed out. "What really made them furious," he said, "was when we started talking about closing the loopholes for private jets!"

If these policy shifts were designed in part to win the Kochs' support, they succeeded. By July, David Koch not only embraced Romney but threw a $75,000-per-couple fund-raiser for him at his Southampton estate. Romney and Koch were described as exuding a "confident glow" as they and their wives descended the stairs following a private half-hour chat before the other guests arrived. A few weeks later, Romney chose Ryan as his running mate. The pick was opposed by Romney's campaign consultant, Stuart Stevens, and proved baffling to Obama because of the unpopularity of Ryan's extreme budget plan. But conservative donors, including David Koch and his wife, Julia, had lobbied for Ryan. It was one more indication that an invisible wealth primary was shaping the discourse and the field long before the rest of the country had the chance to vote.

With two of the largest fortunes in the world at their disposal—together worth an estimated $62 billion by 2012—Charles and David Koch were perfectly positioned to take advantage of the growing importance of money in American politics. Yet the presidential campaign still proved difficult for them to manage. With the eclipse of the party professionals by outside funders, virtually any novice with enough cash, including other donors in their own circle, could now disrupt the process.

As the presidential race began, Sean Noble was arguing to anyone in the Koch fold who would listen that it was time to "pull the trigger" on Newt Gingrich. The former Speaker of the House from Georgia had reinvented himself as a long-shot Republican presidential candidate. Even some of the conservatives who had been part of Gingrich's revolution in the House in the 1990s were privately begging the Koch operatives to act before Gingrich did irreparable damage to the other Republican candidates and the party. Gingrich was a brilliant force of entropy, dazzlingly eloquent on some occasions, utterly daft on others, and ruthlessly destructive to anyone in his path. For him, politics was total war, and he had the scars to prove it.

In preparation, Noble's firm quietly produced what it hoped was a lethal television ad using footage from a 2008 ad showing Gingrich sitting on a dainty love seat with Nancy Pelosi, agreeing that they needed to fight global warming. On the Republican side, it would have proved pure poison. But Noble couldn't get authorization to air it. The hesitation appeared related to the addition of Sheldon Adelson, the enormously wealthy casino mogul, to the Koch circle.

Sheldon Adelson, whom President George W. Bush once reportedly described as "this crazy Jewish billionaire, yelling at me," wasn't exactly the Kochs' type. He was a hard-right foreign policy hawk who was focused on ensuring the security of Israel. He had been a Democrat, but he shared the Kochs' antipathy toward labor unions, Obama, and redistributive income taxes. "Why is it fair that I should be paying a higher percentage of taxes than anyone else?" he once complained. Perhaps more important, with a fortune estimated in 2011 at $23.3 billion, the seventy-eight-year-old chairman of the Las Vegas Sands Corporation brought a lot of chips to the table. He could potentially increase the power of the Koch donor network exponentially. The Kochs had repeatedly invited Adelson to join their group but gotten nowhere. So when he finally showed up for the first time at their January 2012 summit in Indian Wells, California, they were not eager to trash his favorite candidate, who happened to be Gingrich.

"There were a lot of them who were pretty unhappy with Sheldon," a Koch confidant says, "but Newt pushed all his buttons." The odd couple had been friends for decades, bonding in the 1990s when Gingrich helped Adelson prevail in a bitter war to keep his casino operation, unlike the others in Las Vegas, union-free. They also shared a deep commitment to Israel's hard-line conservatives, especially its prime minister, Benjamin Netanyahu, with whom an associate says Adelson often spoke several times a week. Adelson had lavished millions of dollars on Gingrich during his precipitous ups and downs. Calling himself "just a loyal guy," Adelson continued that support after Gingrich was forced to resign from office in 1999 amid ethics charges and an insurrection within his own ranks. Long after the center of political gravity had shifted elsewhere, Adelson continued to loan Gingrich his private jets and contributed nearly $8 million to the nest of ventures that kept Gingrich employed.

But there was one touchy Israel-related issue on which the old friends disagreed. Adelson had long sought clemency for Jonathan Pollard, the Jewish American spy convicted of passing state secrets to Israel, who was serving a life sentence in federal prison. In the past, Gingrich had called Pollard "one of the most notorious traitors in U.S. history" and scuttled a Clinton-era deal to release him. If freed, Gingrich warned, Pollard might "resume his treacherous conduct and further damage the national security of the United States." But in December 2011, as Gingrich was heading into the Iowa caucuses in desperate need of cash, he switched his position. In an interview with the Jewish Channel, he announced that he now had "a bias in favor of clemency" for Pollard. Within weeks, Adelson donated $5 million to Gingrich's sputtering campaign, which otherwise in all likelihood would have fizzled out.

Adelson's cash temporarily revived Gingrich, unleashing a chain of unintended consequences. The pro-Gingrich super PAC used the casino magnate's money to purchase more than $3 million in advertising time in South Carolina. Then it aired a half-hour video called "King of Bain: When Mitt Romney Came to Town" that eviscerated Romney as a greedy, "predatory corporate raider." After the video was attacked, Gingrich called on the super PAC to take it down but not before he amplified the message by denouncing Bain Capital, the private equity company that Romney had co-founded, as "rich people figuring out clever ways to loot a company."

No left-winger could have made the case against high finance more convincingly. Romney became the face of "vulture capitalism," which was depicted as heartlessly cannibalizing what was left of the country's middle class. When Gingrich was finished with Bain, he went on to demand that Romney release his tax returns. As Noble had feared, the consequences of Gingrich at full throttle were disastrous for the Republicans.

Gingrich's attack on capitalist excess was underwritten by one of the richest men in the world whose international gambling empire was at that moment under federal criminal investigation for laundering money and foreign corrupt practices. Eventually, according to court testimony, Adelson's company paid a $47 million out-of-court settlement in the money-laundering case for failing to report a $45 million transfer of cash it made on behalf of a Chinese-Mexican businessman who was under investigation for drug trafficking. In another case, Adelson's former chief executive officer accused the mogul's subsidiary in Macao of consorting with organized crime figures and making excessive payments to a local official that might breach laws prohibiting U.S. citizens from engaging in corrupt practices overseas. Adelson described the allegations as "delusional and fabricated." But the legal cloud did little to enhance the image of the Koch network or the GOP. Instead of shoring up the Republican ticket, big money tainted the brand, prolonged the primaries, pushed the candidates to adopt their donors' pet issues, and, all in all, did the Democrats' work for them.

Romney did nothing to mitigate the "Richie Rich" caricature. After insisting that "corporations are people" and saying, "I like being able to fire people," he revealed details of a $250 million blind trust crammed with offshore investments in tax havens ranging from Switzerland to the Cayman Islands. His description of the $374,000 he made in speaking fees in 2010 as "not very much" sealed his image as hopelessly out of touch with ordinary Americans. The snapshot showing how the 1 percent lived became more toxic still when, under pressure from Gingrich, Romney released his tax returns, revealing that he had paid an effective tax rate of 14 percent on income of $21.7 million. It was less than half the rate paid by many middle-class wage earners. Gingrich trounced Romney in South Carolina, winning his first primary and proving that while the American public admired success, it also believed in fairness.

By the time the Romney campaign woke up to the threat posed by Gingrich, defeating him soundly in Florida, the damage had already been done. "With those attacks on Bain, he laid down the blueprint for Obama," lamented a conservative in the Kochs' circle.

Foster Friess, the multimillionaire mutual fund manager from Wyoming and longtime member of the Kochs' donor circle, was creating chaos, too. As Romney was trying to finish off Gingrich, Friess was spewing cash into a super PAC promoting Rick Santorum, a former senator from Pennsylvania who shared his zealous Christian conservatism. The nearly $1 million spent by Santorum's super PAC in Iowa vaulted him from footnote status into first place, assuring that his candidacy would continue far beyond its natural political shelf life. Friess, who seemed to love the spotlight almost as much as Santorum, joined the candidate in making a series of pronouncements about reproductive and gender issues that shocked many women. In the midst of an interview with the NBC correspondent Andrea Mitchell, for instance, Friess explained why he and Santorum took issue with the contraceptive coverage for women included in Obama's health-care plan. "Back in my day, they used Bayer aspirin for contraceptives," joked Friess. "The gals put it between their knees and it wasn't that costly." Mitchell, whose professional command was ordinarily unshakable, stammered, "Excuse me? I'm just trying to catch my breath from that, Mr. Friess, frankly."

By the time Santorum and Gingrich bowed out of the presidential race in the late spring, Friess had contributed $2.1 million and Adelson and his wife over $20 million to the campaigns of their respective favorites. The Democrats were ecstatic at the damage inflicted by the rogue donors. "We were killing them on contraception," says Jim Messina, Obama's campaign manager. "And we were winning on tax issues for the first time since 1996." Steve Schmidt, a Republican political operative, suggests that the shift from broad-based party funding to hugely wealthy outside donors turned the race into "an ideologically driven ecosystem." The candidates, he says, were "like these football players with their sponsors' names on their jerseys. If you have a single person responsible for your nomination, you owe them everything. You can say not, but it's determinative."

Jim Margolis, co-founder of GMMB, the campaign consulting company that worked for Obama's reelection, suggests that Romney would have fared better as a moderate, but his radical backers prevented it. "Romney's best strategy would have been to give Obama a golden watch and say basically, 'We all had such hope, he tried, but he didn't get it done. I can. I'm Mr. Fix-It. I know how to create jobs.' But Romney never successfully did that. Instead, he ran to the right." The Tea Party in 2010, and the donors behind it, stirred what Margolis calls "this supercharged Republican primary electorate. We didn't know how it would play out, but the likelihood of a moderate, appealing candidate emerging from this? Instead, they had Herman Cain, Michele Bachmann, Rick Santorum, and Newt Gingrich! That was a problem for Romney."

As the general campaign got under way, Obama too had to worry about rich donors. He had been itching to make economic fairness the center of his presidential campaign. But some of his advisers worried that populism was a dangerous force to play with in an era when both parties were increasingly reliant on hugely wealthy patrons. Obama, though, had sought the presidency in part because he hoped to alter the relationship between powerful financial interests and those who govern. "One of the reasons I ran for President," he had said, "was because I believed so strongly that the voices of everyday Americans—hardworking folks doing everything they can to stay afloat—just weren't being heard over the powerful voices of the special interests in Washington."

The Occupy movement had further emboldened him. So he decided to kick off his reelection campaign at the end of 2011 in the tiny town of Osawatomie, Kansas. There, in the place where Theodore Roosevelt had delivered a fiery speech in 1910 demanding that the government be "freed from the sinister influence or control of special interests," he tried to tackle the thorny issue of America's growing economic inequality.

Obama denounced the "breathtaking greed" that had led to the housing market's collapse, as well as the Republican Party's "you're-on-your-own economics." He also had some stinging words for big money's influence on politics. "Inequality distorts our democracy," he warned. "It gives an outsized voice to the few who can afford high-priced lobbyists and unlimited campaign contributions, and it runs the risk of selling out our democracy to the highest bidder."

The words were ringing. The audience cheered. The problem, though, was that no matter how keenly Obama wanted to address economic inequality, he was going to have to turn to his party's own billionaires and multimillionaires for help. Soon, in fact, Obama would set a record for the number of fund-raisers attended by an incumbent president. He continued to speak out, even directly to the donors, telling one small gathering of moguls that included Microsoft's co-founder Bill Gates, the richest man in America, "There are five or six people in this room *tonight* that could simply make a decision—this will be the next president—and probably at least get a nomination, if ultimately the person didn't win. And that's not the way things are supposed to work." But like it or not, Obama was, as one top progressive donor, the former head of the Stride Rite shoe company Arnold Hiatt, put it, "in a bind."

In an early 2012 meeting in the Roosevelt Room, his campaign manager, Jim Messina, shocked the president by sharing the bad news that they now expected outside Republican spending against him to reach $660 million.

"How sure are you?" Obama asked.

"Very sure," replied Messina.

Obama had reserved some of the harshest words of his presidency for the *Citizens United* ruling, saying that he couldn't "think of anything more devastating to the public interest." So he had steadfastly refused to encourage supporters to form an "outside" super PAC that could accept unlimited contributions on his behalf. "I think we need to switch our position," Messina said. "Until people understand it's important to you, they're not going to give."

Soon after, Obama bowed to the new economic reality and reversed himself. His campaign began encouraging supporters to give to the pro-Obama super PAC, Priorities USA. It wasn't the first time Obama had been rendered a hypocrite in order to raise funds. In 2008, after championing campaign-finance reform in the Senate, he broke his own pledge to accept public financing as a presidential candidate. Obama admitted that he suffered "from the same original sin of all politicians, which is: We've got to raise money." But he insisted that he would fight to reform the system: "The argument is not that I'm pristine, because I'm swimming in the same muddy water. The argument is that I know it's muddy and I want to clean it up."

The extent to which the same moneyed interests tainted both parties, though, became clear after Priorities USA aired its first television ad. It was an emotional tirade from a steel mill worker whose plant was closed down by Bain. "He'll give you the same thing he gave us: nothing. He'll take it all," the worker said of Romney. The Obama campaign then underscored the powerful message from the super PAC with its own ad, calling Romney a "job destroyer" and his firm "a vampire."

At the time, a number of thoughtful economists and academics from both ends of the political spectrum were deeply concerned about the finance industry's impact on the country's growing economic inequality. While high-earning executives particularly in the finance industry were prospering, wage earners were stagnating. Experts ranging from former Treasury secretary Lawrence Summers to the neoconservative theorist Francis Fukuyama worried that the trend was threatening the middle class and overwhelming the political system.

Yet when Obama's ads broached these crucial issues, Wall Street–linked Democrats erupted in anger. Steven Rattner, who had made millions at the investment bank Lazard Frères and whose wife was the former finance director for the Democratic Party, denounced the ads as "unfair." Harold Ford Jr., a former Democratic congressman from Tennessee who had migrated to Wall Street, protested that "private equity is a good thing in many, many instances." Cory Booker, the mayor of Newark, New Jersey, who was a rising star in the party and who had numerous supporters in the finance industry, went on national television and, to the fury of the White House, said "this kind of stuff is nauseating to me on both sides."

Bill Clinton dealt the final blow. In an interview on CNN,

he said, "I don't think we ought to get into the position where we say this is bad work—this is good work." From 2006 until 2009, Chelsea Clinton, the daughter of the former president, worked as an associate at Avenue Capital Group, a $14 billion private equity and hedge fund firm. Marc Lasry, co-founder of Avenue Capital, was a major Clinton supporter as well as a $1 million investor in a fund managed by the Clintons' son-in-law, Marc Mezvinsky. The Clinton administration had been rife with Wall Street tycoons. Now, as the Obama administration was teeing up Romney's rapacious business record as his key disqualification, Clinton summarily announced that Romney's "sterling business career crosses the qualification threshold." (At the time, Hillary Clinton reportedly disapproved of her husband's comment, privately saying, "Bill can't do that again.")

In response, the Obama campaign tailored its message more carefully. For the most part, rather than hammering Romney's wealth directly, it relied on sly symbolism to address the touchy issue of class. "There was too much blowback, so we used cues," says Margolis. "We showed him standing next to Trump's private jet."

Regardless of what the donor class thought, the anti-Bain ads proved among the most effective of the campaign. When nervous Obama campaign aides prescreened the ads in focus groups, "they kept telling us to relax! 'Stop asking if it's unfair,'" Margolis recalls. Evidently, the broad public was deeply uneasy about the winner-take-all ethic of corporate America. Yet, according to the Princeton University professor of politics Martin Gilens, because of the outsized influence that the affluent exert over the political process, "under most circumstances the preferences of the vast majority of Americans appear to have essentially no impact."

The perception gap between the donor class and the rest of the country was unceremoniously exposed in September when *Mother Jones* revealed a secret recording made that May by a member of the waitstaff at a high-end fund-raiser for Romney. Outrage spread as the public eavesdropped on Romney assuring wealthy supporters gathered for cocktails at a mansion in Boca Raton, Florida, that the votes of 47 percent of the population weren't of concern to him.

Romney's assertion came in response to a question about how he planned to "convince everybody you've got to take care of yourself." The subtext seemed to be that the country was rife with freeloaders. "My job is not to worry about those people. I'll never convince them they should take personal responsibility for their lives," Romney replied. "There are 47 percent of the people who will vote for the president no matter what." As he described them, they were people who were "dependent upon government, who believe they are victims, who believe government has a responsibility to care for them, who believe they are entitled to health care, food, to housing, you name it." These were "people who pay no income tax," he said, and so "our message of low taxes doesn't connect." He seemed to be implying that nearly half the country consisted of parasites.

This was no slip of the tongue. Romney was expressing what *The Wall Street Journal* described as the "new orthodoxy" within the Republican Party. In a new twist on the old conservative argument against government aid for the poor, it denigrated nearly half the country as what the *Journal* called "Lucky Duckies" freeloading off the rich. This startling theory held that because many members of the middle class and working poor received targeted tax credits, such as the earned income tax credit and the child tax credit, which reduced their income taxes to zero, they were "a nation of moochers," as the title of a book written by a fellow at the Wisconsin Policy Research Institute put it.

Behind the theory were several nonprofit organizations tied to the Kochs and other wealthy ideologues, including the Heritage Foundation and AEI. Foremost perhaps was the Tax Foundation, an antitax group founded in opposition to Roosevelt's New Deal that had been resurrected by Charles Koch's cash and directed for some time by Wayne Gable, the president of the Charles Koch Foundation and head of Koch Industries' Washington lobbying operation. As Scott Hodge, president of the Tax Foundation, explained it simply, there were "two Americas: the nonpayers and the payers."

Critics immediately pointed out that the theory ignored the many other taxes paid by lower- and middle-income Americans, including sales taxes, payroll taxes, and property and gas taxes, which took a disproportionately large share of their income. The theory also overlooked the unique circumstances of retirees, students, veterans, and the unwillingly unemployed. And it completely ignored the many tax breaks disproportionately enjoyed by the wealthy, from mortgage and charitable deductions to the preferential treatment for unearned income that kept Romney's income taxes at an effective rate of 14 percent. But the flattering distinction between "makers" and "takers" advanced by conservative think tanks and scholars had won great favor in wealthy, conservative circles. In fact, some conservatives who opposed virtually every other tax increase had started calling for new taxes on meager earners, ostensibly for the country's civic good. As *Slate*'s David Weigel cheekily wrote, "Republicans have finally found a group they want to tax: poor people."

The Blackstone billionaire Stephen Schwarzman made this argument nine months before Romney was caught saying essentially the same thing. When asked in a Bloomberg television interview if, given the dire state of the economy, his own taxes should be raised, Schwarzman, who was one of the most vigorous defenders of the carried-interest loophole, suggested that, to the contrary, the poor needed to pay more. "You have to have skin in the game," he said. "The concept that half of the public isn't involved with the income tax system is somewhat odd, and I'm not saying how much people should do, but we should all be part of the system." In addition to its political obtuseness, the comment betrayed complete ignorance of the history of the income tax, which began as a tax only on the 0.1 percent and was never designed to target the poor.

At the time, Schwarzman's comment got little attention. But when the rest of the nation learned from Romney's remarks that the superrich considered nearly half of them free-loaders, the reaction was explosive. Obama's internal polling numbers, which had hovered steadily in the range of 48 to 50 percent, shot up to 53 percent over Romney. The damage was even more pronounced in battleground states, where Romney's numbers plummeted. Within days, polls showed that fully 80 percent of the country had heard about the remark—more, one pollster said, than knew of the existence of North Korea.

The Obama campaign delightedly held its fire while Romney tried to explain but never disavowed it. Finally, after ten days, Obama's team went on the air with a new television ad slamming the 47 percent gaffe. It was not the original version the campaign had created. The first version, which never aired, cast Romney's remark against a backdrop of impoverished Americans whose woeful portraits seemed borrowed from Walker Evans or from Robert Kennedy's tour of Appalachia. But in the version that aired, the poor had been banished, replaced by the middle class. The ad now featured female factory workers wearing protective eye gear, a Latino construction worker near a ladder, redolent of upward mobility, and steely-eyed retired veterans in VFW hats. This wasn't just about the poor. By parroting his donors, Romney had cast the election, the "Mother of All Wars," as a fight between a tiny, privileged clique and virtually everyone else.

For the most part, the Kochtopus was more sensed than seen during the campaign, but one month before the election its elaborate funding mechanism came perilously close to exposure. In California, the Fair Political Practices Commission, the state's campaign ethics watchdog, demanded to know who was behind a suspicious $15 million donation aimed at influencing two controversial California ballot initiatives. One initiative would raise taxes on the wealthy, and the other would curb labor unions from spending money on politics. The donor purported to be an obscure Arizona nonprofit called Americans for Responsible Leadership, but California officials were not convinced this was the whole story. At the eleventh hour, they launched an investigation to learn more, because the state's stringent campaign laws required full donor disclosure.

Soon California authorities began to uncover an extraordinary dark-money shell game involving many of the same donors, operatives, and front groups associated with the Kochs. Overseeing it was Sean Noble, the Kochs' outside political consultant. His group, the Center to Protect Patient Rights, had passed the money from undisclosed individuals to the obscure Arizona nonprofit, which had sent it on without the donors' names to California. In between, there was a shuffle back and forth to another nonprofit in Arlington, Virginia, Americans for Job Security. As a result, the identities of the original sources of the contributions were masked. Among them was Charles Schwab, the Koch network regular, whose chatty e-mail to Charles Koch surfaced, asking for "several million" dollars for the California fight and promising to catch up on the golf course after the election. "I've committed an extra 2 million today making my total commitment 7 million," Schwab wrote. "I must tell you that Sean Noble from your group has been immensely helpful to our efforts."

The Kochs, according to one adviser, "panicked" as California investigators began unraveling Noble's money operation, which was entwined with their own. "They did it wrong, and they thought they had legal liability," he said. Details started emerging, such as a deposition from a California political consultant snared in the investigation who described how the scheme had begun with "some donors who were part of

Koch" who wanted to wage an antilabor fight in California, like the one in Wisconsin. "They liked the Koch model," the consultant, Tony Russo, explained, so they suggested that he work with Noble, whom Russo identified as the Kochs' "outside consultant."

After a lengthy investigation, Ann Ravel, the head of the California Fair Political Practices Commission, blasted the daisy chain of front groups as "definitely money laundering." The agency eventually imposed a record-breaking $1 million fine to settle the case. It exposed a "nationwide scourge of dark money nonprofit networks hiding the identities of their contributors," Ravel said in a public statement that also noted that the groups involved were tied to "the 'Koch Brothers' Network.'"

Koch Industries officials leaped in, stressing that the settlement had stipulated that the lawbreaking was "inadvertent, or at worst negligent," and that the Kochs had not personally donated money to influence the California ballot initiatives. Further, they argued, Noble was merely an independent contractor. "There is not a Koch *network* in the sense of we control these groups, I don't understand what that means," Mark Holden, the company's general counsel, told *Politico*'s Vogel, who pointed out that, to the contrary, Charles Koch had referred to "our network" himself, in his invitation to the 2011 donor seminar.

Following the embarrassing California investigation, which went on into late 2013, the Kochs began to ease Noble out. By then, Noble, the sunny avatar of small-town America, had left his wife for an office colleague and stirred additional bad publicity by charging almost $24 million for his and his firm's services in 2012. This was more than $1 for every $6 that the Center for Patient Rights spent, according to ProPublica. As the investigation grew in California, the Koch world expertly distanced itself. "They've spun it really well," said one of Noble's friends, who spoke on condition that he not be identified because he, too, feared retribution. "They've worked it hard. The truth? The guy who the billionaires hire to direct the money got caught breaking the law. Is he guilty? It's not Sean who is the problem—it's the enterprise—it's an illegal enterprise!"

In the final stretch of the campaign, it became clear that the presidential race was so close that the outcome would likely depend on voter turnout. Nowhere was this truer than in the state of Ohio, without which Romney couldn't rack up enough electoral votes to win. Here, too, the Kochs and other conservative philanthropists played a little-detected role.

Controversy about allegations of voter fraud had built to a boiling point all summer. Each side accused the other of dirty tricks, further poisoning and polarizing the political process. The chairman of the Republican National Committee, Reince Priebus, accused Democrats of "standing up for fraud— presumably because ending it would disenfranchise at least two of its core constituencies: the deceased and double voters." Democrats accused Republicans of deliberately reviving racist voter suppression tactics predating the civil rights movement. Bill Clinton declared, "It's the most determined effort to limit the franchise since we got rid of the poll tax and all the other Jim Crow burdens on voting." Impartial experts, meanwhile, like Richard Hasen, a professor of election law at the University of California in Irvine, regarded the allegations of fraud as the real fraud. After searching in vain to find a single case since 1980 when "an election outcome could plausibly have turned on voter impersonation fraud," he concluded the problem was a "myth."

Nonetheless, the alarmism resulted in legislative initiatives aimed at requiring voters to produce official photo IDs in thirty-seven states between 2011 and 2012. It also led to a national outbreak of mysterious citizen watchdog groups calling for crackdowns on election fraud. One such group, the

Ohio Voter Integrity Project, policed voter rolls for "irregularities" and then persuaded local election authorities to send summonses to suspect voters requiring them to prove their legitimacy at public hearings. Teresa Sharp, a fifty-three-year-old lifelong Democrat from the outskirts of Cincinnati, who received one such summons, discovered at the hearing that the self-appointed watchdog group had mistaken her address for a vacant lot. "My first thought," recalled Sharp, who is African-American, "was, Oh, no! They ain't messing with us poor black folks! Who is challenging my right to vote?"

The national outbreak of fear over voter fraud appeared a spontaneous grassroots movement, but beneath the surface there was a money trail that led back to the usual deep-pocketed right-wing donors. To target Sharp, for instance, the Ohio Voter Integrity Project had relied on software supplied by a national nonprofit, True the Vote, which itself was supported in different ways by the Bradley Foundation, the Heritage Foundation, and Americans for Prosperity.

True the Vote described itself as a nonprofit organization, created "*by* citizens *for* citizens," that aimed to protect "the rights of legitimate voters, regardless of their political party." But its founder, Catherine Engelbrecht, a Houston Tea Party activist, was guided by Hans von Spakovsky, a Republican lawyer and fellow at the Heritage Foundation who had made a career of challenging liberal voting rights reforms. Heritage had an ugly history on the issue. The think tank's founder, Paul Weyrich, had openly admitted, "I don't want everybody to vote." In 1980, he told supporters, "As a matter of fact our leverage in elections quite candidly goes up as the voting populace goes down."

Spakovsky's most recent book, *Who's Counting?*, which was filled with incendiary claims about voter fraud, was published by Encounter Books, a Bradley Foundation grantee, and co-authored by John Fund, another Heritage Foundation fellow. True the Vote, meanwhile, had received Bradley Foundation funds. Americans for Prosperity also gave the organization and the voter fraud issue a boost by featuring both Fund and Engelbrecht at its political events.

If the aim was to intimidate voters like Sharp, though, in her case, it backfired. When her name was called at the hearing, Sharp, who was accompanied by six other members of her family, walked to the front, slammed her purse and papers on the table, and asked, "Why are you all harassing me?" Later she said, "It was like a kangaroo court. There were, like, ninety-four people being challenged, and my family and I were the only ones contesting it! I looked around. The board members and the stenographer, they were all white people. The lady bringing the challenge—she was white." Sharp concluded, "I think they want to stop as many black people as they can from voting."

On Election Day, to the surprise of Romney and his backers, Democratic voters turned out in far bigger numbers than the Republicans expected. The Koch network had spent an astounding $407 million at a minimum, most of it from invisible donors. The operatives running the enterprise believed they were able to accurately anticipate how the vote would go, and right until the polls closed on November 6, they, like the Romney team, were convinced victory was at hand.

Sean Noble, who was already under a cloud because of the California campaign-finance scandal, was so sure of success that on Election Day he sent out a memo to the donors telling them that soon the rest of the country would know the good news that they already did, which was that Romney would be the next president. But around 4:30 that afternoon, Frank Luntz called. He said the exit polls didn't look right. But neither Noble nor anyone else among the big donor groups believed it yet.

At 11:12 p.m., NBC News called Ohio for Obama, projecting him as the election's winner. When Fox News followed suit, Karl Rove, who was a Fox News analyst as well as the founder of the American Crossroads independent campaign operation, threw a fit on the air. He had talked the rich into contributing $117 million to his super PAC, and many, many more millions in dark money, and had confidently assured them of a historic victory. It was "premature" for Fox to call the race, he insisted. Fox's number crunchers, however, held their ground. Romney had lost.

"What happened? We had bad data," a Koch insider conceded after it was over. They had counted on an electorate less diverse than the one that swept Obama into office in 2008. Instead, the 2012 voters were even more diverse. While the proportion of the electorate that was white and old fell, the participation by Hispanic, female, and young voters rose. Black voters, meanwhile, held steady, casting an overwhelming 93 percent of their votes for Obama. The America that the conservative donors were counting on was out of touch with the reality.

In a postelection phone call to his biggest contributors, Romney explained it a little differently. The problem, he said, was that Obama had in essence bribed supporters with government services. "What the president's campaign did was focus on certain members of his base coalition, give them extraordinary financial gifts from the government, and then work very aggressively to turn them out to vote."

Obama chuckled upon hearing of Romney's analysis. "He must have really meant that 47 percent thing," he told his aides.

In Bentonville, Arkansas, a few days later, Senator John McCain's private cell phone interrupted a meeting with Walmart's top executives by mechanically announcing the name of a caller trying to reach him. "Mitt Romney!" it squawked. "Mitt Romney!" Looking a little startled, McCain fished the phone out of his pocket and answered, rising to leave the room so that he could speak in privacy. When McCain returned, he explained to the curious executives that Romney had wanted advice on how to cope with losing the presidency. "I told him the first time, I did it all wrong," McCain related. "My wife talked me into taking a vacation in Tahiti. Worst Goddam mistake I ever made. The second time," he went on, "I just went right back to work. It was fine. I told him, 'Go back to work.'" The only problem, someone cracked, was that Romney, like those loafers in the 47 percent, had no job.

Commentators leaped to the conclusion that 2012 proved that money had little or no influence on elections. *Politico* changed the heading for a series it had been running on money in politics from "The Billion-Dollar Buy" to "The Billion-Dollar Bust?" With a final tally of approximately $7 billion in traceable spending on the presidential and congressional campaigns, it was the most expensive election in American history by far. One donor alone, Sheldon Adelson, who had vowed to spend "as much as it takes," had dumped nearly $150 million, $92 million of which was disclosed, and had still come up short. Approximately $15 million of that had reportedly gone to the Kochs' group, Americans for Prosperity.

All in all, super PACs and independent groups that could take unlimited contributions had spent a staggering $2.5 billion and, it seemed, changed nothing. Obama would remain in the White House, the Democrats would continue to dominate the Senate, and Republicans would continue to control the House.

Defeat on this scale did not sit well with the Kochs or their donors. "The donors were livid," recalls one adviser. Disappointed but ever persistent and methodical, Charles Koch sent out an e-mail to his network informing them that the next donor seminar would be postponed from January until April while he and his operatives analyzed what went wrong. "Our goal of advancing a free and prosperous America is even more difficult than we envisioned, but it is essential that we continue, rather than abandon, this struggle," he wrote.

The media's box score approach to politics, however, overlooked the many more subtle ways that money had bought influence. Hugely wealthy radicals on the right hadn't won the White House, but they had altered the nature of American democracy. They had privatized much of the public campaign process and dominated the agenda of one of the country's two major political parties. David Koch, in fact, attended the Republican National Convention as an alternate delegate, a sign of how much the party had changed. (Arguably he had changed too. At the convention, he gave an interview supporting gay marriage, demonstrating that on this issue he had come far from the day when he had participated in the scheme to blackmail his brother. The Kochs did not, however, put their financial clout behind promoting gay marriage, and David's private view had no visible influence on the Party.)

On a raft of other issues, though, including climate change, tax policy, entitlement spending, and undisclosed campaign contributions—which the Republican Party platform now embraced in a reversal from the past—the preferences of the Kochs and their political "partners" had prevailed. There was no more talk of strengthening the Clean Air Act, mockery of "Voodoo Economics," support for "compassionate conservatism," or expanding Medicare drug coverage, as there had been under the Bush presidencies. Government was a force for evil, not public good.

Contrary to predictions, the *Citizens United* decision hadn't triggered a tidal wave of corporate political spending. Instead, it had empowered a few extraordinarily rich individuals with extreme and often self-serving agendas. As the nonpartisan Sunlight Foundation concluded in a postelection analysis, the superrich had become the country's political gatekeepers. "One ten-thousandth" of America's population, or "1% of the 1%," was "shaping the limits of acceptable discourse, one conversation at a time."

Obama won, but he had few illusions that he had vanquished big money. "I'm an incumbent president who already had this huge network of support all across the country and millions of donors," he told a few supporters. It had enabled him to, as he put it, "match whatever check the Koch brothers want to write." But, he warned, "I'm not sure that the next candidate after me is going to be able to compete in that same way." Messina too was worried. "I think they erred badly with their strategy," he said. "But I don't think they're going to make the same mistake twice."

CHAPTER THIRTEEN

The States: Gaining Ground

THE DAY AFTER THE ELECTION, NO ONE WAS HANGING BLACK crepe at the Republican Party's state headquarters on Hillsborough Street in Raleigh, North Carolina. In Washington, pundits were proclaiming that Obama's reelection proved the failure of big money, but in North Carolina, Republicans were toasting its triumph at the state level. The REDMAP plan that Ed Gillespie had described at the Kochs' donor summit eighteen months earlier had worked remarkably well. Republicans had cemented their control of the state legislature and redrawn the boundaries of the congressional districts in North Carolina so artfully that despite getting fewer votes than the Democrats, they had won more congressional seats. The same pattern was repeated in enough other states that the Republicans were able to hold on to the House of Representatives, despite a bigger 2012 turnout nationwide for Democrats. It was a strange anomaly but not an accidental one.

For the Koch machine, North Carolina had become something of a test kitchen.

"A few years ago, the idea we had was to create model states," Tim Phillips, the president of Americans for Prosperity, explained in 2013. "North Carolina was a great opportunity to do that—more so than any other state in the region. If you could turn around a state like that, you could get real reform."

Phillips declined to say how much the Kochs' political organization had spent in North Carolina to help conservatives take power. "It was significant" is all he would say. "It was one of the states in which we were most active."

If the first phase of the project had been achieved by the

Republican takeover of North Carolina's state assembly in 2010, the second began in February 2011, when Tom Hofeller, a white-haired black belt in the dark art of carving congressional districts, or gerrymandering, as it was known, showed up at the Republican Party headquarters on Hillsborough Street.

There, a back room had been set aside for mapmaking.

The new census on which the congressional districts would be based hadn't even been released yet. But Hofeller was nothing if not thorough. The advent of computers had turned redistricting into an expensive, cynical, and highly precise science. Hofeller, the foremost practitioner on the Republican side, had professionalized the vast ideological sorting of the country into warring partisan camps. On his laptop was a program called Maptitude that contained the population details of every neighborhood, including the residents' racial makeup.

In the past, Hofeller had worked for the Republican Party. But by 2011, he was a private contractor, working for big outside money. Many of the financial details remained shrouded. But according to documents contained in a later lawsuit, he would eventually make ten trips to North Carolina to consult with local Republicans on how to create the largest number of safe seats possible. For his services, Hofeller would earn more than $166,000.

The process was closely guarded, and access to the room was tightly controlled. But at least one well-known figure was allowed into the inner sanctum. Art Pope, the multimillionaire discount chain store magnate who was the state's top political donor and a longtime ally of the Kochs', became a frequent adviser.

"We worked together at the workstation," one of the technical experts, Joel Raupe, said in a later legal deposition. "He sat next to me." Pope was a nonpracticing lawyer and held no elected office in the state, but the Republican leadership in the state legislature had quietly appointed him "co-counsel" to the politically sensitive project.

Gerrymandering was a bipartisan game as old as the Republic. What made it different after *Citizens United* was that the business of manipulating politics from the ground up was now heavily directed and funded by the unelected rich. To get the job done, they used front groups claiming to be nonpartisan social welfare groups, funded by contributions from some of the world's largest corporations and wealthy donors like the Kochs. The big outside money flowing into the most granular level of politics was transformative. "The Kochs were instrumental in getting the GOP to take over state legislatures," observed David Axelrod, Obama's erstwhile political adviser. "The GOP is top-down, but the Kochs had a different plan, which was to organize the grass roots. It's smart. There's no equivalent on the Democratic side," he admitted. "They're damn good organizers."

According to a report by ProPublica, Hofeller and his team were hired for the job by a dark-money group called the State Government Leadership Foundation. This was actually an offshoot of the group that Gillespie had used to run REDMAP, the Republican State Leadership Committee. But unlike the main group, the offshoot was a 501(c)(4) "social welfare" organization that could conceal the identities of its donors. Adding one more layer of security to the operation in North Carolina was a state-level dark-money group calling itself Fair and Legal Redistricting for North Carolina.

The work, like the funding, was stealthy. Hofeller kept a PowerPoint presentation on his computer with admonitions such as "Make sure your security is real." "Make sure your computer is in a PRIVATE location." He warned, "Emails are the tool of the devil." He also stressed that those working with him should "use personal contact or a safe phone!" "Don't reveal more than necessary." "BEWARE of nonpartisan, or bipartisan, staff bearing gifts," he added. "They probably are not your friends."

In theory, redistricting was supposed to reflect the fundamental democratic principle of one person, one vote. The shifting U.S. population was supposed to be equally distributed in accordance with the new census figures, across all 435 of the country's congressional districts. In a charade of fairness, Republican legislators overseeing the process in North Carolina crisscrossed the state to hold public hearings, gathering comments and suggestions from citizens about how the lines could best be drawn. "What we are here for is to basically hear your thoughts and dreams about redistricting," the chairman of the state senate committee in charge of the process told a crowd in Durham. In reality, however, Hofeller later admitted under oath that he never bothered to read the transcripts of the public testimony.

By the time Hofeller's team was done, the new map severely reduced the number of congressional seats that Democrats could win. To achieve that, the operatives had packed minority voters into three districts that already had a high concentration of African-American voters. This left more of the surrounding territory white and Republican, and the Democrats in those areas stranded. In effect, the new map had resegregated the state into congressional districts in which minority voters could dominate their own neighborhoods but were unlikely to see their party gain majority power in the state.

Progressive groups immediately filed suit, alleging that the new maps violated the Voting Rights Act, which prohibits discriminatory elections. Republican officials defended the maps as fair. Here, too, however, a flood of undisclosed cash spent by dark-money groups affiliated with Pope and other members of the Koch network influenced the course of events.

The case was headed to the state's supreme court where the Republicans held a 4–3 majority, making it likely that the Republican redistricting plan would get a friendly hearing. But before that could happen, the judges were up for reelection in 2012, and conservatives worried that one Republican incumbent appeared likely to lose. His Democratic challenger seemed poised to tip the court's political balance toward the Democrats, imperiling the Republican redistricting plan.

But a sudden wave of outside cash rescued Paul Newby, the Republican judge, just in time. Outside groups spent more than $2.3 million helping him, an unheard-of sum in such a judicial race. The money trail was dizzyingly complex, making it all but impossible for ordinary citizens to follow, but among those contributing were Gillespie's group, the Republican State Leadership Committee; Pope's company, Variety Wholesalers; and the Kochs' organization, Americans for Prosperity. The money paid for a barrage of media ads that touted the Republican judge's toughness on crime.

On Election Day, Newby was narrowly reelected. Soon afterward, the state supreme court upheld the Republican-led redistricting plan. In 2015, however, the U.S. Supreme Court ordered it to reconsider the case on the grounds that the minority-packed districts were racially discriminatory. But by then, the North Carolina delegation had become ensconced in the House of Representatives, where it added to the Republican majority as it mounted a new wave of radical resistance to the Obama administration's policies.

"The other side has killed us at that stuff," admitted Steve Rosenthal, a Democratic strategist with ties to the labor movement. By channeling donors' money to largely overlooked state and local races, Republicans succeeded not only in advancing their political agenda but in wiping out a generation of lower-level Democratic office holders who could rise in the future. And North Carolina was not the only place this happened. Successive midterm losses in 2010 and 2014 cumulatively cost the Democrats more than nine hundred legislative seats and eleven governorships, according to an analysis by the Democratic National Committee.

Gillespie's REDMAP plan had proved a stunning success. For years, North Carolina had been a politically divided, or "purple," state. It had backed Barack Obama's election in

2008 but not in 2012, when, seemingly overnight, it turned a deep shade of crimson. That November, Republicans added to their previous gains by winning the governorship and veto-proof majorities in both houses of the general assembly. It was the first time since Reconstruction that the Republican Party had complete control of the state's government. And thanks to Hofeller's expert maps, Republicans also now dominated the congressional delegation, whose makeup went from seven Democrats and six Republicans to nine Republicans and four Democrats in 2010.

But no one benefited more from the election than Art Pope. It transformed him from a backroom kingmaker in North Carolina into a very central public power. Almost as soon as Pat McCrory, the new Republican governor, was sworn in, he stunned many in the state by appointing his benefactor, Pope, to be the state's budget director. Voters had years before rejected Pope's one bid for statewide office, his run for lieutenant governor in 1992. The state legislature had also turned down repeated bids by Pope for appointive jobs, including membership on the state university system's board of governors. Pope was widely respected but not beloved. Richard Morgan, a Republican state legislator with whom he had a falling-out, described Pope as unpopular with colleagues because his attitude was "my way, or everyone else is wrong."

Now Pope was arguably the second most powerful official in North Carolina. As budget director, he had the governor's ear, a supermajority in both legislative chambers, and massive authority over which government functions would and would not get funded. Cutting government spending had long been his dream. Morgan recalled that as a state legislator Pope had spent long hours analyzing the numbers. "When he was done, there wasn't a bone buried in the budget Art hadn't dug up and chewed on." Now he had the chance to remake the whole state.

It is unusual for those wielding plutocratic power in America to exercise it directly, according to Jeffrey Winters, the political scientist specializing in oligarchy. Direct rule by the superrich invites a dangerous amount of scrutiny. Those who have used their vast fortunes to secure public office in the United States, like Michael Bloomberg, the former mayor of New York City, typically have made an effort not to appear to be ruling *as* oligarchs or *for* them. Pope clearly sensed the peril. He took care to say that he would waive the usual salary and only stay in office for a year. But questions about self-interest arose almost immediately. As North Carolina took a whiplash-inducing lurch in favor of the haves at the expense of the have-nots, it stirred a heated debate about the influence of big money in the state's politics in general and about the motives and financial designs of Art Pope in particular.

Within a few months, the legislature had overhauled the state's tax code and budget from top to bottom. On almost every issue, the legislature followed the right-wing playbook that had originated in two think tanks, the John Locke Foundation and the Civitas Institute, which were founded by Pope and largely funded by the Pope family's $150 million John William Pope Foundation. Critics described Civitas as Pope's conservative assembly line and a powerful force pushing the state's politics ever further to the right. Pope rejected the description. "It's not my organization," he protested. "I don't own it." The Pope family foundation, however, had supplied Civitas with more than 97 percent of its funding since its founding in 2005—some $8 million—and Pope sat on its board of directors. It also had supplied about 80 percent of the John Locke Foundation's funding. A good bit of the remainder came from tobacco companies and two Koch family foundations.

In fact, starting in the 1980s, Pope and his family foundation had invested $60 million in the systematic development of a conservative infrastructure in North Carolina that functioned as a "conservative government in exile," according to Dee Stewart, a Republican political consultant in the state.

The think tanks were 501(c)(3) organizations, enjoying

the same tax-exempt status as churches, universities, and public charities. Legally, these organizations were barred from participating in politics or lobbying to any substantial degree. Yet the lines were a blur. Top officers at the Pope-linked think tanks, for instance, cycled back and forth into Republican campaigns and Americans for Prosperity, where Pope was a director. The think tank personnel wrote model bills, which they previewed for legislators, and boasted of their clout in the general assembly. Pope was proud of the achievement, telling the conservative Philanthropy Roundtable, "In a generation, we've shifted the public-policy debate in North Carolina from the center-left to the center-right."

Besides the $60 million that Pope and his family foundation put into this ideological infrastructure, they gave more than $500,000 to state candidates and party committees in 2010 and 2012. In addition, Pope's company, Variety Wholesalers, gave nearly $1 million more to outside groups running independent campaigns during that period. In the state of North Carolina, Pope was, as one of his former political advisers, Scott Place, put it, "the Koch brothers lite."

The agenda this money was behind became apparent once the Republicans won control of North Carolina's general assembly. In a matter of months, they enacted conservative policies that private think tanks had been incubating for years. The legislature slashed taxes on corporations and the wealthy while cutting benefits and services for the middle class and the poor. It also gutted environmental programs, sharply limited women's access to abortion, backed a constitutional ban on gay marriage, and legalized concealed guns in bars and on playgrounds and school campuses. It also erected cumbersome new bureaucratic barriers to voting. Like the poll taxes and literacy tests of the segregated past, the new hurdles, critics said, were designed to discourage poor and minority voters, who leaned Democratic. The election law expert Richard Hasen declared, "I've never seen a package of what I would call suppressive voting measures like this." The historian Dan T. Carter, who specialized in southern history at the University of South Carolina, noted that when friends around the country asked if things in North Carolina were as bad as they looked from the outside, he was forced to answer, "No, it's worse—a lot worse."

Republicans claimed their new policies allowed residents to "keep more of their hard-earned money." But according to a fact-checking analysis by the Associated Press, the working poor were in line to pay more while the wealthiest gained the most. The North Carolina Budget and Tax Center scored the changes and found that 75 percent of the savings would go to the top 5 percent of taxpayers. The legislature eliminated the earned-income tax credit for low-income workers. It also repealed North Carolina's estate tax, a move that was projected to cost the state $300 million in its first five years. Yet the benefits of this tax break were so skewed to the wealthiest few that only twenty-three estates would have been big enough to qualify as of 2011, because the existing law already exempted the first $5.25 million of inheritance from taxation. (The Pope-funded Civitas Institute had first proposed many of these top-weighted tax cuts, with the assistance of its special adviser, Arthur Laffer, the controversial inventor of supply-side economics.)

At the same time, the legislature cut unemployment benefits so drastically that the state was no longer eligible to receive $780 million in emergency federal unemployment aid for which it would otherwise have qualified. As a result, North Carolina, which had the country's fifth-highest unemployment rate, soon offered the most meager unemployment benefits in the country.

The state also spurned the expanded Medicaid coverage for the needy that it was eligible for at no cost under the Affordable Care Act. This show of defiance denied free health care to 500,000 uninsured low-income residents. A study by health experts at Harvard and the City University of New York projected that the legislature's obstruction of these benefits would cost residents between 455 and 1,145 lives *a year.*

Art Pope was fond of the libertarian saying "There is no such thing as a free lunch," and in North Carolina his budget proved him right. To make up for the projected billion-dollar-a-year shortfall created by the many new tax cuts he helped to deliver, something had to give. So for savings, the legislators turned to the one institution that had distinguished North Carolina from many other southern states—its celebrated public education system.

The assault was systematic. They authorized vouchers for private schools while putting the public school budget in a vise and squeezing. They eliminated teachers' assistants and reduced teacher pay from the twenty-first highest in the country to the forty-sixth. They abolished incentives for teachers to earn higher degrees and reduced funding for a successful program for at-risk preschoolers. Voters had overwhelmingly preferred to avoid these cuts by extending a temporary one-penny sales tax to sustain educational funding, but the legislators, many of whom had signed a no-tax pledge promoted by Americans for Prosperity, made the cuts anyway.

North Carolina's esteemed state university system also took a hit. Ideological warfare infused the fight. Pope's network had waged a long campaign to slash spending, with employees of the John William Pope Center for Higher Education Policy, another Pope-created nonprofit, accusing the university system of becoming a "niche for radicals," describing the public funding as "a boondoggle," and demanding that the legislature "starve the beast." The center dug up professors' voting records in an effort to prove political bias. Once the Republican majority took over the legislature, it quickly imposed severe cuts that were projected to cause tuition hikes, faculty layoffs, and fewer scholarships, even though the state's constitution required that higher education be made "as free as practical" to all residents.

Bill Friday, a revered former president of the University of

North Carolina, confided not long before he died in 2012 that he was afraid the changes would put higher education out of reach for many poor and middle-income families. "What are you doing, closing the door to them?" he asked. "That's the war that's on. It's against the role that government can play. I think it's really tragic. That's what's made North Carolina different."

At the same time that Pope's network fought to cut university budgets, he offered to privately fund academic programs in subjects he favored, like Western civilization and free-market economics. A $500,000 gift that Pope made to North Carolina State University, for instance, funded lectures by conservatives. "I'm pretty sure we would not invite Paul Krugman," a professor who picked the speakers and was affiliated with the John Locke Foundation, acknowledged. Some faculty saw Pope's donations as a bid to buy academic control. "It's sad and blatant," said Cat Warren, an English professor at North Carolina State. Pope, she said, "succeeds in getting higher education defunded, and then uses those cutbacks as a way to increase leverage and influence over course content."

The John Locke Foundation also sponsored the North Carolina History Project, which aimed to reorient the state's teaching of its history by providing online lesson plans for high school teachers that downplayed the roles of social movements and government while celebrating what it called the "personal creation of wealth." In a similar vein, Republicans in the state senate passed a bill requiring North Carolina's high school students to study conservative principles as part of American history in order to graduate in 2015. The bill stressed the "constitutional limitations on government power to tax and spend." "It's all part of Pope's plan to build up more institutional support for his philosophy," said Chris Fitzsimon, director of NC Policy Watch, a liberal watchdog group.

But Pope became a lightning rod as his profile grew. The NAACP began holding weekly "Moral Monday" protests in the state capital against North Carolina's turn to the right and eventually began picketing the chain stores owned by Pope's company, Variety Wholesalers.

Even some Republicans in the state accused Pope of going too far. Jim Goodmon, the president and CEO of Capitol Broadcasting Company, which owned the CBS and Fox television affiliates in Raleigh, said, "I was a Republican, but I'm embarrassed to be one in North Carolina, because of Art Pope." Goodmon had deep ties to the state's conservative establishment. His grandfather A. J. Fletcher was among Jesse Helms's biggest backers. But Goodmon described the Pope forces as "anti-community," adding, "The way they've come to power is to say that government is bad. Their only answer is cut taxes." He concluded, "It's never about making things better. It's all about tearing the other side down."

Interviewed in a spare office overlooking a suburban parking lot that served as Variety Wholesalers headquarters in Raleigh, Pope dismissed those who were trying to paint him as extreme as misinformed. "If the left wing wants a whipping boy, a bogeyman, they throw out my name," he protested. "Some things I hear about this guy Art Pope—you know I don't like this guy Art Pope that they're talking about. I don't know him. If what they say were true, I wouldn't like a lot of things about me. But they're just not true."

In a nearly four-hour-long, lawyerly rebuttal, he argued that conservatives like himself were the underdogs in North Carolina and that his expenditures merely represented an effort to balance the score. He said that he was driven not by "narrow corporate interest" but by abstract idealism. He described himself as "politically a conservative" and a "classical liberal, philosophically." He acknowledged that the nonprofit groups he supported took many positions advantageous to his business, such as opposition to minimum wage laws. In fact, critics, like Dean Debnam, a liberal North Carolina businessman, accused Pope of exhibiting "a plantation mentality" by keeping "people working part time . . . He preys on the poorest of the poor, and uses it to advance the agenda of the richest of the rich," he charged. But Pope said he didn't take positions to enhance his bottom line. In the tradition of John Locke, he said, he just believed that society functioned best when citizens were rewarded with the wealth that their hard work produced.

Pope, who credited a summer program run by the Cato Institute for first exposing him to free-market theories, argued that the country's growing economic inequality was not a worry because "wealth creation and wealth destruction is constantly happening." All Americans, he said, had a fair chance at success. Citing Michael Jordan and Mick Jagger as examples, he asked, "Why should they be deprived of that money—why is that unfair?" He noted, "I'm not envious of the wealth that Bill Gates has," and added, "America does not have an aristocracy or a plutocracy."

The poor, he argued, were largely victims of their own bad choices. "Really, when you look at the lowest income, most of that is just simply a factor of age and marriage. If you're young and single—and God forbid if you're young and a single parent, and don't have a high school education—then your earnings will be low, and you'll be in the bottom twenty percent."

The constellation of nonprofit groups supported by Pope's fortune echoed this tough-luck message. For instance, a researcher at the Civitas Institute asserted that the poor in America lived better than "the picture most liberals like to paint." The researcher Bob Luebke cited a Heritage Foundation study showing that the poor often had shelter, a refrigerator, and cable television. "The media obsession with pervasive homelessness also appears a myth," he declared. John Hood, a bright protégé of Pope's who moved from the John Locke Foundation to become head of the John William Pope Foundation in 2015, stressed that "the true extent of poverty in North Carolina and around the country is woefully overestimated." Where poverty did exist, he asserted, it largely resulted from "self-destructive behavior."

Gene Nichol, the director of the Center on Poverty, Work, and Opportunity at the University of North Carolina School of Law, pointed out that one-third of the state's children of color lived in poverty, meaning they started at the bottom, long before they were old enough to make choices of their own. But Pope's network successfully pressured the university to eliminate the Center on Poverty in 2015 after Nichol criticized Republican policies.

Pope's own experience of poverty was limited. He grew up in a wealthy household, attended a private boarding school before the University of North Carolina and the Duke School of Law, and joined his family's discount store business, which was started by his grandfather and expanded by his father. But Pope often stressed, "I am not an heir." He explained that his father had demanded that he and his siblings buy stakes in the family-owned business. Like Charles Koch, and many others in their donor network, Pope believed that he had advanced to the helm of the company on his own merits. Those who knew Pope confirmed that he worked extremely hard and was obsessively frugal. But he also received many advantages from his parents, including hundreds of thousands of dollars in campaign contributions.

Scott Place, who served as campaign manager during Pope's one bid for statewide office, his unsuccessful 1992 run for lieutenant governor, recalled one transaction vividly, when Pope's father made a donation to his campaign. "He had his checkbook, and he was stroking the check. He said, 'How much?' Art says, 'Well, I guess $60,000.' The dad bitched. I was standing, thunderstruck. I said, 'That's a HUGE check!' The father responded, 'Well, it's Art's inheritance. I guess he can do whatever the hell he wants to with it.' It wasn't like, 'Go get 'em, son,'" Place recalled. "It was more like, 'Take the money and get out!'"

Before the campaign ended with Pope's defeat, records show that Pope's parents made uncollected "loans" to him of approximately $330,000, which, adjusted for inflation, would be more than half a million dollars today.

Place said of Pope, "He thinks that if you're poor, you're just not working hard enough. It's all about free enterprise. He probably did grow his daddy's business, and he is smart and politically shrewd. But he wasn't just born on third base. He started out within an inch of home plate." Place suggested, "Anybody can be politically effective if they have got almost a blank check."

David Parker, the chair of the North Carolina Democratic Party, accused Pope of glossing over the fact that he was born privileged. "All this talk of Protestant work ethic," he said, "but he made his money the old-fashioned way: his mother bore a son." He added, "We're all prisoners of Art Pope's fantasy world."

The ideological machine that Pope bankrolled in North Carolina was unusually powerful, but just one part of the multimillion-dollar system of interlocking nonprofit organizations conservatives had built in almost every state by the time Obama was reelected president. Because they were partial to federalism and suspicious of centralized power, the emphasis was natural. From the Civil War on through the civil rights movement, states' rights had been a conservative rallying cry, particularly in the South. Historically, it had often been bound up in racial animosities, with local jurisdictions resisting federal interference. Then, during the Reagan years, the movement took on a pro-corporate cast. While conservative business leaders such as Lewis Powell and William Simon organized

corporate interests to counter the liberal public interest movement nationally, conservative allies set up similar organizations at the state and local levels. As one leader of this effort,
Thomas A. Roe, an anti-union construction magnate from
Greenville, South Carolina, reportedly declared to a fellow
trustee at the Heritage Foundation during the 1980s, "You
capture the Soviet Union—I'm going to capture the states."

Roe went on to found the State Policy Network in 1992, a
national coalition of conservative state-based think tanks. By
2012, the network had sixty-four separate think tanks turning out cookie-cutter-like policy papers, including at least one
hub in every state. In North Carolina, for instance, both of
the think tanks founded by the Pope fortune were members.
The organization's president, Tracie Sharp, described each as
"fiercely independent." But behind closed doors, she likened
the group's model to the global discount chain store Ikea. She
told eight hundred members gathered for an annual meeting in
2013 that the national organization would provide them with a
"catalogue" of "raw materials" and "services" so that local chapters could assemble the ideological products at home. "Pick
what you need," she said, "and customize it for what works best
for you."

In 2011, the State Policy Network's budget reached a sizable $83.2 million. Coordinating with the think tanks were
over a hundred "associate" members that included conservative
nonprofit groups like Americans for Prosperity, the Cato Institute, the Heritage Foundation, and Grover Norquist's Americans for Tax Reform, which the Kochs also helped to fund.

Adding clout to the Right's reach at the state level was the
American Legislative Exchange Council. Weyrich's brainchild
had grown impressively since the 1970s, when Richard Mellon
Scaife had provided most of its start-up funding. Critics called
it a conservative corporate "bill mill." Thousands of businesses
and trade groups paid expensive dues to attend closed-door
conferences with local officials during which they drafted

model legislation that state legislators subsequently introduced as their own. On average, ALEC produced about a thousand new bills a year, some two hundred of which became state law. The State Policy Network's think tanks, some twenty-nine of which were members of ALEC, provided legislative research.

ALEC was in many ways indistinguishable from a corporate lobbying operation, but it defined itself as a tax-exempt 501(c)(3) "educational" organization. But to its allies, ALEC touted its transactional achievements. As one member-only newsletter boasted, ALEC made a "good investment" for companies. "Nowhere else can you get a return that high," it said. To avoid appearing bought off, lawmakers made sure not to mention the corporate origins of the model bills. But as the former Wisconsin state legislator (and later governor) Tommy Thompson admitted, "Myself, I always loved going to these [ALEC] meetings because I always found new ideas. Then I'd take them back to Wisconsin, disguise them a little bit, and declare that 'It's mine.'"

The Kochs were early financial angels of this state-focused activism. Koch Industries had a representative on ALEC's corporate board for nearly two decades, and during this time ALEC produced numerous bills promoting the interests of fossil fuel companies such as Koch Industries. In 2013 alone, it produced some seventy bills aimed at impeding government support for alternative, renewable energy programs.

Later the Kochs presented themselves as champions of criminal justice reform, but while they were active in ALEC, it was instrumental in pushing for the kinds of draconian prison sentences that helped spawn America's mass incarceration crisis. For years among ALEC's most active members was the for-profit prison industry. In 1995, for instance, ALEC began promoting mandatory-minimum sentences for drug offenses. Two years later, Charles Koch bailed ALEC out financially with a $430,000 loan.

In 2009, the conservative movement in the states gained

another dimension. The State Policy Network added its own "investigative news" service, partnering with a new organization called the Franklin Center for Government and Public Integrity and sprouting news bureaus in some forty states. The reporters filed stories for their own national wire service and Web sites. Many of the reports drew on research from the State Policy Network and promoted the legislative priorities of ALEC. Frequently, the reports attacked government programs, particularly those initiated by Obama. The news organization claimed to be a neutral public watchdog, but much of its coverage reflected the conservative bent of those behind it.

Professional journalists soon took issue with the Franklin Center's labeling of its content as "news." Dave Zweifel, editor emeritus of *The Capital Times* of Madison, Wisconsin, called the group's Web site in the state "a wolf in disguise" and "another dangerous blow to the traditions of objective reporting." The Pew Research Center's Project for Excellence in Journalism ranked Franklin's reports as "highly ideological." But Franklin's founder, Jason Stverak, was undeterred. He told a conservative conference that his organization, whose financing he refused to disclose, planned to fill the vacuum created by the economic death spiral in which many of the "legacy media" found themselves at the state level all over the country.

Cumulatively, these three groups created what appeared to be a conservative revolution bubbling up from the bottom to nullify Obama's policies in the states. But the funding was largely top-down. Much of it came from giant, multinational corporations, including Koch Industries, the Reynolds American and Altria tobacco companies, Microsoft, Comcast, AT&T, Verizon, GlaxoSmithKline, and Kraft Foods. A small knot of hugely rich individual donors and their private foundations funded the effort, too.

Much of the money went through DonorsTrust, the Beltway-based fund that erased donors' fingerprints. Fewer than two hundred extraordinarily rich individuals and private foundations accounted for the $750 million pooled by DonorsTrust and its sister arm, Donors Capital Fund, since 1999. Many were the same billionaires and multimillionaires who formed the Koch network.

This relatively small group of contributors to DonorsTrust provided 95 percent of the Franklin Center's revenues in 2011. The big backers behind DonorsTrust and Donors Capital Fund also put $50 million in the State Policy Network's think tanks from 2008 to 2011—a sum that goes far at that level. Whitney Ball, who ran DonorsTrust, and who was also a director on the State Policy Network's board, explained that during the Obama years, conservative donors saw "a better opportunity to make a difference in the states."

In the autumn of 2013, fallout from the conservative make-over of North Carolina reached far beyond state boundaries. An obscure Republican freshman congressman from one of the newly gerrymandered districts helped set in motion the process that led to the shutdown of the federal government. The episode became an object lesson in the way that the radicalized donor base in the Republican Party was polarizing politics to an extent that would have been almost unthinkable just a few years earlier.

Until his election in 2012, Mark Meadows had been a restaurant owner and Sunday-school Bible teacher in North Carolina's westernmost corner. Previously, the rural, mountainous Eleventh Congressional District had been represented by a former NFL quarterback and conservative Democrat named Heath Shuler. But gerrymandering had removed so many Democrats from the district that Shuler retired rather than wasting time and money on what was clearly a hopeless race, all but handing over the seat to Meadows.

After only eight months in office, Meadows made national headlines by sending an open letter to the Republican leaders of the House demanding they use the "power of the purse" to kill the Affordable Care Act. By then, the law had been upheld by the Supreme Court and affirmed when voters reelected Obama in 2012. But Meadows argued that Republicans should sabotage it by refusing to appropriate any funds for its implementation. And, if they didn't get their way, they would shut down the government. By fall, Meadows had succeeded in getting more than seventy-nine Republican congressmen to sign on to this plan, forcing Speaker of the House John Boehner, who had opposed the radical measure, to accede to their demands.

Meadows later blamed the media for exaggerating his role, but he was hailed by his local Tea Party group as "our poster boy" and by CNN as the "architect" of the 2013 shutdown. The fanfare grew less positive when the radicals in Congress refused to back down, bringing virtually the entire federal government to a halt for sixteen days in October, leaving the country struggling to function without all but the most vital federal services. In Meadows's district, day-care centers that were reliant on federal aid reportedly turned distraught families away, and nearby national parks were closed, bringing the tourist trade to a sputtering standstill. National polls showed public opinion was overwhelmingly against the shutdown. Even the *Washington Post* columnist Charles Krauthammer, a conservative, called the renegades "the Suicide Caucus."

But the gerrymandering of 2010 had created what Ryan Lizza of *The New Yorker* called a "historical oddity." Political extremists now had no incentive to compromise, even with their own party's leadership. To the contrary, the only threats faced by Republican members from the new, ultraconservative districts were primary challenges from even *more* conservative candidates.

Statistics showed that the eighty members of the so-called Suicide Caucus were a strikingly unrepresentative minority. They represented only 18 percent of the country's population and just a third of the overall Republican caucus in the House.

Gerrymandering had made their districts far less ethnically diverse and further to the right than the country as a whole. They were anomalies, yet because of radicalization of the party's donor base they wielded disproportionate power.

"In previous eras," Lizza noted, "ideologically extreme minorities could be controlled by party leadership. What's new about the current House of Representatives is that party discipline has broken down on the Republican side." Party bosses no longer ruled. Big outside money had failed to buy the 2012 presidential election, but it had nonetheless succeeded in paralyzing the U.S. government.

Meadows of course was not able to engineer the government shutdown by himself. Ted Cruz, the junior senator from Texas, whose 2012 victory had also been fueled by right-wing outside money, orchestrated much of the congressional strategy. A galaxy of conservative nonprofit groups funded by the party's big donors, meanwhile, promoted Meadows's petition while also organizing a state-based campaign of massive resistance to Obamacare so fierce it was likened to the southern states' defiance of the Supreme Court's 1954 decision in *Brown v. Board of Education*. Like the segregationists, they refused to accept defeat.

Much of America was taken by surprise by such radical action. But conservative activists had been secretly drawing up various sabotage schemes for some time.

The raw anger behind this radicalism was evident in an address given by Michael Greve, a law professor at George Mason University, at an American Enterprise Institute conference in 2010. Greve was the chairman of the Competitive Enterprise Institute—an antiregulatory free-market think tank in Washington funded by the Bradley, Coors, Koch, and Scaife Foundations, along with a roster of giant corporations— and a fervent opponent of Obamacare. "This bastard has to be killed as a matter of political hygiene," he declared.

"I do not care how this is done, whether it's dismembered,

whether we drive a stake through its heart, whether we tar and feather it and drive it out of town, whether we strangle it," he went on. "I don't care who does it, whether it's some court some place, or the United States Congress. Any which way, any dollar spent on that goal is worth spending, any brief filed toward that end is worth filing, any speech or panel contribution toward that end is of service to the United States."

The radical resistance didn't end after the Supreme Court upheld the law in the spring of 2012 and the public reelected Obama that fall. Instead the right wing regrouped. As *The New York Times* later reported, a "loose-knit coalition of conservative activists" began gathering in secret in Washington to plot how else they could disrupt the program. The meetings produced a "blueprint to defund Obamacare" signed by some three dozen conservative groups who called themselves the Conservative Action Project. Their leader was the former attorney general Edwin Meese III, an aging standard-bearer of the conservative movement who held the Ronald Reagan chair at the Heritage Foundation, served on the board of directors at the Mercatus Center at George Mason University, and was a frequent attendee at the Koch donor summits. One scheme was the initiative that Meadows eventually championed, to hold up congressional funds for the health-care program.

Another scheme was a massive "education" campaign to stir noncompliance with the federal law, both on the part of state officials, like those in North Carolina who refused to set up insurance exchanges, and by citizens. Freedom Partners Chamber of Commerce, the Koch network's "business league," financed much of the fight. It used its youth-oriented front group, Generation Opportunity, to post online advertisements featuring a tasteless cartoon version of Uncle Sam jumping between the legs of a young woman undergoing a gynecological exam to spread fear about the government's interference in private health-care matters. (The Kochs' front group seemed to have no such qualms about government intrusion into reproductive health issues.) The organization also sponsored student-oriented protests at which mock Obamacare insurance cards were burned like draft cards during the Vietnam War. The disinformation campaign spread fear and confusion. News reports reflected a widespread belief, particularly in desperately poor areas, that the government was setting up "death panels."

In the summer and fall of 2013, as Meadows was gathering co-sponsors for his open letter, Americans for Prosperity spent an additional $5.5 million on anti-Obamacare television ads. Asked about this later, Tim Phillips stressed that his group merely wanted to repeal rather than defund the health-care law. But either way, he acknowledged that the Kochs' political organization was not giving up. It planned to spend "tens of millions" of dollars on a "multi-front effort" against the law, he said.

As part of that effort, Americans for Prosperity pressured states to refuse the free, expanded Medicaid coverage included in the program, which meant denying health-care coverage to four million uninsured adults. They also pressured state officials across the country into refusing to set up their own health-care exchanges, as anticipated by the law. Meanwhile, the Cato Institute and the Competitive Enterprise Institute promoted the theory that it was illegal for the federal government to step in where the states failed to act—an interpretation of the law contradicted by both the Republican and the Democratic legislators who drafted it. This nonetheless formed the basis for the second legal challenge to the Affordable Care Act to reach the Supreme Court, *King v. Burwell,* which in the summer of 2015 also proved unsuccessful.

(The Kochs and their allies had already played a largely unnoticed role in quietly financing the first legal challenge to the health-care law to reach the Supreme Court. Officially, the lawsuit was brought by the National Federation of Independent Business. But the NFIB was talked into signing up as the plaintiff at a Heritage Foundation event in 2010. Afterward, the Kochs' organization Freedom Partners, DonorsTrust, Karl Rove's dark-money group Crossroads GPS, and the Bradley Foundation all helped to fund the NFIB.)

Phillips maintained that the conservative groups were vastly outspent in the health-care fight by the law's supporters. "It's David versus Goliath," he claimed. But according to Kantar Media's Campaign Media Analysis Group, which tracks spending on television ads, $235 million was spent on ads demonizing the law in the two years following its passage. Only $69 million was spent on ads supporting it.

In the run-up to the government shutdown, the Heritage Foundation played a major role too. In 2013, Senator Jim DeMint of South Carolina had resigned his Senate seat to become president of the organization, and under his leadership it became an increasingly radical and aggressive faction within the Republican Party. As part of the new aggressiveness under DeMint, Heritage created a dark-money 501(c)(4) arm called Heritage Action that could engage directly in partisan warfare, into which the Koch network put $500,000. (John Podesta, the head of the liberal Center for American Progress, came up with this new wrinkle, which he called a way to create "a think tank on steroids." In 2010, Heritage copied it.)

Heritage Action stunned Republican moderates by attacking those who declined to sign Congressman Meadows's open letter to "defund Obamacare." The internecine warfare was so heated that Heritage Action was kicked out of a Republican congressional caucus in which the think tank had long been welcome. But the pressure tactics were "hugely influential," David Wasserman, a nonpartisan expert for the respected *Cook Political Report,* told the *Times.* "When else in our history has a freshman member of Congress from North Carolina been able to round up a gang of 80 that's essentially ground the government to a halt?"

After the 2012 election political leaders in both parties had expressed hope that the partisan battles would subside so that the government could finally tend to the serious economic, social, environmental, and international issues demanding urgent attention from the world's richest and most powerful nation. Speaker of the House Boehner made it clear to the extremists in his party that it was time to back off. "The president was reelected," he reminded them. "Obamacare is the law of the land."

Yet less than a year later, the country was held hostage in another futile fight over Obamacare. As congressional leaders met with Obama at the White House on October 2, 2013, in what turned out to be an unsuccessful effort to reach a deal that could avert the disastrous shutdown, Obama pulled the Speaker aside.

"John, what happened?" the president asked.

"I got overrun, that's what happened," he replied.

A bipartisan compromise eventually enabled the government to reopen. Boehner, in a rare moment of candor for Washington, then singled out the real people responsible for the meltdown. Self-serving, extreme pressure groups, he said, were "misleading their followers" and "pushing our members in places where they don't want to be. And frankly I just think they've lost all credibility."

But if their fortunes were radicalizing American politics from the roots up, the Kochs and Art Pope saw it as progress. In North Carolina, Pope had a message for his growing chorus of critics: "I am not going to apologize for making the decisions on how I spend my generation's money."

CHAPTER FOURTEEN

Selling the New Koch: A Better Battle Plan

AS THE HOUSELIGHTS DIMMED AND THE INTRODUCTORY COUN-try music faded to an expectant hush, four aging white men in dark business suits appeared from behind the curtains in a large auditorium and one by one took their turns at the lectern to prove that they were in fact, as the title of the program that day advertised, "the smartest guys in the room."

It was March 16, 2013, and at the annual Conservative Political Action Conference the heads of Washington's most influential conservative think tanks—the closest thing the movement had to wise men or witch doctors—were gathered on one stage to diagnose how the election of 2012 had gone so wrong and deliver a cure. Edwin Feulner was there, with a dapper gold pocket square, the grand old man of the Heritage Foundation. So was Lawson Bader, the bald and bearded leader of the scrappy Competitive Enterprise Institute. John Allison was there too, looking every inch the southern banker he had been until recently, before leaving the helm of BB&T for that of the Cato Institute. The scene-stealer, though, was Arthur Brooks, the president of the American Enterprise Institute.

Gaunt, with a salt-and-pepper beard, a receding hairline, and the heavy black-rimmed glasses of an intellectual, Brooks had traded an earlier career as a French horn player for a job hitting just the right conservative notes. He had a knack for phrasing and timing and for boiling down complicated mate-rial into engaging and accessible nuggets, as he did that day.

"There's only one thing you need to know," Brooks said about 2012. "I know it makes you sick to your stomach," he added. But one statistic, he said, explained why conservatives had lost: only a third of the public agreed with the statement that Republicans "care about people like you." Further, only 38 percent believed they cared about the poor.

Conservatives had an empathy problem. This mattered, Brooks explained, because, as a recent study by Jonathan Haidt, a psychologist at NYU's Stern School of Business, had shown, Americans universally agreed with the statement that "fairness matters." In a nod to his conservative audience, Brooks repeated, "I know it makes you *sick* to think of that word 'fairness.'" But Americans, he said, also universally believed that "it's right to help the vulnerable."

Unfortunately, in the view of the American public, Brooks explained further, the Democrats were "the 'fairness guys.' They're the 'helping-the-poor' guys. Who are we? We're the 'money guys'!"

If conservatives wanted to win, he exhorted his audience, they had to improve their image. It wasn't a policy problem, he assured everyone. Conservative policies, he maintained, still offered the best solutions. It was a messaging problem. To persuade the public, they needed more compassionate packaging. "In other words," Brooks said, "if you want to be seen as a moral, good person, talk about fairness and helping the vulnerable." He added, "You want to win? Start fighting for people! . . . Lead with vulnerable people. Lead with fairness! . . . Telling stories matters. By telling stories, we can soften people. Talk about people, not things!"

Some sharp-eyed conservatives, such as Matthew Continetti, gently mocked Brooks's prescription, suggesting that "maybe it's also the content of the message" that was a problem. Perhaps, he suggested archly in *The Weekly Standard*, the public wasn't wrong to question whether "corporate tax reform" of the type backed by the business elite "would allow the poor to operate on a level playing field with Alcoa and Anheuser-Busch." But as the Kochs assessed the damage after 2012 and began planning their next moves, they embraced Brooks's advice.

They then launched what was essentially the best public relations campaign that money could buy. Underlying it all was the simple point that Brooks had stressed. If the "1 percent" wanted to win control of America, they needed to rebrand themselves as champions of the other "99 percent."

By supplying the research necessary for this political makeover, Brooks was providing one of the key services for which AEI and the other conservative think tanks in Washington were founded. "Conservative think tanks, which are almost exclusively funded by very wealthy people, are the front line of the income-defense industry," observed the political scientist Jeffrey Winters. Brooks, in his CPAC session, put it another way. As he faced an audience filled with the defeated foot soldiers of the conservative movement, he said, "We in the think tanks assist you. We run the idea guns to you!"

After the humiliating presidential defeat of 2012, there was no doubt that the Kochs and the other outsized spenders in their club were in desperate need of new ammunition. Opponents had vilified them relentlessly. One Koch Industries employee recalled, "We had such serious image problems and morale problems, when you said 'Koch,' you might as well have said you work for the devil."

These problems worsened at the start of 2014 as Harry Reid, the Democratic majority leader in the U.S. Senate, began attacking the Kochs almost daily from the Senate floor for, as he put it in one outburst, "trying to buy America. It's time that the American people spoke out against this terrible dishonesty of these two brothers, who are about as un-American as anyone that I can imagine."

Many would have backed down in the face of such public pressure, but the Kochs were determined to double down. "We're going to fight the battle as long as we breathe," David Koch had declared in *Forbes*.

Around the time that Reid began his attacks, the Kochs hired a new chief of communications, Steve Lombardo, a for-

mer chair of Burson-Marsteller's U.S. public affairs and crisis practice in Washington, who had previously burnished the
image of tobacco companies, among others. At the time, they
were still in the midst of a rigorous postmortem, trying to pin-
point where their political operation had gone wrong.

The Republican National Committee was also assessing
its failings. In an unusually candid and self-critical public exe-
gesis, it found among other things that out-of-control spending by outsiders was overwhelming the candidates, giving rich
donors too much influence. "The current campaign finance
environment has led to a handful of friends and allied groups
dominating our side's efforts. This is not healthy. A lot of centralized authority in the hands of a few people at these outside
organizations is dangerous for our Party," it warned.

The Kochs' analysis was kept secret, but in May 2014 a
hint of their thinking surfaced when *Politico* got ahold of a
"confidential investor update" sent by Americans for Prosperity
to its big donors. It tracked closely with Arthur Brooks's view
that the problem had more to do with packaging than content.
"We consistently see that Americans in general are concerned
that free-market policy—and its advocates—benefit the rich
and powerful more than the most vulnerable in society," the
memo from Americans for Prosperity lamented. "We must
correct this misconception."

Soon after, more information leaked out. On June 17,
2014, a young, little-known blogger and Web producer named
Lauren Windsor, who hosted an online political news program
called *The Undercurrent,* began posting a series of audiotapes of
the secret sessions that had taken place just days before, during the Kochs' semiannual donor summit. Windsor had been
libertarian herself. But she had lost her job in the 2008 financial crash and, with it, her faith in free markets. By the time
the Kochs and their circle gathered at the St. Regis Monarch
Beach resort outside Laguna Beach, California, on Friday,
June 13, Windsor had become a crusader against the cor-

rupting influence of big money in politics. Working with an unnamed source who attended the conference, she was eager to spill the Kochs' secrets. The tapes she began revealing didn't disappoint.

A number of news stories resulted from these tapes. But as it turned out, there was at least one more that Windsor didn't release because of its poor audio quality. If anything, it provided an even more stunning picture of the scope and audacity of the Kochs' designs on the country, as well as their effort during this period to recast themselves, in order to appear less threatening.

On Sunday, June 15, the donors came together in the Pacific Ballroom of the five-star oceanfront resort for a confidential post-lunch seminar titled "The Long-Term Strategy: Engaging the Middle Third." As he took the floor, Richard Fink, who was introduced as Charles Koch's "grand strategist," provided a fascinating and at times startling tour through the new political plan. In some ways, no one in the Koch empire was more on the hook for the failures of 2012 than Fink, the brothers' longtime consigliere. Fink was executive vice president and a director of the board of Koch Industries, as well as a board member of Americans for Prosperity. After the election, he had thrown himself into the kind of unsparing internal review for which the company was known. It included an analysis of twenty years of research into political opinions, based on 170,000 surveys taken both in the United States and abroad, as well as many meetings and focus groups. Its conclusion, Fink told the donors, was that if they were to win over America, they needed to change.

"We got our clocks cleaned in 2012," Fink began. "This is a long-term battle." The challenge, he said he had learned, was that the country was divided into three distinct parts. The first third already supported the Kochs' conservative, libertarian vision. Another third, the liberals, whom he referred to as "collectivists," using the old John Birch Society term, were beyond the Kochs' reach. "The battle for the future of the country is who can win the hearts and minds of the middle third," Fink said. "It will determine the direction of the country."

The problem, he said, was that free-market conservatives had lost the all-important "middle third." This segment of the American population tended to believe that liberals cared more about ordinary people like themselves. In contrast, he said, "big business they see as very suspicious . . . They're greedy. They don't care about the underprivileged."

Assuming that he was among friends, Fink readily conceded that these critics weren't wrong. "What do people like you say? I grew up with pretty much very little, okay? And I worked my butt off to get what I have. So," he went on, when he saw people "on the street," he admitted, his reaction was, "Get off your ass and work hard, like we did!"

Unfortunately, he continued, those in the "middle third"—whose votes they needed—had a different reaction when they saw the poor. They instead felt "guilty." Instead of being concerned with "opportunity" for themselves, Fink said, this group was concerned about "opportunity for other people."

So, he explained, the government-slashing agenda of the Koch network was a problem for these voters. Fink acknowledged, "We want to decrease regulations. Why? It's because we can make more profit, okay? Yeah, and cut government spending so we don't have to pay so much taxes. There's truth in that." But the "middle third" of American voters, he warned, was uncomfortable with positions that seemed motivated by greed.

What the Koch network needed to do, he said, was to persuade moderate, undecided voters that the "intent" of economic libertarians was virtuous. "We've got to convince these people we mean well and that we're good people," said Fink. "Whoever does," he said, "will drive this country."

Fink was brutally honest about how unpopular the right-wing donors' views were. "When we focus on decreasing government spending," he said, and "decreasing taxes, it doesn't do it, okay? They're not responding, and don't like it, okay?"

But, he pointed out, if anyone in America knew how to sell something, it should be those in the Koch network. "We get business—what do we do?" he asked. "We want to find out what the customer wants, right? Not what we want them to buy!"

The Kochs' extensive research had shown that what the American "customer" wanted from politics, alas, was quite different from their business-dominated free-market orthodoxy. It wasn't just that Americans were interested in opportunity for the many, rather than just for themselves. It also turned out, Fink acknowledged, that they wanted a clean environment and health and high standards of living, as well as political and religious freedom and peace and security.

These objectives would seem to present a problem for a group led by ultrarich industrialists who had almost single-handedly stymied environmentalists' efforts to protect the planet from climate change. The extraordinary measures that the Kochs and their allies had taken to sabotage the country's first program offering affordable health care to millions of uninsured citizens might also seem to be problematic. Their championship of tax breaks for heirs, hedge fund managers, offshore accounts, and other loopholes favoring the rich, along with their opposition to welfare, the minimum wage, organized labor, and funding public education, also would seemingly fly in the face of the middle third's interest in widening opportunity.

These political problems would seem to have been compounded by new statistics showing that the top 1 percent of earners had captured 93 percent of the income gains in the first year of recovery after the recession.

But rather than altering their policies, those in the Koch network, according to Fink, needed a better sales plan. "This is going to sound a little strange," he admitted, "so you'll have to bear with me." But to convince the "middle third" of the donors' good "intent," he said, the Koch network needed to reframe the way that it described its political goal. What it needed, he said, was to "launch a movement for well-being."

The improved pitch, he said, would argue that free markets were the path to happiness, while big government led to tyranny and fascism. His reasoning went like this: Government programs caused dependency, which in turn caused psychological depression. Historically, he argued, this led to totalitarianism. The minimum wage, he said, provided a good example. It denied the "opportunity for earned success" to 500,000 Americans who, he estimated, would be willing to work for less than the federal minimum standard of $7.25 per hour. Without jobs, "they've lost their meaning in life," said Fink. This, he warned, had been "a very big part of the recruitment in Germany during the '20s." Thus, he argued to an audience that included many of the country's billionaires, minimum wage laws could be described as leading to the kinds of conditions that caused "the rise and fall of the Third Reich."

Freedom fighters, as Fink labeled the donors, needed to explain to American voters that their opposition to programs for the poor did not stem from greed, and their opposition to the minimum wage wasn't based on a desire for cheap labor. Rather, as their new talking points would portray it, unfettered free-market capitalism was simply the best path to human "well-being."

Charles Koch had expressed similar sentiments in a recent interview with the *Wichita Business Journal*. In it, he said, "The poor, okay, you have welfare, but you've condemned them to a lifetime of dependency and hopelessness." Like Obama, he said, "We want 'hope and change.' But we want people to have the hope that they can advance on their own merits, rather than the hope that somebody gives them something." In the same interview, Koch described, without any self-consciousness, how he had recently promoted his son, Chase, to the presidency of Koch Fertilizer and how at "every step, he's done it on his own." The possibility that his son, like he and his brothers, Richard Mellon Scaife, Dick DeVos, and the Bechtel boys, to name just a few in his network, might have benefited from a job in the family's business or a huge inheritance, rather than having been "condemned . . . to a lifetime of dependency and hopelessness," because "somebody" had given "them something," seemed not to have crossed his mind.

To "earn the respect and good feeling" of those whose support they needed, Fink went on to explain during his talk, the Kochs would also form and publicize partnerships with unlikely allies. This would counteract critics who claimed they were negative or divisive. For instance, he told the donors, they were going to hear about the Kochs' partnerships with the United Negro College Fund and with the National Association of Criminal Defense Lawyers, the latter of which they had been financially supporting for several years. Later that afternoon, in fact, Fink was joined in another panel discussion, titled "Driving the National Conversation," with Michael Lomax, president of the United Negro College Fund, along with Norman Reimer, executive director of the National Association of Criminal Defense Lawyers. Fink explained that by reaching across the partisan divide, the Kochs could present their group as offering America "a positive vision." He said it would demonstrate that "the other side creates divisiveness, but we solve problems."

There were in fact more than a few connections between the defense bar and the Koch network. A surprising number of the donors had been ensnared in serious legal problems. Not only had the Kochs faced environmental, workplace safety, fraud, and bribery allegations; many others in their group had legal issues too. At that moment, Renaissance Technologies, the hedge fund co-directed by Bob Mercer, who had become an increasingly active member of the Koch network, was still under investigation by the Internal Revenue Service for avoiding more than $6 billion in taxes between 2000 and 2013. In a 2014 Senate inquiry, Democratic senator Carl Levin denounced the company's accounting as a "pretty stunning bit of phony and abusive tax machinations." A company spokesman acknowledged the complicated accounting method but maintained it was "appropriate under current law."

Meanwhile, SAC Capital, Steven Cohen's huge hedge fund, had been under criminal investigation for years while its managing director, Michael Sullivan, belonged to the Koch network, performing as a featured speaker at one seminar. In the end, neither Cohen nor Sullivan was charged with criminal wrongdoing, but after eight SAC employees pleaded guilty to or were convicted of insider trading, the government accused Cohen of turning "a blind eye to misconduct" and in a settlement slapped his firm with a $1.8 billion fine, the largest such fine in history.

In his own remarks at the donor summit, Reimer described the criminal justice system as "overly abusive, overly inclusive" and suggested that "there probably isn't a single person in this group who doesn't have a friend, a relative or a co-worker, a neighbor, someone you care about who hasn't been caught up in the criminal justice system in this country." He was closer to the mark than he probably knew.

As hoped for, these bipartisan moves soon stirred positive headlines outside the Kochs' tight circle, creating exactly the kind of image overhaul they had in mind. Obama's senior adviser, Valerie Jarrett, surprised those familiar with the Kochs' full record by inviting Mark Holden, the general counsel of Koch Industries, to meet with her and other top officials about the issue in the White House, enabling the Kochs to appear above "divisiveness," just as Fink had planned. Particularly effective was their joining an alliance for criminal justice reform with a number of progressive groups, including the

Center for American Progress. Washington's premier liberal think tank regarded the partnership as a means of adding financial and political clout to the cause of poor and minority inmates. But the Kochs had long had other kinds of perpetrators in mind. The platform of the Libertarian Party in 1980—the year David Koch ran on its ticket—called for an end to the prosecution of all tax evaders. The Kochs also objected vociferously to the many environmental crimes with which they had been charged.

Holden acknowledged in an interview that the Kochs became active in criminal justice reform when the Clinton Justice Department charged Koch Industries in 2000 with environmental crimes. "It was hell," recalled Holden. He said Charles Koch saw the prosecution as "government overreach" and grew concerned more generally about the issue.

But far from an abusive prosecution of the powerless, the 2000 case was initiated by the Koch employee in Corpus Christi, Texas, who blew the whistle on the company for trying to cover up the fact that it was, as she put it, "hemorrhaging benzene"—a known carcinogen—into the air. This was the case that David Uhlmann, the prosecutor and later law professor, had described as "one of the most significant cases ever brought under the Clean Air Act." The company was not falsely accused. It paid a $20 million fine, thereby avoiding jail time for its employees. The ability of the Kochs to spin this fifteen years later into a campaign for bipartisan, populist social reform—one aimed at weakening the government's prosecutorial powers—was a masterful bit of self-promotion.

Holden, who had been a prison guard early in his career, spoke feelingly in public about the country's over-incarceration of underprivileged prisoners. Whether the Kochs truly shared his views or merely saw criminal justice reform as a means of weakening the government's hand against corporate crime, and whitewashing their own image, remained to be seen. Skeptics pointed out that the Kochs continued to support numerous candidates—including Scott Walker, whom David Koch named in 2015 as their favorite presidential candidate until he dropped out—who had records on criminal justice issues that completely belied the Kochs' professed concern. They also noted that the Kochs only championed a corporate campaign against "check the box" forms, requiring job seekers to disclose prior criminal convictions, after Koch Industries got in trouble with the federal government for failing to reveal its own criminal record.

Nonetheless, the $25 million grant from Charles's foundation to the United Negro College Fund just before the June 2014 summit began was winning them positive headlines. "Increasing well-being by helping people improve their lives has long been our focus," said Charles in a prepared public statement about the donation.

His use of the new buzz phrase "well-being" seemed almost offhand. But during another session at the summit that June, a speaker explained to the donors just how deliberate and politically disarming the term was. James Otteson, a conservative professor of political economy at Wake Forest University, called it "a game changer." In fact, he told the donor group that he was planning to build a "well-being" center at Wake Forest, where he already was executive director of the BB&T Center for the Study of Capitalism.

One anecdote, he said, illustrated "the power of framing" free-market theories as a movement to promote well-being. He recounted that a colleague, whom he described as a prominent "left wing political scientist" who "rails" against Republicans and capitalism, had been so entranced by the idea of studying the factors contributing to human well-being that he had said, "You know, I'd even be willing to take Koch money for that." Upon hearing this, the donors laughed out loud. "Who can be against well-being? The framing is absolutely critical," Otteson exclaimed.

The idea of sugarcoating antigovernment, free-market ideology as a nonpartisan movement to enhance the quality of life had clear advantages. And Otteson's success at penetrating academia with the approach was especially encouraging to the group. The growing emphasis on academia as a delivery system for the donors' conservative ideology and as a long-range strategy to change the country's political makeup was, in fact, another major focus of the donor summit.

As the Olin and Bradley Foundations had demonstrated, and as Charles Koch's early blueprint for advancing libertarianism showed, winning the hearts and minds of college students had long been a core strategy on the right. That weekend, Kevin Gentry, the conference's emcee, who was vice president for special projects at Koch Industries and vice president of the Charles Koch Foundation, described academia as "a great investment" and "an area—for this group—this seminar network—that is a significant competitive advantage" and an important component of the Kochs' ambitious designs.

As Ryan Stowers, vice president of the Charles Koch Foundation, recounted to the donors, in the 1980s, when Charles Koch and Richard Fink first tried to use Hayek's model of production as a means of manufacturing political change, it seemed far-fetched to try to convert academia into a source of free-market ideology. There were so few free-market scholars in America, Stowers said, that Charles could barely find enough to hold a conference. But with "courage, investment, and leadership," from Charles and the other donors, he said, "we've built a robust, freedom-advancing network" of nearly five thousand scholars in some four hundred colleges and universities across the country.

A breakthrough, Stowers related, was the creation of some two dozen privately funded academic centers, the flagship of which was the Mercatus Center at George Mason University. As a 2015 report by one of the nonprofits connected to Art Pope explained, private academic centers within colleges and universities were ideal devices by which rich conservatives could replace the faculty's views with their own. "Money talks loudly on college campuses," it noted. As an example, the report profiled the trailblazing record of John Allison, the former Cato Institute chairman, who had overseen grants to sixty-three colleges when running the BB&T bank. All of these programs were required to teach his favorite philosopher, the celebrator of self-interest Ayn Rand.

But as earmarked grants proliferated, controversy over academic freedom grew, increasing the need for slicker marketing. By 2014, the various Koch foundations alone were funding pro-corporate programs at 283 four-year colleges and universities. At Florida State University, where a Koch foundation grant in 2008 gave the foundation a say on faculty hires, criticism erupted into a public fight. Students complained that the Koch influence was nefarious and omnipresent. Jerry Funt, an undergraduate, said that in the public university's introductory economics course, "We learned that Keynes was bad, the free-market was better, that sweatshop labor wasn't so bad, and that the hands-off regulations in China were better than those in the U.S." Their economics textbook, he said, was co-written by Russell Sobel, the former recipient of Koch funding at West Virginia University who had taught that safety regulations hurt coal miners. The textbook, which Funt described as arguing that "climate change wasn't caused by humans and isn't a big issue," had been given an F by an environmental group. But when critics raised objections, the Kochs defended their purchase of influence over public universities as merely providing "fresh" college thinking.

The Kochs were also directing millions of dollars into online education, and into teaching high school students, through a nonprofit that Charles devised called the Young Entrepreneurs Academy. The financially pressed Topeka school system, for instance, signed an agreement with the organization which taught students that, among other things, Franklin Roosevelt didn't alleviate the Depression, minimum wage laws and public assistance hurt the poor, lower pay for women was not discriminatory, and the government, rather than business, caused the 2008 recession. The program, which was aimed at low-income areas, also paid students to take additional courses online.

At the June summit, Stowers stressed to the donors that this "investment" in education had created a valuable "talent pipeline." Assuming the thousands of scholars on average taught hundreds of students per year, he said, they could influence the thinking of millions of young Americans annually. "This cycle constantly repeats itself," he noted, "and you can see the multiplier effect it's had on our network since 2008."

In summation, Gentry stressed to the donors, "So you can see, higher education is not just limited to an impact on higher education." The students were "the next generation of the freedom movement," he said. "The students that graduate out of these higher-education programs populate the state-based think tanks and the national think tanks." And, he said, they "become the major staffing for the state chapters" of the "grassroots" groups. Those with passion were encouraged to become part of what he called the Kochs' *fully integrated network.* At this point, he paused and said, "I got to be careful how I say this." He paused again. "They populate our *program.*"

The reason Gentry had to be careful was that the Kochs described their educational activities to the IRS as nonpolitical charitable work, qualifying them for tax breaks and anonymity. Yet what Gentry was describing could scarcely be more political. It was a full-service political factory. As he addressed the donors, cajoling them to "invest" more, he couldn't resist adding further detail. "It's not just work at the universities with the students," he went on. "It's building the state-based capabilities, and *election* capabilities, and *integrating* this talent pipeline. So you can see how this is useful to each other over time. No one else has this infrastructure. We're very excited about doing it!"

Evidently, the donors were enthused, too. By the time the

summit ended on June 17, the Kochs had set a fund-raising goal of $290 million. It was an audacious and, at the time, unprecedented sum for any outside group to spend in a midterm election.

"I know on the one hand this is crazy; $290 million is an extraordinary figure," Gentry acknowledged, shortly before the final pledges were made. But he told the secret gathering, "We've come a long way from where we were seven or eight years ago." He added, "You know, we're trying to do this in a businesslike way for you all, because, literally, you all are our investors."

Eight days later, the Charles Koch Institute hosted what it called its Inaugural Well-Being Forum at the Newseum in Washington. Among the panelists was Professor James Otteson from Wake Forest. In an online essay, Charles explained that his foundation's "Well-Being Initiative" aimed to "foster more conversation about the true nature of well-being." Displayed prominently beneath his byline was a quotation from Martin Luther King Jr. No mention was made of King's vision of well-being, which included labor unions, national health care, and government employment for those needing jobs.

Among the five members on the advisory board to Charles Koch's new Well-Being Initiative was Arthur Brooks, whose discovery that conservatives needed to be seen as more caring had deeply influenced the Kochs. By then, Brooks had moved beyond an earlier book he had written—which, like Mitt Romney, divided Americans into "makers" and "takers"—and turned out a new one that defined free enterprise as a path to happiness. Unhappiness, according to Brooks, "had a strong link" to "economic envy," such as the kind of thinking that pushes for higher taxes on the very rich. *The New York Times* deemed Brooks's theories on this print-worthy enough to publish in its opinion section. Evidently, the new well-being trope was gaining traction.

As they recast themselves in public as nonpartisan reformers, the Kochs' increasingly aggressive private political machine geared up for the 2014 election. The ultimate prize was control of the U.S. Senate. If Republicans could capture the majority in the upper chamber and hold on to the House, they would dominate Congress, controlling the legislative agenda and creating a formidable roadblock to President Obama.

But the Kochs had reached an important conclusion during their post-2012 autopsy. "They decided that the Republican Party's infrastructure wasn't worth a damn, and if they wanted it to be done better, they'd have to do it themselves," said the Koch Industries employee who had described the company's image problems during this period.

It might seem a radical and troubling step for a couple of billionaire businessmen who had never been elected to any office, and had no formal allegiance to anything other than their massive, private multinational company, to decide to supplant one of the country's two political parties. But in his interview with the *Wichita Business Journal,* Charles shrugged it off nonchalantly. Asked why he was so involved in politics, he likened himself to the golfer Lee Trevino, who, he said, explained his reason for winning tournaments by saying, "Well, somebody has got to win them, and it might as well be me." Charles added, "There doesn't seem to be any other large company trying to do this, so it might as well be us. Somebody has got to work to save the country." Far from being some sort of evil Svengali, he said his primary role at Americans for Prosperity was this: "I write a check." He added, "Listen, if I could do everything that's attributed to me, I would be a very busy boy."

As the Kochs' donor network poured a record amount of money into the 2014 midterm elections, Charles continued to portray himself, and probably to think of himself, as a disinterested patriot. In an op-ed piece in *The Wall Street Journal* that spring, he described himself as involved in politics only reluctantly and recently. Dating his activism to the founding of the biannual donor seminars, he asserted that he'd only been politically engaged for a decade. But after tallying up the $7 million or so that the Kochs had poured into politics more than a decade earlier, the nonpartisan fact-checking group Politi-Fact judged his claim to be "false."

A longtime associate who declined to be named, exclaimed, "He has been trying since the 1970s to get his Libertarian Revolution going!" Charles might have started as a bookish idealist who disdained conventional politics, but at each step of the way he had learned from his failures and moved closer to the center of power. He was disciplined and methodical. After 2012, for instance, he had systematically studied not only his own side's weaknesses but also the other side's strengths. "He's learned a lot from the Democrats, particularly about using grass roots," said the associate. "For Charles, politics is another form of science—just dealing with people, not molecules."

Inside the Obama White House, as the 2014 midterm elections approached, David Simas, director of the Office of Political Strategy and Outreach, began to suspect that the Kochs had reverse engineered the data analytics that the Obama effort used in 2012. The implications, a White House official said, were, in a word, "huge."

Computers had transformed the business of winning elections into a rapidly changing high-tech competition for massive amounts of voter data. Realizing that its data operation had fallen woefully behind in 2012, the Koch network took serious remedial action. Freedom Partners, as the Koch donors now referred to themselves, quietly made a multimillion-dollar investment in i360, a state-of-the-art political data company, which then merged with the Kochs' troubled data collection effort, Themis. Soon the operation had hired a hundred staffers and assembled detailed portraits of 250 million U.S.

consumers and over 190 million active voters. Field workers for the Kochs' many advocacy groups were armed with hand-held devices on which they constantly updated the data. Their political operatives could then determine which voters were "persuadable" and bombard them with personalized communications aimed at motivating them to vote or to stay home.

The Kochs' development of their own data bank marked a pivotal moment in their relationship with the Republican Party. Until then, handling the voter files had been a core function of the Republican National Committee. But now the Kochs had their own rival operation, which was by many accounts easier to use and more sophisticated than that of the RNC. Several top Republican candidates started to purchase i360's data, even though they were more expensive, because they were better. With little other choice, in 2014 the RNC struck what it called a "historic" deal to share data with the Kochs. But the détente was reportedly strained. By 2015, the acrimony had broken out into the open as Katie Walsh, the chief of staff at the RNC, all but accused the Kochs of usurping the Republican Party.

In an extraordinary public rebuke, she told *Yahoo News*, "I think it's very dangerous and wrong to allow a group of very strong, well-financed individuals who have no accountability to anyone to have control over who gets access to the data when, why and how."

Michael Palmer, the president of i360, punched back, say-ing, "We believe that a robust marketplace . . . is a healthy way to advance past the single monopoly model that has failed the Republican Party in recent presidential elections." Having embraced the Kochs' free-market ideology and their right to spend unlimited money, the Republican Party was now ironi-cally finding itself sidelined and perhaps imperiled by the rapa-ciousness of its own big donors. Alarmed, a source "close to the RNC" told *Yahoo*, "It's pretty clear that they don't want to work with the party but want to supplant it."

If in 2012 the Kochs had rivaled the Republican Party, by

2014 they had in many ways surpassed it. "They're building a party from outside to take over the party—they're doing it by market segments—it's like a business plan," observed Lisa Graves, the head of the Center for Media and Democracy, a liberal watchdog group that studied the mechanics of political manipulation.

Americans for Prosperity had expanded its ground game to 550 paid staffers, with as many as 50 in a single pivotal state like Florida, as *Politico* reported. Other Koch-backed advocacy groups, such as Generation Opportunity and the LIBRE Initiative, planted grassroots organizers wherever there were hotly contested elections. The Koch constellation also added Aegis Strategic, an organization that aimed to recruit and train candidates. This way the Koch network could avoid the kinds of flaky misfits who had plagued Republicans in 2012. As he watched their progress, Axelrod was impressed. "They aggressively corrected the problems they had last time with terminal foot-in-mouth disease," he said. "It showed."

On November 4, 2014, the investors of the Koch network finally got their money's worth. Election Day proved a Republican triumph. The GOP picked up nine seats in the Senate, winning full control of both congressional chambers. Beltway pundits proclaimed President Obama a "lame duck" whose presidency they said was, for all intents and purposes, over. From this point on, they predicted, he would be largely relegated to playing defense against conservatives' efforts to roll back everything his administration had done before.

The election was as big a victory for ultrarich conservative donors as it was for the winning Republican candidates. As the *Times* noted, the conservative outside groups had "retooled and revamped" during the previous year and a half and emerged as the preeminent forces in the election. There had never been a costlier midterm election, nor one with more outside money.

And the largest overall source fueling this explosion of private and often secret spending was the Koch network. All told, it poured over $100 million into competitive House and Senate races and almost twice that amount into other kinds of activism.

Four years into the *Citizens United* era, the numbers were more numbing than shocking. The only suspense in each election cycle was the factor by which the spending had multiplied over the previous one. Mark McKinnon, a centrist political consultant who had advised both Republicans and Democrats, declared, "We have reached a tipping point where mega donors completely dominate the landscape."

A few of the biggest spenders were now Democrats, like the California hedge fund magnate turned environmental activist Tom Steyer. The $74 million he spent trying to elect candidates who pledged to fight global warming made him the largest disclosed donor in 2014. While this added some ideological diversity, it did nothing to dilute the concentration of wealth that now influenced elections. The 100 biggest known donors in 2014 spent nearly as much money on behalf of their candidates as the 4.75 million people who contributed $200 or less. On their own, the top 100 known donors gave $323 million. And this was only the disclosed money. Once the millions of dollars in unlimited, undisclosed dark money were included, there was little doubt that an extraordinarily small and rich conservative clique had financially dominated everyone else.

"Let's call the system that *Citizens United* and other rulings and laws have created what it is: an oligarchy," declared McKinnon. "The system is controlled by a handful of ultra-wealthy people, most of whom got rich from the system and who will get richer from the system."

From the Republic's earliest days, the wealthy had always dominated politics, but at least since the Progressive Era the public, through its elected representatives, had devised rules to keep the influence in check. By 2015, however, conservative legal advocates, underwritten by wealthy benefactors and aided by a conservative majority on the Supreme Court, had led a successful drive to gut most of those rules. It was no longer clear if the remaining checks on corruption were up to the task. It had long been the conceit in America that great economic inequality could coexist with great social and political equality. But a growing body of academic work suggested that this was changing. As America grew more economically unequal, those at the top were purchasing the power needed to stay there.

Among the new power brokers, few if any could match the political clout of the Kochs. The reach of their "integrated network" was unique. One reflection of their singular status was their relationship with the new majority leader of the Senate, Mitch McConnell. Only a few months before assuming that position, McConnell had been an honored speaker at their June donor summit. There, he had thanked "Charles and David" and added, "I don't know where we would be without you." Soon after he was sworn in, McConnell hired a new policy chief—a former lobbyist for Koch Industries. McConnell then went on to launch a stunning all-out war on the Environmental Protection Agency, urging governors across the country to refuse to comply with its new restrictions on greenhouse gas emissions.

Three of the newly elected Republicans who joined the Senate in 2014 had also attended the secret Koch meeting in June, where they, too, had gushed over their sponsors. The leaked tapes of the event caught Joni Ernst, for instance, who had previously been, by her own account, a "little-known state senator from a very rural part of Iowa," crediting the Kochs with transforming her, like Eliza Doolittle, into a national star. "Exposure to this group and to this network and the opportunity to meet so many of you," she said, were what "really started my trajectory."

Charles Koch's trajectory had been a longer climb, but it was hard not to marvel at how far he, too, had come from the days when he had haunted the John Birch Society bookstore in Wichita and teetered with the Freedom School and the Libertarian Party on the outermost fringe of political irrelevance. The force of his will, combined with his fortune, had made him one of the most formidable figures in modern American politics. Few had waged a more relentless or more effective assault on Americans' belief in government.

He and his brother had built and financed a private political machine that had helped cripple a twice-elected Democratic president and begun to supplant the Republican Party. Educational institutions and think tanks all over the country promoted his worldview, doubling as a talent pipeline. A growing fleet of nonprofit groups mobilized public opinion behind his agenda. The groups trained candidates and provided the technological and financial assistance necessary to run state-of-the-art campaigns. The money they could put behind their chosen candidates was seemingly limitless. Congressmen, senators, and presidential hopefuls now flocked to their secret seminars like supplicants, eager to please them in hopes of earning their support.

Rare was the Republican candidate who wouldn't toe the Kochs' line. John Kasich, the iconoclastic governor of Ohio, prompted an angry walkout by some twenty donors at the Kochs' April 2014 summit for criticizing the Koch network's position against Medicaid expansion. In answer to Randy Kendrick, who had questioned his pro-Medicaid position, Kasich retorted, "I don't know about you, lady. But when I get to the pearly gates, I'm going to have an answer for what I've done for the poor." He added, "I know this is going to upset a lot of you guys, but we have to use government to reach out to people living in the shadows." The Kochs never invited Kasich back again.

Donald Trump, the New York real estate and casino magnate whose unorthodox bid for the Republican nomination flummoxed party regulars, was also left off the Kochs' invitation list. In August 2015, as his rivals flocked to meet the Koch donors, he tweeted, "I wish good luck to all of the Republican candidates that traveled to California to beg for money etc. from the Koch Brothers. Puppets?" Trump's popularity suggested that voters were hungry for independent candidates who wouldn't spout the donors' lines. His call to close the carried-interest tax loophole, and talk of the ultrarich not paying its share, as well as his anti-immigrant rants, made his opponents appear robotically subservient, and out of touch. But few other Republican candidates could afford to ignore the Kochs.

Among their most astonishing feats, the Kochs had succeeded in persuading hundreds of the other richest conservatives in the country to give them control over their millions of dollars in contributions, in effect making them leaders of a conservative billionaires' caucus. Most of the other partners, as they called themselves, were silent. Their names rarely if ever appeared. When, in response to criticism, the Kochs invited the media to cover snippets of their summits, they insisted that the reporters agree not to name the other donors. Yet this secretive, unelected, and unaccountable club was changing the face of American politics.

Charles Koch denied he had ever given any dark money. "What I give isn't 'dark.' What I give politically, that's all reported," he told CBS News in a 2015 interview. "It's either to PACs or to candidates. And what I give to my foundations is all public information." Perhaps he believed it, but during the previous five years alone, he, his brother David, and their allies had contributed over $760 million to mysterious and ostensibly apolitical nonprofits such as the Freedom Partners Chamber of Commerce, the Center to Protect Patient Rights, and the TC4 Trust. From there the money had been disbursed to dozens of other nonprofits, some of which were little more than mailboxes, which had then spent the funds promoting the donors' political interests both directly in elections, and indirectly in countless other ways. As for the transparency of Charles Koch's foundations, two of them had made grants of nearly $8 million between 2005 and 2011 to DonorsTrust, whose stated purpose was to mask the money trail.

"It's extraordinary. No one else has done anything like it," said Rob Stein, the Democratic activist who tried to create a progressive counterweight called the Democracy Alliance. "It takes an enormous amount of money, and many years, to do what the Kochs have done. They're deeply passionate. They're disciplined, and they're also ruthless."

In an interview, Brian Doherty, libertarianism's historian, said of the Kochs, "There are few policy victories you can lay directly at their feet." But he suggested that "if you look at the larger eco-system of libertarianism they were absolutely key." Because of them, he said, "the general sense of valuing Free Markets—the intellectual zeitgeist—now recognizes libertarianism in a way it never did twenty years ago."

Less than a decade later, the influence of the Kochs and their fellow "radicals for capitalism" extended well beyond just zeitgeist. They still might not have been able to take credit for many positive legislative accomplishments, but they had proven instrumental in obstructing those of their opponents. Despite the radicalism of their ideas, which had developed in a direct line from the John Birch Society, the Kochs had fulfilled Charles's 1981 ambition not just to support elected politicians, whom he regarded as mere "actors playing out a script," but to "supply the themes and words for the scripts."

By 2015, their antigovernment lead was followed by much of Congress. Addressing global warming was out of the question. Although economic inequality had reached record levels, raising taxes on the runaway rich and closing special loopholes that advantaged only them were also nonstarters. Funding basic public services like the repair of America's crumbling infrastructure was also seemingly beyond reach. A majority of the public supported an expansion of the social safety net. But leaders in both parties nevertheless embraced austerity measures popular with the affluent. Even though Americans overwhelmingly opposed cuts in Social Security, for instance, the Beltway consensus was that to save the program, it needed to be shrunk.

Obama's Affordable Care Act had survived, and polls showed that it was growing in popularity. But after nonstop battering, and the Obama administration's own serious fumbles, its reputation, and Obama's, had been damaged, even though the country's health-care costs and medical coverage, like the economy as a whole, were far better off than before he took office. Unemployment was down, and incomes and markets were up. Yet faith in government reached new lows. Obama could make progress on his environmental and other goals by taking executive actions, but in Congress ambitious new programs were out of the question.

Equally hopeless, it seemed, was campaign-finance reform. An overwhelming bipartisan majority of Americans disapproved of the amount of money in politics and supported new spending restrictions. Yet the Republican Party was now overrun by minority views, including opposition to virtually all limits on campaign spending, that seemed outlandish when the Kochs expressed them in 1980.

The radical rightists in Congress had gained so much sway by September 2015 that they effectively forced the resignation of House Speaker John Boehner, whom they had threatened to depose for not acceding to their latest demands. Leading the charge against Boehner had been Representative Mark Meadows, the North Carolina Tea Party Republican whose election had been greased by gerrymandering and other help from dark-money groups. On his way out, Boehner took a parting shot at "false prophets" and "groups here in town" who "whipped people into a frenzy believing they could accomplish things that they know, they know are never going to happen."

Conventional political wisdom measured power on the basis of election outcomes, chalking up 2012 as a loss for the Kochs, 2014 as a win, and 2016 as a test whose results remained to be seen. But this missed the more important story. The Kochs and their ultra-wealthy allies on the right had become what was arguably the single most effective special-interest group in the country.

The Kochs hadn't done it on their own. They were the fulfillment of farsighted political visionaries like Lewis Powell, Irving Kristol, William Simon, Michael Joyce, and Paul Weyrich. They were also the logical extension of the legacies of earlier big right-wing donors. John M. Olin, Lynde and Harry Bradley, and Richard Mellon Scaife had blazed the path by the time the Kochs rose to the pinnacle of their power.

During the 1970s, a handful of the nation's wealthiest corporate captains felt overtaxed and overregulated and decided to fight back. Disenchanted with the direction of modern America, they launched an ambitious, privately financed war of ideas to radically change the country. They didn't want to merely win elections; they wanted to change how Americans thought. Their ambitions were grandiose—to "save" America as they saw it, at every level, by turning the clock back to the Gilded Age before the advent of the Progressive Era. Charles Koch was younger and more libertarian than his predecessors, but, as Doherty observed, his ambitions were if anything even more radical: to pull the government out "at the root."

The weapon of choice of these wealthy activists was philanthropy. The early concerns that private foundations would become undemocratic forces of elite political power were long forgotten a century later. Leapfrogging beyond a failed political experiment by the liberal Ford Foundation in the late 1960s, the conservative rich created a new generation of hyper-political private foundations. Their aim was to invest in ideology like venture capitalists, leveraging their fortunes for maximum strategic impact. Because of the anonymity that charitable organizations provided, the full scope of these efforts was largely invisible to the public. The conservative philanthropists were, as Edwin Meese once said of Scaife, the "unseen hands."

As they began to gain ground, their war spread from "beachheads" in academia and law to corporate front groups purporting to represent public opinion. At each step, they hired the smartest and slickest marketers that money could buy, policy entrepreneurs like Frank Luntz who were skilled at popularizing the agenda of wealthy backers by "framing" their issues in more broadly appealing terms. As their efforts grew increasingly political, the funders continued to cloak these projects under the mantle of philanthropy. Few of the sponsors of this radical reorientation of American thinking were known to the public. Some carved their names in the institutions they built or attached them to the academic chairs they underwrote. But they rarely ran for office, and when they did, they even more rarely won. They exercised their power from the shadows, meeting in secret, hiding their money trails, and paying others to front for them. The dark-money groups masquerading as "social welfare" organizations during the Obama era were merely the latest iteration of a privately funded, nonprofit ideological war that had begun forty years earlier.

These political philanthropists defined themselves as selfless patriots, motivated by public, not private, gain. In many instances, they were likely sincere. Almost all gave generously not just to political projects but also to the arts, sciences, and education and, in some cases, directly to the poor. But at the same time, it was impossible not to notice that the political policies they embraced benefited their own bottom lines first and foremost. Lowering taxes and rolling back regulations, slashing the welfare state, and obliterating the limits on campaign spending might or might not have helped others, but they most certainly strengthened the hand of extreme donors with extreme wealth. "Giving back," as Peter Buffett, the son of the legendary billionaire financier Warren Buffett, observed, "sounds heroic." But he noted, "As more lives and communities are destroyed by the system that creates vast amounts of wealth for the few," philanthropists were frequently left "searching for answers with their right hands" to problems that they had "created with their left." Whether their motives were virtuous or venal, in the course of a few decades a handful of enormously rich right-wing philanthropists had changed the course of American politics. They created a formidable wealth defense movement, which had become a sizable part of what Buffett dubbed "the charitable-industrial complex."

Much as they had achieved by 2015, there was still a major item on the Kochs' shopping list: the White House. Anyone paying attention knew that 2014 was just a trial run for the presidential race in 2016. Phil Dubose, the former Koch Industries manager who spent twenty-six years working for the Kochs before testifying against them in court, had no doubt that they now had their sights on all three branches of government. "What they want is to get their own way," he said. "They call themselves libertarians. For lack of a better word, what it means is that if you're big enough to get away with it, you can get away with it. No government. If it's good for their business, they think it's good for America. What it means for the country," he added, speaking from his modest home in rural Louisiana, "is it would release the dogs. The little people? They'd get gobbled up."

On the last weekend of January 2015, as was their custom, the Kochs again convened their donor summit at a resort in

Rancho Mirage, outside Palm Springs, California. Marc Short, the president of Freedom Partners, acknowledged that "2014 was nice, but there's a long way to go." To get there, according to one ally, that weekend Charles and David Koch each pledged to give $75 million. If so, their contributions would still represent a mere fraction of the network's new fund-raising goal announced that weekend. This time, the Koch network aimed to spend $889 million in the 2016 election cycle. The sum was more than twice what the network had spent in 2012. It rivaled the record $1 billion that each of the two major political parties was expected to spend, securing their unique status as a rival center of gravity. The Kochs could afford it. Despite their predictions that Obama would prove catastrophic to the American economy, Charles's and David's personal fortunes had nearly tripled during his presidency, from $14 billion apiece in March 2009 to $41.6 billion each in March 2015, according to *Forbes*.

To Fred Wertheimer, Washington's battle-hardened liberal crusader against political corruption, the sum was almost beyond belief. "Eight hundred and eighty-nine million dollars? We've had money in the past, but this is so far beyond what anyone has thought of it's mind-boggling. This is unheard of in the history of the country. There has never been anything that approaches this."

Wertheimer was a public interest lawyer who had been waging an uphill battle to stem the rising tide of money in politics since the Watergate days. From his perspective, the country's democratic process was in crisis. "We have two unelected multibillionaires who want to control the U.S. government and exercise the power to decide what is best for more than 300 million American people, without the voices of these people being heard." He added, "There is nothing in our constitutional democracy that accepts that two of the richest people in the world can control our destiny."

As was clear from the more than $13 million a year that Koch Industries spent lobbying Congress, the Kochs had enormous financial stakes in the U.S. government. The idea that they and their allies were spending nearly $1 billion for completely selfless reasons strained credulity. Of course, money wasn't always the determinant of American elections, but there was little doubt that if the American presidency was on the auction block in 2016, the Kochs hoped to make the winning bid.

In an interview with *USA Today,* another instance in which he said that all he wanted was to "increase well-being in society," Charles Koch bristled at the idea that he was motivated by an interest in boosting his bottom line. "We are doing all of this to make more money?" he asked. "I mean, that is so ludicrous."

Some of course might have used the same adjective to describe the two-decade-long legal battle that he and his brothers waged against each other after each inheriting hundreds of millions of dollars, in order to get a bigger share. But sharing was never easy for Charles Koch. As a child, he used to tell an unfunny joke. When called upon to split a treat with others, he would say with a wise-guy grin, "I just want my fair share—which is all of it."

In many ways, the research on this book began three decades ago when I arrived in Washington to cover Ronald Reagan's presidency for *The Wall Street Journal*. During the intervening years, I've interviewed countless political players in all forms of public life, from presidents to voters, and watched as American politics increasingly has been shaped by an ever-rising tide of private money. This book is based on hundreds of interviews conducted during the past five years with a wide range of sources spanning from the main characters and their family members, friends, and ideological allies to their business associates and political competitors.

In an ideal world, every interview would be conducted on the record. Several of the sources to whom I owe the most, however, have asked to have their names withheld. I apologize in advance to readers for not being able to fully identify these sources, but where possible I have tried to indicate their expertise and outlook, and where not possible I have tried to be scrupulous in vetting their accounts for accuracy. I also regret that several of the major characters in this saga were unreachable. Some, such as Richard Mellon Scaife, provided access to some of their papers, while others, such as Charles and David Koch, declined to participate or, like John M. Olin and Lynde and Harry Bradley, had long since passed away.

Dozens and dozens of other named sources, though, took time from their busy lives, and in some cases risked reprisal, to help me tell this story. I am immensely grateful to all of them. I also am hugely indebted to the authors of the hundreds of outstanding books, articles, studies, and news stories on which I drew. At the risk of accidentally leaving some out or of bogging readers down, I have tried to give credit in the text or the notes.

In addition, I want to give special thanks to those on whose writing I leaned most heavily. There is no way that I could have written this book without the path-blazing work of the Center for Media and Democracy, the Center for Public Integrity, the Center for Responsive Politics, Democracy 21, ProPublica, Mike Allen, Neela Banerjee, Nicholas Confessore, Clayton Coppin, Brian Doherty, Robert Draper, Lee Fang, Michael Grunwald, John Gurda, Mark Halperin, Dale Harrington, John Heilemann, Eliana Johnson, John Judis, Robert Kaiser, Andy Kroll, Chris Kromm, Charles Lewis, Robert Maguire, Mike McIntire, John J. Miller, Kim Phillips-Fein, Eric Pooley, Daniel Schulman, Theda Skocpol, Jason Stahl, Peter Stone, Steven Teles, Kenneth Vogel, Leslie Wayne, Roy Wenzl, and Bill Wilson.

Many, many others were essential to this enterprise as well, but none more so than my brilliant editor at Doubleday, Bill Thomas; my ever-resourceful literary agent at ICM, Sloan Harris; and the amazing team at *The New Yorker* that shepherded into print the original 2010 article on the Koch family that inspired this book: David Remnick, Daniel Zalewski, and the heroic checking department. I owe huge thanks also to those who helped with the book's exhausting research and fact-checking: Andrew Prokop and Ben Toff. There are no others with whom I'd rather share a foxhole.

NOTES

INTRODUCTION

6   As a former member: Charles Koch was an acolyte of Robert LeFevre, whom Brian Doherty, the libertarian author of *Radicals for Capitalism: A Freewheeling History of the Modern American Libertarian Movement* (Public Affairs, 2007), described in an interview with the author as "an anarchist figure who won Charles's heart." For more on LeFevre, see chapter 2.

7   For the most part: During Ronald Reagan's presidency, which I covered for *The Wall Street Journal,* there were constant divisions between the establishment Republicans and the conservative purists, whom many in the Reagan White House still regarded with suspicion as outliers.

7   George Soros: See Jane Mayer, "The Money Man," *New Yorker,* Oct. 18, 2004.

7   "The Kochs are on a whole": Jane Mayer, "Covert Operations," *New Yorker,* Aug. 30, 2010.

9   "there was a sense": John Podesta, interview with author.

10   "the mercantile Right": Craig Shirley, interview with author.

10   "It was obvious": Matthew Continetti, "The Paranoid Style in Liberal Politics: The Left's Obsession with the Koch Brothers," *Weekly Standard,* April 4, 2011.

12   "When W. Clement Stone": Dan Balz, "'Sheldon Primary' Is One Reason Americans Distrust the Political System," *Washington Post,* March 28, 2014.

12   "We're not a bunch": Continetti, "Paranoid Style in Liberal Politics."

12   Participants at the summits: See Kenneth R. Vogel, *Big Money: 2.5 Billion Dollars, One Suspicious Vehicle, and a Pimp—on the Trail of the Ultra-rich Hijacking of American Politics* (Public Affairs, 2014), for an excellent account of the Koch seminars.

13   In order to foil: Michael Mechanic, "Spying on the Koch Brothers: Inside the Discreet Retreat Where the Elite Meet and Plot the Democrats' Defeat," *Mother Jones,* Nov./Dec. 2011.

13   "There is anonymity": Vogel, *Big Money.*

13   the combined fortunes: Known participants at Koch seminars worth $1 billion or more as of 2015 valuations include the following:

     Charles Koch: $42.9 billion
     David Koch: $42.9 billion
     Sheldon Adelson: $31.4 billion
     Harold Hamm: $12.2 billion
     Stephen Schwarzman: $12 billion
     Philip Anschutz: $11.8 billion
     Steven Cohen (represented by Michael Sullivan): $10.3 billion
     John Menard Jr.: $9 billion

Ken Griffin: $6.5 billion
Charles Schwab: $6.4 billion
Richard DeVos: $5.7 billion
Diane Hendricks: $3.6 billion
Ken Langone: $2.9 billion
Stephen Bechtel Jr.: $2.8 billion
Richard Farmer: $2 billion
Stan Hubbard: $2 billion
Joe Craft: $1.4 billion
Elaine Marshall, whose fortune was estimated at $8.3 billion in 2014, dropped off *Forbes*'s list of billionaires in 2015. When her estimated 2014 worth is added to the cumulative fortunes of the known participating billionaires during the Obama presidency, the total tops $222 billion.

14   The gap between: Jacob S. Hacker and Paul Pierson, *Winner-Take-All Politics: How Washington Made the Rich Richer—and Turned Its Back on the Middle Class* (Simon & Schuster, 2010), says in 2007 that the top 1 percent of earners took home 23.5 percent of the country's income, when capital gains and dividends were factored in.

14   Liberal critics: See Chrystia Freeland, *Plutocrats: The Rise of the New Global Super-rich and the Fall of Everyone Else* (Penguin, 2012), 3.

14   "We are on the road": Paul Krugman, speaking in an interview with Bill Moyers about Thomas Piketty's book *Capital in the Twenty-First Century*. "What the 1% Don't Want Us to Know," BillMoyers.com, April 18, 2014.

15   "Wealth begets power": Joseph E. Stiglitz, "Of the 1%, by the 1%, for the 1%," *Vanity Fair*, May 2011.

15   Thomas Piketty: Thomas Piketty, *Capital in the Twenty-First Century*, trans. Arthur Goldhammer (Belknap Press/Harvard University Press, 2014).

16   "disconnect themselves": Mike Lofgren, "Revolt of the Rich," *American Conservative*, Aug. 27, 2012.

16   Only one full guest list: The list was published by the Web site *Think-Progress*, on October 20, 2010, in a news story by Lee Fang. In 2014, *Mother Jones* published an additional partial list.

17   vulture fund: See Ari Berman, "Rudy's Bird of Prey," *Nation*, Oct. 11, 2007, regarding the New York State legislature enacting legislation to aid his pursuit of repayment. In addition, Singer sought help from the U.S. courts in pressuring Argentina to repay him at a profit for bonds on which the country had defaulted.

18   In the wake of the 2008 market crash: According to David Carey and John E. Morris, *King of Capital: The Remarkable Rise, Fall, and Rise Again of Steve Schwarzman and Blackstone* (Crown Business, 2010), "The catalysts that spurred Congress to action were Schwarzman's birthday gala and the looming Blackstone IPO, say people who followed the congressional discussions."

19   three domestic servants soon sued him: Christie Smythe and Zachary Mider, "Renaissance Co-CEO Mercer Sued by Home Staff over Pay," *Bloomberg Business*, July 17, 2013.

19   The sum was so scandalously large: Ken Langone, whose wealth *Forbes*

estimated at $2.9 billion as of 2015, argued that Grasso's pay was reasonable, an argument that eventually prevailed in court.

19   "if it wasn't for us fat cats": Mark Halperin and John Heilemann, *Double Down: Game Change 2012* (Penguin, 2013), 194.

19   "an even wealthier man": "Richard Strong's Fall Came Quickly," Associated Press, May 27, 2004.

20   "prepaids done slightly differently": David Cay Johnston, "Anschutz Will Cost Taxpayers More Than the Billionaire," *Tax Notes: Johnston's Take*, Aug. 2, 2010.

21   By 2009, DeVos's son: "DeVoses May Pay a Price for Hefty Penalty; Record Fine Presents Problems; Lawyers Say They Will Appeal," *Grand Rapids Press*, April 13, 2008.

21   "largest private hoard": Daniel Fisher, "Fuel's Paradise," *Forbes*, Jan. 20, 2003.

22   Later, Massey was bought: In 2015, Alpha Natural Resources, the country's fourth-largest coal company, filed for bankruptcy protection.

22   Harold Hamm: Josh Harkinson, "Who Fracked Mitt Romney?," *Mother Jones*, Nov./Dec. 2012.

23   Further, in the summer of 2008: Koch Industries argued that it was in compliance with the trade ban because it had used a foreign subsidiary to help Iran build the largest methanol plant in the world. By using offshore employees as a cutout, Koch Industries adhered to the letter of the law while evading the intent of a U.S. trade ban that had been in place since 1995. Asjylan Loder and David Evans, "Koch Brothers Flout Law Getting Richer with Secret Iran Sales," *Bloomberg Markets*, Oct. 3, 2011.

24   Paternalistic and family-owned: For an excellent history of Bechtel, see Sally Denton, *Profiteers: Bechtel and the Men Who Built the World* (Simon & Schuster, forthcoming).

24   But when a former company pilot: In 2010, Stewart, his wife, daughter, and two others were killed in a helicopter crash that investigators reportedly believed was caused when his five-year-old daughter, who was sitting in the cockpit, kicked the controls.

25   He understood how to sell: Sean Wilentz, "States of Anarchy," *New Republic*, March 30, 2010.

27   In hopes of staving off: TARP details come from Hank Paulson, *On the Brink: Inside the Race to Stop the Collapse of the Global Financial System* (Headline, 2010), chaps. 11–13.

28   Among the groups now listed: On October 1, 2008, the day of the Senate vote, Senator John Thune's office released a list of groups that supported the bailout, and AFP was on that list: http://www.thune.senate.gov/public/index.cfm/press-releases?ID=8c603eca-77d3-49a3-96f5-dfe92eacda06.

28   A source familiar: In his book, *Democracy Denied* (BenBella Books, 2011), Phil Kerpen, who was a top Koch operative at Americans for Prosperity, admitted that although he "hated the bill," "I was genuinely frightened that our financial system would disintegrate."

29   "the fight of their lives": Bill Wilson and Roy Wenzl, "The Kochs' Quest to Save America," *Wichita Eagle*, Oct. 15, 2012.

29   "like to slice and dice": Barack Obama, Keynote Address, Democratic National Convention, July 27, 2004.

CHAPTER ONE: RADICALS

34   Koch fought back: The most thorough account of the legal issues appears in Clayton A. Coppin, "A History of Winkler Koch Engineering Company Patent Litigation and Corruption in the Federal Judiciary." Unpublished. Commissioned by Koch Industries, shared with author.

34   "The fact that the judge": Koch family associate in interview with author.

34   But by 1932: Alexander Igolkin, "Learning from American Experience," *Oil of Russia: Lukoil International Magazine*, 2006.

34   Fred Koch continued to provide: The reference to one hundred units is attributed to the "Economic Review of the Soviet Union" as quoted in a report titled "Why the Soviet Union Chose the Winkler-Koch Cracking System" by Clayton A. Coppin, commissioned by Koch Industries.

35   Wood River Oil & Refining: Koch Industries' Web site, History Timeline.

35   "enjoyed its first real": Charles G. Koch, *The Science of Success: How Market-Based Management Built the World's Largest Private Company* (John Wiley & Sons, 2007), 6.

35   During the 1930s: Fred Koch's business trips to Germany were described by a family member.

35   Archival records document: Rainer Karlsch and Raymond Stokes, *Faktor Öl* [The oil factor] (Beck, 2003).

35   "agent of influence": Davis was never charged with criminal wrongdoing. After he died in 1941, a Justice Department investigation implicating him was covered up, according to Dale Harrington, *Mystery Man: William Rhodes Davis, American Nazi Agent of Influence* (Brassey's, 1999), 206.

35   The president of the American bank: Ibid, 14. Charles Spencer of the Bank of Boston refused to have anything to do with the deal. Instead, he foisted it off on lower officers at the bank who were less scrupulous.

36   "Gentlemen, I have reviewed": Ibid., 16.

36   personally autograph a copy: Ibid., 16.

36   "deeply committed to Nazism": Ibid., 18.

36   "produce the high-octane gasoline": Ibid., 19.

37   "was hugely, hugely important": Peter Hayes, interview with author.

37   "Winkler-Koch benefited directly": Raymond Stokes, interview with author.

37   "Although nobody agrees": Fred Koch to Charles de Ganahl, Oct. 1938, in Daniel Schulman, *Sons of Wichita: How the Koch Brothers Became America's Most Powerful and Private Dynasty* (Grand Central, 2014), 41–42.

39   The nanny's iron rule: Descriptions of the nanny are based on interviews with a knowledgeable source who asked not to be identified in order to maintain ongoing relations with the family.

40   "My father was fairly tough": Bryan Burrough, "Wild Bill Koch," *Vanity Fair*, June 1994.

40   "a real John Wayne type": John Damgard, interview with author.

40   Koch emphasized rugged pursuits: Interview with Koch family cousin.

41   "By instilling a work ethic": Charles G. Koch, *Science of Success*, 9.

42   "Father wanted to make": Maryellen Mark, "Survival of the Richest," *Fame*, Nov. 1989.

42 Clayton Coppin: Coppin worked at the Program in Social and Organizational Learning, based at George Mason University, which was largely funded by the Koch family.

43 Portia Hamilton: Hamilton was a 1940 graduate of Columbia University who wrote popular newspaper columns on psychology suggesting that child's play and Rorschach tests could shed light on inner turmoil. In one column, "Troubled Little Minds," *Milwaukee Sentinel,* April 3, 1949, she described a little girl who received "too much love" from her parents and grandparents.

44 His mother made clear: Wayne, "Survival of the Richest."

44 "I pleaded with them": Brian O'Reilly and Patty de Llosa, "The Curse on the Koch Brothers," *Fortune,* Feb. 17, 1997.

44 "I hated all that": Charles Koch reminisced about his school years in an interview with Jason Jennings, posted on Koch Industries' Web site.

44 Eventually, Culver expelled him: The expulsion is described by both Wayne, "Survival of the Richest," and Coppin's unpublished study commissioned for Bill Koch, "Stealth: The History of Charles Koch's Political Activities, Part One," a copy of which was shared with the author.

44 As punishment, Charles's father: Charles Koch, interview with Jennings. Charles Koch's reminiscence of his father, from interview with Jennings.

44 "Father put the fear": O'Reilly and de Llosa, "Curse on the Koch Brothers."

44 "Charles spent little": Coppin, "Stealth."

44 "There was a lot of strife": Coppin, interview with author.

45 "I think he thought": Roy Wenzl and Bill Wilson, "Charles Koch Relentless in Pursuing His Goals," *Wichita Eagle,* Oct. 14, 2012.

45 "As soon as we arrived": Elizabeth Koch, "The World Tour Compatibility Test: Back in Tokyo, Part 1," *Smith,* March 30, 2007, http://www.smithmag.net.

45 "staring down that dark well": Elizabeth Koch, "The World Tour Compatibility Test: Grand Finale," *Smith,* May 3, 2007, http://www.smithmag.net.

45 "When you are 21": Kelley McMillan, "Bill Koch's Wild West Adventure," *5280: The Denver Magazine,* Feb. 2013.

46 "Never did such good advice": O'Reilly and de Llosa, "Curse on the Koch Brothers."

48 "you won't be very controversial": Lee Fang, *The Machine: A Field Guide to the Resurgent Right* (New Press, 2013), 100.

48 "utterly absurd": FBI memo, March 15, 1961, addressed to C. D. DeLoach (assistant FBI director), uncovered through a Freedom of Information Act request filed by Ernie Lazar.

48 An alphabet soup: Fang, *Machine,* 97.

49 "collectivists": Charles Koch, "I'm Fighting to Restore a Free Society," *Wall Street Journal,* April 2, 2014.

49 "a very intelligent, sharp man": Fang, *Machine,* 96.

49 "the spirit of Moscow": Ibid., 102.

50 Instead of winning: Some conservatives have argued that Goldwater's candidacy clarified and strengthened the GOP, but others, like Michael Gerson in "Goldwater's Warning to the GOP," *Washington Post,* April 18,

2014, regard his candidacy as disastrous for Republicans, partly because it repelled future generations of minority voters.

50   Before the emergence: Fang, *Machine.*

50   "it bordered on anarchism": Rick Perlstein, *Before the Storm: Barry Goldwater and the Unmaking of the American Consensus* (Nation Books, 2009), 113.

51   "there are certain laws": Wenzl and Wilson, "Charles Koch Relentless."

51   Early on, the Internal Revenue Service: Coppin, "History of Winkler Koch," 29.

51   He remained vehemently opposed: Wilson and Wenzl, "Charles Koch Relentless."

51   Among other strategies: Gary Weiss, "The Price of Immortality," *Upstart Business Journal,* Oct. 15, 2008; "Estate Planning Koch and Chase Koch (Son of Charles Koch): Past, Present, and Future," *Repealing the Frontiers of Ignorance,* Aug. 4, 2013, http://repealingfrontiers.blogspot.com.

51   "So for 20 years": Weiss, "Price of Immortality."

52   he arranged to pass his fortune: In his letters, Fred Koch described his concerns about children given family fortunes at young ages who disowned their fathers, according to Coppin.

52   "It was pretty clear": Gus diZerega lost touch with Charles and eventually abandoned his right-wing views, becoming a political science professor and writer on spiritual and other matters. He nonetheless credits Charles with opening his mind to political philosophy, which set him on the path to academia.

52   "LeFevre was an anarchist figure": Brian Doherty, interview with author.

53   As the journalist: Mark Ames, "Meet Charles Koch's Brain," *NSFWCorp,* Sept. 30, 2013. See also George Thayer, *The Farther Shores of Politics: The American Political Fringe* (Simon & Schuster, 1967). As also recounted by Donald Janson, "Conservatives at Freedom School to Prepare a New Federal Constitution," *New York Times,* June 13, 1965, LeFevre claimed in a memoir that he took dictation from saints, drove at sixty miles per hour for twenty miles with his eyes shut, and left his physical body behind while traveling through the air to Mount Shasta, where he met Jesus Christ.

53   The school taught a revisionist version: The description of the Freedom School's curriculum is based on interviews with three former attendees, including Gus diZerega, the other two of whom asked to remain anonymous.

54   bastion of "ultraconservatism": Janson, "Conservatives at Freedom School to Prepare a New Federal Constitution."

54   Charles Koch was so enthusiastic: Clayton Coppin believes that the elder Fred Koch agreed to Charles's request that he attend the Freedom School for a week in exchange for Charles's agreement to support the John Birch Society.

55   Charles was so incensed: "Toe the line" is based on the recollection of a source close to the Kochs.

55   James J. Martin: Martin wrote for the Institute for Historical Review's publication, *The Journal of Historical Review,* and his book *The Man Who Invented "Genocide": The Public Career and Consequences of Raphael Lemkin* was published in 1984 by the Institute for Historical Review. In an inter-

view with the author, Deborah Lipstadt, author of *Denying the Holocaust: The Growing Assault on Truth and Memory* (Plume, 1994), said, "One cannot be officially affiliated with the IHR and regularly publishing in its pages if one is not a Holocaust denier."

55 "It was a stew pot": Gus diZerega, interview with author.

55 As Angus Burgin describes: Angus Burgin, *The Great Persuasion: Reinventing Free Markets Since the Depression* (Harvard University Press, 2012), 88.

56 Hayek touted it as the key: Phillips-Fein writes, "The great innovation of Hayek and von Mises was to create a defense of the free market using the language of freedom and revolutionary change. The free market, not the political realm, enabled human beings to realize their liberty . . . [T]he free market, not the welfare state, was the true basis of meaningful opposition to fascism." Kim Phillips-Fein, *Invisible Hands: The Making of the Conservative Movement from the New Deal to Reagan* (Norton, 2009), 39–40.

56 By the time LeFevre died: In 2010, a spokesman for Koch Industries tried to distance the family from the Freedom School, insisting Charles and David had never been LeFevre's "devotees," as I described them in the 2010 *New Yorker* story "Covert Actions." The spokesman said, "In fact they have had no contact with him since the 1960's." However, as Mark Ames first reported, Charles Koch sent LeFevre a friendly letter in 1973 asking for LeFevre's approval of his plan to personally take over another libertarian organization to which LeFevre had ties, the Institute for Humane Studies.

57 The private life of the younger Frederick: Deposition of William Koch.

59 "homosexual blackmail attempt": O'Reilly and de Llosa, "Curse on the Koch Brothers."

59 "Charles' 'homosexual blackmail'": Schulman, *Sons of Wichita*, 130. Schulman describes the blackmail scheme as taking place after the senior Fred Koch died, but that is not the way it is described in Bill Koch's deposition.

59 wealthiest man in Kansas: See Coppin, "Stealth."

60 Koch Industries acquired the majority share: The Kochs bought the Pine Bend Refinery from J. Howard Marshall II, whose family members became virtually the only outside investors in Koch Industries, retaining a 15 percent share. Marshall became tabloid fodder at the age of eighty-nine for marrying Anna Nicole Smith, who at the time was a memorably zaftig twenty-six-year-old stripper and *Playboy* model.

60 "This single Koch refinery": David Sassoon, "Koch Brothers' Activism Protects Their 50 Years in Canadian Heavy Oils," *InsideClimate News*, May 10, 2012.

61 "Here I am one of the wealthiest": Leslie Wayne, "Brothers at Odds," *New York Times*, Dec. 7, 1986.

61 "an iron hand": Bruce Bartlett (an economist who formerly worked for the National Center for Policy Analysis, a Dallas-based think tank that the Kochs funded), interview with author.

61 In 1983, Charles and David bought out: Schulman, *Sons of Wichita*, 142.

62 Unlike his brothers, Frederick preferred: Among Frederick Koch's donations was a $3 million gift to restore the Swan, a Shakespearean theater

in Stratford-upon-Avon. He attended the opening, at which Queen Elizabeth personally officiated, but requested that she not mention his name.

63   He lived lavishly: Rich Roberts, "America 3 Win No Bargain Sail," *Los Angeles Times,* May 17, 1992.

63   He, too, barely spoke: Bill Koch broke his silence to speak with Charles at his twin David's birthday party and at a visit to Bohemian Grove, the exclusive men's social retreat in Northern California.

63   "in a fifty-fifty deal": See Louis Kraar, "Family Feud at Corporate Colossus," *Fortune,* July 26, 1982.

64   "When you're the only one": Weiss, "Price of Immortality."

64   "the cheapest person": *Park Avenue: Money, Power, and the American Dream,* PBS, Nov. 12, 2012.

65   "It's going to cost them": Interview with author. For more on David Koch's resignation from WNET's board, see Jane Mayer, "A Word from Our Sponsor," *New Yorker,* May 27, 2013.

65   Later clashes: The Oil, Chemical, and Atomic Workers union called a strike at Koch's Pine Bend Refinery that lasted nine months starting in January 1973. According to Coppin, "Stealth," "If he could have Charles Koch would have eliminated the union from his refinery."

66   "Ideas do not spread": Charles Koch, "The Business Community: Resisting Regulation," *Libertarian Review,* Aug. 1978.

66   Around the same time: Coppin, "Stealth," describes the conference and quotes from the papers given there at length.

69   The brothers took an even: Charles Koch "liked the idea of being in control of things even though he is not recognized as being in control," David Gordon, a fellow libertarian activist, told *Washingtonian* magazine. Luke Mullins, "The Battle for the Cato Institute," *Washingtonian,* May 30, 2012.

69   "David Koch ran in '80": Grover Norquist, interview with author.

70   But at the Libertarian Party convention: Marshall Schwartz, "Libertarians in Convention," *Libertarian Review,* Nov. 1979.

71   "It tends to be a nasty": See Mayer, "Covert Operations."

71   "They weren't really on my radar": Richard Viguerie, interview with author.

CHAPTER TWO: THE HIDDEN HAND

73   "the leading financial supporter": Robert Kaiser, "Money, Family Name Shaped Scaife," *Washington Post,* May 3, 1999, A1.

74   "You fucking Communist": Karen Rothmyer, "Citizen Scaife," *Columbia Journalism Review,* July/Aug. 1981.

74   In 2009, however: Richard Scaife shared a copy of his memoir with the author and authorized the use of all requested material, other than a small portion dealing with a litigious divorce, some details about which do not appear here.

75   "Nowadays there are no": Lionel Trilling, *The Liberal Imagination: Essays on Literature and Society* (Viking, 1950), xv.

75   "He's the originator": Christopher Ruddy, interview with author.

75   In 1957, *Fortune* ranked: Rothmyer, "Citizen Scaife."

76   "How beautifully he summed up": Richard Mellon Scaife, "A Richly Conservative Life," 282.

76   "a gutter drunk": Kaiser, "Money, Family Name Shaped Scaife."

77   "My father—he was suckin'": Burton Hersh, *The Mellon Family: A Fortune in History* (Morrow, 1978).

77   "a lightweight": Kaiser, "Money, Family Name Shaped Scaife."

77   "My political conservatism": Scaife, "Richly Conservative Life," 20.

77   "He was concerned": Ibid., 21.

78   "Alan Scaife was terribly worried": Kaiser, "Money, Family Name Shaped Scaife."

78   "From top to bottom": Isaac William Martin, *Rich People's Movements: Grassroots Campaigns to Untax the One Percent* (Oxford University Press, 2013), 25.

79   His Union Trust bank: Ibid., 34.

79   In an effort to win: Ibid., 45. Mellon argued that if taxes were lowered on the rich, they would be less inclined to invest in tax-exempt bonds, thereby spurring greater revenue for the Treasury and, coincidentally, for financial institutions like the Mellon Bank.

79   Sixty years later: The Gerald R. Ford Library contains a June 11, 1975, memorandum from Bob Golden, of the American Enterprise Institute, to Dick Cheney, at the Ford White House, to which is attached a copy of an academic paper by Jude Wanniski on which is scrawled the title "Santa Claus Theory."

79   Once in public office: John B. Judis, *The Paradox of American Democracy: Elites, Special Interests, and the Betrayal of the Public Trust* (Routledge, 2000).

79   "cut the tax rates on the richest": Isaac William Martin, *Rich People's Movements*, 64.

79   Not only did his economic theories: Judis, *Paradox of American Democracy*, 46.

80   "I don't know what": Scaife, "Richly Conservative Life," 61.

80   "equality of sacrifice": See Kenneth F. Scheve Jr. and David Stasavage, "Is the Estate Tax Doomed?," *New York Times*, March 24, 2013. They note that "equality of sacrifice" was a term used by John Stuart Mill and grew from the nineteenth century into an argument in favor of progressive taxation, particularly in financing wars.

81   "When I can't sleep": Scaife, "Richly Conservative Life," 6.

81   "making each other totally miserable": Robert Kaiser and Ira Chinoy, "Scaife: Funding Father of the Right," *Washington Post*, May 2, 1999, A1.

83   "The first priority": Scaife, "Richly Conservative Life," 43.

83   "Isn't it grand": Ibid., 46.

85   Today, they are commonplace: John D. Rockefeller met secretly with President William Taft in an effort to get his support for the creation of the Rockefeller Foundation, but regardless of the effort the U.S. Senate rejected the idea in 1913, according to Rob Reich's paper "Repugnant to the Whole Idea of Democracy? On the Role of Foundations in Democratic Societies" (Department of Political Science, Stanford University, for the Philanthropy Symposium at Duke University, Jan. 2015), 5.

86   "represent virtually by definition": See Ibid, 9.

86   By 1930, there were approximately: Ibid., 7.
86   "completely irresponsible institution": Richard Posner likens perpetual charitable foundations to hereditary monarchies. He suggests that they may be a useful form of self-taxation by the rich but also questions why they should enjoy tax breaks, particularly in the case of foundations run by businessmen who are simultaneously polishing the image of their companies. See "Charitable Foundations—Posner's Comment," *The Becker-Posner Blog,* Dec. 31, 2006, http://www.becker-posner-blog.com.
87   "The result": Scaife, "Richly Conservative Life," 66.
87   "advance ideas that I believe": Ibid., 58.
87   "This was the beginning": Ibid., 70.
88   Carrying out this attack: In *The Rise of the Counter-establishment: From Conservative Ideology to Political Power* (Times Books, 1986), Sidney Blumenthal made the term "counter-establishment" famous and for the first time told much of the early intellectual history of the movement.
89   "Attack on American Free Enterprise System": For more on the origins and impact of Lewis Powell's memorandum, see Phillips-Fein, *Invisible Hands,* 156–65.
89   "We didn't have anything": Pierson's comments were made in a panel discussion with Gara LaMarche at an Open Society Institute forum, Sept. 21, 2006.
90   "lay siege to corporations": Staughton Lind, quoted in Phillips-Fein, *Invisible Hands,* 151.
91   Powell's defense of the tobacco companies: See Jeffrey Clements, *Corporations Are Not People* (Berrett-Koehler, 2012), 19–21.
91   Income in America: Isaac William Martin, *Rich People's Movements,* 155.
92   Powell called on corporate America: Some have questioned whether too much has been made of Powell's memo. Mark Schmitt of *The American Prospect* wrote in 2005, "The reality of the right is that there was no plan, just a lot of people writing their own memos and starting their own organization."
92   "single-minded pursuit": Phillips-Fein, *Invisible Hands,* 164.
92   "tax-exempt refuge": For more on Buchanan's memo, see Jason Stahl, *The Right Moves: The Conservative Think Tank in American Political Culture Since 1945* (University of North Carolina Press, forthcoming), 93.
93   "the artillery": James Pierson comments at Open Society Institute's Forum, Sept. 21, 2006.
94   One of them: Feulner was a member of the Mont Pelerin Society, an Austrian economics club that Hayek co-founded and attended and that was almost entirely underwritten by American businessmen.
94   described himself openly as a "radical": David Brock, *Blinded by the Right: The Conscience of an Ex-conservative* (Crown, 2002), 54.
94   After reading Powell's memo: Lee Edwards, *The Power of Ideas: The Heritage Foundation at 25 Years* (Jameson Books, 1997).
94   "I do believe": See Dan Baum, *Citizen Coors: A Grand Family Saga of Business, Politics, and Beer* (William Morrow, 2000), 103. Weyrich added, "Coors is the kind of guy who thinks you can write your congressman and get something done."
95   Convinced that radical leftists: Ibid.

479   NOTES

96   Scaife's money soon followed: Before founding Heritage, Feulner had worked at the Center for Strategic and International Studies, which was almost single-handedly funded by Scaife in its early years, so he would have recognized Scaife's potential as a backer.

96   "Coors gives six-packs": Kaiser and Chinoy, "Funding Father of the Right."

96   "free from any political": Judis, *Paradox of American Democracy*, 122.

96   "The AEIs and the Heritages": Ibid., 169. Leaders of conservative foundations such as William Simon might have perceived themselves as merely providing political balance and copying the activism of liberal foundations, but the political scientist Steven Teles pointed out in an interview with the author that there were key differences. The boards of the earlier establishment foundations such as Ford tended to be centrist, while those at the new conservative foundations like Olin tended, he says, to be "ideologically-aligned" and more likely to embrace grant making as a form of movement building.

97   "a scholarly institute": Adam Curtis, "The Curse of Tina," BBC, Sept. 13, 2011.

97   The Sarah Scaife Foundation: Martin Gottlieb, "Conservative Policy Unit Takes Aim at New York," *New York Times*, May 5, 1986.

98   "As you well know": L. L. Logue to Frank Walton (Heritage Foundation), Nov. 16, 1976, folder 16, Weyrich Papers, University of Montana.

99   "'big business' pressure organization": Jason Stahl, "From Without to Within the Movement: Consolidating the Conservative Think Tank in the 'Long Sixties,'" in *The Right Side of the Sixties: Reexamining Conservatism's Decade of Transformation*, ed. Laura Jane Gifford and Daniel K. Williams (Palgrave Macmillan, 2012), 105.

99   Powell and others: See Stahl, *Right Moves*. Stahl describes the way that the conservative think tanks upended the notion of expertise with the concept of political balance. He also describes the Ford Foundation's donation to AEI.

99   fight criticism that it was liberal: In 1976, in a move that rocked staid philanthropic circles, Henry Ford II resigned in protest from the board of the foundation bearing his family name, arguing that it wasn't sufficiently pro-business.

100   "That was quite the heist": The note from the friend to William Baroody Jr. is described in Stahl, *Right Moves*.

100   "Funders increasingly expect": Steven Clemons, "The Corruption of Think Tanks," Japan Policy Research Institute, Feb. 2003.

100   "We've become money launderers": Claudia Dean and Richard Morin, "Lobbyists Seen Lurking Behind Tank Funding," *Washington Post*, Nov. 19, 2002.

101   "socialism out and out": Phillips-Fein, *Invisible Hands*, 174.

101   "I saw how right-wing ideology": Brock, *Blinded by the Right*, 77.

101   "the unseen hand": Many of these details are drawn from Michael Joseph Gross, "A Vast Right-Wing Hypocrisy," *Vanity Fair*, Feb. 2008.

101   "I don't think he had": Kaiser, "Money, Family Name Shaped Scaife."

102   "With political victory": Ibid.

102   "We did what comes naturally": Gross, "Vast Right-Wing Hypocrisy."

102 According to Scaife's son: Ritchie denied the marijuana anecdote, but Scaife confirmed it in ibid.

102 "Ritchie loves Dick": Ibid.

103 "Wife and dog missing": Ibid.

104 "had particularly in mind": Edwards, *Power of Ideas*.

104 "can order people done away with": John F. Kennedy Jr., "Who's Afraid of Richard Mellon Scaife?," *George*, Jan. 1999.

106 "the development of a well-financed cadre": Cited in Nicholas Confessore, "Quixotic '80 Campaign Gave Birth to Kochs' Powerful Network," *New York Times*, May 17, 2014.

106 Koch Industries had just become: Ibid.

106 Its start-up funding: Michael Nelson, "The New Libertarians," *Saturday Review*, March 1, 1980.

107 "I said my bank account": Ed Crane, interview with author.

107 "Ed Crane would always call": Mullins, "Battle for the Cato Institute."

107 "serve as a night watchman": Schulman, *Sons of Wichita*, 106.

108 In fact, after Watergate: Stahl, in *Right Moves*, quotes an AEI official making this argument to business leaders after Watergate.

108 list of the Heritage Foundation's sponsors: Box 720, folder 5, Clare Boothe Luce Papers, Library of Congress.

108 "that the think tanks": Piereson comment, Open Society forum.

108 Americans' distrust of government: Judis, *Paradox of American Democracy*, 129.

109 The labor movement: For an excellent, detailed description of labor's congressional setbacks, see Hacker and Pierson, *Winner-Take-All Politics*, 127.

109 "We are basically a conduit": Phil McCombs, "Building a Heritage in the War of Ideas," *Washington Post*, Oct. 3, 1983.

109 "ALEC is well on its way": George Archibald to Richard Larry, Feb. 3, 1977, Weyrich Papers.

110 "the Golden Rule": See Alexander Hertel-Fernandez, "Funding the State Policy Battleground: The Role of Foundations and Firms" (paper for Duke Symposium on Philanthropy, Jan. 2015).

110 Weyrich was particularly adept: Randall Balmer, a historian of American religion, argues in his book *Redeemer: The Life of Jimmy Carter* (Basic Books, 2014) that the conventional wisdom, which holds that the backlash against *Roe v. Wade* created the Christian Right, is wrong. Instead, he suggests, it was evangelicals' opposition to integration that truly launched the movement. Weyrich, he suggests, brilliantly seized on evangelicals' anger at Jimmy Carter's refusal to grant tax-exempt status to Bob Jones University because it had an explicit whites-only admissions policy.

110 According to Feulner: Dom Bonafede, "Issue-oriented Heritage Foundation Hitches Its Wagon to Reagan's Star," *National Journal*, March 20, 1982.

110 He slashed corporate: Congress cut the effective federal income tax rate on the top 1 percent of earners from 31.8 percent in 1980 to 24.9 percent in 1985. In contrast, Congress raised the effective rates on the bottom four-fifths of earners from 16.5 percent to 16.7 percent. It wasn't a big tax increase for the vast majority of Americans, but it was a substantial tax cut for the wealthy. As a result, from 1980 to 1985, after-tax income in the top 5 percent of earners increased, while it decreased for everyone else, accord-

ing to Judis, *Paradox of American Democracy,* 151. See also Daniel Stedman Jones, *Masters of the Universe: Hayek, Friedman, and the Birth of Neoliberal Politics* (Princeton University Press, 2012), 265.

111 Scaife, who by then had donated: Ed Feulner describes the scope of Scaife's giving in the Luce Papers.

111 "I was lucky": Scaife, "Richly Conservative Life," 22.

CHAPTER THREE: BEACHHEADS

112 uprising at Cornell University: An excellent report on the protest appears in Donald Alexander Downs, *Cornell '69: Liberalism and the Crisis of the American University* (Cornell University Press, 1999).

112 "the most disgraceful": David Horowitz, "Ann Coulter at Cornell," Front PageMag.com, May 21, 2001.

113 "The catastrophe at Cornell": John J. Miller, *A Gift of Freedom: How the John M. Olin Foundation Changed America* (Encounter Books, 2006).

113 "saw very clearly": John J. Miller, *How Two Foundations Reshaped America* (Philanthropy Roundtable, 2003), 16.

114 "These guys, individually": Lizzy Ratner, "Olin Foundation, Right-Wing Tank, Snuffing Itself," *New York Observer,* May 9, 2005.

114 Each side would argue: James Pierson, for instance, who regards hugely well-endowed, establishment nonprofit organizations such as the Ford Foundation as liberal, argues that the Right has been routinely outspent by the Left.

115 "saving the free enterprise": Olin's general counsel was Frank O'Connell, a labor lawyer who was famously tough on unions.

115 Olin followed closely: This account of Olin's history draws extensively on Miller, *Gift of Freedom.*

117 In the summer of 1970: E. W. Kenworthy, "U.S. Will Sue 8 Concerns over Dumping of Mercury," *New York Times,* July 25, 1970, 1.

117 Subsequently, the Justice Department: The Olin Corporation dumped mercury into a landfill known as the 102nd Street site, which was also used by the Hooker Chemicals and Plastics Corporation.

117 Eventually, the Olin Corporation: The maximum fine for each of the seven misdemeanor convictions was $10,000, thus the maximum fine in total was $70,000. "Olin Fined $70,000," Associated Press, Dec. 12, 1979.

118 For decades, Saltville: "End of a Company Town," *Life,* March 26, 1971. See also Tod Newcombe, "Saltville, Virginia: A Company Town Without a Company," Governing.com, Aug. 2012.

118 "They all knew the dangers": Harry Haynes, interview with author.

119 Dangerous levels of mercury: Virginia Water Resources Research Center, "Mercury Contamination in Virginia Waters: History, Issues, and Options," March 1979. See also EPA Superfund Record of Decision, Saltville Waste Disposal Ponds, June 30, 1987.

120 *Life* magazine produced: "End of a Company Town."

120 "It's a ghost town": Shirley "Sissy" Bailey, interview with author.

120 "Common sense should have": Stephen Lester, interview with author.

121 "It is possible": James Pierson, e-mail interview with author.

121   "The Olin family": William Voegeli, e-mail interview with author.

121   "My greatest ambition": Quoted in Ratner, "Olin Foundation, Right-Wing Tank, Snuffing Itself."

122   "with definite left-wing attitudes": John M. Olin to the president of Cornell, 1980, in Teles, *Rise of the Conservative Legal Movement*, 185.

122   "It was like a home-study course": Miller, *Gift of Freedom*, 34.

122   By the late 1960s, Ford: James Piereson describes the Ford Foundation's leading role as liberal activist philanthropists in an incisive essay, "Investing in Conservative Ideas," *Commentary*, May 2005.

123   "almost identical": Miller, *How Two Foundations Reshaped America*, 13.

123   "Since the 60's, the vast bulk": William Simon, *A Time for Truth* (Reader's Digest Press, 1978), 64–65.

124   "What we need": Miller, *Gift of Freedom*, 56.

124   "Capitalism has no duty": Simon, *Time for Truth*, 78.

125   "They must be given grants": Miller, *Gift of Freedom*, 57.

125   "Joyce was a true radical": Ralph Benko, interview with author.

126   "because they were emulated": Teles, *Rise of the Conservative Legal Movement*, 186.

126   "The only way you're going": Miller, *How Two Foundations Reshaped America*, 17.

126   "the most influential schools": James Piereson, "Planting Seeds of Liberty," *Philanthropy*, May/June 2005.

127   Princeton's Madison Program: Miller, *Gift of Freedom*.

127   "a savvy right-wing operative": Max Blumenthal, "Princeton Tilts Right," *Nation*, Feb. 23, 2006.

127   "perhaps we should think": Piereson, "Planting Seeds of Liberty."

127   the CIA laundered: Most of the CIA funds arrived from an organization called the Dearborn Foundation. The Olin Foundation then disbursed the funds to a Washington, D.C.–based organization called the Vernon Fund.

127   the press exposed the covert propaganda: In 1967, *Ramparts* magazine blew the cover on the covert CIA program. Additional reports revealed that the CIA had been secretly funneling money through as many as a hundred private foundations in the country that were acting as front groups and passing the money on covertly to Cold War anti-Communist projects. Some of the money was spread to domestic groups such as the National Student Association. Liberal organizations, including teachers' unions, acted as fronts too.

128   Soon the Olin Foundation was investing: Miller, *Gift of Freedom*.

128   "a wine collection": James Barnes, "Banker with a Cause," *National Journal*, March 6, 1993.

129   "Lott's claimed source": Adam Winkler, *Gunfight: The Battle over the Right to Bear Arms in America* (Norton, 2011), 76–77.

129   Another Olin-funded book: See Jane Mayer and Jill Abramson, *Strange Justice: The Selling of Clarence Thomas* (Houghton Mifflin, 1994), for a more thorough analysis of Brock's role in the confrontation between Thomas and Hill.

130   "If the conservative intellectual movement": Miller, *Gift of Freedom*, 5. Also Miller's defense of Lott's research as "rigorous," 72.

130   "On the right, they understood": Steve Wasserman, interview with author.

131 "John Olin, in fact, was prouder": Miller, *Gift of Freedom.*
131 "I saw it as a way": Jason DeParle, "Goals Reached, Donor on Right Closes Up Shop," *New York Times,* May 29, 2005.
132 "If you said to a dean": Teles, *Rise of the Conservative Legal Movement,* 189.
132 "was considered a marginal": Ibid., 108.
132 In 1985, however, the foundation: Miller, *Gift of Freedom,* 76.
133 "the most important thing": Paul M. Barrett, "Influential Ideas: A Movement Called 'Law and Economics' Sways Legal Circles," *Wall Street Journal,* Aug. 4, 1986.
133 "the most successful": Teles, *Rise of the Conservative Legal Movement,* 216.
133 "taking advantage of students' financial need": Alliance for Justice, *Justice for Sale: Shortchanging the Public Interest for Private Gain* (Alliance for Justice, 1993).
134 A study by the nonpartisan: Chris Young, Reity O'Brien, and Andrea Fuller, "Corporations, Pro-business Nonprofits Foot Bill for Judicial Seminars," Center for Public Integrity, March 28, 2013.
134 Federalist Society: The $5.5 million figure from Olin represents funding over two decades, as reported by Miller, Gift of Freedom, 94.
135 All of the conservative justices: For a more complete index of influential members of the Federalist Society, see Michael Avery and Danielle McLaughlin, *The Federalist Society: How Conservatives Took the Law Back from Liberals* (Vanderbilt University Press, 2013).
135 "it possibly wouldn't exist": Miller, *How Two Foundations Reshaped America,* 29.
135 "one of the best investments": Miller, "A Federalist Solution," *Philanthropy,* Fall 2011. Irving Kristol was among the earliest fund-raisers for the Federalist Society.
135 a key $25,000 investment: The Olin Foundation eventually donated a total of $6.3 million to the Manhattan Institute.
136 "It was a classic case": Charles Murray, interview with author.
136 Critics said it overlooked: For a fuller analysis of *Losing Ground,* see Thomas Medvetz, *Think Tanks in America* (University of Chicago Press, 2012), 3.
136 "It took ten years": Ibid., 5.
137 Among them was the *Dartmouth Review:* Louis Menand, "Illiberalisms," *New Yorker,* May 20, 1991.
137 ABC correspondent Jonathan Karl: Karl was the first network television journalist invited by the Kochs to moderate a political panel discussion during a seminar for their donors, which he did in January 2015. ABC's decision to participate in the otherwise-closed event stirred criticism and controversy but created a precedent when the *Politico* columnist Mike Allen moderated a candidates' forum at a Koch fund-raising conference in August 2015, accepting an invitation that the CNN correspondent Jake Tapper turned down on principle.
137 "We've got money": Many details regarding the history of the creation of the Bradley Foundation are drawn from John Gurda's *Bradley Legacy,* which was commissioned by Michael Joyce and published in 1992 by the Lynde and Harry Bradley Foundation.

138 During the next fifteen years: Patricia Sullivan, "Michael Joyce; Leader in Rise of Conservative Movement," *Washington Post,* March 3, 2006.

138 At least two-thirds: According to James Barnes, "Banker with a Cause," *National Journal,* March 6, 1993, 564–65, well over two-thirds of the $20 million that the Bradley Foundation doled out each year went to "conservative intellectual" support.

138 Continuing the strategic emphasis: Katherine M. Skiba, "Bradley Philanthropy," *Milwaukee Journal Sentinel,* Sept. 17, 1995.

138 "Typically, it was not just": According to Bruce Murphy, Joyce spent $1 million subsidizing Murray's writing of *The Bell Curve.* Murphy, "When We Were Soldier-Scholars," *Milwaukee Magazine,* March 9, 2006.

139 "the chief operating officer": Neal Freeman, "The Godfather Retires," *National Review,* April 18, 2001.

140 "package for public consumption": "The Bradley Foundation and the Art of (Intellectual) War," Autumn 1999, was a twenty-page confidential memo prepared for the foundation's November 1999 board meeting, a copy of which was obtained by the author.

140 The event that multiplied: Allen-Bradley's trustees had initially valued the company at $400 million, although they later enlarged the valuation, according to a wonderful article on the sale of Allen-Bradley by James B. Stewart, "Loss of Privacy: How a 'Safe' Company Was Acquired Anyway After Bitter Infighting," *Wall Street Journal,* May 14, 1985.

140 The deal created: Ibid.; Gurda, *Bradley Legacy,* 153.

140 "symbol of a military": Peter Pae, "Maligned B-1 Bomber Now Proving Its Worth," *Los Angeles Times,* Dec. 12, 2001.

140 Rockwell waged a strenuous: Winston Williams, "Dogged Rockwell Bets on Reagan," *New York Times,* Sept. 30, 1984. The B-1 would prove useless until 2001, when, after the government spent an additional $3 billion retrofitting the planes, they were finally deployed for conventional use in Afghanistan. A Congressional Research Service report in 2014, however, described the planes as "increasingly irrelevant."

141 "teetered on the edge": Gurda, *Bradley Legacy,* 92.

142 "Karl Marx was a Jew": Bryan Burrough, *The Big Rich* (Penguin, 2009), 211.

142 "the two major threats": Gurda, *Bradley Legacy,* 115.

142 In 1966, a federal judge: Ibid., 131.

144 "deprive future generations": Rich Rovito, "Milwaukee Rockwell Workers Facing Layoff Reach Agreement," *Milwaukee Business Journal,* June 27, 2010.

144 "the most polarized": See Craig Gilbert, "Democratic, Republican Voters Worlds Apart in Divided Wisconsin," *Milwaukee Journal Sentinel,* May 3, 2014.

144 leaving Milwaukee: For more on Milwaukee, see Alec MacGillis's insightful piece, "The Unelectable Whiteness of Scott Walker," *New Republic,* June 15, 2014.

145 "overarching purpose": In a 2003 speech at Georgetown University, Michael Joyce said, "At Olin and later at Bradley, our overarching purpose was to use philanthropy to support a war of ideas to defend and help recover the political imagination of the [nation's] founders."

CHAPTER FOUR: THE KOCH METHOD

146   "He wasn't always": Doreen Carlson, interview with author.

146   "He was practically swimming": Ibid.

147   "I was a young guy": Tom Meersman, "Koch Violations Arouse Concerns," *Minneapolis Star Tribune*, Dec. 18, 1997.

147   Afterward, numerous scientific studies: David Michaels, *Doubt Is Their Product* (Oxford University Press, 2008), 76, provides an excellent discussion of benzene, illustrating the oil industry's efforts to block its regulation.

147   Four federal agencies: A list of agencies classifying benzene as a carcinogen appears in Loder and Evans, "Koch Brothers Flout Law Getting Richer with Secret Iran Sales."

147   "I didn't even know": Meersman, "Koch Violations Arouse Concerns."

147   "socialistic": Charles Koch's 1974 speech as cited in Confessore, "Quixotic '80 Campaign Gave Birth to Kochs' Powerful Network."

148   "I'm looking for some accountability": Meersman, "Koch Violations Arouse Concerns."

149   "We should *not* cave": Charles Koch, "Business Community."

149   "unceasingly advance": Ibid.

150   "Libertarianism is supposed to be": Tom Frank, interview with author.

150   "The refinery was just hemorrhaging": Loder and Evans, "Koch Brothers Flout Law Getting Richer with Secret Iran Sales."

150   Rather than comply: At first, the company had installed a new antipollution device, but when it proved deficient, instead of addressing the problem, the company disconnected the apparatus and falsified the record.

151   Defenders of Koch Industries: John Hinderaker, a frequent defender of the Kochs, calls Barnes-Soliz "a poor employee who, anticipating termination, asserted false claims against her employer in order to set up a lawsuit," in his Oct. 6, 2011, entry on PowerLineBlog.com.

152   "The government's case": David Uhlmann, interview with author, and additional comments from him in Sari Horwitz, "Unlikely Allies," *Washington Post*, Aug. 15, 2015.

152   For her whistle-blowing: Barnes-Soliz's account is derived from Loder and Evans, "Koch Brothers Flout Law Getting Richer with Secret Iran Sales."

152   According to two statements: Carnell Green, interviews with Richard J. Elroy, Sept. 18, 1998, and April 15, 1999; a copy of Elroy's report was obtained by the author.

153   soil samples were later taken: According to the analysis done by Cirrus Environmental's laboratory, one sample contained 180 parts per million of mercury and the other 9,100 parts per million. The legal limit is 30 parts per million. Green's OSHA complaint went nowhere because it was filed past the deadline, according to his statement.

154   "Green was just a nice": Jim Elroy, interview with author.

154   "They're always operating": Schulman, *Sons of Wichita*, 216; Angela O'Connell, interview with author.

154   "repeatedly lied": Schulman, *Sons of Wichita*, 215.

155   "for the next four or five years": Author interview with David Nicastro.

155   In court papers: Filings relating to a 1997 petition for a protective order,

Charles Dickey et al. v. J. Howard Marshall III, describe Koch Industries as "among the best clients" of the private investigative firm Secure Source, run by Charles Dickey and David Nicastro. "Over the past three years they performed numerous investigations for Koch Industries and its numerous entities," a filing on behalf of the firm states. By 2000, the firm had been dissolved following a legal settlement between the partners.

155 "They lie about everything": Angela O'Connell, interview with author.

156 "There were times": Schulman, *Sons of Wichita*, 226, gives a full account of these cases.

156 These misdeeds paled: A vivid and meticulously researched account of the Smalley case appears in ibid., 211.

157 Koch Industries offered Danny: Ibid., 214, writes that Smalley "wanted the opportunity to sit on the witness stand" so that he could make "Charles and David Koch understand just what they had taken from him."

157 "I'm not saying": Ibid., 218.

157 An investigation: The information about the National Transportation Safety Board report is based on Loder and Evans, "Koch Brothers Flout Law Getting Richer with Secret Iran Sales."

157 "Swiss cheese": Ibid.

158 "Koch Industries is definitely responsible": Schulman, *Sons of Wichita*, 219.

158 "They said, 'We're sorry'": "Blood and Oil," *60 Minutes II*, Nov. 27, 2000.

159 "quietly enraged": Senate committee member, interview with author.

159 In fact, the other companies: The allegation that other companies turned Koch Industries in is according to a former official involved in the Senate investigation.

159 His specialty had been: Elroy had compiled much of the evidence against Koch Industries, using two-hundred-millimeter lenses to photograph Koch employees as they gathered oil from scattered wells, and then he went door-to-door, he said, saying, "I'm from the FBI, and I want to talk to you about the oil you've been stealing. Are you taking it down the road and selling it?" He said that many replied, "No, the company makes us do it." The company's lawyer adamantly denied his allegations.

160 According to the Senate report: The November 1989 report by the Special Committee on Investigations of the Select Committee on Indian Affairs of the U.S. Senate documents that a Koch employee "went so far as to interview the ex-wife" of a Senate investigator and that "Koch also attempted to look into the backgrounds of Committee staff."

160 Kenneth Ballen: Ballen established a nonprofit organization, Terror Free Tomorrow, to which William Koch made a contribution in 2007, but had no personal relationship with any of the Kochs during the period when the hearings were under way.

160 "It wasn't like politics": Kenneth Ballen, interview with author.

160 Don Nickles: Nickles received large campaign contributions from Koch Industries over the years; see Leslie Wayne, "Papers Link Donations to 2 on Senate Hearings Panel," *New York Times*, Oct. 30, 1997. In 2014, Koch Industries' Public Sector division hired Nickles's lobbying company to fight campaign-finance reform; see Kent Cooper, "Koch Starts Lobbying on Campaign Finance Issue," RollCall.com, June 9, 2014.

161 "We don't know who": Wick Sollers, interview with author.

161   "It's very intimidating": Robert Parry, "Dole: What Wouldn't Bob Do for Koch Oil?," *Nation*, Aug. 26, 1996.

161   "I did not want my family": "Blood and Oil."

162   Nickles recommended the appointment: The previous U.S. attorney had resigned.

162   "You can say this": Author interview with Nancy Jones.

163   "not even aware": Nickles's and Leonard's denials were obtained by Phillip Zweig and Michael Schroeder, "Bob Dole's Oil Patch Pals," *Business-Week*, March 31, 1996. The U.S. Bureau of Indian Affairs, like the grand jury, found no actionable wrongdoing stemming from the Senate's report. However, *BusinessWeek* notes that key members of the Osage tribe, who had defended Koch Industries, later felt they and the Bureau of Indian Affairs had been duped. The magazine reported that "Charles O. Tillman Jr., principal chief of the Osage tribe, wrote in a Nov. 29, 1994, letter to Senator John McCain (R-Ariz.), a member of the investigative committee: 'We are left with the inescapable conclusion that the Bureau of Indian Affairs was more concerned with putting a lid on your committee's findings than in providing us with the truth.'"

163   "I was surprised": Zweig and Schroeder, "Bob Dole's Oil Patch Pals."

163   "You have to have intelligence": Burrough, "Wild Bill Koch."

164   "It was to find anything": Republican operative, interview with author.

165   Becket Brown International: See Gary Ruskin, "Spooky Business: Corporate Espionage Against Nonprofit Organizations," Nov. 20, 2013.

165   "That blows my mind": Barbara Fultz, interview with author.

166   "They were just mis-measuring crude": Phil Dubose, interview with author.

167   He denied defrauding: "If the producers believe your measurements are not as accurate as somebody else's, they're going to take volume away from you," Charles Koch testified. "Tulsa Okla. Jury Hears Last Day of Testimony in Oil-Theft Trial," *Tulsa World*, Dec. 11, 1999.

168   "It was the first time": Phil Dubose, interview with author.

168   although in 2010 the company: "Toxic 100 Air Polluters," Political Economy Research Institute, University of Massachusetts Amherst, 2010, www.peri.umass.edu/toxicair_current/.

168   In 2012, the Environmental Protection Agency's database: See the EPA's Toxic Release Inventory data bank, 2012. The company's ranking among the top thirty for all three forms of pollution was described by Tim Dickinson, "Inside the Koch Brothers' Toxic Empire," *Rolling Stone*, Sept. 24, 2014.

170   "disgusting": James Huff, interview with author.

170   "surprised": Harold Varmus, interview with author.

171   "involved in improper payments": Loder and Evans, "Koch Brothers Flout Law Getting Richer with Iran Sales."

171   "It is beyond spectacular": See Mayer, "Covert Operations."

CHAPTER FIVE: THE KOCHTOPUS

172   "What a jackass": Bill Wilson and Roy Wenzl, "The Kochs' Quest to Save America," *Wichita Eagle*, Oct. 13, 2012.

172   "creepy when you have to deal": Ed Crane, interview with author.

173 As Fink later described it: A version of Richard Fink's paper "The Structure of Social Change" appeared under the title "From Ideas to Action: The Roles of Universities, Think Tanks, and Activist Groups," *Philanthropy* 10, no. 1 (Winter 1996).

173 the Kochtopus: According to David Gordon, a libertarian at the Von Mises Institute, who was involved at Cato during its early years, the name was coined by Samuel Edward Konkin III, whom he describes as an "anarcho-libertarian."

174 "so brutalized by the process": W. John Moore, "The Wichita Pipeline," *National Journal,* May 16, 1992.

174 "corporate defense": Parry, "Dole."

174 "It was the investigation": Brian Doherty, interview with author.

174 "Establishment" politician: David Koch's views on Bob Dole, according to his brother Bill, as quoted in Parry, "Dole."

174 Dole reportedly helped: For more on the Kochs and Dole, see the excellent piece by Zweig and Schroeder, "Bob Dole's Oil Patch Pals."

175 Had it passed: For more on the legislative wheeling and dealing, see Center for Public Integrity, *The Buying of the President* (Avon Books, 1996), 127–30.

175 Koch Industries did succeed: Dan Morgan, "PACs Stretching Limits of Campaign Law," *Washington Post,* Feb. 5, 1988.

175 "I've always believed": Charles Green, "Bob Dole Looks Back," *AARP Bulletin,* July/Aug. 2015.

175 "I see the White House": William Rempel and Alan Miller, "Donor Contradicts White House," *Los Angeles Times,* July 27, 1997.

176 The conservative Republican: In his history of Charles Koch's "Stealth" political operation, Coppin writes, "It was believed by members of the investigating committee that Koch Industries used economic Education Trust and Citizens for the Republic as front organizations to hide Koch's paying for the anti-Docking ads."

176 the Federal Election Commission: Elizabeth Drew, *The Corruption of American Politics: What Went Wrong and Why* (Carol, 1999), 56.

176 Carolyn Malenick: Malenick acknowledged that the scheme had pushed the envelope in new ways but insisted that Triad merely balanced the money spent legally by labor unions. The notion that labor had a spending advantage was commonplace among conservatives, although, according to Drew (Ibid.), in 1996 business outspent labor by as much as twelve times. See the FEC judgment against Malenick: http://www.fec.gov/law/litigation/final_judgment_and_order_02CV1237.pdf.

177 What made the Koch family's: Of course, liberals give huge quantities of money, too. Their most prominent donor during these years, the financier George Soros, runs the Open Society Foundations, which have spent as much as $100 million a year in America. Soros has also made huge private contributions to various Democratic outside groups, triggering fines for campaign-finance violations in 2004. But the causes Soros backs—such as decriminalizing marijuana and strengthening civil liberties—don't benefit his fortune in obvious ways according to Michael Vachon, his spokesman, who argues that "none of his contributions are in the service of his own economic interests." For more on Soros, see Mayer, "Money Man."

177 "unprecedented in size": See Charles Lewis et al., "Koch Millions Spread Influence Through Nonprofits, Colleges," Investigative Reporting Workshop, July 1, 2013.

177 "My overall concept": Moore, "Wichita Pipeline."

178 "Who else would give": Teles, *Rise of the Conservative Legal Movement,* 239.

178 "In recent years": Moore, "Wichita Pipeline."

179 the Kochs' multidimensional political spending: See Mayer, "Covert Operations."

179 Only the Kochs know: Private foundations are legally required to publicly disclose their grants, but the recipients have no obligation to disclose the identities of their donors. Thus if the recipients pass the donations to secondary groups, the money trail becomes obscured.

180 "a shell game": Koch associate, interview with author.

181 Rothbard called the putsch: David Gordon, "Murray Rothbard on the Kochtopus," LewRockwell.com, March 10, 2011.

181 "cannot tolerate dissent": The Rothbard memo is described in Schulman, *Sons of Wichita,* 156–57.

182 "staunchly anti-regulatory center": Al Kamen, "I Am OMB and I Write the Rules," *Washington Post,* July 12, 2006, A13.

183 "a lobbying group disguised": Coppin, "Stealth," pt. 2.

183 "Of all the teachers": *The Writings of F. A. Harper* (Institute for Humane Studies, 1979).

183 Anxious at one point: Charles's micromanagement at IHS and the Cato Institute is described in a richly reported article by Mullins, "Battle for the Cato Institute."

184 "all human behavior": Robert Lekachman, "A Controversial Nobel Choice?," *New York Times,* Oct. 26, 1986.

184 "libertarian mecca": Julian Sanchez, "FIRE vs. GMU," Reason.com, Nov. 17, 2005.

184 Liberals, however, regarded: According to the Mercatus Center's Web page, it "does not receive financial support from George Mason University or any federal, state, or local government." Yet Mercatus is headed "by a faculty director who is appointed by the provost of George Mason University."

185 "almost a Marxist faith": Daniel Fisher, "Koch's Laws," *Forbes,* Feb. 26, 2007.

186 "In that, I echo Martin Luther": Charles Koch, acceptance speech for the Richard DeVos award, at the Council for National Policy in Naples, Fla., Jan. 1999. Cited in Fang, *Machine,* 120.

186 "He thinks he's a genius": Ed Crane, interview with author, 2010. Crane's comment on Charles Koch appeared unattributed when first published in *The New Yorker,* but when asked, Crane confirmed to David Koch that he was the source, a fact that has been widely published since.

186 "Richie exploited MBM": Cato official interview with author. Richard Fink declined to be interviewed, according to Steve Lombardo, a spokesman for Koch Industries.

187 "Koch has been constantly": Thomas McGarity, interview with author.

187 The EPA, she argued: Susan Dudley, the Mercatus fellow who concocted the pro-smog argument against the Clean Air Act, became the head of the Office of Information and Regulatory Affairs in the George W. Bush

administration, overseeing the development and implementation of all federal regulations.

189 By 2015, according to an internal list: The colleges and universities with programs subsidized by Koch family foundations as of August 2015 appear here: http://www.kochfamilyfoundations.org/pdfs/CKF UniversityPrograms.pdf.

189 "After a whole semester": Heather MacDonald, "Don't Fund College Follies," *City Journal* (Summer 2005).

189 Charles Koch's foundation gave additional: IRS 990 forms for the Charles G. Koch Charitable Foundation; Lee Fang, "Koch Brothers Fueling Far-Right Academic Centers at Universities Across the Country," *Think-Progress,* May 11, 2011.

189 The foundation required the school: According to the Charles Koch Foundation grant, "Prior to the extension of any offer for the Donor Supported Professorship Positions [professors hired with Koch grants], the Dean of the College of Business and Economics, in consultation with professor Russell Sobel or his successor, shall present the candidate's credentials to CGK Foundation." In addition, the foundation insisted on the right to withdraw funding from any professor hired by its grant who displeased it.

189 The Kochs' investment: For more on the Kochs' coal interests, see http://www.kochcarbon.com/Products.aspx.

190 "Are workers really better off": Evan Osnos, "Chemical Valley," *New Yorker,* April 7, 2014.

190 "We support professors": John Hardin, "The Campaign to Stop Fresh College Thinking," *Wall Street Journal,* May 26, 2015.

190 "entire academic areas": John David, "WVU Sold Its Academic Independence," *Charleston Gazette,* April 23, 2012.

191 "Even great ideas": Charles Koch's 1999 speech at the Council on National Policy, ibid.

191 "What we needed was a sales force": Continetti, "Paranoid Style in Liberal Politics."

CHAPTER SIX: BOOTS ON THE GROUND

196 In a revealing private letter: DeMille Foundation correspondence appears in Sophia Z. Lee, *The Workplace and the Constitution: From the New Deal to the New Right* (Cambridge University Press, 2014), chap. 3. The first quotation is from Donald MacLean (DeMille Foundation) to Joseph C. Fagan (Wisconsin State Chamber of Commerce), Oct. 13, 1954. The second quotation is from MacLean to Reed Larson, Aug. 15, 1956.

196 Although the Kochs were the founders: See Dan Morgan, "Think Tanks: Corporations' Quiet Weapon; Nonprofits' Studies, Lobbying Advance Big Business Causes," *Washington Post,* Jan. 29, 2000.

198 "I can't prove it": Dan Glickman, interview with author.

198 "Our belief is that the tax": "Politics That Can't Be Pigeonholed," *Wichita Eagle,* June 26, 1994.

198 CSE's ads: David Wessel and Jeanne Saddler, "Foes of Clinton's Tax-Boost Proposals Mislead Public and Firms on the Small-Business Aspects," *Wall Street Journal,* July 20, 1993, A12.

198   "They can fly under the radar": Morgan, "Think Tanks."

198   "The split was about control": Dick Armey, interview with author.

200   Phillips was not charged: Phillips's organization, the Faith and Family Alliance, passed cash to Abramoff's gambling clients on at least one documented occasion.

200   "Grover told me Ralph": Bruce Bartlett, interview with author.

201   "I'm gonna be for that guy": Tim Phillips, transcript of an unpublished interview with the documentary filmmaker Alex Gibney, April 19, 2012.

201   "I was intrigued by the idea": Ibid.

CHAPTER SEVEN: TEA TIME

203   a former futures trader: Rick Santelli was a vice president of Drexel Burnham Lambert.

204   The immediate provocation: The Homeowner Affordability and Stability Plan was a temporary relief package for homeowners facing an $8 trillion loss in housing wealth after the market's alarming 2008 collapse.

204   Ross, a personal friend: Ross in October 2014 hosted a party to celebrate David Koch. Mara Siegler, "David Koch Celebrated by Avenue Magazine," *New York Post*, Oct. 2, 2014.

204   His private equity company: For more on Ross's interests in home mortgages, see Carrick Mollenkamp, "Foreclosure Tsunami Hits Mortgage-Servicing Firms," *Wall Street Journal*, Feb. 11, 2009.

204   Critics would later point out: Before Obama took office, Bush's Treasury secretary, Henry "Hank" Paulson, had already spent $125 billion on bank bailouts, and an additional $20 billion was in the pipeline.

205   "The Boston Tea Party": Michael Grunwald, *The New New Deal: The Hidden Story of Change in the Obama Era* (Simon & Schuster, 2012), 280.

205   "It was the guy in Chicago": Fink's protestations were made to *The Wichita Eagle* as well as to the *Frum Report*'s Tim Mak. He acknowledged the Kochs had been asked to fund the Tea Party, but he said none of the activists' proposals met their standards, which required well-defined goals and measurable timelines and benchmarks.

205   "I've never been to a tea-party event": Andrew Goldman, "The Billionaire's Party," *New York*, July 25, 2010.

205   "Oh, *please*": Elaine Lafferty, "'Tea Party Billionaire' Fires Back," *Daily Beast*, Sept. 10, 2010.

205   "a new strain of populism": Mark Lilla, "The Tea Party Jacobins," *New York Review of Books*, May 27, 2010.

206   "mass rebellion": Theda Skocpol and Vanessa Williamson, *The Tea Party and the Remaking of Republican Conservatism* (Oxford University Press, 2012).

206   "The problem with the whole libertarian movement": Jane Mayer, "Covert Operations," *New Yorker*, Aug. 30, 2010.

208   "I think that's actually": Wilson and Wenzl, "Kochs' Quest to Save America."

208   "a never-ending campaign": Vogel, *Big Money*, 42.

209   "If we had run more ads": See Frank Rich, "Sugar Daddies," *New York*, April 22, 2012, on Simmons's quotation, which was derived from an inter-

view with *The Wall Street Journal*'s Monica Langley, "Texas Billionaire Doles Out Election's Biggest Checks," March 22, 2012.

209   "There was a growing sense": Daschle interview with *Frontline*, "Inside Obama's Presidency," Jan. 16, 2013.

209   "nothing more, and nothing less": Daniel Schulman reports, for instance, that the brothers were involved on such a detailed level in Americans for Prosperity, they employed the outside political operatives who created the group's ads. Schulman, *Sons of Wichita*, 276.

210   "Bankers, brokers and businessmen": Charles G. Koch, "Evaluating a President," KochInd.com, Oct. 1, 2010.

210   "prolonged and deepened": Charles Koch's disparagement of the New Deal appears in Charles Koch, "Perspective," *Discovery: The Quarterly Newsletter of the Koch Companies*, Jan. 2009, 12.

211   The company that syndicated: Kenneth Vogel of *Politico* broke the story of the payments to Limbaugh, Mark Levin, and Glenn Beck. Kenneth P. Vogel and Lucy McCalmont, "Rush Limbaugh, Sean Hannity, Glenn Beck Sell Endorsements to Conservative Groups," *Politico*, June 15, 2011.

211   "We're not here to cut deals": Grunwald, *New New Deal*, 142.

212   "If the Purpose of the Majority": Ibid., 142–43.

212   "In the past, it was rare": Steve LaTourette (who retired at the end of the 2012 session), interview with author.

213   "What they said": Grunwald, *New New Deal*, 145.

214   "It was stunning": Ibid., 190.

215   "They turned on Obama so early": Bill Burton, interview with author.

216   Five years later, a survey: Justin Wolfers, "What Debate? Economists Agree the Stimulus Lifted the Economy," *New York Times*, July 29, 2014.

217   TaxDayTeaParty.com: Fang, *Machine*, 32.

217   The founder of the Sam Adams Alliance: Fang, in ibid., describes Rich as the founder of the Sam Adams Alliance. Rich declined to respond to interview requests.

218   Rich in particular: See, for instance, Russ Choma, "Rich Rewards: One Man's Shadow Money Network," OpenSecrets.org, June 19, 2012.

218   He almost invariably declined: Howard Rich failed to respond to several attempts I made to reach him for comment as well.

218   "My 32 years": Marc Fisher, "Wisconsin Gov. Scott Walker's Recall: Big Money Fuels Small-Government Fight," *Washington Post*, March 25, 2012.

218   But after the referendum succeeded: Dan Morain, "Prop. 164 Cash Trail Leads to Billionaires," *Los Angeles Times*, Oct. 30, 1992.

219   "the Kochian deep pockets": Sarah Barton, The Ear, *Rothbard-Rockwell Report*, July 1993.

219   "a prairie fire of populism": Timothy Egan, "Campaign on Term Limits Taps a Gusher of Money," *New York Times*, Oct. 31, 1991.

219   "I ignited the spark": Ibid.

220   But an investigation: Bill Hogan, "Three Big Donors Bankrolled Americans for Limited Government in 2005," Center for Public Integrity, Dec. 21, 2006.

220   "We're not going to be shut up": Jonathan Rauch, "A Morning at the Ministry of Speech," *National Journal*, May 29, 1999. In the summer of 2008:

Eric Odom provided his own account of these events, insisting the Tea Party was a spontaneous outpouring but ignoring the issue of who funded the Sam Adams Alliance or Rob Bluey. Odom, "The Tea Party Conspirators and the Real Story Behind the Tea Party Movement," *Liberty News,* Aug. 30, 2011.

220 "a card-carrying member": Ben Smith and Jonathan Martin, "BlogJam: Right-Wing Bluey Blog," *Politico,* June 18, 2007.

220 They sent out Twitter messages: All summer long, as oil and gasoline prices hit highs, energy industry moguls including Larry Nichols, chairman of the giant Oklahoma oil and gas company Devon Energy, who attended the Kochs' donor summits, had been pushing hard to expand offshore drilling. Several other Koch network members, including the Las Vegas casino owner Sheldon Adelson, Dick Farmer of Cintas, and Stan Hubbard of Hubbard Broadcasting, were also involved, funding a pro-drilling front group called American Solutions, run by Newt Gingrich.

222 He noted that Americans for Prosperity: Lee Fang's early report questioning whether the Tea Party was an "Astroturf" movement manufactured in Washington led the way in getting the press to look more closely. His first major story was "Spontaneous Uprising?," *ThinkProgress,* April 9, 2009.

222 "It was very much a put-up job": Thomas Frank, interview with author.

222 "I was a member of the Tea Party": Peggy Venable, interview with author.

224 "spent hours and hours on the phone": Dick Armey, interview with author.

225 "We thought it would be a useful tool": Dick Armey, interview with author about Glenn Beck payments. See also Vogel and McCalmont, "Rush Limbaugh, Sean Hannity, Glenn Beck Sell Endorsements to Conservative Groups."

225 Beck, whose views were shaped: Sean Wilentz, "Confounding Fathers," *New Yorker,* Oct. 18, 2010.

225 "That rant from Santelli": Frank Luntz, interview with author.

225 "In an atmosphere primed": John B. Judis, "The Unnecessary Fall," *New Republic,* Aug. 12, 2010.

226 professed to be discomfited: A source who spoke at length with Fink shared his thinking with the author.

226 "the most radical president": Continetti, "Paranoid Style in Liberal Politics."

227 "It was hard for me to believe": "Obama's Interview Aboard Air Force One," *New York Times,* March 7, 2009.

228 forced to refund $32 million: Purva Patel, "Woodforest Bank to Hand Back $32M in Overdrafts," *Houston Chronicle,* Oct. 13, 2010.

228 Daschle was expected to become: Daschle was named to serve a dual role as HHS secretary and White House health czar but was forced to withdraw due to a controversy about unpaid taxes in early February.

229 She and a handful of other multimillionaires: The ballot initiative, which had been drafted by the Goldwater Institute, was narrowly defeated in November 2008.

230 "What organizations are doing this?": Eliana Johnson, "Inside the Koch-Funded Ads Giving Dems Fits," *National Review Online,* March 31, 2014.

232 "I can't tell you": Kim Barker and Theodoric Meyer, "The Dark Money Man," ProPublica, Feb. 14, 2014.

232 Fact-checkers later revealed: "Dying on a Wait List?," FactCheck.org, Aug. 6, 2009.

233 "If you want an assassination": Peter Hart, interview with author.

233 "The think tanks became the creators": Frank Luntz, interview with author.

233 In playing this role: In his book *Rich People's Movements*, Isaac William Martin describes the historic role of "policy entrepreneurs."

234 a conservative idea hatched: For more on Republican support of the individual mandate, see Ezra Klein, "A Lot of Republicans Supported the Individual Mandate," *Washington Post*, May 12, 2011.

235 "We knew we had to make": Johnson, "Inside the Koch-Funded Ads Giving Dems Fits."

235 "create a movement": Amanda Fallin, Rachel Grana, and Stanton Glantz, "To Quarterback Behind the Scenes, Third-Party Efforts: The Tobacco Industry and the Tea Party," *Tobacco Control*, Feb. 2013.

236 it had mocked Al Gore's environmental jeremiad: Antonio Regalado and Dionne Searcey, "Where Did That Video Spoofing Gore's Film Come From?," *Wall Street Journal*, Aug. 3, 2006.

236 Pretty soon: David Kirkpatrick, "Groups Back Health Reform, but Seek Cover," *New York Times*, Sept. 11, 2009.

237 "This year has been really": Dan Eggen, "How Interest Groups Behind Health-Care Legislation Are Financed Is Often Unclear," *Washington Post*, Jan. 7, 2010.

237 "public education programs": Ken Vogel, "Tea Party's Growing Money Problem," *Politico*, Aug. 9, 2010.

237 "We met for 20 or 30 years": Bill Wilson and Roy Wenzl, "The Kochs' Quest to Save America," *Wichita Eagle*, Oct. 3, 2012.

238 Not only had he been invited: Mark Holden, the general counsel to Koch Industries, described Noble as "an independent contractor" and "a consultant" to the company, in an interview with Kenneth Vogel, *Big Money*, 201.

238 "pack the hall": Lee Fang, "Right-Wing Harassment Strategy Against Dems Detailed in Memo," *ThinkProgress*, July 31, 2009.

238 "We packed these town halls": Johnson, "Inside the Koch-Funded Ads Giving Dems Fits."

239 "couldn't have done it": Grover Norquist, interview with author.

240 "I thought on health care": One of the few in the media to question whether the Tea Party protests were, as he put it, "orchestrations of incivility" rather than a brand-new widespread movement was Rick Perlstein, who warned in an essay in *The Washington Post*, "Conservatives have become adept at playing the media for suckers." He argued that "the tree of crazy," as he called the far-right protesters, was ever present in American politics, but in the past a more robust press corps, as well as more responsible conservatives, such as William F. Buckley, had "unequivocally labeled the civic outrage represented by such discourse 'extremist'—out of bounds." See Rick Perlstein, "Birthers, Health Care Hecklers, and the Rise of Right-Wing Rage," *Washington Post*, Aug. 16, 2009.

240 "wasn't really tracking": David Axelrod, interview with author.

240 When fewer than sixty-five thousand: Some dispute the crowd estimate.

240 Membership in the Liberty League: See Kevin Drum, "Old Whine in New Bottles," *Mother Jones*, Sept./Oct. 2010.

241 330,000 activists: Devin Burghart, "View from the Top: Report on Six National Tea Party Organizations," in *Steep: The Precipitous Rise of the Tea Party*, ed. Lawrence Rosenthal and Christine Trost (University of California Press, 2012).

242 It was hard not to notice: Lee Fang first noted the similarity between the pageantry at the Defending the American Dream Summit and that at presidential nominating conventions. Fang, *Machine*, 121.

CHAPTER EIGHT: THE FOSSILS

244 "The change wrought": National Security Strategy, Washington, D.C. (Office of the President of the United States, 2010), 8, 47.

244 "we face risks": American Association for the Advancement of Science, Climate Science Panel, "What We Know," 2014.

244 Mann wasn't particularly political: Mann told Neela Banerjee, "I started out as a scientist who didn't think there was much of a role to play in public policy." Banerjee, "The Most Hated Climate Scientist in the US Fights Back," *Yale Alumni Magazine*, March/April 2013.

245 "What we didn't take into account": Michael Mann, interview with author.

245 "it's like the switch from whale oil": Ibid.

246 He owned, by one count: Fisher, "Fuel's Paradise."

246 Only the U.S. government: Neela Banerjee, "In Climate Politics, Texas Aims to Be the Anti-California," *Los Angeles Times*, Nov. 7, 2010.

247 "unleash what became known": Daniel Yergin, *The Quest: Energy, Security, and the Remaking of the Modern World* (Penguin, 2011), 328–29.

247 The Kochs, too: For more on the Kochs' fracking investments, see Brad Johnson, "How the Kochs Are Fracking America," *ThinkProgress*, March 2, 2012.

248 If the world were to stay: See "Global Warming's Terrifying New Math," by Bill McKibben, *Rolling Stone*, July 19, 2012. He explains that scientists believe the earth can tolerate the burning of roughly 565 more gigatons of carbon dioxide by mid-century, but that informed estimates place the currently untapped carbon reserves at 2,795 gigatons.

249 As early as 1913: The history of the oil depletion allowance is described in Robert Bryce, *Cronies* (PublicAffairs, 2004).

249 As Robert Caro recounts: "A new source of political money, potentially vast, had been tapped," Caro writes, "and Lyndon Johnson had been put in charge of it." Robert Caro, *The Path to Power* (Vintage Books, 1990), 637.

249 "the deep-tissue insecurity": Bryan Burrough, *The Big Rich: The Rise and Fall of the Greatest Texas Oil Fortunes* (Penguin, 2009), 204.

250 "the restoration of the supremacy": Ibid., 138.

250 Cullen's political ambitions: Ibid., 220, bases his assertion that Cullen was the largest contributor in 1952 on research by the University of North Carolina professor Alexander Heard.

250 "to succeed in politics": Ibid., 210.

251 What he discovered: Fighting the science of climate change was not the

only issue these groups and candidates focused on, but it was the single issue they all had in common.

251 His research showed: The Kochs outspent ExxonMobil in their funding of nonprofit groups, not politicians.

251 "kingpin of climate science denial": See "Koch Industries, Secretly Funding the Climate Denial Machine," Greenpeace, March 2010.

251 "campaign to manipulate": Robert J. Brulle, "Institutionalizing Delay: Foundation Funding and the Creation of U.S. Climate Change Countermovement Organizations," *Climate Change* 122, no. 4 (Feb. 2014): 681–94.

253 Between 1999 and 2015: Whitney Ball died in August 2015, and in a tribute that appeared in *National Review,* James Piereson wrote that from its founding in 1999 DonorsTrust had given away $750 million. Donors Trust announced that Lawson Bader, CEO of the Competitive Enterprise Institute, who had been vice president of the Mercatus Center at George Mason University, would succeed her.

254 "We just have this great big unknown": Andy Kroll, "Exposed: The Dark-Money ATM of the Conservative Movement," *Mother Jones,* Feb. 5, 2013.

255 "There's a better scientific consensus": As quoted by Ross Gelbspan, "Snowed," *Mother Jones,* May/June 2005, and requoted by Michaels, *Doubt Is Their Product,* 197.

255 the plan was the brainchild: Chris Mooney, *The Republican War on Science* (Basic Books, 2006), 83.

255 "central cog": "Global Warming Deniers Well Funded," *Newsweek,* Aug. 12, 2007.

256 Leading the charge: Fred Seitz had previously distributed $45 million from R. J. Reynolds to scientists willing to defend tobacco. Fred Singer had attacked the EPA's assertion that secondhand smoke was a health hazard. The financing for Singer's work was a grant from the Tobacco Institute, a group supported by cigarette companies. The money was filtered, though, through a nonprofit organization called the Alexis de Tocqueville Institution. Singer's work on secondhand smoke took place during the 1990s. Tax records show that between 1988 and 2002, the Alexis de Tocqueville Institution received $1,723,900 from the Bradley, Olin, Scaife, Philip M. McKenna, and Claude R. Lambe Foundations.

256 "yet, for years the press": Naomi Oreskes and Erik M. Conway, *Merchants of Doubt* (Bloomsbury Press, 2010), 9.

256 As late as 2003: Poll numbers attributed to Theda Skocpol, *Naming the Problem: What It Will Take to Counter Extremism and Engage Americans in the Fight Against Global Warming* (Harvard University, Jan. 2013).

257 It quickly drew criticism: Dr. Steven C. Amstrup, chief scientist with Polar Bears International and a U.S. Geological Survey polar bear project leader for thirty years, explained that estimates of the size of the polar bear population in past decades were nothing more than guesses, but their grim future was a certainty if nothing was done to preserve their habitat, which he said was undeniably "disappearing due to global warming." Further, in 2008 polar bears became the first vertebrate species listed under the Endangered Species Act as threatened by global warming. See also Michael Muskal, "40% Decline in Polar Bears in Alaska, Western Canada Heightens Concern," *Los Angeles Times,* Nov. 21, 2014.

257 "There are more polar bears": Ed Crane, interview with author. For more on the polar bear controversy, see "Koch Industries, Secretly Funding the Climate Denial Machine."

258 Without disclosing it: See Justin Gillis and John Schwartz, "Deeper Ties to Corporate Cash for Doubtful Climate Researcher," *New York Times,* Feb. 22, 2015.

258 Yet from that moment on: Mann and his co-authors had been openly cautious about their findings, noting that because there were no temperature records kept a thousand years ago, they had been forced to use "proxy" methods, which included less than optimal techniques such as studying ice cores and tree rings.

258 Koch Industries' political action committee: Between 2005 and 2008, KochPAC made federal contributions totaling $4.3 million, in comparison with ExxonMobil's $1.6 million, according to FEC reports.

258 The company's expenditures: Koch Industries spent $857,000 on lobbying in 2004, which grew to $20 million by 2008, according to the Center for Public Integrity. See John Aloysius Farrell, "Koch's Web of Influence," Center for Public Integrity, April 6, 2011.

259 As the Harvard political scientist: Skocpol, *Naming the Problem.*

259 At the time, Morano was working: When he promoted the "Swift Boat" story questioning John Kerry's Vietnam War record, Morano worked as a reporter for Cybercast News Service, a project of the Media Research Center, which the Scaife family foundations funded, among others.

259 "You've got to name names": See Robert Kenner's 2014 documentary film, *Merchants of Doubt.*

259 "We had a lot of fun": Ibid.

259 "the 'climate con'": Banerjee, "Most Hated Climate Scientist in the US Fights Back."

260 "State political veterans": Tom Hamburger, "A Coal-Fired Crusade Helped Bring Bush a Crucial Victory," *Wall Street Journal,* June 13, 2001.

260 "case study in managing": Barton Gellman, *Angler* (Penguin, 2008), 84.

260 Cheney used his influence: The *Los Angeles Times* broke the story of Cheney's influence on the fracking exemption, noting that his former company Halliburton had interests in fracking. Tom Hamburger and Alan Miller, "Halliburton's Interests Assisted by White House," *Los Angeles Times,* Oct. 14, 2004.

261 In all, the Bush energy act: The subsidies were tallied by Public Citizen, "The Best Energy Bill Corporations Could Buy," Aug. 8, 2005.

261 41 percent of the American public: Gallup poll; see Skocpol, *Naming the Problem,* 72. Gore's acclaim is described in Eric Pooley, *The Climate War* (Hachette Books, 2010).

262 "Climate denial got disseminated": Skocpol, *Naming the Problem,* 83.

262 the climate problem was real: McCain made these comments in the second presidential debate; see Pooley, *Climate War,* 297.

264 leases on over a million acres: Steve Mufson and Juliet Eilperin, "The Biggest Foreign Lease Holder in Canada's Oil Sands Isn't Exxon Mobil or Chevron. It's the Koch Brothers," *Washington Post,* March 20, 2014.

264 Koch Industries alone: The 300 million tons of carbon dioxide figure comes from Brad Johnson, "Koch Industries, the 100-Million Ton Car-

bon Gorilla," *ThinkProgress,* Jan. 30, 2011, and is cited in Fang, *Machine,* 114.

265 "The Earth will be able": Goldman, "Billionaire's Party."

265 Rather than fighting global warming: For an excellent report on Koch Industries' lobbying, see Farrell, "Koch's Web of Influence."

265 "The Obama budget proposes": Fang, *Machine,* 115.

266 "I rode more hot-air balloons": Jim Rutenberg, "How Billionaire Oligarchs Are Becoming Their Own Political Parties," *New York Times Magazine,* Oct. 17, 2014.

266 Reams of faxes arrived: Kate Sheppard, "Forged Climate Bill Letters Spark Uproar over 'Astroturfing,'" *Grist,* Aug. 4, 2009.

266 Later one of the disruptive members: See Fang, *Machine,* 176.

267 Mike Castle: Pooley, *Climate War,* 406.

267 "go ask the unicorns": Ibid., 393.

267 The process wasn't pretty: For an authoritative account of the cap-and-trade fight in the House, see ibid.

268 Quietly funding it: See Steven Mufson, "New Groups Revive the Debate over Climate Change," *Washington Post,* Sept. 25, 2009.

268 As soon as Obama's EPA: For more on the dispute, and a statement by John Nielsen-Gammon, Texas's state climatologist, see David Doniger, "Going Rogue on Endangerment," *Switchboard* (blog), Feb. 20, 2010.

269 One posted a report: Marc Sheppard, "UN Climate Reports: They Lie," *American Thinker,* Oct. 5, 2009.

269 "A miracle has happened": The Web site on which the contrarian wrote was Climate Audit.

269 "The blue dress moment": Chris Horner, "The Blue Dress Moment May Have Arrived," *National Review,* Nov. 19, 2009.

270 "a crucial tipping point": Tim Phillips was speaking about the Climategate leaks at the Heritage Foundation on October 26, 2010, as reported by Brad Johnson, Climate Progress, Nov. 27, 2010. Phillips did all he could to exploit the situation, staging an Americans for Prosperity protest in Copenhagen outside the United Nations conference on climate change, where he declared, "We're a grassroots organization . . . I think it's unfortunate when wealthy children of wealthy families . . . want to send unemployment rates in the United States to twenty percent." See Mayer, "Covert Operations."

270 The facts, when fully understood: Neela Banerjee provides a very clear and detailed analysis of the leaked e-mails in her profile of Mann, "Most Hated Climate Scientist in the US Fights Back."

272 As Mann recounts in his book: Mann writes that the Southeastern Legal Foundation demanded information from the National Science Foundation about its grants to him and his colleagues at Penn State. The Landmark Legal Foundation, he writes, sued to obtain personal e-mails he sent to colleagues at other schools who had collaborated on his hockey stick research. Michael E. Mann, *The Hockey Stick and the Climate Wars* (Columbia University Press, 2012), 229.

272 "a vicious S.O.B.": Vogel and McCalmont, "Rush Limbaugh, Sean Hannity, Glenn Beck Sell Endorsements to Conservative Groups"; John

Goodman, "Talk Radio Reacts to Politico on Cain; Mark Levin Criticizes Ken Vogel," *Examiner*, Nov. 2, 2011.

272 "I don't know why": "Levin to Female Caller: 'I Don't Know Why Your Husband Doesn't Put a Gun to His Temple,'" *Media Matters*, May 22, 2009.

272 "and the other advocates": Mark Levin, *Liberty and Tyranny* (Threshold, 2010), 133.

275 Almost half of those polled: Cited in Kate Sheppard, "Climategate: What Really Happened?," *Mother Jones*, April 21, 2011.

275 "I have come to conclude": Ryan Lizza, "As the World Burns," *New Yorker*, Oct. 11, 2010.

276 "Gridlock is the greatest friend": Kenner, *Merchants of Doubt*.

276 "The influence of special interests": Lizza, "As the World Burns."

CHAPTER NINE: MONEY IS SPEECH

279 One associate said: A social acquaintance of David Koch's, interview with author.

280 "difficult to see": Richard Posner, "Unlimited Campaign Spending—A Good Thing?," *The Becker-Posner Blog*, April 8, 2012.

280 "it gave rich people": Jeffrey Toobin, "Republicans United on Climate Change," *New Yorker*, June 10, 2014. Also see his "Money Unlimited," *New Yorker*, May 21, 2012.

281 In a growing backlash: See Elizabeth F. Ralph, "The Big Donor: A Short History," *Politico*, June 2014.

284 After news of their involvement: Dale Russakoff and Juan Williams, "Rearranging 'Amway Event' for Reagan," *Washington Post*, Jan. 22, 1984.

284 "They're not a business": "Soft Soap and Hard Sell," *Forbes*, Sept. 15, 1975.

285 In 1980, Richard DeVos: In "Rearranging 'Amway Event' for Reagan," Russakoff and Williams write that "DeVos, former finance chairman of the Republican National Committee, gave $70,575 in independent expenditures; Van Andel, former chairman of the U.S. Chamber of Commerce, chipped in $68,433."

285 By 1981, their titles: Ibid.

285 DeVos, the son of a poor: See Andy Kroll's excellent piece on the DeVos family, "Meet the New Kochs: The DeVos Clan's Plan to Defund the Left," *Mother Jones*, Jan./Feb. 2014.

285 The scandal exploded: Kitty McKinsey and Paul Magnusson, "Amway's Plot to Bilk Canada of Millions," *Detroit Free Press*, Aug. 22, 1982.

286 In 1989, Amway paid: Ruth Marcus, "Amway Says It Was Unnamed Donor to Help Broadcast GOP Convention," *Washington Post*, July 26, 1996.

286 "We were losing": Russakoff and Williams, "Rearranging 'Amway Event' for Reagan."

286 The DeVos family nonetheless: For statistics on the DeVos's spending, see Kroll, "Meet the New Kochs."

286 "There's not a Republican president": Ibid.

286 "a little-known club": David Kirkpatrick, "Club of the Most Powerful Gathers in Strictest Privacy," *New York Times*, Aug. 28, 2004.

287 "the doers": On March 22, 2005, Paul Weyrich said on C-SPAN (http://www.c-span.org/video/transcript/?id=7958) that the Council for National Policy, "in the words of Rich DeVos, brings together the doers with the donors."

287 Her father, Edgar: Jeremy Scahill, *Blackwater: The Rise of the World's Most Powerful Mercenary Army* (Nation Books, 2007), 78.

287 "the world's most powerful": Erik Prince, a swashbuckling former navy SEAL officer, soon ran into professional legal trouble. He eventually moved abroad and changed the company's name to escape its reputation as an international outlaw after its guards were charged with murder for gunning down seventeen civilians during the Iraq War.

288 "a spending edge": John David Dyche, *Republican Leader: A Political Biography* (Intercollegiate Studies Institute, 2009).

288 "Money, money, money": John Cheves, "Senator's Pet Issue: Money and the Power It Buys," *Lexington Herald-Leader,* Oct. 15, 2006.

288 "If we stop this thing": Michael Lewis, "The Subversive," *New York Times Magazine,* May 25, 1997.

289 "The relationship between": Marcus Owens was interviewed by Jon Campbell, who first wrote about the unusual relationship between Bopp and the James Madison Center in "James Bopp Jr. Gets Creative: How Does the Conservative Maestro of Campaign Finance Fund His Legal Work?," Slate.com, Oct. 5, 2012.

289 "Soft money": Betsy DeVos, "Soft Money Is Good: Hard-earned American Dollars That Big Brother Has Yet to Find a Way to Control," *Roll Call,* Sept. 6, 1997.

290 In 2004, Democratic-aligned outside groups: Trevor Potter, "The Current State of Campaign Finance Laws," *Brookings Campaign Finance Sourcebook,* 2005.

290 Leading the pack: For more on Soros's spending in the 2004 presidential election, see Mayer, "Money Man."

290 "was really Jim": David Kirkpatrick, "A Quest to End Spending Rules for Campaigns," *New York Times,* Jan. 24, 2010. Theodore Olson, a far better litigator than Bopp, argued the crucial oral argument in front of the Supreme Court.

291 "We had a 10-year plan": Ibid.

291 With his shaggy gray: Stephanie Mencimer, "The Man Who Took Down Campaign Finance Reform," *Mother Jones,* Jan. 21, 2010. Mencimer recounts that in 2008 the U.S. District Court judge Royce Lamberth "actually laughed at Bopp."

291 Clint Bolick, a pioneer: See Teles, *Rise of the Conservative Legal Movement,* 87.

292 While polls consistently showed: According to a poll conducted by ABC News on February 17, 2010, eight out of ten Americans surveyed opposed the Supreme Court's *Citizen United* decision.

292 "I would not have been": Bradley Smith, interview with author.

293 The litigation, meanwhile: Robert Mullins, "Racine Labor Center: Meeting Place for Organized Labor on the Ropes," *Milwaukee Business Journal,* Dec. 23, 1991.

293 He had been the Senate's premier: In 2002, Senators Russell Feingold and

John McCain, Republican of Arizona, co-authored the Bipartisan Campaign Reform Act, known as McCain-Feingold, which *Citizens United* largely undid.

293   "This Supreme Court decision": "Changes Have Money Talking Louder Than Ever in Midterms," *New York Times*, Oct. 7, 2010.

294   "not true": Technically, *Citizens United* said nothing about what foreign corporations could do, so some nonpartisan fact-checkers said Alito was right to object to Obama's description of the ruling as opening the doors to foreign spending. But the *Citizens United* decision did open a way for U.S. subsidiaries of foreign corporations to spend unlimited sums in American campaigns.

294   "It unshackled the big money": David Axelrod, interview with author.

CHAPTER TEN: THE SHELLACKING

295   Although Brown was a low-profile: See Brian Mooney, "Late Spending Frenzy Fueled Senate Race," *Boston Globe*, Jan. 24, 2010. The total spending by Brown and his opponent, Martha Coakley, in the Senate race was roughly equal, but while Coakley benefited from a large amount of cash from conventional Democratic Party committees, Brown got no money from GOP committees. The $2.6 million in contributions he got from outside conservative groups, which was almost $1 million more than Coakley got from outside spending groups, played a crucial role in filling this gap.

296   Two of the most active: According to Steve Leblanc's report for the Associated Press, Feb. 19, 2010, the American Future Fund spent $618,000 against Martha Coakley, and Americans for Job Security—a group that would receive $4.8 million from the Center to Protect Patient Rights in 2010—spent $460,000 on ads against Coakley. Together with the U.S. Chamber of Commerce's $1 million in last-minute ads, those three groups made up the bulk of the $2.6 million spent by conservative outside groups in the last twelve days of the campaign.

296   "We thought we had it won": Participant who spoke on the grounds that he not be identified, interview with author.

297   Its clients ranged: Ed Gillespie said he never supported the individual mandates, even though his firm represented the coalition of companies that suggested the plan. See James Hohmann, "Ed Gillespie's Steep Slog to the Senate," *Politico*, Jan. 13, 2014.

297   Within weeks, he set out: Vogel, *Big Money*, 47, describes the meeting at the Dallas Petroleum Club in greater detail.

298   "People call us": Ken Vogel, "Politics, Karl Rove and the Modern Money Machine," *Politico*, July/August 2014.

298   "It was all conceived": Glenn Thrush, "Obama's States of Despair: 2010 Losses Still Haunt," *Politico*, July 26, 2013.

299   By the end of 2010: See Olga Pierce, Justin Elliott, and Theodoric Meyer, "How Dark Money Helped Republicans Hold the House and Hurt Voters," ProPublica, Dec. 21, 2012.

299   "It was three yards": See Nicholas Confessore, "A National Strategy Funds State Political Monopolies," *New York Times*, Jan. 12, 2014.

299 In the previous decade: The $40 million spending figure is according to an analysis of tax records by Democracy NC, a progressive government watchdog group.

300 "He was a terrible candidate": Bob Geary, interview with author, which first appeared in Jane Mayer, "State for Sale," *New Yorker*, Oct. 10, 2011.

300 "I'm not a charismatic": Art Pope, interview with author, which first appeared in ibid.

301 Under his guidance: See Ted Gup, "Fakin' It," *Mother Jones*, May/June 1996. He writes that homemade-looking placards were in fact FedExed to the smokers' rights groups from the tobacco company executives in Winston-Salem, North Carolina.

301 In 1994 alone: Peter Stone describes the organization of smokers' rights groups in his piece, "The Nicotine Network," *Mother Jones*, May/June 1996.

302 In 2012, he pleaded guilty: Ellis pleaded guilty in June 2012 to a felony charge of making an illegal campaign contribution. In the plea deal, he received four years of probation and was fined $10,000. He says it is his understanding that following the probationary period, in 2016, further adjudication may dismiss the charge.

302 "The grass roots was designed": Jim Ellis, interview with author.

302 At a second Capitol Hill rally: Sam Stein, "Tea Party Protests—'Ni**er,' 'Fa**ot' Shouted at Members of Congress," *Huffington Post*, March 20, 2010.

303 "You know they're gonna": Halperin and Heilemann, *Double Down*, 13.

303 "We made a deliberate": Johnson, "Inside the Koch-Funded Ads Giving Dems Fits."

304 About a third of this: The forms showed TC4 sending money to what accountants call "disregarded entities," so that instead of appearing to go to CPPR, it went to two phantom limbs called Eleventh Edition LLC and American Commitment. See Viveca Novak, Robert Maguire, and Russ Choma, "Nonprofit Funneled Money to Kochs' Voter Database Effort, Other Conservative Groups," OpenSecrets.org, Dec. 21, 2012.

304 Previously, they had given: The main such "social welfare" group the Kochs supported prior to 2010 was Americans for Prosperity, which they only moderately funded during the Bush years. Instead, they had donated mostly to what the IRS defined as charitable organizations, or 501(c)(3)s, for which they could take tax deductions and which were more strictly barred from electoral politics.

305 For example, at the end of 2010: The Center for Responsive Politics first reported on the fact that the Center to Protect Patient Rights reported no spending on politics in its 2010 IRS 990 tax form. Kim Barker did an excellent, extensive report later, "How Nonprofits Spend Millions on Elections and Call It Public Welfare," ProPublica, Aug. 18, 2012, describing the phenomenon in further detail.

305 Yet it granted $103 million: These spending figures cover the years 2009 to 2011 and include the TC4 Trust.

305 In 2006, only 2 percent: These sums were calculated by the Center for Responsive Politics and exclude spending by party committees.

305 "The political players": Barker, "How Nonprofits Spend Millions on Elections and Call It Public Welfare."

306 Some joked that they attended: Steven Law said several attendees, including himself, "went so they could tell their friends they went to Karl Rove's house." Joe Hagan, "Goddangit, Baby, We're Making Good Time," *New York,* Feb. 27, 2011.

306 "the birthplace of a new": Vogel, *Big Money,* 49.

306 Working closely with both: Bloomberg reported, for instance, that in 2009 and 2010 the health insurance industry secretly funneled over $86 million into the U.S. Chamber of Commerce for attack ads. Drew Armstrong, "Health Insurers Gave $86 Million to Fight Health Law," Bloomberg, Nov. 17, 2010.

306 "there wasn't one race": Vogel, *Big Money,* 53.

307 "in order of the likelihood": Eliana Johnson, "Inside the Koch-Funded Ads Giving Dems Fits," NationalReview.com, March 31, 2014.

308 Efforts to track down: Jim Rutenberg, Don Van Natta Jr., and Mike McIntire, "Offering Donors Secrecy, and Going on Attack," *New York Times,* Oct. 11, 2010.

308 "has no purpose": Mike McIntire, "Under Tax-Exempt Cloak, Political Dollars Flow," *New York Times,* Sept. 23, 2010.

308 In addition, Noble directed millions: In 2010, Noble's CPPR distributed $31 million—just under half of its funds—to five conservative groups that then spent similar amounts on TV ads targeting fifty-eight House Democratic candidates. The groups were the American Future Fund ($11.6 million), the 60 Plus Association ($8.9 million), Americans for Job Security ($4.8 million), Americans for Tax Reform ($4.1 million), and Revere America ($2.3 million). CPPR provided at least one-third of the budget raised by each of those five groups that year. CPPR's next-largest expenses were $10.3 million for "communications and surveys" and $5.5 million to Americans for Limited Government, which sent out mailings attacking House Democrats.

309 "For the first time": Pooley, *Climate War,* 406.

309 "The Koch brothers went after me": Rick Boucher, interview with author.

311 McCarthy was an old hand: Larry McCarthy declined to comment.

311 "Larry is not just": Floyd Brown, interview with author, which first appeared in Jane Mayer, "Attack Dog," *New Yorker,* Feb. 13, 2012.

311 "serial offender": Geoff Garin, interview with author, which first appeared in ibid.

312 "a war": Jonathan Alter, "Schwarzman: 'It's a War' Between Obama, Wall St.," *Newsweek,* Aug. 15, 2010.

312 "You have no idea": James B. Stewart, "The Birthday Party," *New Yorker,* Feb. 11, 2008.

313 A 2007 *Wall Street Journal* profile: Henry Sender and Monica Langley, "How Blackstone's Chief Became $7 Million Man," *Wall Street Journal,* June 13, 2007.

313 The media sensation: Even business publications ran columns blasting the loophole. See Martin Sosnoff, "The $3 Billion Birthday Party," *Forbes,* June 21, 2007.

313   over $6 billion a year: Randall Dodd, "Tax Breaks for Billionaires," Economic Policy Institute, July 24, 2007.

314   "Hedge funds really need": Asness's open letter was written earlier, in May 2009, and was criticizing Obama for demonizing hedge funds for not going along with his administration's attempt to restructure Chrysler. See Clifford Asness, "Unafraid in Greenwich Connecticut," *Business Insider,* May 5, 2009.

315   "the closest thing": Andrew Miga, "Rich Spark Soft Money Surge—Financier Typifies New Type of Donor," *Boston Herald,* Nov. 29, 1999.

315   According to later reports: See Michael Isikoff and Peter Stone, "How Wall Street Execs Bankrolled GOP Victory," NBC News, Jan. 5, 2011.

315   eleven were on *Forbes*'s list: They were as follows:
      Charles Koch: $44.7 billion
      David Koch: $44.7 billion
      Steve Schwarzman: $11.3 billion
      Philip Anschutz: $11 billion
      Ken Griffin: $7 billion
      Richard DeVos: $5.8 billion
      Diane Hendricks: $3.6 billion
      Ken Langone: $2.9 billion
      Steve Bechtel: $2.7 billion
      Stan Hubbard: $2 billion
      Joe Craft: $1.4 billion

316   "target-rich": Paul Abowd, "Donors Use Charity to Push Free-Market Policies in States," Center for Public Integrity, Feb. 14, 2013.

316   By the end of the meal: Kenneth Vogel and Simmi Aujla, "Koch Conference Under Scrutiny," *Politico,* Jan. 27, 2011.

317   "one hell of a wake-up call": See Sam Stein, "$200 Million GOP Campaign Avalanche Planned, Democrats Stunned," *Huffington Post,* July 8, 2010.

317   "It was clear": Anita Dunn, interview with author.

317   As late as May: David Axelrod, conversation with author, May 2010.

318   "dropped on me": Bruce Braley, interview with author, which first appeared in Mayer, "Attack Dog."

319   In 2010, Americans for Prosperity: See Fang, *Machine,* 174. He describes attending the 2010 Conservative Political Action Conference and seeing attendees taught to use video cameras "to harass Democratic officials until their inevitable outbursts were caught on tape." He writes that several conservative groups held training sessions in the ambush video technique, according to attendees at their functions, including Americans for Prosperity, FreedomWorks, and American Majority.

320   Only in 2011 did it surface: See Ben Smith, "Hedge Fund Figure Financed Mosque Campaign," *Politico,* Jan. 18, 2011. Smith credits his colleague Maggie Haberman with figuring out the money trail.

321   "I voted to help build": Mayer, "State for Sale."

322   Pope was instrumental: The racially charged ad was produced by the North Carolina Republican Party. Pope said that he was not involved in its creation, but he and three members of his family gave the Davis campaign a $4,000 check each—the maximum individual donation allowed by state

law. Pope told ProPublica that his $200,000 donation to Real Jobs NC was not for the REDMAP operation, or redistricting work. A lawsuit filed after the election concerning the redistricting effort, however, revealed that Pope consulted on how the borders were drawn. See Pierce, Elliott, and Meyer, "How Dark Money Helped Republicans Hold the House and Hurt Voters."

323   "We didn't have that before 2010": Mayer, "State for Sale."
323   "Those ads hurt me": Ibid.
324   "If you put all of the Pope groups": Ibid.
324   "People throw around terms": Art Pope, interview with author, which first appeared in Mayer, "State for Sale."
326   "The Obama team": Thrush, "Obama's States of Despair."
326   "We lost all hope": David Corn, *Showdown: The Inside Story of How Obama Fought Back Against Boehner, Cantor, and the Tea Party* (William Morrow, 2012), 44.
327   The conventional wisdom: See a more detailed description of the debate over blaming dark money in ibid., 40.
329   "a 5,700-square-foot, eight-bedroom house": Jonathan Salant, "Secret Political Cash Moves Through Nonprofit Daisy Chain," Bloomberg News, Oct. 15, 2012.

PART THREE: PRIVATIZING POLITICS

331   "There's class warfare all right": Ben Stein, "In Class Warfare, Guess Which Class Is Winning," *New York Times*, Nov. 26, 2006.

CHAPTER ELEVEN: THE SPOILS

333   whose donor network had spent: The figure $130.7 million represents the 2009–2010 spending by the Center to Protect Patient Rights ($72 million), the TC4 Trust ($38.5 million), and Americans for Prosperity ($38.5 million), deducting the money passed back and forth among these three nonprofits to avoid double counting, as reported by the groups' IRS filings.
333   "Charles and David Koch no longer": Tom Hamburger, Kathleen Hennessey, and Neela Banerjee, "Koch Brothers Now at Heart of GOP Power," *Los Angeles Times*, Feb. 6, 2011.
335   those with massive financial resources: Freeland, *Plutocrats*.
335   "The more Republicans depend": Lee Drutman, "Are the 1% of the 1% Pulling Politics in a Conservative Direction?," Sunlight Foundation, June 26, 2013.
335   "radicalization of the party's donor base": For more on the implications of the "rise of the radical rich," as Frum terms it, see David Frum, "Crashing the Party: Why the GOP Must Modernize to Win," *Foreign Affairs*, Sept./Oct. 2014.
335   "took the biggest leap": Skocpol, *Naming the Problem*, 92.
336   Now the new Republican leadership: The contributions and influence of the Kochs over the committee were first detailed by Hamburger, Hennessey, and Banerjee, "Koch Brothers Now at Heart of GOP Power."

336   signed an unusual pledge: Lewis et al., "Koch Millions Spread Influence Through Nonprofits, Colleges."

336   "No Climate Tax" pledge: See Eric Holmberg and Alexia Fernandez Campbell, "Koch Climate Pledge Strategy Continues to Grow," Investigative Reporting Workshop, July 1, 2013.

337   By then, the 1980 Superfund law: For more on the defunding of the Superfund program, see Charlie Cray and Peter Montague, "Kingpins of Carbon and Their War on Democracy," Greenpeace, Sept. 2014, 26.

338   "rejected in a class action suit": See "Crossett, Arkansas—Fact Check and Activist Falsehoods," KochFacts.com, Oct. 12, 2011.

338   "All along our street": David Bouie was interviewed in Robert Greenwald's film, *Koch Brothers Exposed*, produced by Brave New Films.

338   Two years earlier: See "The Smokestack Effect," *USA Today*, Dec. 10, 2008.

338   Of this total output: See EPA's Toxic Release Inventory databank. By 2013 Koch Industries had improved its standing so that it ranked as the country's tenth-largest toxic polluter, out of eight thousand companies required by law to register with the EPA.

338   "The investment banks": Continetti, "Paranoid Style in Liberal Politics."

338   Another defender: The University of Kansas political science professor Burdett Loomis told the *Washington Post*, "I'm sure he would vigorously dispute this, but it's hard not to characterize him as the congressman from Koch." See Dan Eggen, "GOP Freshman Pompeo Turned to Koch for Money for Business, Then Politics," *Washington Post*, March 20, 2011.

339   Within weeks, Pompeo: *The Washington Post* first wrote about Pompeo's championing of the Kochs' legislative priorities. Ibid.

339   Koch Industries' lobbying disclosures: See the Sunlight Foundation's Influence Explorer data, http://data.influenceexplorer.com/lobbying/?r#aXNzdWU9RU5WJnJlZ2lzdHJhbnRfZnQ9a29jaCUyMGluZHVzdHJpZXM=.

339   "naked belly crawl": Robert Draper, *When the Tea Party Came to Town* (Simon & Schuster, 2012), 180.

340   "It hurts to be tossed out": Robert Inglis, interview with author.

340   "an unconstitutional power grab": Fred Upton and Tim Phillips, "How Congress Can Stop the EPA's Power Grab," *Wall Street Journal*, Dec. 28, 2010.

340   "a wish list": Leslie Kaufman, "Republicans Seek Big Cuts in Environmental Rules," *New York Times*, July 27, 2011.

340   "rips the heart out": "A GOP Assault on Environmental Regulations," *Los Angeles Times*, Oct. 10, 2011.

341   Contrary to the partisan hype: Solyndra went bankrupt, as did several other firms supported by the huge government loan guarantee program, but as National Public Radio reported, despite $780 million in losses from defaults on loans, the program made $810 million in interest, yielding a $30 million profit. Jeff Brady, "After Solyndra Loss, U.S. Energy Loan Program Turning a Profit," NPR, Nov. 13, 2014.

341   A huge investor: Dixon Doll's firm, DCM, invested in Abound Solar.

341   "like night and day": Hamburger, Hennessey, and Banerjee, "Koch Brothers Now at Heart of GOP Power."

341   "If you look": Coral Davenport, "Heads in Sand," *National Journal,* Dec. 3, 2011.

342   "citizen's arrest": Kenneth P. Vogel, "The Kochs Fight Back," *Politico,* Feb. 2, 2011.

343   "spumed and sputtered": Golf partner of the Kochs, interview with author. The Kochs laying blame on the media for death threats and the need for bodyguards is based on author interviews with two of their interlocutors.

343   "They somehow thought": Vogel, "Kochs Fight Back."

343   Michael Goldfarb: See Jim Rutenberg, "A Conservative Provocateur, Using a Blowtorch as His Pen," *New York Times,* Feb. 23, 2013. See more at http://rightweb.irc-online.org/profile/center_for_american_freedom/#_edn13.

343   Later, he founded: When the Kochs signed him on, Goldfarb was vice president of a public relations firm called Orion Strategies, LLC. *The Washington Free Beacon* was published by a nonprofit organization that hid its donors, called the Center for American Freedom. Its chairman was Goldfarb. Its 990 IRS disclosure shows that the Goldfarb-led nonprofit reported paying one for-profit vendor for public relations work: his own firm, Orion Strategies, LLC.

343   "Do unto them": See Matthew Continetti, "Combat Journalism: Taking the Fight to the Left," *Washington Free Beacon,* Feb. 6, 2012.

344   "I mean no disrespect": Eliza Gray, "Right vs. Write," *New Republic,* Feb. 22, 2012.

344   "tactics that have helped": See Kenneth Vogel, "Philip Ellender: The Kochs' Unlikely Democratic Enforcer," *Politico,* June 14, 2011.

345   "a wake-up call": Liz Goodwin, "Mark Holden Wants You to Love the Koch Brothers," *Yahoo News,* March 25, 2015.

346   It's uncommon for a private detective: In a story about the company's unusually aggressive dealings with reporters, in which *The Washington Post* described me as "the Kochs' Public Enemy No. 1," their spokesmen said only that the brothers had "no knowledge" of the plagiarism allegations made against me. See Paul Farhi, "Billionaire Koch Brothers Use Web to Take on Media Reports They Dispute," *Washington Post,* July 14, 2013.

347   This time the sender: Friess later said he had no involvement in the proposed investigative story on me.

350   "intellectual ammunition": See Schulman, *Sons of Wichita,* 320, which quotes Robert Levy, then Cato's chairman, describing David Koch's telling him that he wanted more "ammunition" for Americans for Prosperity and to support the Republican Party.

350   If anything, the Kochs' ham-fisted reaction: Kenneth Vogel and Tarini Parti, "Inside Koch World," *Politico,* June 15, 2012.

350   The bidding during the final: Interview with a guest at the resort during the seminar weekend.

351   "There's a lot of sharp knives": Halperin and Heilemann, *Double Down,* 346.

352   Tea Party leaders: See Skocpol and Williamson, *Tea Party and the Remaking of Republican Conservatism.*

352   While rich free-market enthusiasts: For more on the differences in the

policy preferences of the rich and others concerning entitlement spending, see Martin Gilens, *Affluence and Influence: Economic Inequality and Political Power in America* (Princeton University Press and Russell Sage Foundation, 2012), 119.

352   It was an intriguing idea: Chapter 7 of the House of Representatives' ethics manual bans all "unofficial office accounts" including "in-kind contribution of goods and services for official purposes." Specifically, members are prohibited from accepting "volunteer services" from paid political consultants "pertaining to the development and implementation of [the member's] legislative agenda."

352   Much of it moved: Overseeing the project at TC4 Trust, and later at a subgroup called Public Notice, was the same operative, a former Bush administration press officer named Gretchen Hamel, who had given a presentation at the January 2011 Koch seminar titled "Framing the Debate on Spending."

352   The TC4 Trust was little more: OpenSecrets.org did the groundbreaking reporting on the TC4 Trust. See, for instance, Novak, Maguire, and Choma, "Nonprofit Funneled Money to Kochs' Voter Database Effort, Other Conservative Groups."

353   "It wasn't about developing policy": Ed Goeas, interview with author.

353   As President Obama worked up: Paul Ryan's eventual pitch, which was found misleading by several nonpartisan fact-checkers, claimed that it was Obama, not he, who planned to cut Medicare. In reality, Obama's healthcare act anticipated steady increases in Medicare spending but predicted a future reduction in the *rate* of increase, thanks to projected savings. Obama critics soon echoed the line of attack, though. Rush Limbaugh, for instance, claimed on his radio show, "Paul Ryan doesn't rape Medicare to the tune of $500 billion! Your guy did!"

354   "When oligarchs control": Neera Tanden, interview with author.

354   A 2008 study: For the study of the four hundred top taxpayers and tax rates during the twentieth century, see James Stewart, "High Income, Low Taxes, and Never a Bad Year," *New York Times*, Nov. 2, 2013.

354   Fully 60 percent: A concise and illuminating report on capital gains taxes, from which the statistics here are drawn, is Steve Mufson and Jia Lynn Yang, "Capital Gains Tax Rates Benefiting Wealthy Feed Growing Gap Between Rich and Poor," *Washington Post*, Sept. 11, 2011. They note that 80 percent of capital gains during the previous twenty years went to just 5 percent of Americans, of which half were among the wealthiest 0.1 percent of the population.

355   Soon, though, those at the very top: Jeffrey A. Winters, *Oligarchy* (Cambridge University Press, 2011), 228.

355   "tax-cutting spree": See Hacker and Pierson, *Winner-Take-All Politics*, 48.

355   "Our goal": Charles Koch, "Business Community."

356   "Wealthy people self-tax": Friess as quoted by Freeland, *Plutocrats*, 246–47.

356   "I agree with": Charles Koch's speech to the Council for National Policy, Jan. 1999.

356   "This is false": Leon Wieseltier, interview with author.

357   According to one 2006 report: Public Citizen and United for a Fair Economy, *Spending Millions to Save Billions: The Campaign of the Super Wealthy*

to Kill the Estate Tax, April 2006, http://www.citizen.org/documents/EstateTaxFinal.pdf.

357 One member of their network: Cris Barrish, "Judge Shuts Down Heiress' Effort to Alter Trust with Adoption Plot," *Wilmington News Journal,* Aug. 2, 2011.

358 "It used to be": Corn, *Showdown,* 76.

359 "failed to withstand": Barry Ritholtz, "What Caused the Financial Crisis? The Big Lie Goes Viral," *Washington Post,* Nov. 5, 2011.

361 "right-wing lunacy": Noam Scheiber, *The Escape Artists: How Obama's Team Fumbled the Recovery* (Simon & Schuster, 2011).

361 According to a *New York Times* analysis: These projections of the fallout from cuts in Ryan's budget refer to its 2012 iteration and appeared in Jonathan Weisman, "In Control, Republican Lawmakers See Budget as Way to Push Agenda," *New York Times,* Nov. 13, 2014.

362 "Robin Hood in reverse": See Jonathan Chait, "The Legendary Paul Ryan," *New York,* April 29, 2012.

362 "the most courageous": David Brooks, "Moment of Truth," *New York Times,* April 5, 2011.

362 "The right had succeeded": See Freeland, *Plutocrats,* 265. She writes, "In April and May of 2011, when unemployment was 9 percent, . . . the five largest papers in the country published 201 stories about the budget deficit and only sixty-three about joblessness."

363 "We made a mistake": Bob Woodward, *The Price of Politics* (Simon & Schuster Paperbacks, 2013), 107.

364 A Democratic underdog: The race in New York's Twenty-Sixth Congressional District was won by the Democrat, Kathy Hochul.

364 But the House Republicans: See Draper, *When the Tea Party Came to Town,* 151.

364 "*We* led": Ibid.

364 The donors were excited: The assertion that the donors felt their investment was worth it is based on an interview with someone familiar with their thinking, who asked not to be identified.

364 "an apocalyptic cult": Thomas E. Mann and Norman J. Ornstein, *It's Even Worse Than It Looks: How the American Constitutional System Collided with the New Politics of Extremism* (Basic Books, 2012), 54.

365 "deal with it as adults": Naftali Bendavid, "Boehner Warns GOP on Debt Ceiling," *Wall Street Journal,* Nov. 18, 2010.

365 "if we don't solve": Frum, in "Crashing the Party," describes Stanley Druckenmiller's position as "amazing" and radical.

365 "delay tough decisions": In addition, Koch-backed advocates had long argued against closing the carried-interest loophole. In 2007, when Congress debated closing it, Adam Creighton, a Koch fellow at the Tax Foundation, a research group supported by Charles Koch, argued that "this is not going to raise tax revenue at all."

366 "they start wetting their pants": Stephen Moore, former Club for Growth president. Matt Bai, "Fight Club," *New York Times Magazine,* Aug. 10, 2003.

366 The president and Boehner: In the grand bargain, Obama would agree to cut spending in exchange for the debt ceiling extension and for the

Republicans "cleaning out the garbage" in the tax code, as Boehner put it. Boehner wouldn't agree to raise tax rates, but he would agree to eliminate some tax loopholes.

366   He was among the House's top: See Alec MacGillis, "In Cantor, Hedge Funds and Private Equity Firms Have Voice at Debt Ceiling Negotiations," *Washington Post*, July 25, 2011.

366   So although one study: The 2006 study is cited in Hacker and Pierson, *Winner-Take-All Politics*, 51.

366   "Boehner begged David": Author interviews with family adviser, a congressional source, and Emily Schillinger.

367   "With no basis in fact": Mann and Ornstein, *It's Even Worse Than It Looks*, 23.

367   Cantor later told: Ryan Lizza, "The House of Pain," *New Yorker*, March 4, 2013.

369   "I think he came in truly trying": Neera Tanden, interview with author.

CHAPTER TWELVE: MOTHER OF ALL WARS

370   Or so they thought: Brad Friedman, "Inside the Koch Brothers' 2011 Summer Seminar," *The Brad Blog*, June 26, 2011.

370   *The New York Times*'s resident: Nate Silver, "Is Obama Toast? Handicapping the 2012 Election," *New York Times Magazine*, Nov. 3, 2011.

371   "Wouldn't it be easier": Halperin and Heilemann, *Double Down*, 345.

372   Four years later: For more on Christie's record, see Cezary Podkul and Allan Sloan, "Christie Closed Budget Gaps with One-Shot Maneuvers," *Washington Post*, April 18, 2015, A1.

372   "Who knows?": Friedman, "Inside the Koch Brothers' 2011 Summer Seminar."

372   Christie had campaigned: See Joby Warrick, "Foes: Christie Left Wind Power Twisting," *Washington Post*, March 30, 2015.

375   From the start: Freedom Partners made grants of $1 million or more in 2012 to the following groups:

    Center to Protect Patient Rights: $115 million
    Americans for Prosperity: $32.3 million
    60 Plus Association: $15.7 million
    American Future Fund: $13.6 million
    Concerned Women for America Legislative Action Committee: $8.2 million
    Themis Trust: $5.8 million
    Public Notice: $5.5 million
    Generation Opportunity: $5 million
    Libre Initiative: $3.1 million
    National Rifle Association: $3.5 million
    U.S. Chamber of Commerce: $2 million
    American Energy Alliance: $1.5 million

375   David Koch's group: Technically, the Kochs' spokesmen insisted that David Koch was only chairman of the Americans for Prosperity Foundation, but in his introduction of David Koch during the June 2011 seminar

Kevin Gentry seemed to describe him simply as "chairman of Americans for Prosperity."

377 For the Koch network: The Koch Industries PAC donated $43,000 to Walker's gubernatorial campaign, and David Koch donated $1 million to the Republican Governors Association in 2010.

378 Some, like the liberal: John Podesta, the founder of the Center for American Progress, in 2015 signed on as the chairman of Hillary Clinton's presidential campaign.

378 "the big government": See Jason Stein and Patrick Marley, *More Than They Bargained For: Scott Walker, Unions, and the Fight for Wisconsin* (University of Wisconsin Press, 2013), 37.

378 The Bradley Foundation: See Patrick Healey and Monica Davey, "Behind Scott Walker, a Longstanding Conservative Alliance Against Unions," *New York Times,* June 8, 2015. The paper reported that in 2009 the Bradley Foundation gave a grant of $1 million to the Wisconsin Policy Research Institute and provided one-third of the budget of the MacIver Institute, both of which drew up lists of proposals for the incoming governor, at the top of which was curbing the power of the state employee unions. The MacIver Institute had numerous ties to the Wisconsin chapter of the Koch advocacy group Americans for Prosperity. Three members of the MacIver Institute's board also served as directors of Americans for Prosperity in Wisconsin. One of these, David Fettig, was a Koch seminar attendee as well.

378 "one of the most powerful": Daniel Bice, Bill Glauber, and Ben Poston, "From Local Roots, Bradley Foundation Builds a Conservative Empire," *Milwaukee Journal Sentinel,* Nov. 19, 2011.

379 As a college dropout: In 2010, an offshoot of Americans for Prosperity calling itself Fight Back Wisconsin organized Tea Party rallies across the state featuring Scott Walker, who was then Milwaukee county executive. Later, the secretly funded group helped him get out the vote. Meanwhile, in a bit of philanthropic back-scratching, the Bradley Foundation in 2010 gave $520,000 to the Americans for Prosperity Foundation.

379 "We go back": Adele M. Stan, "Wall Street Journal Honcho Shills for Secret Worker 'Education' Program Linked to Koch Group," *Alternet,* June 3, 2011.

379 Once in office: See Michael Isikoff, "Secret $1.5 Million Donation from Wisconsin Billionaire Uncovered in Scott Walker Dark-Money Probe," *Yahoo News,* March 23, 2015. Laurel Patrick, Walker's press secretary, issued a strong denial to *Yahoo News* concerning any favoritism shown Menard. She denied that the governor had provided any special favors for Menard and said Walker was "not involved" in the decision to award his firm tax credits, which were approved by the Wisconsin Economic Development Corporation for expansions of existing facilities in order to create jobs. (She also noted that Menard's firm had been awarded $1.5 million in tax credits in 2006 under Democratic Gov. James Doyle. State records show these were reduced to $1 million when the company failed to meet its full job-creation requirements.)

380 According to a 2007 profile: See Mary Van de Kamp Nohl, "Big Money," *Milwaukee Magazine,* April 30, 2007.

380 One employee described: Ibid.

381 That case was followed: See Bruce Murphy, "The Strange Life of John Menard," UrbanMilwaukee.com, June 20, 2013. Donald Trump's wife, Melania, also filed a separate $50 million suit against John Menard, claiming damages from his cancellation of a promotional deal with her line of skin care products. Menard's lawyers described the Trump deal as void.

382 Soon after the governor: Diane Hendricks donated $10,000, the maximum allowable amount, to Walker's campaign in 2011, while her company donated $25,000 to the Republican Governors Association. In 2012, she donated $500,000 to fight the effort to recall Walker. In 2014, she donated $1 million to Wisconsin's Republican Party.

382 Thanks to complicated accounting: According to an account by Cary Spivak, "Beloit Billionaire Pays Zero in 2010 State Income Tax Bill," *Milwaukee Journal Sentinel,* May 30, 2012, the tax director for Hendricks's company, ABC Supply, described her zero personal state income tax payment as an anomaly, stemming from the reclassification of her company from an S corporation, in which she had paid the taxes, to one in which the company paid the $373,671 state tax bill for the second half of 2010.

382 Walker unwittingly lent: The prank phone caller was Ian Murphy. For his account, see "I Punk'd Scott Walker, and Now He's Lying About It," *Politico,* Nov. 18, 2013.

383 After Walker triumphed: See Adam Nagourney and Michael Barbaro, "Emails Show Bigger Fund-Raising Role for Wisconsin Leader," *New York Times,* Aug. 22, 2014.

383 According to one tally: See Brendan Fischer, "Bradley Foundation Bankrolled Groups Pushing Back on John Doe Criminal Probe," Center for Media and Democracy's PR Watch, June 19, 2014.

384 "We will not step back": Schulman, *Sons of Wichita,* 304.

385 "The secret of my influence": Novak, Maguire, and Choma, "Nonprofit Funneled Money to Kochs' Voter Database Effort, Other Conservative Groups."

385 "Koch has been targeted": Matea Gold, "Koch-Backed Political Network Built to Shield Donors," *Washington Post,* Jan. 5, 2014.

385 This consolidation of power: Total traceable election spending by all candidates, parties, and outside groups reached $7 billion, while the amount spent by independent groups and super PACs reached $2.5 billion, of which $1.25 billion came from traditional PACs and $950 million came from super PACs with unlimited contributions. In comparison, $1.576 billion was spent by the Democratic and Republican Parties, according to the Federal Election Commission's report "FEC Summarizes Campaign Activity of the 2011–2012 Election Cycle," April 19, 2013. Spending by "outside political committees" topped party spending for the first time, according to the FEC commissioner Ellen Weintraub's statement, Jan. 31, 2013.

385 On its own: I reached the sum of $407 million by adding up disclosures, but Matea Gold, in her excellent post-2012 feature on the Koch network's spending, cites the figure $400 million. See Gold, "Koch-Backed Net-

work, Built to Shield Donors, Raised $400 Million in 2012 Elections," *Washington Post*, Jan. 5, 2014.

386   *Politico*'s Kenneth Vogel: See Vogel, *Big Money*, 19.

386   No previous year: For statistics on the increasing concentration of dona-tions, see Lee Drutman, "The Political 1% of the 1% in 2012," Sunlight Foundation, June 24, 2013.

386   "the financial engine": Hayley Peterson, "Internal Memo: Romney Court-ing Kochs, Tea Party," *Washington Examiner*, Nov. 2, 2011.

387   There he delivered a keynote: For details of Romney's budget speech, see Donovan Slack, "Romney Proposes Wide Cuts to Budget," *Boston Globe*, Nov. 5, 2011.

388   "They're the ones that suffer": "Quotes from Charles Koch," *Wichita Eagle*, Oct. 13, 2012.

388   "These guys all talk": Dan Pfeiffer, interview with author.

388   "confident glow": Schulman, *Sons of Wichita*, 341.

389   "Why is it fair": For George W. Bush's comment about Adelson, and Adelson's comment on income taxes, see the groundbreaking piece by Connie Bruck, "The Brass Ring," *New Yorker*, June 30, 2008.

390   The odd couple had been friends: See Vogel, *Big Money*, 79.

390   "a bias in favor": Jewish Channel, Dec. 9, 2011.

390   Within weeks, Adelson donated: Sheldon Adelson said of Gingrich's statement, "Read the history of those who call themselves Palestinians, and you will hear why Gingrich said recently that the Palestinians are an invented people." By the time Adelson's money arrived, Gingrich had finished fourth in Iowa, and he was about to be buried in New Hampshire. Adelson later pressed Romney to switch his position on Pollard, but Rom-ney resisted. Romney did, however, sit next to Adelson at a fund-raiser in Israel at which he suggested that Palestinians were culturally inferior to Israelis.

391   "delusional and fabricated": Chris McGreal, "Sheldon Adelson Lectures Court After Tales of Triads and Money Laundering," *Guardian*, May 1, 2015.

393   "We were killing them": Jim Messina, interview with author.

393   "an ideologically driven": Steve Schmidt, interview with author.

395   "There are five or six people": Obama spoke in February 2012 at the home of the Costco co-founder Jeff Brotman according to Vogel, *Big Money*, vii.

395   "in a bind": Arnold Hiatt, interview with author.

395   In an early 2012 meeting: Messina's conversation with Obama as described in Halperin and Heilemann, *Double Down*, 314.

396   Experts ranging: Summers and Fukuyama expressed their concerns in a fascinating essay by Thomas Edsall, "Is This the End of Market Democ-racy?," *New York Times*, Feb. 19, 2012.

397   "Bill can't do that": Hillary's private disapproval is recounted in Halperin and Heilemann, *Double Down*, 381.

397   "under most circumstances": Gilens, *Affluence and Influence*, 1.

398   "new orthodoxy": Jonathan Weisman, "Huntsman Fires at Perry from the Middle," *Wall Street Journal*, Aug. 21, 2011.

399   "Republicans have finally found": Dave Weigel, "Republicans Have Finally Found a Group They Want to Tax: Poor People," *Slate*, Aug. 22, 2011.

401   "They did it wrong": Koch Industries adviser who asked not to have his name disclosed because he continues to work with the company. Interview with author.

401   "some donors who were part": Deposition of Tony Russo, State of California Fair Political Practices Commission Investigative Report, Aug. 16, 2013.

402   "There is not a Koch *network*": Vogel, *Big Money*, 201.

402   This was more than $1: See Barker and Meyer, "Dark Money Man."

404   "My first thought": Teresa Sharp, interview with author.

404   "I don't want everybody to vote": Ari Berman, *Give Us the Ballot: The Modern Struggle for Voting Rights in America* (Farrar, Straus and Giroux, 2015), 260.

404   Spakovsky's most recent book: Encounter Books was founded in 1998 with a $3.5 million grant from the Bradley Foundation to publish "serious non-fiction." In an interview with the author, Hans von Spakovsky denied that he was motivated either by racial discrimination or by partisan gain. "I believe in having fair elections," he said. "My interest is in making sure that the person who people vote for the most wins." See Jane Mayer, "The Voter-Fraud Myth," *New Yorker*, Oct. 29, 2012.

404   True the Vote, meanwhile: True the Vote was forced to return the funds it received from the Bradley Foundation after the IRS had not yet granted the organization tax-exempt status.

406   "What the president's campaign": Romney's November 14, 2012, call to his contributors is described in Halperin and Heilemann, *Double Down*, 468.

407   Approximately $15 million: Peter Stone first revealed the size of the Adelsons' contributions to Americans for Prosperity in his piece "Watch Out, Dems: Sheldon Adelson and the Koch Brothers Are Closer Than Ever," *Huffington Post*, June 14, 2015.

407   "Our goal of advancing": According to Robert Costa, "Kochs Postpone Post-election Meeting," *National Review Online*, Dec. 11, 2012, Charles Koch's e-mail to his donor network said, "We are working hard to understand the election results, and, based on that analysis, to re-examine our vision and the strategies and capabilities required for success."

408   David Koch, in fact: Charles Koch continued to maintain, "I'm neither Republican nor Democrat," even though his political operation was fused with that of his brother.

408   "One ten-thousandth": Drutman, "Political 1% of the 1% in 2012."

408   "I'm an incumbent president": Vogel, *Big Money*, viii.

CHAPTER THIRTEEN: THE STATES

410   The same pattern was repeated: This mathematically odd outcome had only occurred twice before in the past century.

410   "A few years ago": Tarini Parti, "GOP, Koch Brothers Find There's Nothing Finer Than Carolina," *Politico*, May 11, 2013.

410   Phillips declined to say: Nationally, the Koch network's main bank, Freedom Partners, poured $32.3 million into Americans for Prosperity in 2012. But how much of this went into North Carolina remained undisclosed.

411 For his services: The State of North Carolina paid Hofeller an additional $77,000 as well.

411 "We worked together": Raupe is quoted in an excellent ProPublica investigative piece by Pierce, Elliott, and Meyer, "How Dark Money Helped Republicans Hold the House and Hurt Voters."

412 "The Kochs were instrumental": David Axelrod, interview with author.

412 According to a report: Pierce, Elliott, and Meyer, "How Dark Money Helped Republicans Hold the House and Hurt Voters."

412 "Make sure your security": See Robert Draper, "The League of Dangerous Mapmakers," *Atlantic*, Oct. 2012.

413 In reality, however: Hofeller's failure to read the public hearing transcripts was attributed by ProPublica to court documents, and ProPublica noted that Hofeller declined to comment further.

413 But before that could happen: The Democratic challenger was Sam Ervin IV, a rising star who shared the name of his famous grandfather, a former North Carolina senator who won national acclaim during the Watergate hearings.

414 The money trail: ProPublica traced over $1 million back to Gillespie's Republican State Leadership Committee. Pope's company, Variety Wholesalers, contributed some of this cash. The RSLC's role was hidden behind a new group that sprang up, calling itself Justice for All NC. This group in turn donated $1.5 million to a super PAC called the North Carolina Judicial Coalition.

414 Successive midterm losses: Nicholas Confessore, Jonathan Martin, and Maggie Haberman, "Democrats See No Choice but Hillary Clinton in 2016," *New York Times*, March 11, 2015.

415 Almost as soon: Pat McCrory attended events for Americans for Prosperity before declaring his candidacy for governor in 2012, and once he did declare, AFP spent $130,000 in mailers benefiting his campaign.

415 "my way, or everyone else": Richard Morgan, interview with author, which first appeared in Mayer, "State for Sale."

415 "When he was done": Ibid.

415 It is unusual: Winters, *Oligarchy*, xi.

416 "conservative government in exile": Matea Gold, "In NC Conservative Donor Sits at the Heart of the Government He Helped Transform," *Washington Post*, July 19, 2014.

417 Yet the lines: Jack Hawke, a Republican political operative, for instance, moved back and forth between the presidency of the Civitas Institute and the campaigns of the Republican governor Pat McCrory.

417 "the Koch brothers lite": Scott Place, interview with author.

417 "I've never seen": Lynn Bonner, David Perlmutt, and Anne Blythe, "Elections Bill Headed to McCrory," *Charlotte Observer*, July 27, 2013.

418 "No, it's worse": Dan T. Carter, "State of Shock," *Southern Spaces*, Sept. 24, 2013.

419 So for savings: See ibid.

419 The assault was systematic: Spending on public schools in North Carolina was reduced to $7.5 billion in 2012–2013 from $7.9 billion in 2007–2008, despite the state's rapidly growing population, according to Rob Chris-

tiansen, "NC GOP Rolls Back Era of Democratic Laws," *News Observer,* June 16, 2013.

420   "What are you doing": Bill Friday, interview with author, which first appeared in Mayer, "State for Sale."

420   "I'm pretty sure": Stephen Margolis (the former chair of NC State's economics department), interview with author. See ibid.

420   "It's sad and blatant": Mayer, "State for Sale."

420   "constitutional limitations": David Edwards, "NC GOP Bills Would Require Teaching Koch Principles While Banning Teachers' Political Views in Class," *Raw Story,* April 29, 2011.

421   "I was a Republican": Jim Goodmon, interview with author, which first appeared in Mayer, "State for Sale."

421   opposition to minimum wage laws: In an interview with the author, Roy Cordato, a vice president at the John Locke Foundation, argued that "the minimum wage hurts low-skilled workers, by pricing them out of the market," and that concern about worker exploitation was "the kind of thinking that comes from Karl Marx." In Cordato's view, "any freely made contracts among consenting adults should be legal," including those involving prostitution and the sale of dangerous drugs. He said he supported child-labor laws but opposed what he called "compulsory education" for minors.

422   "a plantation mentality": Dean Debnam, interview with author, which first appeared in Mayer, "State for Sale."

422   "wealth creation and wealth destruction": Ibid.

423   "He had his checkbook": Scott Place, interview with author.

424   David Parker: interview with author, which first appeared in Mayer, "State for Sale."

425   "You capture the Soviet Union": Ed Pilkington and Suzanne Goldenberg, "State Conservative Groups Plan US-Wide Assault on Education, Health, and Tax," *Guardian,* Dec. 5, 2013.

425   "Pick what you need": See Jane Mayer, "Is Ikea the New Model for the Conservative Movement?," *New Yorker,* Nov. 15, 2013.

425   In 2011, the State Policy Network's budget: See "Exposed: The State Policy Network," Center for Media and Democracy, Nov. 2013. The report is thorough and well documented and makes the point on page 3 that the organization helped to spread the Kochtopus's "financial tentacles across the states."

426   On average, ALEC produced: For ALEC's track record on introducing bills, see Cray and Montague, "Kingpins of Carbon and Their War on Democracy," 37.

426   "Nowhere else can you get": The quotations from the ALEC members' newsletter and from Thompson appear in Alexander Hertel-Fernandez, "Who Passes Businesses' 'Model Bills'? Policy Capacity and Corporate Influence in U.S. State Politics," *Perspectives in Politics* 12, no. 3 (Sept. 2014).

426   Two years later: For more on ALEC, see ALECExposed.org, produced by the Center for Media and Democracy.

427   "a wolf in disguise": Dave Zweifel, "Plain Talk: 'News Service' Just a Wolf in Disguise," Madison.com.

427   "legacy media": Jason Stverak spoke about the "vacuum" at a Heritage

Foundation conference, "From Tea Parties to Taking Charge," April 22–23, 2010.

427 Much of the money went through: For one of the best analyses of the finances of DonorsTrust, see Abowd, "Donors Use Charity to Push Free-Market Policies in States."

428 The big backers: See "Exposed: The State Policy Network," 18.

428 "a better opportunity": Abowd, "Donors Use Charity to Push Free-Market Policies in States." According to "Exposed: The State Policy Network," 19–20, inadvertent disclosures by just two State Policy Network think tanks, in Massachusetts and Texas, revealed major deposits from Koch Industries and the Koch family foundations. David Koch's personal contribution of $125,000 in 2007 to the Massachusetts-based member of the State Policy Network, the Pioneer Institute, showed that he was the single largest donor to the group that year. A similar mistaken disclosure by the Texas Public Policy Foundation revealed that Koch Industries contributed over $159,000 to the think tank in 2010, while one of the Koch family foundations contributed over $69,000.

429 "historical oddity": See Ryan Lizza, "Where the G.O.P.'s Suicide Caucus Lives," *New Yorker,* Sept. 26, 2013.

430 Big outside money: Kenneth Vogel, in *Big Money,* 211, makes much the same point, writing, "Nearly eleven months after the biggest of the big-money mostly failed to get its way at the ballot box, the shutdown battle was proof that the 2010 and 2012 spending sprees were having more impact than ever on the way American government functioned."

430 A galaxy of conservative: Todd Purdum, "The Obamacare Sabotage Campaign," *Politico,* Nov. 1, 2013.

430 "This bastard has to be killed": Linda Greenhouse, "By Any Means Necessary," *New York Times,* Aug. 20, 2014.

431 "loose-knit coalition": Sheryl Gay Stolberg and Mike McIntire, "A Federal Budget Crisis Months in the Planning," *New York Times,* Oct. 5, 2013.

431 The meetings produced: In his article "Meet the Evangelical Cabal Orchestrating the Shutdown," *Nation,* Oct. 8, 2013, Lee Fang notes that the Conservative Action Project was closely affiliated with the secretive Council on National Policy and had been meeting in Washington since at least 2009.

431 Freedom Partners: Stolberg and McIntire, "Federal Budget Crisis Months in the Planning," suggested that Freedom Partners spent $200 million in the fight against health care, but this figure represents other spending by the group as well.

432 News reports reflected: Jenna Portnoy, "In Southwest Va., Health Needs, Poverty Collide with Antipathy to the Affordable Care Act," *Washington Post,* June 19, 2004.

432 As part of that effort: The figure of four million uninsured adults blocked by the states refusing to expand Medicaid comes from the Kaiser Family Foundation. Rachel Garfield et al., "The Coverage Gap: Uninsured Poor Adults in States That Do Not Expand Medicaid—an Update," Kaiser Family Foundation, April 17, 2015.

432 Meanwhile, the Cato Institute: See Alec MacGillis's profile of the Cato

Institute's Michael Cannon for a revealing look at the think tank's behind-the-scenes role. MacGillis, "Obamacare's Single Most Relentless Antagonist," *New Republic,* Nov. 12, 2013.

432 This nonetheless formed: See Robert Pear, "Four Words That Imperil Health Care Law Were All a Mistake, Writers Now Say," *New York Times,* May 25, 2015.

432 But the NFIB was talked: The NFIB called itself "America's leading small business association," and in previous years most of its funding had come from its small-business members. But starting in 2010, the year it agreed to act as the plaintiff in the court challenge, outside money from some very big fortunes started filling its coffers. In 2012, the year the case reached the Supreme Court, as CNN first reported, the NFIB received more money from Freedom Partners than from any other single source. In addition, from 2010 until 2012, DonorsTrust supplied over half of the budget for the NFIB's legal center. The Bradley Foundation donated funds, too.

The combined millions of dollars in contributions paid for some of the most brilliant litigators in the country to advance arguments that Josh Blackman, a conservative law professor who wrote *Unprecedented,* a book on the case, admitted seemed "crazy" in the beginning. Yet because of the efforts of a few activists bankrolled by wealthy ideological entrepreneurs, the challenge went from the fringe to one vote short of victory in the Supreme Court. For more, see Blackman, *Unprecedented: The Constitutional Challenge to Obamacare* (PublicAffairs, 2013).

433 "It's David versus Goliath": Stolberg and McIntire, "Federal Budget Crisis Months in the Planning."

433 $235 million was spent: For Kantar Media statistics on ad spending, see Purdum, "Obamacare Sabotage Campaign."

433 "When else in our history": Stolberg and McIntire, "Federal Budget Crisis Months in the Planning."

434 "The president was reelected": Boehner, interview with Diane Sawyer, ABC News, Nov. 8, 2012.

434 "John, what happened": See John Bresnahan et al., "Anatomy of a Shutdown," *Politico,* Oct. 18, 2013.

434 "I am not going to": Art Pope, interview with author.

CHAPTER FOURTEEN: SELLING THE NEW KOCH

436 "maybe it's also the content": Matthew Continetti, "The Double Bind: What Stands in the Way of a Republican Revival? Republicans," *Weekly Standard,* March 18, 2013.

437 "Conservative think tanks": Jeffrey Winters, interview with author.

437 "We're going to fight": Daniel Fisher, "Inside the Koch Empire," *Forbes,* Dec. 24, 2012.

437 Around the time that Reid: See John Mashey, "Koch Industries Hires Tobacco Operative Steve Lombardo to Lead Communications, Marketing," DeSmogBlog.com, Jan. 10, 2014.

438 "The current campaign finance": Republican National Committee, Growth and Opportunity Project, March 13, 2013, 51.

438   "We consistently see": See Kenneth Vogel, "Koch Brothers' Americans for Prosperity Plans $125 Million Spending Spree," *Politico*, May 9, 2014.

441   These political problems: See Annie Lowrey, "Income Inequality May Take Toll on Growth," *New York Times*, Oct. 16, 2012.

442   "The poor, okay": See Bill Roy and Daniel McCoy, "Charles Koch: Business Giant, Bogeyman, Benefactor, and Elusive (Until Now)," *Wichita Business Journal*, Feb. 28, 2014.

444   Michael Sullivan: Asked whether Steven Cohen and Michael Sullivan contributed money to the Kochs' political efforts, Mark Herr, a spokesman for Point72, Cohen's new hedge fund, said, "We don't comment or offer guidance on political donations."

444   Obama's senior adviser: Holden met in the White House with Jarrett, the domestic policy director, Cecilia Muñoz, and the White House counsel, W. Neil Eggleston, on April 16, 2015. Subsequently, Obama defended the Kochs' involvement on criminal justice reform issues, though he disparaged them not long afterward for opposing government support for renewable energy. Charles Koch described himself as "flabbergasted" by the president's criticism.

445   "It was hell": Goodwin, "Mark Holden Wants You to Love the Koch Brothers."

445   "hemorrhaging benzene": Loder and Evans, "Koch Brothers Flout Law Getting Richer with Secret Iran Sales."

446   Nonetheless, the $25 million: Some liberal groups, like AFSCME, criticized the United Negro College Fund for taking money from the Kochs, whom it accused of breaking public employees' unions that had provided employment to many minorities.

447   As a 2015 report: Jay Schalin, *Renewal in the University: How Academic Centers Restore the Spirit of Inquiry*, John William Pope Center for Higher Education, Jan. 2015.

448   By 2014, the various Koch foundations: The number 283 comes from ibid., 17.

448   "We learned that Keynes": Jerry Funt, interview with author.

448   Russell Sobel: Sobel became a teacher at the Citadel after abruptly leaving West Virginia University in 2012. Sobel was also a visiting fellow at the South Carolina Policy Council, part of the State Policy Network, and was affiliated with the Mercatus Center, the Cato Institute, the Fraser Institute, the Tax Foundation, and programs partly funded by grants from the Kochs at Troy University in Alabama and Hampden-Sydney College in Virginia.

448   But when critics raised: See Hardin, "Campaign to Stop Fresh College Thinking."

448   Young Entrepreneurs Academy: *The Huffington Post* published a news-making story on the Kochs' incursions into high schools. See Christina Wilkie and Joy Resmovits, "Koch High: How the Koch Brothers Are Buying Their Way into the Minds of High School Students," July 21, 2014.

450   Displayed prominently: Beneath his byline, Charles appended a quotation from Martin Luther King Jr.: "We are caught in an inescapable network of mutuality."

450   No mention was made: In his essay on the Well-Being Initiative, Charles Koch offered some of his own theories on the topic. As he saw it, the world had been divided for 240 years between those who believed government could make one happy and those who sought fulfillment through self-reliance. The split began with the French Revolution, continuing through the Russian Revolution, and on through tyrannical states like North Korea, he said. He contrasted these "collectivists" with the United States, whose founders, he said, "chose a very different path."

But two American historians who read his essay found it full of factual flaws. Rather than opposing the French Revolution, Founding Fathers like Thomas Jefferson greatly admired it. Moreover, as the Princeton professor Sean Wilentz noted in an interview with the author, the U.S. Constitution was inspired by the European Enlightenment and calls for the government to "promote the general welfare." Further, the Georgetown University professor Michael Kazin noted that far from being laissez-faire, the federal government had been intervening in support of public welfare since before the Civil War, often in aid of businesses. "The Koch version of history is a complete fairy tale," he said in an interview with the author.

450   By then, Brooks had moved: See Chris Young, "Kochs Put a Happy Face on Free Enterprise," Center for Public Integrity, June 25, 2014, which was the first report describing their embrace of "well-being" as a public relations gambit.

451   "Well, somebody has got to win": Roy and McCoy, "Charles Koch."

452   But after tallying up: Louis Jacobson, "Charles Koch, in Op-Ed, Says His Political Engagement Began Only in the Last Decade," PolitiFact.com, April 3, 2014.

453   The Kochs' development: The Democratic National Committee had undergone a somewhat similar transformation a decade earlier when about a hundred investors, including George Soros, combined forces to fund the creation of a nonparty political data and analytical firm called Catalist. In contrast to i360, Catalist was a co-op, formed by constituent groups in the progressive political sphere, such as labor unions and environmental groups. It was owned by a trust, and if it were sold, its charter required its investors to donate any profits to charity.

453   "I think it's very dangerous": See Jon Ward, "The Koch Brothers and the Republican Party Go to War—with Each Other," *Yahoo News,* June 11, 2015.

454   "They're building a party": Lisa Graves, interview with author.

454   Americans for Prosperity had expanded: See Mike Allen and Kenneth P. Vogel, "Inside the Koch Data Mine," *Politico,* Dec. 8, 2014.

454   "They aggressively corrected": David Axelrod, interview with author.

454   "retooled and revamped": See Nicholas Confessore, "Outside Groups with Deep Pockets Lift G.O.P.," *New York Times,* Nov. 5, 2014.

455   "We have reached": Mark McKinnon, "The 100 Rich People Who Run America," *Daily Beast,* Jan. 5, 2015.

455   A few of the biggest: Tom Steyer's organization was called Next Generation.

455   The 100 biggest known donors: According to *Politico,* 501(c) groups dis-

closed $219 million in campaign spending to the Federal Election Commission, 69 percent of which was by conservative groups. But this *disclosed* spending was a fraction of all of the 501(c) political spending during the 2014 midterm elections. One single Koch-backed 501(c) group, Americans for Prosperity, alone spent $125 million. See Kenneth Vogel, "Big Money Breaks Out," *Politico,* Dec. 29, 2014.

456   As America grew more: See Eduardo Porter, "Companies Open Up on Giving in Politics," *New York Times,* June 10, 2015, who writes that "unbridled spending" could create the "nightmare situation" where "those at the pinnacle of American society purchase the power needed to preserve the yawning inequities of the status quo."

456   Among the new power brokers: Koch Industries spent over $13 million lobbying Congress in 2014, as well as making over $3 million in political action committee contributions, according to OpenSecrets.org. https://www.opensecrets.org/lobby/clientsum.php?id=D000000186&year=20, https://www.opensecrets.org/pacs/lookup2.php?strID=C00236489&cycle=2014.

456   Soon after he was sworn in: See Lee Fang, "Mitch McConnell's Policy Chief Previously Lobbied for Koch Industries," *Intercept,* May 18, 2015.

456   Three of the newly elected: The other two freshman Republican senators expressing thanks at the Kochs' 2014 June summit were Colorado's Cory Gardner and Arkansas's Tom Cotton.

457   John Kasich, the iconoclastic governor: Neil King Jr., "An Ohio Prescription for GOP: Lower Taxes, More Aid for Poor," *Wall Street Journal,* Aug. 14, 2013; and Alex Isenstadt, "Operation Replace Jeb," *Politico,* June 19, 2015.

458   "What I give isn't 'dark'": Charles Koch interview with Anthony Mason, *CBS Sunday Morning,* Oct. 12, 2015. Yet as Paul Abowd revealed in his investigative report on DonorsTrust, "Donors Use Charity to Push Free-Market Policies in States," Center for Public Integrity, Feb. 14, 2013, "The Knowledge and Progress Fund, a Wichita, Kansas–based foundation run by Charles Koch . . . gave almost $8 million dollars to Donors Trust between 2005 and 2011. Where the funds ended up is a mystery." In addition, he reported, the Charles G. Koch Foundation also filtered small grants through DonorsTrust.

458   "over $760 million": This figure is according to Robert Maguire, an investigator at the Center for Responsive Politics. This included $64 million to groups in the Koch network, such as the American Future Fund, 60 Plus, and Americans for Prosperity in 2010, $407 million to the network in 2012, and pledges of $290 million to the network in 2014, according to Peter Stone's report, "Koch Brothers Unveil New Strategy at Big Donor Retreat," *Daily Beast,* June 13, 2014.

459   "It's extraordinary": Rob Stein, interview with author.

459   "There are few policy victories": Brian Doherty, interview with author.

459   "actors playing out": Ibid.

460   Even though Americans: Just 6 percent of Americans wanted Social Security cut, according to Lee Drutman, and a slight majority wanted the program's benefits increased; see Drutman, "What Donald Trump Gets About the Electorate," *Vox,* Aug. 18, 2015.

460 "false prophets": John Boehner's interview with John Dickerson on *Face the Nation*, CBS News, Sept. 27, 2015.

463 "Giving back": Peter Buffett, "The Charitable-Industrial Complex," *New York Times*, July 26, 2013.

463 Anyone paying attention: Confessore, "Outside Groups with Deep Pockets Lift G.O.P.," *New York Times*, Nov. 5, 2014.

463 "What they want": Phil Dubose, interview with author.

464 To get there: The information on the Kochs' pledges of $75 million is based on an interview with one source who is politically allied with them on several projects.

464 This time, the Koch network: James Davis, a spokesman for Freedom Partners, emphasized that the $889 million budget covered not just electoral spending but the whole universe of ideological spending by the Koch network, including think tanks, advocacy groups, voter data, and opposition research.

464 "Eight hundred and eighty-nine million dollars": Fred Wertheimer's interview with the author. Wertheimer's nonprofit organization Democracy 21 had been supported by grants from George Soros's Open Society Foundations. Wertheimer had nonetheless criticized Soros's use of big money on elections.

464 As was clear: According to OpenSecrets.org's tally of lobbying records, Koch Industries spent $13.7 million on lobbying in 2014, https://www.opensecrets.org/lobby/clientsum.php?id=D000000186&year=2014.

465 "We are doing all of this": Fredreka Schouten, "Charles Koch: We're Not in Politics to Boost Our Bottom Line," *USA Today*, April 24, 2015.

INDEX